A HISTORY OF
THE EAST INDIAN ARCHIPELAGO

LONDON : HUMPHREY MILFORD
OXFORD UNIVERSITY PRESS

NUSANTARA

A HISTORY OF
THE EAST INDIAN ARCHIPELAGO

BY

BERNARD H. M. VLEKKE

HARVARD UNIVERSITY PRESS
CAMBRIDGE · MASSACHUSETTS
1943

PRINTED AT THE HARVARD UNIVERSITY PRINTING OFFICE
CAMBRIDGE, MASSACHUSETTS, U.S.A.

PREFACE

Nusantara — Empire of the Islands — is a little-known name for that area of the southwestern Pacific which politically is known as the Netherlands Indies and geographically as the East Indies or Indonesia. This Malay term, *Nusantara*, was first used by Ki Hadjar Dewantoro, the founder of the Taman Siswa movement in Java. Although it has never gained wide recognition — and probably never will — it has been chosen as the title for this history of the Netherlands Indies as a tribute to those men and women of Indonesia who, like Dewantoro, understand that a sound development of national civilization must be based upon respect for and exchange of ideas with other cultures, and who have striven to make the Indonesian world, admirably located at the crossroads of three of the principal currents of human civilization, a place where, in spite of Rudyard Kipling's pessimistic prognostics, East and West may finally meet.

This history is intended to be an introduction into the study of the development of Indonesian civilization and of the effect of three hundred years of Dutch influence on the Malay world. In the footnotes extensive bibliographic references have been given to facilitate further studies, and the author will consider himself amply rewarded for his efforts if he succeeds in evoking genuine interest in this particular field of historical research.

Students of Sanskrit and Old Javanese may find fault with the transcription of some of the names and terms of the early period of this history. For technical reasons it is impossible to give the correct transcription of some of the Sanskrit vowels and consonants. The prevailing conditions have prohibited the cutting of the necessary new types. In some instances I have preferred to follow the transcription introduced by earlier writers or commonly accepted in geographical or historical textbooks. It seems more desirable to establish a definite tradition in the transcription of Indonesian names than to aim at the greatest possible exactness from the philological point of view; consequently, I have written Ma*dj*apahit but *J*ohore, *J*a*c*atra but *Dj*ocja*k*arta.

I am greatly indebted to all those who helped me in completing this work, first of all to the Director, Librarians, and assistants of the Harvard University Library. Sometimes I must have almost exhausted their patience with my daily and never-ceasing requests for books.

The Hon. Charles O. van der Plas, Chairman of the Netherlands East Indian Commission, now at Melbourne, Australia, kindly assisted me with his expert advice. I thank the Director and Staff of the Netherlands Information Bureau in New York, who gave me their full support and supplied me with much valuable information. I profited greatly by the advice of Professor Raymond Kennedy of Yale University, who was so kind as to read the manuscript. Dr. Sydney Fairbanks assisted me in preparing the maps. Yet this book could never have been completed if it had not been for the interest taken in my work by Professor Taylor Starck of Harvard University and Mrs. Taylor Starck, whose encouragement and advice helped me to continue and complete the task I had undertaken. To them I am most grateful for all they have done for me in these trying years of war.

I feel indebted to the Harvard University Press for the willingness with which the publication of my work was undertaken and to the members of the staff of the Press for their valuable assistance, by which they have relieved me of many tiresome details.

The larger part of this book was written during the months of 1941 and 1942 when the Japanese invaded the archipelago. To write about the glories of the Indies at the moment of their downfall was a nerve-racking task for me, and therefore for my wife. To her I dedicate the work now that it has been completed and that world events seem to point toward a better future.

B. H. M. Vlekke

Cambridge, Massachusetts
August 24, 1943

CONTENTS

ILLUSTRATIONS

MAPS

ABBREVIATIONS

BKI	*Bijdragen van het Koninklijk Instituut*
CD	"Corpus Diplomaticum Neerlando-Indicum"
ENI	*Encyclopedie van Nederlandsch Indië*
ENI Aanv.	*Encyclopedie van Nederlandsch Indië: Aanvullingen*
IG	*Indische Gids*
KS	*Koloniale Studiën*
Krom, HJG	Krom, *Hindoe-Javaansche Geschiedenis*
Krom, IHJK	Krom, *Inleiding tot de Hindoe-Javaansche Kunst.*
Linsch. V.	Linschoten Vereeniging
Stapel, *Gesch.*	Stapel's *Geschiedenis van Nederlandsch Indië*
TBG	*Tijdschrift van het Bataviaasch Genootschap*
VBG	*Verhandelingen van het Bataviaasch Genootschap van Kunsten en Wetenschappen*

INTRODUCTION

THE GEOGRAPHICAL BACKGROUND

THE NETHERLANDS EAST INDIES, with a land area of nearly 735,000 square miles, are about twice as large as the state of Texas. But if we figure the enormous inland seas among the islands, the area is much larger. From west to east, that is, from the western point of Sumatra to the Dutch–Australian boundary in New Guinea, the distance is nearly 3000 miles. In American geography this would equal the distance from San Francisco to the Bermuda Islands. From north to south the width of this land-and-sea surface measures about 1300 miles, or, compared again to the western hemisphere, a distance equal to that from Buffalo, New York, to Key West, Florida. Hence the total land and sea area of the Indies, and we take the name here in its geographic, not in its political meaning, amounts to nearly four million square miles. This is a million square miles more than the solid block of land that forms the continental United States of America without Alaska.

At the extreme west of the group of islands lies Sumatra, spreading from northwest to southeast and covering about the same extent of territory as the combined states of Virginia, North and South Carolina, and Georgia. The west coast of Sumatra is mountainous. The eastern part consists mostly of plains which, near the sea, change into swamps and marshes. To the southeast of Sumatra, separated from this island by the narrow Sunda Strait, which at some places is only about twenty miles wide, lies the island of Java, of the same size as the state of New York and extending nearly 750 miles from west to east. North of Java and east of Sumatra is Borneo, somewhat larger than Texas, of which one fourth forms part of the British empire, with the remainder under Netherlands rule. Whereas Java is wholly under cultivation, Borneo is nine-tenths covered with jungle. At the extreme east of the archipelago, New Guinea forms a transition to the Australian world. It is the second largest island of the world — Greenland holding the first rank — but at the same time one of the least civilized territories on earth. About half of it, equalling the combined area of Wisconsin, Illinois, and Indiana in size, belongs to the Netherlands Indies. Between Borneo and New Guinea's eastern boundary lies the "Great East," a scattered group of islands, of which Celebes is the largest island and the small Spice Islands of the Moluccas the most famous part.

South of this group the chain of the Lesser Sunda Islands spreads between Java and the Australian continent. Thus, the East Indies are a land bridge between the two great continents of Asia and Australia, and the logical deductions seem to be, first, that the western islands must resemble Asia in vegetation and animal life while the eastern group must be likewise related to Australia and, second, that the intermediate islands will present a transition between those two continents, so different in nature.

If we look more closely at the map we see that the seas between the Asiatic continent and the islands of Sumatra, Borneo, and Java are extremely shallow, nowhere more than two hundred feet deep, while further to the east we find the enormous depth of 20,000 feet. The conclusion is apparent. The islands named must have been separated from the mainland in recent times, or at least in what geographers call recent times, namely after the last glacial period, an uncertain number of thousands of years ago. When the huge masses of ice that covered part of the earth in that period melted, the sea level rose about 200 feet and the lowlands of southeastern Asia were submerged. Thus the islands of Sumatra, Borneo, Java, and Bali came into existence. Modern geography has now explained this geological development, but the true story seems to have been preserved all along in native tradition. Jan Huyghen van Linschoten, the first Netherlander who gave a description of the Far East, relates a story that circulated among the Malays in the sixteenth century, telling that the Peninsula and Sumatra had formed one vast continent many centuries ago.[1] Both science and legend make it plain that these western islands must show a close resemblance to Asia rather than to Australia in botanic and animal life. The flora and fauna of Java on one side and Sumatra and Borneo on the other show a certain difference, however.

The curious construction of the mountain masses of the East Indies further corroborates the thesis of science and the legendary story concerning the origin of the islands. From Asia the mountains come down in several parallel ranges. The first of the ranges which form the southern part of the Malay Peninsula may be traced through the Java Sea, where the islands of Bangka and Billiton present the worn remnants of its mightiest tops, and it seems to be continued in the southwestern mountain chain of Borneo. The second range comes down

[1] J. H. van Linschoten, *Itinerario*, ed. by H. Kern for the Linschoten Vereeniging (The Hague, 1910), I, 74.

from Burma, forms the northern part of the Peninsula, and then stretches in a solid wall through Sumatra, of which it forms the backbone. South of Sumatra the range bends eastward, the turning point being formed by the only too well known island volcano of Krakatau. From Java this mountain chain runs eastward and forms the Lesser Sunda Islands, cut up again and again by deep intervals, and approaches the Australian continent. From the mountains the rains and rivers brought down soil which filled up part of the shallow sea and formed the coastal plains of the three islands.

In the eastern part of the East Indian archipelago, the Arafura Sea presents the same aspect as the Java Sea in the west. It is shallow and dotted with many islands. Here again we have the remnants of a continent which once connected Australia and New Guinea. It is no wonder that those two have so much in common in our day, especially in animal life. They are, for instance, the home of the marsupial animals, which are found only in this part of the world. It seems, however, as if the vast continent of Australia had opposed itself like an insurmountable barrier to the Asiatic mountain range which was thrust at it like a dagger through Java and the Sunda Islands. The dagger struck on solid stone and the point bent inward, first to the north through the smaller islands of eastern Indonesia and then back to the west through the southern Moluccas. It is as if two enormous masses of the earth clashed together in this part of the archipelago, and in the shock the strangest deformations came into existence. Volcanic eruptions deformed the island world still more. Thus we find high mountains rising straight out of the sea, and close at hand sea depths with a difference of twenty to thirty thousand feet within a hundred miles. Strangest of all are the two islands of Celebes and Halmahera, which look one like a giant, the other like a pigmy spider crawling out into the sea. Strange as their form is, their flora and fauna are still stranger. In many respects they form a world of their own, distinct from the Asiatic as well as from the Australian type.

The archipelago is one of the most volcanic areas in the world. From the northwestern part of Sumatra through Java and the Sunda Islands and then upward through the Moluccas toward the Philippines, the volcanoes succeed each other in an uninterrupted line. Eruptions and earthquakes are so frequent that in some regions they have determined the style of architecture. The Seismographic Institute of Batavia registers usually two or three minor earthquakes a day. In this region the surface of the earth is still in the period of formation. Islands come up and islands disappear. Most famous of all volcanoes is Krakatau, which before 1883 was an island 2000 feet high and was then destroyed by an eruption that threw up enormous masses of water and steam. The eruption of 1883 was so terrific that part of the ashes that were thrown out circulated two or three times around the world before settling.

Thus, in a geographic sense the archipelago does not form a unity. There is only one characteristic common to its parts: their location near the equator assures an abundant rainfall. In some parts, especially in those close to the equator such as western Sumatra, central Borneo, and central New Guinea, there is a yearly precipitation of over one hundred and sixty inches. The western islands have hardly a single day without rain, while Buitenzorg, near Batavia, may boast of having the world maximum of thunderstorms, 322 a year. There is little seasonal differentiation. "Winter" and "summer" are words without a meaning in the Indies. However, even in the lowlands it is never so hot as the summer in the Middle West of the United States. Since 1866 temperatures have been registered at Batavia, the oldest meteorological station in the tropics. Never in those seventy-five years has the temperature risen above ninety-six degrees, which is twenty-five degrees less than the highest temperature noted in Idaho. On the other hand the temperature has never sunk below sixty-six, which is equal to the average summer temperature for both Portland, Oregon, and Portland, Maine. The humidity, however, particularly in the evening, combines with the complete absence of winds to give the sensation of unbearable heat. The monotony of the climate, especially in the western part, and the persistence of heat throughout the nights are extremely trying.

Everywhere on earth where rainfall is continuous and abundant throughout the year, and where temperature is high, the soil will be covered by dense tropical forests. Such a forest is one of the worst enemies of human activity. Open spaces, cleared at great effort, fill up again in two or three years. Because of its tropical vegetation, those parts of the islands are best fitted for human occupation where the rain is not too abundant but is sufficient to prevent droughts, and where the soil by erosion of volcanic materials has become fit for intensive agriculture. These circumstances happen to exist in central Java. It is not purely accidental that this island became one of the greatest centers of Indonesian civilization. Here the Hindus built their most beautiful monuments, here was the residence of the mightiest Javanese sultans, and here the first Dutch rulers chose to establish their center of government. The density of the population, nearly 850 people to the square mile, is nowhere greater than in Java, where seventy per cent of the total number of the inhabitants of the East Indies is concentrated.

The history of the East Indies is, therefore, mainly the history of Java. Sumatra also has had great importance throughout history, especially its eastern and northern districts. The interiors of Borneo and Celebes, however, have no history at all, since only the coastal districts were drawn into the sphere of Javanese and Sumatran influence.[2] The Moluccas drew the attention of the whole world for a few centuries but now play a passive role.

In this book the term East Indies, or Indonesia, will be used to indicate the whole complex of territories which nowadays form the Netherlands Indies. It is not quite correct from a geographic point of view. The Philippines undoubtedly also belong to the island world of Eastern Asia, but historically they are only loosely connected with it. It is impossible, however, to exclude the Malay Peninsula, which has shared with the Indies all the vicissitudes of peace and war until the present day.

[2] Here "history" is understood of course as "a record of man and his accomplishments based on written documents." In this sense the interiors of Borneo and Celebes were, at the beginning of the nineteenth century, still in a prehistoric period.

A HISTORY OF
THE EAST INDIAN ARCHIPELAGO

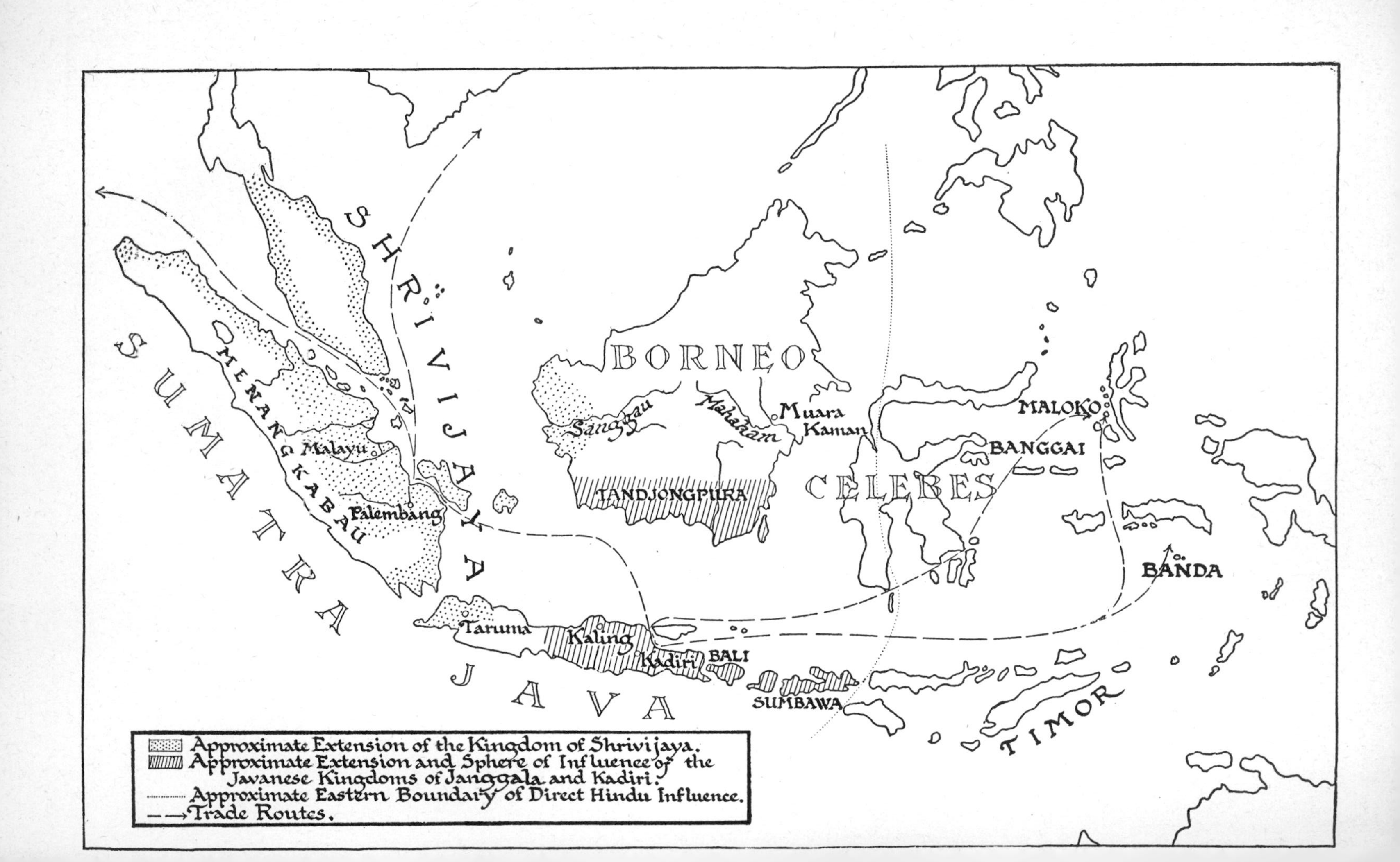
SHRIVIJAYA
SUMATRA
MENANGKABAU
Malayu
Palembang
BORNEO
Sanggau
Mahakam
Muara
Kaman
TANDJONGPURA
CELEBES
MALOKO
BANGGAI
BANDA
Taruma
Kaling
Kadiri
BALI
JAVA
SUMBAWA
TIMOR
Approximate Extension of the Kingdom of Shrivijaya.
Approximate Extension and Sphere of Influence of the Javanese Kingdoms of Janggala and Kadiri.
Approximate Eastern Boundary of Direct Hindu Influence.
Trade Routes.

CHAPTER I

THE DAWN OF HISTORY

THE ISLANDS of the Indies lie across the main sea lanes between eastern and southern Asia. In a stepping-stone territory like this one naturally expects to find a racially mixed population. The racial mixture of the Indies is especially interesting because of the coincidence that at least three of the principal races of mankind inhabit the adjacent continents.

Anthropological discoveries have added not a few complications to the study of the racial problem in the island group. It is quite possible that Java must be considered the home of one of the earliest races of mankind. In 1890 Dr. Eugene Dubois found some remains of a skeleton which apparently could not be classified as that of either an ape or a man.[1] The learned discussions of the remains of the "Pithecanthropos erectus" (the name suggested by Dr. Dubois) produced no definite conclusions. In recent days remains which perhaps are still older have been found near Modjokerto in Java. These have been given the name "Homo Modjokertensis" by Dr. G. H. von Koenigswald, who first described them and who placed both types as far back as the Middle Pleistocene age.[2] Pithecanthropus and Modjokertensis form a race apart in the history of mankind. The case is different with the next generation. Between 1931 and 1934 the remains of eleven skulls were found near Ngandong in East Java. These skulls showed the same characteristics as those of the famous "Neanderthal man" found in Europe.[3] The anthropologists place them nearly 40,000 years back in history. It is very doubtful, however, that the Indonesians of historic times are descendants of these prehistoric races.[4]

[1] See Eugene Dubois, *Pithecanthropus erectus, eine menschenähnliche Übergangsform aus Java* (Batavia, 1894). Most of the discussions on the subject are summed up in L. J. C. van Es, *The Age of Pithecanthropus* (The Hague, 1931).

[2] G. H. R. von Koenigswald, "Die fossilen Säugetierfaunen Javas," in *Verhandelingen der Koninklijke Akademie van Wetenschappen*, vol. XXXVIII, no. 2 (Amsterdam, 1935).

[3] On the discovery of the Ngandong skulls, see W. F. F. Oppenoorth, "Een nieuwe fossiele mensch van Java," in *Tijdschrift van het Aardrijskundig Genootschap*, Tweede Reeks, deel XLIX (1932), pp. 704 sq.

[4] An excellent survey of the prehistoric period in Indonesia is given by A. N. J. Thomassen à Thuessink van der Hoop, "De Praehistorie," in *Geschiedenis van Nederlandsch Indië*, I, 8–111, published under the direction of F. W. Stapel, Amsterdam, 1938,

There are several theories on the ethnological development of Indonesia. The archipelago is a chaos from the linguistic as well as from the racial point of view. Several hundred languages are spoken in the islands, and often several languages are in use on a single small island. The inhabitants of one small area may be of widely different racial types. In New Guinea, for instance, dwarf-like people with an average height of only four feet five inches may live close to tribes whose men have an average height of as much as five feet six inches. In one village the people have a distinctly Semitic appearance, the older men closely resembling the bearded Assyrian kings of the monuments of Nineveh, while the people of the next village are of an unmistakably negroid type. There is not a single island, however small, where the population is not racially mixed to a great extent, and on all the larger islands we find primitive tribes living side by side with people of a high degree of civilization. One of the most remarkable aspects of the problem is that on every one of the larger islands there exists a marked difference between the inhabitants of the coastal areas and those of the interior.

The brothers P. and F. Sarasin, well-known explorers of the interior of the island of Celebes, formulated a plausible theory to explain this difference between the tribes of the interior and the coastal population. This theory has been further developed by later anthropologists.[5] The theory of the brothers Sarasin is that the original population of the archipelago belonged to a race of dark skin and small stature, and that this race originally inhabited the whole of southeastern Asia. That area was then one solid block of land. The ice never covered the East Indian islands, of course, but at the end of the period the level of the sea rose

---

and later. (Four volumes of this history had been published up to May 1940, covering the history of the Indies from the earliest times until 1790.) Another survey of the period is that by P. van Stein Callenfels, "Korte Gids voor de Praehistorische Verzameling [of Batavia]," in *Jaarboek van het Koninklijk Bataviaasch Genootschap*, II (1934), 69–106. An annual bibliography of Indian archeology is published by the Kern Institute of Leyden.

Thomassen ("De Praehistorie," p. 110) gives the following chronology of the early prehistoric period:

Homo Modjokertensis	600,000 years back
Pithecanthropus	300,000 years back
Skulls of Ngandong	40,000 years back.

[5] For the theory of the brothers Sarasin, see P. and F. Sarasin, *Die Weddas von Ceylon und die sie umgebenden Völkerschaften* (Wiesbaden, 1892–93) and *Versuch einer Anthropologie der Insel Celebes* (Wiesbaden, 1905). A survey of the anthropology of the Indies has been given by J. P. Kleiweg de Zwaan, *De rassen van den Indischen Archipel* (Amsterdam, 1925), and in an English version, *The Anthropology of the Indian Archipelago and Its Problems* (Weltevreden, 1929). For Java, see D. J. H. Nyessen, *The Races of Java* (Weltevreden, 1929), and *Somatical Investigations of the Javanese* (Bandung, 1930). An extensive study of Indonesian ethnology by Professor Raymond Kennedy of Yale University is in course of preparation.

so high that the South China Sea and the Java Sea came into existence and separated the volcanic mountain area of Indonesia from the mainland. Scattered remnants of the original population are supposed to have maintained themselves in the inland districts, while the newly formed coastlands were populated by new immigrants. The Sarasins call the descendants of the original race the Vedda-people, after one of the best-known tribes belonging to the group, that of the Vedda in Ceylon. To the same group they attribute the Hieng tribes of Cambodja, the Miao-tse and Yao-jen of China, and the Senoi of the Malay Peninsula. In the archipelago they include the wild forest peoples of Sumatra, the Kubu, Lubu, and Mamak in the same group with the Toala of Celebes.

The immigration of the Malays forced these aborigines to take refuge in the jungles. Even today the people of these tribes are shy and rarely seen unless visited in their abodes in the wilderness. Most anthropologists distinguish two different groups within the Malay race. The Sarasins called them "Proto-" and "Deutero-Malays." The Proto-Malays, the ancestors of perhaps all the peoples now considered to belong to the Malay-Polynesian group that spreads from Madagascar to the farthest eastern islands in the Pacific, are supposed to have immigrated into the archipelago from southern China. In China a region which approximates the present province of Yunnan was their original home, and from there they migrated into Indo-China and Siam and thence into the archipelago. They may well have brought with them the neolithic civilization of which many traces have been discovered in the islands. If this supposition is correct, their arrival would have to be dated about three thousand years before the beginning of our era.

The descendants of the Proto-Malays were in their turn pushed inland by the arrival of new immigrants, the Deutero-Malays. This second wave of Malay immigration also had its origin in northern Indo-China and adjacent areas. The Deutero-Malays are identified with the people who introduced iron tools and weapons into the island world. Through a study of the development of civilization in Indo-China we are able to fix a date for this event too: the immigration must have taken place between three and two hundred years before Christ.[6]

[6] For the chronology of the neolithic period, see Thomassen van der Hoop in Stapel, *Gesch.* I, 108–111, and P. van Stein Callenfels, "Bijdrage tot de chronologie van het neolithicum in Zuid Oost Azie," in *Oudheidkundig Verslag*, 1926. See also articles by van Koenigswald and Thomassen in the *Tijdschrift van het Bataviaasch Genootschap*, vol. LXXV (1935), and in a volume published by the Oudheidkundige Dienst in 1932: *Hommage du Service archéologique des Indes Néerlandaises au premier congrès des préhistoriens d'Extrême Orient à Hanoi* (Batavia, 1932).

Naturally Proto- and Deutero-Malays mixed freely; it is therefore extremely difficult, now, to distinguish between the two racial groups among the Indonesians. To the Proto-Malays seem to belong the Gajo and Alas people of northern Sumatra and the Toradja of Celebes.

Nearly all the other peoples of the Indies, with the exception of the Papua of New Guinea and adjacent islands, belong to the Deutero-Malay group. New racial groups have arisen because of the frequent intermarrying of the Indonesians with the later immigrants. Millions of Hindus, Chinese, and, finally, Europeans have come to the islands in the course of history, sometimes penetrating far into the interior, as is the case in Java and in some parts of Sumatra; sometimes only fringing the coastal districts, as in Borneo and Celebes. The Malay-Polynesian people belong to the great seafaring races of the world and this fact, too, naturally led to further intermingling of the tribes.

The already confusing picture is further complicated by its linguistic aspects. The Malay language forms part of the Indonesian language group, which in its turn belongs to the group of the Austronesian languages, also called the Malay-Polynesian languages. The relationship is as follows:

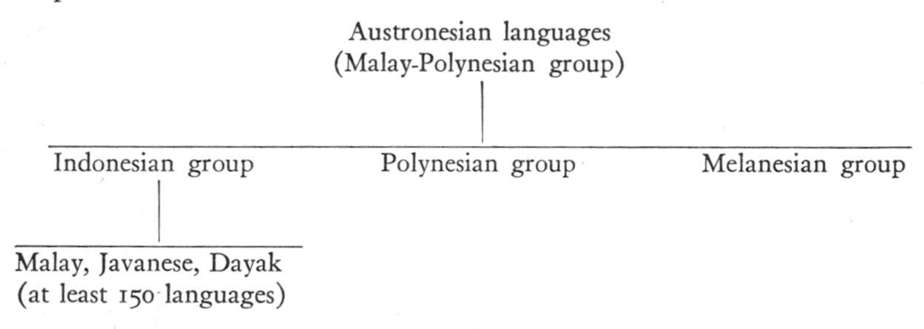

Apart from all other languages spoken in the Indies stand the North Halmahera-Papua group spoken in the interior of New Guinea and in the northern part of the island of Halmahera.

This survey plainly shows that the linguistic division does not coincide with the racial division. Researches into the racial and linguistic characteristics of the Papuan peoples will have to be continued for a long time before we can draw safe conclusions. For the purpose of the present work, however, we do not need to investigate this problem; we are concerned with the *history* of the Indies, and are therefore little concerned with the peoples of New Guinea and other backward areas who until very recently were still living in the prehistoric neolithic period.

The Malay language, which gave its name to the whole southeastern

Asiatic language group, is actually spoken only in parts of Sumatra and the adjacent Malay Peninsula and is the mother tongue of only a few of the sixty million people of the East Indies. This language received an artificial stimulus, however, when after the fifteenth century the traders of all the Indonesian ports used to meet in Malacca, and the language of that city became therefore the *lingua franca* of the Indonesian seas.[7] From that time on the knowledge and use of the Malay tongue spread over all parts of the archipelago and gave that heterogeneous area at least a superficial aspect of unity.

There is, however, a deeper unity that binds together nearly all the tribes and peoples of the East Indies. This unity derives from the common basic elements of their civilization.

Archeological researches have brought to light some of the aspects of early Indonesian civilization. More results have been obtained through the study of comparative ethnology and philology. It has been the privilege of the late Prof. J. H. Kern [8] to have elucidated the early period of Indonesian history through his philological researches. In his book *Linguistic Materials for the Determination of the Country of Origin of the Malay Peoples* (1889) he sought to determine the original vocabulary of the Malay language through the elimination of all later imported terms. By this process he hoped to be able to discover the objects, trades, and customs that had been known to the original Malays.

His researches revealed that the principal means of existence of the Malay people at that early stage was agriculture, and a highly developed type of agriculture, for it included the cultivation of rice on irrigated fields (*sawahs*). This does not mean that all Malay groups, wherever they settled, preserved this particular type of agriculture, but that it was known among them and was applied wherever circumstances were

[7] Remarkable in this connection is the statement of Jan Huyghen van Linschoten quoted below, Chapter IV, note 2.

[8] Johan Hendrik C. Kern (1833–1917) was born at Poerworedjo in the Indies and studied in the Netherlands. After his graduation from the University of Leyden he lectured at the *Gymnasium* (Latin School) of Maastricht. At the age of twenty-nine he had already gained such repute as a Sanskrit scholar that he was called to Queens College in Benares (India) as a professor of that language. Two years later he became professor of the same language in the University of Leyden. He extended his studies to the old Indonesian languages, especially the old Javanese, and was the first to translate a number of old Indonesian inscriptions. His work is collected in his *Verspreide Geschriften* (15 vols., The Hague, 1913–28). The "Taalkundige gegevens ter bepaling van het stamland der Maleisch-Polynesische volken" mentioned in the text was first published in the Verslagen en Mededeelingen van de Koninklijke *Akademie van Wetenschappen, afdeeling Letterkunde*, Derde Reeks, vol. VI (1889). It is reprinted in Volume VI of Kern's collected works.

favorable. This happened to be the case in eastern Java among other places. Climatic conditions and the extreme fertility of the soil helped the old Javanese, descendants of common Malay stock, to preserve and further develop their cultural inheritance. In other parts of the archipelago the Malay settlers were forced by circumstances to return to the system of cultivating rice on *ladangs* (in Java called *gaga*, dry fields prepared by the burning down of the forest). Wherever this happened the progress of civilization was slow, for under this system the fields could be used only a few years and the farmers were then forced to migrate from one part of the forest-covered hills to another. Where, however, cultivation on irrigated fields prevailed, a definite social order came into existence; for this form of agriculture requires the close co-operation of all the inhabitants of each separate village under common leadership. This factor has determined the social organization of the people of Java and many other parts of the archipelago until the present day.

Kern's researches proved that the otherwise very heterogeneous peoples of the Indies had a basically uniform social organization which reached its highest development in Java. From this point comparative sociology and ethnology could carry on their own investigations into the problem. These showed that the original Malay (in the widest sense of the term) village was, and still is in many parts of the archipelago, a democratic community with joint responsibility of the members of the community for the common welfare and the public order. Many traces of this old form of social organization are still preserved in the Javanese *desa* of our day.[9]

The desa consists of a group of farmhouses and barns with their yards.[10] Each house is surrounded by a hedge, and another hedge surrounds the whole village. Primitive gates give access to the village. As the houses are scattered among trees and gardens, the village seen from a distance looks like a patch of woods in the midst of the ricefields. In a broader sense the desa includes also the fields, the fishponds, the ad-

[9] *Desa* is the term used for the village in Java, Madura, and Bali. In the other territories of the archipelago different names are used: *gampong*, *kuta*, *nagari*, etc. *Kampong* or *gampong* is used by the Europeans in the Indies to indicate any Indonesian settlement. *Nagari* has been taken over into the Dutch language under the form of *negorij* and then means hamlet.

[10] For a short description of the Javanese desa and its institutions see *Encyclopedie van Nederlandsch Indië* (second edition, The Hague–Leyden, 1917 and later), vol. 1, under "desa," and for the village of the islands outside Java, the same volume under "dorp." See also C. Lekkerkerker, *Land en Volk van Java* (Groningen–Batavia, 1938), 1, 567–578. All books on the property rights of the soil also deal with some of the main characteristics of the Indonesian village organization.

jacent forests and uncultivated grounds. The farmlands were originally the property of the community or tribe. The members of the community who had by their own efforts brought tracts of uncultivated land under cultivation gained a personal right to those particular fields but, even then, their rights remained subject to the superior right of the community as a whole to dispose of the soil in the common interest. With the passage of time and the progressing social organization this limited right of property developed into full ownership or else disappeared altogether. The latter happened when a number of communities had been grouped together into a larger unit under a hereditary monarch, as happened for instance in part of Java. The king then became the sole and absolute proprietor of all land, a system which has been by turns adopted and rejected by the European rulers of the Indies.[11]

Everywhere there remain many traces of the original social organization. The most remarkable one is the joint responsibility of all members of the community for the common welfare. This includes the obligation to help each other in time of distress and to bear jointly the responsibility for crimes and offenses committed on village soil if the actual perpetrators are not discovered.[12]

The headman of the village is now usually elected by the village people or appointed by the authorities. Undoubtedly the original custom was to elect the headman according to tribal law. This does not mean his election by individual vote, a western system still hardly understood even by the more civilized villagers of Java, but his recognition by common consent as the leader and what we might call "keeper of traditions and customs."

All these forms of social organization were basically identical over the whole archipelago and among the multifarious tribes and peoples. But from both Kern's philological and Wilken's and others' ethnological researches we know that in many other respects also the people of the Indies form basically one social group which in the course of time will develop into a great and united nation.[13]

[11] This principle was adopted by T. S. Raffles during the British administration of Java (1811–1816). He based his tax system upon it, and this system afterwards was maintained by the Dutch. The principle was definitely abandoned in 1870, however, in favor of the exclusive ownership of the soil by the Indonesian people (see Chapters XI and XII).

[12] The Netherlands administration introduced, of course, the principle of individual responsibility.

[13] George A. Wilken (1847–1891), a Netherlander born at Menado, Celebes, was an official of the Indies government and one of the greatest of Indonesian ethnologists. In his youth he planned to become an officer but could not pass his examinations! He suc-

In our day nearly sixty-three of the seventy million inhabitants of the archipelago are Mohammedans, while two millions are Christians. The remaining five millions are divided among the various native cults. Many of the original native beliefs still survive, however, among both Mohammedans and Christians. Animism is at the bottom of all religious conceptions of the Indonesian people. According to this original belief, all manifestations of nature are the consequences of the work of supernatural forces, mostly evil spirits who must be appeased with offerings and whose anger must be avoided with the utmost prudence. The main elements of this primitive Indonesian religion are the following:[14]

First, a pantheistic belief that everything and every living being has its "soul," its "life-energy," which is the same for all but may be stronger in one than in another and more concentrated in one part of the human body than in another. The practices of cannibalism and headhunting have no other purpose than to appropriate the "life-energy" of a slain enemy. Objects with a peculiar form are often considered to have extraordinary virtue and therefore are specially cherished.

Second, the belief in the existence of a personal soul that attends the human being through life. The soul survives the body and after death is supposed to remain in the neighborhood of the places where the body lived. The soul does not withdraw from the community of the living but continues to take an interest in communal life. Consequently, the souls of the deceased may be angered when their descendants give up the old traditions or fail to fulfill their duties toward the spirits. Ancestor worship is always one of the strongest forces in the maintenance of old customs and traditions.

Thus, the tribes of the Indies, with the exception of some of the aboriginal minorities and the numerically weak group of the Papuas, are basically one people, and even the minorities just mentioned differ little in matters of religion and customs. From the beginning the Javanese, that is, the inhabitants of central and eastern Java, were most favored by circumstances and consequently developed a higher degree

---

ceeded, however, in passing the examinations for the civil service of the Indies and later became a professor of ethnology after having received an honorary degree from the University of Leyden, a very rare honor in the Netherlands, at the age of thirty-seven. His works have been edited in four volumes by F. D. E. Ossenbruggen (Semarang–The Hague, 1912).

[14] See Albert C. Kruyt, *Het Animisme in den Indischen Archipel* (The Hague, 1906), and the article by the same author in ENI, vol. II, under the heading "Heidendom."

of civilization. The inhabitants of West Java, the Sundanese,[15] of the same stock as the Javanese, remained more backward. To the east, the inhabitants of Bali were drawn into the sphere of influence of Java, and indeed the history of Bali has always been connected with that of the larger island to the west. Madura, northwest of Java, also shared all the vicissitudes of Javanese history, but its poorer soil hindered the development of the agricultural communities and progress in civilization. The degree of civilization reached in Sumatra was nearly the same as that in West Java. The fact that the larger part of Celebes, Borneo, and the Lesser Sunda Islands is backward in civilization does not necessarily lead to the conclusion that there was an absolute stagnation of cultural development in that area for thousands of years. Some progress in civilization may have been made, and also the reverse may be true. It is one of the myths of popular history that the trend of civilization must always be progressive, never retrogressive. We shall see that in the Indies there is historical evidence to prove the contrary.

At the beginning of our era the primitive Indonesian civilization described in the preceding paragraphs was still untouched by foreign influences. The tribes and even the races were many, but the civilization was fundamentally the same, although East Java, Bali, and South Sumatra may have been ahead of the other parts of the archipelago. The Indonesians were a people of rice-farmers and fishermen, organized in small, democratic communities. The religious beliefs of the Indonesian peoples were primitive and did not call for places of public worship except under the open sky where the deified forces of nature were immediately present.

Some monuments not unlike the menhirs of France and England have been found in Java and in the Lesser Sunda Islands (Sumba). These monuments undoubtedly were built as tombs for chiefs and important people. All over Java other primitive constructions in the form of terraced hillsides have been discovered. On these terraces there are small stone pyramids, and those of West Java are even adorned with sculptures. Similar constructions still exist in southern Sumatra. The exact significance of these monuments is of course a matter of conjecture. Interesting theories have been formulated regarding their builders, among others by the British archeologist William J. Perry, who sees in these stone constructions the traces left by a hypothetical

[15] The Sundanese call their dialect "mountain talk," which indicates that originally they lived in the mountain districts of the Preanger (southwestern Java), whence they spread to the north shore.

migratory people, "the Children of the Sun." To this same people he attributes the stone monuments of France, England, Indonesia, and America.[16]

For us it is sufficient to know that often the same places that served for worship in the primitive period served for the same purpose, though for other deities, in later stages of civilization and sometimes are still places of worship, even in Java. This proves that there has been a continuity of civilization.

The primitive Indonesians at the beginning of our era undoubtedly knew little of the outside world, but the reverse was equally true. The oldest report on Indonesian affairs is found in the annals of the emperor Wang Mang of China.[17] This emperor of the Han dynasty sent an embassy to a country referred to as "Huang-tche," which has been identified with Atjeh [18] or at least some part of Sumatra. The Chinese embassy was sent out to acquire a rhinoceros for the Imperial Zoological Garden, and it is true that this interesting creature could have been acquired in Sumatra. Better evidence, however, may be found in the fact that numerous specimens of Chinese ceramics of the Han period have been found in southern Sumatra, western Java, and eastern Borneo. This undoubtedly indicates that there existed regular connections between China and these islands.

Another report, this time of A.D. 132, and again from a Chinese source, reveals more interesting information.[19] It says that a king of "Ye-tiao" sent an embassy to the emperor of China to offer tribute. We must not attach too much importance to the expression "to offer tribute," for the Chinese were accustomed to regard every present sent to His Celestial Majesty as a token of submission. The name "Ye-tiao"

[16] For a discussion of this problem and the opinions of Perry see N. J. Krom, *Hindoe-Javaansche Geschiedenis* (first edition, The Hague, 1926), pp. 40–44. Perry's book *The Children of the Sun* was published in New York in 1923. A different view of this megalithic civilization is presented by Thomassen van der Hoop, in Stapel, *Gesch.* I, 98 sq. He points out that these megalithic monuments are still being constructed and venerated in several parts of the archipelago, for instance on the islands of Nias, Flores, and Sumba.

[17] Wang Mang ruled China first as a regent and later in his own name between the first year of our era and A.D. 23, and his reign forms a period of transition from that of the first to that of the second Han dynasty.

[18] In this book the Dutch spelling "Atjeh" will be used in preference to the English spelling "Achin," in order to make the references to Dutch literature more easily understood.

[19] Most references to the archipelago in Chinese sources have been collected by W. P. Groeneveldt and published in the *Verhandelingen van het Bataviaasch Genootschap van Kunsten en Wetenschappen*, vol. XXXIX, part I (1876). A second edition appeared in the *Miscellaneous Papers Relating to Indo–China and the Indian Archipelago*, second series, vol. I (1887), later supplemented by some references published in the periodical *T'oung Pao*, vol. VII (1896).

has been explained as a Chinese transcription of "Yavadvipa," and the name of its king, given in the Chinese text as "Tiao-pien," as a transcription of the Sanskrit name "Devavarman." The latter seems rather dubious, but the first transcription is generally accepted.

This name gives us a clue to further information on the early history of the Indies. "Yavadvipa" is a Sanskrit name which means "Millet Island" and is found in the Hindu epic of the *Ramayana*. The epic mentions "Yavadvipa, adorned by seven kingdoms, the Gold and Silver Island, rich in gold mines" as one of the most remote parts of the earth. Beyond that the epic knows only the mountain "Çiçira, visited by Gods and demons." [20]

The Prakrit version of the name is "Iabadiu." In this version the name was known to the Greek geographer Ptolemy (of Alexandria, A.D. 160), who may be remembered as the first western author who ever wrote about Indonesia. Apparently he drew his information from the same sources as the author of the *Ramayana*. It is noteworthy that the particular passage of the epic in which Indonesia is mentioned belongs to late interpolations and dates from the same period as Ptolemy's book. Ptolemy is more exact than the author of the *Ramayana* and distinguishes between a "Gold-" and a "Silver-land" both of which he locates on the continent of southeastern Asia. Next to these countries he places the "Golden Peninsula" and near this the "five Barousai Islands, the three Sabadeibai Islands, where cannibals live, and the island Iabadiu, which means Millet Island." On the island of Iabadiu is a city named "Silver City."

It is not difficult to recognize in the Golden Peninsula the Malay Peninsula and in the islands the archipelago of Indonesia. The description, although vague, is accurate enough to convince us that it was obtained from seafaring people who had actually visited the archipelago and this, in its turn, establishes the existence of trading connections between India and Indonesia as early as the first century of our era.

The *Ramayana* mentions seven kingdoms in Yavadvipa. Were these kingdoms autochthonous Indonesian kingdoms? It is not impossible. Some of the titles of high dignitaries in the Hindu-Javanese kingdoms of the eighth century are pure Indonesian. Consequently the titles must have been in use before the arrival of the Hindus. This would imply an organized Indonesian state before the arrival of the Hindus. In most

[20] See Krom, HJG, p. 59. On the text of Ptolemy, see the same work, pp. 53–54. Professor Krom, the greatest authority on Hindu–Javanese history, published a second edition of his book in 1931 and wrote the section on the Hindu–Javanese period in the *Geschiedenis van Indië* of F. W. Stapel (I, 119–298). In this later work (1938) he revised many of his opinions as given in HJG.

cases, however, the early Indonesian states were certainly founded by immigrants from India. The Hindu immigration, which took place between the beginning of our era and the eighth century, definitely shaped the cultural development of Indonesia. For seven centuries a continuous stream of immigrants moved from west to east along the coasts of southern Asia. The immigrants probably were never very numerous, but the movement continued over such a long period that it finally deeply influenced Indonesian civilization and, to a lesser extent, Indonesian languages. From a racial point of view its influence was negligible, except perhaps in some parts of Java.

The later legends of Java personified that movement. They attributed the first social and political organization of Java to a legendary prince, Aji Saka, who was said to have come from India.[21] He was believed to have taught the people of Java the art of writing and to have given them their chronology. It is doubtful whether these immigrants were really princes or conquerors. Probably they were simple merchants or political refugees. They intermarried with the Indonesians and would have been quickly absorbed by the original population had not the immigration constantly brought new blood from India. The descendants of the Hindus and the Hinduized Indonesians formed the upper class of the new society, while the lower class remained purely Indonesian. The newcomers imposed many Sanskrit words upon the Malays but never were numerous enough to supplant the native language by their own tongue.[22]

The Hindu immigration exerted its greatest influence in Java and Sumatra. Traces of Hindu civilization have also been found in Borneo and Celebes (farther east the Hindus hardly penetrated). Once Hindu-Indonesian states had been organized in Java, the Moluccas were visited from these states. The character of the early Hindu-Indonesian civilization,[23] its religion and its oldest political organizations, are known to

[21] Many of the legends of the Javanese were inserted by Thomas Stamford Raffles in his *History of Java* (London, 1817, 2 vols.). Raffles did not command any information taken directly from medieval Javanese sources, and consequently, in the purely historical sections of his work, was led completely astray by the misinformation he received from some Javanese men of letters who derived their knowledge from modern Javanese writings, the so-called *babads*. For a discussion of the historical value of the babads, see Hussein Djajadiningrat, *Critische beschouwing van de Sadjarah Banten* (Haarlem, 1913), and C. C. Berg, "Javaansche Geschiedschrijving," in Stapel, *Gesch.* II, 7–148.

[22] For a more popular and, at the same time, more recent survey of the Hindu-Indonesian period, see the series published by W. F. Stutterheim: vol. I — *De Hindu's* (Groningen-Batavia, 1932); vol. II — *Hinduisme in den Archipel* (*ibid.* 1932); vol. III — *De Islam en zijn komst in den Archipel* (*ibid.* 1935).

[23] The Hindu period of Indonesian history is usually called the Hindu-Javanese period.

us through a number of inscriptions found in the western part of the archipelago. These inscriptions are the oldest historical documents in the Indies. They are written in Indian script and in one or another of the Indian languages.

The oldest inscriptions have been found in East Borneo at a place now called Muara Kaman, a hundred miles inland on the Mahakam river. Muara Kaman is now a rather desolate village lying in the midst of swamps and jungles. The district is scarcely populated. Only in recent years, since the discovery of coal and oil deposits nearer the coast, has this part of Borneo begun to attract attention. The inscriptions apparently are survivals of an early Hindu settlement that did not succeed.

Since the four inscriptions of Muara Kaman are the oldest literary monuments of the East Indies, a translation of one of them may prove of interest:

> The famous prince Kundungga the Eminent had a son, the renowned Açvavarman, the founder of a dynasty, who is comparable to Amçuman. Three sons he had who were like three sacrificial fires. The most excellent of these, renowned for the power of his asceticism and for his self-control, is His Majesty Mulavarman, the Lord and King who brought offerings of much gold. In remembrance of these offerings this sacrificial pillar has been erected by the principal ones of those who have been twice born.[24]

This inscription may be the work of a Hindu, but it may just as well be the work of an Indonesian who had completely mastered the Hindu language and adopted Hindu civilization. Some evidence in favor of this latter possibility may be found in the names mentioned in the inscription. Mulavarman is a Hindu name; Kundungga, however, may well be an Indonesian name.[25] Açvavarman is undoubtedly Hindu, and this prince, although second in the line of succession, is mentioned as the founder of the dynasty. These facts suggest a gradual assimilation to Hindu culture of an already existing Indonesian kingdom.

The evidence concerning the religion of the ancient Indonesians provided by these inscriptions is of more interest than the genealogy of their kings. Mention of the sacrificial pillar points to the existence of the custom of sacrificing animals to a deity. King Mulavarman's religion, therefore, must have been Brahmanist, since Buddhism does not allow animal sacrifice. Sacrificial pillars, however, are extremely rare in

---

As the Hindu civilization was by no means limited to Java, I prefer to speak of Hindu-Indonesian culture.

[24] I follow the translation given by N. J. Krom in HJG, p. 67 (first ed.).

[25] Professor Krom (HJG) does not care to decide whether the name Kundungga is originally Indonesian or Hindu.

India proper, while they are a common part of the appurtenances of the Old-Indonesian cults. Thus we may conclude that around A.D. 400, the period in which the inscriptions were written, an Indonesian kingdom roughly assimilated to Hindu culture existed in East Borneo.

There must have been other kingdoms in this condition in the archipelago at that time. A rock at the foot of the mountains south of Batavia (Java) has preserved for us a beautiful inscription written in clearly designed characters. The inscription is carved in the rock next to the imprints of two human feet, said to be the imprints of the feet of "the powerful ruler, the illustrious Purnavarman, king of Taruma, whose footsteps are like those of Vishnu." Not far from this spot the king's elephant has also left his footprints. A second imprint of the royal feet is accompanied by somewhat menacing language:

> These feet of the Illustrious Protector who is devoted to his duty, the incomparable Prince, His Majesty Purnavarman, who formerly ruled over Taruma, may trample upon the cities of his enemies and bring help to his faithful allies.

Thus we know that king Purnavarman of West Java was one of many kings of the island among whom many wars were fought and alliances concluded. But we know still more of the enigmatic king Purnavarman. His name is connected with the oldest public irrigation work of which we know in Java, a canal which was completed in twenty-one days, if we may believe the inscription, although it was not less than seven miles long.[26]

Near Palembang, in southern Sumatra, a statue of Buddha has been found which dates back perhaps to the second century after Christ. Later a Hindu-Indonesian kingdom existed with Palembang as a capital, and we deduce from these facts that southern Sumatra was one of the earliest Hindu settlements in the archipelago.

Chinese sources speak of still another Hindu kingdom which they call "P'o-li." In this kingdom some modern scholars recognize Bali, and it seems to be beyond doubt from other evidence that this small island was another point of attraction for the earliest Hindu immigrants.[27]

From which part of India did these immigrants come? The script they introduced into the islands of Indonesia was the Pallawa script, which originated in southeastern India. Other indications point to the same section. Most of the immigrants followed the Brahmanist reli-

[26] The inscriptions are given after the Dutch version by Prof. N. J. Krom, HJG, pp. 75–77.

[27] Poli has also been identified with other parts of the Indies, northern Atjeh or West Borneo, for instance. The most probable identification, however, remains Bali.

THE BOROBUDUR

Gate giving access to the three highest terraces of the Borobudur where the Dhyani-Buddhas stand.

gious rites, but there were Buddhists among them, although only in small numbers. For this we have the testimony of a Chinese Buddhist pilgrim who, in the year 414, visited the islands. This pilgrim, Fah-Hien, noted sadly that nearly all the inhabitants of the islands were pagans or heretics — that is, Buddhists of a philosophy different from his own.

Thus, around A.D. 400, the Indies had found their place in the cultural world of Asia. Relations had been established with neighboring countries and these relations were to undergo no fundamental change for ten centuries to come. New currents of civilization and new religions were always to come to the Indies from the west, never from the north. India — and beyond India, Arabia, Persia, and Europe — were to be sources of Indonesian cultural life. What the Indonesians obtained from these sources they blended with their own traditions and civilization.

Chinese culture, although rich and flourishing, never gained any real influence in Indonesia, but politically and economically the ties with China were often to be more important than those with India. The Chinese chronicles of the fifth and sixth centuries note a number of Indonesian embassies to the court of the emperor. These embassies brought and received presents. In China they were gracefully received as emissaries from vassals paying homage. The Indonesian princes cared not at all what interpretation the Chinese put upon this form of intercourse but exploited it as a convenient method of trading with China.

For a while the Indies were a center of theological learning, and thither the Chinese Buddhists went to discuss the philosophy of their creed and to collect manuscripts. A change had come over Sumatra shortly after Fah-hien had visited it and turned away in disgust from the "heretics." This change had been the work of a royal prince of Kashmir, Gunavarman, who in imitation of the Buddha had become a monk and had gone to teach the true way of salvation to foreign nations. Shortly after 420 he went to Indonesia, where he visited Java and Sumatra. There he converted many of the princes to Buddhism, and after his visit the upper classes of these countries seem to have remained Buddhist for several centuries, although they changed their adherence to a type of Buddhism other than that preached by Gunavarman.

Gunavarman also visited China as a missionary and thus promoted religious ties between India, Indonesia, and the Celestial Empire. The Chinese theologians were inspired by an ardent desire to see the places where the Buddha had lived and taught. A trip to India took several years, and, naturally, the pilgrims stopped on their way in Sumatra or Java, where they often spent many months. The most famous of these pilgrims is I-tsing, who undertook the voyage in the last quarter of the seventh century. When he decided to visit the "tree of knowledge" in India he looked for companions, but his friends shrank from the dangers of the voyage. This inspired him to write the following poem:

> During my travels I passed through several myriads of stages,
> The fine threads of sorrow entangled my thought a hundredfold.
> Why was it, pray, you let the shadow of my body alone
> Walk on the boundaries of five regions of India?

On his way home he stayed for several months at Sumatra, of which he gave the following account:

> Many kings and chieftains in the islands of the Southern Ocean admire and believe [in Buddhism] and their hearts are set on accumulating good actions. In the fortified city of Bhoga, Buddhist priests number more than one thousand whose minds are bent on learning and good practices. They investigate and study all the subjects that exist just as in the Middle Kingdom [Madhya-deça in India]; the rules and ceremonies are not at all different. If a Chinese priest wishes to go to the west in order to hear [lectures] and read [the original texts] he had better stay here one or two years and practice the proper rules and proceed to Central India.[28]

Theology and philosophy must have been flourishing in Sumatra in I-tsing's time, for he collected so many manuscripts for transcription that he had to go back to China to get more paper and ink — the Indonesian books were probably written on palm leaves. After his return he completed his transcriptions and finally he was able to take nearly four hundred different Buddhist texts to China.

I-tsing's pilgrimage took place between A.D. 671 and 692. The story of his travels makes it perfectly clear that in his time there must have been frequent communication by ship between India and China via Malaysia. The Chinese chronicles record an increasing number of Indonesian embassies to the Imperial Court. The kingdoms that sent these later embassies, however, were no longer the same kingdoms, as we know by the inscriptions of the fifth century.

According to the Chinese sources, the political situation of the archipelago was about the following:

In Sumatra there were two kingdoms. The northern one was that of Malayu. Its capital was located on the site of the present town of Djambi on the Batang river. The southern and more important one

[28] English translation by J. Takakasu in his book, *A Record of the Buddhist Religion as Practised in India and in the Malay Archipelago* (Oxford, 1896).

was that of Shrivijaya, of which Palembang was the captial. It is evident from the Chinese reports that Shrivijaya gained control over Malayu and a number of other ports and territories in Sumatra and the Malay Peninsula. In time it became the great naval power of western Indonesia.[29]

In Java there were certainly two and probably three kingdoms. That of Taruma, the state of king Purnavarman, continued to exist, although under another name. The historical evidence we have concerning this western Javanese kingdom is of the scantiest, but time and again we find incidental remarks about it in the annals of Shrivijaya and Central Java. The continuous existence of a western Javanese state with rather close commercial relations with the neighboring Sumatran state of Shrivijaya seems, therefore, a safe conclusion to draw.

There is no doubt at all about the existence of a kingdom in Central Java in I-tsing's time. We know the name of that kingdom. The Chinese give it as "Ho-ling," which transcribed in its Indonesian form is "Kaling." "Kaling," or "Kalinga," is also the name of a Hindu state on India's East coast. "Kling" is at the present time the Indonesian name for the people of India. Therefore, the Central Javanese kingdom mentioned by the Chinese of the seventh century was undoubtedly a Hindu state, founded in Java. The Javanese legends of later centuries and the legendary genealogy of the Javanese princes of the sultanate of Mataram (and consequently of the present sultans of Djocja and Surakarta) place a prince Sanjaya on the throne at the beginning of Javanese history. That prince was said to have been a great conqueror who subjected Bali, Sumatra, Cambodja, and even India and China to his rule. After his death he was deified, and the descendants of the "Divine Sanjaya" still enjoyed special privileges as late as the year 1100. The most definite information we have about this prince is, however, an inscription found near Tjanggal (district of Kedu) which tells us that king Sanjaya in the year 732 erected a monument at that place. Thus we are sure that Sanjaya is more than a mythical figure. The inscription even refers to the territory of Kunjarakunja [30] as the homeland of Sanjaya's people.

[29] On Shrivijaya see, besides the works of Krom, G. Coedès, "Le Royaume de Çrivijaya," in *Bulletin de l'École Française de l'Extrême Orient*, XVIII (1918), 6; Gabr. Ferrand, "L'Empire sumatrais de Çrivijaya," *Journal Asiatique*, 1919, 1922, and 1932; J. Ph. Vogel, "Het koninkrijk Çrivijaya," BKI, LXXV (1919), 26 sq.; and J. H. Moens, "Çrivijaya, Yawa and Kataha," TBG, LXXVII (1937), 317–487. For prehistoric Sumatra see F. M. Schnitger, *Forgotten Kingdoms of Sumatra* (Leiden, 1939).

[30] According to Krom (Stapel, *Gesch.* I, 154), Kunjarakunja is the area around the mountain of Agastyamalai (formerly named Kunjara) and along the river Tamraparni, in the utmost southern point of India.

The Chinese sources seem to indicate the possibility of the existence of a third kingdom in Java, in the eastern section, south of the present city of Surabaya. The best evidence for the existence of this kingdom is, however, obtained from the further development of Hindu-Indonesian civilization in Java.

Whereas the Chinese reports on Java and Sumatra become more explicit, Borneo is hardly mentioned. There is a scarcity, too, of archeological evidence. Few samples of Hindu-Indonesian art or of Sanskrit inscriptions have been found in Borneo after the earliest cited. That the kingdom of Mulavarman and other hypothetical Hindu states on the island had disappeared together with the traces of Hindu immigration is not a necessary conclusion from this lack of archeological material. In the district where in the fifth century Mulavarman had ruled, the kingdom (or sultanate, after conversion to Islam) existed in later centuries. The chronicles of the sultans of Kutei mention the existence of a realm of Muara Kaman (Mulavarman's district) as late as the seventeenth century. We presume that the small Hindu settlements that were founded in this and other parts of Borneo and, perhaps, in southern Celebes and on some of the Lesser Sunda Islands, have been completely absorbed by the original Indonesian population. The forms of Hindu civilization disappeared and the political organizations alone continued to exist in rather primitive form.

Thus we must concentrate our attention on Java and Sumatra for the greater part of the Hindu-Indonesian period. Between these two islands there existed important differences.

Existing inscriptions prove that Shrivijaya had become an important commercial and naval power. These inscriptions are written in the usual Pallawa script. The language, however, is no longer Sanskrit but Old-Malay. Apparently the process of absorption of the Hindu immigrants by the original population had made considerable progress in Sumatra also. The religion of the Hindu-Sumatrans of Shrivijaya was Buddhism. Buddhism is divided into two main sects, that of the Hinayana and that of the Mahayana (of the Great and of the Little Vehicle).[31] We know for certain that in the seventh century the

[31] The two sects are also known as the Northern and the Southern Church. The Southern Church prevails in Indo-China, Burma, and Ceylon, the Northern Church in Nepal, Tibet, China, and Japan. According to the old chronicles of Buddhist church history there were eighteen schools of Buddhism, while the tradition of the Northern Church knows of twenty schools. A first schism took place about one hundred years after the death of the Buddha, at the council of the Buddhist church at Waiçali. Two groups originated from this council, the Theravadins and the Mahasanghikas. The former represented the original Hinayana. Another sect, derived from this group, was the Sar-

Hindu-Sumatrans followed the path of the Hinayana. In the middle of the seventh century several of the greatest theologians of the school of the Mahayana visited Sumatra, and their presence must have had a great influence on the people of Shrivijaya. Within fifty years they had been converted to the doctrine of the Great Vehicle.[32]

Java presents a totally different picture. The language of Sanjaya's inscription is Sanskrit. His religion is Shivaism, one of the two types of Brahmanism. His inscription, of the year 732, glorifies Shiva, Brahma, and Vishnu. Shiva is mentioned first, and Shivaism always remained the form of Brahmanism professed in Java. To Shiva were dedicated the temples whose ruins are still standing on the Dieng plateau in central Java.[33]

The Dieng plateau is high up in the Prahu mountains. It is nearly 6,000 feet high but not more than 8,000 feet long and 2,500 feet wide.

---

vastivada with its center in Kashmir. It was this form of Hinayana that gained influence in the archipelago. The other group that originated from the council of Waiçali, the Mahasanghikas, became the forerunner of the Mahayana. The Mahasangha claimed that it restored the original ideals of Buddhism and presented a reaction to the monastic ideals of the Theravada.

The adepts of the Hinayana, professed by the Southern Church, seek salvation in the form of a complete renunciation of life which may be obtained through virtue and contemplation. It leads away from the world. The Mahayana aims at combining activity in life with the pursuit of holiness and recognizes besides the Buddha in heaven many saints on earth. These Buddhists expect the story of Buddha to be repeated several times before earthly life has completed its course. The purpose of life is no longer to seek to return to nothingness and absorption into the universal spirit but to be an emanation of the Buddha in life. To obtain this degree of holiness one must imitate the Buddha in his works and qualities. The personification of these qualities is another step toward the development of polytheism. Besides Buddha, six Dhyani-Buddhas, the Meditative Buddhas, are venerated. Corresponding to the Buddhas on earth they are the real Buddhas, those in the sphere of ideas. Each of the six rules a particular period of history and each has some of his qualities embodied in a female companion. A later development made the achievement of sanctity easier through offering a short cut. Secret knowledge was believed to exist which, through certain formalities and spells, could bring about the desired state of perfection. This is called Tantrism and is now found mainly in Tibet.

[32] See also C. M. Pleyte, "Bijdrage tot de kennis van het Mahayana op Java," in *Bijdragen van het Koninklijk Institut*, vols. LII and LIV (1901 and 1902), and F. M. Schnitger, "Enkele oudheidkundige opmerkingen over het Tantrisme op Java," BKI, vol. XCII (1935).

[33] An inventory of all Hindu antiquities in the Indies, with bibliography, has been published by the Oudheidkundige Dienst in Nederlandsch Indië, under the direction of N. J. Krom, in its Reports of 1914, 1915, and 1923, published at Batavia in 1915, 1918, 1923, respectively. For a description of the monuments of ancient Java and for a discussion of the problems connected with the history of Hindu-Javanese art, see N. J. Krom, *Inleiding tot de Hindoe-Javaansche Kunst*, 3 vols. (first ed. The Hague, 1919, second ed. *ib.* 1926). For the history of Balinese art, see W. F. Stutterheim, *Oudheden van Bali* (Singaradja, 1930), and by the same author, *Indian Influences in Old Balinese Art* (London, 1935).

Because of its altitude its landscape is quite different from the normal equatorial type. It is one of the few places in Java where the temperature may go below the freezing point. The plateau was formed by a volcano the crater of which was slowly filled up. Once it may have been a lake, for even now the rain would submerge the whole plateau if it were not for a drainage system built in recent times. That the same problem was solved by the Hindus in the eighth century is proved by the discovery of a drainage canal built of stone and dating back to the period of construction of the temple. Stone staircases gave access to the plateau. In these awe-inspiring surroundings the old Javanese worshipped their gods, and it is quite probable that the Dieng had already been a place of worship long before the first Hindu arrived.

The exact models for Hindu-Indonesian architecture must be sought in India, for it should be remembered that the art of the Dieng plateau is purely Hindu. We have not yet been able to locate the place of origin of these models. The only indication we have is the inscription of King Sanjaya which points to the utmost southern point of India. The temples themselves are simple structures of classic beauty. The Indonesian style which appears later in so many monuments and their decorations is of a totally different character from that of these temples. In the neighborhood of the temples, foundations of houses have been found, and these houses, in contrast to the temples, must have been of a pure Indonesian type. Houses of the same type are found and are still built in the principalities of Java in our day. One single statue confirms the Shivaitic character of the temples. It represents Shiva in the figure of Bhatara Guru, the "Divine Teacher." [34]

In the years immediately following the construction of the temples of Dieng a great change must have taken place in central Java. The successor of Sanjaya apparently belonged to another dynasty. The new king professed another creed, and his inscriptions are written in another script. The script, the religion, and the names of places and deities all point towards the same province of India as the country of origin of this dynasty, namely towards Bengal.

The university of Nalanda was one of the principal centers of Mahayana-Buddhism. This creed must have been introduced into Java

[34] Shiva, the "destroyer" who represents the forces of nature that destroy in order to create anew, is sometimes represented as the Mahadeva, the "Great God" with four arms and riding the bull Nandi. As Bhatara Guru he is represented as a bearded old man. Shiva's goddess is Devi, *the* goddess, who is also called Durga, the unapproachable. Their son is Ganeça, the elephantman, the god of wealth. Statues of Ganeça are frequent in the Indies. Vishnu, the god of light, is mostly represented riding the Garuda, the man-eagle.

in the second half of the eighth century, but in Java it cannot have been a mere conversion of the people, or rather of the aristocracy, to another creed as was the case in Sumatra. The efflorescence of art that took place directly after the arrival of the new dynasty and the introduction of the new script can only be explained by the fact that at this time a new wave of immigration spread over Indonesia and especially over Java. This alone would explain the purity of the sculpture and architecture in which the classic models of India are meticulously followed.

The new dynasty is known as that of the Shailendra. In later years it also ruled in Shrivijaya. For a long time historians explained its development as a conquest of Java by the princes of that Sumatran kingdom. This seems highly improbable. Sumatra has no monumental works of architecture like those built in Java during the Shailendra period. In Sumatra the Old-Malay tongue had already superseded the Sanskrit. The new script [35] remained limited to central Java and to this particular period. The only explanation for the presence of the Shailendra in Sumatra is that the dynasty was transplanted to that island, perhaps through a royal marriage, shortly before it was overthrown in Java.

Greatest of all monuments of the Shailendra period (between 760 and 860) is the Borobudur. This monument, situated not far from the present city of Djocjakarta, covers the upper part of a hill which has been shaped into a series of terraces. The floors and retaining walls of the terraces have been faced with stone. The top of the hill has been flattened and thus made to look like the flat roof of an enormous building. On the center of this "roof" there stands a "stupa" containing, or supposed to contain, a statue of Buddha. Around this central statue there are numerous smaller stupas of stone fretwork in which are found statues of Dhyani-Buddhas. The walls of the terraces are covered with sculptures.[36]

[35] The pre-Nagari script from which the Nagari, still used in India, developed.

[36] The Borobudur itself is an enormous *stupa,* a type of massive stone monument which the Indians erected on the sacred spots the Buddha had passed during his earthly life. These stupas were also used as shrines for reliquaries. A stupa always has a rectangular base. On top of this a half globe is constructed which in its turn is crowned by a *pajong,* the sunshade which in India indicates royal rank. The Borobudur is probably a shrine, but the relics may well be buried inside the hill where they are safe from all sacrilegious attempts to remove them.

The monument is also a *mandala,* i.e., a magic mystic representation of the universe. For this see P. Mus, in *Bulletin de l'École Francaise de l'Extrême Orient,* XXXII (1932), 267 sq., and H. Zimmer, *Kunstform und Yoga* (Berlin, 1926). See next note.

The Borobudur has been cleaned of all vegetation that grew on it in the course of the centuries. Some parts are in ruins and a number of statues have been removed to be put in museums or even to be presented to foreign princes, as happened when the king

The building is so enormous that the construction must have taken at least ten years. The artists remain nameless, of course, but from their work it is perfectly clear that they followed definite models brought over from India. Each set of reliefs illustrates a story connected with Buddhist tradition, and the literary sources for this, too, came from India. There are no fewer than four hundred statues, and fourteen hundred sculptures in relief adorn the walls of the terraces.

The sculptures are a textbook in stone of Mahayana doctrine. The lowest wall of the sanctuary displays gruesome stories of hell and of the sufferings of a life outside salvation. Then the Buddha comes as a savior and in the guise of a white elephant approaches his future mother. He is born as the prince Siddartha, who also is called Gautama. He is the son of the Queen Maya and from the moment of his birth he is in full possession of all his faculties. He goes humbly to school with other children, even though he knows more than his teachers. As a young man he surpasses all his comrades in strength. A picture of the Borobudur shows him grasping the tail of a dead elephant with his toe and throwing the huge body over seven walls. Gopa, the proud princess who alone of all girls could sustain the light from his eyes, becomes his wife. Prince Gautama rejoices in life but is miraculously preserved from all evil because he is the Bodhisattva, he who is going to be a Buddha. The sight of old age, of sickness and death make him give thought to salvation. A monk shows him the way to follow, but his father, the king, who notices his preoccupation, surrounds him day and night with joy and music. However, the prince had understood the baseness of sensuality, revealed to him in his harem of 84,000 women. His decision is taken, and with the help of the gods he escapes to begin a new life. Living in abstinence and meditation the Bodhisattva finally attains the bodhi, the real and only wisdom, and becomes a Buddha. He goes to Benares and there starts "turning the wheel of the law," that is, teaching his dogma.

The story of the Buddha's life prepared the pilgrim to realize the ephemeralness of earthly life. Fortified by the example of the great teacher he studied the stories of Gautama's former lives in which the Bodhisattva prepared to become a Buddha, for, according to Buddhist belief, the soul is reborn as many times as is necessary to obtain perfec-

---

of Siam visited Java in 1896. Numerous studies on the Borobudur have been published. The main work is N. J. Krom, *Barabudur, Archeological Description*, 2 vols. (The Hague, 1927). For a list of literature up to 1926, see Krom, IHJK, I, 39, to which must be added: "Bahadur Chand Shastri, the identification of the first sixteen reliefs on the second main wall of Barabudur," in BKI, LXXXIX (1932), 73 sq.

RELIEFS OF THE BOROBUDUR

tion. Hence the Borobudur depicts the virtues practiced by the Bodhisattva in his former lives and those which will be practiced by the future Bodhisattvas.

As long as the pilgrim walked from terrace to terrace on the lower levels, he was surrounded by an abundance of sculptures and decorations suggesting the amenities of earthly life. As soon as he stepped onto the circular terraces above — three circular terraces form the upper section of the building while the four lower ones are rectangular — he found himself suddenly in another world. Here the serene simplicity of the supernatural rules, here are no ornaments and no sculptures. In closed ranks the Dhyani Buddhas are meditating. Each statue is protected by a simple open stupa. On the highest terrace of all rises a single enormous stupa, enclosing — invisible to the human eye — that which stands for the Buddha himself — empty space — for the Buddha is the beginning, the center, and the end of all life.[37]

Not far from the Borobudur are other religious buildings of the same period, among them the Tjandi Mendut, a temple of perfect architecture with a huge but wonderful statue of the Buddha. The kings of the Shailendra dynasty must have been true patrons of the arts, in contrast to the kings of Shrivijaya, whose fleets in the same period plundered the coasts of southeastern Asia.

Kaling was not the only kingdom in Java. There was another one in eastern Java, and it may well be that the royal successors of the Shivaitic Sanjaya, driven from central Java by the invasion of the Buddhists from Bengal, had found refuge in that region of the island. It seems well established that it was a king of eastern Java who after the downfall of the Shailendra took possession again of central Java. With the return of these kings, Shivaism also returned.

The Shailendra period is that of the purest Indian art that ever existed in Java. Later, Indonesian elements came more and more to the fore. This development was already apparent in literature during the Shailendra period. One of the princes of this royal house ordered the translation of the Sanskrit poem *Amaramala* into the native tongue of Java. Unfortunately this poem survives only in a very corrupt form. The bilingual culture of the Javanese upper class in this period is fur-

[37] The stupa on top now contains a statue of Buddha which does not belong there. Apparently an obliging Javanese district ruler, expecting a group of European archeologists for the exploration of the monument, put the statue in to spare his guests a disappointment. See Krom, IHJK, I, 392. If we include the hidden (buried) structural base with its reliefs picturing the effect of Karma and the large stupa on the top, there are *ten* terraces which correspond with the ten *bhumis* or stages of the spiritual path of the Bodhisattva.

ther attested by the Sanskrit–Old-Javanese glossary which was added to the translation.[38] The upper class already spoke Javanese but still studied the Sanskrit as the mother tongue of their civilization.

Between the fifth and the ninth century there were two centers of Hindu-Indonesian civilization, Palembang and central Java. In the following period central Java dropped back into obscurity and was replaced by East Java.

[38] See Kern, *Verspreide Geschriften*, IX, 273 sq., and H. H. Juynboll, *Supplement catalogus van Javaansche en Madoereesche handschriften te Leiden*, vol. I (Leiden, 1907).

CHAPTER II

THE MEDIEVAL PERIOD OF INDONESIAN HISTORY

NEAR Prambanan, on the boundary between the present principalities of Djocjakarta and Surakarta and not far from the ruins of the Buddhist temples of the Shailendra period, an enormous complex of more recent temple ruins has been found. In one of these buildings, a statue is preserved. It is the statue of Durga, the "unapproachable," the goddess who is one of the personifications of Devi, the consort of Shiva.

The natives no longer know the significance of this statue. They have given it the name of "Lara Djonggrang," "slender maiden," and have connected it with the legend of a princess changed into stone by the curse of a rejected lover. In spite of the ignorance of the modern natives and of the fact that all Javanese now profess the Islamitic faith, the centuries-old veneration of the statue continues. The simple Javanese people go to the ruins to offer money, fruit, and flowers to the goddess. Professor Krom, the most distinguished student of Hindu-Javanese history, once noticed that two goats were brought to the temple by a farmer as an offering.[1] This farmer certainly was unaware that more than ten centuries ago the goat had been a favorite sacrificial animal for offering to Durga and that he, a Moslem, was following an old Hindu rite practiced by his ancestors.

The whole complex of buildings is now known by the name of Lara Djonggrang. In ancient times it was surrounded by an outer wall of irregular construction enclosing an area about 1200 feet square. Inside this outer wall another wall included a square measuring 700 feet on each side. Four entrances facing directly north, west, east, and south led to three terraces each about three feet above the preceding one. On the three terraces, which surrounded another inner square, three rows of small temples were built. Each of these 156 buildings contained a single room of about fifty square feet. Inside the inner square three larger temples stood on the east side and three smaller ones just opposite. The open spaces left on the north and south sides between these two rows of temples were broken by the construction of two little sanctuaries.

[1] Krom, IHJK, I, 444.

The three larger temples were dedicated to the trinity of the Brahmans — Vishnu, Shiva, and Brahma. The three smaller buildings on the west side probably contained the statues of the sacred animals on which the gods were believed to ride. The temples of the gods were decorated with sculptured works representing scenes from the Hindu epic, the *Ramayana*.[2]

What was the purpose of the numerous small temples around the inner square? Each of these has a small pit inside at the center of the floor and in some of these pits ashes and remains of offerings have been discovered. This whole temple complex must have been a huge mausoleum in which the main temple may have served as the tomb for the king while the small temples served for the interment of the dignitaries of the empire and were dedicated to the special gods who protected the separate districts of the state.

The question now arises: of which state and which kings is this the mausoleum? Lara Djonggrang is so near the temples of the Shailendra period that all the buildings, those of the older as well as those of the younger period, must have been built within the precincts of a single city. There are indications, however, that when the more recent temples were built the older part of the city was already decreasing in importance. A royal palace has been discovered among the ruins of the older city, but quite close to it lie quarries from which the materials were drawn for the construction of the mausoleum. This would suggest that at the time of the construction of the mausoleum the palace must have been deserted. The name of the king who built Lara Djonggrang is known, and he calls himself a king of Mataram. We also know that the dynasty to which he belonged was supposed to descend from King Sanjaya, the predecessor of the Shailendras, and once more took up the title of "kings of Mataram," formerly used by that prince. Sanjaya had been Shivaist, and the new dynasty also was Shivaist. This Shivaitic mausoleum of Lara Djonggrang was built near the deserted palace of the Buddhist Shailendra. It probably was constructed at the beginning of the tenth century, that is to say, not more than forty years after the downfall of the Shailendra dynasty.

From all these facts and from the development to come we gather that after the disappearance of the Shailendra, the Shivaist descendants of Sanjaya, who had taken refuge in East Java after the invasion of the Buddhist, have come back to central Java. There is no proof, however, that these political changes were accompanied by violence. No-

[2] See W. F. Stutterheim, *Rama-legenden und Rama-reliefs in Indonesien*, 2 vols. (München, 1927).

where have the buildings been destroyed by fire or deliberately ruined. That the new kings of Mataram came from the eastern part of the island may be deduced from the fact that shortly after the construction of the monuments of Lara Djonggrang the residence of the monarchy was moved to East Java, to the same part of the island where the oldest inscriptions of the new kingdom have been found.[3]

After the withdrawal of the kings of Mataram to East Java, the central part of the island falls back into obscurity. Java was, at that time, still very thinly populated. There was plenty of arable land, and all people who for one reason or another preferred to be in the neighborhood of the kings may have migrated with the court from middle to eastern Java. The first king after the withdrawal of the court to the east was Sindok (around 925). With him a new dynasty is considered to begin, and this dynasty continued to rule until 1222. The history of this period (between the reign of Sindok and his last successor, Kertajaya, 925–1222) is of importance for two reasons. The first is that the transfer of the royal residence to the east caused a further weakening of the Hindu influence in government, religion, and art and a rapid increase in importance of the native Indonesian elements in these affairs. The Hindu element did not receive any considerable reinforcement after that last wave of immigration that had brought the Shailendra and the builders of the Borobudur. In East Java it had always been less strong than in Central Java. From the eleventh century on, the Hindu-Indonesian civilization was definitely more Indonesian than Hindu.

The second reason for the importance of this period is that apparently the kings of East Java paid far more attention to overseas affairs than to those of the island itself. It marks the beginnings of the trade connections of Java with the Moluccas to one side and with Sumatra and the Peninsula to the other. The island of Bali, settled by Hindu immigrants at an early date, now begins to play an important part in Javanese history. Bali seems to have formed part of the East Javanese kingdom, although on Java itself the territory of King Sindok and his next successors extended only over the valley of the Brantas river, west of Surabaya and west and east of the Kawi mountains.

Prominent among the kings of East Java of this dynasty is Dharmavamça (±985 — ±1006). This king is the first historical person of the Indonesian islands of whom we have more than a dim vision. He

[3] For Old-Javanese inscriptions and their translation see "Oud-Javaansche Oorkonden," transcribed by Dr. J. Brandes, edited by Dr. N. J. Krom, in VBG, vol. LX, pts. 1 and 2 (Batavia, 1913); and H. Kern, *Verspreide Geschriften, passim.*

ordered the codification of the Javanese laws and fostered the growth of Javanese literature. He had some of the old Sanskrit texts translated into Javanese and these texts form the oldest prose literature which we possess in that language. Dharmavamça, like other founders of states — such as Alfred the Great and Charlemagne — found his greatest fame in the promotion of learning and social order. Like Charlemagne, who ordered the epics of his people written down in their own language, Dharmavamça saw to it that a Javanese version of the Hindu epic *Mahabharata* was composed. It was a prose version with interpolations of Sanskrit verses. It can hardly be called an important literary work, but as the oldest product of Javanese literature, aside from the charters issued by the chanceries, it is of the greatest interest.[4]

Dharmavamça, like the other empire-builders mentioned, knew how to combine diplomacy and warfare with cultural activity. Under his rule Javanese authority over Bali was established. From that time the princes of Bali began to look toward eastern Java as the petty German princes of the eighteenth century looked toward Paris and began to imitate their more powerful neighbor wherever possible. Even the old Balinese language was banished from their chanceries in favor of the Javanese language.[5]

Dharmavamça also forced a principality on the west coast of Borneo to recognize his overlordship. This state must have been small and weak, for we are told that it possessed only one town. The value of this acquisition was probably strategic, for king Dharmavamça planned a great enterprise, no less than the destruction of the old empire of Shrivijaya and his own supremacy over all the islands.

The Sumatran kingdom under the House of Shailendra had kept control over Sumatra's east coast, over the adjoining islands, and over the Peninsula. It waged successful wars against Cambodja and controlled the South China Sea. To the west it maintained friendly relations with the kingdoms of India.[6] One of the Shailendra kings must actually have held territory in India, for he donated a village near Negapatnam, on the southeast coast of India, to a Buddhist convent. The renown of the kingdom of Shrivijaya reached even the Arabian empire, where it was known as the country from which tin, gold, ivory,

[4] Editions of the *Adiparva* and *Virataparva* by H. H. Juynboll (1906 and 1917), of the *Bishmaparva* by J. Gonda in the *Bibliotheca Javanica*, vols. 7 and 7A (Batavia, 1936 and 1937).

[5] Krom, HJG, p. 226.

[6] Shrivijaya was still Mahayana Buddhist and in regular connection with Bengal. Students from Sumatra went to the university of Nalanda in Bengal, and for their convenience the kings of Shrivijaya founded a students' home in that town.

spices, precious wood, and camphor were traded all over Asia. Even the parrots from the Sumatran forests had the reputation of being particularly clever. An Arabian author of the tenth century noted gravely that the birds were able to speak, if they were taught, Arabic, Persian, Greek, and Hindustani.[7] From the reports of the Arabian and Chinese authors it is evident that in the tenth century Shrivijaya was at the crossroads of important sea lanes. The Arabians themselves probably never visited Sumatra in these times, but they traded in the ports of India's west coast, where the district of Gujerat with its great city of Cambay, already prominent in the time of Ptolemy, became once more prominent. The merchants of Gujerat made trading voyages to Sumatra and even as far as Canton in China. To get a clear picture of their widespread activities one must remember that after they had accepted the Mohammedan religion they were referred to indiscriminately by historians as Gujerats and as Arabs.[8] While Cambay was the great western port of this trade movement, Canton was the eastern port. In 971, when order and peace had been restored in China by the first emperor of the Sung dynasty, the port of Canton was opened for the traders from the south, and among those who used to frequent it were men from Kedah on the Peninsula, from Java, West Borneo, the Philippines, and Shrivijaya.[9]

The power of King Dharmavamça of East Java seems negligible if compared to that of his rival in Palembang. Nevertheless, Dharmavamça decided to subjugate Palembang. In a furious onslaught he carried the war into the central part of that Sumatran empire and for several years during the last decade of the tenth century the throne of Shrivijaya was in constant danger of being overthrown. We know no details, but Dharmavamça's attack must have been beaten off, and Shrivijaya's retaliation, though delayed, was merciless. Its army, reinforced by its vassals from the Peninsula, swept over Java, took the capital, and set fire to the *Kraton*, the royal palace.

After the death of Dharmavamça the power of the Javanese kingdom

[7] Reported by Ibn-al-Fakih (902). For all reports on the East Indies in Arabian and Persian sources, see Gabr. Ferrand, *Relations de voyages et textes géographiques arabes, persanes et turques relatifs à l'Extrême Orient du VIIme au XVIIIme siècles*, 2 vols. (Paris 1913–1914). The report of Ibn-al-Fakih quoted above may be found in vol. I, p. 56.

[8] On the terms "Arabic" and "Arabians" in early Indonesian history see C. Snouck Hurgronje, *Arabië en Oost Indië*, Oration at the University of Leyden (Leiden, 1907), p. 13.

[9] On trade relations between China and the East Indies see W. W. Rockhill, "Notes on the Relations and Trade of China with the Eastern Archipelago and the Coast of the Indian Ocean during the Fourteenth Century," in the periodical *T'oung Pao*, vols. XV and XVI (1914 and 1915).

was crushed and the various local potentates made themselves supreme in their districts. The empire appeared to have disintegrated and the old realm of Shrivijaya, now for the first time called Sumatra, appeared to be the dominant power in the islands.[10] The House of Shailendra, however, was showing its old splendor for the last time. In the first quarter of the eleventh century it became the center of the Northern Church of Buddhism. Buddhism had already lost ground in India and had been persecuted in China. Palembang became its last refuge, and the head priest of that kingdom its ranking scholar. Disciples from many parts of Asia now came to study on the banks of the Musi river, and among these students was Atisha, who founded a reformed Buddhist church in Tibet. The kingdom of Shrivijaya seemed prospering, but disaster struck suddenly.

A daring king from India's east coast appeared with a strong fleet on the Musi river. He attacked the unprepared kingdom, seized the city, captured the king, and looted his treasures. The conquest was carried out in perfect *blitzkrieg* style. Moving rapidly to the north the invader took Malayu and from there sailed to the Peninsula, where such terror had fallen upon the vassals of Shrivijaya that all capitulated with hardly a show of resistance. The brief occupation of Atjeh, on Sumatra's northern point, and a looting expedition to the Nicobar Islands on the way home, completed the program of invasion.

The House of Shailendra, though struck a staggering blow, survived the disaster and continued to exist for nearly three centuries more, but, even though it managed to extend its authority for a time over the whole island of Sumatra, it never recovered its ancient power. One of the consequences of the weakening of Shrivijaya was the revival of the Javanese kingdom under one of the most remarkable kings of Indonesian history, Airlangga, the son-in-law of the murdered Dharmavamça. This prince has left us, in a long inscription, the story of his amazing adventures. When he came from Bali, where his father was merely a local potentate, and tried to take possession of the throne of Java he naturally was opposed by the local rulers, who preferred the continuation of chaos to vassalage under a strong king.

Airlangga, like King Alfred of England, was obliged to live in hiding in the forests. The long years spent in solitude among the hermits of the woods and mountains were no lost time for the prince, for during

[10] For a discussion of the origin of the name Sumatra and other problems of early Sumatran history, see G. P. Rouffaer in his articles in BKI, vol. LXXIV (1918), "Oudheidkundige Opmerkingen," and vol. LXXVII (1921), "Was Malakka emporium voor 1400 A.D., genaamd Malajoer?"

PRAMBANAN

One of the minor temples of the inner square of the Lara Djonggrang temple group (built *circa* 900 A.D.).

them he gathered physical and moral strength to accomplish his task. To this period of abstinence and exercise in self-control the Javanese ascribed his ultimate success. Self-control practiced in conformance to Brahmanistic teaching naturally strengthened Airlangga's will-power, but to the theologians of Indonesia his experience meant more. They saw in it a period for the accumulation of the secret knowledge and power which they believed present in everything on earth and which finds its highest expression in the conscious use by initiates of the magic force. The use of this higher power was in itself no evil. Evil lay only in the misuse of it. Magic power was believed to be possessed by those persons in whom the gods chose to be reborn. The art of using it could be learned through study and its strength could be augmented by the practicing of asceticism. The practice of the secret doctrines of self-education could make man into superman, and the possession of this power was therefore revealed to all by the success an individual achieved in his own life. Sometimes the magic power ran so strong that it could not be controlled and restricted to the narrow confines of normal life but drove the man who possessed it to defy all recognized rules and laws. Such a man was not considered a criminal; rather his aberrations were accepted as a sign that he needed wider scope for his powers and that possibly it was his destiny to become a leader of men.

At first Airlangga's authority was limited. He ruled only over the district in the neighborhood of Surabaya, and many local potentates resisted his claims to overlordship; but, by making full use of the opportunity offered by Shrivijaya's weakness, Airlangga succeeded in conquering all his enemies and reuniting eastern Java under his rule. Further his ambition did not go. Towards Palembang he took a conciliatory attitude, and the friendship between the kings of Shrivijaya and East Java was sealed by the marriage of the king of Sumatra to a Javanese princess. Although Airlangga's authority did not extend very far, his reputation was so great that less powerful monarchs tried to imitate the magnificence of his court.

West Java had remained a backward country sinces the early days of Hindu immigration. It had not been influenced by the civilization of its eastern neighbor. In Airlangga's time, a king of Sunda (another name for West Java) presents himself in an inscription under a glorious but rather cumbersome name which we give for the reader's edification: *Çri* (prince) *Jayabhupati Jayamanahen Vishnumurtti Samaravijaya Çakalabhuvanamandaleçwaranindita Haro Govardhana Vikramottunggadeva.*[11] Scholars have long discussed the exact significance

[11] Krom, HJG, p. 225.

of all these beautiful titles. The problem has not been wholly solved but it is undeniable that His Majesty's name was very pretentious, for it included claims to territories where quite definitely others had control. The title is actually an imitation — in rather bad taste — of that of his more powerful eastern neighbor and for this reason was even couched in the Javanese instead of the Sundanese tongue. It is amusing to find the name of this mighty king of Sunda in another document among the vassals of Sumatra!

Airlangga's name is connected with the composition of one of the oldest and finest pieces of Javanese literature, the *Arjunavivaha*, a story taken from the old Indian epic the *Mahabharata*. This section of the epic was chosen for Javanese adaptation because it can be interpreted as the story of King Airlangga himself in the allegoric form of the life of the saint Arjuna.[12]

Arjuna was an ascetic who through a long life of seclusion had attained such a degree of spiritual power that the gods themselves asked his assistance in their struggle against an invincible demon. Before they intrusted this tremendous task to him, the gods tested his self-control and asceticism. Arjuna withstood all their temptations, then challenged the demon and destroyed him. The similarity with Airlangga's own early life is obvious. The end of the story had to be changed, however, for in the epic Arjuna was ill rewarded by the gods and subjected to the ignominious humiliation of being changed into a eunuch-dancer at the court of a voluptuous king where he had to endure a new period of trial for thirteen years. This of course did not accord with Airlangga's high position. Moreover, to compare a king who was at the height of power to a dancer and buffoon would have been equivalent to invoking disaster and humiliation upon his head. The proper application of the sacred text of the story was believed to have the power of bringing happiness to the king. This belief was probably the reason for the composition of the epic by the Javanese poets, for by being compared to the great ascetic, Arjuna, the king would come to share in the qualities of the legendary hero just as, if he were compared to a buffoon, he would lose dignity and authority.

So the end of the Arjuna legend was changed in the Javanese version in such a way that the holy man was rewarded by the gods with the highest favors, among which was the privilege of enjoying for six months the company of those same beautiful maidens whose advances

[12] On this epic and its significance, see C. C. Berg, "De Arjunawiwaha, Er-langga's levensloop en bruiloftslied," BKI, XCIX (1938), 19 sq. Also Raden Poerbatjaraka, BKI, LXXXII (1926), 181.

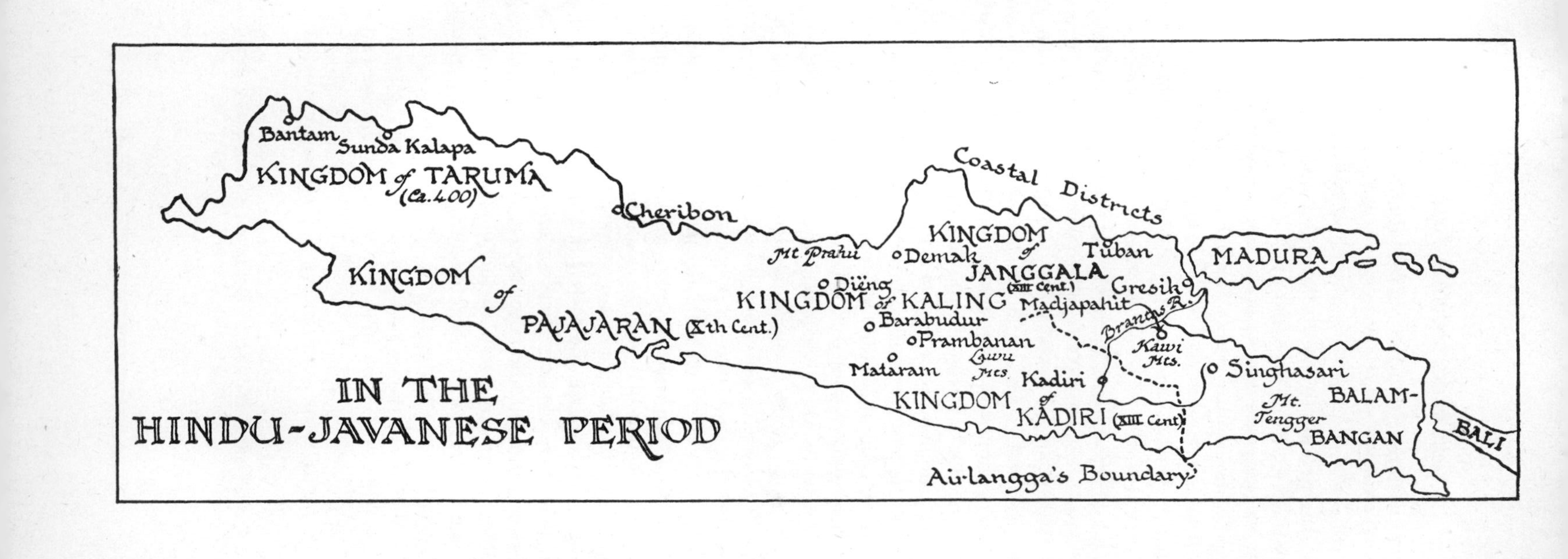
Bantam
Sunda Kalapa
KINGDOM of TARUMA (Ca. 400)
Cheribon
KINGDOM of PAJAJARAN (Xth Cent.)
Coastal Districts
Mt Prahu
Demak
KINGDOM of JANGGALA (XIII Cent.)
Tuban
Gresik
MADURA
Dieng
KINGDOM of KALING
Madjapahit
Brantas R.
Barabudur
Prambanan
Mataram
Luwu Mts.
Kadiri
Kawi Mts.
Singhasari
KINGDOM of KADIRI (XIII Cent.)
Mt. Tengger
BALAM-BANGAN
BALI
Air-langga's Boundary
IN THE HINDU-JAVANESE PERIOD

he had sternly rejected during his period of trial. This, from our point of view, is a rather strange privilege for an ascetic, but in the opinion of the Javanese it was one certain to be accepted in good part.

There is something peculiarly Javanese in the version of the Hindu poem which directs our attention to another interesting aspect of Javanese life. It is apparent from some of the texts that there existed in Airlangga's time another version of the same story that seems to have been used for representation in the Javanese theater, especially for the *Wayang*, the shadow theater.[13] For the theater, the stories taken from the Hindu epics are not merely translated into the Javanese language but are also adapted to the Javanese life and mentality. In the theater the heroes are accompanied by typical Javanese buffoons, whose part in the play is only vaguely indicated in the texts so that there are ample opportunities for the performer to demonstrate his own wit. Later, these Javanese buffoons appear also on the sculptured walls of the temples where the stories of the old Indian heroes are depicted.

The great promoter of the Javanese literature, King Airlangga, never relinquished the idea of returning to a life of solitude. He finally succeeded in freeing himself from many of his royal duties and in taking up again the life of contemplation while retaining his royal rank. The new title found on the inscriptions of this period, "His Majesty the Most Reverend," reveals this combination of spiritual and worldly dignities, the possession of which enabled him to control the ecclesiastical as well as the temporal affairs of his kingdom.

The two churches, the Buddhistic and the Shivaitic, had continued to exist side by side in perfect peace. We may call them churches, for in both cases the worship of the gods was well organized in definite institutions. Both had priesthoods. The priests of Shivaism formed a class apart in the rigid caste system of that religion. Buddhism does not recognize caste divisions, but its priests and monks were distinguished from the faithful laity by their greater knowledge, which during the slow deterioration of their religion came to mean merely a greater acquaintance with magic formulae. Both priesthoods had ac-

[13] The shadow theater has been the favorite entertainment of the Javanese throughout their history. For whole nights the Javanese villagers will sit and absorb these performances. The plays are given by professional men who chant the story of the heroes to the accompaniment of an orchestra of a special Javanese type, the *gamelan*. The Javanese *wayang* seems to be original Indonesian — see articles of W. H. Rassers in BKI, LXXXI (1925), 311, and LXXXVIII (1931), 317 — but other scholars accept the possibility of introduction from India. According to Rassers the wayang is part of the old ancestor worship of the Indonesians. See also J. Kats, *Het Javaansch tooneel: I. Wajang Poerwa* (Weltevreden, 1923; only one volume published). An older book on the same subject is G. A. J. Hazeu, *Bijdrage tot de kennis van het Javaansch tooneel* (Leiden, 1897).

quired considerable wealth, and whole villages had been granted to the temples, convents, and shrines. These estates destined to the upkeep of the sacred buildings were free from taxes and other onerous obligations. The church could have become such a power as to threaten the authority of the king. This danger was cleverly averted by Airlangga, who brought both priesthoods under government control by appointing royal superintendents and by making the priests themselves royal officials.

At Belahan, about thirty miles south of Surabaya, there have been discovered the ruins of a mausoleum that contains a wonderful statue of the god Vishnu riding his man-eagle Garuda. The mausoleum is the resting place of Airlangga's ashes and the statue is probably a portrait of this remarkable man. The veneration in which the king was held by his people is attested by the fact that the statue that represents him has the attributes of Vishnu, the god of Life and Light.

King Airlangga had brought the Javanese state to new life, but in spite of that his name was often cursed by his successors, who were driven to the use of the most demoniac devices to restore what he had broken by making a wrong use of secret knowledge. It is an historical fact that after Airlangga's death (1045?) the unity of the East Javanese kingdom was destroyed. According to the Javanese chronicles the king himself had decided to divide his realm between his two sons. The chronicles say that the king ordered a wise monk named Bharada, who was said to be so well versed in the forces of the supernatural world that he could fly through the air, to draw the boundaries between the two parts. Counter-magic hindered the completion of the monk's work, but the curse of division and eternal strife had been laid upon the country.[14]

The division of the realm is said to have taken place in 1041, and the two parts of the kingdom are known in Javanese history as the kingdoms of Kadiri (or Daha) and of Janggala. The latter rapidly fell apart and is of little importance. Kadiri, however, must have been an important state, although we are very poorly informed about its internal history. In the Javanese legends the kingdom of Kadiri appears as the ideal realm of chivalry, like King Arthur's realm in European legends. Of all its kings, King Jayabhaya (1130–1160) is best remembered because tradition attributes to him the prophecies about Java's downfall and future greatness that still circulate among the people. There is no proof whatsoever that these prophecies have anything to do with the

[14] For an explanation of this legend and of its significance for Javanese history, see C. C. Berg in his "Javaansche Geschiedschrijving," Stapel, *Gesch.* II, 34.

historic King Jayabhaya.[15] This king has another claim on our gratitude, however, because of his service to literature. He ordered the composing of the *Bharatayuddha*, a translation of a part of the *Mahabharata* into Javanese. The poet was not content with a mere translation but rewrote the whole epic, transposing its story into Javanese surroundings and adapting it to Javanese customs and mentality. As the *Brata-Juda* it is still one of the popular literary works of Java.

Kadiri must have rapidly developed into a sea power of the first rank. It is reported to have controlled Bali and several others of the Lesser Sunda Islands and to have exercised sovereignty over the southwestern coast of Borneo and the southern part of Celebes. Thus, a second empire of the seas came into being besides the Sumatran kingdom of Shrivijaya. For the time being, both powers had their sphere of influence, and between them only a kingdom in West Borneo remained as an independent power of some significance.

This development of Kadiri's naval power was related to a change in the general situation of the archipelago in the twelfth century. Commerce was developing quickly. A growing number of traders came from the west and visited the islands, either to buy pepper, spices, and precious wood or to rest before continuing their trip from the archipelago to China. Many of these traders were Mohammedans, and to the Chinese all Mohammedans were Arabs. Thus came into existence the accounts of extensive Arabian shipping and trading all over southern and eastern Asia. In reality, there were very few, if any, natives of Arabia among these traders. An isolated tombstone found in Leran, not far from Surabaya, reveals in an inscription in Arabic letters that there a young Islamitic woman had been buried in the year 1102, but this is no proof that she was Arabian by birth or even by descent.[16] The Arabic language is the ritual language for all Mohammedans, just as the Latin is for the Roman Catholic Church. Hence, the use of Arabic on a tombstone indicates only that there a follower of the prophet is buried, nothing else. The Mohammedans who came to the Indies and China in the twelfth century were from Hindustan, where the city of Cambay in Gujerat still maintained its tradition as a shipping center. From the ninth century on, commerce had brought a number of Persian merchants to Gujerat. In this manner Islam had been introduced and by the thirteenth century had gained the upper

[15] On King Jayabhaya and his prophecies, often quoted in our days because they foretold "a short period of domination by people of a yellow race," see G. W. Drewes, *Drie Javaansche Goeroe's* (Leiden, 1925).

[16] On this inscription, see P. Ravaisse, "L'Inscription coufique de Léran à Java," TBG, LXV (1925), 668 sq.

hand in that part of India. These Gujerats made more and more frequent calls at Indonesian ports. The spices from the Moluccas thus found an ever expanding market, for they were brought in great quantities to Europe via Egypt and Venice.

Through this revival of commerce, even the old kingdom of Shrivijaya seemed to gain new strength. Its fleets appeared off the coast of Ceylon and Madagascar, where its sailors found, to their great amazement, tribes whose language they could more or less understand.[17] These far-flung expeditions might be called piratical as well as commercial. Actually there was little difference, since piracy was only another way of acquiring the goods wanted for sale at home. The more neglected parts of Sumatra and Java also participated in the general prosperity. The territories on both sides of Sunda Strait began to gain importance as producers of pepper, which became an increasingly important merchandise. Indeed for centuries pepper remained the main product of Indonesia, and the pepper trade was at the base of the prosperity of Venice, as well as that of the Dutch East India Company.

Since the Moluccas were the main producers of spices, they soon became a place of political importance. Until the twelfth century they had taken practically no part in the affairs of Indonesia, for the original inhabitants of the Moluccas knew little about the market value of the clove and nutmeg that grew abundantly on the steep hillsides of the volcanic islands. The Chinese and Arabs had some information about these islands but never visited them before the fifteenth century. Finally sailors and traders came from other islands to collect the clove and nutmeg. Some of these people settled along the coasts, and the primitive inhabitants withdrew into the interior after some disagreeable experiences with the shrewd and hardfisted newcomers.[18] In the new settlements, the richest merchant automatically became the leader, and after a while such a leader took the title of raja or king. Before the twelfth century no political organizations existed on the Moluccas, and it is probable that the rise of the first local government was closely connected with the extension of Javanese shipping to the islands, for from the beginning of Moluccan history its first state, the kingdom of Ternate, was a vassal state of one of the Javanese kingdoms.

The period of the Javanese Middle Ages, as we may call the years between 1045 and 1222, ended with the downfall of the kingdom of

[17] According to Edrisi, as quoted by G. Ferrand, *Relations*, I, 173.

[18] We have no historical records of the foundation of the kingdom of Ternate but may suppose that the development was analogous to that in other parts of the archipelago, where a similar situation existed in historic times.

Kadiri and the reuniting of East Java into one state. The story of these events is told in one of the most important historic documents of Java we have, the *Pararaton* or the Book of Kings.[19] This book was composed in four different periods, and it is therefore somewhat incoherent in composition. Some parts of the narrative are very explicit and detailed, while other parts are only dry summaries of events. The first chapters tell the story of Angrok, the founder of the kingdom of Singhasari. This place, Singhasari, now a little village, is situated north of Malang on that part of the island where Java narrows considerably to form its eastern peninsula. To the east and the west of the village are high mountains. Between the mountains is the valley of Malang, formed by the river Brantas, which flows directly south between the gigantic Tengger massif to the east and the high Kawi mountains to the west. When the river nears the south coast, it turns suddenly west and then north and, circling around the Kawi, forms in this way, west of the mountain, a second larger valley in which Kadiri is situated. The river finally flows into the sea through an enormous delta opposite the island of Madura. The fertile valley of the Brantas is now one of the most densely populated districts on earth, and Surabaya at the mouth of the river is one of the most important trading ports of the Indies. The two valleys of Kadiri and Malang were respectively the centers of the two successor states, Kadiri and Janggala, created by Airlangga's division of the realm.

The Book of Kings tells us in great detail the story of Angrok, who succeeded in reuniting most of the two states. It is a strange story.

[19] Edited by J. Brandes in VBG, vol. XLIX (1896) and, in a second revised edition, by N. J. Krom, VBG, LXII (1920). Krom discusses the composition of the *Pararaton* in the first chapter of his *Hindoe-Javaansche Geschiedenis*. He distinguishes four parts which have been combined into one chronicle, namely: (1) the history of Angrok, the first king of Singhasari; (2) a chronicle of the kings of Singhasari and Madjapahit; (3) two romantic stories on the foundation of the empire of Madjapahit (the story of prince Vijaya and of Gajah Mada); (4) notes on the royal family of Madjapahit taken from official records. In its present form the *Pararaton* was composed some time after 1481, but several parts date from the middle of the fourteenth century. The language is medieval Javanese, which is already distinct from the Old-Javanese.

Compare, however, C. C. Berg's discussion of the basic ideas of Javanese historiography and their application in the composition of the *Pararaton*, in Stapel, *Gesch*, II, 15 sq. Berg explains that historiography, like poetry and drama, was a literary means of conjuring the spiritual forces of the ancestors and of the past for the benefit of the living generation. From this point of view he explains the omissions in the chronicles and the predilection shown by the chroniclers for certain kings and facts. See C. C. Berg, "Een vleugje licht in een duister verhaal," BKI, XCVIII (1939), 1 sq.; *id.*, "Opmerkingen over de chronologie van de oudste geschiedenis van Madjapahit," BKI, XCVII (1938), 135 sq., and Raden Poerbatjaraka, *De dood van Raden Wijaya, den eersten koning en stichter van Madjapahit* (Leiden, 1926). For Krom's researches, see TBG, LX (1921), 86 sq.

Once a criminal who lived in Singhasari offered himself for sacrifice to the gods, hoping to secure through their favor a rebirth into a better position in life. The gods granted his wishes. Brahma became his father by a peasant woman, Shiva adopted him as a son, and Vishnu was incarnated in his body. His name was Angrok, which means "He who upsets everything." The young man started on a career of crime. He committed theft, murder, rape, and every sort of violence, not out of baseness of mind, but because the magic power received from the gods ran too strong in him to be controlled. He had to find an outlet for his superhuman strength; the laws of men were not made for him. The Brahmans understood his true nature and taught him how to use supernatural forces, in which he became a master. When he fell in love with the queen of Singhasari, he obviously had the right to eliminate the king. Queen Dedes was herself a woman of such spiritual energy that only a man like Angrok would be the right partner for her. Nevertheless, this lawbreaker-by-divine-inspiration saw fit to ask the advice of the Brahmans, who became somewhat embarrassed, for they had to combine their respect for the law with their adoration of this great magician. One of them found a wonderful answer. "Angrok, my son," he said, "a Brahman may not approve of your plan to kill another man and take his wife, but do as you think best. Be on your guard for the king is strong. Choose a good sword. Go to my friend Gandring, the smith. With a sword made by him, you won't need to stab twice." The advice was plain enough. Angrok went to the smith, ordered a sword, and, irritated because the smith was a bit slow, tried out his new weapon on its maker. Dying, Gandring put a curse on the sword. "Through this sword you shall die, you, your children, and your children's children. Seven kings shall die by this single sword."

Frightened by this prophecy, Angrok decided that he would pour favors and wealth upon the smith's family as soon as he became king. He hoped thus to soothe the anger of the murdered man's spirit and to preserve his dynasty — a laudable purpose for a son of the gods — but he did not succeed.

He showed himself a clever murderer, for he lent his new weapon to a friend, who was very proud of it and showed it everywhere. Then he took it secretly away, killed the king, and left the sword in the body. The friend was executed as the murderer, while Angrok married the queen and ascended the throne. This is a bad record for a man whose memory was presented to the people for veneration as that of the savior of the state. But perhaps there is some underlying truth in the story.

The new king, although probably of humble origin, was pure Javanese in descent, without a single drop of Hindu blood in his veins. He could not look back upon generations of noble ancestors, therefore the story gave him gods for parents. Moreover, his ascent to the throne marked a reaction against the earlier state of affairs. The very name Angrok, "He who upsets everything," is historically apt. Before his time, the descendants of the Hindu immigrants had formed the upper classes, to which the Indonesians gradually obtained access. With ascent to the throne this process was suddenly completed.

Such a usurper — history offers many such examples — once he has upset everything in his path, is always careful in dealing with established institutions. Having no traditions himself, he needs the coöperation of those who have. Napoleon Bonaparte, for example, was careful to secure the help of the Church and of the aristocracy in France after the Revolution had made him dictator. Angrok's tactics were the same, for he sought the support of the Buddhist and Shivaitic clergy. He then recognized their rights and ensured their incomes so that magic power on the one hand and vested interests on the other coöperated very efficiently.

His neighbor, the king of Kadiri, was not so clever. This king, Kertajaya, tried to emulate Angrok in his manifestations of supernatural power. As soon as he had become sufficiently experienced in the art, he demanded that the priests of his realm should offer him the *sembah*, or high salute, which is made only by vassals to their sovereign. In other words, King Kertajaya fomented a quarrel between church and state. The clergy of both sects asserted their ancient privileges and refused this request. Kertajaya then tried to cow them into submission by exhibiting some of his magic tricks, such as appearing with four arms and three eyes like Shiva, or sitting on the sharp point of a spear. But the monks knew a good deal about those things themselves and were not impressed. They fled to King Angrok and implored his help, which was, of course, just what that adventurer wanted. He immediately began a "holy war." As a defender of the rights of the clergy, he found wide support. Nevertheless, the decisive battle was bitterly contested. Even the sober words of the chronicle recall the fury of the fighting. Kadiri was defeated (1222). Its king, despairing of the efficiency of his magic force, committed suicide. His pages then killed his horse and themselves, that they might follow their master into the other world and serve him there. Thus King Angrok came to rule over both states, and the unity of the greater part of the nation was restored. The conquest of the remaining parts of Janggala — Singhasari being only one of its districts — followed. The magic force of Bharada, the divider, was excelled by the greater power of Angrok, the restorer. After that, his name as king was "Rajasa," "Conqueror," or "Amurva-bhumi," "He who gives form to the world."

However, neither glory nor power could save Rajasa from his doom. His stepson, the child of Queen Dedes and the murdered king, discovered who had killed his father. He got hold of the sword that had been cursed by Gandring and gave it to a friend who with it slew the king. The ungrateful prince then used the sword to strike down his friend.

The new prince knew that violent death also awaited him. Of course it would have been useless — in the Javanese conception — to try to destroy the magic weapon; this would only have hastened his death. First, he fought with fate; afterwards he resigned himself to it, gave up all precautions, and himself handed the sword to the man who was destined to be both his murderer and his successor. Three kings had now died by the same weapon, while the violent deaths of four more princes of Singhasari had been predicted. In blood and fire the realm had been founded, and in blood and fire it was destroyed.

Such is the dramatic story of this kingdom, as told by Javanese historians. The records show that Singhasari must have been rich and that some of the wealth of the spice islands and of the west-east trading movement of southern Asia must have flowed into the royal treasuries. A statue, apparently representing the goddess Prajnaparamita, deity of highest wisdom, is in reality a portrait of Queen Dedes, the wife of King Angrok. The queen's strong features and the characteristic lines of her mouth — just a trifle derisive — make it difficult for us to believe that she played the passive and rather subservient role in Angrok's story which the Book of Kings ascribes to her.[20]

The remains of two temples near the capital show the last examples of the classic style of Hindu-Javanese art. One of these is of exceptional construction. It is a tower temple of several stories in height, but it never was completed. The ornamental decoration had just been started, when for some unknown reason the work was stopped. The cause may have been the death of the king who ordered the construction or the sudden catastrophe which befell the kingdom of Singhasari.

These monuments show that there had been a new development in Javanese art. The style is the same as of old, but a new spirit breathes through it, for King Angrok's ascent to the throne had allowed the native element to come to the fore at the expense of the Hindu style.

[20] A reproduction of the statue in Krom's IHJK, deel III, plate 54.

This does not mean that there took place a degradation of the art, but rather the contrary. The simplicity and beautiful harmony of the older constructions are somewhat lacking, but the richness and delicacy of the decoration have improved. It has become more elaborate and is more skillfully executed. The sculptures show a direct influence of original Javanese models and ideas. In the reliefs of the Tjandi Dago — the burial temple of another of the Singhasari kings — the heroes are always followed by their servants and buffoons, plump, distorted and ridiculous-looking creatures, types we know from the Wayang. Through these details we note the gradual transformation of Hindu models into Javanese forms.

The difference between Buddhism and Shivaism disappeared more and more. Buddha, the Dhyani-Buddhas, the Bodhisatvas, and their female companions are like Shiva, his companions and his wives and daughters, the personifications of the divine and magic powers of nature. The sculptures of the Tjandi Dago set forth a series of stories which had very little to do any more with the original Buddhist beliefs. If it were not for the statues of the gods, we should not recognize it as a Buddhist temple. It became quite customary for the kings to have their ashes divided between a Shivaitic and Buddhist mausoleum. In this way, they satisfied the clergy of both churches and made sure of the other world in both directions. They would never have shown themselves so impartial if they had been cognizant of a real difference between the two religions. The last king of Singhasari, Kertanagara, simplified matters by bringing both religions together in one building. The lower floor was dedicated to Shiva and the upper floor to Buddha. The only floor that was accessible to the public was the lower one. Does this indicate that Buddhism was still the religion of a limited group?

The last king of Singhasari, Kertanagara (1268–1292), was known as a man initiated in the most secret knowledge.[21] The *Pararaton* has little to say about him, except that he was a drunkard and that he loved palm wine above everything else. The wine caused his downfall, the chronicle says, for he was surprised and killed by his enemies during one of his orgies. The blame for his death was laid upon his chancellor, who is said to have encouraged the king to indulge his vices. He later shared the fate of his master, but was lucky enough to have a chance to die as a man, sword in hand on the battlefield. There are other sources concerning the reign of this king and they tell a quite different

[21] For Kertanagara, see Berg's comparison between the two medieval Javanese chronicles describing his reign, the *Pararaton* and the *Nagarakertagama* ("Javaansche geschiedschrijving," Stapel, *Gesch.* II, 26 sq. and 65 sq.).

story. One of them is the *Nagarakertagama*, a poem in praise of King Hayam Wuruk, composed in 1365 by the head of the Buddhist clergy, Prapanca. It is panegyric, but contains invaluable information on the religious and social conditions during the last part of the Hindu period in Java.[22] The author of this poem has a totally different view of King Kertanagara and has nothing but praise for him, calling him a saint and an ascetic, free from all passion. He does not deny that the king drank a good deal of palm wine, but explains that drinking was part of his duty.

There must be some truth in the story of the priest Prapanca. It is impossible that King Kertanagara was nothing but a drunkard. His armies conquered a great part of the archipelago, and he prepared the way for Java's hegemony over all the islands. In his ambition to conquer far-away countries, he may have overlooked danger lurking nearer home, but it was not a matter of sheer negligence and profligacy. King Kertanagara believed still more than his predecessors in the power of magic. He was so interested in spiritual affairs that he studied the philosophy and theology of Buddhism thoroughly and himself composed a book on religious institutions. Buddhism seems to have attracted his interest more than Shivaism, and he devoted most of his time to that special type of Buddhism which deals with magic and demons. The adherents of this sect believed that the world was passing through the worst of all periods. Demoniac powers were rampant and had to be conjured. Where contemplation failed, ecstasy alone could succeed in bringing forth such energy as might conquer the forces from hell. Physically and psychically, human nature had to expand beyond its normal limits. Alcohol and sexual excesses might break the narrow limits of normal life and make the body capable of necessary psychic exertions. Thus, in the view of this perverted Buddhism, drinking and profligacy were not sins, but virtues. King Kertanagara followed the rules of this "ascetic system," which may be summarized as indulgence in vice without inner passions. The orgies that shocked the chronicler

[22] The *Nagarakertagama* exists in only one manuscript, discovered on the island of Lombok when in 1894 the Netherlands troops occupied the residence of the chieftains of Tjakranagara. J. Brandes published the original text (in Balinese script) in VBG, vol. LIV (1902). J. H. Kern translated the whole poem and published it in BKI (also in Kern's *Verspreide Geschriften*, vols. VII and VIII). Kern's translation was republished by Krom in 1919 in a separate volume. The poem gives a description of a trip undertaken by King Hayam Wuruk and the places visited by him. Among the descriptions of sanctuaries, festivals and so on, numerous historical references are inserted. See N. J. Krom, "Eenige opmerkingen over den Nagarakertagama," TBG, LXVII (1928), 375 sq. and Raden Ng. Poerbatjaraka, "Aanteekeningen op de Nagarakertagama," BKI, LXXX (1924), 219 sq.

of the Book of Kings were intended to make the king's soul free for his sacred work. He was killed while drinking with his priests and monks, who died with him. This circumstance makes it still more probable that the orgy was actually a religious ceremony.

Kertanagara learned through his studies of the existence of special, perhaps secret, Buddhist sects. Into one of those he was initiated. Strengthened by the magic forces in which he believed, he set out to accomplish the political unification of Java and afterwards of the archipelago. He had succeeded to a fair extent when he was struck down dramatically by a revolution from within. Perhaps it was a revolution against his religious policy, but we do not know.

The whole of Java, even the distant western parts, seems to have recognized his sovereignty. Kertanagara was not afraid of military revolts, but he feared the demoniac forces that might destroy his work of unification. In his mind he identified one of those demons with a personality in the history of Java. This force from hell was none other than the soul of Bharada, King Airlangga's most trusted spiritual adviser. Bharada had been the man who divided Airlangga's kingdom into two separate states, using supernatural force to determine the boundaries. Thus he impersonated the demon of political division. Once Kertanagara had recognized his enemy, he devoted all his energy to suppressing his power. He had his own statue, with the outward appearance of a meditative Buddha, erected on the exact spot where, according to tradition, Bharada had lived. He went carefully through all the ceremonies of conjuring this evil force, and the inscription on the statue tells us that this pious act had been accomplished for the "benefit of the king and the royal family, and the unity of the kingdom." So it represented a direct challenge to the demon of division. The same statue now adorns one of the parks of Surabaya, where the Javanese gave it, in spite of the high veneration in which they hold it, the name of "Djaka Dolog," which means "the fat boy." [23]

In the meantime, events of tremendous importance had taken place in Sumatra. Te senescent empire of Shrivijaya was falling apart. Piratical tribes of the Malay Peninsula had taken over control of the South China and Java Seas. Their daring enterprises took them to the coast of India, where the local princes had the greatest difficulty in beating them back. Their power was not equal to their audacity, and

[23] Raden Ng. Poerbatjaraka, "De inscriptie van het Mahaksobhyabeeld te Simpang (Soerabaya)," BKI, LXXVIII (1922), 426 sq.; and N. J. Krom, in *Mededeelingen Kon. Akademie van Wetenschappen te Amsterdam, afd. Letterkunde*, v, 2 (1917), 306 sq.

in a short while they were brought under the supremacy of the kings of Siam. Kertanagara saw his chance and sent a Javanese force to attack Sumatra by land and sea. The former kingdom of Malayu, north of Palembang, was conquered and reorganized as a vassal state. The Javanese troops penetrated far into the interior and erected at the foot of the mountains a monument that glorified the conquest of Kertanagara. For the first time, the mountain tribes of Sumatra were drawn into the political sphere of the kingdoms on the coast. They organized a state of their own, and their legends contain stories about a defeat which they claim to have inflicted upon the Javanese. This defeat is improbable; on the contrary, it is likely that only through the downfall of Shrivi-jaya and the expeditions from Java did the backward mountain territories get an opportunity to develop into the new state of Menangkabau.[24] Long afterward, when the mountaineers of Sumatra had accepted the Mohammedan religion, they preferred to forget the humble origin of their state and concocted for their kings a wonderful genealogy which made them the descendants of Iskandar — which is the Mohammedan version of Alexander the Great. King Alexander was said to have had three sons whom history does not know, but who became, in the tradition of Menangkabau, respectively the Sultan of Turkey, the Emperor of China, the Maharajah dhi Raja ("great king of kings") of Menangkabau. After that, the tribal chiefs of inner Sumatra used to address the rulers of China and Turkey as their brothers.

The conquest of Malayu was a great success for King Kertanagara. Shortly afterward, he extended his power over southwestern Borneo and some districts of the Peninsula. Bali and several islands of the Moluccas were also conquered. In spite of these great successes, however, the local resistance in Eastern Java continued. The chronicler mentions several "criminals" who were punished by the king. These were, of course, rebellious vassals. One of them finally succeeded in his rebellion. This was the prince of Kadiri, who managed to entice the royal army far from the capital and then surprised the defenseless city and killed the king (1292). The fact that Kertanagara refused to believe all reports concerning the rebellion and went calmly on with his religious orgies suggests that after all he put more earthly passion into the ceremony than was intended by his religious teachers.

This was Kadiri's revenge for the defeat suffered at the hands of

[24] Krom, HJK, p. 333, and ENI, under "Menangkabau, history." Archeological discoveries in this area may bring out many unknown facts.

Angrok, but the success was ephemeral. The armies of Singhasari were still holding the field on Sumatra and Bali and in the northern portions of the island of Java itself. They were ready to return and to restore the kingdom. But the unexpected happened. Great changes were at hand in the islands of Indonesia.

CHAPTER III

GAJAH MADA, FOUNDER OF THE JAVANESE EMPIRE (1331–1364)

THE TIME when the fate of the Indonesian Archipelago could be decided by the Indonesians alone had passed. New rulers were seated upon the throne of the Celestial Empire in Peking. In the second half of the thirteenth century China had been completely conquered by Kublai Khan, the prince of all Mongols. With a new ruler, a new period began in the relations of China with neighboring countries. For centuries, the Chinese emperor had been satisfied by the verbal declarations of respect which had been sent from Burma, Indo-China, and Indonesia. Those declarations had been accompanied by presents consisting largely of products of the islands, from rhinoceroses to parrots and from gold to nutmeg. Kublai Khan desired more from his vassals than token tribute. He asked for actual obedience, and the enormous size of his army enabled him to send military expeditions in all directions. Burma was conquered and devastated, Korea occupied, and Japan threatened with an invasion. The kings of Indo-China saw the storm coming and looked for allies. Kertanagara, king of Singhasari, proud of his magic power and his victorious armies, offered help, but in vain. Indo-China was overrun. Chinese ambassadors came to the court of Singhasari asking for explanations and summoning Kertanagara to appear in person at the Imperial Court in Peking. For years the Javanese king avoided a definite answer to this unpleasant request, but in 1289, when he had exhausted all possible subterfuge, he gave up pretending friendship, arrested the ambassadors, and sent them home with mutilated faces. The Great Khan's fury can easily be imagined, and he swore to punish the outrageous behavior of Singhasari's king.

Why did Kertanagara refuse in such a brutal way? Had he come to the conclusion that the Khan was only bluffing and did not possess the power that he pretended to have? In 1281 an enormous Chinese armada had been annihilated when it attempted the invasion of Japan, and a few years later a Chinese army had been exterminated in Indo-China. Kertanagara had perhaps heard of those defeats, and such defeats may have indicated to him that the Khan lacked the inner strength and magic force which Kertanagara believed himself to possess. It was an omen that the gods were not with the Mongols. Now Kertanagara's brutality left the Khan no choice. He had to send an expedition to vindicate his reputation.

It took several years to prepare the fleet and the army. In 1292 a thousand ships with an army of 20,000 men sailed for the south. The emperor followed modern tactics. He tried to rally the support of Kertanagara's own vassals by proclaiming his friendly feelings towards the people and the country of Java. He made known that he had no other intentions than to punish the king's impertinence. It took the Chinese ships some months to reach Java. When they arrived, they discovered that the king was dead and his power broken.[1]

After Kertanagara's death, chaos reigned in Eastern Java. The crown prince, Vijaya, was deserted by nearly all his vassals and had to flee to Madura. Further escape was impossible, and therefore the young prince submitted to great humiliation. He offered his submission to the murderer of the late king, the prince of Kadiri, and tried to win his favor. In time he received a district on the river Brantas, where he built a village to which the name of Madjapahit (which means "bitter fruit") was given. A Madurese follower of the prince who picked a fruit while working at the new settlement and threw it away because it was too bitter is said to have given the village its name. Prince Vijaya gained slowly a number of secret supporters from the vassals of Kadiri. One of these was a Madurese prince, an arch-conspirator who, through all of the vicissitudes of Javanese politics, managed to serve his own interests in a profitable way. Together they planned to use the Chinese armada for their own purpose, the destruction of Kadiri.[2]

When the generals of the Great Khan arrived at the mouth of the Brantas river and heard of Kertanagara's death, they learned that the successor of this king, Prince Vijaya, would be glad to recognize the emperor's sovereignty but needed the support of the Chinese army to overthrow the usurper, Kadiri. They accepted these proposals. Fleet and army moved upstream, defeated Kadiri's troops, and conquered the capital. In full confidence, the generals spread their troops over the country, which they believed completely subdued. Too late they dis-

[1] The reports of the commanding Chinese generals have been inserted in the official history of the Yuan dynasty and may be found in Groeneveldt's Notes, VBG, XXXIX, 20 sq.

[2] On the story of the foundation of Madjapahit, see the articles of Poerbatjaraka and Berg, quoted in the preceding chapter, and C. C. Berg, "Een nieuwe redaktie van den roman van Raden Wijaya," BKI, LXVIII (1931), 1 sq., and, by the same author, "Opmerkingen over de chronologie van de oudste geschiedenis van Madjapahit," BKI, XCVIII (1938), 135 sq.

covered the treachery of Vijaya, who destroyed several Chinese detachments in surprise attacks and maneuvered the invaders into such an unfavorable position that a withdrawal to the fleet and return to China seemed the only solution. They thought it unwise to take further risks, as the honor of the Great Khan had already been avenged. A permanent occupation had never been their intention. The generals overlooked the fact that now the only result of the expedition was that the son of the man whom they had come to punish had been restored to power. This Chinese intermezzo inaugurated the history of the last and most glorious kingdom of Java, the empire of Madjapahit.

At the very time that the new kingdom was starting on its glorious career, the first signs of its later downfall appeared on the horizon. In the year of Kertanagara's death, the first Europeans appeared in the Indonesian Archipelago — the Venetian Marco Polo, with his father and uncle. Their story is too well known to be repeated here, and forms in reality only a part of the Great Khan's attempts to establish close relations between China and the outer world. The Polos did not come to Indonesia as European traders or missionaries, but as ambassadors of the Khan of Mongolia and China. They saw only the northeastern coast of Sumatra, where they had to stay for a few months while waiting for favorable weather (1292). Marco Polo was disgusted with the uncivilized conditions prevailing among the "cannibals" of the district, but the visit gave him the opportunity to inquire about the geographic and economic conditions on the other islands. His description remains vague and does not differ essentially from older Chinese and Arabic reports, except for one single point which is of the highest importance: he noted that the inhabitants of the little town of Perlàk on the northern tip of Sumatra had been converted to Islam.[3]

It was still the only Islamitic place in the archipelago. Thus, we know exactly when and where the Mohammedan religion entered the East Indies. It started on its course at the same moment as the kingdom of Madjapahit, which it was to destroy two centuries later. The oldest Mohammedan inscription on Sumatra dates from the year 1297, five years after Marco Polo's visit. It exists in the village of Samudra, one hundred miles northwest of Perlàk on the Sumatran coast, and it is the epitaph on the tombstone of the sultan Malik-al-Saleh, the first Mohammedan ruler of that once-famous port. This tombstone gives us an unexpected amount of information about the early Mohammedans of

[3] Marco Polo explicitly states that Islam had been introduced into Sumatra by Mohammedan merchants "who in great numbers frequent these ports," see ed. Yule-Cordier (London, 1903), II, 284.

Indonesia. The stone, with the inscription ready made, was imported from Cambay in India.[4] This trading center had finally been conquered by Mohammedan rulers in the middle of the thirteenth century. It is therefore plausible that merchants from this port were the first propagandists for Islam on Sumatra. This opinion is confirmed by the similarity between the Indian and the Indonesian forms of Mohammedanism. In both cases, Islam was strongly influenced by the Indian tendencies towards mysticism. Here it may be added that only twenty years after the first propagation of Islam, the first missionary of the Catholic Church arrived in Indonesia — the Franciscan Odorico di Pordenone, who traveled all over Asia but never got so far as settling down and beginning the preaching of the gospel. His observations are very superficial and inaccurate and do not add to our knowledge of mediaeval Indonesia.[5]

To these two new elements in Indonesian history — the arrival of the first Europeans and the first successes of Islamitic propaganda — a third must be added. From this period come the oldest reports of definite Chinese settlements on the islands.[6] There was no Chinese immigration in the normal sense of this word, for most of the colonists were shipwrecked sailors. Small islands on the coast of Borneo had been occupied by groups of Chinese soldiers who had been left behind on the expedition of 1293, and a gang of Chinese pirates is mentioned at the same time at the mouth of the Musi river, which once had been the stronghold of Shrivijaya. The Chinese intermarried with native women but passed on their own civilization to their children, who thus remained distinct from the mass of the Indonesian people. Thus the elements that were going to give to the Indies their present outward aspect of civilization, Islam and Chinese and European penetration, were already in existence when the Hindu-Javanese period reached its political summit.

The last efflorescence of Hindu civilization on Java lasted hardly one century. The kingdom of Madjapahit was founded in 1293 by King Vijaya, and it lost its significance with the death of his grandson,

[4] J. P. Moquette, "De eerste vorsten van Samoedra Pase," in *Rapport van den Oudheidkundigen Dienst* (1913), pp. 1 sq. A survey of the introduction of Islam into the Indies is given by R. A. Kern in Stapel, *Gesch.* I, 305–365.

[5] For Odorico's travels, see Yule-Cordier, *Cathay and the Way Thither* (Hakluyt Society, London, 1913), II, 146.

[6] The history of the Chinese immigration into the Indies is still to be written. Some information may be found in W. J. Cator, *The Economic Position of the Chinese in the Netherlands Indies* (Oxford, 1936), while P. J. Veth in his *Borneo's Westerafdeeling*, 2 vols. (Zalt Bommel, 1854–1856) and in his *Java*, second ed., 4 vols. (Haarlem, 1896–1907) gives additional material.

Hayam Wuruk, in 1389. But these kings were not the true founders and rulers of the empire, the history of which is closely connected with the name of Gajah Mada, the *patih* or prime minister of Hayam Wuruk. This man is the most interesting political figure of Javanese history, and there is some reason for honoring his memory even in our day, for he was the first of all to succeed in unifying the whole archipelago under one authority.

Gajah Mada started on his career as an officer of the royal bodyguard. The second king of Madjapahit was a weak man and was continually threatened by revolts. Once he had to flee from his capital and all seemed lost until Gajah Mada saved the situation. He crushed the rebellion amongst the soldiers of the guard and escorted the king to a safe hiding place. Thereupon he himself returned to the camp of the rebels and spread a rumor that the king was dead. After he had carefully studied the reaction of the common soldiers in the rebellious army, he organized a counter-revolution and restored the king to power. Promotion to one of the highest civil offices was the reward for his courageous conduct. In 1331, he ascended to the highest position, that of *patih* or omnipotent prime minister. It was a much diminished empire over which he received control. Southwestern Borneo was the only outlying possession that was left, Sumatra and Bali were lost, and in the eastern peninsula of Java the royal authority was hardly recognized. Against these Javanese rebels Gajah Mada directed his first military expedition. In a short while he returned victorious, and after his return to the court took a solemn oath in the presence of the royal family and high officials that he would never enjoy *palapa* (we do not know whether this is a special type of food or a special type of income) until all islands of the archipelago were subjected to his master, the king. The whole court thought the oath ridiculous and amused itself at the expense of the prime minister. Gajah Mada resented the mockery and derision of the courtiers; from that time, his decision was unalterable: he would conquer all the islands or die. Thus he became the first conscious empire-builder of Indonesia. He managed to keep the confidence of his king and to lead his armies from victory to victory until the desired goal had been practically attained. His work constitutes the real significance of Madjapahit. Never before had the islands been united under one government, nor did this happen again until the Netherlanders completed their conquest.

Gajah Mada considered himself the continuator of the work of King Kertanagara, whose reputation was whitewashed in the *Nagarakertagama*, the official panegyric of the empire. Certainly this literary work could never have been composed without the approval of the omnipotent prime minister. It is noteworthy too that in 1351 he dedicated by order of the king — an order inspired by himself — a temple to the memory of the prime minister and the priests who had died with Kertanagara in the same catastrophe. He even continued the work of the "king magician" in conjuring the demons of division by building a new temple on the old boundary line which formerly had divided the two parts of the realm. It may well be that Gajah Mada shared the religious opinions of Kertanagara, and that he intended to complete the work that had been begun by that prince.[7]

First of all, Bali felt the force of the Javanese army. After that, the minister directed his troops against Sumatra. Military action was supported by diplomatic activity. A young prince of Malayu who lived at the court of Java was taken back to his native country and put on the throne as a vassal of Madjapahit. This young man had learned Gajah Mada's lessons only too well. He extended his dominion from the plains of Sumatra to the mountain districts of Menangkabau and moved his residence to that less accessible territory. As King Adityavarman he ruled practically as an independent prince and laid the base for the future greatness of that kingdom. A number of Hindu ruins in central Sumatra date from his time.

The other districts of central and northern Sumatra considered it wise to follow the example of Menangkabau. They sent embassies to the king of Madjapahit and paid him tribute. In internal affairs, they remained practically independent, but the seas were controlled by the Javanese fleet, which put a check on the ruthless piracy of the Malays. The small Mohammedan kingdoms of the northern point of Sumatra also recognized the Javanese overlordship. This did not, however, interfere with the expansion of the Mohammedan belief from Sumatra's north coast over the Peninsula, a slow but continuous progress.

The expedition to Sumatra brought the coast of Borneo also under Gajah Mada's control, and the Javanese fleets were occupied for a time in chasing Chinese pirates from the west coast of the island. As the reputation of Java began to spread over the islands, the local princes hastened to send embassies and to recognize the authority of that country. The subjection of the "Great East," a term that covers all islands east of Borneo, was easy. Mention is made of an expedition to Sum-

[7] On Gajah Mada, see, besides the books of Krom and Kern's *Nagarakertagama*, the articles of F. M. Schnitger, "Gadjah Mada, Rijksbestierder," in *Nederlandsch Indië, Oud en Nieuw*, XVI (1931–1932), 289 sq., and C. C. Berg, "Arya Tadah and de Gadjah Mada gelofte," BKI, XCVIII (1939), 253 sq.

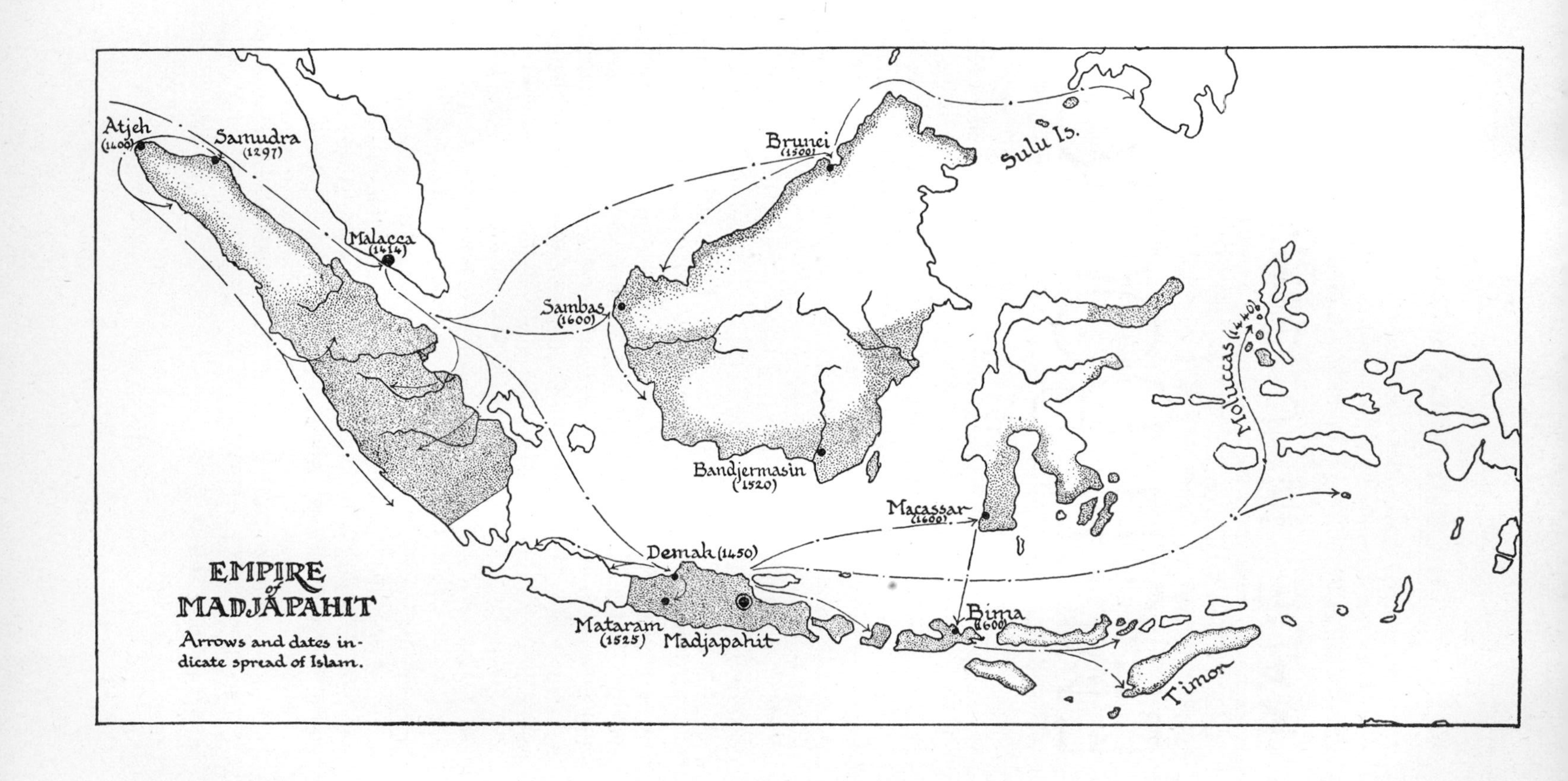
EMPIRE of MADJAPAHIT
Arrows and dates indicate spread of Islam.
Atjeh (1400)
Samudra (1297)
Malacca (1414)
Brunei (1500)
Sulu Is.
Sambas (1600)
Bandjermasin (1520)
Macassar (1600)
Moluccas (1440)
Demak (1450)
Mataram (1525)
Madjapahit
Bima (1600)
Timor

bawa, east of Bali and Lombok. Macassar, on the southern point of Celebes, paid tribute and so did the island of Timor. The princes of the Moluccas, descendants of merchants and adventurers who had come from the western islands, depended on Java for their commerce, and they probably considered it both an advantage and an honor to be recognized as the vassals of the great empire of Madjapahit. It was a justification of their rather dubious royal pretensions. They gave to the Javanese officials a long list of territories which they considered their dependencies, including New Guinea and the far southeastern islands, but their connections with those districts were probably limited to irregular visits of their ships and some desultory trading with the natives.

One of the last territories to come under Java's control was Palembang. A successor state to the empire of Shrivijaya existed here and was conquered by the Javanese in 1377. Vainly the king of Palembang had looked for help from China. Speculating on the centuries-old relations between the two states, he had offered the overlordship of his country to the Chinese emperor, who graciously accepted and sent ambassadors to reinvest him solemnly as king of Shrivijaya. But the embassy from Peking came too late. Its members found Javanese troops already in possession of Palembang, and were ignominiously put to death, an insult which the ruler of the Celestial Empire did not dare or did not care to avenge.

Palembang was not treated in the same way as the other conquests of Java. It was not permitted to continue its existence as a vassal state but was made into a province governed by Javanese elements. The rapid downfall of the city and the complete disappearance of its monuments suggest a deliberate neglect of its interests.

It is difficult to obtain a clear idea of the real organization of the vast Javanese empire. We have a long list of its vassal states transmitted to us by the poet Prapanca. Curiously enough, among them the kingdom of Sunda is not included. Concerning the relations between these states our chronicles tell us a dramatic story which throws an interesting light on Gajah Mada's political views.

The young king, Hayam Wuruk, wished to marry the daughter of the king of Sunda. After some negotiations conducted by the prime minister, an invitation was sent to the king of West Java to come with his daughter to Madjapahit, where the wedding was to be celebrated. With a great number of followers, the king of Sunda arrived at the capital. He camped north of the city on a large field where the noblemen of Madjapahit used to hold their games and tournaments. The

Sundanese were proud that a daughter of their King was to be the official Queen of the mightiest Empire of Indonesia. For them, the wedding meant the inauguration of an alliance between the two kingdoms, in which the poor state of Sunda might share some of the wealth of its eastern neighbor. Then the prime minister, cold and disdainful, stepped in to wreck all their hopes. From the beginning he had been an opponent of thc marriage, which he considered below the dignity of his master. He made the Sundanese understand that he would merely allow them to deliver their princess to the royal harem as a tribute from a vassal king to his overlord. Instead of a wedding, simply a ceremony of acceptance would take place, in which His Majesty, the king of Madjapahit, would graciously agree to accept the princess as one of his many wives.

The Sundanese, proud of their independence, refused. Once more Gajah Mada commanded them to surrender the princess. In the meantime he brought his troops together. Escape was impossible. The noblemen of Sunda preferred death to dishonor, and as further delay would only have made their situation worse, decided to attack at once. Their king was among the first to fall, but his warriors continued the battle, driving back the Javanese several times. Unable to break through the ring of steel that surrounded them, they made at last a desperate assault on Gajah Mada himself and his retinue. This was the end. The old war-lord mercilessly cut his way through the ranks of the Sundanese. None of them escaped. There are two versions of what happened to the princess. The first says that the king married her, but not as his official queen, and that she died shortly afterwards. The other version is given by the romance in which this story still circulates on Java and Bali. This story holds that the princess killed herself on the battlefield beside her father's body. After this massacre, rancor and hostility existed between the two parts of Java, and Sunda never submitted to Gajah Mada's hated authority.[8]

Over the rest of Indonesia the prime minister became the virtual ruler, though the conquest of Palembang was not completed until thirteen years after his death. Gajah Mada enjoyed the privilege of remaining in office until his death, a rare privilege for prime ministers in Oriental kingdoms. There were of course plots to overthrow his regime, but they brought only bad luck to the plotters.

The poet Prapanca has left us a record of all of the possessions of the

[8] The story of the Sundanese princess in romantic form appears in "Kidung Sunda," edited by C. C. Berg in BKI, LXXXIII (1927), 1 sq. (Javanese text with Dutch translation and notes).

empire of Java. The outer districts he calls disdainfully "the rural districts," in contrast to the metropolitan territory of eastern Java. He cannot find enough words of praise for this central part of the empire. The mountains and forests, he says, were as safe for all wanderers as the parks of a city. The list of the "rural districts" given by him is amazingly long. We hear of a number of kingdoms the very existence of which was unknown before. How did those states come into existence? The question is easily answered if we consider what is really meant here by "king" and "state."

There were only a few "kings" in Indonesia, if we take this word in its modern sense. Besides the kingdom of Madjapahit, there were those of Sunda and Malayu. All the other princes and kings were only local chiefs of districts without a definite authority or a well-defined territory. This holds good not only for the Hindu period of Indonesian history, but also for the periods of Portuguese and Dutch domination. Those local chiefs might derive their authority from one of two different sources; either they were originally the headmen of a native tribe that had progressed in culture and wealth, or they were descendants of successful traders. A knowledge of the origin of the two different types of kingdom is highly important for an understanding of the social structure of modern Indonesia. The tribal chiefs of the less-developed groups of the population had about the same right to a royal title as the chiefs of those American Indian tribes who were described as "kings" by the famous Captain John Smith at the beginning of the seventeenth century. A few years ago identical institutions still existed in the interior of Borneo and Celebes. A modern scholar [9] gives the following characterization of these institutions: The head of a village assumes his function by reason of his greater sense of responsibility and his knowledge of the local customs, so that he can give advice on all matters when called upon. He has to be a man of words and deeds who knows how to defend his people and how to lead them in warfare. A few of the younger members of the clan act as his assistants. By the time the head man becomes too old, it is evident who is to be his successor, and the transfer of authority takes place gradually and without difficulty. The head man has no power to force anybody to carry out an

[9] In the book, *The Effect of Western Influence on Native Civilization*, edited under the direction of B. J. Schrieke (Weltevreden, 1929), A. C. Kruyt described the native institutions of the people of Central Celebes before they came into contact with the western world. In the chapter on Borneo, A. W. Nieuwenhuis described the antithesis between the original Dyak population of the interior of the island and the Malay sultanates along the coast, which sultanates may be considered typical for the second type of native kingdom described in the paragraphs above.

order; this is done by the pressure of public opinion. The head man is the incarnation of this opinion, and if anyone does not wish to submit to the will of the community, the only choice left to him is to move to another village. In this way, the community maintains discipline among its members, who are dependent upon one another. They have to respect one another's rights, because there is no place to go when their own group ousts them. Another restraining influence is the fear of black magic. The spirits of the ancestors are watching the community and avenge on the entire group every revolt against tradition. In this way, the clan-members think and do as others have thought and done since time immemorial. Imagine such a community brought into contact with the outside world and the head man transformed into a hereditary chief, but under maintenance of the sacred traditions, and one has a true picture of most of those kingdoms which are mentioned by Prapanca or by the Portuguese and Dutch traders.

The other type of petty king is quite different. The usual story is as follows: A Malayan trader from Sumatra, the Peninsula, or Java comes to one of the less civilized islands. He establishes a trading post on an island off the coast at the mouth of a river or upstream at the junction of several branches of a river. He is much shrewder than the natives; he knows what merchandise the outside world wants, and he secures a monopoly. He collects followers and slaves and organizes a bodyguard, which only too often is merely a gang of criminals. He begins to exact toll from passing ships and to levy tribute from the native tribes, and he fights off all competition. The natives who have the bad luck to fall under his control degenerate into poverty, and probably the descendants of the founder of the state degenerate into profligacy. He among those potentates who manages to gain control over a few other posts becomes a king.

This development accounts for the clear distinction that exists between the inhabitants of the coast of Borneo and the interior. It explains the transformation which took place in the population of the Moluccas. Most of those petty kings had no real power. They hastened to submit to a superior force, especially when submission gave the chance to do some profitable trading. To make themselves more important, they took good care to present themselves as the rulers of the native tribes of their districts, over which their authority was, in fact, very limited. Their position always remained very uncertain; hence the rapid rise and fall of so many of those states. With endless internecine wars, a slow process of crystallization took place which would have resulted eventually in the establishment of a smaller number of organized states, but was interrupted when the Portuguese, and after them the Dutch, got control of the seas and stopped the wars. Thus several hundreds of those embryonic kingdoms were preserved for our times.

Gajah Mada kept good record of the names and location of all the vassals of Madjapahit. Those who failed to present their annual contribution were "visited" by a Javanese fleet. Prapanca mentions expressly that several admirals won fame in these expeditions. This control of the sea, and therefore of commerce, caused the submission of many of the merchant kings, simply because they were afraid of being ousted from trading. Gajah Mada must have had sound business ideas. The Javanese practically monopolized the spice trade. Navigation was still in its primitive stage of hopping from one port to another along the coast, and this made several stops at the ports of Java necessary and gave the prime minister full opportunity to control all commerce. Long after Madjapahit had lost its glory, the Javanese traders maintained their control of the navigation between the peninsula and the Moluccas.

The maintenance of a large fleet was one of the means of controlling the outer possessions. Gajah Mada found another one by which he supervised the Javanese officials in the different parts of the empire. The following is the story given by our poet-historian:

> A rule was set for the learned priests who went to foreign countries [that is, outside Java] that they could not participate in any commerce to their own profit, for it would be of great disadvantage to the world, but they could be sent by the king to places where the true belief of Shivaism should be maintained and preserved from deterioration. The Buddhists had not the same rights; they were limited in their actions. The western part of the Empire was forbidden to them, but they might freely visit the eastern districts. The work of the priests who traveled east and west made good progress, thanks to the help of the king's officers.[10]

This is Prapanca's story. Does he mean that the officers of the king helped the Shivaitic missionaries in the propagation of their faith? Certainly not! Those priests were special missionaries, who, by a royal order, controlled the officers and the vassals of the empire. Combined with this, they looked after the maintenance, eventually the restoration, of the Shivaitic sanctuaries. Propagation of the faith in our sense of the word was unknown to the Shivaists. They adhered strictly to the caste system. The Brahmans, the highest class of society, looked down with abhorrence on the common people, especially on subjected tribes,

[10] All quotations from the *Nagarakertagama* are translated from Kern's Dutch version (*Verspreide Geschriften*, vols. VII and VIII).

who, for their political inferiority alone, were grouped among outcasts. Contact with these lower beings imperiled the purity of the Brahman priest. This caste system was not maintained in Indonesia with the same harshness as in India, but the distinction did exist.

A curious anecdote from Prapanca's panegyric reveals the more tolerant Indonesian point of view in all matters of caste and rules of purity. The poet himself was a Buddhist priest but had a strong tendency towards syncretism, that is, the combination of the essences of the two religions in a common creed. He describes a royal dinner party in Madjapahit. The meat of buffalo, deer, sheep, and bird was freely enjoyed by all, but the forbidden meat of dog, donkey, mice, and frogs was eaten by many of the common people, "who," Prapanca says, "in their gluttony did not care about the commands of the gods." Thus, the king saw no objection to offering the forbidden food he would not himself eat to others who had fewer scruples. For a Brahmanist, his attitude was very lenient; a high-caste Hindu would have shrunk even from the sight of such dreadful things. To be sober is one of the first rules of both religions, but Prapanca relates pleasantly the most awful scenes of drunkenness at the royal court, and there is no question this time of a religiously inspired debauchery. It was plainly enough excessive drinking for the sake of drinking.

All these considerations together give us the certainty that a Shivaitic priest did not think of missionary work when he went out to the other islands. That he took care of the sanctuaries was quite another matter. This was not done for the sake of the believers who might visit those temples, but for the contentment of the gods who might become angry and take revenge if their dwelling places were neglected. One difficulty remains; why was the western part of the empire forbidden to them? Was there any danger that the presence of those Buddhist priests in Sumatra might revive in the old territory of Shrivijaya the traditional antagonism against Java? Or, and this is perhaps more likely, was the prime minister afraid that the contact between the Javanese Buddhists and their Sumatran colleagues might make the former more aware how far they had fallen away from their original creed, which could imperil the nearly attained unification of the two Churches? There was never any religious persecution in the old times in Indonesia. The Shivaists took from the Buddhist belief a number of philosophical and ethical conceptions, but these conceptions were for the few who were initiated into the higher grades of wisdom.

Gajah Mada's death in 1364 made the king despair, if we may believe Prapanca. He called all the members of the royal family into a solemn council of state, where the great man's succession was discussed. After long deliberation, it was decided that the burden of government of such a large empire was too heavy for a single man. Four ministers were appointed, among whom Gajah Mada's work was divided. This meant, of course, that the king himself had to take a hand in government affairs, if only as coördinator for the four departments. This may have been too heavy a strain on his majesty's energy, for a few years later he selected one of his ministers to be prime minister again with complete control over all matters of state. The division of the government among four ministers guaranteed a better administration, but the presence of a prime minister guaranteed an easy life for the king. It had another advantage; it freed his majesty from all direct contact with the dirty affairs of daily life, which, after all, were beneath his dignity. Prapanca gives us an idea of what was considered by the old Javanese courtiers a truly royal way of living, and we must bear in mind that he wrote this with the approval of the prime minister:

> Truly King Hayam Wuruk is a great potentate. He is without cares or worries. He indulges in all pleasures. All beautiful maidens in Janggala and Kadiri [the two parts of East Java] are selected for him, as many as possible, and of those who are captured in foreign countries, the prettiest girls are brought into his harem.

Under those circumstances a prime minister who did the work was certainly indispensable!

Prapanca is again the well-informed author who explains the ethical rules and the religious conceptions of his time. He had succeeded to the position of superintendent of the Buddhist priesthood. He had studied the theological books of both religions and had undoubtedly taken part many a time in the public religious discussions of the two clergies. He begins his poem with a confession of his creed, which is unfortunately worded in very obscure terms. We must not look, however, for mere logic in his theological explanations, for, to a true adherent of the Mahayana belief, reason often brings forth obscurity and logical thinking does not bring insight, but confusion. The first lines of the poem run as follows:

> Praise to the god of all gods, the most unthinkable of all unthinkable things, yet present in this world in incarnation. He is Shiva-Buddha, immaterial, yet connected with the material. He is present everywhere, he is Vishnu for the Vishnuists, he is the Individual Soul for the philosophers, in the books on the art of love he is god of love, and for the others the god of wealth.

Shiva-Buddha, Vishnu, the gods of wealth and love — they are all different forms of one Being, according to our poet. What were his ideas about this Being? He does not answer this question, but other Buddhists of his creed did answer it, with the solution that this Being is empty space, nothing, and that the whole world is in reality nothing. It is non-existent. The learned Buddhist poet was apparently an adept of a vague pantheism, but on the other hand he makes it quite clear that for him everything divine was incarnated in his king. Thus, the king could do no wrong, neither constitutionally, as in Great Britain, nor in reality. The king does not need to worry. He may do anything. It is a privilege to die for the king, even if it is only to please his majesty's whims. This theory is expounded by Prapanca in the story of a royal hunting party.

The hunters of the king surround a forest. They set fire to the woods and scare all animals out of their hiding-places by shouting and yelling. The animals group together deep in the forests and hold a meeting. The deer and other timid beasts propose to flee, while the buffaloes, boars, and rhinoceroses prefer to fight. Then the tiger, king of the forest, gives his decision: "Let us distinguish between the good and the bad ones among our attackers. The low-class people will flee from us. The priests of the three sects we shall fight, but the king you must not resist, should he want to kill you, for he has the power to kill all creatures. Shiva is incarnated in him, and he who dies by his hand will see all his sins forgiven. Such a death brings more blessing than even the suicidal self-sacrifice in the holy lakes. My reward for such a holy deed will be that I shall be reborn, not as a beast, but as a human being." The wild beasts turn around and attack the hunters. The first line of soldiers (who were used for beating up the game) begin to kill the deer, but the wild boars charge furiously and drive them ignominiously from the field. One after the other they are struck down. Other soldiers come armed with heavy spears, killing the deer, but then the rhinoceroses attack in force. Left and right the soldiers flee, losing many dead. Some climb trees, others ascend steep rocks, but when they fall down, they are caught by the beasts. Now the members of the court intervene and fight off the rhinoceroses. In the general enthusiasm, even Shivaitic and Buddhist priests take up arms, forgetting that it is their duty to be good to all living creatures. When they point their spears at the animals, punishment follows immediately. Growling tigers appear, and the ecclesiastical gentlemen flee for their lives, pursued by the beasts. Then the king, fearless on his battle car, kills the tigers and puts an end to the hunting, having killed more of the game than all the others together.

This story gives an exact idea of the consideration in which the different classes of society were held. Apparently the Renaissance Cardinals of Rome were not the only ecclesiastics who could not forsake the worldly pleasures of hunting parties.

The king's only duty was to take care that he followed strictly the rules set for the veneration of the gods and that he contented his ancestors. If he did so, he might enjoy life to his heart's content. It was the prime minister's work to decide which rites and dedications might be necessary for the conservation of the state, for this was undoubtedly the basic idea of all worshipping. To fulfill these religious duties and to participate in the magic strength of his ancestors, the king had to travel around his kingdom visiting all sanctuaries. Thus he could keep in touch with the spiritual forces, while the prime minister managed the earthly business. Such a royal cortege was an unorganized crowd of men riding on horses and elephants, of vehicles drawn by mules and oxen, and stately carriages, in which the royal harem accompanied its lone husband. And wherever the cortege passed, it was a heavy burden for the inhabitants, who had to bring cattle, rice, and vegetables for the royal table and the innumerable followers. When the king stayed for a few days in the same place, the neighborhood had to provide the royal pleasures also, Prapanca tells us. Beautiful women and "the choice of the virgins" were brought to his camp. The poet relates how the king visited a Brahmanist recluse in the forest, where he "reposed and left the young girl anchorites languishing and enamored. For them he was the god of love who had come down from heaven to seduce." Not only was everything the king did right, but, in Prapanca's opinion, being loved by the king was participating in the strength of the gods.

Both churches now simply formed part of the state institutions. The superintendents of the clergy were high state officials, of course. As in the early Middle Ages in Europe, the art of reading and writing was known to a relatively small number of individuals, and of those, most belonged to the clergy. Therefore, it was the duty of the priests and monks to take care of the archives. Each convent and each temple had its own charters and documents. Gajah Mada had a general survey made of these papers, and documents that had been lost were replaced by new copies. A general survey of laws and customs was made, and this codification remains one of the greatest achievements of the prime minister. Fixed rules existed for the internal administration, which was entrusted to some of the closest relatives of the king.

Some interesting lines from Prapanca's epic show us that the administrative system was nearly identical with that which existed in the nineteenth century and is still partly in use. This is his description:

TEMPLE OF SINGHASARI

Built (*circa* 1280 A.D.) by King Kertanagara but never completed because of the sudden collapse of the kingdom.

> From a great celebration at the royal court, all the village elders and all of the *wadanas* [district chiefs] returned home, having taken leave of the king. This was the last exhortation given them by the king's uncle: "Serve faithfully your Lord and King! Take care to neglect nothing that may add to the welfare of your district; take good care of the bridges, the roads, the waringins, the houses, and the sacred monuments, that our ricefields and all that is planted may flourish, be protected, and well tended. Look after the dikes of the sawahs, that the draining water does not run off and the people have to leave for better sites. And, if people have to move to another place, let them follow the royal ordinances on the extension of the village fields. Take care that the kitchens (the number of families) are registered and the lists controlled the last day of each month."

One who has had the opportunity to attend the monthly meetings of the wadanas of a district at the meeting-hall under the leadership of a Javanese regent in our days will have heard the same admonitions repeated time and again.

The village chiefs have ruled the desa (village) until the present day. The district chiefs, the wadanas, continue to rule their districts as in Hayam Wuruk's time. They are grouped now under regional hereditary chiefs. So they were in the fourteenth century. Only the territorial princes, who ruled larger units as vassals of the king of Madjapahit, have disappeared in modern times. Thus the native village rule has been preserved throughout the centuries, even though some details needed changing in our times for economic and educational reasons. But many of the age-old customs still exist. The waringins, the shadow-spreading fig trees, are still considered the holy trees in Java villages. In the royal ordinance they are mentioned in one breath with the houses and temples. The temples were the dwelling-places of the gods, the houses those of living men, and the high and large trees were believed to give shelter to the souls of the deceased. To cut down the waringins would bring the vengeance of the spirits upon the village.

The Javanese village is in some ways a perfect social unit. The administration of the island must therefore be developed from this basic unit. This was of course obvious to the mediaeval kings of Java, for they continued to collect taxes in agricultural products from the villages, not from the individuals. The kings rewarded their faithful servants by granting them the income of one or more villages, which had to supply food and labor to their lords. In exchange, the villages were liberated from the general taxes. Other villages were ordered to take care of sanctuaries and of the priests that served them.[11] The Euro-

[11] This institution still survives in the 182 so-called free communities (*vrije desa's*) in Java and Madura which have special administration and special duties recognized by the Netherlands East Indian Government. Some details may be found in the articles of

pean administration never attempted a radical change in this native system. A break in tradition such as happened in western Europe during the French Revolution never took place in the Javanese institutions.

The Empire of Madjapahit had become a great Asiatic power. The capital had developed accordingly and had grown from a village to a city of several hundred thousand inhabitants. People from all over the country flocked there in the hope of finding work or simply of living on the charity of the king and of the *grands seigneurs*. The courtiers had around them thousands of followers. The royal stables, with their numerous elephants, horses, oxen, and exotic animals, needed swarms of attendants. The city existed by and for the kings, and therefore little is left of its glory, except some ruins of the temples, the city walls, and the gates. Most of the buildings were of perishable material, since even the stone buildings were made of native bricks. Earthquakes, the climate, and the abundant vegetation did away quickly with these monuments once the city was deserted.

The poet Prapanca describes the wonders of the capital. The city wall was of red brick, thick and high. Through the gate at the west side the visitor entered a wide plaza, in the center of which was a deep pool of clear water. Around the plaza were several rows of tall trees. Among these the policemen walked up and down, controlling this outer court. At the north side was the beautiful main gate with its decorated iron doors. This gate led to the field for the tournaments, in the center of which stood a pavilion for the king. One side of this field was a hall for audiences and for the meetings of the royal council. On the other was a meeting place where the Shivaitic and Buddhist priests held discussions and arranged the offerings. When the king came to attend the sacrifice, the whole plaza was carpeted with flowers. The poet does not find words enough to describe the splendor of the buildings, to tell of the cages full of innumerable birds, of the soldiers who stand guard, of the continuous stream of visitors who bring presents to the king. Around the plaza the royal princes had their quarters, and to the northeast was the residence of Gajah Mada, "patih of Madjapahit, brave, wise in counsel, reliable, honestly subservient to the King, eloquent in his argumentation, honest, moderate, alert, and firm when he maintains the orders of His Majesty." Thither the king went, if we may believe Prapanca, in his vehicle drawn by dogs and lions (leopards?). Those two types of animals, he notes gravely, do not mix, but a great number

L. W. C. van den Berg, "De Mohammedaansche geestelijkheid en de geestelijke goederen op Java en Madoera," BKI, XXVII (1882), 1 sq., and "Het Inlandsch Gemeentewezen op Java en Madura," BKI, LII (1901), 135.

of servants keep them in their places and all people look at them in great amazement!

On the plaza, the king amused himself with the contests and war games of his noblemen. There he invited thousands of his followers to dinner. The buffoons went around, making jokes and dancing. The whole company joined in singing and listened in obligatory admiration when his majesty himself gave a song. "The delightful singing of the prince," Prapanca says, "was admired by all. It was lovable as the call of the peacock sitting in a tree, sweet as a mixture of honey and sugar, touching as the scraping noise of the reeds." It would be too monotonous in this world if there were no variety in musical taste. But the courtiers were delighted. They asked for a further display of the royal artistic talents. The king's uncle played the gamelan, the queen put on a funny wig and sang, and the king himself gave a masquerade, accompanied by the young men of the court.

Those days without worries did not last long for Madjapahit, however. The mighty empire was the work of a few men, and after their death it collapsed.

CHAPTER IV

MOHAMMEDANS AND PORTUGUESE

At the end of the thirteenth century, a Javanese nobleman fled from his home country and came to the little fishing and trading port of Singapore. Still pursued by enemies, he moved on along the west coast of the Peninsula and installed himself in the insignificant village of Malacca. His small number of followers mixed with the original Malay population, and Malacca became a place of refuge for the pirates who infested the straits between Sumatra and the Continent, straits which were called after the town of Malacca as soon as the little fishing village had grown into a commercial metropolis. The favorable geographic position of the town secured for it a rapid development, thanks to the ability of its rulers.[1] The coastal district in which it was situated had been for a long time under the control of the kingdom of Siam. For a while Madjapahit had superseded the Siamese authorities, but after the sudden and unexpected collapse of the Javanese empire the overlordship of Siam was restored.

The downfall of Madjapahit had been a catastrophe in true Oriental style. As in so many Oriental kingdoms, harem stories had been at the bottom of the affair. King Hayam Wuruk had no "official" son. His sons by lower class women were considered legitimate, but to have no right of succession. Only a daughter had been born to the official Queen. Rather than leave his son by another woman in a position of inferiority, he decided to divide his kingdom, ruining the work of unification which had been accomplished by his ancestors. Thus the demon of division was set free again. The consequences really seemed to confirm the theories of devilry and witchcraft that had been so prominent in the minds of Kertanagara and Gajah Madah. They had endeavored to keep down the evil forces of division, and they had spared no trouble to strengthen the mystic forces of unity. Now by a reckless act King Hayam Wuruk destroyed their work, and immediately the empire collapsed. A period of internal strife followed, and at this token of the wrath of the gods the petty kings of the islands turned away from Madjapahit and transferred their allegiance to a stronger

[1] For the first years of Malacca's history, see G. P. Rouffaer, "Was Malakka emporium voor 1400 A.D., genaamd Malajoer?" BKI, vol. LXXVII (1921).

power. Java was divided, reunited, redivided, and finally reduced to a state of political chaos. The local rulers regained their independence, and what was spared by the wars was ruined by famine. Thus the population was reduced to a miserable condition of living. The seas of the archipelago became infested with pirates. It was a great opportunity for reckless adventurers.

Prominent among them was the first ruler of Malacca. He understood perfectly the art of checking one potential aggressor by another. When Madjapahit had been eliminated, Siam became the most dangerous enemy. But against Siam he secured the help of China. Thus he gained some time to build up the strength of his little kingdom. In the beginning he made his profits by plundering the merchant ships that sailed from India to Indonesia. The merchants quickly discovered that the best safeguard against his attacks lay in a voluntary stop at the port of Malacca and a payment of customs duties. When they found that this port was conveniently located, midway between India and China and within easy reach of the traders from Java, it proved to them an even more convenient emporium than Palembang had been. In a few years it became the principal port of the archipelago. When two centuries later a Dutchman wrote for the first time on the trade of Malacca, he explained that from this place the Malayan language had originated and spread over all the islands.[2]

It was lucky for the first ruler of Malacca that he founded his kingdom exactly at the moment when the empire of China rose to power once more under the dynasty of the Ming Emperors. In 1368, China had been freed from Mongol domination, and fourteen years later the empire was completely restored under the first emperor of the House of Ming. This dynasty started on a definite policy of conquest in the southern seas, continuing the work of the great Kublai Khan. Ambassadors were sent to Indo-China, the Peninsula, and the islands to request submission, and a war fleet followed to force recalcitrants to surrender. The ruler of Malacca was quick to grasp his chance. Since the Chinese meant business this time, and resistance was impossible, the best policy seemed to be to submit at once, thus securing the help of the emperor

[2] Jan Huyghen van Linschoten in his *Itinerario*, I, 73, reports a local tradition of the Malays of Malacca according to which the beginnings of the city dated back "only a few years" before his time (last quarter of the sixteenth century), and originated in the gathering of fishermen of all nations at that particular spot, where they decided to build a town and "to develop their own language, taking the best words from all languages of the neighborhood." Once the town, because of its favorable situation, became the principal port of southeastern Asia, "its language called the Malay came to be considered the most polite and the fittest of all languages of the Far East."

against possible opponents. It is no wonder that the Chinese action in the archipelago met with amazing success. The ambassadors traveled from port to port, explaining politely and persuasively their mission and requesting from the local rulers a personal visit to the capital of China to present tribute. For a few years there was a rush towards Peking. The first to go was the king of Puni (either West Borneo or Brunei), who arrived at the imperial court with a remarkable request. He asked the Emperor, the Overlord of all Eastern Asia, to release him from paying the tribute he owed to Madjapahit and allow him to pay it directly to China, a favor which was graciously granted. Those local potentates must have been shrewd diplomats. By a single move, this king of pirates and headhunters secured independence from Java, official recognition as a king, and Chinese support in his quarrels. The rajas of Malacca had the same success in Peking, and obtained an imperial order to the king of Siam that he should leave Malacca undisturbed. On their trip through the archipelago, the Chinese ambassadors also visited Madjapahit, where they had the bad luck to get mixed up in a local battle in which one hundred and fifty of their followers were accidentally killed. They reported to Peking, and Madjapahit had to pay a heavy fine, which it dared not refuse. In Sumatra the embassy found Palembang in the power of a Chinese pirate chief, who played the king within this old city. They arrested him and sent him to China, a fact which proves that the imperial authority was well respected.[3]

Under Chinese protection Malacca flourished. The name of the second prince of Malacca was Muhammad Iskandar Shah, which indicates that he was a Moslem. The title Shah points to Persia and was probably given to him by Persian merchants. Thus we know that Malacca was converted to Islam in the first decade of the fifteenth century. The tombstones of the first Moslem rajas were imported from Gujerat. When all bits of information are patched together, the whole story of the conversion becomes plain. The merchants from Gujerat had frequented the growing commercial center and had imported their religion, creating in this way a market for that curious piece of merchandise the nicely carved tombstone with inscriptions in the Arabic language. It must have become fashionable among the first Indonesian adherents of the Prophet to have their memory perpetuated on their gravestones in the newly introduced holy script and language, just as for a long time it was fashionable in occidental countries to have a Latin

[3] For a discussion of this Chinese intervention in the affairs of the archipelago, see Krom, HJG, ch. xiii, based on the studies of Rouffaer, Groeneveldt, Ferrand, and Rockhill, quoted above.

inscription on one's grave. The Gujerats got the material for the stones cheaply. They simply took them from the Hindu temples, which they had learned to despise as monuments of idolatry. But the same fate befell the same stones once more, when the Portuguese used them for the construction of Malacca's fortress, without respect for the hated Moslem religion.

Mohammad Iskandar Shah ascended the throne in 1414. Islam had spread at that time along the northeast coast of Sumatra, but had nowhere penetrated into the interior. It rapidly conquered the coastal district of the Peninsula. The first Arabic grave in Java (at Gresik, north of Surabaya) dates from 1419. It is the grave of Malik Ibrahim, whom popular belief has made into an apostle and the saint of the Moslem religion. Modern scholars deciphered the inscription on his tombstone and concluded that he was a wealthy Persian merchant who probably made his money in the spice trade. There is some truth in a legend like this, which makes an unknown Persian trader into an apostle. We do not know whether this man Malik was specially influential in the spreading of Islam; we do not know the names of the real apostles of that creed; but it is beyond doubt that the new religion was propagated by a great number of merchants from the western coasts of the Indian Ocean, even if those merchants must remain nameless for us. The propagation of Mohammedan doctrines followed exactly the trading and shipping routes of southeastern Asia. They were brought from Gujerat to the Peninsula, from Malacca to Eastern Java, and from there to the principal islands of the Moluccas. From these central points they spread along the coast of the islands. The interior was converted centuries later, or has never been converted at all. Only where the old Hindu immigration had created organized states in the interior could Islam expand rapidly. This development makes it probable that Islam was first confessed in the principal ports by small groups of foreigners, enterprising men who had great resources and many slaves at their disposal. Thus the old story of the traders who became kings was repeated once more, and this time not only in the less civilized parts of the archipelago, but also on Java.

The kingdom of Madjapahit had lost all power in the last quarter of the fifteenth century, and a prince of Kadiri finally conquered the capital, which fell rapidly into ruin.[4] The petty princes on the coast were glad to marry their sons and daughters to the children of the rich

[4] The fall of Madjapahit is commemorated in many legends. For a discussion of facts and legends, see G. P. Rouffaer, "Wanneer is Madjapahit gevallen?" BKI, 6 ser. v (1899), 111 sq.

foreign merchants and became in that way attracted to Islam. In a few decades, the Javanese aristocracy of the coastal districts had gone over to the new belief. This meant no break with the old traditions and customs, such as the wayang performances, which continued to be enjoyed by the people even if they were not in accordance with the rules of the Koran. In the beginning, Islam meant little more for the masses of the people than a change in the name of the Supreme Being from Shiva-Buddha to Allah. On one of the oldest Mohammedan graves we still find Shivaitic symbols. Slowly the people of Java have been educated by Moslem missionary work to a stricter conception of the Mohammedan belief, a work that has been strongly influenced from Mecca and is still continuing.[5]

The introduction of Islam made the difference between the Malayan traders who lived on the coast of Borneo and Celebes and the native tribes in the interior still greater than it had been. For these traders, the chapter on the spreading of the Holy Word was one of the most interesting parts of the Koran. If directed against pagans, the propagation of the faith by the sword was not only justifiable but even highly laudable. This was a wonderful expedient, to combine piety and piracy, and the petty kings on Sumatra's north coast grasped the opportunity. To the merchant kings in the Moluccas it gave a chance to secure salvation by expanding their commercial sphere of interest. Malacca, too, profited by the same system, but when commercial interest demanded it the princes of that city made little distinction between Moslem and Kafir (infidels). The only power that might have checked this movement was the Chinese Empire, but the Ming dynasty had declined in strength as quickly as it had risen (±1450).

This was the state of affairs when the first Portuguese arrived in Indonesia in the beginning of the sixteenth century. With them they brought another holy war, that of the Christians of Spain and Portugal against the Moors of Africa. The idea of the Crusade was always and everywhere present in the mind of the Portuguese conquistadores. It influenced all their colonial activities. They started on their distant expeditions with the express intention of carrying the Crusades into the territory of the enemy. The direct attack on Africa was difficult, and therefore the Portuguese planned to attack the Moors in the rear by sailing towards Africa's south coast. These enterprises carried them

[5] The early history of Islam on the island of Java is rather confusing. An excellent survey, based on recent studies, may be found in C. Lekkerkerker, *Land en volk van Java* (Groningen-Batavia, 1938), I, 309 sq. See also D. A. Rinkes, "De Heiligen van Java," TBG, vols. LII–LV (1910–1913).

much farther than they had originally intended, but wherever they went they found "Moors" to fight, for to them all believers in Islam were "Moors" and enemies. There is something great in this conception, something that seems more noble because more disinterested than the motives which later brought the British and the Dutch to Indonesia. But if we look at the details of the campaign, there is little left of the glamor of chivalry.[6]

Vasco da Gama reached the coast of India in the spring of 1498. A few years later he returned to the Indian seas with the definite order from the king of Portugal to stop all Arabian shipping between Mesopotamia and India. By fierce fighting he secured control over the western half of the Indian Ocean for his king. This work was later completed by the greatest of all conquistadores, Alfonso de Albuquerque, who in the six years of his governorship, 1509–1515, opened the seas of the Far East to the Portuguese merchants. He arrived in India at the moment when the first ship that had been sent exploring to Malacca returned from its voyage. The crew had had unfortunate experiences with the sultan of Malacca. First they had been received very kindly, and later they had been attacked without any warning. Several men had been taken prisoner. It may be that the Javanese merchants, who must have suffered heavy losses because of the repercussions of the Arabian-Portuguese war, were anxious to block further extension of European sea power. They insisted that the intruders should be punished immediately. The sultan of Malacca was dependent on these merchants for his income and therefore consented.

Albuquerque heard of these events after he had conquered the city of Goa, the conquest of which gave the maritime empire of Portugal a bridgehead on the continent. He decided that Malacca should be its second bridgehead, and in 1511 sailed eastward. Thus began a holy war in Indonesia between Moors and Crusaders, in which the champions of Islam remained victorious. With its first blow, the Portuguese fleet

[6] For an older survey of Portuguese activities in the East Indies and for the literature on the subject, see P. A. Tiele, "De Europeeërs in den Indischen Archipel," in BKI, 4 ser. I (1877), 321 sq., continued in the volumes of 1879, 1880, 1881, 1882, and 1884. A discussion of the Portuguese contemporary literature on the subject appears in G. P. Rouffaer, "Wanneer is Madjapahit gevallen?" BKI, 6 ser. VI (1899), Appendix I (pp. 145–197). The two volumes of F. C. Danvers' *The Portuguese in India* (London, 1894) deal also with the affairs of the East Indies, but are based almost entirely upon Portuguese information. The author apparently did not consult the numerous publications of documents from Dutch archives and therefore his exposition of the Dutch-Portuguese war in the years between 1600 and 1661 is not satisfactory.

Of the Portuguese contemporary historians, the books of Duarte Barbosa and Antonio Galvao have been published in English versions by the Hakluyt Society.

struck down the newly-founded empire of Malacca, but three other kingdoms were ready to keep the green banner of the Prophet waving in the archipelago — the sultanates of Atjeh in northern Sumatra, of Demak in Eastern Java, and of Ternate in the Moluccas.

The fire of the crusades was strong enough in Albuquerque to make him capture and loot all Mohammedan vessels he could find between Goa and Malacca. Thus he fought the Moors while he served the Portuguese commercial interests. But it is one of the first examples of those terrible blunders which Europeans can make if they try to conquer nations of which they have insufficient knowledge. Albuquerque did not know how important a position the Gujerat merchants had held for centuries in the archipelago, and that all their relatives and friends from Atjeh to the Moluccas would hear in a few weeks that the Portuguese were pirates and could not be trusted. Nevertheless, Albuquerque, who was a true leader, succeeded in establishing Portuguese authority over the trading routes of Asia, although he had still more trouble with his own officers than with the Malayans.

He collected a fleet of nineteen ships manned by 800 Portuguese sailors and soldiers for his expedition to the East. This force was small in numbers compared with the native armies, but far superior in equipment. When the troops landed near Malacca, the sultan asked for negotiations. Albuquerque demanded payment of the war expenses and permission to build a Portuguese fort in the town. These conditions the sultan could not accept without losing his independence. It would be an act of submission quite different from the homage he used to pay to the Emperor of China. Upon his refusal the Portuguese attacked. The first assault was successful but not decisive. Some of the Portuguese officers protested against the continuation of the expedition. The extremely unhealthful climate of Malacca was a good pretext for a withdrawal, for the place was so fever-ridden that one of the first Netherlanders to describe it wrote, "The Europeans who survive it may thank our Lord for such a miracle."

Albuquerque silenced the opposition, however, and on August 10, 1511, led his soldiers to a second attack, which made him master of the city.[7] He was not strong enough to encircle it, and hence he could not hinder the Sultan from withdrawing with his court and his troops to a place farther south on the coast from where he continued the war.

Malacca was now a Portuguese city. Albuquerque immediately

[7] For an account by an eyewitness, see Giovanni da Empoli, "Lettera mandata a Lionardo suo padre del viaggio di Malacca," in *Archivio storico Italiano, Appendici*, III (1846), 19–91.

started the construction of a fortress. The graves of the Mohammedans were ruthlessly destroyed to obtain building materials. The inhabitants, particularly the Oriental merchants, were far from satisfied with the political change, and Albuquerque made his second mistake by the summary execution of the leading Javanese trader for an alleged plot against the Portuguese rule. Having full confidence in the strength of the Portuguese fleet, the admiral did not care much about the opinions of the Indonesians, whom he hoped within a few years to oust completely from the international trade. He immediately organized expeditions to Siam, to China, and to the Moluccas.

These Spice Islands had become legendary in Europe as the principal source of Oriental wealth. Clove and nutmeg were their products.[8] Clove, the dried flower-bud of the clove tree, is mentioned for the first time in Occidental literature in a Greek report of the seventh century. In Europe during the Middle Ages this spice was sold at tremendous prices, but its high price had little to do with the cost of production or the available quantity. The cultivation of clove-tree orchards requires little work, and the tree continues to bear fruit for three quarters of a century, which fully compensates for the long period of growth before producing flowers — nearly twelve years. It was the cost of transportation that made the spices so expensive, and the high risks of the long sea voyages in the small native barks. The islanders of the Moluccas did not profit so much from the trade as the Javanese and Gujerat traders, if they were lucky enough to bring a number of cargoes safely to the western coast of India. A hundredweight (about 112 pounds) of cloves cost only one or two ducats in the Moluccas, but were sold for ten or more in Malacca. Farther to the west the prices rose accordingly. Magellan's ship *Victoria* was the first to bring a shipload of clove directly from the Moluccas to Europe, where it was sold at a profit of 2500 per cent. The clove grew originally only in the small islands of Ternate, Tidore, Halmahera, and a few others.[9]

The nutmeg was the principal product of Amboina and the Banda Islands. The tree begins to bear fruit after ten years. At sixty years it

[8] A description of the production of spices in the archipelago is given in ENI, under "Kruidnagelen," "Nootmuskaat." See also R. H. Crofton, *A Pageant of the Spice Islands* (London, 1936); I cannot concur in the opinion expressed by the author (p. 23), who follows here the opinion of many earlier writers, that in Europe the demand for spices was far greater in the Middle Ages than in modern times. The production of spices in our day by far exceeds that of earlier periods. Only *relatively* did the spices play a more important role in the Middle Ages, with their limited variation in diet, than they do now.

[9] For an early Dutch description of spice production, see Linschoten, *Itinerario*, vol. II, ch. lxii sq.; and G. Rumphius, *Amboinsch Kruydboeck* (7 vols., 1741–1755).

stops producing, but occasionally may reach the age of a hundred years. It is no wonder that the Bandanese like to compare the growth of the nutmeg tree with that of man. During the last century, clove has been planted in several other parts of the world, but the production of nutmeg is still limited to the Indonesian archipelago. The Portuguese hoped to secure a monopoly on the export of these spices. Yet they could not make huge profits unless they eliminated all middlemen and brought the spices directly to Europe. The maintenance of such large profits, however, depended on the quantity of spice they could transport. The supply was abundant, more than at that moment the peoples of Europe were able to buy. If the Portuguese intended to keep the prices high, they had to secure a monopoly and to restrict export. This meant war with the Javanese traders and made necessary permanent policing of the sea routes between Indonesia and Arabia. The Portuguese began this task with enthusiasm. Every pound of nutmeg taken away from the Moslem traders was a blow at the prosperity of the trading cities of Syria and Egypt, which were under the political authority of the Sultan of Turkey. This meant loss of income for the Padishah in Constantinople, and thus would be of advantage to the Christians who had to fight the Turkish fleets on the Mediterranean. So it was at once a laudable and a profitable undertaking to throw the Moslems out of business.

The first thing to do was to obtain the friendship of the spice producers. Without their help, the whole scheme was doomed. Unhappily these producers had been converted to Islam only twenty years earlier. This made the problem a very complicated one, which the Portuguese failed to solve.[10] Albuquerque sent his lieutenant, Antonio D'Abreu, with three ships, from Malacca to the Moluccas in the last days of the year 1511. D'Abreu had definite orders to abstain from all military action and to present himself as a trader. The little fleet was preceded by the Malayan bark of a native trader, who promised to prepare the

[10] The best survey of the complications in which the Portuguese became involved in the Moluccas because of their double role as merchants and crusaders has been given by C. Wessels S.J., *De Geschiedenis der R. K. Missie in Amboina, 1546–1605* (Nijmegen-Utrecht, 1926), also a French translation: *Histoire de la Mission d'Amboine* (Louvain, 1934). Wessels continued his researches in his articles: "De eerste Franciscaner missie op Java, 1584–1599" in *Studiën*, CXIII (1930), 117 sq.; "De Katholieke Missie in Noord Celebes en de Sangi eilanden, 1563–1605," *Studiën*, CXIX (1933), 365 sq.; "Eenige aanteekeningen betreffende het bisdom en de bisschoppen van Malakka 1558–1838," *Historisch Tijdschrift*, XII (1933), 204 sq.; and "Uit de missiegeschiedenis van Sumatra en Atjeh in de 16e en 17e eeuw," *Historisch Tijdschrift*, XIX (1939), 5 sq. These articles derive much of their importance from the extensive researches by the author in Roman archives, some of which are not accessible to the public.

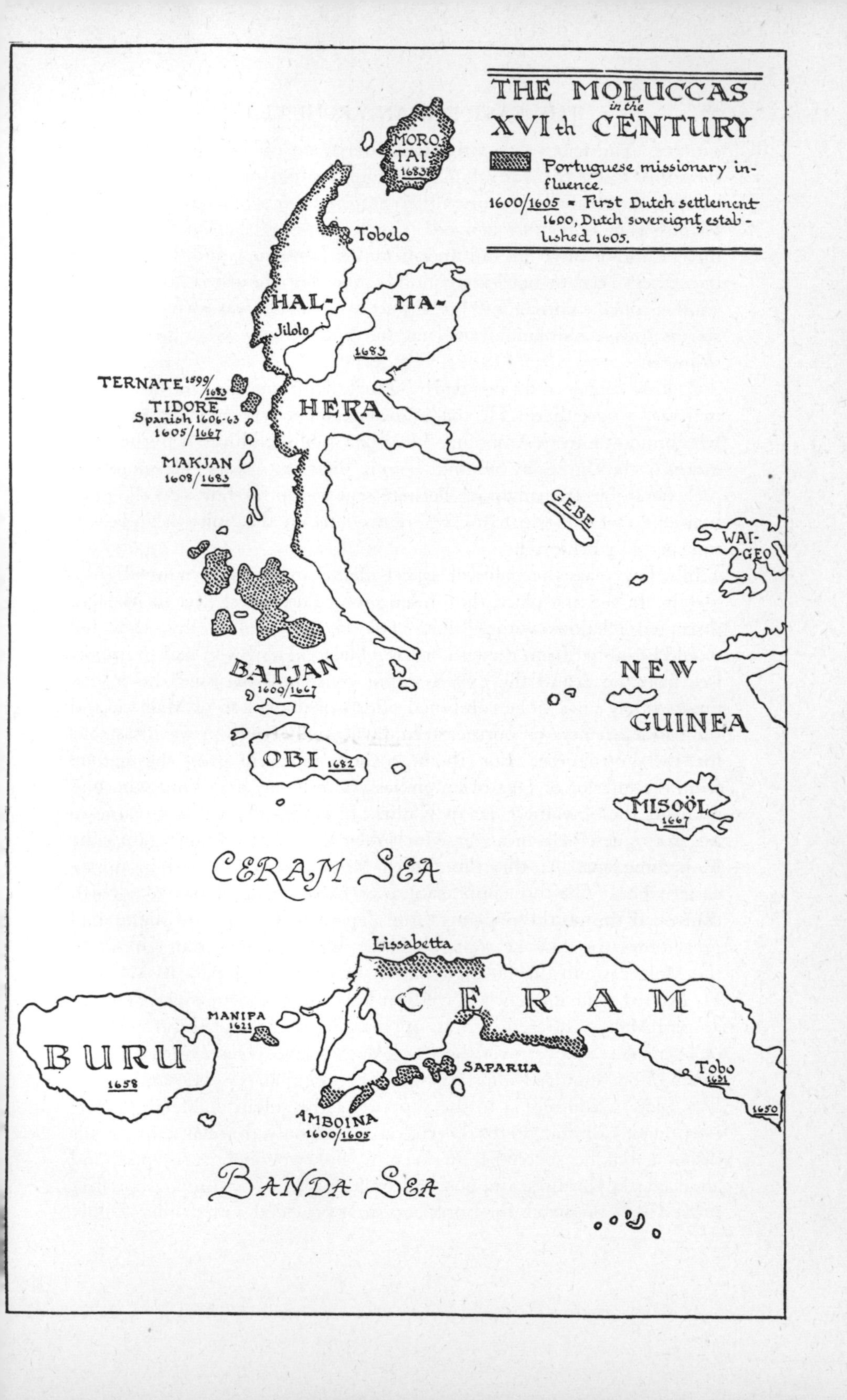
THE MOLUCCAS in the XVI th CENTURY
Portuguese missionary influence.
1600/1605 = First Dutch settlement 1600, Dutch sovereignty established 1605.
MORO TAI 1683
Tobelo
HAL- MA- HERA
Jilolo
1683
TERNATE 1599/1683
TIDORE
Spanish 1606-63
1605/1667
MAKJAN
1608/1683
GEBE
WAI-GEO
BATJAN
1600/1667
NEW GUINEA
OBI 1682
MISOÖL
1667
CERAM SEA
Lissabetta
CERAM
MANIPA
1621
BURU
1658
SAPARUA
Tobo
1651
1650
AMBOINA
1600/1605
BANDA SEA

ground. The first part of the trip offered no difficulty. The port of Gresik in East Java was safely reached, but after this point the difficulties began. D'Abreu lost one of his ships between Java and the Banda Islands. The other two arrived in such condition that he was glad to buy a cargo of clove and nutmeg from the Bandanese and did not even try either Ternate or Tidore. Only one ship returned to Malacca; another one, commanded by Francesco Serrao, was driven by the storms toward Amboina, and not far from this island it was lost in shipwreck.

Captain Serrao could not reach Ternate with his ship, but he himself managed to get there. He made an agreement with a Malayan pirate who brought him to Amboina. Here he established himself in the good graces of the natives by helping them in their petty wars. He soon won such fame that the sultan of Ternate sent a ship for him. So the original object of the trip to make connections on the Spice Islands was unexpectedly achieved.

In a few years the political aspect of the archipelago changed completely. In the first place, the presence of a Portuguese fleet in Malacca disrupted relations with China. The Javanese feared that they too would be ousted from the emporium. Malacca, however, had to import rice from Java, and the exiled sultan constantly harassed the Portuguese supply lines. The combined efforts of the sultan of Malacca and the Moslem rulers of northeastern Java might easily prove disastrous for the Portuguese. For them, a hopeful event was the arrival from the interior of Java of an embassy sent by a pagan king who was probably the Shivaitic ruler of Kadiri. In reality this embassy came to ask Portuguese help in a war which their king was waging against the Mohammedans. At this time three Moslem states existed in northeastern Java. The most important was the sultanate of Demak, which controlled the northern plains from Japara to Gresik. Its sultan had great power because he controlled the shipping lines from Gresik to the Moluccas and the Javanese export of rice from Japara to Malacca. He exerted some influence in western Java and in Palembang. The war around Malacca offered him an opportunity to attempt the restoration of Javanese sea power over the whole archipelago. Hastily he equipped a fleet of one hundred ships, manned by more than ten thousand sailors and soldiers, and sent it to the support of the sultan of Malacca. The Portuguese admiral, Perez D'Andrada, had only thirteen ships at his disposal, but he succeeded in keeping his two opponents apart and attacked the Javanese in good crusader style. The Indonesian fleet proved to be no match for European ships provided with artillery. Only a thunderstorm saved the Javanese from utter destruction. This victory established the reputation of the Portuguese and gave them control of the Indonesian seas. The sultan of Malacca withdrew to the marshy islands of Singapore Strait, where he built a stronghold in the wilderness which became the town of Johore. From here, he continued to harass the Portuguese.

Another sultanate, that of Atjeh, now became prominent. In the fifteenth century it was one of the least important districts on the northern shore of Sumatra.[11] It had been under the control of the local ruler of another district, but at the end of the fifteenth century, for the most part because of the growing importance of the pepper trade, the roles were reversed. Sumatra has always been the only pepper-producing country in the world. As trade with Europe grew, there came an increasing demand for pepper. To establish themselves in this trade, the Atjenese started a series of "holy wars" which gave them control over a large part of the northeastern and northwestern coast of Sumatra. By extending their authority southward along the west coast they made converts for Islam and gained a large share in the pepper trade for themselves. Before the middle of the century they had occupied the coast of the once renowned kingdom of Menangkabau and converted its princes and its people to the Moslem faith. Only the sturdy Bataks on the high plateau around Lake Tobi clung stubbornly to their old traditions. They are the only people of Sumatra of whom the majority are still unconverted to Islam. The Atjenese took up the holy war against the Portuguese, and their successes increased their prestige in the Indonesian world.

Ten years after the conquest of Malacca the Portuguese were still in a precarious situation. To the south, they had to take into consideration the enmity of the sultan of Johore. To the west, Atjeh grew more threatening every year. Nor were their relations with Java encouraging. Many Moslem traders, wishing to avoid the contact with the Portuguese-controlled emporium of Malacca, transferred their headquarters to the small port of Brunei on the north coast of Borneo. A king-merchant had ruled there since the days of Madjapahit, but now the place suddenly gained importance. Traders from China also flocked there. The raja became acquainted with Islam, accepted it, and started immediately a furious campaign to spread his belief. He subdued the

[11] The history of the sultanate of Atjeh is still to be written; only a beginning has been made with the researches in the native sources. See ENI, under "Atjeh"; and Hoessein Djajadiningrat, "Critisch overzicht van de in Maleische werken vervatte gegevens over de geschiedenis van het soeltanaat van Atjeh," BKI, LXV (1911), 135 sq., giving a survey of Malay chronicles dealing with Atjenese history.

northwestern coast of Borneo and the Sulu Islands to the northeast which form a natural bridge between Borneo and the Philippines. Thus the little state of Brunei had just risen to power when in the spring of 1521 a European ship sailed into the harbor, coming from the east. It was Magellan's ship *Victoria*, which had crossed the Pacific Ocean and visited the Philippine Islands. Magellan and his Spaniards were the first to come from America and Asia, but unfortunately in the Philippines the leader and many of his men had been killed by the natives. In Brunei also fighting broke out, and the ship turned east again. It sailed through the Sulu Islands and arrived unexpectedly in the Moluccas, to the great surprise and annoyance of the Portuguese.[12]

The arrival of the *Victoria* made the Portuguese realize that it was high time to strengthen their positions in the Spice Islands. The construction of a fortress with a permanent garrison became necessary, but where should they build it? The princes of both Ternate and Tidore requested them to make their headquarters in their territory. These royal businessmen expected great profits from trading with the Portuguese, from whom they hoped to get higher prices for their merchandise. They knew that they would be brought under the overlordship of the king of Portugal, but did not take this political relationship very seriously. The choice between Ternate and Tidore was difficult for the Portuguese. Finally they chose an alliance with Ternate, which naturally brought them into conflict with the other power. Ternate and Tidore are both very small islands west of Halmahera, but they had extended their authority over a great number of other islands and coastal districts in the Moluccas. The villages of all those islands were grouped into two political alliances, one under the leadership of Ternate, the other under that of Tidore. On both islands Islam had become the official religion, but Ternate had been the first to accept the new faith and its kings were more fanatic. Ternate would not accept non-Islamitic tribes or villages into its political group, while Tidore made no discrimination against them.[13]

The treaties concluded between the Portuguese and the Sultan of Ternate secured for the king of Portugal the monopoly of the clove

[12] For the reports on the voyage of the ship *Victoria*, see Stanley's edition for the Hakluyt Society (London, 1874), especially the references to the visit of the *Victoria* to Borneo (pp. 110 sq.) and the Moluccas (pp. 124 sq.).

[13] Much information regarding the history of the Moluccas in the period immediately preceding the arrival of the Dutch may be found in the huge compilation of François Valentijn, *Oud en Nieuw Oost Indiën* (Dordrecht-Amsterdam, 1724–1726), whose work will be discussed later (Chapter IX, note 17). See also the book of Heinrich Bokemeyer to which we will refer in Chapter VI.

THE ISLAND OF TERNATE
From Fr. Valentijn's *Oud en Nieuw Oost Indiën* (1724–26).

trade. The presence of the Portuguese in the Spice Islands had, however, the effect of increasing the production of spices. Clove-tree plantations were started in the second quarter of the sixteenth century on other islands, such as Amboina and Buru, and to these islands the Javanese merchants had easy access. It required great skill on the part of the Portuguese officials to maintain their position of control as competition on the market grew more and more intense. But skill was a quality that the Portuguese lacked. Their behavior was so rapacious that the great missionary, Saint Francis Xavier, reported later that their knowledge was restricted to the conjugation of the verb *rapio*, "to steal," in which they showed an "amazing capacity for inventing new tenses and participles." [14] It became customary for the viceroy in Goa to deport people of low character to the settlements in the Moluccas. Even the governors of the Moluccas sought only to enrich themselves in the four or five years of their stay in the hope of being able to live in opulence forever afterwards. Antonio Galvao, who governed at Ternate from 1536 to 1540, was the only exception. Of him it was said that the natives regretted his departure. Probably he was the only Portuguese — with the exception of some missionaries — whose departure was ever regretted in the Moluccas.[15]

The Portuguese were less successful on the Banda Islands, where the trading in nutmeg was centered. At that time the Bandanese were organized in several republics, and their system of government was extremely democratic. They were a proud and enterprising people who took a great part in the shipping between the Moluccas and Java. Not only did they resist to the utmost the intrusion of the Portuguese but they would not allow them to build any fortifications on their island or to monopolize the spice trade. For a share in the production of nutmeg the Portuguese had to rely upon normal trading and upon the friendship of the Amboinese, but, after all, a foothold had been gained in the Moluccas, and naturally it was of the highest importance for the officers of the king of Portugal to obtain control of the sea lanes between Malacca and the Moluccas.

The normal route followed the coast of Borneo, crossed the Java sea, where Gresik (the Grissee of the Dutch), near the present Surabaya, was an important stopping place, and went from there along the south

[14] In his letter of January 27, 1545, to Father Rodrigues in Lisbon (quoted by C. Wessels, *Histoire de la Mission d'Amboine*, p. 68).

[15] For a native chronicle of the kingdom of Ternate (composed, however, in the nineteenth century), see P. van der Crab, "Geschiedenis van Ternate in het Ternataansch en het Maleisch" (with Dutch translation), BKI, 2 ser. II (1878), 381–493.

coast of Celebes to the Moluccas. The hostility of the Moslems of northern Java made this route very unsafe for the Portuguese ships. The governor of Malacca was, therefore, very much interested in establishing regular connections with the Shivaitic kings of the interior of Java, one of whom had sent an embassy to Malacca immediately after the conquest of the city. In 1522 a Portuguese ship visited western Java and halted at the port of Sunda Kalapa, the very place where Batavia now is located. The king of this city was still Shivaitic, and eagerly offered to the Portuguese all facilities for the construction of a fortress, hoping to obtain their protection against his Moslem enemies. The city of Bantam, more to the west, had already gone over to Islam. Bantam was an important center for the pepper trade and attracted the attention of the Mohammedan traders from East Java who, as usual, had introduced their own religion. The Portuguese were unable to follow the invitation of the king of Sunda Kalapa immediately. When they returned five years later, entrance to the city was denied to them. It had been conquered by the Moslems of Bantam, under whom it received the name of Jacatra. For nearly twenty years, the Mohammedan rulers refused to enter into trading relations with the hated conquerors of Malacca. Before 1535 the whole of the north coast of Java had been converted to Islam, while in the interior the remnants of the old Shivaitic empire continued to exist some decades longer. The only point where the Portuguese could get into contact with the Shivaists, who sought their friendship in common hatred of Islam, was the extreme eastern point of Java, where Shivaism maintained its freedom for fifty years more.[16] In the meantime, Islam had spread from Bantam over southern Sumatra and from Demak over southern Borneo. This rapid extension of Islam was a serious setback for the Portuguese plans of conquest. The holy war threatened to spread also over the Moluccas, where the Bandanese and the Amboinese, already partly converted, maintained close connections with the sultans of Java.

The only effective counter-policy seemed to be a rapid propagation of the Christian faith. Missionary work had to concentrate on the pagan populations, for wherever Islam had been introduced the chances for the Catholic Mission were very slight.[17] The missionaries who were

[16] We have only scanty information concerning the disappearance of Hinduism in Java and the history of the last Shivaitic states. For a survey containing most of the information at our disposal, see Lekkerkerker, *Land en volk van Java*, I, 292–309.

[17] This explains why so few missionaries succeeded in entering Sumatra, which was controlled by the fanatic sultan of Atjeh. When finally Franciscan fathers were allowed to build a church in the capital of Atjeh (at the end of the seventeenth century), they could not make any conversions and had to limit their efforts to giving assistance to the

sent to the Shivaitic kingdom in Eastern Java came too late. The downfall of this last Hindu-Javanese kingdom was already a certainty. The most dramatic events in the history of this missionary movement happened, therefore, in the Moluccas. The Catholic Church gained a foothold on the island of Amboina, on the northern part of Halmahera, and on some of the smaller islands, but the existence of these communities remained very precarious. Their future depended on the attitude of the Portuguese authorities in the fortress of Ternate. When the military power of Portugal weakened, the missions were attacked by the Moslems, and whenever the governors vigorously maintained the king's authority the natives flocked together around the missionaries to receive baptism. For all these uncivilized tribes religion was synonymous with political power. Many villages embraced Catholicism as a token of their alliance with the Catholic king of Portugal, just as they went over to Islam when they joined his enemies.

As we have said, the Moluccas were divided into two political factions, one under the leadership of the sultan of Tidore, the other under Ternate. Ternate was the enemy of Christianity and therefore the enemy of Catholic Portugal but, at the same time, it was allied with the Portuguese king's officers for commercial purposes. The confusion that resulted from this strange combination may be imagined. The governors did not dare to oppose the sultan of Ternate for fear of losing the profitable monopoly of the clove export. The missionaries protested in Goa and Lisbon against a policy under which the officers supported the enemies of the Catholic Church.[18] The easiest way out of this dilemma seemed to be to concentrate both commercial and religious efforts on the island of Amboina, since this produced clove as well as nutmeg and was not subject to either Ternate or Tidore. Moreover, the establishment of a second base in the Moluccas would give the Portuguese more freedom of action and make them less dependent on the support of far-away Malacca. A great number of villages on Amboina and the neighboring islands were reported to be awaiting the arrival of missionaries. At one time the number of Christians in these parts was estimated to be as high as 70,000. It is true that the reports sent to Rome indicated among the newly converted complete ignorance

---

numerous European captives in the city. This difference between the western and the eastern part of the archipelago was of importance for the future development.

[18] The importance of these political factors is brought out very well by Wessels' studies. He also points out that several of the most prominent Jesuit missionaries were no Portuguese but Italians, who of course had not the same interest in the affairs of the king of Portugal as their Portuguese colleagues. Some of the early Jesuit missionaries were Flemings.

of Christian doctrines. The great St. Francis Xavier had visited Amboina in 1546 and prepared the way for his followers, but the number of priests really necessary for the instruction of the natives was never available. The great majority of these converts fell away from Christianity as rapidly as they had accepted it, as soon as they were threatened by the Mohammedans. The only way out of these difficulties would have been the annihilation of the power of Ternate. Instead of this, the Portuguese governors attempted to compromise with a sultan who outwitted them in every controversy.

Sultan Hairun of Ternate was one of the most remarkable figures of Indonesia in the sixteenth century. When he was arrested by the Portuguese on insufficient grounds he insisted on being sent to Goa to have his whole case investigated, and by this skillful move he forced the Portuguese to reinstate him in his kingdom. This gave him the legal right to appeal to the king of Portugal himself in all differences with the governor of the Moluccas. When the Portuguese decided to construct a second fortress on Amboina, he persuaded them to postpone the construction, and, while he bought the friendship of the officers by giving them full opportunity to enrich themselves, his troops attacked furiously the growing Christian settlements and frightened thousands away from the church. He extended his authority farther and farther until all islands from Mindanao in the north to Amboina in the south paid him tribute. Thus he successfully undermined the Portuguese position in the Moluccas. In 1565 the whole mission was ruined. Several priests were killed, and of the native Christians a number preferred to suffer death rather than go over to Islam. In these circumstances the missionaries appealed to the viceroy in Goa, who sent a fleet to restore order. The fortress on Amboina was now built, and once more the inhabitants of the islands turned to the Church for support. The situation seemed safe, when the governor of the Moluccas by his excessive rapacity caused the ruin of all Portuguese authority. He considered Sultan Hairun's power broken and thought the moment ripe to rob him of his legal share in the profits of the clove trade. Hairun resisted, and war seemed inevitable, when interested intermediaries brought about a reconciliation. With a solemn oath, the renewal of friendship was confirmed. The sultan swore with his hand on the Koran, the governor on the Gospel. Next day, when Sultan Hairun came to visit the Portuguese fortress, he was foully murdered (1570). In a few hours Ternate was in revolt, and the new sultan, Baabullah, swore that he would avenge his father by driving the Portuguese out of the Moluccas. Thus the Portuguese authority was shaken just at the moment that foreign competition began to threaten.

From a political point of view, the Portuguese had made little progress. They had no settlements outside Malacca and the Moluccas. Malacca had been continuously threatened since Atjeh had become an important power. In 1537, in 1551, in 1547, the Atjenese had assaulted the Portuguese stronghold itself. Vainly the governor sought to check this opponent by an alliance with other native states. He established connections with the Bataks, the only pagan tribe that remained in Sumatra. But all his efforts were fruitless.

Notwithstanding the fact that both Portuguese settlements in Malacca and in the Moluccas were continuously threatened, their commercial activity was extended more and more. After 1545, the Portuguese obtained a share in the trading on Bantam, whence every year three and a half million pounds of pepper were shipped to China and to India. They concluded treaties with the sultan of Brunei, with whom they had come into contact when they tried to find a new sea route north of Borneo from Malacca to the Moluccas, thus avoiding the dangerous passage of East Java. The Portuguese gave the name of the city of Brunei to the whole island of Borneo. The new route to the Moluccas also brought about the first contact of the Europeans with the island of Celebes. The Portuguese never realized that the different parts of Celebes, which they had discovered, all belonged to a single island. They believed them to be a group of islands to which they gave the name "the Celebes," a name unknown to the natives and the origin of which can not be traced.

The huge profits made by the Portuguese lured other European nations to Indonesia. The way to India was no secret. The Portuguese used a great number of foreign sailors, and navigation charts could be bought in Lisbon. In 1530 a Frenchman, Jean Parmentier of Dieppe, a man of letters and a geographer and at the same time a well-known merchant, left the coast of Normandy to explore the Indies. Two men of his crew knew the Malayan language and must have served on Portuguese ships. From a sailor's point of view, this trip was a great success, for Parmentier reached Madagascar in four months, and three months later the west of Sumatra. As a commercial enterprise, however, it was a complete failure and it discouraged the French for a long time from further attempts.[19]

[19] For the French attempts to obtain a share in the East India trade, see Tiele, *op. cit.*, *passim.* For Parmentier's voyage, see A. Guibon, *Sur les traces des Dieppois à Sumatra* (1529–1934) (Dieppe, 1936).

More trouble was caused by the Spaniards. The Portuguese government had officially protested against the visit of Magellan's ship to the Moluccas. They considered this an infringement of the Treaty of Tordesillas, concluded June 7, 1494, between the kings of Spain and Portugal, by which the globe was divided into two equal spheres of interest. A congress of experts from both nations deliberated on the affair in 1524, but these men, the best authorities on geography and navigation in the two countries, could not even agree on the exact location of the Moluccas. The Portuguese and Spanish computations differed by about forty-seven degrees.[20]

The Spaniards decided to reassert their claims and sent a fleet of seven ships westward through the Straits of Magellan, but only four of the seven ships managed to work their way through the straits. One of these disappeared somewhere in the Pacific, and while the other two reached Indonesia one was stranded on the coast of Mindanao in the Philippines, where it was lost and the crew reduced to slavery. A single vessel finally reached its goal, but in such condition that it had to be abandoned. The Spaniards had sailed for Tidore, where the sultan received them heartily in the hope of using them against Ternate and the Portuguese. There was peace between Spain and Portugal in Europe, but under the banners of Ternate and Tidore the two nations fought a brisk little war in the Far East, in which a handful of Spaniards proved more than a match for the Portuguese forces. The Portuguese governor of Malacca hurriedly sent some reinforcements, but the expedition brought new surprises to the Portuguese navigators. When they had passed north of Borneo, through miscalculations they missed the Moluccas and landed on the northern coast of New Guinea, which was thus discovered by the Europeans.

However, the Spaniards did not succeed in gaining a foothold on Tidore. All support for them had to come from America, where the famous Hernando Cortez had just conquered Mexico. He equipped three ships, of which only one arrived in the Moluccas, just in time to join in the capitulation of the small Spanish fort. Meanwhile, the governments in Europe agreed upon a new delimitation of the spheres of interest, in which the Spaniards promised to stop their explorations at seventeen degrees east of the Moluccas. Nevertheless, they appeared once more in the Philippines thirty years later and, ignoring all protests, took possession of the islands for King Philip of Spain and founded

[20] A similar discussion in American geography would raise the question as to whether Boston lay on the same degree of longitude as Salt Lake City!

the city of Manila in 1571.[21] So they were firmly established north of the Moluccas when the great revolution against Portugal took place after Sultan Hairun's death.

For five years the Portuguese fortress on Ternate was besieged. The Indonesians did not dare to storm its walls and they were not able to cut off all communication with the outside world, but they never gave the garrison a moment of respite. The fortress on Amboina was deserted, and the last trace of Portuguese authority would have disappeared if it had not been saved by the daring and ruthless Vasconcellos, who rallied around him the native Christians, built a new fortress, and waged war against all Mohammedans in the neighborhood. The story that his soldiers presented him with a great basket filled with the heads of their slain enemies proves clearly enough that they had not broken with all their former head-hunting traditions in accepting the name of Christians. The fortress of Ternate fell in 1574, and in all that time no help had been sent from Malacca or Goa. And thus Portuguese prestige was completely ruined and the Christian communities in the Moluccas were destroyed. Sultan Baabullah's power in Ternate was at its peak. An Italian missionary estimated at seventy-two the number of the islands which recognized the sovereignty of Ternate at that time.

While the Portuguese were losing ground, the Spaniards extended their authority farther and farther south. They put an end to the propagation of Islam by the sultan of Brunei. They were only waiting for the moment when they could take over control of the Moluccas. They would have done so eventually had not a great change in Europe made it unnecessary. In 1580 King Philip II of Spain united Portugal to his throne. He confirmed all the privileges of his new subjects and strictly forbade his officers in the Philippines from interfering in the Moluccas unless the Portuguese asked for help. Thus began a new period in the history of Indonesia.

As a forerunner of the coming of other nations, Sir Francis Drake had appeared in the Moluccas, where he was well received by the sultan of Ternate, who considered him a potential ally against the Portuguese. Moreover, it was also to the sultan's interest that more European nations should trade with the Moluccas, for competition would raise prices, already trebled since the arrival of the Portuguese. Sir Thomas

[21] For the sources of the early history of the Philippines see the *Catálogo de los Documentos relativos a las Islas Filipinas* of Pedro Torres y Lanzas, with the historical introduction by Pable Pastello (Barcelona, 1925 and following), especially the first two volumes.

Cavendish was the second Englishman to visit the Indies, but he only crossed the archipelago from north to south through the Straits of Macassar and of Bali, which were the less frequented parts of Indonesia. James Lancaster, the next visitor from England, lowered the British reputation considerably by his acts of piracy in the Strait of Malacca, and this gave the Portuguese a good opportunity to discredit all foreign Europeans with the natives.[22]

When the Portuguese first went to Indonesia they gained, within a few years, the reputation of being invincible. Fifty years later there was little left of that prestige. By 1585 the situation even seemed hopeless, but a peace treaty concluded with Atjeh in 1587 gave them some respite, at least in the western part of the archipelago. An alliance with the sultan of Tidore and the death of their irreconcilable enemy, Sultan Baabullah, saved the situation for them in the Moluccas. Apparently, however, they had not the energy to rebuild their empire. Even the Catholic missions had to do without their support. In the last years of Portuguese rule a group of Dominican Fathers began proselytizing on the Lesser Sunda Islands, especially on Flores and Timor, where Portuguese merchants used to call twice a year to buy the famous sandalwood, which is valuable for its oil and is used as an aromatic in Hindustan. But the governor of Malacca never thought it worth while to establish his authority over these islands. The missionaries tried to organize their native Christians for their defense but succeeded only partly in preserving them from the influence of the Moslem propagandists from Java. The mission continued to exist, however, into the time of the Dutch East India Company.[23]

Side by side with the already flourishing Mohammedan states of Atjeh and Ternate, Java too seemed to gain new strength. The interior of the island had gone over to Islam, and with this change the districts of central Java which had been so flourishing in the days of the Shailendra seem to have regained their political importance. The name of Mataram again appears in the history of Java. The ruler of this district forced all other princes of Middle and Eastern Java to recognize his

[22] The stories of the first English voyages to the East Indies have been republished by the Hakluyt Society (that of Drake by W. S. W. Vaux, London, 1854; that of James Lancaster by C. R. Markham, London, 1877). For Thomas Cavendish, see R. Hakluyt, *Principal Navigations*, Hakluyt Soc. ed. (Glasgow, 1903–05), XI, 290 sq.

[23] This mission was the origin of the present Portuguese colony of Timor. See the articles by B. C. C. van Suchtelen and G. P. Rouffaer, "De ruine van het oud-Portugeesche fort op Poeloe Ende," "De Dominikaner Solor-Flores Missie, 1561–1638," "Chronologie van de Dominikaner Missie op de Solor eilanden," in *Nederlandsch Indië Oud en Nieuw*, VIII (1923/24), 79 sq., 121 sq., 141 sq., 204 sq., 256 sq.

authority. The coastal districts, weakened by the struggle with the Portuguese, had already lost much of their importance.

The sultanate of Demak had been divided into four separate states. One of these was Padjang, a country in the interior of Central Java. This country was far less densely populated in the sixteenth century than it is now. There was still an abundance of uncultivated land in Java, and the population moved from one part to another, crowding together in those districts where the chances of making a living seemed good. In the middle of the sixteenth century the once prosperous district of Mataram was practically deserted; only three hundred families lived there when the sultan of Padjang granted this district to one of his noblemen.[24] The son and successor of the first ruler of Moslem Mataram was Suta Vidjaja, better known in Javanese legends and history as the *Senopati*, or "commander-in-chief." This title was given to him by the sultan of Padjang, but the sultan was ill requited for his liberality when the Senopati made himself an independent ruler. A period of incessant warfare began in which the Senopati of Mataram extended his authority over all territory between Cheribon in the west and the Shivaitic Balambangan in the East. From the war-stricken districts of the coast the people took refuge in the interior around the Kraton — the palace of the new potentate. Once more Java became an exclusively agricultural state. When the Senopati died in 1601, only the northeastern coastal districts, among which Gresik and Surabaya were prominent, had maintained part of their independence. The Shivaitic princes of Balambangan were on the verge of succumbing to Mohammedan aggression. Refugees who stubbornly refused to accept Islam fled to Bali, thus strengthening in this island the still vigorous Hindu tradition of which it became the last bulwark. Had Java remained united, Bali too would have been conquered by the Moslem. As it was, the new empire of Mataram was constantly torn by wars caused by the endless questions of succession.

In this way the naval power of Java had suffered heavily by the end of the sixteenth century. Its fleets had been repeatedly defeated by the Portuguese, and the very existence of the thriving trading cities on the coast was threatened from two sides, first by the Portuguese, who attempted to ruin their shipping and trading with the Moluccas, and second by Mataram, which aimed at their complete destruction and cared little for commercial interests. To the first Dutch ambassadors

[24] The rise of the empire of Mataram has not yet found its historian. For a survey see P. J. Veth, *Java*, I, 299 sq. For the Javanese traditions, J. J. Meinsma, *Babad Tabah Djawi in Proza: Javaansche Geschiedenis tot 1647 der Javaansche jaartelling* (The Hague, 1874).

to the Imperial Court the ruler of Mataram declared: "You may trade freely in my country without paying any custom duties for I am no merchant like the sultans of Bantam and Surabaya who have to fear your competition." This indicates clearly enough how the political scene had changed in Indonesia by the time the first Dutch ships appeared.

CHAPTER V

TRADERS FROM THE LOW COUNTRIES

On June 5, 1596, four Dutch ships approached Sumatra's west coast. Eighteen days later they reached the port of Bantam in northwestern Java. Hardly had they thrown out their anchors when several Portuguese merchants boarded the ships to salute the newcomers, "showing them all politeness and explaining the conditions of Java to them and exalting the great fertility and wealth of the island." After a short while the merchants took a respectful leave, honored by the Dutch commanders, who fired a salute of three guns.

This is the narrative of the first encounter between the Netherlanders and the Portuguese in the Indies, as it is given by one of the Dutch sailors. They showed each other all friendship and knew how to hide their real sentiments. The dignitaries of the Javanese prince of Bantam paid their visit to the ships next day. They too were friendly and invited the Dutch merchants to trade freely in their port, whereupon a swarm of little boats with Javanese, Chinese, and Gujerat traders surrounded the Dutch vessels on the roadstead. In no time their decks were transformed into a market place. The Dutch narrative continues: "There was nothing missing and everything was perfect except what was wrong with ourselves." [1]

Indeed, there was something wrong with the crews. The voyage had lasted fourteen months, nearly double the necessary time, and of the 249 members of the crews, 145 had died before reaching the East. All these misfortunes came from lack of leadership and insufficient knowledge of navigation. There had been continuous quarreling among the captains and *commiezen* (the merchants in charge of all matters of finance and commerce). One of these malcontents had been put in

[1] Records of many of the sixteenth- and seventeenth-century Dutch voyages have been reprinted or published in the volumes of the Linschoten Vereeniging, the Dutch equivalent of the British Hakluyt Society. Of the journals kept on the first voyage to the East Indies, many editions have been published. The principal one is G. P. Rouffaer and J. W. IJzerman, *De eerste schipvaart der Nederlanders naar Oost Indië*, 3 vols. (The Hague, 1915–1929), being Linsch. V., vols. VII, XXV, and XXXII. J. C. Mollema, *De eerste schipvaart der Hollanders naar Oost Indië, 1595–1597* (The Hague, 1935), gives a complete narrative of the voyage, based upon the materials published by Rouffaer and IJzerman. The quotation is from the journal of Frank van der Does (Rouffaer and IJzerman, II, 293).

chains and had made the whole trip through the Indies locked up in a small cabin. Another of the skippers died in India, probably poisoned by the chief merchant of the fleet, who in his turn was arrested by his own crew. Rough, impertinent, and preposterous conduct brought these first Dutchmen into great difficulties with the Indonesian rulers. Once they nearly lost their ships by their imprudence and another time, because of over-suspicion, they killed a Javanese prince who meant no offense at all, with many of his followers. Most of these mistakes must be attributed to the chief merchant of the fleet, Cornelis de Houtman.

This Cornelis de Houtman had spent many years in Lisbon.[2] He pretended to be well informed on all matters relating to the Indies and to know everything about the navigation of the Eastern waters. On his two trips to the Indies he proved to be a boaster and a ruffian. Nevertheless, he had succeeded in obtaining the support of a group of wealthy merchants in Amsterdam. These merchants had equipped the first expedition to Indonesia. The story of this first trading company with the East Indies has been written many times, and nearly all textbooks repeat the same version of the story, connecting this first expedition with a decree issued by King Philip II of Spain and Portugal closing the port of Lisbon to all traders from England and the Netherlands. Since this decree made it impossible to obtain the spices and other products from the East in Lisbon, the Netherlanders were forced to go to the Indies. This story sounds plausible but is only partly true.[3]

Long before 1594, when King Philip signed the decree of expulsion, the Dutch were sailing the Atlantic Ocean far and wide. They were trading on the west coast of Africa and visiting the West Indies and

[2] The stay of de Houtman at Lisbon is usually interpreted as an act of "economic espionage," committed on behalf of some of the merchants who formed the first company for trading in the Indies. F. W. Stapel, in his lecture on this subject, given for the Congress of Dutch historians in 1936 (*Tijdschrift voor Geschiedenis*, 1936, p. 370), refutes this theory and, in my opinion, with good reasons. His main arguments are that long before Houtman went to Lisbon "to find out the Portuguese secrets about the trade to India," numerous Dutch sailors had taken part in the Portuguese voyages and thus were well acquainted with the problems of the voyage to Asia, and that before Houtman left, accurate Portuguese maps had been reprinted and offered for sale in Amsterdam by Cornelis Claes.

[3] This theory has been propounded by J. F. Furnivall, in his *Netherlands India*, among others, and was the common theory among Dutch historians until a few decades ago. It is perfectly clear, however, that the chief reason why the Dutch began to trade directly in the Indies at the end of the sixteenth century was that for many years Dutch sailors in increasing numbers had been sailing on the India route in Portuguese ships, so that naturally the inclination came to make the voyage for their own profit; that Dutch ships under the Portuguese flag were already sailing to the West Indies; and further, that several enterprising merchants, among whom was Balthasar de Moucheron, had already been exploring the northeast passage in order to reach China.

Brazil, either under their own flag or under that of the Portuguese. For years they had been exploring the northeast passage which would bring them to China along the route north of Siberia. In 1584 a Dutch ship had visited Nova Zembla, and ten years later four ships penetrated into the Arctic seas, from where they hoped to make their way to Eastern Asia. The reason they hesitated to follow the route around the Cape was not fear of the Portuguese but the great difficulties which this route presented for navigation. The Netherlands' geographers were well acquainted with all details of navigation in the Southern Atlantic and in the Indian Ocean. Their great expert on Asiatic affairs was Jan Huyghen van Linschoten, who had lived for many years in Goa and noted carefully all information he could collect. On his return he published his *Itinerario*, a geographical description of the world with all necessary information for the voyages to India or America.[4] Undoubtedly the merchants from the Netherlands would have found their way to the Spice Islands sooner or later. Even a petty German prince, the Duke of Lauenburg, plotted great expeditions to Asia as early as 1592.[5] The decree of King Philip II hastened the development but did not cause it.

The four ships of de Houtman formed the advance guard of great armadas to come. For the Indonesians, they were only passers-by who came and went and were soon forgotten. They had been seen in Bantam, where they concluded a treaty with the Sultan. This is the first treaty ever concluded between Netherlanders and an Indonesian prince, therefore its contents may follow here:

As it pleased God, our Lord, and you, Sirs, that you came to visit us with four ships, and as we have seen the patent letter which His Excellency, Prince Maurice of Nassau, graciously ordered shown to us, by which letter we learn that His Excellency offers all friendship and alliance to us which friendship is to be confirmed by you, we are well content to have a permanent league of alliance and friendship with His Highness the Prince and with you, gentlemen, and we swear to maintain this friendship and alliance and to order all our subjects to do the same.[6]

[4] Jan Huyghen van Linschoten's *Itinerario* has been published many times and in many languages. Only part of his information was obtained through personal observation. In his book he inserted among other information that of Dirk Gerritsz. Pomp, the first Netherlander (as far as we know) who sailed to China and Japan (see Arthur Wichmann, *Dirck Gerritsz. Ein Beitrag zur Entdeckungsgeschichte des 16ten und 17ten Jahrhunderts*, Groningen, 1899).

[5] See for instance the study of J. E. Heeres, "Duitschers en Nederlanders op de zeewegen naar Oost-Indië voor 1595," in *Gedenkboek van het Kon. Instituut voor Taal-, Land- en Volkenkunde van Nederlandsch Indië* (The Hague, 1926), p. 171 sq.

[6] A collection of all treaties between Dutch representatives and Indonesian princes and peoples may be found in the "Corpus Diplomaticum Neerlando-Indicum" of J. E. Heeres,

A few weeks later this friendship was broken by the rude behavior of Cornelis de Houtman. It was soon renewed, but when the Dutch traders departed, their Portuguese opponents felt that they had no need to be afraid of such competition. De Houtman sailed along the north coast of Java. He visited the town of Sunda Kalapa or Jacatra, a place which he considered far more agreeable than Bantam and where twenty years later Batavia was built. North of Surabaya the ships were attacked by Javanese pirates, and so many men of the crew were lost that one of the ships had to be abandoned. On the coast of Madura the natives were friendly, but the Dutch used violence without any reason. The only pleasant experience the unfortunate expedition had in the East Indies was a visit to the island of Bali. Apparently the beauty of this island so appealed to the Hollanders that two men of the crew deserted. From Bali the squadron continued its voyage south of Java and returned to Europe.

There was great rejoicing in Holland, notwithstanding that the expedition had rendered only small profits. The ship-owners understood that a new expedition under better leadership could be a great success. To the Portuguese, the presence of Dutch ships in Asia was a shock. Since 1580 Portugal had been united with Spain under King Philip II. The king of Spain was the irreconcilable enemy of the independence of the Netherlands. From now on, Portugal was involved in the war between King Philip and his former subjects. Thus the Portuguese had to fear not only the competition of Dutch merchants in the spice trade but also open acts of hostility against their settlements in Asia. The viceroy in Goa, Francesco da Gama, took immediate steps to prevent further expeditions of the enemy to the Indies. He equipped two galleons — large sailing vessels — and two galleys, low-built rowing ships of the same type as those used in the Mediterranean. These four ships were formed into a fleet with a number of smaller craft and entrusted to the command of Lourenzo de Brito. The viceroy gave definite orders that this armada should not interfere with native shipping and not mix in wars between the Indonesian princes. He understood clearly that the sympathy and coöperation of the Indonesians were necessary to maintain the Portuguese position in this emergency. But, he chose the wrong commander.[7]

When de Brito arrived at the roadstead of Bantam and asked for the

continued by F. W. Stapel, published as BKI, vols. LVII, LXXXVII, XCI, XCIII and XCVI (1907–1938). The quotation is translated from p. 3 of vol. I of the series.

[7] For a detailed description of the Portuguese reaction on the first Dutch visit to the Indies, see Tiele, in BKI, 4 ser. V (1881), 212 sq.

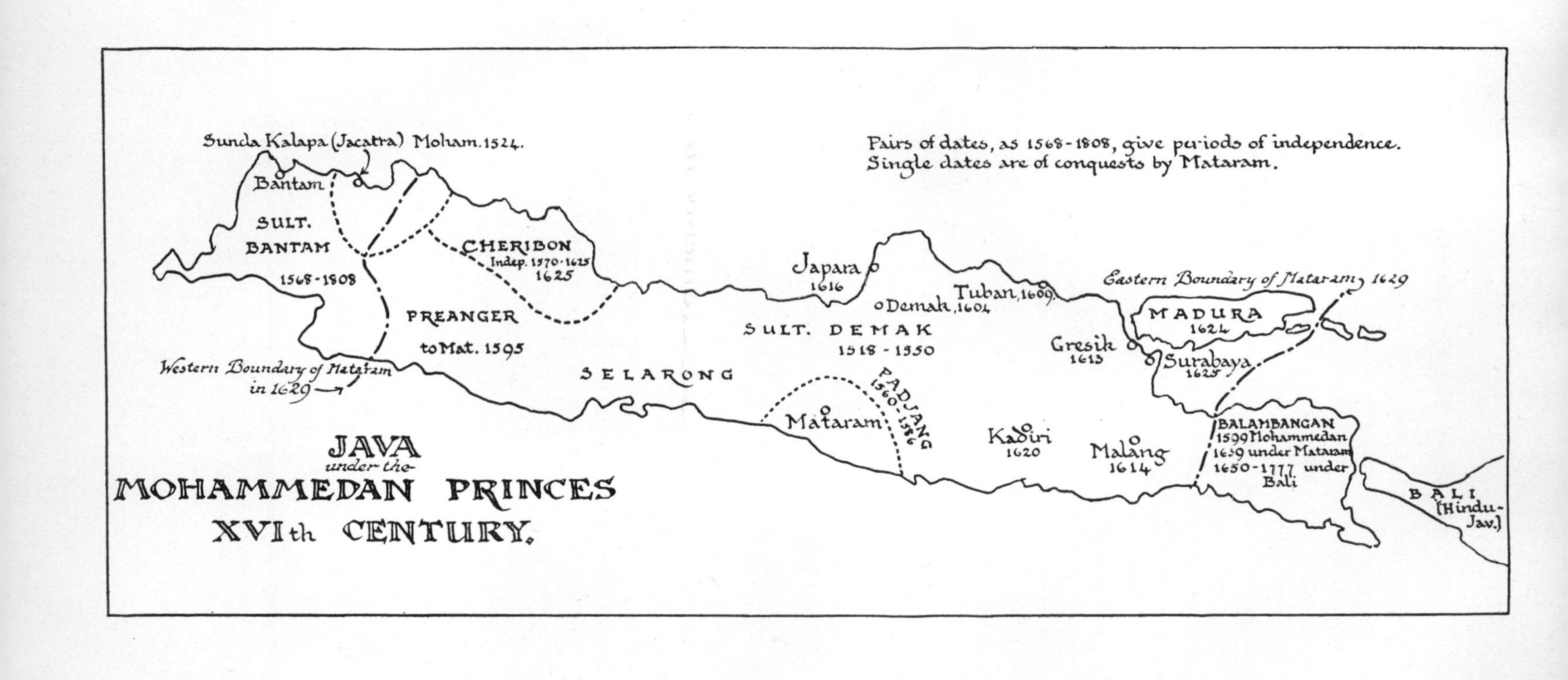
JAVA
under the
MOHAMMEDAN PRINCES
XVIth CENTURY.
Pairs of dates, as 1568-1808, give periods of independence.
Single dates are of conquests by Mataram.
Sunda Kalapa (Jacatra) Moham. 1524.
Bantam
SULT. BANTAM
1568-1808
CHERIBON
Indep. 1570-1625
1625
PREANGER
to Mat. 1595
Western Boundary of Mataram in 1629
SELARONG
Japara
1616
Demak, 1604
SULT. DEMAK
1518 - 1550
Tuban, 1609
PADJANG
1560-1586
Mataram
Kadiri
1620
Malang
1614
Gresik
1613
Surabaya
1625
MADURA
1624
Eastern Boundary of Mataram, 1629
BALAMBANGAN
1599 Mohammedan
1639 under Mataram
1650-1777 under Bali
BALI
(Hindu-Jav.)

Dutch ships, he was told by the Javanese that the enemy had sailed west and was probably to be found near Ceylon. In reality de Houtman was already back in Holland. Don Lourenzo thought it a good idea to teach the prince of Bantam a lesson, so that he should never again communicate with foreign European merchants, whom he called, for convenience's sake, "English pirates." Sir James Lancaster, who had visited the archipelago a few years before, had left a bad reputation and, therefore, the Portuguese considered it good politics to make the Dutch share that reputation. Contrary to his instructions, Don Lourenzo attacked Javanese and Chinese barks and demanded the payment of a huge sum of money from the sultan of Bantam. The resistance of the Javanese, however, was unexpectedly successful. Two of the Portuguese ships were captured, and thus the unfortunate admiral accomplished exactly the reverse of what he was instructed to do. Instead of strengthening the Portuguese prestige, he had ruined it forever. Defeated and discouraged, he withdrew the rest of his fleet to Malacca, where he remained idle when a second Dutch fleet appeared in Indonesian waters.

Immediately after the return of de Houtman the ship-owners of Amsterdam equipped a second fleet, this time of eight ships. Other groups of merchants followed their example, and in the single year of 1598 five expeditions, totaling twenty-two ships, left Holland for Eastern Asia.[8] This fact alone proves sufficiently that it was the spirit of enterprise that brought the Netherlanders to the Indies. Thirteen of these ships took the route around the Cape, while nine attempted the passage through the Strait of Magellan. Of the thirteen ships that sailed east, twelve made the voyage safely. The one that was lost went no further than Dover, where it capsized. Of the nine ships that sailed west, some never succeeded in passing through the Strait of Magellan. One reached Japan, where it was confiscated by the Japanese government. One was captured by the Spaniards in South America, and another one by the Portuguese in the Moluccas. Only a single ship, commanded by Oliver van Noort, reached the Indies, and, returning around the Cape, accomplished the first Dutch circumnavigation of the

[8] For a survey of these expeditions, see J. K. J. De Jonge, *De Opkomst van het Nederlandsch Gezag in Oost-Indië*. The first three volumes (The Hague, 1862–1865) cover the period up to 1610. Although published three quarters of a century ago, this work remains invaluable because of the documents published in the second (and larger) section of each volume. For the journals and documents relating to the early voyages to the Indies, around Africa as well as around America, see Linsch. V., vols. IX, XXI, XXII, XXIV, XXVII, XXVIII, XXXVIII, and XLII. An excellent and very recent survey by H. Terpstra appears in Stapel, *Gesch.* II, 275–461.

world. The two expeditions that sailed west caused to the ship owners a loss of more than half a million guilders. Of the three fleets that took the eastern route one caused heavy losses, the second brought a moderate profit, and only the third one gave rich returns, nearly 100 per cent. This proves that the first voyages of the Netherlanders to the Indies were not so profitable as tradition makes us believe.

The energy of the ship owners seemed inexhaustible, however. Within three years after the return of the first expedition their ships had appeared off the west coast of Sumatra and near Atjeh, they had visited Java and the Moluccas, they were seen off Brunei on Borneo's north coast and off Manila in the Philippines. They had visited the coast of Siam and Indo-China and had attempted to establish connections with the Chinese in Canton. They were seen in Japan in 1600.[9] They were trading in Ceylon in 1602 and explored the northern coast of Australia in 1605.[10] Three squadrons sailed from Holland in 1599 and two more in 1600. In 1601 four expeditions left for the Indies. Together these fleets numbered thirty-one ships, which brings the yearly average of Netherlands ships going out to the East to twelve, a number which far exceeded the Portuguese efforts. With the exception of one, these expeditions had no other aim than commerce. Only van Noort made his circumnavigation of the world into a piratical excursion, in which he did much damage to the Spanish but suffered as much himself. Jacob van Neck, the admiral of the second fleet, reported with satisfaction that great profits had been earned on his voyage, not by injustice or tyrannical oppression, but by honest trading with foreign nations.[11]

Van Neck's fleet had been the first Dutch squadron to visit the Moluccas. Here he had entered into normal trading relations with the natives, bargaining with the harbor masters over the custom duties which he had to pay and exhibiting his merchandise in a storehouse ashore. From morning to night the Dutch sailors were buying and selling. From all over the islands people flocked together to see the mer-

[9] See F. C. Wieder, "De reis van Mahu en de Cordes door de straat van Magelhaes naar Zuid Amerika en Japan" (Linsch. V., vols. XXI, XXII and XXIV, The Hague, 1923–1925). For the Dutch-Chinese relations in the seventeenth century G. Schlegel, "De betrekkingen tusschen Nederland en China volgens Chineesche bronnen," BKI, XLII (1893), 1 sq. and 188 sq. Schlegel's views on the subject have been corrected in the far more complete study of W. P. Groenevelt, "De Nederlanders in China," vol. I, 1601–1624, in BKI, vol. XLVIII (1898). This is the only volume published.

[10] For the first discoveries by the Dutch in Australia, see J. E. Heeres, *The Part Borne by the Dutch in the Discovery of Australia 1606–1765*, text both in Dutch and in English (Leiden–London, 1899).

[11] Stapel, *Gesch.* II, 378.

chandise that was presented: helmets, cuirasses, glass, velvet, and *Norembergerie* (playthings made in Germany). Trading went so well that on the Banda Islands alone two shops were opened. The Asiatic merchants became envious and tried to hinder the commerce by all possible intrigue. Nevertheless, the Dutch had gained such goodwill among the Bandanese that they left several of their men behind, with merchandise worth more than 3800 guilders. The men and the goods were entrusted to the friendship of the natives, who kept their word and protected them until a new fleet came to visit the islands.[12] Another squadron of the same fleet had been welcomed by the sultan of Ternate. Here and on the island of Amboina other trading posts were established. Everywhere the Netherlanders were received with great friendliness. The natives secretly hoped to use them as allies in their war against the Portuguese, but their invitations to join them in offensive action were politely declined by the Dutch admirals. Commerce, not war, had been the aim of the ship-owners and, therefore, the commanders were anxious to avoid all military actions, though one of them openly declared that "where he and his comrades would risk their lives, the directors might well risk their ships and money." [13]

The only places where the Netherlanders were not well received were Atjeh and Madura. In Madura the resentment over de Houtman's brutal behavior made friendly commerce impossible. Atjeh was visited by two ships from Zeeland in June, 1599. The leader of this squadron was again Cornelis de Houtman, hence trouble might have been expected. This time his imprudence proved fatal to himself. He was killed in an attack on his ship in the roadstead of Atjeh. His brother, Frederick, was taken prisoner and spent two years in captivity, where he was in continuous danger of being murdered. Yet he found the opportunity to compose a Malayan-Dutch dictionary and a Malayan translation of Christian prayers.[14]

For the native princes the presence of the Dutch merchants was very advantageous. The competition between the Dutch and the Portuguese and still more between the different Dutch trading companies doubled the prices of pepper, clove, and nutmeg in a few years. The native harbor masters (of whom every village had one or more) raised the port duties every month. The Dutch protested but were always in a

[12] See De Jonge, *op. cit.* and also J. A. van der Chijs, *De vestiging van het Nederlandsch Gezag over de Banda-eilanden* (Batavia–The Hague, 1886).

[13] Jacob van Heemskerck to the chief merchant aboard his ship, De Jonge, *op. cit.*, II, 210.

[14] P. A. Tiele, "Frederik de Houtman in Atjeh," *Indische Gids*, 1881, I, 146 sq.

hurry to obtain a good cargo and, therefore, willing to pay whatever was asked. The profits were large enough to pay even higher prices. Economically, the Dutch held a much stronger position than the Portuguese. Their greater ability as sailors and the better construction of their ships enabled them to carry the spices to Europe at far lower expense than the Portuguese could. If the king of Portugal and Spain intended to maintain his monopoly of the spices, he would have to drive the Netherlanders out by force; but exactly at this moment an English fleet was blockading the port of Lisbon so that no help could be sent to the Indies. At the same time the Netherlands merchants were gradually expanding their sphere of influence.

In September, 1600, a treaty had been concluded between Admiral Steven van der Haghen and the inhabitants of the island of Amboina.[15] It was a formal treaty of alliance against the Portuguese, concluded between Netherlanders and Indonesians on terms of equality. The Dutch promised to construct a fortress on Amboina and to protect the natives, who, in their turn, promised the Dutch a monopoly of the spice trade. This agreement was premature, however. The fortress could not be maintained, and consequently the right of monopoly was not renewed in a following treaty. These first contracts between the Netherlanders and the Indonesians are of great historical importance since they laid the basis for the future political development of the whole archipelago. Some technical difficulties presented themselves in these negotiations. The Indonesians wanted satisfactory information about the power and the personality of the king of Holland before concluding a treaty. Unhappily, there was no king of Holland. Rather than go to the trouble of explaining to the natives the complicated system of government that existed in the Low Countries, the staunch Dutch Republicans, for business reasons, promoted their *stadhouder*, Maurice, Prince of Orange, to the royal rank.

The prince took great interest in the Indian voyages and readily issued letters of recommendation to the commanders of the Dutch fleets. These letters were translated to the native princes—probably in a translation adapted to the circumstances. The King of Bali took the matter seriously enough to respond to the Prince of Orange in a letter written in Balinese, in which he sent his greetings to the "King of Holland" and even expressed his wish that "Bali and Holland should become one."[16] He had been very much impressed by the power of the prince when emissaries of de Houtman had shown him

[15] J. E. Heeres, CD, I, 12.
[16] Agreement of July 7, 1601 (CD, I, 15).

the boundaries of Holland on a map of Europe, boundaries which they put near Moscow and Venice, thus annexing most of Europe for this special occasion! The king of Atjeh was less easily deceived. Some Portuguese merchants who lived in his capital told him that Holland had no king at all but that England was ruled by a queen of whom they did not tell much good. Consequently, the king of Atjeh addressed a letter to Queen Elizabeth, which he sent by some English merchants addressed to the "Queen of England, France, and Holland." Apparently, the geography of Europe was too complicated for these Oriental rulers. To be fair, the same might be said of European knowledge of Asiatic affairs.

In the first years the relations between Netherlanders and Indonesians developed quite satisfactorily. The traders who had stayed at their posts in Ternate, Amboina, and the Banda Islands were held in high esteem by the inhabitants. The king of Bali showed his friendliness toward Admiral van Eemskerk by presenting him with a beautiful girl, a present which the honorable gentleman considered most embarrassing. (His embarrassment grew when the girl refused to leave him and return home.) Difficulties less easy of solution were encountered in dealing with the ruler of Atjeh. Admiral van Caerden, a very reckless and imprudent officer, had been plundering and sinking native trading barks off the coast of Atjeh because he suspected the Atjenese of plotting with the Portuguese to capture his ship. Ruthless as his action had been, it had been surpassed by the still more brutal behavior of the Portuguese authorities. This led finally to an agreement between the king of Atjeh and the Dutch. Admiral Bicker promised to sue van Caerden's company in a Dutch court for the acts of piracy of their officer. In return, the king of Atjeh set free the unfortunate Frederick de Houtman. It is worth noting that the court in Amsterdam condemned van Caerden's company to pay a compensation of more than 50,000 guilders to the Indonesian merchants, and that the sum was actually paid in Atjeh.[17] The king of Atjeh sent two ambassadors to the Netherlands to get more accurate information on the political condition of Europe. These Atjenese were the first Indonesian representatives to visit Holland. They were very well received in Zeeland, and when one of them died in the city of Middelburg he was buried with a great display of official mourning. The other one visited Prince Maurice of Orange in his camp while he was besieging the town of Grave, which gave a good occasion to show the power of the Netherlands army, at that time the best-organized army of Europe, to the

[17] De Jonge, *op. cit.*, II, 234.

Atjenese. After a few years the envoy returned safely to his native country.

Political and economic considerations made the Dutch and Indonesians coöperate in these years. It is certain, however, that the two nations did not understand much of each other. It was a strange company of men who manned those ships to the Indies. Only strict discipline could make them behave even somewhat decently. The Englishman, John Davis, received a very bad impression of them and in his narrative called them cowards "who fled from the natives like mice from cats"; but he had the ill luck to sail on a ship commanded by Cornelis de Houtman.[18] Usually there were too many lawless elements among the crews. Most sailors were unwilling to sign on ships bound for the East Indies. The risks were too great, since normally one fourth of the sailors lost their lives. The ship-owners made the situation worse by sending aboard members of their own families or relatives of their friends whom for personal reasons they wished as far away as possible. In the Indies the crews knew that they were indispensable, therefore they permitted themselves all kinds of impertinence; heavy drinking and fighting followed by mutiny were quite normal. Some of the men ran away and became Mohammedans. Others joined native pirates. Sometimes the captains had to ask the help of the local princes to restore order. It is no wonder that the common sailors were often both feared and despised by the Indonesians. On the other hand, there were better elements, decent sailors who pitied the natives, ill-treated by their shipmates and captains, who had no greater desire than to avoid all unnecessary bloodshed. Some of the admirals treated the enemy with such respect and humanity that they won the admiration of the Portuguese governors. Admiral de Weert risked his life and the success of his expedition by refusing to hand over his Portuguese prisoners to the maharajah of Ceylon. Van Spilbergh sent all men and women whom he found aboard captured Portuguese ships safely home on one of their own vessels, an act of kindness which brought him an official letter of thanks from the governor of Malacca. Admiral van der Haghen negotiated for weeks with the Christians and Moslems of Amboina to bring about a permanent peace between these implacable enemies. An eyewitness tells us how he sat

[18] John Davis' voyage in *Purchas His Pilgrimes* (ed. of 1905/07, Glasgow), II, 308. A series of articles on the conditions existing aboard the ships of the Dutch East India Company (which were slightly better than those prevailing during the first voyages) were published by J. de Hullu in BKI, vols. LXVII (1913) and LXIX (1914). Most of the examples of rough, or, to the other side, exceptionally decent behavior have been taken from the documents published by De Jonge, *op. cit.*

in his cabin for endless hours enduring the oppressive heat, wiping his forehead continuously, never tiring of listening to the complaints and arguments of the Amboinese leaders until he succeeded in bringing about a final reconciliation.

The years 1601 and 1602 brought a turn in the events. The viceroy of Goa decided to reëstablish Portuguese authority in Indonesia. Eight larger and twenty smaller vessels under the command of Furtado de Mendoza sailed from Malacca. After some initial skirmishes with the Atjenese, the fleet headed for Bantam. Accidentally, a Dutch fleet under Wolfert Harmensz, consisting of three large and two small vessels, approached Sumatra from the west at the same time. A Chinese trader had brought them notice of the Portuguese armada. Immediately a council of all officers was called, where the following hardly credible decision was taken: "As the retention of the Port of Bantam is of the highest importance for the United Provinces and their commerce, our ships shall attack the Portuguese fleet with courage, trusting in the help of God Almighty." [19]

Thereupon the five Netherlands ships attacked the thirty Portuguese vessels on Christmas Day, 1601. On December 27 the battle was renewed. With the loss of two ships, the Portuguese were driven from the roadstead of Bantam. In this kingdom the reputation of the Dutch was now well established. From the military point of view it was, however, an ephemeral success. Harmensz had orders to buy spices, not to conquer Portuguese ships. He hurried on to the Moluccas, where his ships scattered among the islands. Consequently, he was unable to help the people of Amboina when they were attacked and badly defeated by Furtado's forces. For commercial reasons, Amboina was left to its fate. This gave the Portuguese a last chance to restore the authority of their king. A pincer movement was planned by the Portuguese against their main enemy in the Moluccas, the sultan of Ternate. From Amboina, Furtado sailed north, and from Manila a Spanish fleet moved south, but this joint attack failed completely because of the exhaustion and demoralization of the Portuguese troops. Discouraged, Furtado returned to Malacca. From there the Portuguese attempted to conquer at least the main strongholds of their mortal enemy, the sultan of Johore. Here, too, they came too late, for a Dutch fleet forced them to return to their base. A general counter-offensive seemed imminent. The sultan of Ternate, now an ally of the Dutch, was more powerful

[19] De Jonge, *op. cit.*, II, 262.

than ever. The people of Banda granted a monopoly of the spice trade to the Dutch merchants, between whom all mutual competition ceased when in March, 1602, the United East India Company was established and received from the States General of the Netherlands a monopoly for all commerce in Asia.

The constitution and the financial organization of the East India Company belongs more to Netherlands than to Indonesian history.[20] A capital of six and a half million guilders was brought together, and a board of seventeen directors instituted. It was eight years more before the board of directors appointed a governor-general who could command in their name in the Indies. The new company took over all factories that had been established in the Indies by its predecessors. Such factories existed at Banda, Ternate, Gresik (north of Surabaya), Patani (north coast of the Malay Peninsula), at Atjeh, Johore, and Bantam. The new company at once equipped fourteen ships for the voyage to the Indies. In the next year thirteen ships more were sent out, and a third squadron of eleven ships left Holland when only two vessels of the former expeditions had returned. Thirty-eight ships were equipped in three years. These mighty, heavily armed fleets were not only destined for commerce. The charter of the East India Company gave full power to this corporation to act in behalf of the States General of the Netherlands and to exercise all rights of sovereignty. The directors ordered Admiral van der Haghen, who commanded the second

[20] In 1693 the Directors of the East India Company gave orders to their legal councilor, Pieter van Dam, to compose a full description of the administration and trade system of the Company. Van Dam completed his work after eight years. Of the eight huge folio volumes which he filled with his minutely detailed description, seven are still preserved in the State Archives at The Hague. By order of the Netherlands Department of Education, F. W. Stapel undertook the publication of Van Dam's *Beschrijvinge* (so far five volumes have been published, The Hague, 1927–1939). Based mainly on Van Dam is the book of G. C. Klerk de Reus, *Geschichtlicher Ueberblick der administrativen, rechtlichen und finanziellen Entwicklung der Niederländischen Ost-Indischen Compagnie* (Batavia, 1894). There are numerous other works on the organization of the Company, for instance, S. Van Brakel, *De Hollandsche Handelscompagnieën der zeventiende eeuw* (The Hague, 1908). Most illuminating of all, however, is the small book by W. M. Mansvelt, *Rechtsvorm en geldelijk beheer bij de Oost Indische Compagnie* (Amsterdam, 1922). F. W. Stapel, in the third volume of the *Geschiedenis van Nederl. Indië*, published under his direction, gives a detailed description of all the commercial activities of the Company in Asia. In fact, this volume is rather a history of the East India Company than of the East Indies. Compare with Mansvelt's book H. Dunlop, *De Oost-Indische Compagnie in Perzië* (The Hague, 1930), being Rijks Geschiedkundige Publicatiën, vol. LXXII, Introduction. On the founding of the Company and its charter, see J. A. van der Chijs, *Geschiedenis der Stichting van de Vereenigde Oost Indische Compagnie*, second ed. (Leiden, 1857).

of their expeditions — that of thirteen ships — to attack the Portuguese at all their strongholds in Mozambique, in Goa, and in Malacca, and to avenge the attack on the allied nation of Amboina.[21]

The counter-attack met with unexpected success. The Portuguese were driven from Johore. The main fleet under the personal command of van der Haghen appeared before Amboina, where, to the great surprise of the Dutch admiral, the Portuguese fortress capitulated without firing a shot. The same year saw the fall of the Portuguese fortress on the island of Tidore. In vain the Portuguese had sought the aid of English traders, to whom they even promised their stock of spices in exchange for powder and ammunition. The conquest of the fortress of Amboina gave to the East India Company its first territorial possession in the archipelago. In February, 1605, Admiral van der Haghen concluded a treaty with all the villages of Amboina, Islamitic as well as Christian, in which these villages recognized the suzerainty of the States General of the Netherlands. Monopoly of trade was, of course, included in the treaty. A remarkable clause promised freedom of religion to all, Moslem, Catholic, and Protestants. Unfortunately this promise was kept for only a few months.[22]

The following year the offensive was continued by an attack on Malacca. An agreement was made with the sultan of Johore which provided for an offensive and defensive alliance and a monopoly of trade. By the terms of this treaty, if the town of Malacca were conquered, it should belong to the Dutch company. The attack, however, was beaten off, and Malacca continued to be Portuguese for thirty-five years more. The confidence of the sultan of Johore in his Dutch allies was weakened, but this was a minor detail compared with the disaster that overtook the Dutch forces in the Moluccas, where a Spanish fleet from the Philippines destroyed the power of the sultan of Ternate and conquered the Dutch trading posts. Thus war was waged between the European nations in the archipelago with uncertain result. The whole territory had entered upon a period of transition in which the future fate of the Indonesian peoples was to be decided.

[21] Instruction to Admiral van der Haghen, De Jonge, *op. cit.*, III, 146–147.

[22] Heeres, CD, I, 31. Paragraph III of the treaty guarantees freedom of religion and its public exercise.

CHAPTER VI

JAN PIETERSZOON COEN, THE FOUNDER OF THE DUTCH COMMERCIAL EMPIRE

UNTIL THE BEGINNING of the seventeenth century, the presence of the Europeans in the Indonesian Archipelago had wrought little change in the political constellation of the area. The same sultanates that had played an important role before the arrival of the Portuguese continued to do so during the whole of the sixteenth century. The sultans of Malacca alone had been forced to move their capital to the newly founded city of Johore. Their old rivals, the sultans of Atjeh, had profited by this change and had taken over the leadership in the Mohammedan world of northwestern Indonesia. The only major political event within the native world, however, had occurred in central Java, where the empire of Mataram had definitely superseded the smaller sultanates of the northeastern coast. Surabaya alone, of all these small commercial kingdoms, continued to offer resistance against the powerful rulers of central Java. This caused a continuous series of wars from which the princes of Mataram always emerged victorious.

These wars must have had a great influence on the development of Java. Before 1600 the sultans of the coastal states had had a strong navy at their disposal. The Dutch narrators who describe the last struggles between Surabaya and Mataram tell us that the emperor was greatly superior on land but could not organize a fleet strong enough to defeat his opponents on sea. After the victory of Mataram, Javanese sea power had disappeared. Sultan Agung, the grandson of the founder of the empire, who from 1613 ruled Mataram, many times showed his contempt for all matters of commerce.[1] The welfare of his country and

[1] For this attitude of the Indonesian princes see F. De Haan, *Priangan*, 4 vols. (Batavia, 1910–1912), III, 24–25. Especially remarkable is the haughty statement by the sultan of Bantam (1624), that if Prince Maurice of Orange [then *stadhouder* of Holland and commander-in-chief of the Dutch Republic] were there, he would send ambassadors to him as to a brother [i.e., a prince of equal rank], but he could not debase himself so far as to send envoys to the governor-general, who was only the chief of a group of merchants. The susuhunan of Mataram despised not only the Dutch but also the other Javanese princes as "merchants." The Chinese court of course took a still more haughty attitude. When Commander Reyersen in 1623 obtained a promise from the governor of Fukien that an embassy would be sent to Batavia, this official entrusted the mission to an employee of low rank (Groenevelt, *op. cit.*, p. 242), or, according to Schlegel's translation, "to a young student" (*op. cit.*, p. 12).

especially its foreign trade was no matter of concern to him. He gave the representatives of the East India Company many trading privileges, chiefly in the hope of securing their assistance against his enemies. Thus the decline of Javanese trading was not caused solely by the competition and the violent methods of suppression of the Portuguese and Dutch merchants, but by the policy of Java's own rulers as well.[2] As long as Surabaya and other coastal districts retained part of their independence, there were Javanese traders in the Moluccas and Celebes. The Javanese also continued trading with Malacca until this city was conquered by the Dutch. The rise of Mataram, however, shifted the center of political, cultural, and economic life from the coast to the middle of Java and thus became jointly responsible for the decline of Javanese commerce. In Bantam, where the sultans took a different attitude, commerce continued to flourish during the larger part of the seventeenth century.

The internal Javanese wars were accompanied by devastations and forced migrations of the people. All this caused eastern and central Java to become once more a purely agricultural state. It was because of its abundant supply of rice that the Dutch merchants were interested in trading with Mataram. Besides, they saw here a good market for the cheap cotton they imported from India. The emissaries of the Company who visited the interior of the island on their voyages to the court of the emperor noted carefully the products sold in the market places. It is to be wished that they had been interested also in the cultural aspects of Javanese life.[3]

The unification of the major part of Java led naturally to a revival of the arts which gave evidence again of the deep roots of the old traditions of Javanese civilization. From the beginning of the seventeenth century dates the *Babad Tanah Djawi*, a historical composition prob-

[2] See the remarks of Sultan Agung quoted in the preceding note. In the period of historiography in which it was customary to blame Europeans and civilization in general for all evils that ever had come over non-European peoples (as, for instance, at the end of the eighteenth century, under the influence of Abbé Raynal's *Histoire philosophique et politique des deux Indes*), the devastation of Java's coastland by the armies of Mataram was simply ignored. Typical of this type of historiography of the Indies is John Crawfurd's *History of the Indian Archipelago*, 3 vols. (Edinburgh, 1820); see, for instance, III, 149 and 220 sq.

[3] The first ambassadors to the court of Mataram were Gaspar van Zurck and Balthasar van Eyndhoven (1614). The reports of this and other early embassies have been published by De Jonge, *op. cit.*, IV, 16, 57, 88. Between 1646 and 1655 yearly embassies were sent, which, in the opinion of the susuhunans, were a token of recognition of Mataram's overlordship over Batavia. Several of these embassies were led by Rijkloff van Goens, who later became governor-general of the Indies; see J. W. IJzerman, "Het aantal hofreizen van Rijklof van Goens," in BKI, LXVI (1912), 246 sq.

ably written for the glorification of Sultan Agung and his dynasty.[4] The author was evidently well versed in the historical literature of Java. We may even say that he was *too* well versed in the old literature, for he knew exactly which texts fell in line with the tendency of his book and which did not, and the latter were destroyed by the order of the sultan! This strange way of displaying interest in history can be explained by the purpose of Javanese historiography, which was still imbued with the old belief in the power of unknown supernatural forces that manifest themselves in all matters living and dead. Islam had not changed the Javanese way of thinking in this respect. As the *Arjuna-Vijaya* was composed to strengthen the personality of King Airlangga, so the *Babad Tanah Djawi* was written to reinforce the prestige and the inner forces of the dynasty of Mataram.

In this seventeenth-century chronicle two traditions were combined. First, an effort was made to connect the ancestry of Agung and his grandfather, the Senopatih, with the old kings of central Java, in other words with the rulers of Shivaitic Mataram. Thus it represented a reaction against King Angrok and Kertanagara, who had brought eastern Java to power. The memory of these rulers was deleted from the records as much as possible. At the same time, however, the chronicle took up the tradition of the empire of Madjapahit as the leading, unifying state in the archipelago. Hence King Hayam Wuruk was included in the list of ancestors of Agung, from which his predecessor Kertanagara was banished. Finally, the chronicle brought the tradition into concurrence with the teachings of Islam by substituting Adam for Shiva-Buddha as the ancestor of the royal family!

Restoration of the empire of Madjapahit was the aim of Sultan Agung, but at the same time the Netherlanders began the organization of another empire that was intended to be not only Indonesian but Asiatic. Sultan Agung's dream of conquest could never be realized, for he did not understand the all-important part sea power had to play in schemes like this. His opponent, Governor-General Jan Pieterszoon Coen, was fully aware of it. Sea power alone was going to decide the fate of the Indies.

The three sea powers of Demak, Malacca-Johore, and Ternate had succeeded in defeating the Portuguese. Their victory had been a Pyrrhic victory and had left them completely exhausted. Demak had succumbed under the attacks of Mataram. Johore had hoped to have a chance to regain its former power with the help of the Dutch Com-

[4] Edited by Meinsma, see note 23 of Chapter IV. The significance of the *Babad Tanah Djawi* is discussed by C. C. Berg in Stapel, *Gesch.* II, 69–73.

pany, but when disappointed had finally sought to make peace with its eternal foes in Malacca. Ternate had emerged from the struggle in such hopeless weakness that it had no choice but to accept either the supremacy of the Dutch Company or that of the king of Spain, represented by his governor of the Philippines. Although the situation seemed extremely favorable for an enterprising prince to assume the leadership over the Indonesian sultanates, the emperor of Mataram, who completely lacked sea power, could never undertake this task. Two serious candidates presented themselves for that leadership: in the northwest, Atjeh; in the northeast, the power that would remain victorious in the Moluccas, either Spain or the Dutch Company.

All circumstances seemed to favor the Sumatran princes of Atjeh. Their capital at the island's northern point was a natural halting place for the Europeans coming from the west. This fact helped the princes of Atjeh to concentrate the pepper trade of most of Sumatra in their country and allowed them to organize a monopoly which the European merchants could not ignore. It happened sometimes that Dutch, English, and French ships anchored at the same time in Atjeh's roadstead. Thus the sultan could play off one nation against the other and raise the prices of pepper to his heart's desire. The great profits of this monopoly made Atjeh, or at least the sultan and his principal advisors, rich beyond expectation. Wealth brought power. The rulers of Deli and Indragiri to the southeast and the districts of Kedah and Pahang on the Malay Peninsula were forced to recognize the overlordship of Atjeh. Kedah was already famous for its tin mines, and as the tin deposits of Bangka and Billiton were still little known, this possession gave Atjeh another monopoly. In 1613 the Atjenese troops attacked Johore, burned down the capital, and took the sultan prisoner. After that, Iskander Muda, who ruled Atjeh between 1607 and 1636, controlled the whole northwestern part of the archipelago. He disregarded a former treaty with the Dutch East India Company which had been concluded in a moment of grave danger for the sultanate when a strong Portuguese fleet was preparing for a decisive attack and which would have given a monopoly of trade and a fortified trading center to the Netherlanders. The victory over Johore enabled Iskander to take a stronger attitude towards the Company, but the Dutch, rather than submit to his pretensions, limited their trading with Atjeh as much as possible.[5]

[5] The first treaty between the Company and Atjeh, in which the Company received the right to build a fortified trading post in Atjeh's capital, was concluded on Jan. 17, 1607 (CD, I, 48). Then relations were broken until Nov. 6, 1649, when a new treaty

Atjeh seemed on the point of obtaining control over the narrows between the Malay Peninsula and the coast of Sumatra, and thus of gaining complete supremacy over the native states of the northwestern archipelago. This was only prevented by an alliance of all the small powers in the neighborhood: Portuguese Malacca, Johore, and Patani. Together the allied fleets crushed the power of Atjeh in a great naval battle near Malacca in 1629. Meanwhile the Dutch limited their activities on Sumatra to regular trading connections with the less powerful sultanates of Djambi and Palembang. Both sultanates, being threatened by more powerful neighbors — Djambi by Atjeh to the north and Palembang by Bantam to the south — were looking for support, and this gave the Company the opportunity of playing the role of protector of the independence of smaller nations. The political pattern of the western part of the archipelago was consequently unfavorable to the rapid extension of European influence.[6]

In the northeastern part of the Indies the situation was totally different. The power of Ternate had been broken by the Spanish counterattack of 1606. Spanish and Dutch fortified posts were scattered all over the small islands of the Moluccas. There guerilla warfare continued on land and sea for many years. Ternate, despairing of the future, saw its only chance in a complete Dutch victory which would at least protect it from the Spaniards and Portuguese, who were not only the enemies of its independence but also of its religion. Therefore the sultan decided to recognize the States General of the Dutch Republic as his protectors, promising to pay back to the Company all the expenses of the war as soon as he was restored to his former position (1607).[7] This treaty, combined with the earlier recognition of the

---

was concluded, immediately followed by a third one which gave the Company well-defined rights to a share in the tin trade (CD, I, 529 and 538).

[6] For a long time the Company traded with the Sumatran pepper growers on an absolutely equal footing with the Asiatic merchants. From our traditional histories of early European contacts with Asia we get only too easily the impression that the European powers were predominant in overseas territories as soon as they appeared there, but this is absolutely contrary to the facts. In the Indies the Europeans had to adapt themselves to the Asiatic system of trade. The competition between European and Asiatic merchants led to wars which usually, but not always, resulted in the establishment of European domination. In Japan, European influence has constantly been pushed back since Hideyoshi's days (decree of 1587 against the Portuguese missionaries). The commanders of the Dutch fleets off the Chinese coast readily acknowledged that Chinese shipping was superior to the Dutch because the Chinese ships sailed faster and were more maneuverable than the Dutch (Groenevelt, *Nederlanders in China*, pp. 127–128). See on this subject J. C. van Leur, "Enkele aanteekeningen met betrekking tot de beoefening der Indische Geschiedenis," in *Koloniale Studiën*, XXI (1937), 654, and the dissertation of the same historian, *Eenige beschouwingen over den ouden Aziatischen handel* (1934).

[7] Treaty of May 26, 1607 (CD, I, 51).

suzerainty of the States General by Amboina, made the Netherlanders virtually the dominant power in the Moluccas. It put a heavy burden on the Company, for the Netherlanders were far from successful in their military enterprises. Several times they attempted to crush the Spanish power at its source in the Philippines, but twice their fleets suffered heavy defeat.[8] Disorder and lack of leadership threatened to make the possession of the coveted Spice Islands a loss for the Company. To make matters worse, the people of the Banda Islands became increasingly hostile to the Dutch.

In 1602 the Bandanese had signed a contract which gave the Dutch the monopoly of the nutmeg trade. Shortly afterwards some of the Netherlanders on the island were murdered and the others fled in a native bark to Bantam. Peace had been restored and the contract renewed, but a complete monopoly could not be obtained. The legalistic Directors of the Company held the opinion that by signing the treaty the Bandanese had agreed to limit forever their commercial relations to trading with the Company alone. The Directors requested their representatives in the Moluccas to enforce the contract, but enforcement proved to be impossible. The Bandanese, dependent upon the import of rice from Java and Macassar, refused to give up trading with the merchants from those centers. The native barks that brought food to the islands carried home part of the spices, and these were sold in Macassar to Indian as well as to Portuguese and English merchants. The Dutch Company considered this a breach of contract, and quarrels followed in which failure to understand native customs made the situation worse. Apparently the tropical climate made the Europeans oversensitive. Everywhere they suspected treachery and conspiracies of murder.[9] They despised the Mohammedans and refused to pay any respect to Mohammedan rites. Thus, the slightest difficulty might result in murderous conflict.[10]

[8] On the Dutch attacks on the Philippines, see F. Blumentritt, "Holländische Angriffe auf die Philippinen im 16ten und 17ten Jahrhundert," *Jahrbuch der Ober–Realschule Leitmeritz*, 1880, and, in a Spanish translation, *Filipinas. Ataques de los Holandeses en los siglos XVI, XVII, y XVIII* (Madrid, 1882).

[9] Distrust of all Asiatics was common to all Europeans except perhaps some missionaries, mainly because of lack of knowledge of language and customs. A number of quotations proving this point have been collected by De Haan in his *Priangan*, I, 6, and notes to this paragraph in III, 14, 15. The Asiatics distrusted the Europeans equally and for the same reasons, as is sufficiently proved by the remarks on the Europeans in the Indonesian chronicles of the seventeenth century.

[10] See Van der Chijs, *De vestiging van het Nederlandsch Gezag over de Banda eilanden* and Heinrich Bokemeyer, *Die Molukken. Geschichte und quellenmässige Darstellung der Eroberung und der Verwaltung der Ost-Indischen Gewürzinseln durch die Niederländer* (Leipzig, 1888). These books, written at a time when the reaction against the "planned

Slowly the friendship between Hollanders and Bandanese changed into open hatred. There was another reason for conflict that resulted from the Indonesian system of doing business. The harvest was purchased beforehand, and large sums were advanced to the natives to secure the delivery of the products.[11] At one time the Company had given credits for more than 20,000 guilders to the people of Banda alone. The islanders lived luxuriously and spent the money as fast as they could. Thus they fell into the temptation to sell their products a second time and postpone the delivery of the spices to the Company. Consequently they became more and more involved in debts. The Dutch officials who were responsible to the Directors in Amsterdam blamed the natives instead of the system and called them in their reports "treacherous scoundrels and thieves." They advised collecting the promised spices by force of arms and, if necessary, by conquering the islands. The practice of transferring sovereignty over land and people in payment of debts was not uncommon in the seventeenth century and was followed in Asia as well as in Europe. The difficulty which Dutch and Indonesians had in understanding each other — there were very few Hollanders who learned to speak Malay, and a kind of sailor-Portuguese was the principal means of conversation[12] — helped to create further misunderstandings. Unhappily, other Europeans, in order to profit from this conflict, deliberately stirred up the fire. The Portuguese intrigued from Macassar and the English appeared with their ships in the Banda archipelago.

The English East India Company had been founded two years before the Dutch, but had developed more slowly. As the capital of the English Company was only one eighth of that of the Dutch, the merchants of London followed their more powerful neighbors wherever they went, hoping to profit from the pioneer work of others. The expenses of the war against Spain, by which Indonesian trade was made safe for

---

economy" of former centuries was at a peak, are extremely critical of the Dutch administration of the Moluccas in the time of the Company. It is true that this administration hardly deserved that name and that its record is bad enough, but it is historically incorrect to judge the doings of seventeenth-century merchants in the light of nineteenth-century theories. In general the most bitter critics of the "system" of the Dutch East India Company are the Dutch historians of the late nineteenth century. In several cases their judgment has become biased however.

[11] Advance buying and selling was and still is a regular practice in the East Indies. For the consequences it usually had, see De Haan, *Priangan*, I, 197 sq.

[12] As late as 1664 there came complaints from the sultan of Djambi that none of the Netherlanders at the trading post in his kingdom understood a word of Malay. In 1654 Van Goens declared that his embassy to the court of Mataram had failed because of lack of interpreters. For these and other facts, see De Haan, *Priangan*, III, 13.

the northern nations, were left graciously to the Netherlanders, but wherever the Dutch Company founded a trading post, the English were sure to follow: at Patani, at Djambi, at Jacatra, and in many other places. "From the beginning of the century," a modern British scholar writes, "the English though far inferior in strength had been following the Dutch around the archipelago, pursuing them like gadflies." [13] Wherever the Dutch got into trouble with the Indonesians the British posed as the well-meaning friends of the poor oppressed natives, suggesting to them that they recognize the overlordship of the king of England as the best protection against the "evil Dutch." Nowhere was the competition fiercer than in the Banda Islands, where the Dutch bluntly used their superiority in numbers and in ships and maintained their "right of monopoly" by chasing the English out under lavish display of gunfire. Of course, there was peace and even an alliance between the two nations in Europe — in those times, diplomatic relations were even more complicated than in our days. All quarrels were reported by both sides to headquarters in Bantam, where the two nations, each with their Chinese and Javanese supporters, fought furious battles in the streets. Edmund Scott, in his *Discourse of Java*,[14] noted gravely that "the Flemmings doe carry themselves very rude and disordered in that abundant manner that they are a shame and infamy to Christendomme." But do not take him too seriously, for further on he writes the following wonderful statement that throws a vivid light on the whole situation. "It is to be noted that though we were mortal enemies in our trade, yet in all other matter we were friends and would have lived and died one for the other."

In the Banda Islands, however, the two neighbors were shooting at each other for the sake of business. The Dutch chased the English out, but this improved the situation only a little. The governors-general for the Dutch Company — an office instituted by the Directors in 1610 — saw only one possibility of effectively securing the monopoly — conquest of the islands by force of arms; but this proved a difficult task, and so the policy of wavering and hesitating continued for some years more. The Company had to take into consideration that the conquest of the Banda Islands might involve its fleet in a war with a new power in Indonesian affairs, Macassar.

[13] Furnivall, *Netherlands India*, p. 27.

[14] On the Dutch-British competition in the Banda archipelago, see the voyages of William Keeling (1607) in Purchas (ed. Glasgow), II, 502–549, and of David Middleton (1609), *ibid.*, III, 90 sq. Edmund Scott's "Discourse" in Purchas, same ed., II, 438–495. His statement on Dutch-British friendship despite competition, *ibid.*, p. 473.

JAN PIETERSZOON COEN: FOUNDER OF BATAVIA

Between Atjeh and Malacca in the west and the Moluccas and the Banda Islands in the east, Java had for a long time held the position of the intermediary power. As the Javanese coastal states declined and were crushed by the attacks of Mataram, the kingdom of Gowa or Macassar in southern Celebes rose into power.[15] For centuries Macassar had been a small trading town, but through the destruction of the ports of eastern Java and through the war in the Moluccas it became the main halting place for Portuguese and native ships traveling between Malacca and the East. In the first years of the seventeenth century Islam was introduced, and as usual this resulted in a series of wars by which the newly converted Mohammedans tried to spread their faith over the neighboring districts and islands. The southern peninsula of Celebes, the east coast of Borneo, and some of the Lesser Sunda Islands were brought under the influence of Macassar. The Portuguese made it their headquarters for the spice trade. The men of Macassar exported the rice of their country to all the islands to the east. The sultans showed a remarkable ability. They followed a cautious policy towards the Europeans, declaring that they had decided to remain neutral in the wars between the Dutch and the Portuguese, and refused permission to construct fortified trading posts in their territory. The Portuguese, who were too weak to have things their own way, submitted to all regulations made by the sultan of Macassar and were accordingly protected by that potentate. The Netherlanders established a factory but met with little success. One of the captains had an unfortunate idea and arrested a group of noblemen from Macassar as hostages for the payment of the debts of the merchants of Macassar. This action resulted in hostility, and since the Company was not strong enough to fight all its enemies at the same time, Macassar remained a center of opposition to the Netherlands until 1667. Portuguese, English, and even Danes [16] were trading from that port, whence a brisk trade with

[15] A native chronicle of the kingdom of Macassar: A. Ligtvoet, "Transcriptie van het Dagboek der vorsten van Gowa en Tello, met vertaling," BKI, XXVIII, being 4 ser. IV (1880), 1 sq. A history of the kingdom of Gowa-Macassar: B. Erkelens, "Geschiedenis van het Rijk Gowa," VBG, vol. L, section 3 (1897). Also, G. K. Niemann, "Mededeelingen over Makassaarsche Taal- en Letterkunde," BKI, X (1863), 58 sq. On early contact with the Dutch: J. W. IJzerman, "Het schip 'De Eendracht' voor Makassar in December, 1616," BKI, LXXVIII (1922), 343 sq.

[16] "Danish" ships are frequently mentioned in the documents. This means, however, only that these ships were sailing with Danish papers and under the Danish flag. Denmark was economically still behind the Netherlands and the towns of Northern Germany. The Danish kings sought to interest Dutch capitalists in Danish enterprises and the Dutch capitalists were eager to make use of this chance to trade in those parts of the world where the Dutch chartered companies held a monopoly. Thus, many of the so-called Danish ships were in reality Dutch ships, manned by Dutch crews but under the Danish flag.

the Spice Islands — "smuggling," the officials of the Company called it — was carried on.

Thus Macassar remained for two thirds of a century a stronghold of international trading. Borneo also remained an area of free trade, but it could hardly be called a stronghold. Its towns and ports were still relatively unimportant. The native princes, of Bandjermasin in the southeast and of Sukadana and Sambas in the west, were looking eagerly forward to the establishment of trading connections with the Europeans, but the officials of the Company did not trust — and this time probably with good reason — these half-civilized rulers. The first experiences of the Netherlanders in these districts had not been very encouraging. Life and death depended too much upon the whims of degenerate princes to make trading safe and alluring. In the Lesser Sunda Islands, however, the Netherlanders gained a foothold in 1613.

Here the Dominican fathers had courageously carried on their mission work under the most difficult circumstances and without any help from the Portuguese government. Portuguese traders from Malacca used to visit Flores and Timor to obtain the precious sandalwood, which was exported to India and China. When a Dutch fleet appeared off the islands of the Solor group and off Flores, the native Christians bravely defended the weak fortresses built under direction of the Dominicans, but they were forced to surrender.[17] Portuguese influence did not disappear completely, however, and regained strength when after a few years the Dutch, disappointed with the results of the trade, withdrew once more from that area. After the withdrawal of the Europeans, the native princes of Macassar and Buton (a small island southeast of Celebes whose prince was a vassal of Ternate) continued to dispute with each other the overlordship of these islands.

See, for the foundation of the first Danish East India Company, Axel Nielsen, *Dänische Wirtschaftsgeschichte* (Jena, 1933), pp. 276 sq. and 283 sq.

[17] For the conquest of the Solor Islands by Ap. Schotte see P. A. Tiele, *Bouwstoffen voor de geschiedenis van de Nederlanders in den Maleischen archipel*, 3 vols. (The Hague, 1886–1890), I, 12 sq. and 80 sq. De Jonge closed his collection of documents on early Dutch history in the Indies with the year 1610. He continued the series with seven volumes on *De Opkomst van het Nederlandsch Gezag over Java* (The Hague, 1869–1878). With three volumes more, M. L. van Deventer brought the narrative down to 1811. His selection of documents on the period of G. G. Daendels aroused much criticism and consequently more volumes were added to the series, giving additional material on Daendels' period of office, published by L. W. G. De Roo (*Documenten omtrent Herman Daendels*, 2 vols., The Hague, 1909). Finally, Van Deventer undertook to continue the series into the nineteenth century; *Het Nederlandsch Gezag over Java sedert 1811*, vol. I, 1811–1820, the only one published, was issued at The Hague in 1891. P. A. Tiele undertook the publication of documents regarding Dutch colonial policy outside Java after 1610. His three volumes mentioned above brought the story down to 1649, but were not continued.

After twenty years of Dutch trading in the Indies the situation was still very unsatisfactory from the point of view of the Directors of the Company. It was true that the Company had gained a foothold on the island of Amboina and a certain authority over the Moluccas, but the competition in the spice market remained fierce, and with the rising prices and especially with the enormous expenses necessitated by the war, profits were still small. During the first eight years of its existence the Company did not pay any dividend to its shareholders. After that the Directors decided to pay a dividend of no less than 162 per cent, but they paid it only partly in cash and most of it in merchandise, chiefly spices. The shareholders had to wait another eight years before the second dividend was distributed. The Directors wrote one letter after the other to their governor-general in the Indies to order that the monopoly of the spice trade be secured by all means, if necessary by force, and that the quantity of production be restricted. In order to prevent smuggling, they even proposed to suppress all native shipping within the limits of Ternate's empire, which meant east of Macassar. They understood that the Asiatic competition from the Chinese and Gujerats who had adapted themselves to the new circumstances was even more dangerous than that of the rival European companies. The first governors-general, however, could not agree with this extreme point of view. They considered a measure of such extreme harshness unjustified and feared a general native uprising.[18]

Thus, the situation in the archipelago around 1615 was unclear. In the northwest Atjeh dominated, and in the northeast the Company represented the strongest power. Mataram, admirably situated in the center of the archipelago and supported by the glory of ancient Madjapahit, might perhaps have taken the lead, but its emperors were too little interested in naval affairs. Yet, as it was, only the rivalry between Mataram and Bantam permitted the Europeans to maintain their trading posts on the coasts of Java. Here, too, their position was highly precarious. The rivalry between Dutch and English further complicated the situation.

One of the English traders, Edmund Scott, has left us a picturesque description of life in Bantam in the first decade of the seventeenth century. The Europeans were always in danger of losing their lives and property in the great fires that ravaged this city of wooden houses every

[18] The first three governors-general (Pieter Both, 1610–1614; Gerard Reynst, 1614–1615; and Laurens Reaal, 1616–1618) did not favor the use of violence in order to obtain a practical monopoly of the spice trade (Stapel, *Gesch.*, III, 96), but this "weakhearted" policy was strongly opposed by Jan Pieterszoon Coen, then director general of commerce (see Colenbrander's biography of Coen, cited in note 22, below, p. 96).

three or four months. Scott had the usual contempt for the natives. Part of the city was inhabited by the Chinese, he says, who worked day and night while the Javanese "lay lazily around." He writes, "They are all poor, for they have many slaves who are still lazier than the masters and which eat faster than their Pepper or Rice growth."[19] It was a city where intrigues, plots, and murders were common, and, accordingly, Scott had no high opinion of its inhabitants. "All the Javans and Chynies are all villains," he wrote.[20] Of course there were continuous quarrels between Dutch and English. Both parties brought their complaints before the *patih* of Bantam and this gentleman grew rich because he accepted bribes from both sides. If it had not been for these quarrels, the Javanese would not have been able to distinguish an Englishman from a "Flemming." Scott and his comrades decided to make this point clear once and for all. On the Coronation Day of Queen Elizabeth they dressed up in their best clothes and held a great parade. There were only fourteen of them, so they marched up and down one after the other, firing their guns and shouting "Hurray," until the whole city rushed out to see the great spectacle. As soon as a large crowd had gathered, the English told the people of Bantam about the glorious Queen Elizabeth and how the poor Flemings had no king or queen at all.[21] We may doubt whether the Javanese understood what they were saying. The prime minister was clever enough to understand that he could profit by this situation through favoring each nation in turn, raising, in the meanwhile, the custom duties and the price of pepper. Finally, the Dutch threatened to move their headquarters to Jacatra where they had already built a small factory.

A total reorganization of the commercial system of the Company seemed indicated. Several proposals for such a reorganization reached the Directors in the second decade of the seventeenth century. Most interesting of these is the "Discourse on the State of India" by the famous Jan Pieterszoon Coen.[22]

[19] Scott, *op. cit.*, p. 440.

[20] *Ibid.*, p. 469.

[21] *Ibid.*, p. 473.

[22] There exist, of course, several biographies of J. P. Coen. The most recent one is that of F. W. Stapel, who made the seventeenth-century history of the Company his special field, in the *Geschiedenis van Nederl. Indië*, edited under his direction, where he devotes sixty-five large pages to Coen's period alone (pp. 117–182). A practically complete collection of Coen's letters and reports has been published by H. T. Colenbrander (*Jan Pietersz. Coen. Bescheiden omtrent zijn bedrijf in Indië*, 5 vols., The Hague, 1919–1923). In a sixth volume published in 1934, the same author gave a detailed biography of the founder of Batavia. The "Discourse" ("Discoers aen de E.Heeren Bewinthebberen touscheerende den Nederlantsche Indischen staet") has been published by Colenbrander in an appendix to this biography (pp. 451–474).

Coen was a young man when he wrote his political program. He was born in 1586 in the small town of Hoorn, one of the seafaring communities on the Zuider Zee, where so may Dutch heroes of the sea were born. Coen received a good education. It was customary for young Dutchmen of the seventeenth century to complete their education by a trip abroad, if possible to France and Italy. Coen visited Rome at the early age of thirteen and took a position in the office of a Dutch merchant in that city, a certain Mr. Visscher, who had Italianized his name to "Pescatore."

Coen stayed six or seven years in Rome, and there learned the Italian system of bookkeeping, which was far more progressive than that followed in the northern countries. He also studied languages, and we are told that he spoke five languages besides his own, French, Italian, Spanish, Portuguese, and Latin. After his return from Rome he accepted an appointment as second merchant on the Company's fleet that sailed in 1607 to the East Indies. It was not a bad position for a young man of twenty-one years who had no experience of Indian affairs. But a man with a knowledge of languages and bookkeeping such as Coen possessed could do better in the Netherlands of the early seventeenth century. Probably his desire to see foreign countries prompted him to accept this position with the East Indian Company. He was animated by the same feelings that induced Linschoten to write twenty years earlier: "My heart is longing day and night for voyages to far-away lands." Thousands of young Dutchmen shared the same sentiment.

The fleet on which Coen sailed had special orders to secure the monopoly on the Spice Islands. Coen witnessed the failure of the expedition and the murder of Verhoeff, the commanding admiral, by the people of Banda. He saw with his own eyes how the English supported the Bandanese in their resistance. These dramatic events he never forgot. In 1610 he was back in Holland, but sailed to the Indies for the second time in 1612. He must have gained the favor of the directors of the Company, for they entrusted to him the command of two ships and gave him the title of chief merchant. When he arrived in the Indies, Governor-General Pieter Both appointed him chief bookkeeper and director of commerce in Bantam. In this capacity the young Coen, twenty-eight years old, wrote his political program.

Coen based his opinion on two arguments: first, that the commerce in the Indies was necessary for the welfare of the Republic of the Netherlands, and second, that the Netherlanders had a legal right to continue this commerce and even to monopolize the trade in many places.

The first argument was easily sustained by the fact that the Netherlands activities deprived the enemy, Spain, of part of its resources, at the same time enriching the home country. Thus the East India Company struck a double blow at the power of the kingdom of Spain.

As to the second argument, Coen derived the legal right to the trade in the Indies from two considerations: that the Dutch had begun their trading in territories where Spain and Portugal held no claims, and that the Netherlanders had acquired a legal title to the territory of Amboina by right of conquest when Spain and Portugal had made unjustified attacks on the "peacefully trading" Netherlanders. The right thus acquired had been further extended by formal treaties with Indonesian nations and princes. From these treaties sprang the right of monopoly in Ternate, Amboina, and the Banda Islands. Hence, the Company had a right to punish the Indonesians who against their oath broke this contract.

Coen considered the position of the Company in the Indies legally well established but politically very precarious. The returns of the spice trade would never be sufficient to cover all expenses. It was impossible to prevent completely the constant smuggling between the Moluccas and Java. The competition of the English was still more dangerous. Coen's advice was to guarantee the interests of the Company by the foundation of Dutch settlements. He developed his political program as follows: Secure complete possession of some territories, for instance, the island of Bakjan in the Moluccas, Amboina, and Banda, and of a fortified port in Bantam or Jacatra; bring groups of Dutch people to these places and give them grants of land and permission to trade in the Asiatic ports; send a fleet strong enough to conquer Manila and Macao, by which conquests the Spanish and Portuguese would be driven from the Philippines and the coast of China. When this had been accomplished, the Dutch colonists and their slaves would be strong enough to defend the acquired possessions. The Company would no longer be dependent on the good will of the king of Ternate and other Indonesian allies. It would have gained such respect among the natives that they would observe faithfully their obligations respecting the monopoly.

The plan was ambitious, but not impossible of execution. The most difficult part would have been the conquest of the Philippines. It is interesting to note that Coen hoped to receive help from the Filipinos, who — if we may believe him — hated the Spanish government. He planned to use thousands of Japanese mercenary soldiers. The emperor of Japan had offered to send as many men as the Company wanted, and Coen wrote: "The Japanese soldiers are just as good as ours." [23]

The Company was not able to send the numerous fleets Coen wanted, but the Directors twice entrusted to him the governorship-general of the Indies. He received this high rank for the first time in 1618 when he was only thirty-one years old. In 1623 he returned to Holland, whence he was sent for the second period of office in 1627. In those years he had further developed his program, but he was not allowed to execute its main point: the settlement of Dutch colonies. In the fifteen years between 1614 and 1629 two diametrically opposed principles were debated by the officials of the Company. The Directors made the final decision in 1626, when they decided on a middle course which determined the development of the Dutch colony in the Indies for the next hundred years.[24]

Coen had further developed his ideas in his reports to the Directors. In his final report at the close of his first period of office, he estimated that during the ten years between 1613 and 1623 the Company had spent 9,396,000 guilders, while the total return cargoes of the fifty-six ships which had sailed to Holland in the same ten years added up to 9,388,000 guilders, leaving a deficit of eight thousand guilders.[25] We can not control these figures, for part of the books of the company have been lost and the accounts were kept in such a way that it is hardly possible to figure out the true financial situation of the Company at any moment. Notwithstanding the losses which the Company was supposed to have suffered, Coen held the opinion that by a reform of the commercial system not only all expenses in India could be covered but a yearly return of five million guilders could be secured from the inter-Asiatic trade and five million more if the trade of China could be drawn into the system. For this purpose Coen needed settlements of Dutchmen who would take in hand the production of the spices. These settlements would be reinforced by colonists from Madagascar, Burma, and China. If there should be no volunteers in these countries to go to the Indies, Coen simply proposed to kidnap the necessary number of individuals. He preferred the Chinese above all others because they were both industrious and unwarlike. His further plans called for the complete annihilation of the native and foreign European shipping in the Indies. To the settlers he proposed to give permission for free shipping and commerce under regulations made by the Com-

[23] "Discoers," Colenbrander, VI, 468: "wandt de Japansche soldaeten soo goet als de onsen sijn." A remarkable statement written down three hundred years before Pearl Harbor!

[24] Decision taken March 29, 1626, see Colenbrander, VI, 372.

[25] Coen's report: Colenbrander, I, 55 sq.

pany. Under this commercial system the silk from Persia, the cloth from India, the cinnamon from Ceylon, the porcelain from China, and the copper from Japan would be exchanged against the spices from the Moluccas and the sandalwood from Timor, all under supervision of the officials of the Company. The profits of the commerce that would center in the port of Batavia would be sufficient to provide for the quantities of spices and pepper that had to be exported to Europe. The consequence of the system would be that the shipping between Europe and Asia would be limited to a few ships a year, but these would be ships laden with a cargo worth millions, while a brisk Dutch shipping and trading would go on all along the Asiatic coast from Persia to Japan.

It is evident that Coen's plans were not limited to the Indonesian Archipelago. He intended to build an enormous Asiatic commercial empire with its capital in Batavia, the city of which he was the founder. He was not interested at all in the political development of the interior of the island. His only concern was to safeguard the few Dutch positions he intended to build up and to maintain complete control of the sea. He was undoubtedly a statesman with great vision and with the imagination and foresight that is characteristic of the true leader of men. Even his narrow-mindedness in other matters and his harshness — we may call it cruelty — helped him to accomplish his great achievements. All his thoughts centered around the great commercial empire he planned to build. He was so sure of the success of his plans that he considered it the directors' own fault if they did not make a profit of millions and, therefore, he felt justified in demanding a reward of tens of thousands for himself, in addition, of course, to his salary. His eternal complaints of being insufficiently paid make not very pleasant reading, but we must consider that he really believed that the Company could make profits ten times higher than it did if the gentlemen in Amsterdam would only accept his advice.

Yet, there is much that remains obscure in his schemes. He never could explain which part of the Asiatic commerce would be reserved for the Company and which part would be entrusted to the settlers. He promised enormous returns without import of capital from Holland, but, on the other hand, he wrote time and again that the Directors ought to send more capital, and his opponents accused him of having increased the expenses in the Indies from six hundred thousand to one million six hundred thousand guilders a year.[26] They pointed out that

[26] Coen's main opponent was the former Governor-General Laurens Reael. The arguments of both sides are summed up by Colenbrander, VI, 333 sq.

it was absolutely necessary for the Company to preserve the friendship of the Indonesians and that the promotion of a favored class of citizens who would enter into an unfair competition with the native traders would call forth a hostile reaction throughout the archipelago. Some settlers had been sent already, but the Company had the worst experience possible with these men.[27]

All opinions agree, however, on one point: that the Company should make its profits from the inter-Asiatic trade, not from the imports and exports from Europe and Asia. It is of the highest importance to see this point clearly, for it gives insight into the basic factors of the economics of Asia in the seventeenth century. The relation between Europe and Asia was not that of home-country and colony in those years. Coen pointed out that the profits from the inter-Asiatic trade would exceed those of the European commerce in the same measure "as these countries of Asia exceed those of Europe in population, consumption of goods, and industry." [28] The quantity of Asiatic products that could be imported into Europe was small and the margin of profits too limited for a trading company such as the Dutch East India Company to maintain its position on these profits.

It is the common opinion that the discovery of the route around the Cape caused the older trading route via Persia and Syria to Italy to fall into oblivion in a short while, but this is contrary to the facts. The trade in spices, transported via Gujerat in India, Ormuz in Persia, and Aleppo in Syria, continued until the beginning of the seventeenth century, that is, until the Dutch conquered the Moluccas and by force

[27] The following are a few quotations from Reael's arguments which bring out a point of view maintained by many people in the Netherlands who were acquainted with Indian affairs — a point of view which is usually neglected in our textbooks. They show that complete disregard of native rights and interests was not common at all, whatever our traditional historiography sustains. Coen urged the sending to the Indies of Dutch colonists who would produce export crops on plantations worked with slaves. Reael declared: "We cannot expect that experienced people, who have knowledge of the Indies, will go overseas to let themselves to be employed as henchmen and guards of a herd of slaves . . . to be the foremen of the 'free-citizens' who mostly are the scum of our nation . . . who by murdering and tormenting of the Indians make the Netherlands nation notorious throughout the Indies as the most cruel nation in the world . . ." (Colenbrander, IV, 618 and VI, 338). "Is it the intention to possess all trade and shipping and even all agriculture in the Indies? If so, how will the Indians be able to make a living? Will you kill them or starve them? You would not find any profit by it, for on empty seas, in empty countries and with dead people little profit can be earned" (*ibid.*, IV, 619 and VI, 339). "With force and violence you will execute your plans to obtain the monopoly of trade in the Indies, which seems such a wonderful thing to you, that you would not shrink back from using all unjust, even barbarous means . . . but by this the Company may be the cause of its own ruin" (*ibid.*, IV, 620 and VI, 340). "The Company must try to augment the native trade" (*ibid.*, IV, 617 and VI, 337).

[28] "Discoers," Colenbrander, VI, 451.

cut them off from all foreign trade connections.[29] The silk trade from Persia via Syria remained active until the eighteenth century, for the cost of transport over the Mediterranean, even including the heavy Turkish custom duties, remained just as cheap as that via the Cape. As long as it existed the Company had to count on the competition of Arabs and Persians in the trade to the West and that of the Chinese in the trade to the North. Most Dutchmen — and they had shown themselves superior to the other Europeans in the Far East — conceded reluctantly that the Asiatics were better and cleverer traders. It was perhaps Coen's principal mistake that he thought that his Dutch settlers could enter into competition with these Asiatics. Nevertheless, his name will be remembered as that of the founder of an Asiatic Empire.

In 1618, when the Directors appointed Coen governor-general of the Indies, the situation was very precarious. The people of the Moluccas were grumbling against the Dutch claims to monopoly. Pepper prices in Bantam were going sky high through the competition of Dutch, English, and Chinese buyers. At Japara the Netherlands trading post was attacked and destroyed by troops of the prince of Mataram; three Dutchmen were killed and seventeen were taken prisoners. Coen decided to bring Bantam to reason first. He stopped all buying of pepper and threatened to move his factory to Jacatra. He had nearly come to an agreement with the Chinese merchants and had forced the price of pepper down 50 per cent when the English intervened. They mustered an important force near Bantam and attacked Chinese ships, an act which Coen believed to be preliminary to an attack on his own ships. He ordered that the storehouse of the Company at Jacatra should be transformed secretly into a dependable stronghold.[30] The prince of Jacatra discovered what was going on and protested, while he asked the English for help. Thereupon Coen moved his headquarters to Jacatra and attacked a battery which had been constructed by the inhabitants opposite the Dutch settlement. The battery was conquered and the English trading post burned down in the same action. This was the beginning of open warfare. Eleven English ships patrolled the roadstead of Jacatra and threatened to cut off all communication

[29] An interesting discussion of these aspects of the European trade in Asia appears in H. Dunlop's *Bronnen tot de Geschiedenis van de Oost-Indische Compagnie in Perzië*, Introduction, p. xxvii sq., lxiii sq.

[30] The literature on the founding of Batavia is abundant. J. A. van der Chijs, *De Nederlanders te Jakatra* (Amsterdam, 1860); J. W. IJzerman, "Over de belegering van het fort Jacatra," BKI, LXXIII (1917), 558–679; F. De Haan, *Oud Batavia*, vol. I (second edition, Bandung, 1935), ch. I.

with the outside world. With his seven ships Coen gave them battle for three hours. Then he resigned himself to giving way temporarily to the superior forces of the enemy. He sailed to the Moluccas, where he hoped to bring more ships together, leaving the garrison in the fort at Jacatra with orders to defend their position to the last. He complained bitterly in his report to the Directors that everything was in danger of being lost because he lacked ships and men, and he dared to write to his superiors in Amsterdam, "I swear that no enemies do more harm to our cause than the ignorance and stupidity existing among you, gentlemen!" [31]

Things at Jacatra went better than he could have hoped. The fortress was saved, not by the heroism of its defenders but because the opponents could not agree among themselves who should claim it after it had been conquered. Both the English and the prince of Jacatra wanted possession of the fortress for themselves, while the king of Bantam was unwilling to leave it to either of them. When the discouraged garrison resolved to capitulate to the prince of Jacatra, troops from Bantam prevented the surrender. The territory of Jacatra was annexed to the sultanate of Bantam, and its prince expelled. The English withdrew in confusion, fearing for their settlements and their goods in the port of Bantam. This gave the Dutch garrison new courage, and between hours of prayer and nights of orgies with wine and women they pledged themselves solemnly to defend the fortress "as long as God will permit." Having taken this brave resolution, the officers discovered suddenly that the fortress had no name. In a meeting of all members of the garrison on March 12, 1619, it was given the name of Batavia "as Holland used to be called in days of antiquity." [32] Thus, the beginning of the city of Batavia was far from glorious. In May 1619 Coen's fleet returned from the Moluccas. On May 28 the governor-general entered the fortress. Two days later he led his troops, one thousand strong, to the attack. With the loss of only one man's life, the town of Jacatra was conquered. It was burned down completely, and the territory where it stood was occupied for the East India Company. Coen immediately ordered the construction of a new, larger fortress and of a small Dutch town, which was built in the next few years in the style of the home country, with canals and bridges. For a long time Coen refused to name his foundation Batavia, but on

[31] Colenbrander, *op. cit.*, VI, 156.

[32] "Batavi" is the name of a Germanic tribe mentioned by Tacitus. In the sixteenth century "Batavia" came to be used to indicate the northern part of the Low Countries in contrast to "Belgium" which then indicated the Low Countries as a whole (the present Holland and Belgium together).

March 4, 1621, the Directors of the Company confirmed the resolution taken by the garrison. This was the official beginning of the capital of the East Indies.

By the conquest of Jacatra and the foundation of Batavia the Netherlanders had acquired control of the seas in the Indies. Coen now declared a blockade of the port of Bantam, and this city, losing its significance as a commercial center, was superseded by Batavia. The English fleet, imprudently dispersed by its commanders, was attacked at several points, and seven ships were taken. The others withdrew to India. The effect of this defeat was the definite destruction of English power in the East Indies. King James I protested in the Hague against the acts of war committed by Coen, and he forced the Directors of the Dutch Company to conclude an agreement with the English company.[33] In 1619 they made a treaty providing for joint commercial and military action, but the alliance remained without practical effect. Coen was obliged to coöperate with the English commanders, but he used a very simple system to sabotage the whole plan. The financial resources of the Dutch Company were eight times larger than those of the British and, consequently, Coen schemed for such expensive expeditions that the English could not afford to take part in them. Once they failed to do their share, Coen had the way free for his own purposes. King James protested vehemently to the ambassadors of the Dutch Republic in London, "Your men have robbed my people of their possessions, you have made war on them, you have killed and tortured several of them. You never considered the benefits you have received from the Crown of England who made and maintained you as an independent nation. You have a man in the Indies who deserves to be hanged. Your people present your Prince of Orange as a great king in the Indies while they picture me as a small ruler and the Prince's vassal. You are masters of the sea wide and large and can do what you want." [34]

For many years the English activities in the Indies were at an end. The famous "massacre of Amboina" of 1623, though often commemorated in the English literature and propaganda of the seventeenth and eighteenth centuries, was merely a dramatic epilogue.[35] It was not even a massacre. Eight Englishmen were executed for an alleged plot to

[33] For Coen's reaction on the report that this treaty had been concluded, see Colenbrander, VI, 159 sq.

[34] Liewe van Aitzema, *Saken van Staet en Oorlog*, 7 vols. (The Hague, 1669–1671), vol. I, book iii, fo. 206.

[35] For a recent discussion based on the documents see F. W. Stapel, "De Ambonsche 'moord,' " TBG, vol. LXII (1923).

seize the fortress of Amboina with the help of a number of the Japanese mercenaries. They had been judged by the court of Amboina, where the procedure had been fairly legal, certainly not more illegal than many other procedures in England or Holland in that century, though it would have been better to postpone the execution of the condemned until the governor-general could have attended personally to the cause. Torture was applied, but this was unhappily normal in those days. The English considered that the execution of their countrymen gave them a good pretext to withdraw with dignity from a position that had become hopeless. They pretended to leave the Moluccas, not because they could not do any profitable business, but in protest against the cruelty of the Dutch officers. For two hundred and fifty years the "massacre of Amboina" kept its propaganda value in Europe. In the Indies it was only one of many bloody episodes in the history of ruthless commercial competition.

Worse things had happened in the Banda Islands. Coen had decided to crush all opposition and to secure the monopoly of the nutmeg trade by the complete conquest of the little archipelago. The Bandanese defended themselves with courage and skill, but their situation was hopeless. The islands were occupied after fierce fighting, and the population practically exterminated. This was an act of cruelty that shocked even the contemporaries. The Directors in Amsterdam shrank back from the consequences of their own orders, and reprimanded Coen, saying that he should have acted with more consideration. A better note was struck by an ex-officer of the Company who wrote, "We must not forget the Bandanese fought for the freedom of their country, exactly in the same way as we have done in Holland for so many years." [36]

[36] "Verhaal van eenige oorlogen in Indië," *Kroniek van het Historisch Genootschap, gevestigd te Utrecht*, XXVII (1871), 511. It may be worth while to give the full quotation in the original: "Wij moetten weeten dat sij voor de vrijheyt van haer landt gevochten hebben, daer wij soo mennighe jaeren lijff ende goet voor opgestelt hebben. Civielder recht had men daer over konnen doen. . . . Maer ten is dat niet geweest, eenige hebben eenen eeuwigen naem willen naer laetten, daer metter tÿt oock well een boucxken als vande Spangiaerden in West Indien van gemaect soude worden." This prophecy realized, see the bitter criticism of van der Chijs in his *Vestiging van het Nederlandsch Gezag op de Banda eilanden*, pp. 115, 148, 153, 158–159. This "Verhaal van eenige oorlogen" is attributed by Stapel to Aert Gijsels, commander in the service of the Company, one of the famous Dutch naval commanders of the beginning of the seventeenth century. From 1611 to 1621 and from 1629 to 1638 he served in the East Indies. After that he joined the navy of the Republic and fought the Spaniards off the coast of Portugal. In 1647 he entered the service of the Elector of Brandenburg, planned an East India Company for this prince and took active part in the development of backward agricultural sections of the principality. The "Verhaal" is evidently written as a criticism of Coen. The same opinion regarding Coen's violent methods and the same understanding of the attitude of

In his second period of office Coen had to confront new dangers that menaced the Netherlands' position in Java. Bantam had lost much of its former strength, but Mataram's power was still growing. In 1622 the troops of Sultan Agung had undertaken an expedition to Borneo where the town of Sukadana had been taken and destroyed. In 1624 his army ravaged the island of Madura, from which forty thousand prisoners were transferred to Java. They were settled in the depopulated area north of Surabaya. Surabaya was the only principality in Eastern Java that was still independent, but it could not escape its doom. Vainly it attempted to make an alliance with Bantam while the sultan of Mataram sent an ambassador to Batavia to ask for the assistance of the Dutch Company. Coen understood that it would be highly prejudicial to the Company's interest if the whole of Java was united under a single ruler, so he refused to enter into the alliance, whereupon the sultan of Mataram conquered Surabaya and then turned his armies against Batavia.

Neither of the two Javanese sultanates had given up its pretensions to the possession of the city and territory of the former Jacatra.[37] Bantam based its claims on the conquest of the district during the siege of 1618, while Mataram derived its pretensions from its alleged position as successor of the mighty empire of Madjapahit, the overlord of all Indonesia.

In the last year of the third decade of the century, both Javanese princes attempted the conquest of the new city. A group of Bantamese

---

the inhabitants of the Moluccas may be found in the "Grondig Verhaal van Amboina," apparently by the same author as the "Verhaal van eenige oorlogen," published in the same volume of the *Kroniek*, pp. 348 sq., 397 sq., 450 sq. (See for instance p. 427.) Still sharper is the judgment of Coen in the "Report of some people who have returned from the Indies" ("Rapport gedaen bij verscheyden persoonen comende uyt de Oost-Indiën") 1622, published in the same volume of the *Kroniek*, pp. 321–339. Here it is said: "Things are carried on in such a criminal and murderous way that the blood of the poor people cries to heaven for revenge. . . . Coen apparently thinks that he has still too many friends."

These quotations may suffice to prove that Coen's policy and methods were not exactly popular among his compatriots in the Indies. The Directors were practically the only ones who supported him, but even they sometimes shrank back from the implacable methods of their governor-general (see Stapel, III, 151).

[37] Coen claimed for the Company all the territory between the sultanates of Bantam and Cheribon and between the Java Sea and the Indian Ocean, but modified his own views later. There is no doubt that the territory of Jacatra originally belonged to the sultanate of Bantam. The Company, however, in a way recognized the claims of Mataram by sending embassies and offering presents to the prince. In the meanwhile it exercised full rights of sovereignty in Batavia and surrounding territory, which it claimed to hold "by right of conquest." This equivocal attitude came to an end, once the Company knew that it did not need fear the power of Mataram. See De Haan, *Priangan*, I, 9–10, III, 19 sq.

warriors forced their way into the citadel of Batavia on Christmas Eve of 1617. Defeated in their attempt, they ran *amok* and escaped after having killed some soldiers of the garrison. Eight months later an ambassador of Mataram presented himself at the gates of the castle and announced the arrival of a large fleet of cargo vessels laden with food and cattle, supplies which the sultan presented to his "friends" of Batavia. The Dutch did not trust this extraordinary display of neighborly love, and they were correct in this view, for the crews of the fleet suddenly attacked the walls of the citadel and were only beaten off with difficulty. This was the beginning of open warfare. The Javanese army stormed the outer fortifications but was completely defeated in a sortie by the garrison. A second Javanese attack undertaken in greater force failed also. The classic Javanese system of besieging a city consisted in cutting the enemy's water supply by closing the river from which the supply was drawn. At Batavia the system failed. For thirty days thousands of the Javanese soldiers toiled to build a dam through the Tjiliwung river, but without success. The commander ordered a last desperate attack, and when this also failed he withdrew, but not before he had executed nearly eight hundred of his unfortunate soldiers in punishment for the defeat. "We would never have believed that such a cruelty was possible," wrote Coen, "if we had not seen with our own eyes the bodies of the executed."

The sultan did not renounce his plans. Preparations were made for an attack by the full military force of his empire. Tens of thousands of his subjects were called to the colors, and slowly an impressive force gathered around Batavia. This army threatened not only the Dutch but also the sultan of Bantam, who, therefore, preferred to ask for peace with the Company. After ten years the blockade of the port of Bantam was lifted and normal commercial relations resumed.

Then as now the supply lines of the armies were all-important in strategy. The ruler of Mataram could not provide his troops with the necessary supplies by overland transport. He had to rely on shipments along the coast, but the transports were exposed to attacks by the greatly superior Dutch naval force. Coen made full use of the opportunity, and two hundred vessels laden with rice were destroyed. When it appeared before Batavia the great army of Mataram was already threatened by famine. The garrison, encouraged by this initial success, resisted bravely. It was composed of soldiers of many races — Dutch, Japanese, Chinese, Indian and Indonesian. The Chinese, who at that time had no great reputation for bravery, distinguished themselves in the fighting. After five weeks the army of Mataram was starving and forced to retreat. "A miserable voyage home this people had. Our patrols followed the army and found everywhere along the roads soldiers who had died from starvation, buffaloes that had died from exhaustion, deserted wagons, weapons, and tools." Only twelve Netherlanders and even fewer Japanese and Chinese soldiers died in the city while the normal trend of life was never disturbed. But Coen never saw the victory which he had prepared by his prudence and courage. A tropical disease caused his death on the night of September 20, 1629. His body was buried with great solemnity in the Town Hall from which it was moved to the church of Batavia when this building had been completed. Long afterwards, when the center of European life in Batavia shifted more to the south, this church was demolished and the exact location of the tomb of the founder of Batavia has been forgotten.[38] Hero worship is not customary among the Dutch, and the stern character of Coen, who never could forget misdeeds even when they resulted from understandable human weakness and whose heart was never softened by the sufferings of his opponents, did not appeal to the imagination of posterity.

His victory over the armed forces of Mataram guaranteed the safety of Batavia. It still remained a question, however, how the relations among the three powers in Java, Batavia, Bantam, and Mataram, would develop and how the other powers of the archipelago, Atjeh and Macassar, would react to this development. The influence of Spain and Portugal, who still had a foothold in Tidore and Malacca, was practically nullified by the superiority of the naval power of the Dutch East India Company.

[38] Report of the Committee of investigation of the burial place of Jan Pietersz. Coen (Batavia, 1936). The results of the investigation are discussed in TBG, LII (1937), 285. The church in which he was buried was torn down in 1733. A storehouse was built on the same lot. The exact location of Coen's grave could not be determined.

CHAPTER VII

GREATEST EXPANSION OF THE EAST INDIA COMPANY

Among the soldiers who came to the Indies during Coen's first period of office was a young man who called himself Theunis Meeuwisz (Anthony son of Bartholomew). Coen noticed immediately that this young soldier was intelligent, well educated, and honest, qualities which, at that time, were only too rare among the Company's servants. Consequently, the young Meeuwisz won rapid promotion. To his great amazement, Coen received a letter from the Directors in which he was warned against "some disorderly young fellows who had gone bankrupt in Holland and had gone to the Indies under false names. Among them there is a certain Anthony Van Diemen who has sailed in one of our ships under the name of Theunis Meeuwisz. Such people should be sent home." [1]

Coen simply ignored the letter. He already knew that the real name of Meeuwisz was Van Diemen and that, in fact, the young man had gone bankrupt and had signed for the Indies under his father's first name, Bartholomew, because the orders of the Company forbade accepting bankrupts for the service. He also knew that Van Diemen had come to the East in the hope of collecting sufficient funds to pay off his debts.

Seven years after his arrival Van Diemen was a member of the Council of the Indies; eighteen years later he was appointed governor-general; and he is remembered in the history of the Indies as one of the most successful and loyal officers of the Company. Coen wanted him for his successor in 1629, but the Council rejected the orders given by the dying governor-general and appointed Jacques Specx, who had gained fame for pioneer work he had done for the Company in Siam and Japan. The choice of the Council was never approved by the Directors in Amsterdam, but it took these gentlemen fully three years to make up their minds to send another governor-general from Holland. Then they selected a member of their own board, Hendrick Brouwer, who, in 1636, was succeeded by Van Diemen. Both Brouwer and Specx tried in vain to restore peace with the sultanates of Bantam and Mataram.

[1] Colenbrander, *Jan Pietersz. Coen*, III, 297.

Sultan Agung of Mataram had been defeated before Batavia, but none of his contemporaries, neither Javanese nor Dutch, had realized the decisiveness of this defeat. Outwardly the empire of Mataram was as strong as ever. Its prestige among the native princes of the archipelago was increasing. In the hope of obtaining trading privileges in exchange, the gentlemen of Batavia themselves thought it a wise policy to recognize eventually the nominal suzerainty of the sultan over their city.[2]

At that time, the fortress of Batavia was still completely isolated from the great Indonesian world that surrounded it. In his ambitious policy Coen had declared all territory between the boundaries of Bantam in the west and of Cheribon in the east, from the Java Sea in the north to the Indian Ocean in the south, to be the domain of the Company, but nobody had recognized this claim, and the Company itself ignored it.[3] In reality the Batavians could hardly leave the city without danger of being killed or kidnaped by Bantamese plunderers. The inhabitants were hindered from farming the land outside the city walls and thus remained dependent upon the import of food from the territory of Mataram. This enabled the sultan to make life difficult for them by arbitrarily stopping or permitting the export of cattle and rice. That his policy caused great inconvenience to his own subjects as well as to the Dutch in Batavia was no matter of concern to him.

Batavia must have been an extraordinary city in those days.[4] The few hundred Dutchmen who formed its aristocracy endeavored to imprint their style and way of living upon this oriental capital. As in Holland, the houses were built in close ranks along canals. They did not have the open galleries that later became an indispensable part of the tropic home, but a protruding section of the roof did nearly the same service. The citadel was built at the seashore, and inside, protected by its walls, was the residence of the governor-general, the members of the Council, and, curiously enough, of the workmen employed at the arsenal. The garrison was numerous, more than twelve hundred men, and paraded every day on the small square before the governor's house. These parades were the only military exercise for the soldiers in peace time, but there was plenty of active duty to keep the army in shape.

[2] For the relations between Batavia and Mataram after 1629, see W. Fruin-Mees, "Waarom Batavia en Mataram van 1629 tot 1646 geen vrede gesloten hebben," TBG, LXVI (1926), 156 sq.

[3] On Coen's claims and the later attitude of the Batavian government in this matter see De Haan, *Priangan*, III, 20 sq.

[4] The best, if not the only, book on the local history of Batavia, at the same time a cultural history of the Dutch in the Indies, is F. De Haan, *Oud Batavia* (second edition, Bandung, 1935) 2 vols., one of text, one of plates.

From the beginning the Chinese formed an important part of the population.[5] The Dutch tried to induce all Chinese merchants in Bantam to migrate to Batavia, but this move was strongly opposed by the sultan of Bantam, who understood that with the Chinese the commerce of Bantam would disappear. In the first year of Batavia's existence the Chinese settlers already numbered eight hundred, and ten years later their number had increased to two thousand. They made a living as traders, visiting the small ports and islands of the archipelago that were too unimportant to be visited by the ships of the Company. They were fishermen and tailors; they were bricklayers and carpenters; so it is no exaggeration to say that Batavia could not have existed without the Chinese. Their main vice was gambling. They indulged in it so passionately that the government decided to reserve one street for their gambling houses and to close this street to all Europeans at night to prevent quarrels and what might come from them.

Like all new settlements, Batavia was a men's town. The Chinese never emigrated with their wives. They married native women or bought slave women and when they returned to China they took their sons — in their conception the only interesting part of the family — with them. Most of them, however, remained in Batavia all their lives and in that case they took good care to educate their sons as Chinese. Thus they remained culturally distinct from the mass of the native population.

In order to make the port of Batavia attractive for foreign traders, the Directors in Amsterdam had given special orders that all Chinese and other Asiatic merchants whose ships might drop anchor in Batavia's roadstead were to be treated with great civility and respect. Once the Chinese had settled in Batavia, however, they became the subjects of the Company. As such they were subject to Dutch laws. The impracticability of this system soon became apparent, and after a few years the government of Batavia consented that matters of minor importance and the complicated affairs of inheritance should be handled by a "captain" of the Chinese, appointed by the governor-general.[6] When Batavia grew in population, the Portuguese system of grouping the

[5] On the Chinese and their share in the building of Batavia, besides De Haan's book, see B. Hoetink, "So Bing Kong, het eerste hoofd der Chineezen te Batavia," BKI, LXXIII (1917), 334 sq., and, by the same author, "Chineesche officieren te Batavia," BKI, LXXVIII (1922), 1–136.

[6] The system of entrusting the supervision over the non-European (better: non-Christian) sections of the population to native heads grew out of the circumstances. The East India Company did not make it a rule until the eighteenth century. The Statutes of Batavia recognized the special position of the Chinese and contained a chapter on the regulation of inheritances among non-Christians.

inhabitants together in separate sections according to nationality was introduced, and in due time each of the national groups was organized under its own chief, also with limited jurisdiction over his subjects.

Discrimination against Asiatics *as such* was unknown. After a few decades many races and nations were represented in Batavia,[7] and marriages between Dutch and natives were common. If baptised, the native and half-caste members of the Dutch families had exactly the same rights as the Dutch. The only restriction put upon them was that the Company prevented as much as possible the emigration of non-Dutch to Holland. According to the prevailing ideas of the period, however, there was a sharp discrimination against all non-Christians, who, unfortunately, formed the majority of Batavia's inhabitants![8] The law strictly forbade the public or secret exercise and teaching of any religion except that of the Dutch Reformed Church. The ordinance was repeated time and again, and the ministers of the Reformed Church insisted upon its enforcement; nevertheless, Chinese and Mohammedans enjoyed practical freedom of religion, if not inside, at least immediately outside the walls of the city. Vainly the ministers protested, but the government replied by requesting them to show more zeal in converting the Indonesians and less alacrity in reprimanding the officers of the Company for their bad morals. All clergymen in the Indies were in the service of the Company and could be deported to Europe any time by simple order, thus the Church never gained considerable influence. When the Consistory of Batavia pointed out to Governor-General Maetsuycker that the Law of Moses forbade the tolerance of non-Christian religions, he simply answered: "The laws of the old Jewish republics have no force in the territory of the Dutch East India Company!"[9]

[7] De Haan (*Priangan*, I, 4) counts, around the middle of the seventeenth century, eleven Indonesian tribes among the inhabitants of Batavia, besides the Dutch, Japanese, Chinese, Pampangers (from Luzon), and "Mardijkers" from Malabar, Coromandel, Arracan, and Bengal. The free non-Christian inhabitants, especially the Indonesians, were only "tolerated"; the Company did not want to assume any responsibility for their well-being, which it would have done if it had considered them its subjects in the legal sense. See a very crude example of this attitude in De Haan, *Priangan*, I, 5. The government of Batavia usually mitigated the harsh instructions of the Directors in Amsterdam.

[8] The testimony of non-Christians was originally not admitted in court. After 1633 their testimony was admitted in some cases in which no Christians were involved. Practice was often less harsh than the legal rule. See De Haan, *Priangan*, I, 4–5, and III, 12–14.

[9] For the history of Protestant missions in the East Indies in the period of the East India Company, see C. A. L. Troostenburg de Bruyn, *De Hervormde Kerk in Nederlandsch Oost Indië onder de Oost Indische Compagnie, 1602–1795* (Arnhem, 1884); *Archief voor de Geschiedenis van de Oude Hollandsche Zending*, vols. V and VI (Utrecht,

A great difficulty in the propagation of the Calvinist creed was the linguistic situation in seventeenth-century Batavia. In some respects the confusion of languages was like that of Babylon. Strangely enough, the common language best known to all inhabitants was the Portuguese. This had been imported by the slaves who were brought from the coast of British India and Ceylon, where the Portuguese authority had existed for a century and a half. The first native Calvinists were former Catholic converts of Portuguese missionaries. The Malayan dialects were so numerous and so widely different that it was useless to preach in Malayan, since only a part of the congregation could understand what was said. Efforts to introduce Dutch instead of Portuguese remained fruitless for nearly a century.[10]

According to Dutch customs all free inhabitants of Batavia were organized into a City Guard divided into companies according to nations. One of the Dutch companies was called that of the "Pennists," because it was composed of the men of the pen, the Company's clerks. After 1630 the Dutch did not take this military duty very seriously, but the companies of the other racial groups marched many times against the enemy when the period of the great wars in Java had come. The last Japanese soldiers disappeared from Batavia when the emperor of Japan broke all relations with the outside world in 1636. The Chinese were free of military duty upon payment of a special tax. During the siege of Batavia they had fought bravely on several occasions, but otherwise they had gained the reputation of always running in the same direction as the enemy, fleeing when he attacked and attacking fiercely when he fled. After all, they had not come to the Indies to fight other people's wars!

All the territory around Batavia had been completely devastated by the incessant wars, and the tropical climate changed the deserted lands in a few years into a dense jungle. So wild was the countryside that

---

1890–91), for the Moluccas; J. Mooy, *Geschiedenis der Protestantsche Kerk in Nederlandsch Indië* (Batavia, 1923–31).

[10] One of the first students of the Malay tongue was Frederik de Houtman, who composed the first Dutch-Malay grammar and dictionary (1603), *Spraeck en Woordboeck in de Maleysche en Madagaskarsche Tale.* In 1612 Albert Ruyl published his *Spieghel van de Malaysche Tale*; see P. A. Leupe, "Albert Ruyl, Maleisch Taalkundige," in BKI, VI (1859), 102 sq. Further is to be mentioned Justus Heurnius, minister of the Reformed Church, who published books on Malay and on Chinese (see J. R. Callenbach, *Justus Heurnius*, Nijkerk, 1897), and greatest of all, Hebert de Jager, the first student of Oriental comparative philology (F. De Haan, "Herbert de Jager," TBG, XLII (1899), 306, and *Priangan*, vol. I, second part, p. 220; F. W. Stapel, "Nog eenige gegevens over Herbert de Jager," BKI, LXXXVIII (1931), 314–317. See also W. M. C. Juynboll, *Zeventiende-eeuwsche beoefenaars van het Arabisch in Nederland* (Utrecht, 1932).

the government of Batavia promised a premium for every rhinoceros killed in the neighborhood of the city, and at the beginning of the eighteenth century the premium might still be paid thirty times in one month. Tiger hunting was still a normal pastime for some of the governors-general. How great has been the progress made in the cultivation of Java may be deduced from the fact that at the present time hardly any tigers can be found on the entire island.

Further to the south, in the mountain districts of Preanger, the situation was no better. Several districts had been depopulated by the armies of the sultan of Mataram in punishment for the rebellious behavior of the local rulers. On one occasion he ordered several thousand inhabitants to be transported to his capital, where all the men, numbering more than twelve hundred, were killed. However, after his attack on Batavia had failed, because his supply lines had broken down, he understood that the first thing to do if he ever wanted to attack the Dutch capital again was to resettle the territories around Bandung and the Tji-tarum River. It is quite probable that Sultan Agung never intended to drive the Dutch from Java completely. There were too many advantages connected with their presence on the island. He accused them, however, of hindering the complete unification of Java under his rule.

Great changes were coming in the political structure of the island. The Javanese chroniclers and the reports of the Dutch ambassadors tell us constantly of murders and mass executions at the court of Mataram ordered by the sultan. Apparently this prince had instituted a reign of terror against his vassals. We have not the necessary documents to form an accurate judgment on the events. It is not unlikely that Sultan Agung was playing the same role in Java that Tsar Ivan the Terrible had played in Russia fifty years earlier, that he was organizing a new system of government through the complete extermination of the nobility.[11]

The coastal districts had been the main centers for opposition against the unification of the island under Mataram. The traders on the coast were unwilling to submit to the rule of the prince of an agricultural state in the interior. Sultan Agung forced the higher noblemen to take up residence in his capital, where they were kept in semi-captivity as hostages for the good behavior of their subjects. Even such powerful rulers as the princes of Cheribon had to submit to the orders of the

[11] We have only a vague idea of what happened inside the empire of Mataram. De Haan collected some of the evidence on this point (*Priangan*, III, 172–175). Veth (*Java*, I, ch. X) is here of far greater help than the new book of Lekkerkerker.

sultan. Recalcitrants were simply exterminated, and with them their families — to make sure against possible revenge. To weaken the coastal rulers still further, their territory was devastated and depopulated. Rijklof Van Goens, Dutch ambassador to the court of Mataram, tells in his journal how he traveled through endless forests as long as he remained on the coastal plains, but found the mountain districts thickly populated. The district of Mataram itself was densely settled. Van Goens estimates the number of villages at three thousand, each inhabited by one hundred to one hundred and fifteen families. This would represent a population of several millions. The highways, or better, muletracks between the coast and the inner plateau, were well guarded. Nobody was permitted to leave the plateau without special permission of the sultan.

His guards also controlled the export of all goods. The Dutch noted the following interesting items of which the export was forbidden: horses, cows, buffaloes, and women.[12]

A further reorganization of the state undertaken by the sultan dealt with the judiciary. Agung, more strictly Mohammedan than his predecessors, endeavored to bring the administration of justice into conformity with the precepts of the Koran. He installed courts the members of which were drawn from the Mohammedan priesthood and entrusted to them all criminal affairs, which until that time had been judged by the king himself or by his representatives. The Koran prescribes also that all matters of marriage and inheritance be entrusted to ecclesiastical courts. The old customs, the *adat*, remained in force for all other affairs. Consequently, the *Suria Alam*, a Javanese code which was composed at this time, presents a mixture of Indonesian and Mohammedan law. Agung's judicial reforms were maintained in substance by the decrees of the East Indian Company when it took over the sovereignty of the larger part of the Island of Java.[13] Another of Agung's reforms was the introduction of a generous tax system. It consisted of export duties on rice and other commodities, of a head tax levied on all proprietors of rice fields, and of a sales tax paid by the people selling in the market. These taxes were very moderate. In a prosperous district such as that of Surabaya they did not yield more than six thousand ducats yearly. For the sultan of Mataram they were sufficient, for he could spend every penny he received for personal expenses and he left the maintenance of all public works and institutions to the district rulers. In comparison with the princes of India,

[12] In De Jonge, *Opkomst*, IV, 295 (Narrative of De Haen's Embassy to Mataram).
[13] See ENI *sub voce* "Rechtswezen" and literature quoted at the end of the article.

however, the wealthiest sultan of Indonesia was a relatively poor man.

After his defeat in the west, Sultan Agung turned his attention for a while to the east. The island of Bali was not yet converted to Islam and had proudly maintained its independence.[14] Its king had even reoccupied the eastern corner of Java, from which the Balinese had been driven by Agung's grandfather. The sultan decided that it was time to destroy this last remnant of Hindu civilization in the archipelago. Before he started on his campaign he wished to be at peace with the Netherlanders in Batavia. He knew that the governor-general had sent an embassy to Bali to propose an alliance. If this scheme was realized, Agung's chances to conquer the little island were gone. He knew that the Netherlanders were eager to have peace, but his dignity did not permit him to propose negotiations, since he had taken the title of "Susuhunan," which means "He to whom everything is subject." Through different diplomatic channels he suggested to the governor-general that he was willing to concede peace in magnanimity and to grant many privileges to the Company, if only the Dutch would consent to ask humbly for negotiations.

The Company's officers in Batavia did not understand the purpose of his diplomatic overtures. They mistrusted the sultan for his "perfidy" and believed that he merely wanted to entrap some of the most prominent Hollanders to be held as hostages and that he might be able to secure better conditions by a definite peace-settlement. The Directors in Amsterdam advised their governor-general to show the sultan "some courtesy," by which they meant, to recognize if necessary his formal overlordship over Batavia. The governor-general sent valuable presents to the sultan, but entrusted these presents to simple messengers and thus deprived His Majesty of Mataram of the satisfaction of receiving high Dutch officials at his court, where he could have made them wait in antichambers for several hours, thus demonstrating his superiority in rank and power. This satisfaction was all he wanted; it was merely a question of prestige, which the Dutch did not understand. Hence the state of war continued between the two powers, with intermittent outbreaks of violence.

[14] Bali owed its independence from Mataram, and, consequently, the preservation of its old beliefs and arts, to the valor of the Balinese warriors, partly descendants from Javanese exiles and therefore stubborn in their opposition toward Islam. The commonly propounded theory that Bali remained free because the Dutch tied the hands of the susuhunan in the west is absolutely incorrect. The Company refused coöperation with the Balinese princes. Commercially the island was of no interest whatsoever for the Dutch, and the government of Batavia did not care whether Mataram ruled there or not. See P. A. Leupe, "Het gezantschap naar Bali in 1633," BKI, v (1856), 1 sq.

The sultan had undoubtedly little respect for the Dutch, whom he despised as "merchants." He never realized the enormous power represented by the Dutch naval superiority and by their economic strength but believed that he could counterbalance the influence of the Dutch by an alliance with other European powers. Malacca was still Portuguese, and lively trading went on between this port and the northern coast of Java. The British in their trading-post of Bantam were also potential allies. Most interesting, however, is Sultan Agung's attempt to establish communications with the powers of the Near East. Some Javanese hadjis, returning from the pilgrimage to Mecca, had brought with them an Arabian Sheik who claimed to be the representative of the "Governor of Mecca." This envoy officially conveyed to the susuhunan the title of "sultan." At the example of Mataram, Bantam and Atjeh also sought connections with Mecca. From this period on, a second Islamitic missionary action started in the Indies. The first period of propaganda had resulted in the spreading of the Mohammedan faith and in a superficial conversion of most peoples of the Indies. The second one aimed at the intensification of Islamitic beliefs and customs in the territory already nominally converted. This second period covers the three centuries that have elapsed since 1640.

Mecca was, of course, the center of religious propaganda, but beyond Mecca lay Turkey, at that time still one of the mightiest empires on earth and a state which could bring strong pressure to bear upon the mercantile states of western Europe. The Dutch especially had many commercial interests in Asia Minor. They had an ambassador at the court of the "Great Turk," the most western of the three great Mohammedan powers which we find mentioned in the Dutch reports as the "Great Turk," the "Great Sophi" (Shah of Persia of the dynasty of the Sefavieh), and the "Great Mogul" (Emperor of India of the Turkish-Mongol dynasty). If these mighty princes could have been persuaded to take an interest in the fate of the Indonesian rulers, they could have checked the rapid growth of European domination. But the intermittent attempts of the Indonesians to arouse that interest never met with any response.

In 1639 Sultan Agung, animated by new Islamitic fervor, decided to begin his "Holy War" against the Balinese believers in Shiva-Buddha. Balambangan, Java's eastern corner, was conquered. The island itself proved nearly inaccessible for a large army, and when the troops of Mataram landed, it was bravely defended. It preserved its independence, and later, the rapid decline of Mataram safeguarded it against further attacks. Agung contented himself with the complete devastation and depopulation of Balambangan. He did not take his setback seriously and, moreover, had the satisfaction of seeing ambassadors from Palembang in Sumatra and Bandjermasin in Borneo at his court to present homage to him as the successor of the great kings of Madjapahit. In this chorus the British joined with a humble request to be allowed to occupy the island of Bangka, a territory over which the authority of the sultan was very dubious.

While Sultan Agung enjoyed his might and glory his fate was sealed by the downfall of the last great Portuguese stronghold in the archipelago. Malacca fell on January 14, 1641.[15] For years the situation of the fortress had been desperate. Atjeh had remained an irreconcilable enemy. The smaller Malayan states, afraid of the naval power of the Company, did not dare to support the Portuguese against the sultan of Sumatra. The blockade of Malacca Strait by the Dutch caused a severe food shortage in the city. In spite of this, when Van Diemen finally decided to attack the defense was so valiant that it took him five months to overcome it. Once conquered, the city quickly lost its importance. Many Portuguese families moved to Batavia, where their language continued to be spoken for more than a century.

The fall of Malacca changed the political situation of the archipelago completely. Mataram could no longer rely upon Portuguese support and had lost its best customer for the rice-export. Atjeh, surrounded by Dutch posts and allies, saw its position imperiled. The prestige of the Dutch rose among the native princes, and consequently the maintenance of the Company's monopoly in spices became increasingly easier.

Meanwhile the general situation on the Spice Islands had grown worse. The system of advancing money to the natives on harvests still to come was continued, and in 1628 the combined debts of the inhabitants of the Banda Islands, Amboina, and the Moluccas amounted to 477,390 guilders. Practically, there was no chance that these debts would ever be paid. The population had become insolvent, and the Company prepared to reap the consequences: it confiscated the means of production and other property of the islanders and reduced them to a condition of bondage. Its attitude was more to be condemned from the humanitarian point of view than from the juridical. The Company always preferred to follow the legal way. Therefore, it bought the consent of the sovereign of most of the islands — of the Sultan of Ternate — by granting him a yearly allowance and then further pro-

[15] P. A. Leupe, "Stukken betreffende het beleg en de verovering van Malakka op de Portugeezen," in *Berigten van het Historisch Genootschap*, vol. VII, part II (1859), pp. 128–428.

ceeded to extirpate the clove trees outside its own territory. The people resisted fiercely, but were subdued by force of arms. The Company made them change their clove-tree gardens into rice fields and sago-tree plantations. The small, mountainous islands could not produce food enough, and the inhabitants were obliged to buy a supplement of rice from the Company. It sold this commodity to them at too high a price, which made the situation still more desperate. Thus the economic system of the Moluccas was ruined and the population reduced to poverty.

The Spanish outpost at Tidore continued to exist until 1663, although, until the treaty of Muenster (1648) finally established peace between Spain and the Netherlands, the shipping connections with the Spanish headquarters in Manila were constantly threatened by the Dutch fleet. Spanish competition in the spice trade was not dangerous to the Company's interests. Much more obnoxious were the brave Malayan sailors from Macassar, who penetrated time and again into the forbidden seas around Banda and Ceram. From the British, Danish, and Portuguese merchants in his capital the king of Macassar bought firearms and other war supplies and with their help he made his state so strong that Governor-General Van Diemen hesitated to interfere with his interests while the Company's ships and soldiers were needed elsewhere.

The main objects of the Company in the archipelago had been achieved, however. Its commercial empire was completed by the conquest of the southern part of India and the island of Ceylon.[16] Here it found an ally against the Portuguese in the king of Kandi. Like many of his colleagues in the East, this king incurred heavy war debts with the Company, but he was rich enough to pay off these debts in regular installments, though in a very strange currency — cinnamon and elephants. The cinnamon trade and the cloth trade of India were now secured for the Company. Its complement was the copper trade of Japan and the spice trade of the Moluccas. When the Japanese government decided to oust all foreigners from the country, it made an exception of the merchants of the Company, who were allowed to continue their activities under strict supervision from the small island of Deshima off the port of Nagasaki.[17] The silk trade from Persia was

[16] For the conquest of the coast of Malabar and Coromandel and the island of Ceylon, see Stapel, *Gesch.* III, 199 sq., 251 sq., 309 sq., and 372 sq.; also H. Terpstra, *De opkomst der Westerkwartieren van de Oost Indische Compagnie* (The Hague, 1918). The *Cambridge History of India* devotes thirty-two pages to Dutch activities on the coasts of Malabar and Coromandel (vol. v, 1929, pp. 28–60, by P. Geyl).

[17] There is an excellent book on the Dutch in Japan in English: C. R. Boxer, *Jan Compagnie in Japan, 1600–1817* (The Hague, 1936). This is based on Dutch and Japa-

flourishing and found its complement in the sugar trade from China, the distribution center of which was the Dutch stronghold on the island of Formosa.[18]

Not content with this marvelous extension of the Dutch enterprises, Van Diemen sought to secure for his Directors the treasures of all those countries that were still unexplored. A legend circulated among the Spanish sailors that east of Japan an island of fabulous wealth had been sighted, the island called "Rica Doro" or "Rich in Gold." By order of Van Diemen, the navigator Maarten De Vries sailed to the northeast, where he visited the Kurile Islands and the east coast of Sakhalin and reached the forty-ninth degree of latitude north, of course without discovering the "golden islands." [19]

More astonishing were the discoveries of Abel Tasman and Frans Visscher, who were sent to explore the "Great Southern Continent," of which some Netherlands ships had seen the western coast. This coast had proved to be extremely inhospitable, widely different from the wealthy and civilized continent of which the sailor's legends told. South of Australia the two Dutchmen sailed from west to east and landed on the island of Tasmania. Proceeding further east they discovered the two islands which they called New Zeeland, after the second seafaring province of the Netherlands. The voyage was highly interesting from a geographical point of view, but economically time and money were wasted. The East India Company was a commercial enterprise, not a company for colonization. Therefore it took no interest in the nearly deserted territories of the Southern Continent it had discovered.[20]

By the middle of the seventeenth century the Company had spread its wings all over the coastlands of Asia. In comparison with the Directors in Amsterdam, the sultan of Mataram was a poor man. "Our Governor General does not bother more about the Sultan than an elephant about a fly," boasted one of the Company's officers; still, the gentlemen in Batavia thought it a wise policy to tolerate the sultan's haughty attitude. They seemed less interested in the interior of Java than in the Kurile Islands and in Tasmania. Only thirty years later

---

nese sources. See also Oskar Nachod, *Die Beziehungen der Niederländischen Ost Indischen Kompagnie zu Japan im siebzehnten Jahrhundert* (Leipzig, 1897). For the eighteenth century, see J. Feenstra Kuiper, *Japan en de buitenwereld in de achttiende eeuw* (The Hague, 1921).

[18] See literature on Formosa quoted in preceding chapter.

[19] P. A. Leupe, *Reize van Maarten Gerritszoon de Vries naar het Noorden en Oosten van Japan* (Amsterdam, 1858).

[20] Tasman's voyage has been reëdited by R. Posthumus Meyjes in the series of the Linsch. V. (vol. XVII, The Hague, 1919). An English translation appears in the series of the Hakluyt Society.

the whole scene had changed, and the Company's troops were marching through the capital of Mataram to restore a fugitive sultan to his throne.

In 1645 both Sultan Agung and Governor-General Van Diemen died. Under Van Diemen's governorship the Company's authority and sphere of influence had been extended from the coast of Persia to that of Japan, and during this same period the new empire had received its legal organization. In 1642 the Statutes of Batavia were published as the code for the Dutch Asiatic territory.[21] The Statutes were composed by "Meester" Johan Maetsuycker, the legal expert of the Council of the Indies. They provided for the administration of justice and for the maintenance of several social institutions, such as Dutch and Chinese orphanages. For all inhabitants of Batavia the Dutch authorities introduced the old Dutch-Roman law. Experience taught that it was necessary to take into consideration the customary law of the Asiatic peoples. Thus, the Chinese were ruled according to their own customs, which had legal force among them, and this was also the case with the Javanese *later* when the jurisdiction of the Company was extended over a larger area in Java.

The Statutes of Batavia originated naturally from a different concept of law from that which lay behind the customs of the people of Java. Its laws and criminal procedure were of a harshness which seems inhuman to us now, but which may be found in all codes of the period. It is pleasant to note at least one brighter spot in the picture, the limitation of the rights of the slave-owners.

The history of slavery in the Indies has been only partly written. It seems evident that the institution of slavery existed in most islands of the archipelago before the arrival of the Dutch, but we do not have a clear picture of the situation. More common than slavery was debt-bondage, which formed part of the customs of all peoples of the Indies. Islam may have contributed to the further extension of slavery. Apparently, on the island of Java slavery was more common in the completely Islamized Bantam than in the empire of Mataram, where the old traditions were much stronger.

Nearly everywhere, however, the rights of the slave-owners were limited, and thus, under the combined mitigating influence of both native customs and Christian ideas, the status of the slaves in Batavia was defined with relative humanity. Most of the slaves belonged to one or the other of the Indonesian peoples, except always the Javanese. Others were descendants of that part of the population of India that

[21] See Van der Chijs, *Nederlandsch-Indisch Plakaatboek*, I, 472 sq.

had come under the influence of Portugal. At the end of the seventeenth century the government of Batavia gave definite orders that natives of Java could not be reduced into slavery and Javanese slaves brought to the city by other Asiatics were considered free.

To all slaves the right of working their way to freedom was guaranteed, and arbitrary violence was strictly forbidden. The atrocities that were permitted and did occur under the laws that regulated slavery in the Caribbean islands were absolutely excluded by the laws enforced among both Indonesians and Dutch in the Indies.

The "Instruction for the Governor General and Council of the Indies" of 1650 further regulated the government of the Company's territories and establishments. Supreme authority was given to the governor-general *and* council.[22] All government in the Netherlands proper was done by council, and the same system was applied to the Indies. Seven of the nine councilors had to be present to make a quorum. In the Indies, however, the necessity for a strong government and the influence of the oriental surroundings made it impossible to maintain the principle of administration by council. The Indonesian princes and peoples regarded the governor-general as the ruler of the Netherlanders in the Indies, and most of the Dutch easily conformed their attitude to that of the Indonesians. The governor-general had no difficulty in reducing the Council to a subordinate position. The councilors became in fact merely the advisers of the governor-general instead of his co-legislators.

The grandiose scheme of Coen to make Batavia the great center of Asiatic trade and to procure by this trade the means of acquiring valuable products for export to Europe seemed to have been realized. From four centers of trading the goods flowed into the storehouses of Batavia — from Persia, from India and Ceylon, from the Moluccas, and from Japan. This system of concentrating all trade in Batavia was rigorously maintained during the seventeenth century. To be sure, nearly a year's delay in transporting the Persian silk could have been avoided by shipping it directly from the Persian ports to Holland instead of sending it first to Batavia and then reëxporting it to Europe. The foundation of the colony of the Cape of Good Hope in 1652 made such direct exports quite feasible.[23] The general accounts of the inter-Asiatic trade continued to be kept in Batavia, however, and thither

[22] Instructions to the governor-general (1650) in Van der Chijs, *op. cit.*, II, 135 sq.

[23] For South Africa, see George McCall Theal, *History of South Africa under the Administration of the Dutch East India Company* (London, 1897); E. C. Godee Molsbergen, *De stichter van Hollands Zuid Afrika, Jan van Riebeek, 1618–1677* (Amsterdam, 1912).

the books of all colonies and establishments were sent for control. The data were incorporated into a general report which was sent to Europe once a year by the so-called "tea- and book-ship," which got its name from the fact that it transported only tea and the many folio volumes in which the general reports were written down.

Coen had planned to entrust the inter-Asiatic trade to free settlers of Dutch origin, but this plan had been rejected by the Directors in Amsterdam, and thus far the Company had succeeded fairly well in keeping the commerce going by means of its own ships. It had been impossible to eliminate the Chinese and Malayan traders completely, and actually the native shipping proved of the highest value for transporting goods from the less-frequented ports to the establishments of the Company. The Gujerats were still doing a thriving business between India and Sumatra, and the Arabs from southern Arabia did their utmost to enter into successful competition with them. The unfortunate Dutch "free citizens" who lived in Batavia and on some of the Moluccas in small numbers were actually less free than the Asiatics and complained bitterly that the High Government favored the Chinese above the Dutch and that much was permitted to the Chinese and the Malays that was forbidden to the Netherlanders. Money lending became their only way of making profits. Money was scarce and the risks were high in the Indies, and this circumstance was expressed in the rate of interest, which was between 12 and 25 per cent a year.

Batavia had been made into an emporium for the whole of Asia. The original capital of the Company (six and a half million guilders) was, of course, insufficient to finance these extensive trading enterprises and adequate military protection for the trading posts and possessions. The original capital was already fully employed in the equipment of the ships that were sent from Holland to the Indies. The Directors faced the difficult task of accomplishing simultaneously several projects, each of which required more money than was provided by the total original capital. These projects were the equipment of strongly armed fleets, the establishment of factories and fortresses in Asia and South Africa, with the necessary personnel and ships, the provision of the capital necessary for the inter-Asiatic commerce, and the setting aside of funds sufficient to pay an occasional dividend to the shareholders in the Netherlands. These gentlemen were already furiously protesting against the financial policy of the Company.[24]

The Directors had distributed an average dividend of 10 per cent a

[24] For the commercial side of the Company's activities, see W. F. M. Mansvelt, *Rechtsvorm en Geldelijk beheer bij de Oost Indische Compagnie* (Amsterdam, 1922).

year during the first thirty years of the Company's existence. This amounted to a total disbursement of 20,000,000 guilders. The shareholders suspected, however, that far greater profits had been made. They did not know that during the same period the Company had incurred a debt of more than 10,000,000 guilders in Holland, which reduced the real profits to an average of 5 per cent a year. Consequently, it is clear that the shareholders received more than they were entitled to according to the figures that could have been found in the books of the Company — books that were kept rigorously secret. Yet, the shareholders were correct in their suspicion that the gross profits had been much larger than the Directors acknowledged. Only, the Directors had not felt justified in distributing the total amount of profits. This puzzling situation can only be explained by an investigation of the system of bookkeeping followed by the Directors.

The East India Company was organized as a firm of ship-owners. The shareholders expected that all profits would be divided immediately and completely when a return fleet with a valuable cargo had come in from the Indies. Each expedition to the Indies was considered a separate commercial enterprise. Under this system it was impossible to build up reserve funds. Yet without reserve funds the commerce in Asia could not be maintained. We have seen that the Directors met this difficulty by completely separating the bookkeeping of the Company in Holland from that used by the Company's representatives in the Indies. They divided all the monies they had in Holland among the shareholders, and even borrowed money to bolster up the dividends, but at the same time they kept huge sums in the Indies for the extension of the trade establishments. Until 1630 the real profits of the Company were very small, but the Directors did their best to keep the shareholders in good humor and gambled on the future, a policy that finally brought good results. As soon as the inter-Asiatic trade began to throw off profits, the financial position of the Company improved. Between 1613 and 1654 these profits amounted to 101,000,000 guilders, while the running expenses for the same period were 76,000,000 guilders. This left a profit of 25,000,000 guilders of which 9,700,000 were sent to Europe and the remaining part kept in the Indies as a working capital for the inter-Asiatic commerce.

The accounts of the Company, consequently, show a quite different picture from that which is given by the routine historical narratives. The "fabulous wealth" which is said to have been drawn by the Dutch from the Indies in the beginning of the seventeenth century amounted actually to the not very fabulous sum of ten million guilders over a

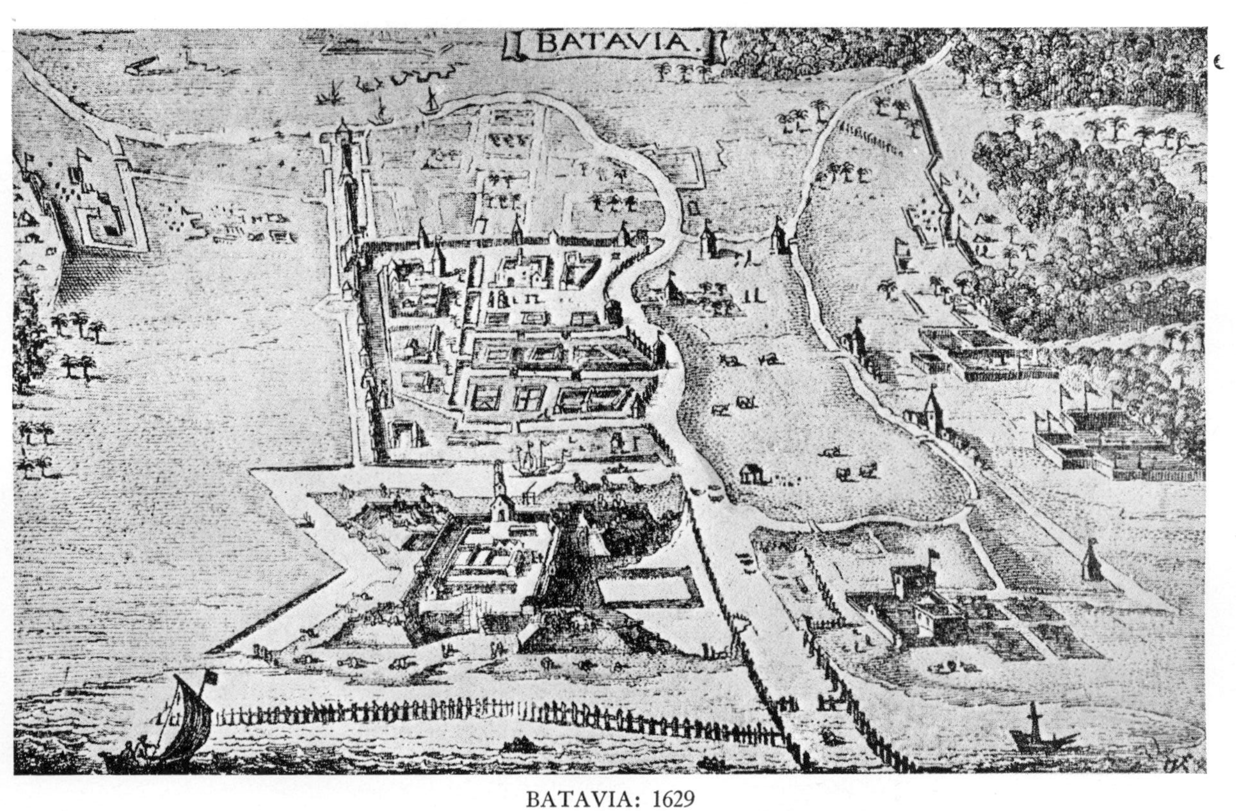

BATAVIA: 1629
From Fr. Valentijn's *Oud en Nieuw Oost Indiën* (1724–26).

thirty years' period. Only a part of these profits was derived from the pepper and spice trade, and consequently, obtained through the rights of monopoly which the East Indian government, by treaty or by force, had acquired. Most of it was obtained through normal trading, unprotected by monopoly, especially in Persia, India, and Japan. Undoubtedly the East India Company contributed to the economic welfare of the Netherlands in the seventeenth century, but this welfare was by no means based on the trade in spices or on the Asiatic commerce. The profits from Asia were always modest if compared with the income the seventeenth-century Netherlanders derived from shipping and trading in Europe.

After 1630, when the situation in Asia was more stabilized and the competition of the British had been eliminated in the archipelago, the profits of the East India Company increased considerably. For a century the Company flourished. Then came a crisis in its affairs. In the eighteenth century the Company began to change from a commercial into an agricultural enterprise, but the period of transition required another hundred years. The first sign of these agricultural activities began to appear shortly after the foundation of Batavia, when the Chinese built the first sugar plantations and sugar mills near that place.[25] In a few years the production rose to a million pounds a year. But in the seventeenth century the value of sugar as an export crop remained low, no more than twelve guilders a hundred pounds. Export to Europe was still unprofitable, but sometimes the skippers of the home-bound vessels needed ballast, and sugar proved to be quite convenient for the purpose. The sudden rise of prices on the European market at the beginning of the eighteenth century changed the whole situation and put the Company upon a new economic basis. When that happened, the government of Batavia already controlled wide inland areas in Java and Ceylon and thus was prepared for the change.

[25] The planting and processing of sugar had been known in the Indies for centuries, but the Chinese around Batavia built it up to an export industry. See De Haan, *Oud Batavia*, I, 323–327.

CHAPTER VIII

DOWNFALL OF THE INDONESIAN STATES

After sixty years of trading in the Indies, years also of continuous warfare, the Dutch East India Company controlled the sea lanes from the Gulf of Bengal and Ceylon to Nagasaki in Japan. Its territorial possessions, however, remained extremely limited. In the Indies, it exercised full sovereignty over only one place, Batavia. It possessed the overlordship of hundreds of small islands in the Moluccas — in fact of all the domains and vassals of the sultan of Ternate — and of some small, rather unimportant island groups in the southeast of the archipelago.[1] To these belonged the Kei and Aroë islands and the Solor group in the Lesser Sunda chain. Far to the northwest, on the Malay Peninsula, it had unrestricted authority over the town of Malacca, now a desolate place that had lost most of its trade to Batavia.

The Directors of the Company were unwilling to extend their authority further than absolutely necessary. They controlled large islands outside the archipelago, for instance Ceylon and Formosa; they maintained hundreds of trading posts from Ispahan in Persia to Nagasaki in Japan, and had founded a relay station for their ships at the southern point of Africa, the future Capetown. Their commercial empire was sufficient for them; they had no ambition whatsoever to transform it into a real empire, extending over vast areas of Asia. Strange as it may sound, the Directors of the Company that gained control over the Asiatic trade were averse to all expansion and schemes of conquest. They were firmly convinced that the Portuguese colonial empire had succumbed because it had been too extensive, or, in the picturesque language of the period, "because there were so many chickens that not all of them could find shelter under the wings of the hen." [2]

This principle of limiting the Company's authority to a few ports and of concentrating on naval power alone made it imperative to avoid

[1] See P. A. Leupe, "De reizen der Nederlanders naar Nieuw Guinea en de Papoesche eilanden in de zeventiende en achttiende eeuw," BKI, XXII (1875), 1 sq., 175 sq., and XXIII (1876), 160; A. Haga, *Nederlandsch Nieuw Guinea en de Papoesche eilanden, 1517–1583*, 2 vols. (Batavia-The Hague, 1884).

[2] De Haan, *Priangan*, III, 225, quoting Philippus Baldaeus, "Naauwkeurige Beschrijvinge van Malabar en Coromandel."

as much as possible becoming involved in the mutual quarrels of the Indonesian princes and the internal conflicts of the individual native states. The government of Batavia was willing to recognize any ruler in the Indies who actually held power over his subjects, whatever his origin or that of his authority might be, as long as such a ruler was willing to fulfill the obligations which his predecessors had undertaken towards the Company. This "foreign policy" of the Company was never more strictly followed than under the governorship-general of Johan Maetsuycker (1653–1678).

Johan Maetsuycker was a lawyer who as the son of Catholic parents had studied at the University of Louvain. When the Directors sought to engage some lawyers to serve as experts with the Council of Justice in Batavia, they could not find a single candidate for this position except Maetsuycker, who was consequently accepted in spite of the fact that he did not meet with the first of all requirements for holding office, either in Holland or in the Indies, namely membership in the Dutch Reformed Church. The Statutes of Batavia were Maetsuycker's work. His exceptional intelligence and diplomatic ability rapidly attracted the attention of Governor-General van Diemen and of the Directors in Amsterdam, and in 1653, although still not a member of the official church, he was appointed governor-general.

For twenty-five years he ruled the colonial empire from the castle of Batavia, never leaving that town except for an occasional hunting party in the jungle close to the city walls. In his general policy he followed scrupulously the ideas of the Directors in Amsterdam who were so well satisfied with his administration that time and again they refused his requests to be discharged from his office. He had nothing of the genius of Coen and shrank back from the far-sighted policy advocated by his most prominent officers, Rijklof van Goens and Cornelis Speelman, who understood that sooner or later a change in the policy of the Company would be necessary and that the Dutch colonial empire would crumble like that of the Portuguese unless it were based upon a solid territorial foundation. Finally, circumstances forced the governor-general to consent to a bolder policy.

Trouble had arisen again in the Moluccas. The Company, fully supported by the sultan of Ternate, had carried through its policy of restricting the production of clove and nutmeg, if necessary by forced extirpation of the trees, and did its utmost to eliminate all competition from native and Chinese traders. The rigorous execution of the orders of the government of Batavia had wrought innumerable hardships upon the inhabitants, especially of Amboina and adjacent islands. One revolt followed another, but the Company's interests were represented here by one of the toughest men of its history, Governor Arnoud De Vlaming, who in a five years' war mercilessly crushed all opposition. Ternate's sultan was reduced to the position of a vassal instead of being respected as the Company's ally. The consequence of this brutal repression was a constant decline of the welfare of the Moluccas.

The economic policy of the Company was not the only cause of unrest in the northeastern archipelago, however. In order to establish its authority on a more solid basis and to gain faithful subjects in the Moluccas upon whom it could rely in case of revolt of the Mohammedans, the Company tried to foster the conversion of the pagan tribes of Ceram and Halmahera to the Calvinist creed, and to rally the Christian inhabitants of Amboina, who had been converted to Catholicism by the Portuguese missionaries, around the Protestant ministers sent from Holland. These attempts were partly successful but aroused the resentment of the Mohammedans, who were strongly supported by the envoys of the king of Macassar, the principal representative of Islam in that area once the sultan of Ternate had offered his submission to the Dutch.[3] Thus the war in the Moluccas had not only economic but also religious causes.

In consequence, the tension between the government of Batavia and the king of Macassar had been increasing constantly. Twice war had been declared (1653–1655 and 1660), but both parties had shrunk back from carrying the conflict to the extreme. Maetsuycker knew that a war against Macassar would entail enormous expenditures for the equipment of a considerable army and he knew too that the Directors in Amsterdam hated to spend their money for the apparently useless conquest of a half-civilized kingdom. Moreover, war had broken out with Portugal in 1651, and although the fleet and troops of the Company under the command of Rijklof van Goens had made sweeping progress on Ceylon and in India, the peace of 1661 had come as a relief.

The king of Macassar, however, seemed to invite disaster. Understandably enough, he prepared for the war against the Dutch which he knew to be inevitable. European traders in his capital, British, Danes, and Portuguese, provided him with artillery and ammunition. Fortifications were built around the town of Macassar, and a fleet of war-

[3] That religion was one of the main causes of the conflicts in the archipelago was the firm conviction of such experienced men of the time as Rumphius and van Goens. See also Tiele, *Bouwstoffen tot de vestiging van het Nederlandsch Gezag*, II, 105.

ships was equipped. This development of native sea power was already sufficiently annoying to Batavia, but even Maetsuycker could no longer avoid taking action when the king continued to give open support to Portuguese merchants in his city and to encourage their trading with the Spice Islands and Timor, which the Company considered to be areas reserved for its own ships exclusively under the treaties concluded with Ternate and the local chieftains. For many years the parsimony of the Directors had been the strongest bulwark of Macassar's independence. Now matters had come to the point where Maetsuycker believed war necessary in order to safeguard the commercial interests of his superiors. An additional reason was that in Europe war had broken out between Holland and Britain. A British squadron had already penetrated into Far Eastern waters, and there were reports that the British had promised assistance to the king of Macassar if he would renew the war against the Company. Actually Dutch ships were attacked, and the "sultan" of Buton (a small island east of Macassar), who was a vassal of Ternate and consequently of the Company, was threatened by a superior Macassar force.

The war against Macassar is more than a mere episode in the endless series of warlike expeditions undertaken by the Company in the Indies. It marked the beginning of a new period. In the three decades between 1650 and 1680, all the major Indonesian states disintegrated. Ternate had been the first to lose its independence, but Macassar, Mataram, Bantam, and even Atjeh followed within a few years. There is undoubtedly a connection between the fact that about 1650 the Dutch Company had definitely established its naval supremacy and the sudden collapse of the Indonesian states. The very nature of these states made a rapid succession of ups and downs in political life unavoidable, but now, for the first time in the history of the archipelago, an outside power, ready to intervene any moment, stood watching the developments; and this outside power was of a character quite different from that of the Indonesian states. It was not subjected to all the vicissitudes through which a sultanate with its never-failing harem intrigues had to go. On the contrary, its government and the succession of its rulers were regulated and stable. It was slow to act, but it never loosened its grip. Too often the Indonesian princes made the mistake of calling upon this foreign power to intervene in their mutual quarrels, and in the civil wars that broke out in each sultanate because of the absence of fixed laws of succession, and although the Company heartily disliked to hazard troops and money in inland wars, it was resolved, once it had become involved in such a war, to see it through and to have its expenses repaid.

Maetsuycker entrusted the expedition against Macassar to Cornelis Speelman.[4] Cornelis Speelman is a typical figure in the history of the Company. From a merchant he became both an admiral and a general, just as the Company itself changed from a trading enterprise into the ruler of a territorial empire. Speelman was born in Rotterdam, and while very young left home for the Indies, where he spent his whole life. He was vigorous and energetic, and the climate of the tropics never hindered him from working if necessary sixteen hours a day. He wrote an enormous number of letters and memoirs. During his campaign against Macassar he composed, between battles, a report on the political and social conditions in southern Celebes that covers eight hundred closely written pages. Intelligent, with a broad knowledge of native languages and customs, without many scruples, willing to risk his life courageously, but also willing to sacrifice other men's lives whenever he thought it necessary, he was an ideal commander for the Indies, where adaptability to all situations was more important than profound strategical knowledge. He repudiated indignantly all charges brought against him that he had abused his position for his own personal profit, although he used all other means to increase his already considerable wealth.[5] In one of his letters, Speelman calls himself "that great professor of Bacchus' pupils," but his iron constitution withstood all excesses and the tropical climate for thirty-seven years, until a combined kidney and liver affliction struck him down at the age of fifty-six, just as he had finally obtained the highest position in the Indies — that of governor-general. This man was the "sword" of the Company in the period when it changed from a commercial to a territorial power, and he was one of the few men who deliberately aimed at changing the character of the Dutch colonial empire.

In 1666 Speelman set out on his campaign against Macassar with a fleet of twenty-one ships and a force of 600 European soldiers. This small force was considerably strengthened by Indonesian auxiliary troops, partly Amboinese under the command of Captain Jonker — a full-blood Amboinese in spite of his Dutch name[6] — and partly a large

[4] The latest biography of Speelman, by F. W. Stapel, "Cornelis Janszoon Speelman," BKI, XCIV (1936), 1–222.

[5] We know that he lent money to Balinese shopkeepers in Batavia, at a rate of 12 and more per cent; see Stapel, *op. cit.*, p. 159.

[6] A biography of Jonker by J. A. van der Chijs in TBG, XXVIII (1883), 351–473, and XXX (1885), 1–234. Like all van der Chijs' historical works, this biography is far from

number of Buginese volunteers led by their prince, Aru Palacca of Boni. The district of Boni borders that of Gowa, the homeland of the king of Macassar. Aru Palacca had been driven into exile by his more powerful neighbor and was seeking revenge. Without his help the conquest of Macassar would have been very difficult.

Speelman's first undertaking was to free the sultan of Buton from the troops of Macassar that were beleaguering him. From Buton he proceeded to the Moluccas, where he negotiated a durable peace between two mortal enemies, the sultans of Ternate and Tidore. Until 1663 Tidore had relied upon the support of Spain, but in that year all Spanish troops had been withdrawn from the Moluccas because the Philippines were threatened with an attack by Chinese pirates. The Dutch had immediately occupied the deserted Spanish forts. This forced the sultan of Tidore to make peace, and by the treaty of 1667 he recognized the overlordship of the Company. Thus, the conquest of the Spice Islands was completed.

Reinforced by troops of Ternate, Speelman returned to the attack upon Macassar. Aru Palacca landed in the district of Boni, where the people immediately revolted against the king of Macassar. It still took four months of hard fighting to make Macassar surrender and its king consent to the treaty of Bongaja (November 18, 1668). Even after this another campaign no less furious than the first one was required before the treaty could be executed. The capital was occupied, and a fortress called Rotterdam after Speelman's birthplace ensured its permanent submission.

The treaty of Bongaja caused a revolutionary change in the political organization of the eastern part of the archipelago. The Company received the monopoly of trade in the port of Macassar and all non-Dutch Europeans were forced to leave the city. Of still greater consequence was the delimitation of Macassar's sphere of interest, which was definitely reduced to the city itself and its near surroundings. Even in this small area the Company exercised its authority and was permitted the fortress Rotterdam, while Dutch coinage was declared to have legal value in the State. All territory ceded by Macassar fell automatically under the control of the Company, even if for practical reasons it was brought under the nominal authority of native princes. Boni, which had been restored to Aru Palacca, and Buton, which had been saved from destruction, became, of course, vassal states of Batavia. The northern and eastern coasts of Celebes were ceded to Ternate, which in

---

impartial and prejudiced against the officers of the Company. A necessary addition is given by De Haan, *Priangan,* vol. I, part II, pp. 228–231.

its turn was now completely under Dutch supervision. The island of Sumbawa, liberated from Macassar, was obliged to accept the overlordship of the Company.

Thus fell the bulwark of Indonesian independence in the eastern part of the archipelago. The attempts to unite the native states against the Dutch had failed. Vainly had the king of Macassar sought alliances with Bantam and Mataram; neither of these states had dared to accept him as an ally.

In the same year that other bulwark of Indonesian independence in the northwest, the sultanate of Atjeh, also crumbled. The growing importance of the tin mines of Perak on the Malay Peninsula, in a district that was subject to the sultans of Atjeh, had caused the Company to take more interest in Atjenese affairs. Until the middle of the seventeenth century this tin had been exported by Gujerat merchants to India. Then Maetsuycker decided upon rather rough measures to secure part of the trade for the Company. He knew that the power of Atjeh had diminished, especially since in 1640 the government of the sultanate had come into the hands of a sultana. Under this rule by women the loosely constructed edifice of the state of Atjeh began to fall apart. Maetsuycker made full use of the opportunity. He renewed the Company's treaties with Atjeh but at the same time fomented revolt against Atjenese rule among the rajas of Sumatra's west coast. A blockade of the Atjenese coast helped to make the rulers of Atjeh aware of the change that had occurred in the political situation of the archipelago. Constant working among the local chiefs on the west coast who already resented the overlordship of Atjeh finally led to the conclusion of the treaty of Painan (July 6, 1663), in which the districts of Indrapura, Tiku, and Padang put themselves under the protection of the Company, which, in its turn, in exchange for an absolute monopoly of trade, promised to guarantee these districts complete independence from Atjeh.[7]

This did not mean that peace and order were immediately established in that area. In those days Sumatra's west coast was a land of romance, or, from a more realistic point of view, the home of incurable pirates and an ideal hunting ground for those who loved wild adventures. Fighting never ceased. The faithful paladins of Meester Johan Maetsuycker, Aru Palacca the Buginese and Captain Jonker the Amboinese, had to fight a campaign in the mountain districts east of Padang before even part of the country had come to rest. The Company was lucky to

[7] W. J. A. de Leeuw, *Het Painansch Contract* (Amsterdam, 1926); H. Kroeskamp, *De Westkust en Minangkabau, 1665–1668* (Utrecht, 1931).

MACASSAR

Siege of the city by the army and navy of the East India Company, commanded by Speelman. From Walter Schultzen's *Ost-Indische Reise* (1676).

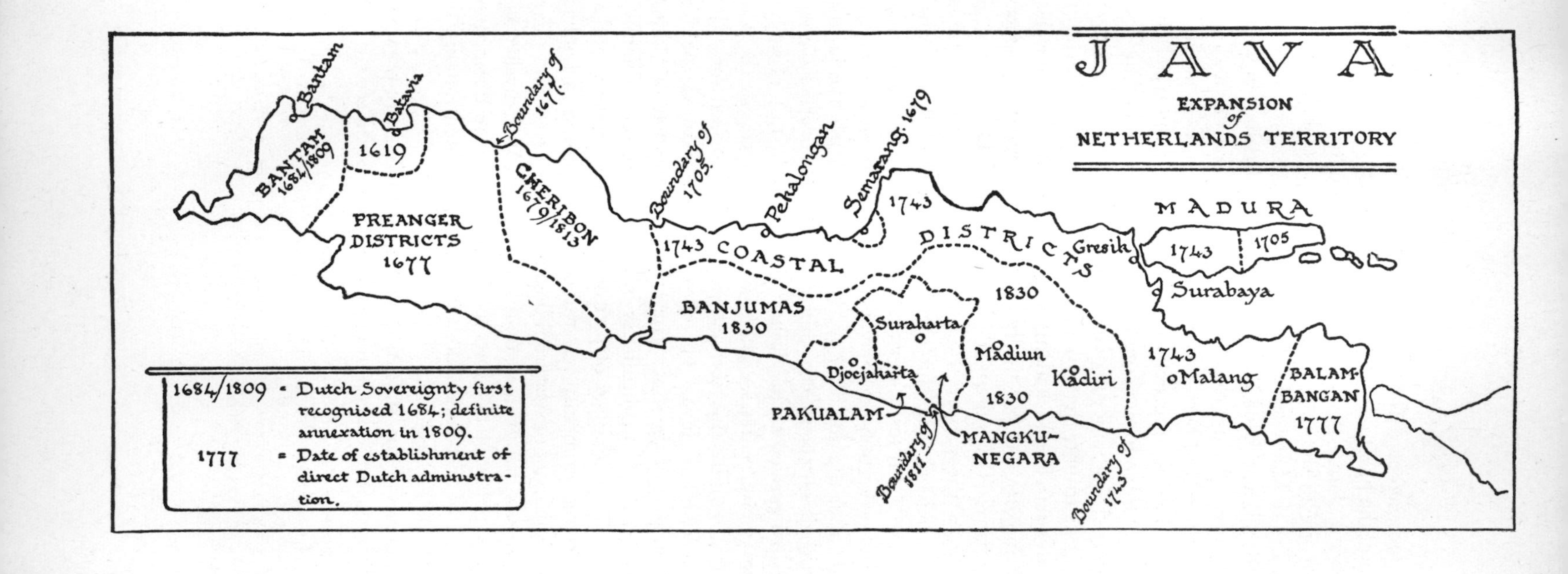
JAVA
EXPANSION of NETHERLANDS TERRITORY
Bantam
BANTAM 1684/1809
Batavia
1619
PREANGER DISTRICTS 1677
Boundary of 1677.
CHERIBON 1679/1813
Boundary of 1705.
1743 COASTAL DISTRICTS
Pekalongan
Semarang. 1679
1743
Gresik
MADURA
1743
1705
Surabaya
BANJUMAS 1830
Surakarta
Djocjakarta
Madiun
Kadiri
1830
1830
PAKUALAM
MANGKU-NEGARA
Boundary of 1811
Boundary of 1743
1743
Malang
BALAM-BANGAN 1777
1684/1809 = Dutch Sovereignty first recognised 1684; definite annexation in 1809.
1777 = Date of establishment of direct Dutch administration.

have a clever agent at Padang, a man who was interested in the people with whom he had to deal and consequently came to know a great deal about them. This agent, Jacob Pits, had collected information on the people living in the interior of Sumatra and notably on the Menangkabau. From Malay chiefs he had learned that a century or more earlier the highlands of Padang had been ruled by kings of Menangkabau, princes who use to call the padishah of Turkey and the emperor of China their "brothers." Descendants of this royal family were still living, and Pits, having obtained the consent of the tribal chiefs, reinstated one of them in the kingdom. This provided the Dutch Company with a very desirable legalization for its authority on the west coast. In return for its trouble the new king ceded to the government of Batavia a small district close to Padang which was reputed to be rich in gold.[8]

Thus Sumatra had practically been brought under the supervision of the Company. The sultans of Palembang and Djambi had granted a monopoly of the pepper trade to the Company and extra-territorial rights to its agents. The chieftains of the islands of Bangka and Billiton had separated their territories from the sultanate of Palembang and had sought the protection of Batavia to maintain their semi-independence.

Shortly after the downfall of Macassar and Atjeh, the Javanese states also lost their independence. For many years Governor-General Maetsuycker had applied all his diplomatic skill to the task of staying out of Javanese internal affairs. There were few places in the Company's commercial empire that seemed less alluring for schemes of conquest than the island of Java. The government of Batavia held an exaggerated opinion of the inner strength of the sultanate of Mataram, and, on the other hand, a ridiculously low opinion of the economic value of the island. That conquest of part or the whole of Java would only be a burden for the Company was the common opinion in Batavia. Thus, when the sultanate of Mataram began to disintegrate and the rivals for the throne sought the help of the Company, Maetsuycker vigorously defended a policy of non-intervention. There were dissident voices in the Council of the Indies, however, and prominent among them was that of Cornelis Speelman.

To understand the sudden downfall of the empire of Mataram we must go back to the beginning of the reign of the second susuhunan.

[8] Pits's creation of a "kingdom of Menangkabau" had of course only an ephemeral existence. The gold mining on Sumatra's west coast never gave great results and was finally abandoned. See Elias Hesse, "Gold-bergwerke in Sumatra 1680–1683," in S. P. L'Honoré Naber, *Reisebeschreibungen von deutschen Beamten und Kriegsleuten im Dienste der Niederländischen Ost- und West-Indischen Kompagnien, 1602–1797*, vol. x (The Hague, 1931).

In 1645 Sultan Agung had died and been succeeded by his son, Amangkurat I, commonly known as Sunan Tegalwangi.[9] This prince has gone down in history as a typical Oriental tyrant. Many are the stories of his monstrous cruelty and his sexual extravagances. The few Dutchmen who had an opportunity to visit his court told gruesome tales of the arbitrariness with which he decided the life and death of his followers and even his relatives. They described the Kraton of the sultan as a huge square enclosed by a wall twenty feet high. During the night, they said, no man was allowed to stay inside the Kraton where sultan Amangkurat slept, the only man amidst 10,000 women. To be fair to that prince we must add that 3,000 of these ladies were old matrons who stood guard — or were supposed to do so — on the walls of the Kraton, and nearly 6,000 were servants who waited on the few hundreds who formed the royal harem.

The Dutch narratives tell further of enormous enclosed meadows near the Kraton where the sultan kept hundreds of rhinoceroses and wild buffaloes and thousands of deer. Here His Majesty went hunting, safe from all the dangers of the wilderness. In outbursts of anger, they say, he was capable of ordering the execution of hundreds of his followers. His own brother, driven to despair by the murder of his friends, ran *amok* with fifty of his followers at the court and killed many of the sultan's bodyguards. Not until he was satisfied with the wild scenes of bloodshed did Amangkurat give the order to strike back and kill his brother. Whole clans of men, women, and children were exterminated because a single member was suspected of treason. On one occasion the sultan sent his *patih*, his prime minister, to accomplish an impossible task and then had him executed because he failed. One report, certainly exaggerated, says that 6,000 persons, Mohammedan priests and their families, were killed within half an hour. But debauchery and brutality reduced the sultan finally to a state of idiocy, and there is a story that in this state he used to wander around his Kraton alone, herding goats as if he were a shepherd.

The story of the Mohammedan priests who were killed by order of the sultan may throw some light on all these apparently senseless acts of cruelty. Amangkurat had revised the administration of justice in his empire. From the Mohammedan priesthood he took away all matters of jurisdiction which his predecessor had given them. Once more all capital crimes were to be judged by the susuhunan himself, who also settled all disputes regarding the delimitation of the rights of his vassals. To curtail the power of these vassals was Amangkurat's

[9] Lekkerkerker, *op. cit.*, p. 338 and Veth, *Java*, II, 1 sq.

next aim. Dutch reports tell us of a complete reorganization of the administration of his empire. The vassals of the coastal districts who had been the most unruly of the susuhunan's subjects were placed under the supervision of four governors who also had the task of controlling the foreign trade. To destroy the last remnants of their independence Amangkurat claimed for himself not only full sovereignty over all lands under his authority but also full ownership of everything existing in those territories. In a conversation with Rijklof van Goens, who had come as an ambassador to the court of Mataram, he pointed out that *his* monarchical power was not limited like that of the Dutch Company but that he could dispose of his empire and all people in it as his private property. This power he delegated to his lieutenants, who had to decide how to put this theory into practice; in other words, had to find out how much they could get out of their subjects without violating too rudely the local customs and traditions.[10]

Amangkurat's policy apparently was only the logical continuation of his father's efforts to establish an absolute and undivided monarchy in Java. But he lacked the great qualities of his father, and when the storm broke loose against his innovations he was not able to hold his own. In 1674 the dissatisfied elements in the empire found a leader in Trunajoyo, prince of Madura. Still the revolt might have been crushed without much difficulty if it had not been for the intervention of other powers. Trunajoyo's revolt came at a moment when the Netherlands and therefore also the East India Company were going through one of the gravest crises of their history. In 1672 war had broken out between the Dutch Republic on one side and France and Great Britain, supported by several German states, on the other. The larger part of the territory of the Republic in Europe had been occupied by the enemy. The downfall of the once powerful Netherlands state seemed imminent. At sea the Netherlanders were able to hold their own, and around Asia the squadrons of the Company even gained a decisive victory over the British.[11] Nevertheless, rumors that the Dutch Republic would surrender shortly, rumors which were eagerly spread by the British merchants, continued to circulate through the Indies. The government of Batavia was forced to take some quite unusual steps and to organize a kind of counter-propaganda by spreading stories that the naval power of the enemies of Holland had been crushed and that the king of France was already suing for peace.

[10] De Haan, *Priangan*, I, 28.

[11] On this war, see C. R. Boxer, "The Third Dutch War in the East," in *The Mariner's Mirror*, XVI (1930), 348 sq.

The enemies of Batavia, however, considered the time ripe for action. Exiles from Macassar were working against the Company in Madura and in Bantam. Trunajoyo's revolt provided them with a wonderful opportunity to gain a foothold on Java and to turn the empire of Mataram into a bulwark against Dutch expansion. Meanwhile, at the other extreme of the island the sultan of Bantam sought to extend his authority over the western provinces of Mataram, which would lead to the encirclement of Batavia by Bantamese territory.

At that time Bantam was ruled by the greatest of its sultans, Abulfatah Agung (1651–1683), who energetically tried to modernize his state and to make it the center of Mohammedan activities in the whole archipelago. He sent his son to make the pilgrimage to Mecca and to proceed from the Holy City to Turkey in order to establish regular connections with the leading power of Islam.[12] At the same time, the sultan and his son introduced some European customs and tried to organize a following of European advisers and adventurers, some of whom actually went over to the Mohammedan faith. The old sultan began the construction of a new residence, the Kraton of Tirtajasa, which, curiously enough, he had built as a small Dutch town, the houses being neatly arranged along a canal.

But his greatest achievement was the organization of a Bantamese overseas trade. Like the king of Macassar, the sultan of Bantam had welcomed to his ports British, Danish, and French traders. With the help of these Europeans he had begun to equip his own ships, which, navigated at first by European skippers, sailed to the Philippines, to Macao, to Bengal, and to Persia.[13] On one of his own ships the crown prince had made the voyage to Mecca. Indian, Chinese, and Arabian merchants flocked to Bantam after they had been driven out of Malacca and Macassar. The merchandise sold in the market of Batavia came partly from the rival port of Bantam, and the pretensions of Sultan Abulfatah rose so high that he demanded a share in the nutmeg trade of Amboina and in the tin trade of the Malay Peninsula, demands which were haughtily refused by the government of Batavia. It was said that never before, not even in the great days of Indonesian shipping that preceded the arrival of the Portuguese, had such extensive trading taken place in an Indonesian port as in Bantam during the

[12] Connections with Mecca became more and more regular. See also C. Snouck Hurgronje, "Een Mekkaansch Gezantschap naar Atjeh in 1683," BKI, XXXVII (1888), 545 sq. For Bantam, N. MacLeod, "De onderwerping van Bantam (1680)," IG, XXIII (1901), 350 sq.

[13] From the documents published by De Jonge, De Haan collected material on the extension of Bantamese shipping; see *Priangan*, III, 238.

years when the East India Company was at the peak of its power.

Successes like this made Abulfatah highly ambitious. He dreamed of gaining supremacy over western Java. He wove his diplomatic nets all over the archipelago. In the Moluccas he intrigued with the sultan of Ternate, Sultan Sibori, commonly known among the Dutch as Sultan Amsterdam. His soldiers attacked Dutch posts on Sumatra. Finally, he wrote letters to the king of Great Britain and to the sultan of Turkey in an effort to obtain them as allies.[14]

With the sultan of Bantam threatening Batavia from the west while Trunajoyo and his Macassar supporters set the land of Mataram afire in the east, the Company had to act. Maetsuycker still tried to limit Dutch intervention to an absolute minimum, but he could not avoid sending a naval force commanded by Speelman against the Macassar auxiliaries of Trunajoyo. It was too late. Although the Company's troops occupied Surabaya and other coastal towns and part of the island of Madura, Trunajoyo succeeded in defeating the army of Susuhunan Amangkurat. Then he established his residence in the old capital of East Java, Kadiri. The energetic Speelman would have liked to march his troops straight into the little-known interior of Java, to Kadiri, in the hope of smashing the power of the usurper before it could take root. He strongly advocated a bold and definite policy, first to restore the power of the susuhunan, who thus would become indebted to the Company, and then to turn against Bantam to put an end to all schemes and pretensions of sultan Abulfatah. But the cautious Maetsuycker would not hear of it. He still considered negotiating with Trunajoyo and hoped to postpone the conflict with Bantam.

Circumstances forced his hand, however. Amangkurat, defeated by the rebels, saw himself suddenly deserted by all his vassals and even by most of his own relatives. Trunajoyo's troops stormed and burned the Kraton of Mataram. The susuhunan's treasures, his crown jewels, his elephants and horses and even his harem, fell into the hands of the new ruler who styled himself the legitimate successor of the great king Hayam Wuruk of Madjapahit, in other words the legitimate heir to the throne of East Java which had been "usurped" by the princes of Mataram. For a short time Kadiri regained its old splendor. In the meantime Amangkurat tried to make good his escape to the coast, to the Dutch settlements. He died of exhaustion on the way. The empire seemed lost for his dynasty. Dying, he advised his son to seek an alliance with the Company.

[14] W. Fruin-Mees, "Een Bantamsch Gezantschap naar Engeland in 1682," TBG, LXIV (1924), 207.

The new susuhunan was a man of weak character. His only hope of restoration lay with the Dutch. In order to obtain their help he did not hesitate to promise the government of Batavia repayment of all war expenses, the monopoly of the importation of cloth and opium, and finally, the cession of a large territory south of Batavia and of the port of Semarang. Even the prospect of acquiring these great advantages was hardly sufficient to overcome Maetsuycker's hesitation. He tried to keep Speelman back from siding definitely with the susuhunan. He made so many objections to the schemes of his commander in chief that Speelman answered: "The only objection I miss in your letter is that perhaps even the sky will fall down from heaven and destroy the whole human race." [15]

We must add that the young susuhunan did his utmost to destroy the confidence which Speelman and others might have had in his character. Instead of coöperating in the reconquest of his empire, he devoted most of his time to silly attempts to recover one of the women of his harem who since being taken prisoner by Trunajoyo had been wandering from one Javanese court to another until she came to Bantam, where the shrewd Abulfatah kept her well guarded in the hope of later making use of her in his diplomatic intrigues.

In 1678, however, with the death of Governor General Maetsuycker on January 4, the conduct of Dutch affairs came into the hands of the more warlike Rijklof van Goens. Speelman was called to Batavia, where he became the most influential member of the Council of the Indies. The Dutch troops, reinforced and commanded by Anthony Hurdt, marched into the interior of Java and, having surmounted incredible difficulties, fought their way to Kadiri. Trunajoyo saved his life but little else. The crown of Madjapahit, recovered by a Dutch officer, was solemnly placed on the head of Amangkurat II by the commander of the Dutch force. Times had changed. Amangkurat's father and grandfather had claimed the overlordship of Batavia and had even demanded a share in the customs duties of that city; Amangkurat II was practically a vassal of the Company.

After the conquest of Kadiri the troops of the Company and of the susuhunan set to work to round up the remnants of Trunajoyo's army. Thus the Dutch first came to know the interior of the island. The Company's allies, Aru Palacca's Buginese and Jonker's Amboinese, were best fitted for this task of pursuing Trunajoyo's guerillas in the jungle-covered mountains of East Java, and Jonker was the one who

[15] De Jonge, *op. cit.*, v, xxxvii. For these events and following years, see H. J. De Graaf, *De moord op Kapitein François Tack, 8 Febr. 1686* (Amsterdam, 1935).

finally forced the usurper to surrender.[16] Once all resistance in East Java had been crushed, the allies marched towards Mataram. The old residence was reduced to ruins. According to Javanese opinion it was now a place of ill omen where the susuhunan could not take up his residence without inviting the forces of evil. Hence a new capital was built, Kartasura, in the valley of the Solo river. In this new residence Amangkurat II was guarded against his enemies by a battalion of the Company's troops (1679).

Mataram thus had practically lost its independence, and Bantam continued to enjoy complete liberty only five years longer. If only the sultan, his family, and his people had remained united against the foreigners they could have defied the Netherlanders much longer, for the parsimony and the caution of the government of Batavia were the best guarantee of their independence. Once more, however, the old story of jealousy and hatred between sultan and crown prince repeated itself. Both Abulfatah and his son, commonly called Prince Hadji (because of his pilgrimage to Mecca) were ardent in their zeal for the Mohammedan faith, but the crown prince showed all friendship to the Netherlanders while the sultan never concealed his violent hatred toward them. During the civil war in the empire of Mataram he had sent his troops to plunder the neighborhood of Batavia and the north coast of central Java. He intrigued with the princes of Cheribon and tried to persuade them to transfer their allegiance from Mataram to Bantam. To secure a hold over the new susuhunan, he returned to that ruler his eagerly awaited lady-love, having first instructed the lady how to influence her lover against the Company. In his kingdom he received all anti-Dutch elements — emigrés from Macassar and Sumatra and Mohammedan fanatics — while British and Danish merchants supplied him with firearms and sent their sailors to serve him as gunners and engineers.

The young sultan was equally fanatic but less courageous than his father. At the same time he was ambitious and wanted the crown for himself. Therefore he sought the friendship of the Netherlanders, and when civil war broke out between the partisans of the two princes, he called in the Dutch. This time there was not a moment of hesitation in Batavia. Van Goens had governed only three years (1678–1681) and had been succeeded in the office of governor-general by Cornelis Speelman (1681–1684). Practically the whole people supported the old Sultan Abulfatah against his son, but the old sultan's troops were no

[16] For these campaigns De Jonge's publications are still among the best. There is still much unpublished material on these events in the archives of The Hague and Java.

JOHAN MAETSUYCKER
Governor-general, 1653–1678.

JOHANNES CAMPHUIJS
Governor-general, 1684–1691.

match for the experienced soldiers of the Company. Once more Jonker's Amboinese secured victory for the Company. Bantam was conquered and Abulfatah taken prisoner. His last supporters were pursued through the unknown mountains of the Preanger, and on this occasion Dutch troops for the first time in history reached the south coast of the island overland.[17]

Both Mataram and Bantam were now under the supervision of the Company. In both states the Company obtained the monopoly of trade for several products. The princes, put on the throne by the troops of Batavia, were heavily indebted to the Company for the reimbursement of its war expenses. The Batavian government stipulated, however, that it would not request payment of these debts as long as the sultans faithfully executed the newly concluded commercial treaties. Thus these sultans were brought into the same condition as the insolvent nutmeg planters of the Moluccas half a century before. There the Company had foreclosed on the estate of the debtors, and the same thing might happen in Java. In this way the kingdoms of Java lost their independence—because of their defective system of government and because of their internal strife. The territories of Bantam and Mataram were now separated by that of Batavia, which was extended southward to the sea, thus including the mountain districts of the Preanger. The princes of Cheribon, promoted from vassals to allies of the susuhunan, officially recognized the protectorate of the Company over their country.

These events had far-reaching consequences. The activities of the British, Danes, and Portuguese came to an end nearly everywhere in the archipelago. The British, driven from Bantam, built a fortress on Sumatra's west coast near Benkulen in 1684. They maintained their position here for one hundred and fifty years.[18]

The Portuguese withdrew to Timor, a poor, desolate part of the archipelago, for the islanders had cut down the greater part of the sandalwood trees, destroying in their greed for immediate profits their source of income. In Timor the Portuguese have maintained a precarious foothold until our day. From all other posts the non-Dutch Europeans, or rather, all Europeans who were not in the service of the Company, were ousted. The monopoly system of the Company now extended over all the islands except Borneo. In Sumatra the Company

[17] De Haan in Volume II of his *Priangan* edited a number of reports on expeditions into the interior of West Java and provided his edition with ample annotations.

[18] P. Wink, "Eenige archiefstukken betreffende de vestiging van de Engelsche factorij te Benkoelen in 1685," TBG, LXIV (1924), 461, and N. MacLeod, "De Oost-Indische Compagnie op Sumatra in de XVII eeuw," IG, XXVIII (1906), 777 sq., 1420 sq.

intervened in the constant quarrels among the sultans of Palembang, Djambi, and Johore, and gradually extended its privileges. Circumstances had wrought a considerable change in the situation of the Company, and some of the prominent members of the Council of the Indies began to see that the whole system of the Company needed to be adapted to these new circumstances.

The Directors remained reluctant to commit themselves to a new policy. They observed, of course, that the profits of the inter-Asiatic trade were going down (the year 1693 was to be the turning point in this development) [19] but they were not worried about this decline, since the prices of all Asiatic products in Europe had risen unexpectedly. After Speelman's death the governorship-general had fallen to the less warlike Johannes Camphuijs (1684–1691), and although the government of Batavia had demanded the cession of the Preanger lands by the susuhunan, it still hesitated to proclaim its own sovereignty in that area. Again circumstances forced the hands of the government and obliged it to adopt a clear and definite policy towards the local potentates of the Preanger and of Cheribon.

The downfall of Mataram, and still more that of Bantam, had caused an immense reaction in the Mohammedan world of the East Indies. People began to talk of the "Holy War" against the "Kafirs." The Java Sea was made unsafe by the pirate fleet of a Menangkabau Malay who called himself Ibn Iskander (descendant of Alexander the Great) and a prophet of Islam.[20] The last supporter of sultan Abulfatah to surrender to the Dutch was Sheik Yusuf, a Macassar priest who had studied in Mecca and was venerated by the people, in Batavia as well as in Bantam, as a saint. Leaflets spread among the population of Batavia and local uprisings in Madura, all directed against the Infidels, made the government of Batavia rather nervous. A few agitators were arrested, but at least one of them had to be released after the great Aureng Zeb, the emperor of India, had filed a strongly worded protest. The jungles of the Batavian Lowlands and of the Preanger mountains hid hundreds of dubious characters and runaway slaves, especially Balinese, who began to style themselves "patriots" and redoubled their activities against more loyal elements. The most dramatic personality among these men was a runaway slave from Bali who had taken the name of Surapati. After having served with the Dutch troops he went

[19] Mansvelt, *Rechtsvorm en Geldelijk Beheer*, p. 95.

[20] See MacLeod, "De Oost-Indische Compagnie op Sumatra," IG, XXIX (1907), 608 sq., 787 sq. De Haan gives, as usual, an excellent survey of the known facts in *Priangan*, III, 323 sq.

over to the rebels because of an insult he had suffered from a Dutch officer who, newly arrived from Holland, had no experience with Indonesian soldiers. With his followers this Balinese, Surapati, terrorized the land south of Batavia and then fled to the court of Susuhunan Amangkurat II. This prince, who owed his throne to the Dutch and was certainly not a fanatic Moslem, intrigued with all parties and offered refuge to Surapati. He entered into correspondence with Iskander the prophet, and when a special embassy was sent to his court, he allowed Surapati to attack and kill the ambassador and many of his escort. After that Surapati escaped to the utmost eastern corner of Java where he began to conquer a kingdom of his own.

If Speelman had been living, there would have been drastic action by Batavia. But his successors feared a general revolution; they did not feel sure any more of their own native troops, especially after proof had been found that even the brave Captain Jonker was involved in a conspiracy against the Company. The Council of the Indies, having carefully weighed the arguments pro and contra, decided upon the arrest of the old Amboinese warrior, which for Captain Jonker was sufficient excuse to take up arms against the government he had helped to make all powerful in the Indies. In the resulting fight he was killed.

In 1703 Amangkurat II died. His death might have been the sign for another civil war in Mataram and possibly for the falling apart of the empire. This time the Company, now represented in Batavia by Governor-General Willem van Outhoorn (1691–1704), decided to intervene and to put a prince of their own choice on the throne.

Kartasura was occupied without much difficulty and the new susuhunan, Pakubuwono I, installed. From central Java the expedition was continued against Eastern Java, where Surapati fell in battle. To secure order, all foreign elements were forced to leave the island of Java. Thousands of Balinese, Madurese, and Macassars who had been making a living as mercenaries in the service of Javanese noblemen and princes were obliged to return to their homeland.

A new treaty between the Company and the susuhunan, concluded October 5, 1705, settled all points concerning the status of western Java which remained in doubt. From now on the Company would have full, unlimited overlordship of the land west of the districts of Tegal and Banjumas. Cheribon's relations with Mataram came to an end; in the future it was to be a fief of Batavia. The remaining part of Mataram came under control of the Company as far as trade and commerce were concerned. The Company had finally become master of Java.

CHAPTER IX

NEW ASPECTS OF INDONESIAN LIFE

WITHIN fifty years after the founding of Batavia a new type of Indonesian had been added to the multifarious tribes and peoples of the Indies. To this new Indonesian type Dr. De Haan has given the name of "Homo Bataviensis," the Indian Hollander. In his book *Oud Batavia* he describes how, under the influence of the tropical climate and the oriental surroundings, "Homo Batavus" or native Dutchman, an industrious, stubborn and high-tempered individual, developed into "Homo Bataviensis," a lazier but not less clever and still more high-tempered type.[1] "Homo Bataviensis" represented of course only a very small percentage of the population of the Indies. It is impossible to estimate the exact number of the European inhabitants of Batavia in the sixteenth and seventeenth centuries, but probably they never numbered more than five to ten thousand. These few thousands, however, held a predominant political and economic position in the Indies.

The development from Batavus into Bataviensis was a difficult and a painful one. Most Hollanders who arrived in Batavia did not have the time to become members of that interesting group of mankind. They died a few months after their arrival. It is no exaggeration to say that the chances of survival of a soldier in modern warfare are several times as good as that of a Hollander who intended to make his home in Batavia in the "good old times." When J. P. Coen returned to the Indies, he lost within a few weeks his child, his mother-in-law, and his brother-in-law.[2] Of those who survived, however, a great number made the Indies their permanent home. In Holland they often had belonged to the poorer classes and they had come to the Indies as sailors and soldiers, hoping to make their fortune in Asia. Only a few succeeded in doing so, and for these, once they had become high officials in the Far East, a return to Holland was not alluring. In the Indies they lived

[1] The name "Homo Bataviensis" is an invention of Dr. F. De Haan, whose book *Oud Batavia* is indispensable for those who want to acquire a thorough knowledge of seventeenth and eighteenth-century Indonesian history.

[2] Reliable figures on the mortality in Batavia during the seventeenth and eighteenth century are not available. De Haan, *Oud Batavia*, pp. 685 and 702, correctly rejects the fantastic figures of Raffles, *History of Java* (one million dead between 1730 and 1752 alone!).

like princes; in Holland they were common citizens, jealously excluded from the ruling caste of oligarchic regents who controlled the Republic. Moreover, many Dutchmen legally married Indonesian women, and for unknown reasons the Directors discouraged the emigration of Indonesians to Europe. Others had vested interests in the East. The descendants of these *blijvers* [3] formed the nucleus of the population of Batavia.

Most of the foreign visitors who came to Batavia in the seventeenth century and at the beginning of the eighteenth could not find words of praise enough for the city. A British sailor describes it as follows in the year 1718:

> Large canals run through several streets of Batavia whereby it is rendered both neat and cool. On each side of this canal is planted a row of fine trees that are always green, which, with the beauty and regularity of the buildings, make the streets look very agreeable so that I think this city (for the bigness) one of the neatest and most beautiful in the whole world.[4]

In other reports, however, it is called straightforwardly a pest hole and a place of death! This may be explained by the second part of the description of the same British sailor:

> There are also two large piers that run about half a mile into the sea and serve to drain all the canals and the inland water that run through the city. About one hundred slaves [5] are employed in taking up the mud and in scouring the space between these piers which otherwise would soon be choked up with what is washed out of the city and country. At the mouth of this place are many alligators or crocodiles, and if a dead dog or any other carcass comes down the stream it goes not far to sea but is immediately devoured by them.

It will be sufficient to add that the famous explorer, Captain James Cook, saw a dead ox lying for days in one of the canals.

The first building which the newly arriving Batavians saw from the sea was a castle, a rectangular building with four bastions.[6] It was a creation of Coen and looked formidable enough, but the walls had suffered so much that in the eighteenth century the garrison was forbidden to fire too many salutes from its batteries lest the walls crumble

[3] The "blijvers" are the Europeans who make the Indies their permanent home, the "trekkers" those who intend to return to Europe as soon as circumstances permit.

[4] Daniel Beeckman, *A Voyage to and from the Island of Borneo and the East Indies* (London, 1718), p. 24.

[5] This work was first done by criminals who had been condemned to hard labor but later by Javanese peasants in *heerendienst* (compulsory labor instead of payment of taxes). The Batavians with a kind of grim humor called these poor fellows the "mud-Javanese" (De Haan, *Priangan*, III, 369–370, and Oud Batavia, p. 197).

[6] Map and minute description in *Oud Batavia*, pp. 116 sq.

under the shock! Inside, not only the garrison, but also the governor-general, the members of the Council, the high officials, and a number of employees of the Company had their quarters, all stuffed together in a small square of approximately 450 feet on a side. Within this limited space, inclosed by walls twenty feet high, the officers of the Company, the most powerful colonial government of its time, held their meetings, received embassies of mighty empires, kept their commercial accounts, judged and executed criminals, stored the goods and treasures of the Company, and finally — for they were merchants after all — sold cloth by the yard and beer by the barrel to the public. It must have been very hot within these walls in the Batavian climate with its average of eighty-two degrees day and night. Yet the gentlemen wore bravely their heavy European clothes and the ladies their tight-laced dresses to grace the dances and receptions of his excellency the governor-general. No breeze from the sea could penetrate the narrow gangways. The kitchens and the storehouses helped to make the air still more odoriferous, but nobody complained. Those who managed to survive the first months of their stay in the Indies were tough individuals. Mr. Van Outshoorn enjoyed these surroundings for sixty years undamaged. Mr. Johan Maetsuycker managed to keep his wits for twenty-five years while ruling the Empire from the musty, ill-smelling castle of Batavia, without ever leaving that miserable small town.

"Homo Bataviensis" was normally very much afraid of fresh air because he feared, always and everywhere, catching cold. Differences in temperature are slight in Batavia, only two or three degrees day and night, but it has been proved that such a climate makes the human body more sensitive and, consequently, more subject to colds. It has *not* been proved, however, that the preventive measures against colds taken by the old Batavians were the most efficient ones. The well-trained Batavian of the year 1700 closed his house, doors and windows, at nine o'clock in the morning to keep the sea wind out. The sea wind brought all kinds of evil smells from the muddy coast, and bad smells were considered dangerous.[7] The Batavian closed his windows to keep the wind out and lowered his curtains to keep the heat out. Opinions were divided as to whether it was advisable to open doors and windows at dusk, but during the night they had to be closed for the night air was extremely dangerous. Thus, the Batavian withdrew about eleven

[7] For sanitary conditions in Batavia, see De Haan, *Oud Batavia*, pp. 684 sq. See also D. Schoute, *De Geneeskunde in den dienst der Oost Indische Compagnie* (Amsterdam, 1928). Governor-General van Imhoff after his arrival in the Indies wrote that he did not feel well and had to recover from "the evil consequences of the sea air"!

o'clock into his bedroom, where he protected his sensitive body by heaping pillows around him in his bed. Then he drew the curtains around his four-poster to keep the mosquitoes out. Nevertheless, he managed to survive the night.

The Batavian took care of his health in his own way. He could not be convinced that cleanliness of the body and hence frequent bathing was important for his health. He did not follow the example of the Javanese, who dive into water whenever they get a chance, but as the latter did not care whether they bathed in the sea or in a mud puddle, the example may not have been very alluring. As late as 1775 an order of the High Government forbade forcing the soldiers of the garrison to take a bath once a week.

The Dutch women, who were nearly all born in the Indies, had less aversion to the water than their husbands who came from wet and rainy Holland. Many houses built along the canals had a little bath house over the water, and from there the ladies unblushingly dived into the general public bathtub, a custom which was vainly forbidden by Van Imhoff, not because he thought the habit indecent, but because the canals were used as sewers and were, therefore, *rather* filthy.

The gentlemen had other means of protecting their health. They started the day by drinking a fair-sized glass of gin on an empty stomach. "Our nation must drink or die," wrote Coen in 1619.[8] The same medicine was taken several times during the day and at night before retiring. It is no wonder that the distilling of *arak* has been called the principal industry of Batavia. Batavian arak gained a reputation all over Asia. "Our men were hugging each other and blessing themselves that they had come to such a glorious place for punch," wrote the British captain Woodes Rogers at the beginning of the eighteenth century.[9] Captain Cook reported as a remarkable fact that the only sailor aboard his ship who had not fallen sick during his stay in Batavia was an old man of more than seventy years who had been constantly drunk. Thus the preventive qualities of alcohol seemed proved beyond doubt! Another preventive was smoking. The Batavian smoked from the moment he arose till he tumbled again into his four-poster, heavy with alcohol and sleep. Those were the golden days when good Dutch cigars were sold a thousand for three dollars and when even the Havanas cost only ten dollars a thousand. But the Batavians preferred their pipes to the cigars. They smoked their pipes

[8] Colebrander, *J. P. Coen*, I, 459 (letter of Aug. 5, 1619).

[9] Woodes Rogers, *A Cruising Voyage around the World*, ed. G. E. Manwaring (London, 1928), p. 286.

when they attended funerals and when they rode in parade as the proud city guards of Batavia, and of course they smoked their pipes when sitting during the evening in front of their houses enjoying the "fresh" air from the canals.

It would be wrong, however, to conclude that the Batavians only drank, smoked, and slept, and did not work. James Cook wrote in 1770, "It is hard to find in Batavia a Chinese who is idle, and a Dutchman or Indonesian who is working." [10] But this statement is not in conformity with others made by the same gentleman.

Two groups must be distinguished among the citizens of Batavia: the servants of the Company and the so-called free citizens. The first were under the direct orders of the High Government in every respect. Coen, the dictator, even went so far as to order a candidate for the ministry of the church to proceed to Bali and choose a wife among the girls of that island. The second group was called that of the "free citizens," who actually had no freedom at all. They were practically confined to the small space of the town of Batavia and its near surroundings. More trades were forbidden than allowed to them. Hence we find a remarkable difference in degree of activity between the two groups.

The Company's servants worked like slaves, especially during the seventeenth century. The founding of an empire is no easy job. History shows that in the Dutch East Indies for ten generations men toiled, suffered, and died — died by the thousands — before the empire really began to take shape. The Company's clerks, a few hundred ill-paid, badly nourished, fever-stricken young men, rose at five-thirty A.M., started working at six A.M., and continued at their writing desks until six P.M. with a short interruption of thirty minutes for breakfast and a pause of two hours for dinner. There was no rest after dinner; work continued in the tropic heat. If there was much work, candles were lighted shortly after six and the writing went on. They wrote shelves-full of folio volumes, and they wrote beautifully. They were not allowed to leave the castle except on Wednesday and Sunday afternoons, and even then they had to be home at seven P.M. There was little recreation afterwards, and they withdrew to the dormitory, the attics of the moist, hot office building. Discipline was very strict. Several times, of course, young men tried to take an evening off without permission, and there were some complaints about scandalous behavior. By the order of the governor-general, insubordinate elements were pun-

[10] James Cook, *Voyages*, 2 vols. (London, 1842). The quotation is from I, 314. For description of Batavia, see I, 299 sq.

ished by their own colleagues. Punishment consisted of a good beating with a heavy stick! The governor-general himself set the example in working. He gave his first audience at six o'clock in the morning and continued working until six P.M., with only short intervals. He had not a single day of vacation in the whole year and hardly ever left Batavia.

The workmen of the Company had no easier life. The shoemakers were ordered to finish one pair of shoes a day under penalty of being jailed. The carpenters and shipbuilders of the Company's wharves were still so efficient at the end of the eighteenth century that James Cook, who had his ship overhauled in the port, wrote: "There is no marine yard in the world that is better than that of Batavia." [11]

The life of the free citizens was different. They were so limited in their activities that they had to make their living by money lending and similar economic activities which of course left them plenty of spare time. Nearly all free citizens were ex-servants of the Company, and Batavia's society was one of new rich with much tasteless display of wealth. It was considered a sign of prosperity to have many slaves and to leave all work and worries, even the education of the children, to the servants. For the few men who tried to make a living in a free profession, life was very hard. This fact was experienced by a son-in-law of the great Rembrandt, a certain Cornelis Suythoff, who himself was a painter. He did his best to live by his art, but for additional income he had to resort to other practices, some of which were forbidden by the laws of the Company. This nearly brought him into prison, but the authorities changed their minds and helped him out of his troubles by appointing him — the warden of the prison! [12]

The easy way of living did not improve the standards of civilization of the citizens of Batavia. From babyhood the children were left to the care of slave women. The boys might get some instruction from private teachers, but the girls hardly learned anything, often not even the Dutch language. They picked up a mixture of Malayan, Portuguese, and Dutch, which remained their only means of expression for the rest of their lives.[13] All girls and women were addicted to the native habit

[11] Cook, *Voyages*, I, 298.

[12] Details on Cornelis Suythoff, taken from notary archives in *Priangan*, II, 183, n. 1. In 1671 or 1672 Suythoff came to the Indies; in 1682, by order of the Directors, he was impeached for transgression of the monopoly rights of the Company. The charge was quietly dropped, and on Feb. 5, 1683, Suythoff was appointed a warden of the prison. He died in 1691.

[13] De Haan (*Oud Batavia*, p. 406) gives some beautiful examples of this Batavian Portuguese. The following is an interesting example of language policy in the seventeenth century: "Undoubtedly the general use of the Dutch instead of the Portuguese

of chewing betel. This made their teeth look reddish brown and their lips black. Even when they went to church they were accompanied by slave girls who carried the prayer book, the betel box, and the spittoon. This last equipment was often made of gold or silver but it remained a spittoon. If there had not existed such a sharp political division between Dutch and Javanese, the Batavians would have been assimilated to the native population in a few decades through the rapid Javanization of the women. The constant influx of native Dutchmen counteracted this tendency.

For two centuries the Batavian families continued to lead the same unbearably tedious life. There were few diversions except the arrival and departure of the Company's vessels. There were few subjects of conversation except the unimportant events in the small town. The people played cards and they practised a little music, but even this was often left to the slaves and it is perhaps better not to investigate into the quality of the music.[14] Yet Batavia had its own style in works of art. The houses of its citizens were beautifully furnished by masterpieces of Dutch Javanese craftsmanship, and there was a growing interest in painting. Some citizens possessed seventy and more paintings, some of which may have been the work of famous seventeenth-century artists.

The Batavians cared less for science. There were a few men who devoted their time to the study of Indonesian biology, but they were exceptions.[15] This is rather surprising, for the Directors in Amsterdam were often interested in these things and ordered samples of rare plants and seeds to be brought to the University of Leyden, while they encouraged experiments in foreign plants in the Company's territory.[16]

For the promotion of missionary work, the Company encouraged

---

language would help to strengthen the foundations of our state here, but there seems to be little chance to realize this change, for the Portuguese have firmly established themselves here and are too well liked by our own people. We will not neglect to use all suitable means to change this undesirable state of affairs, as recommended by you." (Letter of G. G. Maetsuycker to the Directors, Nov. 28, 1676, in De Jonge, *op. cit.*, VI, 157.)

[14] See De Haan, *Oud Batavia*, p. 604, a notice of 1830: "For sale a slave woman, expert laundry woman and harpist."

[15] The earliest study of Indian botany by an official of the Company is that of Jacobus Bontius (1592–1631), whose writings were published by G. Piso in his *De Indiae utriusque re naturali et medica Libri XIV* (Leyden, 1658). More important than Bontius' work is that of Hendrik A. Rheede van Drakesteyn (1637–1691), *Hortus Indicus Malabaricus*, 12 vols. in fo. (Amsterdam, 1678–1698). George E. Rumphius, *Herbarium Amboinense* we have already mentioned.

[16] See later in this chapter the references to Nicolas Witsen. The Directors often ordered plants for the Botanic Garden of Leyden or Amsterdam.

translations of the Bible and other books into the Malay language. Most of these books were printed in Holland. In Batavia there was no freedom of the press — it existed nowhere on earth in that period — and publishers and printers had only a very poor chance of making a living among the Batavienses. Ex-servants of the Company published valuable books on the Indies, and the public in Holland must have been interested in Indonesian affairs, for otherwise the printing and publication of such an enormous work as the series of folio volumes of François Valentijn on the antiquities and the political situation of the Indies would have been impossible.[17] The industrious Abraham Rogerius composed his famous book "The Open Door to the Hidden Heathendom," the earliest, but a very accurate, account of South Indian Hinduism.[18] In a preceding chapter we mentioned Justus Heurnius, who managed to compose a Dutch-Chinese-Latin Dictionary with the help of a Chinese who had learned some Latin from a Portuguese priest in Macao. Herbert De Jager, too, spent part of his time in Batavia. Unfortunately nearly all his manuscripts have been lost.

Batavia had its poets, like every other seventeenth-century town. The quality of the poetry usually was very low; it hardly deserved more than the name of rhyming.[19] The most interesting figure among the Batavian poets was Jacob Steendam, who also has gained some reputation in history as the first poet of that other emporium founded by the Dutch, New York. He lived for some time in the small settlement on the Hudson River, where he composed a long poem in praise of the Colony of New Netherland. When New Netherland was conquered by the British, Steendam returned home, but a few years later he left for the East Indies. In Batavia he was appointed superintendent of the orphanage, and here he published his poems on Batavian life.[20]

[17] François Valentijn wrote his *Oud en Nieuw Oost Indiën*, 5 vols. in fo. (Dordrecht, 1724–1726), a huge compilation from different sources (Livinus Bor and Rumphius on the history of Amboina, see F. De Haan in *Rumphius Gedenkboek*, p. 17 sq.) from Governor-General Camphuijs' history of the founding of Batavia, and others which he prefers not to mention. Among his informants was Jan Frederik Gobius, whose work we mention later (De Haan, *Priangan*, I, sect. 2, pp. 270–280). Dr. De Haan draws a far-from-flattering picture of Valentijn, who seems to have been a very ambitious and unscrupulous man. His work remains indispensable, but in consulting it we must bear in mind the author's character. We can not attach the same value to Valentijn's own writings as to the sources which he reproduced.

[18] Abraham Rogerius, *De Open Deure tot het Verborgen Heydendom*, first published in Amsterdam 1651, and republished for Linsch. V. by W. Caland (vol. x, The Hague, 1915).

[19] On Dutch poetry in the Indies, see De Haan, *Priangan*, II, 732 sq. For books printed in the Indies, J. A. van der Chijs, *Proeve eener Nederlandsch Indische Bibliographie (1659–1870)* (Batavia, 1875).

[20] On Steendam as the first poet of New Netherland, see H. C. Murphy, *Jacob Steen-*

The Calvinist Church — the only one that was permitted to exist in Batavia — did not exercise the cultural influence that might have been expected. The ministers were not very enthusiastic in spreading the maxims of Christianity among the native population. On the contrary, they showed a remarkable racial prejudice against native clergymen. One of the suburbs of Batavia still bears the name of Meester Cornelis, a diligent clergyman of Bandanese descent, who for many years tried in vain to be admitted as a minister of the church. Even the mighty protection of Governor-General Maetsuycker could not break the resistance of the narrow-minded ecclesiastics. After two centuries nearly the whole native Christian population of Batavia had been absorbed by its Mohammedan surroundings, which is certainly a bad record for a small city where often twelve ministers of the gospel were exercising their functions.[21] The Company maintained some schools for the education of the children of the poor and of the slaves, which in the seventeenth century may be called a rare and highly laudable undertaking. The wealthier citizens sent their children to private schools kept by former boatswains, carpenters, or soldiers — schools that were not too good but probably not much worse than those of Europe in the same period. The Directors in Holland urged the East Indian government to provide more schools, especially Latin schools, and their arguments sound strangely modern: "The schools are the nursery-gardens of the commonwealth," they wrote in 1661. "Many people send their children from the Indies to Holland to be educated in the home country. This is not to the interest of the Company, because it tends to deplete the colony of these elements who have been born in the East and naturally look upon the Indies as their real fatherland." [22] But the Latin schools of Batavia never existed for long. The local environment was not suitable to higher learning.

This was the way of life of the Batavian citizens under the paternal rule of the Dutch East India Company, represented by the governor-general and the city council. This city council, an institution of an oligarchic character,[23] took its task seriously, and consequently the

dam, Noch Vaster, A Memoir (The Hague, 1861). A biography of Steendam appears in S. Kalff, "Vroegere Koloniale Poëzie," IG, XXIX, 2 (1907), 1459–1476, and 1624–1635.

[21] For a contemporary criticism of the Batavian ministers of the church, see Cornelis Chastelein, "Invallende Gedachten," written in 1705, publ. in TBG, III (1855), 74. On Cornelis Senen, commonly called Meester Cornelis, see De Haan, *Oud Batavia*, p. 98.

[22] De Jonge, *op. cit.*, VI, lxx–lxxi; J. A. van der Chijs, "De Latijnsche scholen van 1642 en 1666 alsmede het Seminarium van 1745 te Batavia," TBG, X (1861), 163 sq. Most of the pupils of the Latin School of 1666 were "Mardijkers" (see note 24, below).

[23] The city government of Batavia was organized by the ordinances of Aug. 15, 1620,

members took good care of themselves. We still have in the archives the bills presented by the janitor of the town hall for his expenses in providing the council with sweet stuff, wine, coffee, and tea during its morning meetings!

Among the non-Dutch elements of the Batavian population were the descendants of Portuguese immigrants from Malacca (hence a Batavian street was called "Rua Malacca"), the descendants of former slaves, mostly imported from the coast of India and called "Mardijkers" by the Dutch,[24] and the Chinese. The Mardijkers had a bad reputation. They were Christians, and therefore free from the obligation to wear their national costumes like the other Asiatics. "They wear so-called European costume," one of the contemporary Dutchmen writes, "but without shirt, socks or shoes. They parade, dressed up like a quack's monkey at a country fair, and are the shrewdest and most self-conceited of Batavia's inhabitants."[25]

The Chinese were of far greater importance to the colony. Without their help the Company could never have accomplished its task. On the other hand, the Chinese prospered through the protection of the Company. Most of them came to Batavia penniless immigrants.[26] Some of them started their career by buying goods from the Company on credit and selling these goods far below cost if necessary, with the sole purpose of getting some ready money. Then they began to speculate, and if they were successful they paid their debts; if not, they disappeared. Until 1740 the Chinese lived all over the city among the Europeans. They had their own officers, who were supposed to rule them according to their own customs, but gradually these customs were influenced by the Dutch laws, a change which was of particular advantage to the Chinese women, who saw themselves legally promoted to personalities with their own rights. Normally the Chinese were obedient and easily governed citizens, but they could not be kept from building their booths and shacks straight across the street in the fashion of an oriental bazaar. This was of course contrary to the

---

Aug. 18, 1620, June 16, 1625, and the Statutes of 1642 (Van der Chijs, *Plakaatboek*, I, 62, 65, 126, and 475). In case of a vacancy the members of the Council made a list of candidates in double numbers from whom the governor-general selected the new member.

[24] "Mardijker" is a Dutch transformation of "Mahardika," freedman. Mardijk is a small place near Dunkirk. These places had an evil reputation with the seventeenth-century Netherlanders because they were the ports from which the Spanish privateers were equipped who caused inestimable damage to Dutch shipping.

[25] Chastelein, "Invallende Gedachten," TBG, III, 74–75.

[26] On the Chinese in Batavia in the eighteenth century, see J. Th. Vermeulen, *De Chineezen in Batavia en de troebelen van 1740* (Leiden, 1938).

Dutch sense of neatness, and several times the Council had the streets cleared of all these fantastic products of Chinese architecture.

The Indonesians, numbering perhaps twenty thousand in the eighteenth century, and divided into national groups, lived outside the city walls. There we find Balinese, Buginese, Macassars, Malays, and others, but for many decades after the founding of Batavia hardly any Javanese. The government could not forget the surprise attacks made by the troops of Mataram in 1628, and would not allow Javanese too close to the city walls. Gradually this heterogeneous population developed into a new Indonesian national group, distinct from the Sundanese of West and the Javanese of East Java, with the Malay, the *lingua franca* of the archipelago, as their native tongue. From a few thousand at the end of the seventeenth century their number grew to a million in 1940.[27]

In the days of the Company this Indonesian population outside the city walls was of importance as a pool of military reserves. All inhabitants of Batavia were subject to military services when called upon. In the endless wars which the Company carried on on the coastlands of Asia, between Formosa and Ceylon, the battalions formed by the Balinese, Buginese, and Amboinese gained a great reputation on a hundred battle fields.

Batavia's greatest prosperity coincided with the end of the seventeenth and the beginning of the eighteenth century. In that time the small town seethed with the activities of the Dutch and Chinese, and the streets were filled with people dressed in the most exotic and colorful costumes. The European citizens never went out without their escort of slaves, one of whom carried the *pajong* or sunshade. The governor-general had his escort of dragoons and halberdiers. Whereever his carriage passed, all passers-by had to stop and bow respectfully to his excellency. Only Governor-General Van Riebeeck had the exotic idea of taking along an escort of beautifully dressed slave girls riding on donkeys when he drove out to his country house outside the city. The historian Valentijn writes, "No city is more beautiful than Batavia at night. During the evening young people go out in boats on the canal playing instruments and singing."[28] There were other aspects of Batavian life. The inns had to close at nine o'clock, but this left plenty of time for the sailors to get drunk and start quarrels. The streets were not safe after dark, and the police were not too well

[27] Lekkerkerker, *Land en Volk van Java*, I, 224 and 505.

[28] Valentijn, *Oud en Nieuw Oost Indien* (*Beschrijving van Batavia*), IV, 365–366.

organized. During the night, patrols of the city guard of the garrison and nightwatchmen went through the city, but too often they mistook each other for thieves and gangsters. These mistakes were naturally the cause of innumerable fights. In the first decades of Batavia's existence, hardly a week passed without one or more of the slaves running amok, thus causing a little excitement in the tedious trends of normal life. With the improvement of conditions in the city, these outbreaks of violence occurred less and less frequently.

It was of great advantage to Batavia that a definite peace had been concluded with Bantam in 1684. The neighborhood of the city became safer, a condition to which the institution of a field police contributed considerably. These police consisted, of course, of the faithful Amboinese and Balinese. The citizens began to build their country houses upstream. They could not go far and had to remain in the neighborhood of the river, for there was no other means of communication. It was another century before the Dutch began to settle in the cooler and more healthy hill districts of the Preanger.

In the year 1732 Batavia suffered two heavy blows that caused its decline for the next century. The government had ordered the digging of a new canal quite a distance outside the city. Suddenly the greater part of the inhabitants of two Indonesian settlements close to the new canal fell ill, and from them the sickness spread to Batavia. The death rate rose to a terrific height, and stayed high for the next century. Foreign visitors who had come to Batavia and made friends there often did not find a single one of them alive when they returned half a year later from a trip through the archipelago. From the symptoms of the disease, we may safely conclude that the plague was malaria, but it remains unexplained why this disease appeared so suddenly, or, at least, why it spread so suddenly after 1731 and whether the digging of the new canal had something to do with it or not. Contemporary physicians tried in vain to discover its cause. They blamed the sea air and the land air in turn. They imported Spa or Seltzer water from Europe to avoid drinking the dirty river water, and finally they even began to consider the very existence of the filthy canals as unhealthful. Yet the Indonesians, who took no thought of the quality of drinking water, were less afflicted than the Europeans. The Chinese remained practically free from the disease. Since the Chinese drank large quantities of tea, the belief spread that tea was a medicinal beverage, an opinion which the Directors in Amsterdam were quick to exploit. They spread leaflets among the people in Holland advocating the drinking of tea for better health, and advising a consumption of forty cups a day! [29]

Batavia, once the pearl among the European settlements in the Orient, got the reputation of being one of the most unhealthful places on earth. "Death means nothing here," wrote James Cook when he stayed for several months in Batavia in 1770. "The only comment on the death of a fellow citizen is: well, he owed me nothing, or I must get my money from his executors." [30] Those who could move out of the city to the more healthful countryside did so. Even the governor-general broke with tradition, and after 1741 he refused to reside in the castle. It is understandable that the old parts of Batavia became more desolate every year, which fact inspired a learned German professor at the beginning of the nineteenth century to the somber prophecy: "Since no repairs are made, Batavia will not exist for long." [31]

The second cause of Batavia's decline was a sudden and unexpected demonstration of energy by the Directors. As long as the Company had existed it had been paying its servants in the East impossibly small salaries.[32] The consequences had been that everybody looked for extra profits and found the means of making them in extortions, smuggling, and private trading, in transgression of the Company's monopoly. The Directors were perfectly well aware of all these abuses. They saw some of their officials who never had received more than a few thousand guilders a year as salary return to Holland after twelve or fifteen years with a capital of hundreds of thousands of guilders. Everybody knew, for instance, that the regular income from illicit trading by the Company's representative in Japan was thirty thousand guilders a year. The departure of the homeward-bound fleet from Batavia was the greatest event of the year in that city. A thousand affairs had to be settled privately between the skippers and sailors on one side and the settlers on the other side. The goods smuggled to Europe often exceeded in value the regular shipments for the Company. Governor-

[29] On the tea trade with China in the beginning of the eighteenth century, see J. De Hullu, "Over den Chineeschen handel der Oost Indische Compagnie in de eerste dertig jaren van de 18e eeuw," BKI, LXXIII (1917), 32 sq., and M. Vigelius, "Stichting der factorij van de Oost Indische Compagnie te Kanton," TG, XLVIII (1933), 168 sq.

[30] James Cook, *Voyages*, I, 303.

[31] Dr. F. Junghuhn (one of the most famous botanists of the Indies) quoted by De Haan, *Oud Batavia*, p. 709.

[32] In the eighteenth century a captain of the East Indian army received 100 guilders monthly with 50 guilders for board and lodging. A soldier had 10 guilders monthly all together (Klerk de Reus, *Geschichtlicher Ueberblick*, etc., p. 110). A governor of East Java received 2400 guilders yearly, but different emoluments (legal and illegal) raised that income to 100,000 guilders a year.

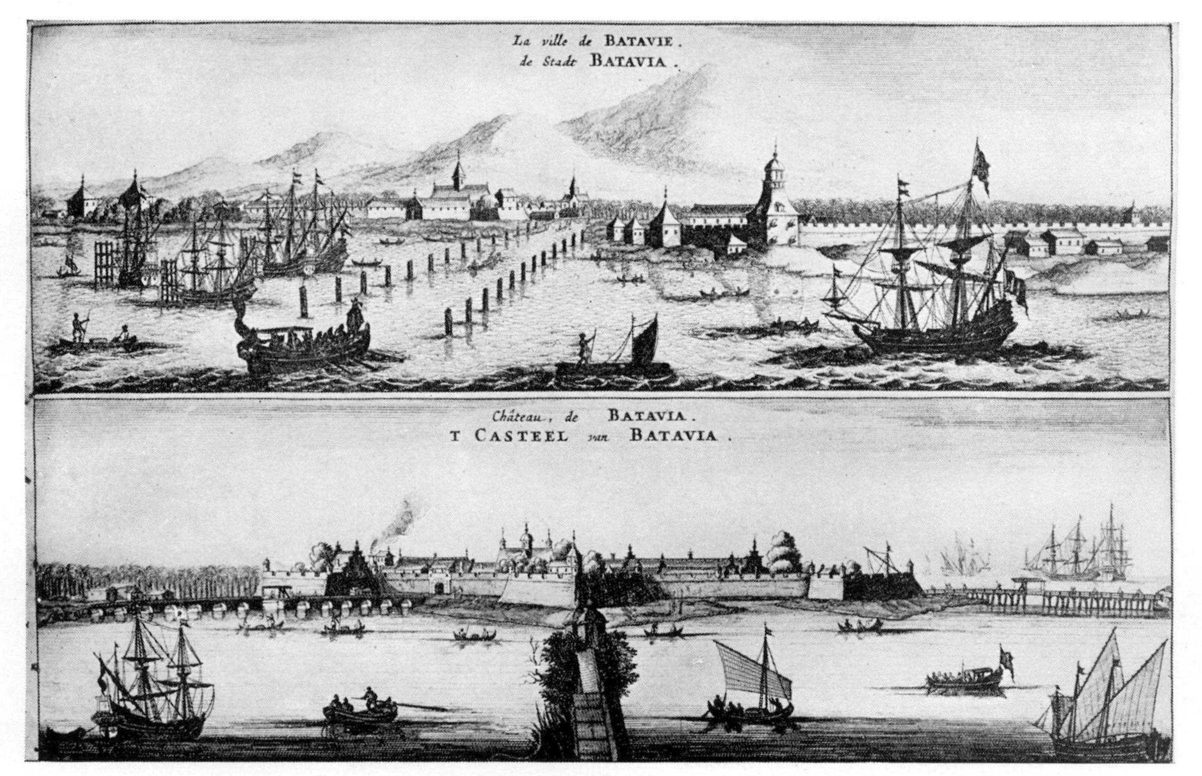

BATAVIA DURING THE EIGHTEENTH CENTURY

General Zwaardecroon had twenty-six men executed at the beginning of the eighteenth century for transgressing the laws of the Company, but to no avail. Fifty years later, in 1731, the Directors decided to set an example and ordered the immediate deposition and forced return to Holland of Governor-General Durven, of the director-general of the Asiatic commerce, of two members of the Council of the Indies, and of a number of other high officials.[33] For a while the smuggling ceased, but this ruined hundreds of Batavians who thereby lost their main source of income.

The Batavian, continuously confronted with death, permanently ill of malaria, and, moreover, suddenly deprived of part of his revenue, got into an extreme state of nervousness. This fact should be taken into account when we read the story of the awful massacre of the Batavian Chinese that occurred in 1740. As early as 1721 the citizens had been stirred up by strange stories about a Javanese conspiracy, said to have been organized by Peter Erberfelt, an Indian-born citizen of German-Siamese descent. This man and a number of others were executed after trial by the Batavian court.[34] In 1740 another story began to circulate, that the Chinese planned to revolt and intended to capture Batavia by surprise. It was rather astonishing that the Chinese should have planned this undertaking, for they had always been the favorite subjects of the Batavian government on account of their industry, peacefulness, and quiet behavior. In the last few years, however, a great number of poor Chinese immigrants had arrived in Batavia who after their arrival had been unable to find employment. The government had limited the number of immigrants and arranged a quota system, but this law was constantly circumvented by the Chinese, who knew the weak spot in the Company's governmental system, the underpayment of its employees. Thus too many came in, and those who could not make a living in a decent way started plundering in the country districts around the capital.[35]

The government decided to deport all superfluous Chinese to Ceylon and South Africa. When the embarkations began, a story was circu-

[33] A. K. Gijsberti Hodenpijl, "Het ontslag en het opontbod van den G. G. Diederik Durven op 9 October 1731," BKI, LXXIII (1917), 178 sq. Durven had started gold mining in areas of Java where no minerals existed at all and by maneuvers like this robbed the Company of enormous sums (*Priangan*, I, 233 sq.).

[34] Probably Erberfelt himself was a victim of a plot in which even G. G. Zwaardecroon may have been involved. See L. G. W. De Roo, "De Conspiratie van 1721," TBG, XV (1867), 362 sq. and *Priangan*, I, sect. 2, p. 210.

[35] A recent compilation of all known facts in J. Th. Vermeulen, *op. cit.* For documents, see De Jonge, *op. cit.*, IX, 923 sq. See also B. Hoetink, "Ni Hoekong Kapitein der Chineezen te Batavia in 1740," BKI, LXXIV (1918), 447 sq.

lated among the Chinese that this was only a trick of the government to get its victims in its power and that afterwards the unhappy Chinese would be thrown overboard in midocean! The Company has some bad deeds on its record, but it never even thought, of course, of committing this crime. The poor Chinese, however, became desperate. Armed groups gathered in the neighborhood of the city and began to attack the outposts. There is little proof that their compatriots within the city walls planned to join their rebellion, but the nervousness of the Dutch citizens may be imagined, and the government rightly decided to order a search for weapons in all Chinese houses. When the search started, fire broke out and then the government lost control. Sailors, soldiers, Dutch citizens and their Indonesian slaves rushed out into the streets and began to kill the Chinese wherever they met them. Several thousands died in the catastrophe. The government seemed helpless or unwilling to stop the massacre before the worst had happened. Afterwards the members of the Council of the Indies tried to put all responsibility on the governor-general, who in his turn, and correctly, held the opinion that for all acts of government the governor *and* the Council were responsible. The Directors in Amsterdam ordered the arrest of the governor-general when he returned to Holland, and an investigation followed that lasted for years, without definite results.[36]

The countryside around Batavia was rapidly liberated of the marauding troops of Chinese, but the movement had swept along Java's northern coast, and at a certain moment a joint revolution of the Chinese and the Javanese seemed unavoidable. Even the susuhunan was involved in the affair, and the Dutch garrison of Kartasura was annihilated after a surprise attack by the Javanese. After a few years the country came to rest again. The susuhunan left his capital, which had been desecrated by bloodshed and plunder, and transferred his residence to Surakarta, where his descendants rule until the present day. The imprudent move of Susuhunan Pakubuwana II to make an alliance with the rebellious Chinese and to permit the anti-Dutch party at his court to begin war against the Company all but caused the downfall of his empire. Too late he understood that only the protection of the Company could save him from the warlike Madurese and from revolt among his own subjects and even the members of his own

[36] G. G. Valckenier, who undoubtedly was responsible for the fact that no attempt was made to stop the massacre, never had a fair trial. The affair dragged on for nine years while Valckenier was imprisoned in the castle of Batavia and came to an end because of the death of the prisoner.

family. The treaty which he concluded on November 11, 1743, guaranteed him his throne but made him into a mere vassal of the Company.[37]

Thus a revolution that began in Batavia ended by changing the whole political constellation of the island. The first decades of the eighteenth century brought still another change in Javanese affairs. In this period, the first foreign crops of economic importance were brought into the Indies, and the Company began to change from a commercial to an agricultural enterprise. Among the causes of this transformation, one, a seemingly very remote one, must be mentioned: the eighteenth-century Dutch predilection for gardening. Up to our day, the beautiful country sites southeast of Amsterdam have given proof of the widespread interest in horticulture that existed in that time in the Netherlands. One of its aspects was an interest in exotic flowers and plants.

Around 1700 some of the high officials in the Indies shared this hobby of gardening with their compatriots at home. This little group of Batavian horticulturists included two governors-general and several members of the Council.[38] Johan van Hoorn was one of them. On his country estate near Batavia he experimented with many non-Indonesian plants. These included a few small coffee trees that had been sent to him from the southwest coast of India. At the time, Van Hoorn could hardly foresee that his experiments were preparing an economic and social revolution which was going to change the destiny of the people of Java.[39]

Van Hoorn's coffee trees did not prosper in the foreign soil of Java. Zwaardecroon and Chastelein continued the experiments with more success, but without the intervention of Nicholas Witsen their en-

[37] CD, v (BKI, xcvi), 360 sq. The susuhunan declared that he received his sultanate from the hands of the Batavian government and ceded all coastlands of Java to the Company.

[38] This is the group around Governor-General Johannes Camphuijs (1684–1691). Pieter van Hoorn (died 1682) advocated large-scale colonization; his son, Johan, became under the guidance of Cornelis Speelman an expert in native affairs. Cornelis Chastelein, another friend of Camphuijs, founded the settlement of Depok. Both Johan van Hoorn and Chastelein took an important part in the promotion of the coffee culture. Camphuijs wrote a history of the founding of Batavia and supplied E. Kaempfer with the material for his famous *Description of Japan*. He also took care that copies were made of Rumphius' *Herbarium* and thus saved it from destruction, and he protected Herbert de Jager, the famous linguist. All these men, who had a more than usual interest for Indian affairs, were landowners. Johan van Hoorn, governor-general from 1704–1709, was the greatest landowner of Batavia. Van Rheede van Drakesteyn worked in the same period. Hendrik Zwaardecroon (governor-general 1718–1725) was the one who provided van Hoorn with young coffee trees from the coast of Malabar.

[39] The first importation of coffee (from Arabia) into Holland was in 1663. Van Hoorn sent a few coffee trees to Amsterdam, whence seeds were sent to the West Indies.

deavors might have remained fruitless.[40] Witsen, burgomaster of Amsterdam and a director of the East India Company, was a man with great general interest in science and archeology. He had that typical eighteenth-century curiosity that prompted him to collect material—often at enormous expense—on widely divergent but always exotic subjects. He sent Cornelis de Bruyn, painter and traveler, to Persia to make drawings of the ruins of Persepolis. For twenty years he collected material for his map and description of Siberia. He was advisor to the Russian court under Peter the Great, and he was the one who in the Indies initiated the cultivation of new export crops, an idea totally foreign to the Company, which until now had relied solely upon the produce of native agriculture. In a way he may be called the founder of the modern Netherlands Indies, and he certainly deserves that title more than Jan Pieterszoon Coen, of whose work only a city and its name survive.[41]

Witsen, who was a relative of Van Hoorn, procured for his friends in Batavia an order by the Directors to continue their effort, with a promise of a reward if their experiments would lead to production of new crops of commercial interest in Java. In 1707 coffee plants were distributed among the district-chiefs around Batavia and in Cheribon. In 1711 the first one hundred pounds of coffee was delivered to the Company's storehouses by Arya Viratana, the Javanese regent of Tjandjur.[42] Nine years later the yearly crop amounted to one hundred thousand pounds, and after twelve years the production amounted to twelve million pounds. The results of Van Hoorn's and Witsen's experiment were amazing, but the Directors considered them frightening. They had set free the forces of nature and they hurriedly made desperate attempts to bring them back under control.

In the obsolescent system of trade of the Company, mass production and selling at low prices in ever-expanding markets could have no

[40] On Nicholas Witsen, see J. Fr. Gebhard, *Het Leven van Mr. Nicolaas Cornelisz. Witsen*, 2 vols. (Utrecht, 1881–82).

[41] In all older works on the history of the East Indies the importance of the period around 1700 has been overlooked. After the thorough researches of Dr. De Haan in the archives of Batavia in the first decade of this century it became possible to gain a better insight into the internal policy of the East Indian government. The older histories, such as that of Clive Day, *The Policy and Administration of the Dutch in Java* (New York, 1904), should be compared with the later Dutch histories. Day's book was at the time of its publication an excellent synopsis of the result of historical studies so far obtained and represents exactly Dutch historical trend during the Liberal period.

[42] The Dutch gave the Javanese district rulers, nearly always members of aristocratic families, the title of "regent" with which in Holland they used to indicate the members of the ruling oligarchic class. In the nineteenth century the title "regent" was officially accepted. Tjandjur is a mountain district, south of Batavia.

place. An expansion of the East Indian commerce would have necessitated an expansion of the capitalization of the Company. Transport of mass products would have increased the general expenses.[43] The Directors wanted only a limited supply of East Indian products which they could sell at high prices, and in order to keep the supply limited, they insisted upon rigorous control over production and strict maintenance of the system of monopoly. The unexpected success of the new coffee plantations shook this whole system to its very foundations. The enormous amount of coffee produced made strict control over the export impossible. Even if the Batavian government were to maintain a whole fleet of patrol ships along the coasts of Java, it could never prevent thousands of pounds being smuggled to the British settlements in Benkulen and the Portuguese posts on Timor. Not that it would have mattered much if a thousand tons of coffee had been smuggled to foreign traders. The Batavian government had a hundred ways of securing the bulk of the production for itself at a cheap price, but this was apparently beyond the understanding of the Directors. Hollanders in the Indies knew better, but they could not make their point of view prevail in Amsterdam.[44]

There was another disquieting aspect to the matter, at least in the opinion of the Directors. In the first years of the new industry, when prices were very high, some of the Javanese district rulers amassed enormous sums of money. They made their subjects plant the coffee but paid them very poorly for their labor, while they themselves received high prices from the Company, up to fifty guilders a picol (125 lbs.).[45] Undoubtedly, economic ties of this kind made the Javanese regents the most loyal vassals the Company could find in the world, but they also made them powerful and self-confident. Here, too, the

[43] There was money enough available among the Dutch bourgeoisie to enlarge the capital of the Company, but the shareholders were opposed to such a move. The Directors knew quite well that the costs of maintenance and equipment of the Company's ships were far too high, and that it would have been more economical to charter ships for the East Indian trade, but were afraid that this would lead to an increase of smuggling.

[44] See Pieter van Hoorn's "Preparatoire Consideratiën ende advys wegens de Nederlandsche Colonie in dese Indische Gewesten" (1675), in De Jonge, VI, 130–147. Chastelein in his "Invallende Gedachten" repeats the arguments of Van Hoorn. G. G. Van Goens and G. G. Speelman shared the same views, while even Maetsuycker seems to have inclined to the same opinion although in his administration he strictly followed the views of the Directors.

[45] In Europe the price of coffee was at that time two guilders a pound. If the Javanese received fifty guilders a picol, they could easily make a living for a whole year by producing a single picol! This gives an idea of the profits made by some of the regents when in the first years of the production they sold thousands of picols to Batavia. In those years their income represented a value equal to that of the income earned by the richest of millionaires in our time.

Directors were unable to take a broad view of the situation. From the beginning of the new period they worried that "the Javanese might become too rich." They did not mean the poor peasants of Java; *those* had little chance of becoming rich; they meant first of all the regents, although these rulers spent their newly acquired wealth still faster than they earned it.[46] The Directors did not consider the possibility that growing welfare in Java might open new markets for the merchandise of the Company. Even if the trade system of the Directors had permitted the introduction of such novel ideas, the limited capital of the Company would have made their execution very difficult.

The Directors, therefore, sought other means of maintaining their traditional policy of commerce. Drastically and arbitrarily they reduced the price of the crude product in Batavia from fifty to twelve guilders a picol. In addition, they ordered a restriction of the plantations. To force prices still further down, the Batavian officials introduced sophisticated distinctions between "mountain picols" of 225 pounds and Batavian picols of 125 pounds. The producers were obliged to deliver the required quantities of coffee in mountain picols but received payment for an identical number of Batavian picols. The difference in weight was explained as a compensation for drying during the transport from the mountain districts to the Batavian storehouses. By manipulating with different types of picols the officials secured ample compensation for their own troubles as well as for the losses of the Company.

It is evident that under these circumstances the Javanese peasants were not very eager to plant coffee. The limited profits, graciously conceded by the Company to the producers, landed in the pockets of the district rulers. For the peasants, the coffee culture brought apparently only extra burdens, no extra income. Consequently it was loathed by the masses of the people. Their unwillingness to coöperate grew so strong that for several years the Company could not even obtain the limited quantities it demanded. The peasants simply neglected the coffee gardens.

Against this opposition the Company found an easy remedy. In the first years of the coffee culture the Batavian government had encour-

[46] "That the Javanese might become too rich" was a fear quite often expressed in the letters of the Company. We must remember that this idea was not peculiar to colonial administrations but the common opinion of the time. See De Haan (*Priangan*, I, 431, and IV, 741), who, among other sources, quotes Voltaire: "Il me paraît essentiel qu'il y ait des gueux ignorants," a point of view wholly shared by the first sultan of Djocjakarta, who held it to be a principle of government that "a poor people is easy to rule" (De Jonge *op. cit.*, vol. XI, Memoir of J. R. van der Burgh, 1780).

aged the planting of coffee trees and had offered to buy the product at a determined price. Although sovereign ruler of the Lowlands and Preanger Districts, the Government when buying the coffee harvest had acted solely in its capacity of commercial agent for the Directors in Amsterdam. But as soon as the Javanese peasants showed unwillingness to continue the production, the Batavian authorities suddenly remembered that, under the existing treaties with Mataram, they possessed sovereign rights over all territory west of the sultanate of Cheribon and that they were also the overlords of that petty principality. In 1677 the Company had acquired the Preanger districts, but the government of Batavia had not shown much interest in its new acquisition. It had not bothered to collect the tributes which the Preanger regents used to pay to Mataram and which were now due to Batavia. For twenty years Batavia left its new territory in the Preanger alone without interfering with its internal affairs.

In 1694 the attitude of the government began to change. In that year it sent a committee composed of two Indonesians and two Dutch officers to the mountain districts with the order to buy — in the open market — and to bring down to Batavia all the yarn it could obtain from native producers. In 1696 the government struck a new note and *demanded* a certain quantity of pepper, yarn, and other commodities of each regency. A reasonable price was set for these products, and it was announced that all goods offered in excess of the demanded quantity would be accepted. This was the first instance of exertion of authority in the Preanger by Batavia and of using her sovereign rights to secure the delivery of certain articles of commerce. The idea was not new, however, for it had been put into practice in the Spice Islands for several decades. Around 1700 the system was still applied with great moderation. The Preanger districts never supplied the demanded quantity of goods, and the government did not bother to enforce its decrees.

The introduction of coffee culture changed the picture. If the regents did not coöperate of their own free will in providing the Company each year with the exact amount of coffee it desired for the European market, they would be forced to deliver this quantity. They would be required to offer it to the Company in the form of tribute (instead of the tribute of rice formerly paid to the susuhunan of Mataram) or they would be obliged, by force of the sovereign authority exerted by the Company, to sell it at a price set by Batavia, and to transport it to the storehouses of Batavia. Here the Company only needed to adopt the principles of the susuhunan, namely that all land and all people in the empire were the property of the ruler. It never bothered, however, to propound definite views on the character or extent of its sovereign rights. Moreover, it never forgot that it was merchant as well as sovereign and, in order to make the transaction still more advantageous, preferred to pay part of the already low price in goods instead of in cash.

A series of decrees set the rules for the new system, which in the historical literature is known as that of the "Contingents and Forced Deliveries." [47] In 1723 coffee was made an article of monopoly, and in the same year the Directors set the amount of the yearly output at four million pounds and the price at twelve and a half guilders a picol. Around 1760 the yearly planting of a given number of new coffee trees was made obligatory. The whole culture was entrusted to the regents, who organized the production in conformity with the requests of the "Commissary for Native Affairs," a Netherlands official appointed by the governor-general. Because of the negligence and indifference shown by the native planters, supervisors were appointed who assisted the regents in organizing the production and controlling the upkeep of the coffee gardens. These supervisors were known as the "coffee sergeants" and from this group of controllers the modern civil service of the East Indies has developed.

The coffee culture has undoubtedly yielded large profits to the Company. In the first half of the eighteenth century coffee remained economically less important than sugar and pepper but in the last quarter of the century it was the principal source of income for the Company, and although its shareholders did not receive much of the profits, these would have been more than sufficient to maintain the Company in a state of prosperity if the management of affairs, both in Amsterdam and in Batavia, had been more efficient. The growing importance of the cultivation of coffee and other export crops [48] coincided with the decline of the inter-Asiatic trade. Both Persia and Japan had, in the eighteenth century, lost much of their importance for that trade. Persia had been torn by wars with Turks and Afghans and civil strife. Commerce had been impeded by the prevailing unstable conditions.

[47] "Contingents" were the tributes offered by the regents to Batavia. For these they received small sums as presents. "Forced deliveries" were the forced sales of products at a set price. In practice there was no difference between the two.

[48] The Company also sought to promote the production of cotton, for which purpose it introduced cotton plants from Bengal, and indigo. The preparation of indigo as practised on Java proved unsatisfactory for the export. Hence there followed an order to the governor of Malabar to send indigo workers from that area and to instruct a few Netherlanders in the method of preparation. An attempt to introduce the silk industry failed completely, but probably only because of neglect on the side of the officials. See *Priangan*, vols. I and III *passim*.

Japan had started on her policy of making herself economically independent of foreign powers. She limited both imports and exports. The trade with India declined when French and British conquerors began to extend European authority over the native states. The Dutch East India Company, too, had to change from a commercial into a territorial power, but the Directors did not understand the trend of events and protested against all deviations from the traditional system. If Witsen had not promoted the coffee culture on Java and thus prepared the ground for a complete reorientation of the Company's economic and political system, the Dutch colonial empire might well have disintegrated beyond repair and have succumbed in the crisis of the turn of the eighteenth century.

So far we have discussed the importance of the coffee culture to the Dutch Company. What did it bring to the people of Java? First of all, it forged a close alliance between the Dutch rulers and the regents of West Java. Some of the regencies of the Preanger had already existed as semi-autonomous districts in the time of Mataram; others had been created by the government of Batavia. The regents were appointed by the governor-general, who, more or less, respected hereditary rights. Their power was curtailed by the obligation to ask the approval of Batavia on the appointment of their *patih's*, or lieutenants. The "coffee sergeants," too, kept an eye on the political gestures of the regents. The strongest check on their independence, however, was their financial liabilities toward the "Commissary for Native Affairs." Like all Indonesians, the regents preferred to sell their agricultural products in advance. At their request the Commissary gave them loans in anticipation of sums they were to receive when the coffee was delivered, and the regents, being very careless in financial affairs and spending much more than they ever might expect to receive, soon found themselves loaded with heavy debts on which they had to pay an interest of one per cent a month. These debts accumulated so rapidly that at the end of the century the whole production of coffee was insufficient to pay the interest alone! Finally the government of Batavia was obliged to annul all debts of the regents and to permit them to make a fresh start.

It is no wonder that, under these circumstances, the regents sought to appropriate all income from the coffee culture for themselves and left practically nothing for the people who really did the work. Following the example set by the princes of Mataram, they considered the peasants as well as the soil their personal property. The people of the Preanger were divided into three classes, the nobility, the personal followers of the regent (the *menumpang*) and the subjects (*tjatjah*). All burdens were loaded upon the shoulders of the unfortunate *tjatjah*. The regents if possible kept their *menumpang* free from forced labor in the coffee gardens that they might cultivate their ricefields and produce food for their chief and his court. Thus only part of the population suffered under the Forced Deliveries, but this section suffered really very heavily.

Much heavier still than the duty of producing the coffee was that of transporting the product to the storehouses of Batavia. At that time there were no roads in West Java. The loads had to be carried to the regency storehouse and then to be transported by caravans of buffaloes to embarkation points on the rivers in the Lowlands. Hundreds of the buffaloes died from exhaustion, and in Batavia hundreds of the Javanese succumbed to the malaria. Yet the coffee culture brought changes for the better in West Java. Under the princes of Mataram the people of the Preanger had been so overburdened with exactions of tributes in rice and other foodstuffs that they never had really settled down, but had continued to move from one mountain valley to another in the hope of shirking the tribute. Consequently, they never had progressed to the more profitable system of cultivating rice on *sawahs*, irrigated fields. Every few years they cleared new fields in the jungle by burning down the forest, and then moved on to another place as soon as the soil became exhausted. This semi-nomadic life hindered progress in welfare and civilization. The coffee plantations tied the people down to permanent settlements. The Company fostered the immigration of new settlers into the thinly populated Preanger, and these immigrants taught the native peasants how to lay out *sawahs* and to install an efficient system of irrigation. Cattle breeding too was encouraged by the government of Batavia. The interests of the coffee culture no longer permitted the petty wars among the regents from which the poor peasants had suffered so much in the days of Mataram, and peace alone was a benefit for the people so great that it far outweighed the burdens of forced cultures. The people of the Preanger hated the forced labor in the coffee gardens, but, although the Company did not maintain strong garrisons in the district, never revolted against the new regime which, after all, had brought them peace and a beginning of impartial justice.

The Batavia of 1750 was a widely different city from that of a century before. The inhabitants were no longer confined to the narrow space within the city walls. Indonesian settlements had sprung up all over the Batavian Lowlands, and scattered among them were the large estates of Dutch-Batavian landowners. Camphuis, Van Hoorn, Chastelein, and their friends had given the Batavian countryside a new aspect. On their estates thousands of Indonesian bondsmen lived who, with hundreds of slaves, toiled in the ricefields and worked in the "gardens," the coffee, cotton, and indigo plantations. On the estates of Camphuis' cultivated friends their fate was far better than that of their compatriots under their own hereditary rulers. There still exists a reminder of the humanity prevailing among the group of men who formed the Indonesian settlement of Depok, once the estate of Cornelis Chastelein. Chastelein was the son of one of the Directors of the Company. At the age of eighteen he had left for the Indies, and he spent his whole life thereafter in or near Batavia. At the time of his death (1714) he was a member of the Council of the Indies and the owner of three large estates in the Batavian Lowlands. One was close to Batavia. Here Chastelein made his first experiments with a coffee garden. On the same terrain Governor-General Daendels founded later his "New Batavia," now the suburb of Weltevreden. The second estate was that of Seringsing, known from the engravings of Cornelis de Bruyn, Witsen's traveling painter who visited Chastelein at the estate. The third was that of Depok. At his death, Chastelein bequeathed this estate to his former slaves who had adopted Christianity, to possess it in common property for themselves and their descendants, and forbade that any part of it should ever be sold or alienated in any other way.[49] Up to the present day the descendants of these slaves are the joint owners of the estate of Depok. The settlement is ruled by a committee elected by all members of the community in the general meeting which is held at least once every year.

The humanitarian ideas of men like Camphuis, Van Hoorn, and Chastelein were the first omens of new times in the Indies. But their era was followed by that of Governor-General Durven, one of the most corrupt officials the Company ever had and by the massacre of the Batavian Chinese. Reforms were urgently necessary but they should have begun at the top, i.e. in the council halls of the Directors in Amsterdam. Unless new ideas should begin to prevail *there*, all attempts of local reorganization in the Indies would remain fruitless. And the Directors, though willing to concede a change of details, would never give up their mistaken commercial policy as a whole. Of the many plans for reform submitted to the Board of Directors during the eighteenth century, not a single one even touched upon the main difficulty.

[49] For Depok see ENI, under headings "Chastelein" and "Depok," where literature is listed.

The best-known of these plans is that of Gustaaf Willem, Baron van Imhoff. This East Frisian nobleman had served the Company in several capacities. After the massacre of the Chinese in 1740 he so violently opposed Governor-General Valckenier (with whom he had a long-standing personal quarrel) that this officer had him arrested and sent to Holland. The Directors, irritated against Valckenier because of the Chinese affair, reversed the situation. They appointed Van Imhoff governor-general and ordered Valckenier, who was on his way home, arrested and sent back to Batavia. This appointment included the approval of Van Imhoff's plan for administrative and commercial reforms in the Indies.[50] The most interesting points of his plan were the voluntary reduction of the Company's commitments in the western section of the Indian Ocean and the settlement of European colonists in the Batavian Lowlands. Van Imhoff definitely wanted the East India Company to concentrate all its efforts on Ceylon and the East Indian archipelago. This reform, if carried through, would have demonstrated the changed character of the Company and accentuated its new position as a territorial rather than a commercial power. The other point was of less consequence. Van Imhoff did not think of a large-scale colonization of Java by Europeans but only of the establishment of a limited number of European-managed farms, where systematically the kind of foodstuffs would be produced which was demanded by the European inhabitants of Batavia. The main purpose of the colonization was to make life cheaper and easier for the people of the city.

Van Imhoff sailed to Batavia on a ship significantly called the *Restorer*. The new governor-general was a true example of the eighteenth-century type of reformer who believed that the outlook of the world and the character of human society could be changed by decree.

Like his colleagues in Europe, whom he preceded by a decade, he undertook more than he could accomplish, and he never allowed himself the time to carry one plan out fully before he started on another. He reorganized the Company's merchant marine, which he sought to improve by introducing military ranks for the skippers and mates. He established a naval academy, reformed the school system of Batavia, transferred the opium trade on Java from the Company to a licensed private association, formed by free citizens of Batavia, and made more liberal regulations for the inter-Asiatic trade by private individuals. He

[50] G. W. van Imhoff, *Consideratiën* (The Hague, 1763); J. E. Heeres, "De Consideratiën van Van Imhoff," BKI, LXVI (1912), 441; A. K. Gijsberti Hodenpijl, "Gustaaf Willem, baron van Imhoff als Gouverneur van Ceylon, 1736–1740," BKI, LXXV (1919), 48 sq.

was indefatigable in his work and published one ordinance after the other, but many of his ideas were very impractical.

Van Imhoff had no objection to breaking with tradition. He was probably the first governor-general to make a public speech, and he was certainly the first in that office to believe in publicity. He even encouraged the publication of a newspaper.[51] This seemed so shocking to the Directors that they hurriedly forbade the dangerous innovation. His most remarkable enterprise was his attempt, undertaken at his sole responsibility, without the knowledge of his Directors, to establish direct trading connections between the Indies and the western hemisphere. Batavia badly needed to import more silver for coinage, and because of a state of war existing between Spain and Great Britain could not obtain it from Mexico through the Philippines or Spain. Van Imhoff therefore decided to send two ships direct to Mexico, and gave the captains instructions to sail to a point between 35 and 36° north latitude (between Monterey Bay and Point Conception in southern California) where they should find a Jesuit mission. With the help of an Irish Catholic priest who happened to be in Batavia and was willing to take part in the enterprise, they were to establish contact with the Spanish authorities. The two ships reached the American west coast much farther south, near the island group Tres Marias, whence they proceeded to Acapulco. All attempts to establish relations with the Spaniards failed. Every Hollander who set foot ashore was imprisoned. The ships were obliged to return to Batavia. Van Imhoff received a sharp rebuke for his imprudent action from the Directors, who, in their turn, had been reprimanded by the States General after severe protests from the Spanish ambassador against Van Imhoff's enterprise. This, it seems, actually represented an infraction of some of the articles of the peace treaty of Muenster between Spain and the Netherlands.[52]

The Directors rapidly lost their friendly feelings for the governor-general whom they had provided with more than the usual authority in the hope that he might be able to reorganize the corrupt East Indian administration. A few years after Van Imhoff's death (November 1, 1750) little was left of his "improvements" except the large country estate which he had founded at the foot of the mountains south of Batavia and to which he had given the rather conventional name of

[51] J. A. van der Chijs, "De Bataviasche nouvelles, 1744–1746 en de Bataviasche Koloniale Courant van 1810–1811," TBG, XI (1862), 192.

[52] A. K. Gijsberti Hodenpijl, "De mislukte pogingen van G. G. van Imhoff tot het aanknoopen van handelsbetrekkingen met Spaansch Amerika," BKI, LXXIII (1917), 502.

"Buitenzorg" (Sans Souci). He had planned the estate as a country residence for the acting governor-general, but the Directors refused to approve of this "luxury" and instead granted the new estate to Van Imhoff personally as a free gift. The property was taken over by the succeeding governor-general, and finally it became customary for the retiring governor-general to transfer it to his successor for a set price. Under the rule of Daendels it was finally turned to the purpose for which Van Imhoff had planned it, and in the beginning of the nineteenth century the famous "Plantentuin," the Government Botanic Garden which has developed into one of the leading botanical institutions of the world, was laid out on its grounds.

CHAPTER X

NETHERLANDERS AND INDONESIANS IN THE EIGHTEENTH CENTURY

THE DOWNFALL of the kingdoms of Macassar, Mataram, and Bantam sealed the fate of the Indies. From 1680 on the Netherlanders controlled the archipelago. Seventy years later, around 1750, only two of the major islands remained free from interference by the dominating power. Those two were Bali and Lombok. Over all the other Indonesian territories and states the Dutch Company, in greater or lesser degree, exerted its authority.[1] Bali and Lombok owed their independence alike to the warlike character of their inhabitants and the economic unimportance of their products. The only merchandise Bali had to offer was slaves. The petty kings of the "paradise of the Indies" caught and sold each other's subjects. In 1778 there lived more than 1300 Balinese slaves and freedmen in Batavia. As long, however, as the Balinese slave hunters did not extend their predatory excursions into the Company's territory, the Batavian government preferred to ignore them. The Balinese clung stubbornly to their Hinduist traditions, and after the downfall of Mataram they no longer had anything to fear from their Mohammedan neighbors. The old customs with all their pageantry, and also with all their cruelties, continued undisturbed.

On Bali and Lombok, Dutch influence did not exist. It was not equally strong, of course, on all the other islands. Around 1750 we can distinguish three different areas of western influence in the archipelago. One extended over the islands of Sumatra and Borneo. Here the presence of the Europeans hardly affected native life. The second area was that of the "Great East," where western influence was strong but far more oppressive than stimulating. Moreover, it remained limited to narrow strips of land along the coasts of the islands. The third was the island of Java, where the Netherlanders penetrated into the interior and, by introducing new means of production, brought considerable change in social and economic conditions.

[1] This authority, everywhere except in Java, was limited to the coastal areas. On the smaller islands, however, actual control of the sea and of the principal ports necessarily included indirect authority over the interior.

The political situation of Sumatra was chaotic. The once powerful sultanate of Atjeh had fallen into a state of anarchy. After the Dutch had broken the Atjenese control over the pepper trade on Sumatra's north and west coast around 1680, the sultans of Atjeh had lost their wealth and consequently the respect of their rebellious vassals. Yet, Atjeh alone of all Sumatran states had maintained its political independence. The inhabitants of Nias and other small islands off the west coast sought the protection of the Dutch against the piratical attacks of the Atjenese. Padang, port to the "Empire" of Menangkabau, was firmly held by the Company. The chieftains of the pagan Bataks, who vigorously maintained their independence from the Islamic Menangkabau, came down from their mountain strongholds to conclude trade agreements with the Dutch.[2] On the east coast the sultanates of Palembang and Djambi continued to exist as vassal states of Batavia. The lowlands north of Djambi were controlled by the sultan of Johore, another ally of the Company, until with the assistance of the Menangkabau they formed a state of their own, the sultanate of Siak.[3]

All these states had conceded to the Company the exclusive right to handle their most important export crops, but here the system of monopoly had not had such disastrous effects as in several other parts of the archipelago. It was less rigorously maintained, if only because the presence of the British in Benkulen and the proximity of the Asiatic continent made its enforcement impracticable. The Sumatran states were certainly less stable than the Javanese sultanates. The authority of the sultans nowhere penetrated far into the interior, where pagan beliefs and tribal organizations still prevailed.[4] The Sumatran sultans were, however, far more fanatical Mohammedans than the princes of Java. Connections with India, where Islam was on the ascendency, were more frequent.[5] But the best safeguard for the inde-

[2] Treaties with the Batak tribes west of Lake Toba were concluded in 1694 and 1698. In 1698 the Dutch commander of the west coast decided to appoint a representative whose task it would be to mediate between the Bataks and the Company (CD, IV, 83 and 143). See E. B. Kielstra, "Onze kennis van Sumatra's Westkust omstreeks de helft der 18e eeuw," BKI, XXXVI (1887), 499.

[3] E. Netscher, "De Nederlanders in Johore en Siak," VBG, vol. XXXV (Batavia, 1870).

[4] See the studies on native institutions by Van Basel, "Radicaale Beschrijving," 1761, partly published by Kielstra in the article quoted above and partly in *Tijdschrift voor Nederlandsch Indië*, vol. IX, and by Coenraad Fr. Hofman (on the Menangkabau, about 1715) published by F. W. Stapel in BKI, XCII (1935), 459 sq. These studies, and others which may still be found in the archives, precede by several decades the great work of W. Marsden, *The History of Sumatra* (first edition, London, 1783).

Hofman clearly states that at his time even the Menangkabau was only superficially Islamized.

[5] Gujerat traders continued to visit Sumatra, especially Atjeh. One of their most important articles of commerce was the tin from Malaya.

pendence of these petty kingdoms was the well-known aversion toward territorial expansion on the part of the Directors of the Company. Only when active interference seemed profitable did Batavia change its policy. This happened to be the case in Bangka and Billiton. On Bangka, tin deposits had been discovered around 1709. Fifty years later Billiton too began to reveal its treasures. Several decades before, the Government of Batavia had already accepted an offer of a chieftain of Bangka to accept Dutch sovereignty (1688), but it had never bothered to put the treaty into effect. Now it secured its rights by treaties with Palembang, another claimant to the sovereignty over the island, and, always faithful to its obsolescent trade policy, sought to limit and monopolize the tin production.[6] Gradually Batavia established its authority over both islands.

Borneo was culturally and economically less developed than Sumatra. The sultanate of Bandjermasin in the southeast corner of the island was the only one of the states of Borneo strong enough to defend itself successfully against the pirate fleets that infested the Indonesian seas. But the place had gained an evil reputation. The Dutch had traded in the port since 1606. In 1669 their representatives were treacherously attacked and murdered. Then the British had tried their luck, but in 1707 their merchants suffered the same fate. In the same period Portuguese missionaries had attempted to penetrate into the interior to preach the Gospel among the pagan Dyaks. They too had been murdered, for the sultans of Bandjermasin feared nothing so much as direct contact between the Europeans and the Dyaks, whom they cruelly exploited and oppressed. Slowly, however, the capital of the sultanate began to gain some importance. After the fall of Macassar it succeeded that port as a meeting point for non-Dutch traders. Portuguese came from Timor, British ships from Benkulen, and a few Chinese junks called yearly. Pepper grown around the town and spices smuggled out of the Moluccas were the main articles of trade. In 1756 the government of Batavia sent a special ambassador and, after the conclusion of a new trade agreement, regained control of the situation.[7]

[6] A native chronicle of Bangka: F. S. A. de Clercq, "Bijdrage tot de geschiedenis van het eiland Bangka," BKI, XLV (1895), 113 sq. and 381 sq.

The total output of Bangka tin was limited to 30,000 picol a year (1875 tons). The present production is 40,000 tons a year. The comparison of these figures gives some idea of the relative significance of the production of the Indies now and a hundred and fifty years ago.

[7] On Bandjermasin: Johan Paravicini, "Rapport over Bandjermasin" (1756), BKI, VIII (1862), 217 sq. J. A. baron von Hohnendorff, "Radicale Beschrijving van Banjermassing" (1757), BKI, VIII, 151 and 213 sq. A modern study: J. C. Noordmann, *Bandjermasin en de Compagnie in de tweede helft der 18e eeuw* (Leiden, 1935).

The other states of Borneo are hardly worth mentioning. The sultans of Sambas, Sukadana, and Kutei led a precarious existence, continually threatened by rivals in their own families and by pirate chiefs who sought to establish a kingdom of their own.[8] In one respect solely they all followed the same policy. They kept the Dyak tribes living upstream on the great Borneo rivers separated from the Europeans. The eighteenth century produced a few interesting studies of native conditions in the interior of Sumatra, but the interior of Borneo remained totally unknown. There is only one interesting feature in the history of eighteenth-century Borneo, namely the founding of a strong Chinese colony in the northwestern sultanate, that of Sambas. Rich gold deposits had been found in the hills east and southeast of the town of Sambas. The sultan, whose Malay subjects showed an intense dislike of hard manual labor, called in hundreds of Chinese miners. These workers organized their "unions," their *kongsis*, and through these organizations made contracts with the sultans for the exploitation of the mines. In twenty years the number of the Chinese had increased to many thousands. To keep these dangerous organizations down, the sultans subjected them to the control of Dyak guardsmen. The vexations and exactions which were the consequence of the system were patiently tolerated by the Chinese until 1770, when their patience was exhausted. A revolution followed; the Dyak guards were exterminated; and from that time the kongsis formed semi-independent republics. In 1855, when Dutch authority was established, the Chinese in Northwest Borneo numbered more than 30,000, all of mixed blood, for as late as 1823 Chinese women were great exceptions in the district.

The history of these kongsis is only a series of feuds between the competing organizations caused by the gradual exhaustion of old mines and the opening of new ones. Once the gold fields ceased to render profits, the Chinese had to resort to agriculture, and thus one of the few foreign Asiatic settlements came into existence in the Indies. This Chinese society was always rather primitive. The settlers exhibited a tenacious attachment to their traditions and Chinese customs, but there was not a trace of higher Chinese civilization.[9] Thus, Chinese infiltra-

[8] One of the most striking examples is that of the founding of the sultanate of Pontianak around 1770 by an Arabian adventurer. The new sultanate soon became the principal power on Borneo's west coast. A treaty with the East India Company assured the new sultans the undisturbed possession of their territory.

[9] On the Chinese settlements in N. W. Borneo: P. J. Veth, *Borneo's Westerafdeeling*, 2 vols. (Zalt Bommel, 1854–1856), I, 297 sq.; J. J. M. de Groot, *Het kongsiwezen van Borneo* (The Hague, 1885); S. H. Schaank, "De Kongsi's van Montrado. Geschiedenis en toestand," TBG, xxxv (1893), 498 sq.

tion achieved more spectacular results in the western section of the archipelago than Dutch domination.

In the "Great East" the situation was exactly the opposite. For the first time perhaps in their history the peoples of the Moluccas were at peace with each other, ever since Admiral Speelman had concluded identical treaties with the sultans of Ternate and Tidore. But here, peace was no better than the state of war. The ordinances of Batavia limited the production of clove and nutmeg to the Banda Islands and Amboina. Outside this territory all spice trees were ordered extirpated, of course with the consent of the sultans of Ternate and Tidore, the official rulers of the Moluccas. In matters like these the Company was meticulously legalistic. To carry out these ordinances yearly *hongi's* were organized, expeditions by fleets of armed proas manned by Amboinese and Bandanese and commanded by Dutch officials. These fleets visited the coasts of islands where the existence of unlicensed spice-tree orchards was suspected. The trees were cut down and the population roughly reminded of the orders of the Company. Thus the production of spices was reduced to one-fourth of that of the times before the Company took control.

The system was evil and the effects horrible. It did not harm the princes and their families, for they received pensions from the Company for their coöperation. Neither did it affect the tribes in the interior of islands like Buru and Ceram. These Alfur tribes never had had any part in the spice production and did not come in direct contact with the Netherlanders until the end of the nineteenth century. The inhabitants of the coastal villages, however, lost their principal means of existence, the spice growing and the inter-island shipping. The population of these villages rapidly diminished and grew apathetic under the sufferings caused by this constant oppression that afflicted them as heavily as the internecine wars of the old days.

The inhabitants of Amboina and the Banda Islands, then, were "privileged," to use the terms of the Batavian documents, with the spice production. This privilege included the obligation to reduce the number of spice trees grown whenever the Company deemed this advisable and, secondly, to buy all foodstuffs from the Company at set, very high, prices. Under these conditions the clove and nutmeg culture was far from alluring. The "privileged" Amboinese and Bandanese lost all interest in the exercise of their privileges. In one century Amboina lost about one-third of its inhabitants. The "free citizens" of Banda [10] were reduced to poverty.

[10] Banda after the conquest by Coen in 1621 was populated by settlers selected among

The Directors of the Company were punished for their misrule by the evil consequences of their own system. When finally the demand for spices in Europe rose, and prices went up, the production could not possibly be increased. The resistance of the inhabitants to establishing new plantations — which perhaps a year later would be ordered cut down — could not be overcome. Jealously the monopoly had been maintained at high cost, and when the demand increased and once more golden times for the spice trade might have been expected, it proved to have been all in vain. The French and British succeeded in planting clove and nutmeg trees in their own colonies in India. The monopoly of spices left only evil memories which at the beginning of the nineteenth century still caused violent outbursts against Dutch authority.

This was the effect of western influence on the Moluccas. The "Great East" included two other groups of islands, Celebes and adjacent islands, and the Lesser Sunda group, from Sumbawa to Timor. A third group, that of the Kei, Tanimbar, and Aroë Islands, with the western coast of New Guinea, was of practically no importance for the Company. There the citizens of Banda were allowed to trade with their own ships, but they preferred to stay in better-known waters, out of reach of the dreaded cannibals of New Guinea.

On the Lesser Sunda Islands, European influence was weak. The large, thinly populated islands were a natural hiding place for pirates and adventurers. There was constant warfare among the local chieftains. A special disturbing element was formed by the "Black Portuguese" of Timor, a clan formed by a French deserter from the Company's service who, like a seventeenth-century Romulus among headhunters, had gathered around him a group of lawless elements and founded a "city." Under the constant threat from these Black Portuguese, the Dutch limited their activities to the southern point of the island where they had their fort "Concordia," a rather inappropriate name among the Timorese, while the real Portuguese, the servants of the king of Portugal, withdrew to the northern point, near the present town of Dilli. Life was primitive in this corner of the archipelago. James Cook relates how in 1770 he met a Dutch official on Timor who, except for some garments he wore and the color of his skin, did not differ in way of living and outward appearance from the Timorese

---

former soldiers, servants, and freedmen of the Company, who received the legal status of citizens. Consequently they were directly ruled by the Company and subject to Dutch laws. The Amboinese, except the inhabitants of the Company's fortresses, were technically allies of the Company and thus ruled according to their own native law.

around him. In 1756 Johan Paravicini, whom we mentioned as ambassador to Bandjermasin, visited Timor and concluded a series of treaties with the local chieftains upon which Dutch authority remained based in that area during the next century.[11]

The extreme northeastern and extreme southwestern corners of the island of Celebes presented two directly opposite aspects of western influence in the Indies. In 1679 Governor Robert Padtbrugge of the Moluccas visited Menado in the district of Minahassa in northern Celebes. The local chiefs of their own free will concluded an alliance with him, and this alliance has remained undisturbed until our day.[12] In the nineteenth century many Menadonese accepted Christianity, and the Minahassa became one of the most westernized parts of the Indies.

In the southwestern corner, discontent among the people of Gowa always threatened to lead to outbursts of violence. The once prosperous town of Macassar was rapidly falling into decay. Its roadstead, seventy years before the meeting place of Chinese, Danish, British, Portuguese, and Malay traders, was now deserted. The harsh orders of the Company had brought all trade and shipping to an end. The dying town was completely dominated by the fortress "Rotterdam" built by order of Admiral Speelman. To the east of Gowa lived the people of Boni, free allies of the Batavian government, but very troublesome allies and inveterate smugglers of spices. The services rendered by Aru Palacca I of Boni, who helped to conquer Macassar, Mataram, and the Menangkabau, had gained for his Buginese a greater freedom of action than many other Indonesian tribes enjoyed, but they certainly abused it.

Buginese pirate fleets swarmed all over the archipelago. They firmly established themselves near Samarinda in the sultanate of Kutei, on Borneo's east coast. They helped the sultans of Borneo's west coast to fight their internecine wars; they overran the sultanate of Johore and threatened the Dutch in their stronghold of Malacca. But they were not the only pirates on the Indonesian seas. There were also the men of Tobelo, a meeting place of freebooters on the northeast coast of Halmahera who raided as far south as Timor. The pirates from the "Papuan Islands," the islands off the coast of New Guinea, made all seas east of Java unsafe for native shipping. Worst of all were the Moros (also called "Illanos") of the Sulu Islands.[13] The Moros had

[11] W. van Hogendorp, "Beschrijving van Timor," VBG, I (1781), 273 sq. J. A. van der Chijs, "Koepang omstreeks 1750," TBG, XVIII (1868), 209.

[12] R. Padtbrugge, "Beschrijving der zeden en gewoonten van de bewoners van de Minahassa" (1679), BKI, XIII (1866), 304, and "Reis naar Noord Celebes" (1677), BKI, XIV (1867), 95.

[13] See article "Zeeroof" in ENI.

fleets of a hundred and more ships, some of them built like the old Roman galleys, with three decks of rowers, armed with several guns, and manned by a crew of a hundred and fifty men. These even dared to attack the heavily armed cruisers of the Company. At the end of the eighteenth century the Moros built a fortress on Sumatra's southern point, which put them in a position to prey on the shipping through Sunda Strait and from where they ransacked the coastal districts of Java, carrying off women and children into slavery.

There must have been a reason for this "outbreak" of piracy all over the seas of the archipelago. It would be easy if we could explain it as one of the evil consequences of the system of monopoly which forced the natives to seek other occupation once they were barred from normal trade and shipping. This explanation is insufficient, however. On the Sulu Islands, main centers of piracy, the Dutch East India Company exercised no influence at all. Moreover, it is hard to believe that the Indonesian seas had been safer in former times when the seapower of the princes of Java and the kings of Macassar still existed. These princes were not much interested in "policing" the seas. The true explanation seems to be that piracy had been rampant among the islands since early days, but that in the eighteenth century the European narrators began to see it as piracy, to distinguish the "pirate" from the "honest trader," while in the sixteenth and seventeenth centuries they had not made the same distinction.

When the Europeans first came to the Indies they had no notion whatsoever of the character of the peoples of the Far East. They did not know what those peoples were interested in, what their customs and their ways of living were. There is an unforgettable story of an Amsterdam Company which in the early days of trading in the Indies exported to Thailand a collection of thousands of Dutch engravings to be sold in the market place of Patani. Among the engravings were Madonnas (to be sold to Buddhists and Mohammedans by order of Calvinist merchants) and Biblical scenes; there were, for classically minded Siamese, prints recording the stories of Livy, and finally, prints with a more general human appeal, a collection of nudes and less decent illustrations.[14] This particular mistake was made only once. It is characteristic of the complete lack of knowledge of Asiatic affairs in the earliest days of the East Indian trade. The first Dutch traders did not understand the language and customs of the Indonesians and there-

[14] J. W. IJzerman, "Hollandsche prenten als handelsartikel te Patani in 1602," in *Gedenkboek van het Kon. Instituut* (The Hague, 1926), p. 84 sq.

fore mistrusted them. For them, as for Edmund Scott, they were "all thieves and villains."

In the eighteenth century Europeans began to understand. If the Dutch of that period did not yet possess an extensive knowledge of Indonesian customs and languages and if they still had not even an inkling of the underlying principles of Indonesian life, they had at least obtained a practical knowledge of Indonesian and especially Javanese affairs. More and more the records of the Batavian government begin to mention "experts on native affairs." In this connection we must mention once more the humanitarian ideas among Governor-General Camphuijs' friends. Johan van Hoorn, especially, took great interest in native affairs.[15] It is logical that, as soon as they began to distinguish between "good" and "bad" Indonesians, they began also to see a distinction between honest traders and pirates, thus applying to the Asiatics ideas that were wholly foreign to them and rather new to the Dutchmen themselves. Western Europe at that time had just begun to learn international law, and one of its points was a clear distinction between "legitimate naval war" and "piracy." There are a thousand examples to be taken from the history of the fifteenth and sixteenth century that prove that then this distinction was not clear in the minds of most seafarers of Europe.[16]

The Indonesian Mohammedans considered every act of violence committed against a non-Moslem a legal act of war. Still farther back, what else were the naval expeditions of the kings of Madjapahit and Shrivi-jaya but large-scale piratical enterprises? If the eighteenth-century Dutch had gone back two centuries in their own history, they would have understood how the Indonesians had no moral objection to attacking "infidels" and kidnapping the children of "heathens." [17] Poverty, religious fanaticism, economic necessities such as that of supplying the slave market, were the factors that, combined, caused the

[15] De Haan, *Priangan*, I, sect. 2, p. 8, compares the "Daghregister" (the Journal of the Batavian Government) of 1678 (which was written by van Hoorn) with those before and after that year and notes that the Register for 1678 gives abundant details on native affairs.

[16] We only mention the piratical excursions of Sir Francis Drake and the exploits of the Dunkirk privateers. On De Houtman's first voyage to the Indies, the crew asked permission to board a Portuguese vessel with a rich cargo, holding that it would be a much easier way of making profits than the far voyage to the Indies.

[17] In the first decades of Dutch shipping around Africa and South America, the captains and crews never had any scruples about kidnapping individuals of savage tribes to take them along to Holland. Of the slave trade on Africa's west coast, which never caused the Europeans pangs of conscience in the seventeenth century, we do not need to speak.

extension of piracy in the Indies. This explains at the same time why it was practically impossible to put an end to it. The Moros of the Philippines, subdued by the Spaniards in 1878, undertook a marauding expedition towards the Moluccas as late as the year 1920. Piracy was simply one of the aspects of social and economic life in the Indies and remained so during a large part of the nineteenth century.[18]

Nevertheless, the Batavian government could have taken far better care of safety on the seas than it did. It did not even provide an adequate protection of the coasts of Java against the slave hunters. This proves once more that the interests of the Company had become largely agricultural and territorial instead of commercial. The war with Britain of 1780–1784, of which we shall speak shortly, further accentuated this development. More and more the Company concentrated all its efforts on Java. Nowhere in the Indies was the influence of western domination so great as here.

We have already spoken about the social conditions in that part of the island that since the end of the seventeenth century had been directly governed from Batavia, the Batavian Lowlands and the Preanger districts. But the vassal states of Batavia, Bantam and Mataram, were also strongly affected by Dutch influence. Both states were disintegrating rapidly. The downfall of Bantam was undoubtedly caused by her disastrous war with the Company in 1684, but for that of Mataram the institutions of that state itself were to blame. In the middle of the eighteenth century the independence of both sultanates received a second heavy blow. The history of all the harem intrigues that prepared the way for renewed civil war and thus for further intervention by the Dutch is not very interesting nor very important. The struggle shows, however, some aspects characteristic of Javanese conditions of the time.

After the treaty of 1684, when all foreign merchants had been driven from her soil, Bantam had suffered terribly. The sultan, his "patih" or prime minister, and part of the nobility had lost their chief source of income, which had consisted in levying all kind of duties on the pepper trade of the European merchants. Compared to Mataram, Bantam was backward and her farmers and countryside poor, but the ruling class had compensated itself by handling the pepper crop and by a shrewd manipulation of the rivalry existing between the Europeans and the Chinese. The overlordship of the Dutch Company and the introduction of the monopoly of trade made an end to their profits. After 1684,

[18] Expedition of Moros in 1920: ENI, IV, 826. TBG gives during the nineteenth century a yearly report on piracy on the East Indian seas.

not even the nobility was permitted to make good profits from the pepper trade. The landowners lost interest in the production and began to prefer the cultivation of food crops. All this led to general discontent and to such political tension that a palace intrigue was sufficient to cause a general outburst, in which religious factors played an important part.

The sultans of Bantam had always been proud of their Moslem orthodoxy. Around 1750 the sultanate was practically ruled by the "Ratu Sjarifa," a daughter of an Arabian spiritual leader who claimed to be a descendant of the Prophet himself. The Ratu Sjarifa represented the Arabian influence which, from the seventeenth century on, was gradually increasing in the Indies and derived its prestige from the Holy City of Mecca, although most Arabian immigrants were merchants from Hadramaut. The revolution that in 1750 broke out in Bantam was, however, directed *against* the Ratu Sjarifa. She was hated for her vexatious demands on the people and, significantly, the rebellious farmers elected as their chief a "Kiai Tapa," a holy hermit who had lived in a sacred cave in the mountains and had for a long time been venerated by the people. This hermit reminds us more of the old Hindu Javanese days of King Hayam Wuruk than of Mohammed and the Koran, an opinion strengthened by the fact that this cave was found to contain many Hindu relics. An old tradition was here still living among the people, and to it they turned in their distress.[19]

The revolt of 1750 caused considerable damage in the Batavian Lowlands which were partially laid waste. After a few years of guerilla fighting the revolt was crushed, but the government of Batavia thought it wise to expel the Sjarifa from the sultanate and to install a new sultan on the throne. By these events the authority of the Company over West Java was strengthened, but conditions in that area did not change and remained bad for the native population.[20]

The other Javanese state, Mataram, retained only a shadow of its former power. In 1705 the Preanger districts, the port of Semarang, and the overlordship over Cheribon had been definitely ceded to the Company. These concessions had been made by Susuhunan Pakubuwana I, who had been elevated to the throne by order of Batavia. Troops of the Company had escorted him to his residence, had crushed the resistance of his opponents — among them the deposed Susuhunan

[19] P. J. Robidé van der Aa, "De groote Bantamsche opstand in het midden van de vorige eeuw," BKI, XXIX (1881), 1–127.

[20] J. De Rovere, "Bantam in 1786," BKI, V (1856), 107 sq. and "Bantam en de Lampongs in 1787," BKI, V, 309 sq.

Amangkurat III — and, finally, had broken the power of Surapati, the brave Balinese *condottiere* who so long had been the backbone of all opposition against the Company. Politically Mataram was still independent, but economically it was already a vassal state of the Company, for the treaty of 1705 had put it under the obligation of delivering at a set price any amount of rice the Company might demand.

After the conclusion of this treaty the Batavian government did its utmost to preserve peace in the sultanate, but it proved to be impossible. Pakubuwana I, his son and successor Amangkurat IV, and his grandson Pakubuwana II, all were continuously struggling against rebellious vassals and members of their own families. The Madurese princes always backed the rebels. The Balinese chieftains took full advantage of the confusion to plunder and devastate the utmost eastern districts of the island. Evidently the Pakubuwana dynasty was hated among the Javanese because of its close alliance with the Dutch. But when in 1740, at the time of the Chinese massacre, Pakubuwana II changed his attitude, proclaimed the Holy War against the Infidels, and ordered the massacre of the Dutch garrison in his capital, he was unpleasantly surprised to see his enemies change sides too and join the Dutch! With the help of the Madurese the Dutch reinstated their garrison in the capital, which was now moved from Kartasura to Surakarta, a few miles from the old site.

The real cause of the disintegration of the empire of Mataram was its inner weakness, not the pressure from the outside. The once powerful sultanate of Atjeh was falling apart in exactly the same way, although there were no foreigners established on its coast. It has always been the common thesis of the historians of a former period that Dutch authority on Java was established by sowing dissension among the native princes, but Batavia could hardly sow more dissension among these princes than existed already because of their mutual rivalry and hatred. After 1705 it definitely was the aim of the Batavian policy to keep Mataram intact. Civil strife and aggression by Madurese and Balinese chieftains could only endanger the profits the Company might otherwise eventually obtain from that country. The endless internecine wars of the princes might even train the peace-loving Javanese peasants to become hardened warriors, a change of affairs which certainly would not be to the advantage of the Dutch.[21]

[21] Raffles, Crawfurd, and other authors of the beginning of the nineteenth century severely criticized the Dutch for their Machiavellian policy, and the accusation has often been repeated (e.g., Day, *op. cit.*, p. 48 and even R. Kennedy, in his excellent book *The Ageless Indies*, New York, 1942, p. 39). In the days of Coen the Company indeed strove to keep Mataram and Bantam separated but in the whole period of the seventeenth and

The treaty of 1743 gave to the Company all coastal districts along Java's north coast, and, in addition to that, the "Eastern Corner," the territory of the former kingdom of Balambangan, and the exclusive control of all seaports of Java. After 1743 Mataram was officially a vassal state of the Company. Shortly before his death, the ruling susuhunan, Pakubuwana II, desiring to secure his empire for his son, ceded all his lands to the Company, which handed them over to the new ruler, Pakubuwana III.[22] The brother of the deceased sultan, Mangkubumi, refused to accept this agreement. For years this prince had been quarreling with his brother about his share in the income from the sultanate. Now definitely ousted from possessions, he "went to the mountains," i.e., gathered his followers around him and started guerilla warfare against the susuhunan. His nephew Mangkunegara, the son of another brother of Pakubuwana II, joined him. Both princes showed such ability in this type of warfare that the combined forces of the Company and the susuhunan were unable to subdue them. The Batavian government grew tired of the endless and costly campaigns on behalf of a susuhunan who was not strong enough to defend his own rights. That prince, on the other hand, knew that he was fully dependent upon the support of the Company. These were the reasons why the three powers concerned finally agreed upon a treaty of reconciliation, concluded on February 13, 1755, at Surakarta.[23] The empire of Mataram was split into two states, that of Surakarta, the ruler of which was to bear the title of Susuhunan Pakubuwana, and that of Djocjakarta, ruled by a Sultan Amengkubuwana. Both states still exist.[24] After

eighteenth centuries not a single war was fought between those two states. Batavia never tried to stir up wars between these or other states. We saw that the Directors acknowledged the overlordship of Mataram over Batavia rather than run the risk of a new conflict.

But Raffles' remark (more will be said about his *History* later) was far from original. In Abbé Raynal's *Histoire philosophique et politique des établissements et du commerce des Européens dans les deux Indes*, one of the most widely read books of Raffles' age, we read (I, 273 of the edition of The Hague, 1774): "[The Dutch] armed the father against the son and the son against the father. The claims of the weak against the strong, and of the strong against the weak, were supported according to circumstances. One day they sided with the monarch, the next with the vassals," etc.—a passage which reminds us too much of certain quotations from the classics to be taken as a piece of original historiography.

On the fear of Batavia that civil war might train the Javanese to become accomplished soldiers, see the Report on the secret deliberations of the Council of the Indies of May 20, 1754, in De Jonge, *op. cit.*, x, 276.

[22] Documents: De Jonge, *op. cit.*, x, 156 sq.

[23] Texts of treaties: De Jonge, x, 298 sq. To understand the system followed by the division of the empire of Mataram the study of G. P. Rouffaer, *De Vorstenlanden*, should be consulted.

[24] The susuhunans from now on accepted the title "Pakubuwana"—"Axis of the

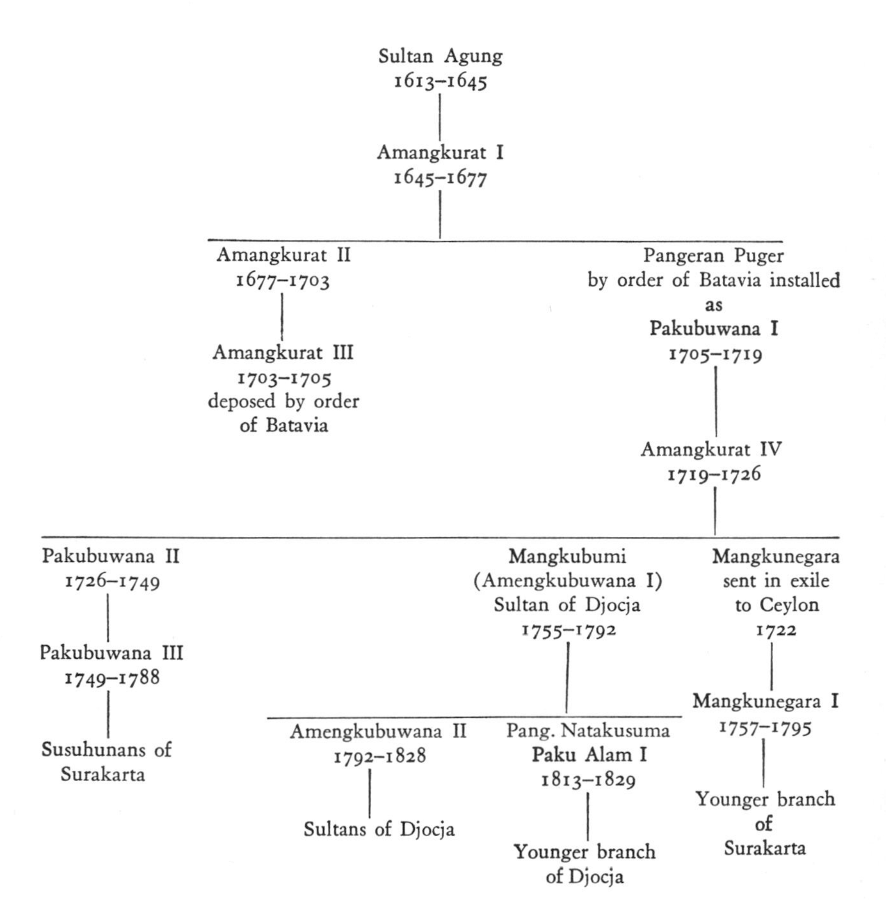

RELATIONSHIP OF THE PRINCES OF SURAKARTA AND DJOCJAKARTA

this settlement the susuhunan was obliged to seek also an agreement with the turbulent and dangerous Mangkunegara, to whom he was forced to cede another section of his state.[25]

After 1755 the Dutch East India Company was the greatest territorial power in Java. The majority of its three and a half million inhabitants were now directly governed from Batavia.[26] The five small native states, Bantam, Cheribon, Djocjakarta, Surakarta, and the Mangkunara Lands, were its vassals, and Dutch residents at the courts of their princes exerted a certain amount of control over their administration. Wars among the princes were forbidden. The Company assumed the protection of East Java against the rapacious Balinese and succeeded in driving the invaders out of its territory, a task which was not completed before 1774. Thus Java was permitted to enjoy a period of relative peace, certainly a great benefit to the poor people, but a benefit bought at a high price, namely, their submission to the administration of the Company and its system of economic exploitation. Admiral Speelman used to speak of the Company's "just and benevolent rule," but its government certainly charged its subjects with heavy burdens.

Nowhere did the advantages of the new situation further exceed the disadvantages than in the "Eastern Corner." After the expulsion of the Balinese plunderers the territory was left nearly empty. Even the valley of the Upper Brantas river, where five centuries before the kingdom of Singhasari had flourished, was reduced to a state of wilderness. A decade after the Dutch occupation this same valley, now the regency of Malang, had become a prosperous coffee-producing district. A stream of immigrants from East Java and Madura came in and overwhelmed the sparse original population. This immigration finally secured this far-away corner of the island for Islam. For centuries Hinduists had maintained themselves in this territory, which in the sixteenth century formed the kingdom of Balambangan. In our days, only the mountain people inhabiting the Tengger massif have retained in a rude and primitive form the original religious conceptions.[27]

The effects of the new political situation in Java were nowhere

---

world." The sultans call themselves "Amengkubuwana" — "He who controls the world." The younger branch of Surakarta holds the title "Mangkunegara" — "He who bears the empire." "Paku Alam" has the same meaning as "Pakubuwana."

[25] By the treaty of Salatiga, March 17, 1754. The Mangkunegara remained under the overlordship of the susuhunan.

[26] For population figures: De Jonge, *op. cit.*, XI, lxxvii. Here the following figures are given: Batavia and Lowlands around 1780, 175,000, Preanger, 60,000, Northeast Coast Government, 1,435,000, Principalities of Mataram, 1,500,000, total, including Bantam and Madura, 3,450,000.

[27] For details on the Tenggerese, see article of G. P. Rouffaer in ENI.

worse than in the small sultanate of Cheribon. Three sultans jointly ruled this principality but actually the whole administration was carried on by the Resident of the Company. The people of Cheribon were subject to compulsory labor service for the Company and were obliged to cultivate coffee and indigo. In addition to this their sultans, feeling secure in their position because of the support of Batavia, thoroughly abused their authority. In order to increase their income they farmed whole villages out to Chinese financiers. These shrewd business men knew how to squeeze every penny out of the poor villagers, but they aroused an immense hatred among the native population. In 1768 discontent had grown so strong that the people begged the government of Batavia to depose the sultans and to establish direct Dutch rule over their territory. They believed that this would protect them from exhortions by the Chinese, for they knew that Batavia did not permit the Chinese even to enter the directly ruled Preanger Districts.[28] The government refused the request, and from that time one revolt in Cheribon followed another. Even after all the Chinese had been expelled from the sultanate, disorders continued.

In the regencies of the north coast, from Tegal to Surabaya, the hard-working and unscrupulous Chinese tried to play the same role as in Cheribon, but the officials of the Company at Semarang and Surabaya kept them under stricter control than Cheribon's sultans did. Nevertheless, here too we find them as farmers of rice fields (which included the labor of the people living near these fields), as farmers of tolls on the highways, and as moneylenders in the villages. These north-eastern regencies were burdened with heavy taxes in the form of contingents and forced deliveries, burdens as heavy as the districts could possibly carry, to use the words of some of the Company's representatives.[29]

In organizing the administration of these territories the Batavian government had to face numerous problems. One of these problems

[28] Here we have one of the instances, unfortunately rare, in which the Company took drastic measures for the protection of the native population. No foreigners, whether Europeans, Mardijkers, foreign Indonesians, or Chinese, were allowed to enter the Preanger districts without written permission of the Government "because the wandering foreign elements cause great inconvenience and damage to the native people." (Resolution of the Council of the Indies of 1696, *Priangan*, III, 437.)

[29] For conditions in northeast Java, see the "Memories van Overgave" van Hartingh, Ossenberch, and others in De Jonge, *op. cit.*, X, XI, and XII. Each governor or resident of the Company wrote (or was supposed to write) a memorandum on the conditions prevailing in his district at the conclusion of his period of office. These "memoirs of transfer" served for the information of his successor. The quotation is from the memorandum of J. R. van den Burgh, 19 September 1780 (De Jonge, *op. cit.*, XI, 440). An identical remark in the "Short Report" of Nic. Hartingh of Nov. 1, 1756 (De Jonge, *op. cit.*, X, 304).

concerned the monetary system. The sultans of Bantam and Mataram used to exert the right of coinage. The Company did the same and imported silver coins from Holland. There was, however, a permanent shortage of coins and coinage materials in the Indies. All gold that was imported immediately disappeared into the treasure chests of the princes. The silver was reëxported, mostly by the Chinese. The situation became really confusing when, besides the Dutch coins and those of Mataram and Bantam, those of Madura and Cheribon and the small lead coins of Palembang and Bali also began to circulate. In 1764 the Batavian government concluded negotiations with the princes of Surakarta and Djocjakarta for a unification of the monetary system, and from that time the Company issued copper coins printed in Batavia. This measure undoubtedly facilitated the conclusion of commercial transactions in Java and was of benefit to the people until the government, forced by circumstances, started on a policy of inflation.[30]

The framework for the administration was provided by the division of the whole territory into regencies. In some districts the ruling families were continued in office and in others the government appointed new officials. Backward districts which began to attract immigrants sometimes were entrusted to Chinese control until they were sufficiently organized to be handed over to the less efficient but also less severe leadership of a native regent.[31] The most difficult problem was that of the administration of justice. Originally Dutch law had been followed in the Company's settlements. The Statutes of Batavia stated that in all cases for which Batavian law did not provide, Dutch customary law, and if this too proved insufficient, Roman law must be followed. We have seen that this rule has always been applied with moderation. Chinese customs regarding probate law had, from the beginning, been respected. These customs, however, although usually *respected*, were not recognized as *law*. In 1708 Governor-General van Hoorn issued two very important decrees. The first instituted a decentralizing of the judiciary by granting the local courts outside Batavia jurisdiction in all affairs in the name of the governor-general and the Council of the Indies. The second one ordered that all criminal and civil affairs in the Preanger districts should be decided by the regents and their courts, who would render justice according to the native laws. The only task of the Dutch officials would be to see to it that justice was rendered impartially and the local laws and customs faith-

[30] See De Jonge, *op. cit.*, XI, lxxix; E. B. Netscher en J. van der Chijs, *De Munten van Nederlandsch Indië* (Batavia, 1863).

[31] An example: memorandum van den Burgh, 1780, De Jonge, *op. cit.*, XI, 421.

fully observed.[32] This decree is historically of the greatest importance, even if in the eighteenth century it was never followed to the letter. In the Preanger there were continuous conflicts of jurisdiction between the Batavian and the regency courts but the principle had been stated that native law would not be superseded by western law.

To the eighteenth-century Batavian rulers it was not very clear, however, what the real contents of native law were. One of the Residents of Cheribon noticed that a zealously Mohammedan sultan before rendering his decision in capital affairs usually asked the advice of the priests, but that a less zealous prince preferred that of "old women." The most capable of the Residents of Cheribon, Jan Frederik Gobius, wrote in 1717: "I always made the judges of Cheribon follow the customs of pre-Mohammedan times and opposed the interference of the priests." These men clearly saw the difference between the Indonesian "adat" (the old native customary law) and the law of the Koran, and deliberately encouraged the former.[33] This was the beginning of the studying of Indonesian law by Dutch scholars which has contributed so much to the preservation of the original character of native society in the Indies.[34]

Thus, the Company's rule over the northern section of Java presented some advantages for the mass of the people, but much depended upon the character of the functionary in office. If he was a rapacious and unscrupulous individual he could make life very hard for the poor people and even for the regents. In this case the Javanese undoubtedly preferred the rule of their native princes above that of the Dutch, especially if the Company gave too much rope to the Chinese tax farmers. "Apparently," wrote Nicolas Hartingh in 1756, "the Javanese prefer being skinned by their own people to being vexed by foreigners."[35] It would be incorrect, however, to conclude from this statement that

[32] The ordinances of 1708 are published in brief form in van der Chijs, *Plakaatboek*, III, 615–617. See the chapter on the Judiciary in De Haan's *Priangan*, I, 405 sq. and IV, 613 sq.

[33] On the studying of native law: C. van Vollenhoven, *De ontdekking van het adatrecht* (Leyden, 1928), also in French translation *Le découverte du droit Indonesien* (Paris, 1933). On J. F. Gobius: *Niew Nederlandsch Biographisch Woordenboek*, 10 vols. (Leiden, 1910), where there are many details, most of them taken from De Haan's *Priangan*, have been put together. Gobius' discussion of native and Mohammedan law has been published by De Haan (*Priangan*, IV, 645–650).

[34] The Batavian Government published a few compendia of Javanese law (that of Cheribon in 1768, of East Java in 1761) but these contained practically only Mohammedan law. These compendia were composed for the convenience of the Dutch courts which were permitted but not obliged to follow the rules of these laws.

[35] Memorandum of Nic. Hartingh, De Jonge, *op. cit.*, X, 313.

the situation of the poor peasants in the Javanese sultanates was much better than that of those in the Dutch territories.

The Javanese chronicles of the second half of the eighteenth century throw a vivid light on conditions existing in these principalities. Of the people they hardly speak. The princes, the "ratus" and "selirs" (the official and the unofficial wives of the princes), their sons and daughters, the patihs and sometimes the priests, are all the chroniclers are concerned with.[36] Decidedly the people exist solely for the princes in the opinion of these chroniclers. Peace, the greatest benefit Dutch rule brought to the people, did not mean anything to the princes. From every page of the chronicles it is clear that peace between the two royal houses was maintained only because of the all-powerful control of Batavia. Sometimes the plundering and burning of villages had already started when the Dutch government abruptly put an end to the game. The first Mangkunegara caused most trouble of all. He showed clearly enough that he was not particularly afraid of Dutch military power and that he would gladly have risked a war if he had not known so well that his uncle, the sultan of Djocja, would have enjoyed the chance to settle some old accounts with his former ally and would have hurried to the assistance of Batavia. In a short time the Dutch officials learned all the tricks of Javanese intrigues and diplomacy. The governor at Semarang even had to settle marriage affairs and to pronounce divorces — a new role for this gentleman, whose real function was that of tax collector and chief merchant for the Company!

We would be glad if our chroniclers, although they do not contain any information about the conditions existing among the mass of the people, would at least inform us about the relations of the Javanese aristocracy with the Europeans and about Javanese opinions on the Netherlanders, but in this respect also our sources are very disappointing. It was not fear that made the authors keep silent on the subject. Their histories were destined for the use of the native princes, and at that time it seemed highly improbable that they would ever come under the eyes of any Hollander, let alone of a Hollander who could read

[36] C. Poensen, BKI, LII (1901), 223 sq. and LVIII (1905), 73 sq., published an abbreviated Dutch version of one of the principal chronicles of Djocja under the titles: *Mangkubumi, Ngayogjakarta's eerste sultan* and *Amangku Buwono II, Ngayogjakarta's tweede sultan.* The chronicle is, however, mainly the story of Natakusuma, younger son of Mangkubumi and founder of the principality of Paku Alam. The whole narrative tends to convey the impression that Natakusuma was the true continuator of the tradition founded by the first sultan of Djocja. From this chronicle most of the details mentioned in the text have been taken.

them. A few stories from the chronicles, however, seem to prove that the Javanese had gone through the same experience as the Dutch, that in the beginning of their association they had not understood anything of Dutch ways of thinking, but that slowly they began to distinguish between "good" and "bad" Europeans, just as the Dutch had learned the difference between "honest" and "treacherous" Indonesians.

Moreover, the Javanese princes felt no need whatsoever for formulating their political opinions in a "program" as we are accustomed to do. Probably they thought it imprudent and foolish to put down such maxims and opinions in writing, but their acts show their mind. The Javanese historian considered it completely superfluous to tell his readers about the "secret motives" of the principal political figures of his narrative. He narrates the acts and the words of the princes and leaves it to the intelligence of the reader to draw the conclusion. Thus the chronicler of Djocjakarta tells us how the first sultan when promoted to the throne had agreed in his treaty with Batavia to provide for the construction of a Dutch fortress in his capital. Twenty-eight years later the walls of the fortress were still unfinished. The sultan kept his stonemasons and his carpenters busy on the construction of palaces and gardenhouses, of waterworks and embellishments of his own residence, and as soon as they had completed something he declared himself much disappointed with the result and ordered it torn down! Immediately the men were set to work on another project. It certainly needed a good deal of stubbornness to keep this game going for twenty-eight years.

Small details sometimes show the prevailing sentiments. A high Dutch official came to the court of Djocja and brought with him a tiger — according to the story, a gigantic specimen with long white hair. He thought to do the sultan a favor by presenting him with this beast, which in every fight with a buffalo had been victorious. To organize such fights was a favorite pastime of Javanese princes. The Hollander noticed immediately that his present caused an unusual excitement at court. In feverish haste an enclosed space was prepared for a fight and the whole court came to see it. This time the buffalo won, and again an unusual display of joy followed. After the combat the Dutch representative found the sultan in the best of moods and could obtain from him whatever he wanted. A note in Raffles' history of Java explains the whole story. He tells us that the Javanese used to compare the tiger in these combats to the Dutch and the buffalo to the Javanese. A Netherlander in possession of an unconquerable tiger was, therefore, the worst possible omen for the future of the Javanese princes, but that this particular tiger was killed by a buffalo of the sultan held great promise!

The Javanese rulers were clever diplomats and shrewd politicians but they often had a hard time understanding the real intentions of the Europeans. We hear of a Javanese prince who had been exiled to Ceylon and who on his return to Java was considered a great expert on dealing with Europeans. He tried to explain to his countrymen the characteristic differences between the Dutch and the British, and his opinion is remarkable enough to transcribe, especially if we bear in mind that it was given around 1780. "The British," he said, "are like the strong rapid current of water, they are persevering, energetic, and irresistible in their courage. If they really want to obtain something they will use violence to get it. The Dutch are very able, clever, patient, and calm. If possible they try to reach their goal rather by persuasion than by force of arms. It may well happen," he concluded, "that Java will be conquered by the British." Thirty years later it happened indeed.

If the chronicles do not give much information on the social conditions and the exact political sentiments, they throw a good deal of light on the religious situation in eighteenth-century Java. They bring out that Hindu beliefs and Hindu traditions were still strong among the people and the aristocracy. Many details which they relate could also have been related of Hayam Wuruk of Madjapahit. Princes and people were equally dominated by the belief in knowledge of secret forces, or magic power as we call it. One of the chroniclers writes that he prefers to pass over in silence certain unpleasant events of the past because he fears to evoke the evil forces that brought them about and that seem to have lost their power. The omnipresence of the souls of the ancestors is recalled on every page. The chronicle itself is written to recall the power and glory of the ancestors and to strengthen its readers through their strength. Mangkubumi himself had passages from the chronicles read to him every day and sought guidance from their contents. Like the Pararaton, these histories tell us of magic spears and swords. Princes derive magic strength from staying days and nights among the graves of the ancestors. One of the most curious, because directly connected with the old Hindu times, is the following story. A crown prince of Djocja insisted upon breaking the old tradition that forbade visiting a haunted place, the "hill of the thousand statues," no other than the famous Borobudur. The tradition held that ill luck would come to him who went up the hill to see a demon locked up in a cage (the Dhyanibuddhas on top!). The prince saw the demon in the cage, but the evil consequences became immediately apparent for he lost all self-control and became a debauchee and the sultan considered it wise and just to have him poisoned to prevent further evils.

Around 1788 the susuhunan fell completely under the influence of certain priests at his court. Later reports have connected the activity of these men with the spreading of new Mohammedan sects, that of the Wahabites for instance, and have explained by their "heretical" character the opposition they encountered from the official Moslem priesthood. It seems more likely that this priesthood saw in the favored priests of the susuhunan heretics of a different type, namely men who mixed Islam with the superstitions of the old Javanese beliefs. Certainly they promised the susuhunan to make him sole master of the island, and they persuaded him that at their magic words the power of Djocjakarta would crumble and that the guns of the Dutch fortress near the "kraton" would melt away and be reduced to nothing. They made their prince believe that they could fly through the air and move under ground at will. It is typical that when the officers of the Company put an end to the incipient revolt and the magicians of the susuhunan were arrested without offering any resistance, the chroniclers explain it by pointing out that Captain Ritman, the commander of the Dutch forces, possessed still greater magic strength than his opponents, that he controlled the forces of nature so well that he made the cannon balls fall apart in the air before they could touch him.

The courts of Djocja and Surakarta were not the right places for arts and sciences to flourish. Islam had brought the Hindu tradition of sculpture to an abrupt end. Architecture, too, had decayed since the downfall of Madjapahit. The civil strife that kept raging among the aristocracy of Java left little opportunity and few resources for the undertaking of monumental works. Later, the Company kept the Javanese workers busy with the production of foodstuffs and export crops which left the princes little opportunity to draft laborers for their own enterprises. Only handicrafts still flourished. The literary traditions of the Hindu period were weakly continued. Islamic learning, with its works on Mohammedan law and theology written in Arabic, competed with native traditions. Historiography was practically the only field where genuine Javanese conceptions were continued.

The picture of eighteenth-century Indonesia would not be complete without a few words about one of the worst of the evil consequences of foreign infiltration into the island world, namely the importation and consumption of opium. The habit of smoking opium existed in parts of the Indies before the first Europeans arrived and probably was imported from Bengal. At that time consumption was probably limited to the population of the principal ports of international trade. During the seventeenth century it spread, especially over Sumatra, Java, and the Moluccas. Sultan Agung of Bantam strictly forbade the import and use of opium in his territory, and after the downfall of the sultanate the Company maintained this prohibition. In Mataram, however, the Company secured the monopoly of the opium trade, and imports of this nefarious drug rose to a hundred thousand pounds a year. In the Preanger districts the Batavian officials sometimes paid the regents partly in cash and partly in opium, but the population apparently did not take to opium smoking, and the imports fell during the whole eighteenth century. On the island of Amboina the import was strictly forbidden by the Company at the urgent request of a number of Amboinese chieftains. The Company certainly had no scruples whatsoever against selling opium to the people, but, on the other hand, it did not try to encourage the consumption, except in a few cases, and even then changed its attitude when the native chiefs protested. It is true that not humanitarian but mainly commercial reasons prompted Batavia to take this attitude. The Company could hardly expect to make great profits from a trade in which the monopoly could so easily be evaded as was the case with the import of opium, where a few hundred pounds constituted a considerable value. Another point of consideration was the vigorous opposition of all leaders of the Indonesian peoples, princes and priesthood, against the consumption of opium. "You know how much money is spent in these parts on opium," wrote Nicolas Hartingh in 1756, "but now sales begin to diminish, mostly because the princes object to it and the common people follow their chiefs." [37]

When the eighteenth century drew to a close, the foundations for a Netherlands administration of the Indies had been laid. A reorganization of the economic and political system of the East India Company was long overdue. Since 1675 the subject had been discussed, but in 1775 still nothing had been accomplished. Then the foundations upon which the Company was built crumbled. New trends of thought undermined the seventeenth-century beliefs in the unquestionable right of the European Christian to exploit pagan nations. Finally, the Netherlands Republic itself, from which the Company derived all its authority, was overrun by foreign powers and made into a vassal state of France, with less freedom of action than was left by Batavia to the princes of Mataram. This is the period of transition in the history of the East Indies, in which upon the old foundations a new political construction was built.

[37] J. C. Baud, "Proeve van een geschiedenis van den handel en het verbruik van opium in Nederlandsch Indië," BKI, I (1853), 73 sq.; and De Haan, *Priangan*, IV, 14 sq. Quotation, De Jonge, *op. cit.*, X, 313.

CHAPTER XI

HERMAN WILLEM DAENDELS, A BATAVIAN NAPOLEON

IN THE SEVENTEENTH CENTURY Batavia was an isolated fortress situated amidst dense jungles and surrounded by hostile peoples, but during the same period it was a center of great naval and economic power. In the eighteenth century the jungles around the city had been changed into rice fields and sugar plantations, and the hostile neighbors had been subdued, but Batavia's power was rapidly declining. The city itself changed when the humanitarianism of men like Camphuijs and Van Hoorn for a while at least mitigated the harshness of Batavian life and rule. Great progress was made indeed between the days of Jan Pieterszoon Coen, who called the Asiatic princes "poor, ignorant fools," and those of Pieter van Hoorn, who wrote a didactic poem on the wisdom of Confucius. Unfortunately the liberal ideas of Camphuijs and his friends found few followers in the next fifty years.

The list of books and pamphlets published in Batavia provides us with a fairly adequate index of Batavian intellectual life.[1] It is true that the government had complete control over the press, for not only were manuscripts censored before publication but the printing machinery itself was the property of the Company and installed within the walls of the castle. The government, however, was mainly concerned with maintaining the commercial "secrets" of the Company. Books describing trade facilities and places and methods of production which might give information to competitors were strictly forbidden. Intellectual life, as far as it existed at all, was as free in Batavia as it was in the Netherlands.[2]

The bibliography of Batavian publication enumerates an endless series of government ordinances and regulations, a number of religious books in Portuguese and Malay,[3] occasional reprints of the commonly used

[1] A bibliography of East Indian books: J. van der Chijs, "Proeve eener Nederlandsch Indische Bibliographie, 1659–1870," VBG, vol. XXXVII (Batavia, 1875), with continuation published in 1879.

[2] Books of "offensive and libelous character" that had been imported were sometimes burned by order of the government. "Offensive and libelous" in this case meant: "injurious to the interests of the Company or to the reputation of its high officials." Van der Chijs, *op. cit.*, under the year 1766.

[3] First edition of a Malay Bible printed in Arabic script, 1756.

Dutch-Malay dictionaries and grammars, and finally, from 1731 on, a yearly almanac with names and titles of the East Indian officials. The monotony of regulations and reprints is occasionally broken by more interesting items, such as, in 1671, Steendam's didactic poem for the youth of Batavia and Pieter van Hoorn's poetic discussion of Confucianism. Two historic works appear on the list: in 1695 a story of the siege of Batavia in 1628, one of Camphuijs' contributions to Batavian arts and letters, and in 1758 a "Short History of the Empire of the Moguls." The first of the two inspired a later Batavian poet, Pieter de Vries, to write a play "embellished with songs, dances and tableaux" and entitled "Jan Pieterszoon Coen, Founder of the Batavian Liberty, a play of war with a joyful ending." In the words "Founder of the Batavian Liberty" (a rather inappropriate title for the grim ruler of 1620) we may imagine we hear a new tone, a faint echo of what was heard in Europe in the same days.

We pass in silence over Batavia's first newspaper, the *Nouvelles* of 1744, as well as an isolated attempt at the promotion of classic learning in the tropics, an edition of *P. Ovidii Nasonis Tristium Libri V* of 1748. Both publications were the outcome of Governor-General van Imhoff's restless activity. The first was suppressed by order of the Directors, the second was too premature to be followed by similar attempts. After 1770 the products of the Batavian rhyming industry began to roll from the government press. Batavia contributed its share to the output of the literary dilettantism of the second half of the eighteenth century. Shortly it would have its dilettante philosophers and moralists, true to the fashion of the age. Willem van Hogendorp, a member of the ruling oligarchic class in the Netherlands who had come to the Indies to restore his fortune, wrote several plays with such interesting titles as "Sophonisba, or happiness of a mother because of the inoculation of her daughters" and "Kraspoekol, or the sad consequences of extreme severity towards the slaves."

New trends of thought had found their way to Batavia and from these new ideas sprang two organizations, the first Lodge of Freemasonry and the Batavian Society of Arts and Sciences.[4] Both societies were founded by one person, Johan C. Radermacher, and both originated in one sphere of ideas, the humanitarianism of the late eighteenth century. Radermacher was the son of a high official at the court of the

[4] On early freemasonry in Batavia, see H. Maarschalk, *Geschiedenis van de Orde der Vrijmetselaren in Nederland, onderhoorige Kolonien en Landen* (Breda, 1872), and J. Hagemann, *Geschiedenis der Vrijmetselarij in de Oostelijke en Zuidelijke deelen des Aardbols* (Surabaya, 1866).

Stadhouder and had gone to the Indies when he was sixteen years old. He rose rapidly — the connections of his family had something to do with it — and at the age of twenty-one he returned to Holland with the rank of chief merchant, one of the higher positions in the service of the Company. In Holland he joined the Society of Arts and Sciences of Haarlem, which became the model for the similar institution in Batavia. After a few years of residence in the home country he returned to Batavia. Here he founded in 1778 the Batavian Society, the first of its kind to be established in a colony in the tropics.[5] The new institution did not aim at the promotion of the arts and sciences for their own sake but to make them serve public utility. The oldest reports published by the Society deal with such problems as sanitary reforms in Batavia, street lights, improvements of roads, the condition of the ports, etc. Although the charter of the Society indicated that "reports on natural history and the antiquities and customs of the Indonesian peoples would be accepted with pleasure," these subjects of study originally took only a secondary place. But even so the mentioning of the history and customs of the native population as a subject of scientific interest was in itself a novelty of great significance. The ruling governor-general, Reinier de Klerk, took great interest in the new foundation and tried to give impetus to the affair by sending a circular letter to all his subordinates advising them to join the Society.

The first Lodge of Freemasons, named "La Choisie," did not last long and was rapidly followed by two others: "La Fidélité Sincère," and "La Vertueuse."[6] We do not know, of course, how seriously the doctrines of Freemasonry were taken by the members of these lodges. The bored Batavians must have thoroughly enjoyed this occasion to bring some diversion into their usually monotonous lives. The fact that the names of the lodges were French is not surprising. During the seventeenth century a number of Frenchmen must have lived in Batavia, for we know that up to 1721 French sermons were regularly delivered in the Batavian churches. After 1721 the custom had been dropped, to be taken up again in 1779 at the request of "many prominent people."[7] Evidently the Batavians shared the then prevailing

[5] P. Bleeker, "Geschiedenis van het Bataviaasch Genootschap," VBG, vol. xxv (Batavia, 1853). Radermacher when leaving for Holland donated a house to the Society and presented to his favored institution a number of objects of interest for natural history, thus laying the foundation for the now famous museum of the Batavian Society. Radermacher with his whole family was killed by Chinese mutineers aboard the ship that was to take him to Holland.

[6] The first Lodge was founded in 1764 and subsisted until 1767. The second and third were founded in 1767 and 1769 and in 1823 amalgamated.

[7] De Haan, *Oud Batavia*, p. 613.

Dutch predilection for the French language and French literature. We know beyond doubt that among the Dutch in the Indies French was better known than English.[8] We may safely conclude that the principal theories of the eighteenth-century French philosophers were well known in Batavia. It remained to be seen how the Batavians were going to respond to the new doctrine of liberty and equality.[9]

The year 1780 brought other affairs to worry about than the problems of philosophy. The Netherlands became involved in the Franco-British-American war. The Stadhouder, Prince William V of Orange, had clung as long as possible to his traditional policy of alliance with Britain, but finally his adherents were out-voted in the State Assemblies by the joint efforts of his oligarchic and his democratic opponents. The democratic wing of the opposition was represented by the "patriots," a movement which sought a reorganization of the Dutch Republic in which the new political ideals would be combined with old Dutch traditions. These "patriots" strove to break down the power of the ruling oligarchy as well as that of the Stadhouder. A downfall of the oligarchy would have involved the East India Company, the Directors of which belonged to the same class. In this the democrats did not succeed, and for the time being the whole attention of all anti-Orangists was demanded for the war with Britain.

The Indies were without an adequate defense against possible British attacks, but only the Company's possessions in India proper suffered from enemy action. Worse was that the British succeeded in blockading so effectively the Dutch ports that all direct communications between the Indies and Holland were cut off. Enormous quantities of tropical products were piled up in the storehouses of Batavia. While these products represented a value of many millions, the Batavian government was in dire need of money. The usual supplies of silver and copper coins from Holland did not arrive, and Batavia was not allowed to sell its products in the open market to procure for itself the necessary amount of cash. Paper money had to be issued. The Directors remained deaf to all pleas from Batavia and insisted upon strict observance of the monopoly which excluded all foreign traders from the Indian ports. By this attitude they dealt a death blow to their own Company. In Holland it could no longer meet its debts and came to the verge of

[8] In the Moluccas negotiations for the surrender of the colonies to the British in the years after 1796 were carried on in French. Dutch officers often could not even read an English letter.

[9] The influence of American events and ideas on the Dutch democratic movement in the last quarter of the eighteenth century was negligible if compared to the French influence. See F. van Wijk, *De Republiek en Amerika* (Leiden, 1921).

bankruptcy. In the Indies it lost its credit. After the war the affairs of the Company were in such a state of confusion that it never recovered.[10]

The peace treaty of Paris of 1784[11] broke the monopoly of Dutch shipping on the East Indian seas. The treaty opened all seas of the archipelago, even the jealousy guarded approaches to the Moluccas, to British shipping. The smuggling of tin and spices now became an easy matter. The British left no doubt about their intentions when in 1788 they occupied the small island of Penang off Kedah on the Malay Peninsula and when, a few years later, they began to explore the coast of New Guinea to find a suitable place for a settlement.[12] Hurriedly the Directors ordered the factual occupation of all ports and coastlands between Celebes and New Guinea, but Batavia with its meagre resources could not think of executing the order.

The British were not the only ones whose competition was feared. The first Dutch Minister to the United States, Pieter van Berckel, soon after his arrival in New York reported that American shipowners were equipping ships for the trade with the East Indies. It is true that this term included the whole of South and East Asia and that most of the American ships were bound for Bombay or Canton, but some scheduled their trips so that they could call at Batavia before proceeding to China. In 1786 the ship *Hope*, equipped by a Mr. Sears of New York, visited Batavia, where parts of its cargo, especially tar, ropes, and other sailing equipment, were sold at great profit. Then for the first time in history the vision rose of direct connections between the countries around the Pacific and a reorientation of the East Indies towards America, a vision which did not seem very alluring to the Directors in Amsterdam and which, if it were realized, they considered catastrophic to the interests of Europe.[13]

[10] For the financial situation of the East India Company at the time of its downfall, see Mansvelt, *Rechtsvorm*, etc., pp. 99–111. Historians have discussed the problem of why the English East I. C. could continue until 1858 while the Dutch Company succumbed in 1799. The chief reason is that the whole structure of the old Dutch Republic, upon which after all the Company was based, collapsed in the period of the Revolution. Nineteenth-century Dutch historians — the sources from which all English writing historians derived their information — misrepresented the facts because they had not thoroughly studied the commercial accounts of the Company as Mansvelt did. On the monetary confusion, see Letter of G. G. Alting of Dec. 31, 1783 (De Jonge, *op. cit.*, XII, 39), and E. Netscher and J. van der Chijs, *De Munten van Nederlandsch Indië* (Batavia, 1863).

[11] The Dutch Republic remained at war with Britain for nine months after France and the United States had concluded peace.

[12] J. De Hullu, "De Engelschen op Poeloe Pinang en de tinhandel der Oost Indische Compagnie in 1788," BKI, LXXVII (1921), 605. P. A. Leupe, "De Engelschen op Nieuw Guinea, 1792–1793," BKI, XXIV (1876), 158.

[13] The ship *Hope*, commanded by Captain Magee, was probably the first American

The East India Company probably could have overcome its difficulties if it had been thoroughly reorganized without consideration for private interests. The ruling oligarchy of the Netherlands could hardly be expected to do this. Thus, it did not mean very much when, between 1783 and 1795, the States General of the Republic gradually curtailed the independence of the Company and sought to make it more fully subordinate to the central government in Europe.[14] This interference had started with the dispatching of a Dutch naval squadron to the Indies in order to reinforce the fleet of the East India Company, which by this time was in a state of total decay. The squadron had arrived too late to take part in the naval operations against the British but it rendered excellent service in restoring a certain degree of safety on the Java Sea and in the Strait of Malacca, where the Buginese pirates already considered themselves the undisputed masters.

The dispatch of the naval squadron was followed by the appointment of a military committee to investigate the state of defense of the Indies, a committee which returned to Holland sorely disappointed and thoroughly disgusted with what it had seen and heard. By this time, however, a counter revolution, backed by Great Britain and Prussia and carried through with the assistance of the Prussian army, had reinstated Stadhouder William V in his former position, including the Directorate-General of the East India Company. Prince William, a good-natured, irresolute man who was afraid of hurting the interests of his followers, decided to give the Company one more chance, and appointed a new committee with the instruction to study a complete reorganization of the Company's system of trade and government. The head of this committee was S. C. Nederburgh, the lawyer of the Company, an intelligent but vain man and a master of intrigue. He left Holland in 1791, spent a year at the Cape of Good Hope, where he introduced minor changes in the government of the colony, and arrived in Batavia in 1793. Here he immediately joined hands with the clique behind the ruling governor-general, Willem A. Alting. Nederburgh and Alting, ably supported by the subtle Johan Siberg, son-in-law of the governor-general, by whom he had been appointed director-general of commerce, rapidly ousted their opponents from all important

vessel to visit Batavia. J. De Hullu, "Over den Opkomst van den Indischen handel der Vereenigde Staten van Amerika als mededinger van de Oost Indische Compagnie, 1786–1790," BKI, LXXV (1919), 281.

[14] Since 1747 the Prince of Orange held the hereditary honorary position of Director General of the East and West India Companies. See: G. J. A. van Berckel, *Bijdrage tot de geschiedenis van het Europeesche opperbestuur over Nederlandsch Indië, 1780–1806* (Leiden, 1880).

offices, thus creating a specially privileged class within the already oligarchic Dutch Indian community. Once more the demands for reform were stifled, but hardly had Nederburgh and his friends firmly established their regime when the whole political construction of the Netherlands and consequently of the Indies was threatened with sudden collapse.

In 1793 the Dutch Republic, following the example of Great Britain, went to war with revolutionary France. Thousands of Dutch exiles, driven from their homes by the Prussian-controlled counter revolution of 1787, joined the armies of the revolution, where they formed a "Batavian Legion." One of the commanding officers of this legion was Herman Willem Daendels, formerly a lawyer in the small town of Hattem in Gelderland. In 1793 the assault of the troops of the revolution was beaten off, but in 1795, in the first days of January, the soldiers of General Jourdan marched over the frozen rivers of Holland and occupied the country without a blow. A few hours before the French troops reached Amsterdam, a bloodless revolution took place by which the ruling oligarchy was removed from office and replaced by the leaders of the democratic movement. The Stadhouder went into exile, and while he found refuge with his relatives in England the stadhouderate was abolished in the Netherlands by decree of the States. The new Dutch government concluded an alliance with the French Republic by which it became involved in war with Great Britain.

A curious situation had arisen. From 1795 until 1810 the Netherlands were practically a vassal state of France with very little freedom of action. Yet the democratic government of The Hague undoubtedly was the lawful government of the Netherlands. The Prince of Orange, residing at Kew near London, could not claim legally to represent the Dutch Republic but he could present strong arguments that his authority over the colonies had not completely been destroyed. In his function as Director-General of the East India Company, a title conferred upon his father with hereditary rights in 1747, he could act to "protect" the colonies from the consequences of the revolution of 1795. In this capacity he issued a circular letter, dated at Kew, February 7, 1795, and addressed to all governors and commanders of the East and West Indian territories and fortresses under Dutch sovereignty, instructing them to admit British troops and administrators and to surrender to them all authority. The British government, he said, had given the solemn promise that once the former political situation had been restored in the Netherlands the colonies would be returned to their legal government.

Batavia now had to choose whether it would follow the Stadhouder or the States General. Nederburgh and Governor-General Alting were strictly conservative and without any sympathy with the new ideals of the revolution. The slogan "Liberty, Equality, Fraternity" had no meaning for them. But the prospect of surrendering the administration of Java to the British had very little allure, and, moreover, Nederburgh belonged to that group of the Dutch oligarchy which had always been opposed to the influence of the Princes of Orange. Thus Batavia decided upon a middle course, namely to maintain its allegiance to the government of The Hague, but at the same time, to resist all liberal trends in the Indies.

After all we have said about the Netherlanders in the Indies we probably would not expect any liberal trend of thought to manifest itself in Batavia. Yet as soon as the news from Holland arrived that a new government had been established upon a democratic basis, things began to move in the Indies.[15] First there was a petition to the High Government, presented by a large group of citzens and employees of the Company. It was composed in rather pompous style but this seems to have been an unavoidable evil in all proclamations of that period. The petition of December 5, 1795, said, among other things:

> We all, citizens and employees of the Company, equally animated by patriotism and love of liberty, have learned with great joy of the peace and treaty of alliance and friendship concluded between the Batave [16] and the French Republics. . . . No occurrence in the history of our Republic has been so blessed and fortunate as that which we have just seen happen. If the pretense of liberty that masked until now the most burdensome oppression of the people has succeeded in making the Netherlands into a republic of fame so great that it was envied by the whole of Europe, what may now be expected once freedom has been established here on the unshakable pillars of equality and fraternity? . . . The High Government informed us of the treaty concluded with France but did not explain whether war with England has resulted from this treaty or not. . . . To every inhabitant of this colony it seems very strange that, while we are threatened by so grave dangers, no preparations are made for defense. Is it a wonder that people become suspicious and that, seeing the example given by that scoundrel and traitor of the Cape of Good Hope,[17] many of us fear for the fate of our city?

The petitioners suspected the loyalty of Nederburgh and Alting. Their immediate demands were very moderate: a celebration of the

[15] F. de Haan, "Jacobijnen te Batavia," TBG, XLI (1899), 103 sq. The petition of Dec. 5, 1795 in De Jonge, *op. cit.*, XII, 359 sq.

[16] After the revolution the name of the Republic of the United Netherlands was changed into that of the "Bataafsche Republiek," which, to avoid confusion with Batavia and Batavians, I transcribe the "Batave Republic."

[17] The governor of the Cape had surrendered his colony to the British.

"liberation" of the Netherlands, the abolishment of all outward distinctions of rank among the employees, and the organization of the defense of Java. Nederburgh conceded the first demand but informed The Hague that the whole movement was nothing but an intrigue stirred up by his personal enemies who were trying to overthrow the government; he lost no time in lashing back at the promoters of the petition, whom he had arrested on various accusations. There was not a single employee of the Company who had never transgressed the trade regulations set by the Directors, and thus the government had a very effective weapon which it could use against any individual in its service who tended to become obnoxious. Nederburgh used this weapon in the most arbitrary way and rapidly silenced the opposition. One offender escaped him, however, and this proved to be the most dangerous one.

At the time of the revolution in the Netherlands, Dirk van Hogendorp, son of Willem van Hogendorp whom we mentioned as the author of several plays, was governor of Java's northeast coast. Dirk van Hogendorp was an intelligent but restless and ambitious man.[18] Before the revolution became known in the Indies he was already working at a report on the reorganization of the system of government. As soon as he learned of the events in the home country, he believed that his time had come and sent a secret report to Holland in which he violently criticized the administration of Nederburgh. To gain the ear of the new rulers of the Netherlands, he profusely expanded on the doctrines of freedom and equality for all human beings, but pointed out, at the same time, that a reorganization of the East Indian government would make the Indies produce more profits for the Netherlands. There is little doubt that he expected this reorganization to be assigned to him, with the rank of governor-general with extraordinary powers. Unfortunately for him, his secret report never reached Holland but fell into the hands of Nederburgh, who without loss of time had the ambitious governor arrested on the usual charge of corruption. Van Hogendorp, knowing his opponent, risked all to escape, and succeeded. Back in Holland, he published his *Berigt*, a small booklet on East Indian affairs in which he defended a radical reform of the very principles upon which the whole political and economic structure in the

[18] D. van Hogendorp, *Mémoires du général Dirk van Hogendorp, publiés par son petit fils* (The Hague, 1887). J. A. Sillem, *Dirk van Hogendorp* (Amsterdam, 1890). To understand his relations with Nederburgh it is important to know that Nederburgh's father, who belonged to the anti-Orangist faction, had been removed from his office in the administration of Rotterdam, to make place for Hogendorp's brother (De Haan, *Priangan* IV, 165, n. 1).

Indies was built.[19] One year later Nederburgh, too, returned to Holland, where he became the leader of the conservative group of colonial experts. The democratic movement in the Indies had been stifled; from now on the conflict of opinions was fought out in the home country.

The East India Company by this time had ceased to exist, and the larger part of its empire had been lost. On March 1, 1796, the Directors surrendered the administration of the Company to a committee appointed by the government. It was decided that the Charter of the Company, which expired on December 31, 1799, should not be renewed. The State was to take over all possessions and all debts of the Company and thus, for the sum of 134 million guilders, the total amount of the debts, it acquired the whole colonial empire with all its resources—definitely a profitable deal.

Once the democratic Batavian Republic had inherited the colonies of the oligarchic Company, it had to define a colonial policy. The Company as a commercial enterprise did not need to bother with principles of government, for its sole aim was commercial profits, but the new State must bring the colonial administration in line with the principles so loudly proclaimed in the home country. The new Committee for East Indian Affairs had indeed written to Batavia that the introduction of the principles prevailing in the Netherlands must be prepared and that the system of liberty and rights of the people must be introduced into the Indies. To this letter of September 5, 1796, the Batavian authorities had given a cautious and very diplomatic answer.[20]

> We must state [they said] that we can hardly imagine in what way a revolution based upon the system of liberty and rights of the people could be introduced into this country without destroying its value for the home country.
>
> Of course we are not well informed on the special principles of the new system . . . but we trust that we may declare that the revolutionary change will not be applied to our relations with the native princes and peoples, for, as the whole existence of this State is founded upon the moral and political conditions actually existing among these princes and peoples, such a change would cause a revolution in this State itself.
>
> Therefore we assume that it is your intention that the new system shall be applied only to the Government of the Company, to its servants and the Dutch citizens. The number of these citizens is, however, very limited, and only a few of them are capable of forming a sound judgment on affairs of importance. The interests of these few citizens can not outweigh those of the Company and they must never jeopardize these more important interests.

The new rulers of the Netherlands were willing enough to take these special interests into consideration. It must have been a great relief for

[19] D. van Hogendorp, *Berigt van den tegenwoordigen toestand der Bataafsche bezittingen* (n. p., 1799).

[20] De Jonge, *op. cit.*, XII, 428–429.

the government at Batavia when it received an answer from The Hague, dated April 27, 1799, in which the Committee for East Indian Affairs made its choice between political theories and practical politics. This letter is of great historical importance, for by this and similar decisions a complete break in the development of political institutions in the Indies was prohibited, a fact which for the time being prevented the realization of many necessary reforms but which, in the long run, also had many beneficial effects. The Committee wrote:

> We persist in the opinion we have always held that the doctrines of liberty and equality, however strongly they may be based on the inalienable rights of men and citizens and however thoroughly they may be introduced into this commonwealth (the Netherlands) and some other European countries, can not be transferred to nor applied to the East Indian possessions of the State as long as the security of these possessions depends on the existing and necessary state of subordination (of the Indonesians) and as long as the introduction can not take place without exposing these possessions to a confusion the effect of which can not be imagined.

The Committee also expressed its compassion for the "miserable fate of the slaves, men and women, born free like us and the rest of mankind," but declared that the abolition of slavery would have to wait "until a higher order of general civilization will permit the amelioration of their fate under the coöperation of all European nations that have overseas possessions."

These statements left little hope that the more liberal ideas defended by van Hogendorp would prevail. In his *Berigt*, published in the same year, 1799, in which the letter quoted above was written, he vigorously protested against the distinction, which made it appear that the people of the East Indies were human beings totally different from those inhabiting Europe. True to the theories of the age, he believed that the free play of economic forces, in the Indies as well as in Europe, would stimulate production and increase the welfare of the population. Consequently he proposed to abolish all forced deliveries and compulsory cultivation of export crops and to replace this source of government income by a head tax levied upon all inhabitants of Java.[21] To stimulate competition among the peasants he advocated the abolishing of communal ownership of farm lands wherever this existed and the introduction of private ownership of the land among the Javanese. These far-reaching reforms were opposed by Nederburgh in his *Considera-*

[21] Hogendorp had served for the Company in Bengal and it is very likely that he derived part of his ideas from the British administration of that province. See later remarks on Raffles and the origin of his tax system.

HERMAN WILLEM DAENDELS
Governor-general, 1808–1811.

tiën and *Verhandeling*, in which he propounded the theory that the people of Java would never make any progress of their own accord "because of their laziness which makes them unfit for any labor except for that which is needed to produce the most necessary foodstuffs."[22] This alleged natural laziness of the people of Java remained the central point of all discussions on theoretical Javanese economy for several decades. If the Javanese peasant really was too lazy to accomplish more work than that absolutely necessary, the rules of western economic life could not be applied to him and compulsory labor which would be to his own benefit as well as to that of his rulers might be justified. If he was not the lazy type of human being Nederburgh depicted in his report, forced labor on special crops was definitely oppressive and unjustified.

This problem was, however, a purely theoretical one. The real problem found its cause in the poverty of the Javanese, which made it impossible to collect an adequate government revenue from normal taxes. Compulsory labor, said the adherents of Nederburgh's opinion, was simply a tax collected in work instead of in cash, and, if properly organized, not more vexatious to the Indonesian peasant than taxes in money to his European colleague. Their opponents did not deny this but contended that the tax in labor never was levied without grave abuses from the side of the collectors, whether Indonesian regents or Dutch officials, and that a free play of economic forces would increase the welfare of the peasants to such an extent that normal taxes soon *would* be sufficient to meet the public expenses. In other words, Hogendorp and his supporters, fully convinced of the veracity of their theory, wanted to draw a bill on the future, while Nedenburgh and his adherents preferred to keep both feet on solid ground. It was not difficult to foresee which side would win.

After the liquidation of the East India Company, the administration of the East Asiatic possessions had been entrusted to a "Council for Asiatic Affairs." In 1802 a new committee was appointed to draw up a "Charter" for the government and commerce of the East Indies.[23] The committee was instructed to plan a system of administration which would provide for "the greatest possible welfare of the inhabitants of

[22] S. C. Nederburgh, "Consideratiën over de Jacatrasche en Preanger Regentschappen," TBG, III (1855), 110 sq. The quotation on p. 122. Nederburgh later developed his ideas once more in his *Verhandeling over de vragen of en in hoeverre het nuttig en noodzakelijk zou zijn de Oost Indische bezittingen van dezen staat te brengen op den voet der West Indische volkplantingen* (The Hague, 1802).

[23] F. W. Stapel, "Uit de wordingsgeschiedenis van het Charter van 1803," BKI, XC (1933), 253 sq.

the Indies, the greatest possible advantages for Dutch commerce, and the greatest possible profits for the finances of the Dutch state." If we may take the order in which the points are given as that of their relative importance in the opinion of the Netherlands government, the instruction was not so conservative as it looked. Both Hogendorp and Nederburgh were members of the committee, but it was Nederburgh who wrote the first draft of the charter and this was subsequently accepted by the committee. None of Hogendorp's reforms were adopted. Forced deliveries and compulsory cultivation of coffee and other products were to be continued. No change would be made in the property rights of the farmlands. Van Hogendorp scored only one success. The committee instructed the government of Batavia to investigate into the conditions of landownership in Java and into the possibility of substituting private property for communal ownership of the soil. Thus Hogendorp may be called, if not the founder, at least the instigator of sociological researches in the East Indies.[24]

The charter never came into force. It was withdrawn by the government in Holland (where governments changed rapidly in the Napoleonic era) and replaced by the Administrative Act of 1806, which was slightly more liberal than the charter. This in its turn was abrogated when the "Batave Republic" ceased to exist and was replaced by the "Kingdom of Holland" with Napoleon's brother Louis as its first — and its last — king.

While in the Netherlands the experts on East Indian affairs discussed the principles of government and native economy, the East Indian government itself endeavored to maintain its independence amidst ever increasing dangers and difficulties. The discussions in Holland had centered around problems which were specifically Javanese, and these were actually the only problems which remained to be solved, for nearly all other territories once belonging to the Company had been lost to the British. In the archipelago, Malacca, Sumatra's west coast, Amboina, and Banda had surrendered at the first summons. The commanding officers were either not prepared or unwilling to resist. After the arrival of a British squadron in the Moluccas, general warfare broke out on the unfortunate islands. The old feuds of Mohammedans against Christians and of Tidorese against Ternatans were revived and set all islands aflame with civil strife and tribal warfare. Of all the fortresses of the Dutch, only Ternate held out against greatly superior

[24] The Charter, with the "Consideratiën en advijs," composed by Nederburgh, is published by P. Mijer, *Verzameling van Instructien, Ordonnancien en Reglementen voor de Regering van Nederlandsch Indië* (Batavia, 1848).

enemy forces.[25] In 1799 a mutiny among the officers of the garrison made a surrender inevitable. On Timor a success was scored when the local commander with the help of armed slaves and tribesmen drove the British from the fortress of Kupang, which they had occupied. Besides Timor, only Macassar, Bandjermasin, and Palembang remained under the authority of Batavia.

The defense of Java itself was totally inadequate. The army numbered no more than 3000 soldiers, of whom only 1000 were Europeans. That a small force like this was sufficient to maintain order in Java shows that the government had the full support of the Javanese princes and regents. Nevertheless, the conquest of Java would have been an easy matter for the British if they had not been fully occupied elsewhere. With the Spanish Philippines and Dutch Java to the east, French Mauritius to the south, and a French army in Egypt to the west, their position in India, where they were involved in difficult wars with Tippu Sahib of Mysore, was rather precarious. The Dutch in Java were among the least dangerous of their enemies, for they lacked the power to take the offensive. To immobilize them completely, a British squadron sailed around Java, destroying the Dutch warships and burning the repair wharves. Thus the last remnants of the once powerful navy of the Company were annihilated.

Peace came in 1802, before a British expedition against Java could be organized. All colonies conquered by Britain except Ceylon were returned to the Netherlands.[26] The peace lasted only one year. Rapidly the British reconquered nearly all the territories which they had just surrendered. Again Java owed its safety from enemy attack to British inaction, not to its own strength. The Batavian government was not especially concerned about the weakness of the defenses of the island. Still balancing between its conservative tendencies and its allegiance to the Hague, it would have preferred to continue in a status of semi-independence, carrying on the administration from day to day with the resources ready at hand.[27] It hoped that the British would refrain from hostilities against Java as long as the Dutch gave no active sup-

[25] On the war in the Moluccas the articles of P. Leupe in BKI, XII (1864), 262; XVII (1870), 215; XXII (1875), 90; XXVII (1879), 202, and the article of J. E. Heeres, "Een Engelsche lezing omtrent de verovering van Banda en Ambon in 1796 en omtrent den toestand daar," BKI, LX (1907), 249 sq.

[26] This treaty naturally freed the British Government of all obligations it might have assumed towards the Prince of Orange when the latter issued the proclamation of Kew in 1795.

[27] J. Hageman, "Geschiedenis van het Bataafsche en Hollandsche Gouvernement op Java, 1802–1810," TBG, IV (1855), 333 sq. and V (1856), 164 sq. O. Collet, *L'Ile de Java sous la domination française* (Bruxelles, 1910).

port to the French. A French general who suddenly arrived at Batavia with a staff of forty officers and declared that he had been ordered by Napoleon Bonaparte to assume command over the allied troops in the Indies was politely refused access to Java and sent back to Mauritius because he could not present the proper credentials issued from the Hague. Governor-General Van Overstraten even called the valiant defense of Timor a "rash and imprudent act which would incite the British to take revenge"! The elevation of Napoleon's brother to the throne in Holland further contributed to the loosening of the ties between Java and the home country. One of the chief officers openly answered a toast to the new sovereign in plain English with a "Damn the king!"

This curious state of semi-independence was made possible by the change in economic relations between Holland and the Indies. The East India Company, with its antiquated system of shipping and trading, could not make ends meet. As soon as Batavia began to sell its products in the open market, to neutral traders who came to get them in the Indies and shipped them at their own risk, the picture was at once reversed. The authorities at the Hague only reluctantly consented to this trade, but Batavia, while writing soothing letters home, made full use of the opportunity. It was a lucky coincidence for Batavia that in the very years during which it was freed from strict supervision by the conservative Board of Directors the prices of tropical products, especially coffee, rose unexpectedly. The revolt of the slaves in Haiti ruined the West Indian coffee production. Java could not produce enough for the demand. In one year (1797), twenty Danish and thirty-one American ships cast anchor in Batavia's roadstead. In 1799 twelve million pounds of coffee were exported. Batavia, however, wanted to sell not only its coffee, but also its pepper, sugar, cloves, and nutmeg. In 1805 there was not a pound of coffee left in the storehouses. The government decided that the time had come to throw the Moluccas open to foreign trade, especially American. To make preliminary arrangements with the mechants in the United States, a special representative was sent to New York. For this task Rogier G. van Polanen, vice president of the High Court of Justice in Batavia, who was well acquainted with the United States, where he had served a term as Minister of the States General, was selected.[28]

[28] References to American trade with Java: De Jonge, *op. cit.*, XIII, 35 (letter from Batavia to Holland of Jan. 31, 1802), 241 (letter of Oct. 24, 1803), 262 (letter of Sept. 6, 1805), 286 (letter of Nov. 15, 1807), 342 (letter of March 19, 1809). On the mission of Polanen: *ibid.*, 356, 471, 489, and 531. L. W. G. de Roo in his supplementary volume to De Jonge–Van Deventer, vol. XIII, publishes numerous letters from and to Van Polanen.

The boom period came to an end as suddenly as it had started. In 1807 Denmark was attacked by the British navy and consequently involved in the war at the side of France. Danish shipping came to an end.[29] In 1807 and 1808 the Embargo Act was passed and supplemented by Jefferson's administration, and all American shipping to foreign countries was abruptly halted. From that time, only a few American blockade runners who felt sure that they could outrun any British warship appeared in Batavia's roadstead. The ten years of prosperity had been sufficient, however, to fill the treasure chest of the government of Java. When Governor-General Wiese surrendered his high office to his successor, there were two million guilders in the treasury of Batavia.[30]

This successor was Herman Willem Daendels. A Bonaparte had come to power in the Netherlands, and from now on military considerations took the first place in the colonial plans of The Hague. Daendels had never been in the Indies, but he seemed to be the right type of man to clean the Batavian stable of Augias, a *new* man who stood outside the cliques and gangs, who knew what he wanted and had an iron hand. From a revolutionary orator, in the days of the "patriots," Daendels had grown into a dictatorial officer of the Napoleonic type. He still spoke in the set phrases of the revolutionary language, but for him they had become mere slogans without inner meaning. On January 1, 1808, he arrived at a small port near Bantam after a difficult and dangerous voyage from Holland via Lisbon and Morocco. The behavior of the new governor-general gave the old-timers one shock after another. Immediately after his arrival he decided to leave the unhealthy and desolate city of Batavia and to move to Buitenzorg. High officials told him that in the prevailing rainy season he would need thirty teams of horses to get there. "I shall use thirty-one teams," said Daendels, and started.

King Louis had given him extraordinary powers which made him independent of the Council of the Indies. Daendels reorganized that Council without any delay and left it only advisory capacity. Then he set to work, slashing at corruption, tearing down and building up the administration, constructing roads and fortresses, in short, doing everything which a self-styled dictator might be expected to do. He accomplished a great deal but incurred the deadly hostility of many

[29] Many of the so-called Danish ships may have been equipped at the expense of the Netherlands State, for we know that the Council for Asiatic Affairs resorted to this means to obtain at least a part of the East Indian produce.

[30] Note of transfer of government to Governor-General Daendels by A. Wiese, De Jonge, *op. cit.*, XIII, 294.

whose interests he hurt, with the result that his silver-tongued successor, Thomas Raffles, was able to take all the credit for the reorganization of Java's government for himself alone while Daendels' memory was burdened with the discreditable aspects of the affair.[31]

One of the first measures taken by the new governor-general was a complete reform of the administration. Until Daendels' time all Dutch territories east of Cheribon had formed a single province, that of Java's northeast coast. The governor of that province because of the numerous "emoluments" connected with his office enjoyed an annual income of one hundred thousand guilders, while, if we may believe Daendels, the government revenue from the territory was practically nil.[32] By decree of August 18, 1808, the province was divided into five prefectures and thirty-eight regencies. All officials received military rank and a suitable salary. Bribery presents from the Javanese regents, special profits, all these abuses had to stop. The difficulty was: where to find the money to pay the higher salaries?

Daendels declared the Javanese regents to be Dutch government officials, in order to safeguard them, he said, against vexatious demands and humiliating treatment from the side of the European officials. It is doubtful whether the regents appreciated the theoretical equality of status with the Europeans they thus acquired, for they paid for it very dearly in loss of income and prestige and especially in freedom of action towards their subjects. There was nothing alluring to them in exchanging the position as semi-autonomous rulers which they had held in the days of the Company for that of civil servant with the rank of lieutenant-colonel in a Dutch-Napoleonic bureaucracy. The sultans of Cheribon were degraded to the rank of regents, a degradation which they fully deserved because of the cruel extortions which they had permitted themselves, but radical interference with hereditary institu-

[31] Daendels' governorship is one of the most debated periods of Dutch administration in the Indies. Van Deventer, in his continuation of De Jonge's series (vol. XIII), amassed so much condemning material that L. W. G. de Roo, having collected other evidence from the same sources, thought it necessary to publish a supplementary volume to the series, *Documenten omtrent Herman Willem Daendels* (The Hague, 1909). Daendels himself, in defense against the accusations (brought among others by N. Engelhardt, *Bericht van den Staat der Ned. O. I. Bezittingen* (The Hague, 1816), published his *Staat der Nederlandsche Oostindische bezittingen onder het bestuur van den G. G. H. W. Daendels* (The Hague, 1814), with two volumes of documents. Raffles, who loved to pose as the liberator of the Indonesians from oppression, found it convenient, of course, to picture the Daendels period of office in dark colors that his own record might seem brighter.

[32] Daendels, *Staat*, p. 39. We must bear in mind that the acting governor of Java's northeast coast was Engelhardt, Daendels' personal enemy. A list of "emoluments" appears in *Staat*, p. 6 note.

tions like this tended to cause apprehension among the Javanese aristocracy. Daendels, who had come to organize the defense of Java, would need the support of the Javanese leaders. But since he was easily deceived by the outward display of servility by those of the Javanese functionaries he met, he was fully convinced that his method of dealing with the native authorities was the correct one.

In his apologetic work, *Staat der Nederlandsche Oost Indische Bezittingen*, Daendels sharply criticized the organization and practice of the judiciary of Batavia. His criticism was undoubtedly justified for, compared to that of modern Netherlands historians, it may even be called mild.[33] The few courts formerly established by the Company were unable to cope with the numerous cases brought before them, and the abuses of judicial authority had gradually become intolerable. "The treatment of prisoners in Batavia's jail was horrible," Daendels said, and he certainly was not tender-hearted. Consequently he undertook a thorough reorganization of the judiciary, which remains one of the most important works he accomplished. The ordinance of 1708 and other decrees of the Company had defined a few principles to be observed by the Batavian courts when dealing with cases in which only non-Christians were involved, and had sustained the judicial power of the Javanese regents, but these ordinances were neither clear nor maintained with consistency. A confusion of jurisdiction among the different courts was the consequence. Native customs and laws might be respected, or might be overruled, exactly as it pleased the European courts. Daendels decided upon a segregation of the different groups of population in matters of justice. He gave every regency, and above the regencies, every prefecture, its own court of justice, composed of Indonesians, with two European members in the courts of the prefecture. These courts would judge in all cases in which natives of Java alone were involved. All cases concerning *foreigners*, i.e. Europeans, Chinese, Arabians, or Indonesians not natives of Java, were to be handled by "Councils of Justice" established at Batavia, Semarang, and Surabaya. The first group of courts would render justice according to Javanese customs and laws, the second according to the existing Dutch-Indian statutes.[34] This system of segregating the

[33] Compare Daendels, *Staat*, p. 15 with *Priangan*, I, 417–419 and IV, 687.

[34] J. Van Kan, *Uit de rechtsgeschiedenis der Compagnie*, 2 vols. (Batavia, 1930–1935); D. J. Mackay, *De handhaving van het Europeeesch gezag en de hervorming van het Rechtswezen onder Daendels* (The Hague, 1861). All these reforms were prepared by the Committee of 1803 and foreseen in the Charter, a fact of great importance in judging the part which respectively Daendels and Raffles had in the modernization of the East Indian administration. Daendels was the first governor-general who permitted public

national groups in matters of justice has been maintained and improved by later administrations. Daendels himself did little more than set down the principle and create the outward organization of the system. He was far too dictatorial to feel bound by his own regulations and showed a marked preference for "administrative justice," i.e., punishment by decree without trial. In justification of his attitude he liked to compare his position as the ruler of an isolated colony to that of the commander of a beleaguered fortress. Even martial law, however, would not permit the arbitrary interference with justice which Daendels allowed himself.

Daendels indeed had extravagant ideas of his position and authority. He simply disregarded the trade-agreements concluded by the East Indian representative in the United States and became involved in personal conflicts with several of his principal officials in Java. Of the Minister of Colonies in Holland he spoke with contempt. He permitted himself what he strictly forbade to his subordinates. Though he enjoyed the enormous salary for that time of 130,000 guilders a year, plus considerable "emoluments," he complained bitterly that he was very poorly paid, and by open abuse of his power he appropriated for himself the estate of Buitenzorg," only to resell it to the government. By this transaction alone he secured a personal profit of 900,000 guilders. This overbearing attitude of the governor-general, who considered himself above the law, irritated Dutch and Javanese alike. Daendels refused to compromise except where it served his own purposes. No one resented this more than the Javanese princes.

The relations between the sultan and susuhunan on one side and the East India Company on the other had been legally perfectly clear; the princes had received their crowns from the Company and after their death their lands returned to the Company to be handed over to their successor. In daily practice, however, the attitude of the Company had been rather deferential to the princes. Its residents at the courts of Djocjakarta and Surakarta acted as if they were the advisors of the sultan and susuhunan, not the representatives of the sovereign power; accordingly they granted the princes first rank at all public ceremonies. The more rationally minded Daendels overthrew this arrangement. He considered this compromise, which flattered the vanity of the Javanese rulers and sustained their self-respect, injurious to the sovereign rights of the Netherlands state. To make it plain to the people of the

exercise of the R. Catholic religion in the Indies (nonconformist Protestants had the same liberty since 1766) but here too, he only executed article 13 of the Instruction for the governor-general, of 1803.

Javanese principalities that supreme authority rested with Batavia, he ordered that the Residents, now called "Ministers," should assume the sign of royalty, the "golden payong" (sunshade), never take off their hats to salute the princes, nor uncover their heads in their presence, etc. The Javanese chronicles reflect a glimpse of what went on in the soul of sultan and susuhunan when these offending novelties were introduced. Their wounded vanity made them rage and fume inwardly. They knew how to hide their feelings in the presence of the representatives of the government, but their wrath promised little good for the future.

Daendels had no more respect for the existing treaties with the Javanese princes than for the feelings of the rulers themselves. From the sultan of Bantam he demanded hundreds of workers for his fortifications along the shore of Sunda Strait. Unwillingness to comply with this demand was considered proof of disloyalty. Renewed demands were met with violence on the part of the people of Bantam, and thus a revolt broke out which could have been avoided. Here Daendels, the sword-rattling general of the Revolution, was in his true element. High on horseback and alone he led the way for his troops in the attack on Bantam, dashing through the groups of armed rebels who, stunned and terrorized, made place for the governor-general. The coastal districts of the sultanate were annexed to the directly ruled territories. The interior subsisted for a few years more as a vassal state.

All these reforms were of great importance. By them the old system of the Company was broken down and the foundations laid for a new one. The real object of Daendels' mission, however, was another. In the "Instruction for the Governor General of His Majesty's Asiatic possessions" issued by King Louis on February 9, 1807, twelve of the thirty-seven articles dealt with military affairs and article 14 made the reorganization of the army the first of his duties.[35] Other matters specially entrusted to his care were: an investigation into the possibility of abrogating the compulsory cultivation of coffee and the forced deliveries, the amelioration of the conditions of life among the native population and, more particularly, the slaves, and finally, the amelioration of sanitary conditions at Batavia, or, if this proved impossible, the removal of the capital to a more healthful district of Java.

It is evident that the first and last items would cause new demands on the treasury while the second and third would tend to reduce the government revenue. This presented a dilemma which Daendels did not even attempt to solve. Although he lacked all personal knowledge

[35] Mijer, *op. cit.*, pp. 347 sq.

of Javanese affairs, he rapidly came to the conclusion that compulsory cultivation must be extended instead of reduced. "The only way to collect taxes from the poor Javanese peasants is to make them work," he wrote to the Minister of Colonies in Holland. "The forced deliveries," he continued, "are not unjust, but all profits must go to the state."[36] Daendels tried hard indeed to secure for the peasants their legal share in the price of the coffee and to curtail the arbitrariness of the regents who sought to keep at least part of the money destined for the peasants for themselves. Exemptions from forced labor in the coffee plantations were no longer permitted. The members of the nobility and the personal followers of the regents were obliged to work side by side with the *tjatjahs*, who so far had carried the burden alone. Daendels figured that this measure would reduce the number of days each individual had to work on the plantations, but at the same time he increased the number of coffee trees each regency had to maintain!

The coffee piled up in the storehouses of Batavia and nobody came to buy it. All neutral trading had been halted. The British blockade became more and more stringent. A curious situation had developed in Java. The Batavian government possessed merchandise to a value of several millions, but no cash. It issued paper money that immediately depreciated, because the government lacked credit while its vassal, the sultan of Djocjakarta, hoarded all the gold he could collect, a treasure of two million guilders. Daendels resorted to a last expedient: the sale of "government domains," a measure which also would serve the ulterior purpose of "modernizing" the economic structure of Javanese society. To understand this, we must realize that Daendels considered the whole of Java, except the territory of the princes, to be "government domain." The East India Company had distinguished between the lands it had obtained by conquest, i.e., the Lowlands around Batavia, and the lands of which the sovereignty had been ceded by the native princes, i.e., the Preanger and Batavia's northeast coast. Daendels, faithful imitator of the French Revolution and Napoleon, ignored such subtle distinctions. Like the ideologists of the Revolution, he knew one great passion, to systematize. For Daendels the sovereign rights of the Netherlands state extended over the whole of Java and were unlimited. To justify the sale of land already populated and cultivated by native farmers he could invoke, if necessary, the theory of the Javanese rulers, that land and people both were the

[36] De Jonge, *op. cit.*, XIII, 325–326.

property of the king; but Daendels did not bother to justify his decisions by theoretical explanations.

The first and most desired result of the transaction would be to bring money into the treasury. The second would be, if we believe Daendels, the promotion of agriculture and industry. The Company had preserved native institutions and closed the country for European enterprise. Daendels, by selling the "domains," claimed to open Java to private enterprise. He imagined all Javanese coastlands already divided up among thousands of large estates, while the mountain area of the west, the Preanger, would remain the government "coffee reservation," and that of the east, the home of the native princes. The Company too had sold land to European planters, but its laws had strictly limited the rights of the landowners over the Javanese bondsmen living on the estates. Daendels abolished these restrictions. "Protection of the native laborer," he said, "only encouraged him in his natural laziness, while it discouraged the western planter."[37] Freedom for both laborer and planter would, according to the economic theory of the age, best serve the interests of society.

Daendels actually sold enormous tracts of land west and east of Batavia. His greatest transaction, however, was the sale of the whole regency of Probolinggo in East Java to a Chinese, Han Ti Ko, for the sum of one million dollars. These, and a few other transactions, were purely speculative enterprises on the part of the buyers. Fortunately Daendels did not rule long enough to carry out his plans to their full extent, which would have resulted in half of the population of Java being reduced to the state of bondsmen *taillable et corvéable à merci*. What the revolution abolished in Europe it introduced into Asia in the name of economic freedom for all.

The dictatorial governor-general who thus attempted to overthrow the whole economy of Java did not forget that the main reason for his presence in the Indies was the deplorable state of the defense of the colony. After the peace of 1802 strong reinforcements had been sent from Europe until the army according to the rolls numbered seventeen thousand men. That number rapidly dwindled because of tropical diseases. Officers were badly needed, and Daendels promoted a number of clerks and citizens of mixed blood (many of whom could not even write or read) to the rank of officer. There were not enough

[37] De Jonge, *op. cit.*, XIII, 390. For a discussion of Daendels' policy and economic principles, see S. J. Ottow, *De oorsprong der conservatieve richting* (Utrecht, 1937), pp. 47 sq., who takes a different view from the traditional one established by the historians of the nineteenth century.

artillerists and arms or equipment. Daendels in feverish activity sought to provide everything, building powder and gun factories and fortresses and coastal batteries. To improve communications, now that the British completely controlled the sea, a highway was constructed from Bantam in the west to Pasuruan in the east. Most of the work was done by peasants, called up for compulsory labor. The highway was completed in a year, but not without great losses in human lives.[38]

Daendels understood that Batavia never could be used as the main center for the defense of the island. Its old castle with its crumbling walls could be smashed from the seas. The climate might kill the soldiers of the garrison before the enemy ever touched the shore. Daendels' instructions had given him permission to move the capital to a healthier district, and one of his predecessors in the governor-ship-general, Van Overstraten, had developed a plan to transfer the residence of the government to the interior of Central Java where the joint forces of the Dutch and the Javanese princes would be able to resist numerically superior enemy forces for a long time.[39] Daendels himself considered the transfer of the capital to Surabaya, which he recognized as a far better base for military operations than Batavia. He ultimately shrank back from the difficulties involved in a complete transplanting of the whole settlement of Batavia, with its storehouses and shiploads of precious merchandise, and decided to move the residential quarters of the city a few miles inland, to the suburb of Weltevreden, formerly one of the estates of Chastelein. Building materials were made available by the demolition of a number of houses, and even of the ancient castle of Coen, in the old section of the city. South of Weltevreden, at Meester Cornelis, a fortified camp was constructed which was to be the main center of defense in case of a British invasion. That invasion would come soon, for Daendels' measures for defense made it imperative for the British to destroy this Dutch-French stronghold before it was too well organized. Daendels, however, was not permitted to conduct the defense. In 1810 Napoleon Bonaparte deposed his brother Louis, the king of Holland, and annexed the Netherlands to the French Empire. Daendels hoisted the French flag in Batavia, although this sign of foreign domination caused great discontent among the old Dutch Indian settlers. Shortly

[38] De Haan, *Priangan*, I, 484 sq. and IV, 897 sq. We must bear in mind that most of the figures of appalling mortality among the Javanese laborers are derived from the writings of Daendels' opponents, Raffles and Engelhardt.

[39] Confidential letter of Van Overstraten, then governor of Java to Nederburgh, May 9, 1796 (De Jonge, *op. cit.*, XII, 400 sq.).

after the annexation of the Netherlands, Napoleon decided to recall Daendels and to replace him by a man of more moderate character. He sent Jan Willem Janssens, who formerly had been governor of the Cape Colony, which he had reached just in time to fight a British invasion and to surrender the colony to the enemy. The same fate befell him once more when he had come to Java.

CHAPTER XII

THOMAS STAMFORD RAFFLES, THE FOUNDER OF SINGAPORE

On August 31, 1810, the Board of the English East India Company wrote to Lord Minto, the governor-general of India:

> We have no hesitation in expressing our entire concurrence in Your Lordship's ideas as to the expediency of endeavouring to expel the enemy from their settlement in the Island of Java, and from every other place which they may occupy in the Eastern Seas. While the Dutch were independent, or at least nominally independent of France, it was neither their interest nor their policy to give us much annoyance from Batavia or their other settlements in those seas. But the case is now materially altered.[1]

The annexation of the Netherlands to the empire of Napoleon and Daendels' attempted reorganization of the Dutch Indian military forces were the direct cause of the British attack on the last Netherlands overseas territory. To the Directors of the English Company (which would have to provide the ships and the troops) the prospect of a campaign against Java had no allure. They did not want the sovereignty over Java, of whose value they held a very poor opinion.

The British government wanted the expedition for strategic reasons, but although it could claim Java for the British crown, it was not interested in the permanent occupation of the island.[2] Accordingly the campaign was planned as that of a punitive expedition, "to expel the enemy from all their settlements, to destroy all their forts, to take possession of all arms and ammunition, and to demolish all the stores and magazines, wishing to leave the possession of these settlements to the occupation of the natives." The men who had to execute these merciless orders held different opinions.

The governor-general of India at that time was Gilbert Elliot, Lord

[1] See the instructions of the Board in M. L. van Deventer, *Het Nederlandsch Gezag over Java en onderhoorigheden sedert 1811*, vol. 1, 1811–1820 (The Hague, 1891). This work was planned as a continuation of the series of De Jonge, but only one volume was published. The instructions are on p. 4, note 1.

[2] "It seems to be understood," wrote Lord Minto on Dec. 6, 1811, "that territories conquered from European powers, although locally situated within the Limits of the Company's privileges . . . are nevertheless acquired exclusively for the Crown" (van Deventer, *op. cit.*, p. 4).

Minto. As a prominent member of the Whig party, Elliot had been one of the leading figures in the attacks on Warren Hastings and his collaborators. "The Whig party," a modern British historian says, "made the occasion a manifesto for their humanitarian sentiments and an exercise in vituperation." There is no doubt about the sincerity of the humanitarianism professed by Lord Minto and his followers, but there is still less doubt about the fact that they made their belief into a slogan for party politics.[3] In preparing his expedition against the Netherlanders in Java, Lord Minto gathered around him a group of men with genuine interest in Indonesian affairs, in the Malay languages, and in the native history and customs — men who certainly shared his humanitarian views, but who also knew that their sole chance of promotion lay in gaining the favor of the prominent Whig politician who was their direct chief. This does not detract from the merits of these men as promoters of the study of Indonesian affairs, but it explains their great display of moral indignation at the injustice committed by others while their own actions were often far from blameless.

One of the most interesting figures among Lord Minto's associates was Dr. John C. Leyden.[4] He was a great student of Malay affairs, but his personality was completely overshadowed by that of a young man whom he recommended to the governor-general, namely Thomas Raffles. A burning ambition and a brilliant intelligence combined to make Raffles the right man to execute Lord Minto's plans for the East Indies. Raffles was not a man of great character, but he was ambitious enough to prefer a reputation in history to an immediate material

[3] Lord Minto (of Roxburghshire, Scotland), member of Parliament 1776–1784 and 1786–1793, moved the impeachment of Sir Elijah Impey. P. E. Roberts (*Cambridge History of India*, v, 246) says "the impeachment frankly was made a party affair." The quotation in the text is from the same volume, p. 310. Historians tend to overlook the fact that men like Leyden (who was a farmer's son of the same county in Scotland where Minto originated) and Raffles were wholly dependent upon the governor of India and practically were forced to share not only his political views but also his ideals, if they ever wanted to receive promotion. Raffles in his *Substance of a Minute* (London, 1814), speaks with great respect of Minto. Lady Raffles, in her *Memoir* (p. 22) began to turn matters around by representing her husband as the original promoter of plans that were in reality those of Lord Minto.

[4] On his life, see W. R. van Hoevell in *Tijdschrift van Nederlandsch Indië*, IX (1847), 43 sq. (after Walter Scott's biography of 1812). He was assistant surgeon in the service of the East India Company, arrived at Madras in 1803, stayed with Raffles at Pulu Penang in 1805, and from here visited Atjeh and other parts of Sumatra. Writings: "On the Languages and Literature of the Indo-Chinese Nations," in *Asiatic Researches* (Marsden's periodical), x, 1808; *A comparative vocabulary of the Burma, Malayan and Thai languages* (Serampore, 1810); "Sketch of Borneo," VBG, vol. VII (1814). His *Malay Annals* were edited by Raffles (London, 1821).

award. To build up that reputation, he worked all his life, first by serving the leading humanitarian statesmen, then by creating, through his writings, an historical legend about his administration in Java, and finally, by a daring but unscrupulous policy of expansion which led to his greatest achievement, the founding of Singapore. And he wrote so well, in such an attractive form, that for a century after his death people continued to judge Raffles by his words instead of by his deeds. Raffles had one great advantage over his predecessors in the colonial administration of the Indies, he knew how to write, how to decorate his narratives with the slogans that would appeal, first to his backers, then, once he had become prominent, to the general public. He knew where to place the words "enlightened government," "rapacious behavior of the Europeans," and "amenity of character of the natives" — expressions that crush a possible opponent before he has uttered a word and immediately associate the personality of the author with everything that is good and noble. These little publicity tricks tend to irritate the historian who otherwise will gladly concede to Raffles the honor of having been one of the most intelligent and active governors that ever ruled in the Indies.[5]

Raffles began his career in the offices of the Company in London — he was in all respects a self-made man — and was appointed to the position of agent of the Company at Pulu Penang in 1805. Here he began his studies of the Malay language, customs and history, and in the course of his studies maintained a frequent correspondence with William Marsden, the author of the *History of Sumatra*, and with Dr. Leyden.[6] When the time for an attack on the Dutch possessions drew near, Lord Minto selected Raffles for the diplomatic preparation of the campaign. The orders from London were to befriend the natives, in

[5] T. S. Raffles was born July 5, 1781, aboard the ship *Ann* of which his father was captain, at Port Morant, Jamaica. In 1795 he entered the service of the East India Company as a clerk, in 1805 he became under-secretary at Penang. He died July 5, 1826, on his estate as Highwood, Middlesex, England. In 1809 Lord Minto appointed him his "Agent with the Malay princes." A good biography of Raffles does not exist, in spite of all the volumes written on him. Lady Raffles published after the death of her husband a *Memoir of the Life and Public Services of Sir Thomas Stamford Raffles* (London, 1830), useful for the documents it contains. In the second edition many important documents have been omitted. The biographies of Demetrius Ch. Boulger (London, 1897), Hugh E. Egerton (London, 1900), and J. A. Bethune Cook (London, 1918), are more panegyrics than historical biographies. Most recent, but also most disappointing, is the biography by R. Coupland, *Raffles, 1781–1826* (Oxford, 1926). The author quotes from many unpublished British sources but apparently was unable to consult Dutch books. His description of the Dutch system in Java is only a repetition — in more exaggerated terms — of Raffles' far from impartial criticism.

[6] *Memoir*, pp. 9 sq.

THOMAS STAMFORD RAFFLES: FOUNDER OF SINGAPORE

order to make the campaign as easy and therefore inexpensive as possible. To this task Raffles devoted himself with great enthusiasm. Using Indonesian merchants as intermediaries, he sent letters to the sultan of Palembang, to the "kings" of Bali, and, with the assistance of the latter, to the susuhunan and the sultan of the Javanese principalities. The answers he received were encouraging, and he took them quite seriously as proofs of sympathy for the British, not realizing that the Indonesian princes who saw the crisis between the two European powers coming nearer, were trying to get footholds in both camps.[7] The sequence of events in Palembang showed this only too clearly.

It is no wonder that in Raffles' eyes the campaign against the French domination in Java took the form of a crusade for the liberation of the Malays from Dutch oppression. Even before the war started, Raffles and his friends were already indulging in an orgy of post-war planning. The following excerpt from one of Dr. Leyden's letters shows their trend of thought:

> [Some people] have succeeded in making some impression upon him [Lord Minto] by talking of accustoming the Malays to independence and all that. The Malays must neither be independent nor yet very dependent, but we must have a general Malay league in which all the Rajahs must be united . . . and these must all be represented in a general Parliament of the Malay states like the Amphitryonic Council of the Greeks, and this Council should meet in the island of Madura or some celebrated ancient place and under the protection of the Governor of Java.[8]

The history of the real Amphitryonic Councils was not very encouraging for those who intended to bring forth a Malay edition of the same institution, but such small matters did not spoil the beauty of the scheme. To make the new regime more acceptable, Raffles even proposed to declare the British governor successor to the kings of Madjapahit!

Ideas like these did not concur with the opinion of the Board of Directors who aimed only at the destruction of Dutch power in the East Indies. Lord Minto fully agreed with his subordinate officers. Immediately after the conquest of Java he reported to the Board the "indispensable necessity of reconsidering that part of the Instructions which enjoined the demolition of the Dutch defenses and the abandonment of that ancient European colony, unarmed, to the vengeance and cupidity of the native tribes," which considerations "rendered the

[7] The Javanese princes did not answer the letters; the Balinese, however, glad at the prospect of a profitable campaign in Java, accepted Raffles' offers (*Memoir*, pp. 32–34).

[8] *Memoir*, letter of Leyden, p. 25.

execution of that order absolutely, because morally, impossible."[9] Lord Minto must have been aware of these considerations before he started on his campaign, and we may assume that he never intended to execute the order. Neither did he share the radical views of Leyden and Raffles. Dr. Leyden asked the latter to urge the Malays to drive out the "cruel and treacherous French and Dutch," but Lord Minto knew that the only possibility for organizing an efficient administration over Java lay in the coöperation of the Dutch, and therefore he did not want to antagonize them unnecessarily — especially since he understood most of them to have been strongly opposed to the French domination.[10]

For the newly appointed Dutch Governor-General Janssens the situation was hopeless from the beginning. His troops were dispersed over the island. Daendels' haughtiness had provoked the resentment of the native rulers and even the loyal Madurese were wavering. A revolt might have been expected, but nothing moved in the Indies until the campaign was brought to a victorious conclusion by the British.[11] With a fleet of nearly a hundred transports and a force of 12,000 soldiers Lord Minto sailed from Malacca. On August 3, 1811, he appeared before Batavia. Six weeks later the campaign was over. After heavy fighting the retrenchments south of Batavia were stormed and taken by the British. The unhappy disposition of the Dutch forces revealed itself. A retreat from Batavia was impossible. Small detachments that attempted to march east along the highway constructed by order of Daendels were intercepted by the British, who could reach Cheribon — where the Dutch had to pass — much more quickly by sea. Governor-General Janssens did his utmost to rally a new force in a strong position south of Semarang, where he hoped to receive help from the Javanese principalities, but only Prang Wedana, the successor of Mangkunegara as "younger prince" of Surakarta, remained loyal to the end. For many years he had received a subsidy from the Batavian government for the upkeep of an auxiliary force, and, in this moment of direst need, he faithfully kept his word, standing by General Janssens when the whole hastily mustered Javanese army dispersed in headlong flight. On September 18, 1811, the capitulation was signed.[12] Java, with its depend-

[9] Van Deventer, *op. cit.*, pp. 5 and 6.

[10] Lord Minto was perhaps informed of a plan formed by a group of Dutch people, with the assistance of the Prince of Orange, to detach Java from the French Empire and to declare it neutral territory for the duration of the war (De Jonge, *op. cit.*, XIII, cxxiv).

[11] On the campaign of 1811: William Thorn, *Memoir of the Conquest of Java* (London, 1815); Bernard, Duke of Saxe-Weimar, *Précis de la campagne de Java, 1811* (The Hague, 1834); G. B. Hooyer, *De krijgsgeschiedenis van Nederlandsch Indië van 1811 tot 1894*, 3 vols. (The Hague, 1895–1897).

[12] General Janssens' report: De Jonge, *op. cit.*, XIII, 545.

encies, Timor, Macassar, and Palembang, became British territory. On Timor and Celebes the transferring of authority did not meet with difficulties, but when British envoys came to Palembang, the sultan informed them politely that he had followed Raffles' advice to drive out the "cruel Dutch," but that he had done so *before* the capitulation (though after the battle of Batavia, when he was sure which side was going to win!) and that, consequently, he had destroyed the Dutch overlordship over his territory before the British had taken over the Dutch rights! He omitted from his narrative any account of how all the Dutchmen and their families, as well as their Javanese servants with women and children, had been foully murdered after their enforced departure. It would have been wiser if he had left some of them alive to testify to the exact date of their expulsion from Palembang, for Raffles now cynically asserted that the murder had taken place immediately *after* the capitulation of Semarang, and that, therefore, the sultan was bound to respect the treaties concluded with the Dutch government. These assertions were followed by a request that he agree to a treaty of monopoly which would give the British the exclusive right to buy the output of the Bangka tin mines. The price offered was 20 per cent lower than that formerly paid by the Dutch! Upon the refusal of the sultan, a British force was sent to avenge the "horrible massacre" of the Netherlanders. The sultan fled inland, carefully preserving the incitatory letters of Raffles that had been the first cause of the trouble. Many years later he presented these to the Netherlands government in defense of his action.[13]

Lord Minto organized the government of Java before returning to Calcutta. He entrusted the lieutenant-governorship to Thomas Stamford Raffles. The Indonesian Archipelago was now completely under the control of the English East India Company and was divided into four administrative units, the governments of Malacca, Benkulen (west Sumatra), Java, and the Moluccas.[14] The situation in Sumatra remained practically unchanged during the period of British rule. Raffles showed considerable interest in the supposed treasures of the former sultan of Palembang, but the treasure hunt proved unsuccessful. As compensation for his disappointment the sultan was forced to cede Bangka and Billiton to the British, who thus controlled the whole tin production of Indonesia.

[13] J. C. Baud, "Palembang in 1811 en 1812," BKI, 1 (1853), 7 sq.

[14] Malacca and Sumatra's west coast had remained under British control since the first conquest in 1796. The Moluccas were reoccupied by the British in 1810. Accordingly, separate government for these territories had already been organized before the conquest of Java.

The Moluccas gained considerably by the change of administration. The system of monopoly was not abolished — the British had no more moral objection to the system than anybody else — but it was applied much more moderately. The English East India Company had not the same financial interest in maintaining the monopoly as the Dutch had had. The British had already succeeded in transplanting clove and nutmeg trees to their own territory in India and preferred to continue these experiments. The Moluccas needed extra protection by troops and ships, and it was quite possible that after the war with Napoleon the territory would be returned to the Netherlands. Consequently the supervision of native shipping was less strict than before under the Dutch. The worst abuses under which the people of the Moluccas had suffered were remedied.

British rule in Celebes and Borneo was not undisturbed. In Celebes there was continuous warfare with the Buginese. These seafarers and pirates were carrying on a profitable slave trade, and Raffles had embarked on his governorship with the determination to oppose as much as possible both slavery and slave trading. This policy antagonized the Balinese, the great providers of Batavia's slave market, too. The Indonesians did not understand of course the humanitarian principles which prompted Raffles to abolish slavery. In Batavia itself the British lieutenant-governor sought to improve the fate of the slaves (which, as we have seen, was far better than that of the West Indian slaves) and by the imposition of special taxes and other means diverted the population from maintaining these servants.[15] The results were mediocre, but these measures remain memorable as the first steps taken against a very objectionable relic of the "good old times."

The old-timers among the Dutch, of course, criticized him for this novelty, and noted with indignation that the anti-slavery apostle consented to some very odd measures taken in favor of a friend of his, measures that seemed explicitly to contradict his theories. These measures concerned the permission given by Raffles to his friend Alexander Hare to "deport criminals and vagabonds" from Java to that gentleman's estate near Bandjermasin in Borneo. A few thousand poor Javanese were transported, most of whom were permitted to return to Java after the restoration of Dutch rule. The measure had undoubtedly been objectionable, and Mr. Hare, a rather eccentric individual, had to

[15] For Raffles' action against slavery, see H. D. Levyssohn Norman, *De Britsche Heerschappij over Java en Onderhoorigheden (1811–1816)* (The Hague, 1857), pp. 157 sq.; for Raffles on the conditions of the Batavian slaves, see his *History of Java*, I, 84 (2nd ed.).

suffer for it, for he was deprived of his estate by the Dutch authorities.[16] They might have taken a more lenient view had it not been for the apparent contradiction between Raffles' complacency toward the arbitrary actions of his friend and his stern judgment of the "inhumane" Dutch methods of dealing with the native people.

Raffles' interference with the non-Javanese territories of his province was of little consequence. He owes his fame in the history of the Indies to his reorganization of the government of Java itself. Here, his work was indeed of great importance and here he achieved lasting results. In his books he speaks quite disdainfully of the administration that preceded his. He exaggerates its "oppressive and cruel" character although he exonerates the individual Netherlander in the Indies from cruelty and baseness of character.[17] This creates the desired effect of contrast between his own administration and that of his predecessors, a contrast like that of a bright morning after a dark night. Raffles was too well informed not to know that a reorganization of the Javanese system of government had been in progress for fifteen years, but he skillfully minimizes its importance. He knew too, that the basic principles of the reform were laid down by Lord Minto, not by himself, and that several of his chief informants and advisors were Dutch, not British, and he acknowledges this in his *Substance of a Minute*.[18] By continually emphasizing, however, the novelty and beneficial character of his reforms, he suggests to the reader that his administration marked the liberation of an amenable people from a centuries-old oppression; and Lady Raffles, by further suppressing part of the evidence in her *Memoir of the Life of Sir T. S. Raffles*, helped to create the historical legend around her late husband which has been faithfully transcribed by generations of historians.[19]

[16] J. C. Baud, "De Bandjermasinsche afschuwelijkheid," BKI, VII (1860), 1 sq. After his expulsion from Borneo Hare moved to the uninhabited Cocos Islands, which after some altercations with the Dutch, were finally annexed by Britain in 1857.

[17] In the introduction to his *History of Java*, I, 4.

[18] "But there is one gentleman, to whom I am, above all, indebted for the happy accomplishment of this important change. I allude to Mr. Muntinghe, whose ability is beyond praise. . . ." (Raffles in his *Substance of a Minute recorded by the Hon. Th. S. Raffles . . . on the introduction of an improved system of internal management and the establishment of a land rental on the Island of Java*, London, 1814, p. 78.)

[19] Compare with the words of Raffles quoted above, the following passage from the *Memoir*: "Some few [of the Dutch] were sufficiently enlightened to perceive the advantages of the new system; two of these, Mr. Cransen and Mr. Muntinghe on this account were regarded by Mr. Raffles with the highest esteem." In other words, Muntinghe was, according to Mrs. Raffles, enlightened enough to see the advantages of a system which according to Mr. Raffles was based upon and made possible by the information given by the same Muntinghe!

The work of the British lieutenant-governor of Java can be divided into three parts, a revision of the treaties regulating the relations of the Batavian government with the Javanese princes, a reorganization of the administrative institutions and the judiciary, and — the most spectacular of his reforms — an attempt at a complete reform of the system of taxes and contributions.

The first of these reforms can hardly have gained for the British rule that sympathy which Raffles claims to have aroused. The policy of Daendels, which had caused such resentment among the Javanese princes, was carried to its full extent. The Dutch Company had deprived them of their political independence but it had left them an outward appearance of sovereignty. Daendels took that away and humiliated them by assigning first rank in all public ceremonies to the representatives of Batavia. Raffles deprived the princes of all freedom in the management of the internal affairs of their states. Bantam, already reduced to half of its former territory by Daendels, ceased to exist as a sultanate. "In the year 1813," wrote Raffles, "the sultan voluntarily resigned the administration of the country into the hands of the British Government, in consideration of an annual pension of ten thousand Spanish dollars."[20] Two years later Cheribon also was annexed, a measure which undoubtedly was of great benefit to the poor people. In the meantime the power of Djocjakarta had been broken. Daendels had been very inconsiderate in the management of the relations with the sultanate. He had deposed the ruling sultan but neglected to banish him from the sultanate. Acting on vague accusations, he had arrested Prince Natakusuma, the ablest of Djocja's princes, whom he subsequently sentenced to death without trial. Fortunately the official to whose guard the prince was entrusted refused to execute the order. It is understandable that under Raffles' administration trouble started again. Matters soon came to a crisis. The kraton of the sultan was stormed by British troops, the sultan taken prisoner, and all his treasures looted.[21] More than 750,000 dollars were divided among officers and soldiers. Each European soldier received thirty-five dollars as his share, a captain as much as 4,900 dollars, and the commanding officer 16,900 dollars, quite a fortune in the early nineteenth century.

Both princes — for the susuhunan was known to have been in secret connivance with the sultan — were punished by a further limitation of

[20] Raffles, *History of Java* (2nd ed.), II, 267.

[21] Lord Minto, the mortal enemy of Warren Hastings, praised the rather rough proceedings of his protégé at Djocja in unequivocal terms (*Memoir*, letter of Minto, Dec. 15, 1812, p. 130).

their territory. They were deprived of the right to maintain troops, except a small bodyguard. In all internal affairs they promised to regulate themselves according to the wishes of the British government, which took over most of their sources of income against the payment of a yearly pension.[22] Djocjakarta's power was still further restricted by the establishment of a second principality within its boundaries. In the same way that the Mangkunegara had held a small territory as a fief of the susuhunan since 1756, the "Paku Alam" was to hold a fief from the sultan of Djocja. The rights of both the younger branches were guaranteed by the Batavian government, so that in reality the overlordship of the susuhunan and sultan was mere form. The first Paku Alam was Prince Natakusuma, who in this way received his reward for his loyalty to Batavia during Dutch and British rule. Thus, in 1812, the present political organization of the four Javanese principalities came into existence.

The second of Raffles' reforms concerned the structure of the administration and the judiciary. Here, too, his work was chiefly a continuation of that of Daendels. To deprive the regents of their last remnant of autonomy, to make them into mere officials under direct control of the administrators of the provinces, now called "Residents" instead of "prefects" or "Landdrosts" as in Daendels' time, was the logical consequence of Daendels' reforms. Raffles made the mistake of overburdening his Residents with administrative functions, and hence the confusion in the administration at the end of his period of office was even greater than before.[23]

Daendels' and Raffles' reforms together, seen as a whole, constituted a complete transformation of the Javanese system of government. These reforms tended to substitute a European for an Asiatic form of administration. We may say also that they replaced a feudal system by a modern organization. Direct rule of the people by paid government officials took the place of indirect rule through the intermediation of hereditary chiefs. In one respect, however, there is a marked difference. Daendels' reforms were modeled on those of Napoleon Bonaparte in western Europe. His ideal was a dictatorial regime working through an efficient bureaucracy. Raffles, true to English tradition, preferred to introduce local self-government as far as compatible with Javanese customs. His informants, the British officials put in charge of the residencies, reported that in many districts of Java the old custom of election of the headman of the village by the people had not yet been

[22] Text of the treaties of 1813: van Deventer, *op. cit.*, pp. 321 and 327.
[23] Norman Levyssohn, *op. cit.*, p. 132.

extinguished. We may doubt whether the information thus obtained was wholly correct, but it provided the lieutenant-governor with the desired material for his reform of local administration. The "Regulation for the more effectual administration of justice in the provincial courts of Java" of February 11, 1814, stipulated (art. VII) that "in each village there shall be a Head-man, to be freely elected by the inhabitants of the village itself from among themselves." We may doubt again whether the elections thus organized were really free. It seemed unavoidable that the centuries-old social institutions of the Javanese people should continue to prevail over the newly introduced foreign system of general elections, but, in spite of all this, Raffles' reform held a great promise for the future. Here indeed he brought an innovation which, at that time, would scarcely have been introduced by even the most liberal of Dutch reformers.[24]

Less successful was Raffles' attempt to reorganize the judiciary. Here he definitely made the mistake of trying to transplant typical British institutions to absolutely foreign soil. The attempt to introduce the jury, an institution unknown in the Netherlands and totally foreign to the Javanese way of thinking, was a complete failure. It was immediately abolished after the return of the Dutch authorities and was never regretted. His other measures for the rendering of justice and especially for the better treatment of prisoners necssarily remained reforms on paper because of lack of time and money to put them into execution. This brings us to the crucial problem of Raffles' administration, the reform of the tax system and finances.

Lord Minto, before leaving Java and transferring the administration to Raffles, had laid down the principles of the tax reform. He had ordered the immediate abolition of all forced deliveries and contingencies and "a fundamental change in the whole system of landed property and tenure." And he added: "The discussion of the subject, however, must necessarily be delayed, till the investigation it requires is more complete."[25] This order was easy to promulgate, but less easy to execute. If the deliveries and contingencies were abolished, the Batavian government lost that part of its income upon which in Raffles' days it had to rely. The produce of the coffee gardens was piling up in the storehouses, but after the promulgation of Napoleon's Continental Blockade and the outbreak of the British-American war, there was no longer a market for it. The old system could not be abolished unless new taxes were introduced, and this, in its turn, involved a revision of

[24] The "Regulation" of 1814: *Substance of a Minute*, p. 217.
[25] Instructions of Lord Minto: *Substance of a Minute*, pp. 5–6.

Batavia's land policy. Nobody could foresee whether the returns from the new taxes would be sufficient for the upkeep of the administration. For this reason, the Dutch committee of 1803 had refused to accept the ideas of Dirk van Hogendorp. From a financial point of view, the reform was a leap into the dark. Raffles was obliged to risk it. The alternative would have been to report to the governor-general of India that his theories were not ripe for practical execution, and this, Raffles knew, would be the end of his career. Hence the inconclusiveness of Raffles' policy, which he sought to cover by a lavish display of noble intentions but for which later Netherlands historians have bitterly criticized him.

In the archives of Batavia, Raffles found the results of an investigation into the conditions of land tenure ordered by Daendels. This investigation had been very incomplete, and consequently Raffles ordered a second, more detailed one. Upon the information thus gathered, he based his reforms. Raffles and his coöperators undoubtedly made many mistakes in their conclusions from the material they had collected, but even now, after a century and more of scientific researches in this field, the authorities on the subject do not agree in their opinions. The worst mistake made by Raffles was that he did not discern that in the different parts of Java the native institutions under the influence of political factors had developed in different ways. Especially in the districts which for centuries had been ruled by the despotic Javanese princes, conditions of land tenure had far deviated from the original Javanese institutions.

Raffles, however, found what he wanted to find in the reports presented to him: a picture of social conditions among the Javanese not unlike those existing among the Indians in Bengal which justified him in introducing a tax system modeled after that followed by the English Company in India. He promulgated a decree based on the theory that all landed property, in fact the whole of the land, by right belonged to the sovereign, that is, to the government of Batavia, according to the Oriental custom "that lands are bestowed upon the several classes of chiefs and public officers provisionally or during pleasure . . . that the actual ownership of the land is vested in the Prince, in short that between the Sovereign and the cultivator there exists no actual right." [26] Thus with a single stroke of the pen Raffles, at least theoretically, deprived all Javanese of their landed property! In his decree (of October 15, 1813) he said: "The Government lands will be let generally to the Heads of Villages. . . . They will re-let these lands to the Cultivators,

[26] *Substance of a Minute*, p. 6.

under certain restrictions, at such a rate as shall not be found oppressive; and all Tenants under Government will be protected in their just rights, so long as they shall continue to perform their correspondent engagements faithfully."[27]

The land rent itself was fixed according to the value of the land and differed from one fourth to one half of the produce. The whole system was worked out by Raffles and his Dutch collaborator Herman W. Muntinghe according to the tax laws existing in Bengal, which also had served Van Hogendorp as the models for his plans. But conditions in Bengal and in Java were different in many respects. In Java, Raffles' theory, in which the rights of sovereignty and of private ownership were confused, could lead to grave consequences. It held, for instance, that all uncultivated land was at the direct and free disposal of the government, an apparent injustice toward the Javanese, who considered large areas of uncultivated land as their land reserve (a fact well known to Muntinghe),[28] to be brought under cultivation as the population increased. If the government decided to sell this land to European or Chinese planters, a landless proletariat, with its accompanying social problems, would grow up in the villages.

It was easier to lay down the rules of the new system than to put them into execution. The system necessitated a complete survey of the Javanese fields. Since the renting out had to be done by contract, rent rolls would have to be kept in each village. The headman of the village was supposed to give extract accounts of the roll to each individual cultivator and to grant receipts for every payment he received. All this was to be done in a country where practically none of the farmers, and only a few of the headmen, could read or write. Since the poor farmers did not have ready money with which to pay their taxes, they sought the help of Chinese money lenders or of their own chiefs, the very people whose influence Raffles had hoped to destroy forever. He had left the regents and headmen control over the working of a certain amount of land in payment for the services rendered by them, and thus the land rent was often only part of the burden of the villager, who had, beside paying that tax, to provide for his own chiefs. Only after many years of organizing could the new system come into full effect. In principle it was more beneficial to the people than the old system, but in the beginning its effects appear to have been oppressive.

[27] "Revenue instructions of Febr. 11, 1814," in *Substance of a Minute*, pp. 181 sq.

[28] See Muntinghe's memoir of July 11, 1817, in S. Ottow, *De Oorsprong van de conservatieve richting*, p. 75. This book, on pages 54–64, gives a sharp, although somewhat exaggerated, criticism of Raffles' policy. It is very useful as a counteragent against the equally exaggerated praise of that policy by Raffles' panegyrists.

A moderate British historian has correctly judged Raffles' reforms when he said: "The reforms of Daendels were for the most part reforms on paper, and this is still more true of the reforms of Raffles because they were even more ambitious." [29]

The financial difficulties of the government of Java were the cause of a grave inconsistency in Raffles' reforms. He definitely excluded the coffee-producing Preanger districts from his new tax system. Here and in the forest districts compulsory production and levying of taxes in the form of labor were continued, as they had been in the days of the Company, though under better control of the administration.[30] Finally, the British lieutenant-governor too resorted to the method of the sale of government lands, that is, of cultivated districts with the peasant population included, to European financiers, and Raffles secured for himself a share in the large estate of Sukabumi, one of the best coffee-producing districts of Java.[31] This was one of his gravest mistakes, which provided Major General R. R. Gillespie, the commanding officer of the British troops in Java, with some of his best arguments when he decided to bring his complaints against the lieutenant-governor before the authorities in Calcutta. From the beginning there had been great difference of opinion and jealousy between the two men, and as soon as Lord Minto, Raffles' protector, had resigned his governor-generalship of India, Gillespie came to the front with his accusations.[32]

The Board of Directors at East India House in London was already far from satisfied with Raffles' administration. The governor had not succeeded in balancing the budget of the new colony — which was hardly *his* fault — and consequently the East India Company was little interested in retaining a colony that cost a great deal of money every year. In 1815 Raffles was recalled, and John Fendall was appointed his successor.[33] As an administrator Raffles had not been a success, but the British interlude in Java's history had cleared away a great deal of the old dust gathered in the days of the Dutch Company, and Raffles

[29] Furnivall, *Netherlands India*, p. 74. The task of surveying the rice fields was of such magnitude that it took seventy years to complete it.

[30] Thus, the so-called "Preanger system" came into existence. This term is used to indicate the special administrative forms under which in the Preanger districts antiquated institutions of levying taxes and administration through the regents were preserved. The regents here even retained some rights of levying taxes for themselves and thus some remnants of their ancient autonomous position.

[31] Furnivall points out that in general Raffles' financial administration was much better than that of his successors (Furnivall, *op. cit.*, pp. 73–74).

[32] See R. R. Gillespie, *A Memoir* (London, 1816), and Norman Levyssohn, *op. cit.*, ch. viii, pp. 301 sq.

[33] John Fendall's administration lasted only from March 11, 1816, until August 19 of the same year.

had been the man who had opened windows and doors so that the wind could blow through the old house. Posterity knows him better as the writer of his *History of Java* than as the governor who introduced the land-rent system.

Raffles' interest in Indonesian languages and customs was genuine. He devoted a great deal of his time and much of his correspondence to matters of purely ethnological interests. To revive the moribund Batavian Society of Arts and Sciences was one of his first undertakings. He read several papers for the Society, which afterwards with the works of other British and Dutch students of Indology were published in its *Verhandelingen*. He encouraged the studying of botany, and the American explorer Dr. Thomas Horsfield became one of his friends.[34] Raffles' own *History of Java*, written in England, is in many respects a remarkable work.[35] Like Marsden's *History of Sumatra*, it was meant to be a full description of the island, its climate, its population, its antiquities, and its history. Marsden's book evidently was the model imitated by Raffles, but while the historian of Sumatra was, first of all, a scholar, the author of the *History of Java* was definitely first of all a politician. His book serves the purpose of all his other undertakings, the ultimate glory of Thomas Raffles himself. Thus it became a curious mixture of scholarly description, apology, and what in modern times we would call intelligent reporting. That reporting is far from impartial,[36] but, brilliant and interesting as it is, it gave publicity to Java and its people in the whole of the English-reading world, for the first

[34] Thomas Horsfield, born May 12, 1773, at Bethlehem, Pennsylvania, first visited Batavia in 1800 as a surgeon aboard an American merchant ship. Two years later he came back to Java and through the Board of the Batavian Society obtained a commission from the governor-general, Siberg, to do research work in the field of pharmaceutic botany. He carried on his researches until 1818, when he decided to join Raffles in Benkulen. When leaving Batavia he took his rich collections, mainly gathered in the service of the Dutch government, along with him and, through the intermediation of Raffles, received an appointment with the India Museum. He died in 1850 in London. Works: treatises in vols. VII and VIII of VBG, *Zoological Researches in Java and the Neighboring Islands* (London, 1824), and others.

[35] The first edition of the *History of Java* in two beautifully printed volumes appeared in London in 1817, a second edition in 1830.

[36] One example: Raffles discussing the construction of roads in forced labor, says, "When completed by his own labor or the sacrifice of the life of his neighbor, the peasant was debarred from their use" (*History of Java*, 2nd ed., I, 220). The same Raffles issued an ordinance forbidding to the Javanese the use of the same roads, "it being only allowed to them to go on the ordinary and long established cartroads as formerly"! (De Haan, *Priangan*, IV, 910.) Raffles in his *History* did not mention this ordinance, of course. It would be relatively easy to collect numerous examples of cases like this, where Raffles blames his predecessors for their inhumane measures and yet maintains these measures and enforces them during his own administration.

time in history. Lady Raffles, in due admiration for the work of her late husband, liked to exaggerate the importance of his writings. Of a letter written by Raffles to Lord Minto in 1811 she says: "The Reader must bear in mind that these Letters were written at a time when scarcely any thing was known either of the literature or of the people, or of the countries of this part of the East,"[37] as if there never had been a François Valentijn who filled huge folio volumes with compact information, or a George Rumphius and Justus Heurnius. But Raffles' work indeed is far more readable and better composed than that of his predecessors, and he approached his subjects with a great sympathy for the native people of the Indies which in most of the earlier works is deplorably missing.

One of Raffles' chief collaborators was John Crawfurd, who served as the Minister of the Batavian government with the Javanese princes. Crawfurd wrote a *History of the East Indian Archipelago* in three volumes, a far less detailed work than that of Raffles but written with great verve and with the fashionable display of humanitarian sentiments and burning indignation for the injustices committed by other people.[38] Many years later Crawfurd revised his *History* and republished it in the form of *A Descriptive Dictionary of the Indian Islands and Adjacent Countries* which contains a great deal of information that is still useful.[39]

When John Fendall was appointed to the lieutenant-governorship of Java, he knew that his position would be a temporary one, for the British government had already decided to return Java to the restored state of the Netherlands. In November 1813, after the battle of Leipzig, a revolt broke out in Holland. The Prince of Orange, William VI, returned to The Hague and first assumed the title of "Sovereign Prince," then, in 1815, that of King of the United Netherlands. On August 13, 1814, the representatives of Great Britain and those of the new kingdom agreed on the stipulations of a treaty which provided for the restitution of all the former Netherlands colonies that had been under Netherlands sovereignty in the year 1803, except the Cape

[37] *Memoir*, p. 39.

[38] Crawfurd's *History* was published at Edinburgh in 1820. It would be an interesting study to see how far authors like Hogendorp, Raffles, Crawfurd, and others of the same opinion in colonial affairs, were influenced by Raynal's *Histoire philosophique et politique*. Hogendorp uses a quotation from Raynal as a motto for his *Berigt* of 1799. The study of Dallas D. Irvine, "The Abbé Raynal and British Humanitarianism," in the *Journal of Modern History*, III (1933), 564 sq., does not throw much light upon this problem. See, however, P. J. Platteel, *De grondslagen der Constitutie van Nederlandsch Indië* (Utrecht, 1936).

[39] The *Dictionary* was published in 1856 in London.

Colony and Demarara.[40] This excluded Ceylon, but called for the restitution of all posts and territories in the archipelago. Here only Benkulen, which had been British since the end of the seventeenth century, remained under the English East India Company. The actual restoration was delayed by the return of Napoleon from Elba. On August 19, 1816, however, the Dutch flag was waving once more over Batavia.

To take over the government in the islands King William sent over three Commissaries General. The chairman of the Committee was C. Th. Elout. The other members were A. Busykens, a naval commander, and G. Baron van der Capellen, who was appointed governor-general and would remain in the Indies after the work of the Committee had been completed. The British officials surrendered the reins of government, but grudgingly, seeking for pretexts of delay in the vain hope that the government in London would change its mind. This delay complicated the already difficult task of the Committee. It gave Raffles, now Sir Stamford Raffles, time to return to the Indies in the capacity of governor of Benkulen before they had completed their task, and immediately after his return he began a diplomatic struggle against the Dutch.

The Commissaries found the government of the Indies in a state of confusion.[41] They were not bound by treaty to accept and continue any of the reforms introduced by the British. Theoretically completely free to return to the system of the Company, they decided at once that the time had come when the Indies should be governed for the sake of its own people and not for that of the Netherlands. They solemnly declared it to be the sole aim of the king "to promote the interests of all his subjects, without any exception." Under these veiled terms they indicated that prejudice of race or class would not be tolerated. This was the principle of the Revolution and of Liberalism. There was no

[40] Documents concerning the negotiation: Van Deventer, *op. cit.*, pp. 25 sq; H. Colenbrander, *Koloniale Geschiedenis* (The Hague, 1926), vol. II, and *Willem I, Koning der Nederlanden* (Amsterdam, 1931), I, 304–315. For a full history with all details, see P. H. van der Kemp, *De teruggave der Nederlandsche koloniën, 1814–1816* (The Hague, 1810), and articles by the same author, BKI, XLVII (1897), 239 sq. and 341 sq.; XLIX (1898), 205 sq.

[41] The studies of P. H. van der Kemp, *Oost Indië's herstel in 1816* (The Hague, 1911), *Het Nederlandsch Indisch bestuur in 1817* (The Hague, 1913, with three continuations), *Java's Landelijk Stelsel* (The Hague, 1916), *Sumatra in 1818* (The Hague, 1920), must be checked against the older work of I. H. J. Hoek, *Het herstel van het Nederlandsch Gezag over Java en onderhoorigheden in de jaren 1816–1818* (The Hague, 1862), and the series of modern studies, conducted under the supervision of Prof. C. Gerretson of the University of Utrecht: P. J. Platteel, *op. cit.*, D. J. P. Oranje, *Het beleid der Commissie Generaal* (Utrecht, 1936), and S. Ottow, *op. cit.*

doubt that the Commissaries were sincere in declaring these maxims of government. It was another question how the matter would work out in practice. The difficulties that presented themselves seemed insurmountable. Both in Europe and in the Indies the state of the Netherlands had to be reorganized. In both parts of the globe the government was in dire need of money, but a large part of the national wealth had been lost during the Napoleonic period, and the new sources of income had not yet begun to produce. The proverbial "fabulous wealth of the Indies" was of no avail, for we have seen that this fabulous wealth consisted almost entirely of the products of agriculture, and mostly of crops introduced or fostered by the Netherlanders. For these crops there was no market over a period of several years. Moreover, the coffee culture had been greatly affected by Raffles' measures of reform. Promotion of the welfare of the Indies could only mean promotion of the production of valuable crops and a more equitable division of the produce among the different coöperating parties. The Commissaries decided, however, that Raffles' tax system was more just than the system of forced labor promoted by Daendels and his predecessors. Hence the land rent was maintained. Over-optimistic adherents to the theory of Liberalism expected a rapid increase in production if the Javanese farmers were left free to handle things in their own way. They were disappointed. Without the assistance of European skill and knowledge, the Javanese seemed unable to develop his farming beyond the production of rice.

Some die-hard Liberals deduced, however, from the solemn declaration of principle issued by the Commissaries that the abolishment of all prejudice of class and race included the abolishment of all restrictions put upon the activities of Europeans as well as those of Indonesians. We know that the Dutch Company had strictly forbidden Europeans to settle or even travel in purely Javanese districts without special permission. Raffles had maintained this restriction. His theory that all land belonged to the government explains sufficiently why. But when the Commissaries declared that the welfare of *all* subjects, without any exception, should be fostered by the king's officers, several enterprising men, among them some Englishmen, some Netherlanders, a Chinese, and even an Armenian, sent requests to the government that they should be allowed to buy tracts of land and to start agricultural enterprises on a large scale. These requests seemed perfectly reasonable. These men asked no privileges. The Javanese were wholly free to follow the same course. Liberty and Equality! Yet, the demands plunged the Commissaries into great embarrassments, for as Van der

Capellen formulated it later: "Measures that if seen at three thousand miles distance apparently are liberal, here prove to be highly illiberal in their effects." If the Commissaries had started selling large tracts of land to non-Indonesian promoters they would have introduced a capitalistic system under which the wealthy landowners would have dominated the native population. The Javanese could not compete in buying land, for not only did they not possess the necessary capital, but the whole idea of acquiring land under the rules of Roman law was foreign to their own conceptions of landed property.

It was useless to buy land if there was no labor available to cultivate it, and the whole population of Java was already occupied in agriculture. Since there remained uncultivated land enough to provide for the natural increase in population, there were not, nor would there be, unemployed farmhands who would have to accept work for wages on the estates. The estate owners would have found difficulty in paying their laborers in wages. Their only recourse was to concede to their laborers small lots on the estates and to allow them to produce their own rice on this territory in return for a certain amount of labor to be spent on the estate. The Javanese settlers were economically weak, the landowners were wealthy, and therefore the labor contract between these two parties could only be in favor of the owner. Thus, the whole system of free contracts would have led — to be sure, by way of a detour — to a restoration of the eighteenth-century estate where Javanese tenants were "corvéable et taillable à merci." "If I must assume," said Van der Capellen, "that in the Netherlands Liberalism is understood to be the protection of European landowners at the expense of the native population, and that the interests of the latter are completely disregarded to give a few speculators and adventurers the chance to succeed in their schemes, then I must declare myself to be an ultra anti-Liberal." [42]

Having considered all the aspects of a possible grant of sale of estates to private capitalists, the Commissaries decided to refuse such requests. They have been called highly inconsistent in their policy, but in reality they stuck to the spirit, if not to the words, of their solemn declaration. Their decision was well-advised, but they had yet to solve the problem of how to increase the revenue of the state. Even after the coffee price had risen on the world market they could hardly make ends meet because at the same time their ambitious program to improve the stand-

[42] Ottow, *op. cit.*, p. 121. We must bear in mind that "liberal" in this connection always is used in its narrower meaning of "adherent of the political and economic theory of the age," i.e. of the early nineteenth-century bourgeois conception of these matters.

ard of living and of culture among Europeans and Indonesians alike caused a spiraling increase of expenses. They founded a new department of government, that of Agriculture, Arts and Education. It is evident that here more than an administrative combination of Agriculture and Education was intended. The task of the new department was to improve agricultural systems by spreading general and professional education and by promoting research work in the field of botany. The first director of this department was Professor Caspar Reinwardt. Professor Reinwardt had been born in Prussia and migrated as a boy to the Netherlands. Here he studied botany and became professor of natural history at the University of Harderwijk — a moribund institution — from which he was promoted to the University of Amsterdam. King William sent him to the Indies. The famous Botanic Garden of Buitenzorg is practically his creation.

The improvement of elementary education in the Indies was a difficult problem. The Company had never interfered with purely Javanese affairs and had limited its educational activities to Batavia proper and a few places in the Moluccas. Elementary education, until the French Revolution, was mostly the concern of the Church. In Java it was in the hands of the Mohammedan priesthood.[43] Professor Reinwardt came to the Indies with definite instructions to investigate the existing school systems and to improve them in accordance with the principles in force in the Netherlands itself: that the state should see to it that everywhere in the country the children should receive proper instruction based upon "the moral principles common to all mankind." It was not so difficult to improve the schools of Batavia, which, although organized for the European children, were thrown open to Mohammedans and Chinese as well. The investigation into the Javanese schools gives us a good idea of what Indonesian education was where it had not been influenced by the Europeans. The Mohammedan priests received only small fees for their teaching, but they did not teach to the Javanese their own language and script, but that of the Koran. Moreover, they taught them how to recite the Koran from the Arabic text — which is quite a different thing from teaching them how to read Arabic texts. Often the reading of the Koran was taught from a Malay translation. Children of the aristocratic class received some instruction in reading and writing their own Javanese language, but this knowledge was handed down in the families from the older to the younger generations and never taught in schools. We see that the intro-

[43] J. A. van der Chijs, "Geschiedenis van het inlandsch onderwijs in Nederlandsch Indië," TBG, XIV (1864), 212 sq. and XVI (1867), 1 sq.

duction of Islam had the same effect on native learning as a conquest by a foreign power. The natural development and spreading of the knowledge of Javanese was hampered by the introduction of a foreign language.

Here the Commissaries could without any difficulty have gained for themselves a great name for generations to come. The fashion of the day was the slogan "equality for all," but it was always understood in this sense: "We, Europeans, people of superior culture, graciously condescend to lift all other peoples of the earth to our standards of learning!" The idea has not wholly disappeared in our day. There are still some Westerners who consider it the greatest benefit they can possibly bestow on colored people to permit them to learn a Western language. If the Commissaries had acted in the same way and organized a few schools where the children of the Javanese aristocrats had been taught Dutch, if they had conceived their task of education to be the transforming as soon as possible of a limited group of Indonesians into people of Dutch language and behavior who could take degrees in Dutch Universities, they probably would have been praised for their "enlightened government." The Commissaries not only neglected this chance to become famous, but even ordered that plans should be made "to spread the knowledge of the Malay, Javanese and other languages among the Europeans!"[44] This was a momentous decision. The Commissaries themselves perhaps did not realize how momentous it was. By ordering "instruction in *Malay*, *Javanese* and *other* languages" they definitely ruled out the possibility that it was their purpose to purvey sufficient knowledge of language to enable the Dutch colonists to communicate with the Indonesians. For that purely practical purpose Malay alone would have been sufficient. The ordinance put the Indonesian and Dutch languages on the same footing, in fact it laid down the principle that the Indonesian language should be the language generally used by *both* Europeans and Indonesians. This language policy has been maintained. Often the Netherlanders have been severely criticized for neglecting to spread their language and culture. Cultural imperialism is, however, much worse than economic imperialism. Of the latter, with all its consequences good and bad, there had been a great deal in the Indies between 1600 and 1870. Of the former, there was none. Once the Indonesians have gained sufficient economic strength to support their cultural activities, they will be able to develop these along their own national lines, unhampered by that varnish of

[44] P. H. van der Kemp, "Uit den tijd van C. P. J. Elout's toewijding aan de Maleische taal," BKI, LXIX (1914), 141 sq.

superficial western forms of thinking and acting which in so many parts of the globe have suffocated the natural development of civilization.

The idealistic plan of spreading education among the peoples of the Indies met, of course, with the greatest practical difficulties. There were no teachers available, neither Dutch nor Indonesian. There were no funds. In the following years of economic exploitation of the Indies by the Netherlands government, the whole scheme was dropped. But Professor Reinwardt had many other vital matters to attend to. One of the sections of his department, for example, was that of Public Health. As director of this branch of government service he led the battle against epidemic diseases. No plague was worse in those days than smallpox. In the territory of Bantam such terror spread among the people that whole villages were deserted as soon as a single case of smallpox occurred in the neighborhood. The government finally succeeded in convincing the people of the advisability of having themselves inoculated, and the progress of the disease was checked.

Their many problems would have given the Commissaries worries enough without the permanent interference of the industrious Raffles, who was stirring up trouble everywhere.[45] Raffles had come back to the Indies a thoroughly disappointed man. The knighthood conferred upon him by the Prince Regent of Great Britain had been only a slight consolation for the reproofs of the Directors of the East India Company. They had permitted him to return to Benkulen, a forlorn post of which the governor-general of India had promised him the governorship. After the lieutenant-governorship of Java this seemed a degradation. He undoubtedly had deserved a better reward. It is amazing that the Directors seemed to have had no interest in making use of the great capacities of a man like Raffles, but perhaps they feared his vaulting ambition. To secure a great name in history lay closer to his heart than to further the financial interest of the Company. Having been rebuked for his progressive system of government, Raffles threw overboard most of his ideals and declared that the people of Benkulen were not ripe for such a liberal administration as that followed in Java. But to look after the pepper plants and small parks of clove trees of Benkulen could not long satisfy the mind of the ever-scheming Raffles.

[45] On Raffles' governorship of Benkulen and the founding of Singapore (besides the general works on Raffles), see H. T. Colenbrander, "Advies over archiefstukken in het India Office te Londen, van belang voor de Indische geschiedenis van 1818 tot 1830," BKI, vol. LXVII (1912), and the articles of P. H. van der Kemp in BKI, XLIX (1898), 1 sq., 205 sq.; L (1899), 1 sq.; LI (1900), 1 sq., 159 sq.; LII (1901), 584 sq.; LIV (1902), 313 sq.; LVI (1904), 1 sq.

He devoted all his time and energy to searching out such loopholes in the treaty of 1814 as would permit him to detach from Batavia a large part of the Indonesian islands. He had soon formed the opinion that under the treaty the Dutch in reality had no claims to Sumatra and Borneo. If he could forestall them in these islands he thought he might still secure the islands for the British.

When a Netherlands Commissary came to take over Padang on Sumatra's west coast, Raffles refused to cede the town. He made a short trip inland and tried to conclude treaties with the chiefs of the Menangkabau, and he took good care to insert in such treaties as he concluded a statement to the effect that the Malayans sought the protection of the British because "they abhorred the Dutch system of oppression." The Dutch had never exerted any authority in the territory concerned, but that did not matter. In March 1818 Raffles had arrived in Benkulen and two months later he had already sent a small detachment of troops to Sumatra's southern point to occupy a village on Sunda Strait, in Dutch territory. The Dutch hoisted their flag side by side with the British and protested officially in Calcutta. By order from Calcutta Raffles was commanded to leave the occupied position. He complained bitterly that the government of Calcutta did not know how important a position it was giving up, that the British *needed* a port on Sunda Strait in order to have some control over that important thoroughfare. It was to no avail. But he had already undertaken another expedition. Muntinghe, in his capacity as Commissary of Batavia, was trying to settle the affairs of Palembang, where the same sultan who had ruled in 1811, the year of the massacre of the Dutch, was still in power. While Muntinghe was negotiating, a small British force marched into the city, straight into the palace of the sultan's son, and hoisted the British flag.[46] They came from Benkulen, crossing Sumatra from west to east (the first Europeans to do so), and pretended that the young sultan had demanded their help. Muntinghe remonstrated, bluntly asked them to haul down the British flag, and, finally, had the whole group arrested and transported to Batavia. Again Raffles protested, but once more the government in Calcutta backed Batavia — Palembang was beyond any doubt included in the territory to be restored by the treaty of 1814 — and the scheme fell through.

In his dispatches to Calcutta and London, Raffles argued that the British government should not permit the political unity of Sumatra to be broken up. The whole island, he declared, should be brought

[46] P. H. van der Kemp, "Palembang en Bangka van 1816–1820," BKI, LI (1900), 331 sq.

under British protection. He found no support. But he did not give up. The treaty of 1814 seemed unclear in regard to the tin-producing island of Billiton. There were no British troops or officials on the island; indeed, it was occupied by a small force of Indonesian allies of the Dutch; but the British, not only Raffles this time but also the government in London, maintained their claim. Raffles urged his colleagues at Pulu Penang to delay the surrender of Malacca and to send a small expedition to western Borneo to establish a claim to that territory. He also put forward a claim to Bandjermasin, a post which had unquestionably been occupied by the Dutch in 1803 but had later been evacuated by Daendels for military reasons.

We have already seen how the Commissaries-General thought it prudent to remove Raffles' friend, Mr. Alexander Hare, from his colony near Bandjermasin. They now hurriedly dispatched a force to reoccupy Pontianak in western Borneo. Another expedition sailed for Malacca. The commander of the latter force did not wait until he received British permission to land, but, claiming the territory to be Dutch under the treaty, landed his troops at once. The British at Pulu Penang had meanwhile intervened in a war of succession in Atjeh and supported the claims of a wealthy merchant of their own city to the throne of that sultanate. Raffles decided that it was time to take a firm stand, lest he lose the diplomatic battle all along the line. He hurried to Calcutta and expounded to Governor Lord Moira the necessity of maintaining a foothold on Malacca Strait for the safety of British commerce from India to China. He argued that the Netherlands government intended to restore completely the system of monopoly and to close the Eastern Seas to all other nations, a policy which they had not the power to follow if they had wanted to. From Calcutta he rushed to Pulu Penang and set out for an expedition through Malacca Strait to look for a suitable place to establish a trading center and port of relay for the shipping to China. He had planned to occupy Johore, but the Dutch had forestalled him once more, and had renewed the treaty of 1785 with the sultan. Raffles' companions then suggested the Karimon islands in Malacca Strait, but these proved to be less suited to the purpose. Raffles turned again to the Rhio islands, which formed part of the sultanate of Johore, and bought from the same sultan, who a few months before had recognized the overlordship of Batavia, the island of Singapore. Here the British flag was hoisted on January 29, 1819.[47] From here Raffles proceeded to Atjeh, where he concluded a treaty

[47] The question of whether the founding of Singapore constituted a violation of the treaty of 1814 is discussed in the articles of Van der Kemp, who opposes the view of

with the actually ruling sultan. He dropped the pretender selected by his colleagues in Pulu Penang — which must have put these gentlemen in an embarrassing position. The new sultan promised to give the English East India Company a privileged position in his territory and to refuse access to all Europeans but the Company's officials.

Thus Singapore was founded, but the Dutch held claims on the territory on which it was built. Should they want to assert these claims, and should they act as promptly as they had in the other instances, there was little chance for Raffles to succeed. By now the British government was thoroughly annoyed with perpetual intrigues of this gentleman. George Canning, Foreign Secretary of the United Kingdom after 1822, wrote to Raffles on a later occasion:

> I cannot deny that your extreme activity in stirring up difficult questions and the freedom with which you committed your Government, without their knowledge or authority, to measures which might have brought a war upon them unprepared, did at one time oblige me to speak my mind to you in instructions of not very mild apprehension.[48]

Raffles, however, hoped to make Singapore flourish in a few years, which would make the British government change its mind, and he succeeded. The port was declared custom free and became a center of Indonesian and European shipping. Vainly some of the Dutch officials urged Governor-General Van der Capellen to follow this example in regard to Malacca.[49] But Batavia let the opportunity pass and limited itself to paper protest instead of taking action by hoisting the Dutch flag beside the British. Raffles, encouraged by this success, continued his "experiments" and occupied the island of Nias near Sumatra's west coast, alleging that the inhabitants had asked for protection against the Atjenese slave traders (Raffles' allies of the day before!). This time he went too far. He received a peremptory order to withdraw the British troops and to deliver Padang to the Dutch. Grudgingly he acquiesced. With Canning's appointment, however, the political situation in Britain changed in his favor. The London government had no longer any intention of giving up the promising settlement of Singapore, but they intended to come to an honorable agreement with the Netherlands, and not simply to seize as much as they could. The Netherlands

---

Boulger, *Life of Raffles*. The date of the founding of the city is given according to Boulger, *op. cit.*, p. 307.

[48] Letter of Oct. 11, 1824 (Boulger, *op. cit.*, p. 276).

[49] In 1818 the Commissaries laid down rules for the future administration of the Indies in the Administration Act ("Regeeringsreglement"), which is published in the collection of P. Mijer (*Verzameling van Instructien*, etc.), pp. 399 sq. Thereupon they handed the reins of government to G. A. Baron van der Capellen as governor-general.

government had the same wishes, especially as Governor-General Van der Capellen was beset by many difficulties.

In Sumatra the sultan of Palembang was waging war against the Dutch, a war that resulted in his expulsion and the annexation of the sultanate to the government territory. In the Menangkabau, the village chiefs made an appeal to the Dutch in Padang for assistance against the warriors of a new Mohammedan sect, that of the "Padris." [50] This sect was founded by some Malays who had made the pilgrimage to Mecca and there had become acquainted with the sect of the Wahabites, then all-powerful in Arabia. Returned home, they found fault with the village institutions of their people. These Malay tribes of the Menangkabau cling to this day to the old matriarchal form of family organization, which is hardly compatible with the commands of the Koran. The zealous pilgrims also objected to the use of tobacco, or worse, opium, and to many other local habits. They started a campaign of reformation, gathered around them a number of adherents, and began to spread their convictions by the sword. Most pilgrims to Mecca traveled via Pedir, a small port on Sumatra's north coast where Islam had first been introduced, and because of this they were called "men of Pedir," which the Dutch, according to the linguistic rule of *lucus a non lucendo*, connected with the Portuguese "Padre" or priest. In the war which resulted from the chiefs' appeal, Dutch soldiers and their Malay allies struggled for years against the fanatic sect. At the same time a local uprising had been caused in the Moluccas by the fear of the inhabitants of Amboina that the former system of monopoly and restriction of production would be restored.[51] Some of the rebels were native Christians, and these seriously called upon their religious teachers, men of their own people, to say an invocation before they attacked and killed a number of Dutch and Javanese government servants! After the revolt had been crushed, Van der Capellen hurried to the Moluccas. He published an ordinance in which all orders of restriction were abolished and a fairer price for the product was promised to the agriculturists. The government maintained for a while the system of monopoly, but Van der Capellen personally urged the king of the Netherlands also to bring to an end this last remnant of the Company's system.

All disputes with Great Britain were settled in 1824 by a second

[50] E. B. Kielstra, "Sumatra's Westkust van 1819 tot 1825," BKI, XXXVI (1887), 7 sq., the first of a series on the history of that section of the Indies up to 1891 (BKI, vols. XXXVII–XLI).

[51] H. A. Idema, "De oorzaken van den opstand van Saparoea in 1817," BKI, LXXXIX (1923), 598 sq.

treaty concluded in London.[52] Singapore had grown into an important emporium and the British intended to keep the town and the territory around it, but, recognizing the claims of the Netherlands to the same territory, the British government proposed to exchange the Malay Peninsula for the district of Benkulen, the British claims to Billiton, and the privileges acquired by Raffles in Atjeh in 1819. Moreover, the British promised not to interfere further with Sumatra or any of the other islands of the archipelago. The Netherlanders promised to respect the independence of Atjeh, but undertook at the same time to protect the shipping around Sumatra's northern point against the Atjenese pirates, two promises that could hardly be kept at the same time.

The treaty of 1824 made an end to the British control over Benkulen. Consequently, Raffles lost his position and returned to England, where he died two years later on his forty-fifth birthday. He had not succeeded in establishing British rule in the archipelago, but his foundation, the city of Singapore, became the main emporium of southern Asia. Raffles had intended that it should be an anti-Batavia. In our time it has been Batavia's citadel.

[52] Colenbrander, *Koloniale Geschiedenis*, III, 26 sq. C. M. Smulders, *Geschiedenis en Verklaring van het tractaat van 17 Maart 1824* (Utrecht, 1856); P. H. van der Kemp, "Geschiedenis van het Londensch tractaat van 1824," BKI, LVI (1904), 1 sq.

CHAPTER XIII

JOHANNES VAN DEN BOSCH AND THE LIBERALS

VAN DER CAPELLEN's period of office had been very unsatisfactory for the Home Government.[1] The public debts of the Indies had increased. The production of export crops had diminished. The European planters were the irreconcilable opponents of the governor-general because he protected the Indonesians. The Liberals at home were indignant because he was reactionary. The king was furious because his governor had concluded a very imprudent contract with British bankers for a loan that put too heavy an obligation on Batavia. During the seven years of his administration Van der Capellen had spent twenty-four million guilders above the government income. There is one excuse for this: the coffee price had dropped suddenly, and consequently Batavia had had to meet a deficit. Coffee is an excellent product for speculators, but its price has not the stability to make it a sound foundation for a governmental budget. Finally, Van der Capellen, meaning well, took steps that unexpectedly caused the outbreak of a great war in Java. He was recalled in 1824 and gave over the reins of government in 1826 when his successor, Du Bus de Gisignies, a Belgian nobleman, arrived.[2] Du Bus governed four years. Those four years were fully occupied by the war against Dipa Negara, prince of Djocjakarta.

In Dipa Negara's career the story of King Airlangga, the hermit on the throne, seemed to repeat itself.[3] Dipa Negara was the elder son of

[1] J. A. Spengler, *De Nederlandsche Oost Indische bezittingen onder het bestuur van den Gouverneur Generaal G. van der Capellen* (Utrecht, 1863); P. H. van der Kemp, "Geschiedenis van het ontstaan van de Nederlandsch Indische lijnwaden verordening van 1824 en het beleid van G. G. van der Capellen," BKI, LXI (1908), 419 sq., and "Mr. C. T. Elout als Minister van Koloniën – zijn veroordeeling van het beleid van den G. G. van der Capellen," BKI, LXII (1909), 1 sq. These studies must be checked against Ottow's "Oorsprong der conservatieve richting," which vindicates the policy of Van der Capellen. See also C. Th. Elout, *Bijdrage tot de kennis van het koloniaal beleid, getrokken uit de papieren van wijlen Mr. C. Elout* (The Hague, 1861).

[2] H. van der Wijk, *De Nederlandsche Oost Indische bezittingen onder het bestuur van den Kommissaris Generaal Du Bus de Gisignies* (The Hague, 1866); W. Th. Coolhaas, *Het Regeeringsreglement van 1827* (Utrecht, 1936).

[3] F. Roorda, "Verhaal van den oorsprong en het begin van den opstand van Dipo Negoro volgens een Javaansch handschrift," BKI, VII (1860), 137 sq.; P. H. van der Kemp, "Dipanegara, een geschiedkundig Hamlet type," BKI, XLVI (1896), 281 sq. In the same volume by the same author, "Brieven van G. G. van der Capellen over Di-

Sultan Amangkubuwana III and he had cherished hopes of succeeding his father, but the authorities of Batavia had preferred to give the throne to his younger brother, who was on his mother's side of nobler birth. Dipa Negara retired from the court and sought consolation in solitude. He strongly disapproved of the dissipated way of life of his brother, and when this prince suddenly died during a feast with his women and friends, he called his death a just punishment from heaven. Wandering around through the country seeking solitude for meditation in sacred caves, Dipa Negara gradually strengthened himself for a decisive struggle with the Netherlanders. His methods of mental preparation were Hinduistic, but he preached strict obedience to the laws of the Koran. He became convinced that Allah had selected him among the princes of Java to restore the power of the Moslem and to drive out the "Kafirs." His reputation among the people grew steadily. Stories were told of a magic sword that had dropped from heaven at the prince's feet. The old tradition of a Prince Liberator who would come to lead the people of Java, a story older than the Dutch occupation, was revived.

Dipa Negara was willing to go to war, but he needed the support of at least part of the aristocracy. His prospects were good, for general discontent had spread through the principalities. After Daendels and Raffles had reduced the territory of the princes it had become increasingly difficult for the susuhunan and sultan to provide their numerous relatives with adequate appanages in land and workers. To compensate for the reduction of the area of land allotted to them, the aristocrats sought to obtain a larger profit per village. They had the means of making this by farming land and workers out to Chinese and European promoters. On several of the leased estates the peasants profited (according to our way of thinking) by the change, for they earned a better income, but they hated to be *forced* to earn a better income. Another cause of discontent was the extortions of the Chinese who had farmed the highway tolls and other government rights. There were stories that they made the Javanese mothers who carried their children on their backs pay toll, because they carried "goods"! The Netherlanders were disliked because they were considered the principal source of all these vexations, but the Chinese were hated and despised. Still the people would never move unless the aristocracy gave the sign for the revolt and the aristocrats profited by the presence of Dutch

panegara's opstand," pp. 533 sq., and also "De economische oorzaken van de Java oorlog," BKI, XLVII (1897), 1 sq.

and Chinese, although they blamed the Batavian government for the reduction of their lands.

Then Governor-General Van der Capellen made the very tactless though well-intentioned decision to which we have referred. On a trip through the principalities he saw the flourishing estates of the Dutch who had farmed the lands of the nobles. He understood that these results were obtained by exacting compulsory labor from the villagers. This went directly against his conceptions of administration, and notwithstanding the great damage that would be suffered by Europeans and Javanese princes alike, he ordered the immediate cancellation of the tenure of the estates. The leaseholders were entitled to an indemnification for all improvements they had introduced on the estates, and the indemnifications were to be paid by the owners, the princes! No wonder that none of the Javanese understood that it really was Van der Capellen's intention to protect the people against extortions. The aristocracy, deprived once more of an important source of income, was now ready for revolt. The people followed their princes. Dipa Negara with a number of followers "withdrew to the mountains," which meant he started guerilla fighting. The people rose and murdered a number of Chinese toll-farmers. All Djocjakarta joined the revolt except the Paku Alam and some of his faithful retainers. But in Surakarta the susuhunan and nearly all of the nobles remained loyal.

This war lasted five years.[4] Dipa Negara avoided pitched battles in which he would have had no chance against the troops of the government, and resorted to guerilla tactics in which he showed himself a master, though he was excelled in the art by his nephew Sentot, the son of a prince who had fallen in a revolt against Daendels. It helped him, of course, that he had the sympathy of the people even in those parts where they did not want to rise openly against the government. The Netherlanders had only a small army at their disposal. This was reinforced by levies from the territory of the susuhunan and of the loyal regents. The susuhunan himself marched against the rebels to show his loyalty to the government. Of further assistance were the princes of Madura, who in recognition of their support received the title of sultan. The men of the Minahassa in Celebes, allies of the Dutch for more than a century and a half, also formed an auxiliary corps. Nevertheless, reinforcements from Europe were necessary, for the soldiers' death rate was high. The victims of disease — the cholera devastated

[4] H. Merkus de Kock, *De oorlog op Java van 1825 tot 1830*, 2 vols. (Breda, 1852/53); P. F. J. Louw en E. S. de Klerck, *De Java oorlog van 1825 tot 1830*, 6 vols. (Batavia-The Hague, 1894/96).

the country in these same years — were many times more numerous than those killed by the enemies. The poor peasants, hindered in harvesting their rice crops by the marching guerilla groups and regular soldiers, suffered horribly. When the outlook for the rebels became hopeless, Sentot went over to the Dutch with all his men. For Dipa Negara nothing was left but to follow this example. He surrendered in 1830 and was sent in exile to Celebes. In the course of the fighting nearly 15,000 soldiers of the government had lost their lives, among them 8,000 Europeans. The number of Javanese who died as a consequence of the war, by sickness and famine as well as by the sword, is estimated at 200,000. Of these hardly one-tenth can have met death on the battlefield.

After the war the territories of Surakarta and Djocjakarta were clearly separated. Both susuhunan and sultan received an annual subsidy in cash as compensation for the provinces that were annexed to the territory of Batavia. The susuhunan, who had been loyal to the government, complained that he had been treated unjustly, but no further resistance developed, and the treaties of 1830 have remained in force until our day. For Batavia the war had, of course, disastrous effects. The already miserable financial position of the government was completely wrecked. Worse was to come. In the same year of 1830 in which the war in Java ended, war broke out in Europe. A revolt of Belgium against the rule of King William I caused an armed conflict in which the Netherlands troops, although they were victorious, were forced to withdraw because of the threats of the governments of London and Paris. For nine years a state of war existed. The Dutch treasury was exhausted both in The Hague and in Batavia, and King William had to look for new sources of income. In this emergency Johannes van den Bosch offered to find that income in the Indies.[5]

Van den Bosch had been in the Indies in the days before Daendels, where he had the bad luck to arouse the anger of this gentleman and had been obliged to leave Java. On his voyage home he had been taken prisoner by the British, and had spent two years in England, but when in 1813 Europe rose against the French domination, Van den Bosch joined the national movement in the Netherlands. He held high military positions in the new Netherlands state, and then retired to

[5] On the origin of van den Bosch's mission to the Indies, see W. A. Knibbe, *De vestiging der monarchie* (Utrecht, 1935). On his work, see J. van den Bosch, *Mijne verrichtingen in Indië (1830–1833)* (Amsterdam, 1864). There is no biography of van den Bosch; see *Niew Nederlandsch Biographisch Woordenboek*, II, 221.

devote his time to problems of social economy. He was very much interested in providing adequate labor for the thousands of paupers who crowded the Dutch cities. The old sources of income from shipping and trading that had existed in the century before had completely disappeared during the French period. The old-fashioned weaving industries of the Netherlands could not compete with the more modern British factories. Thousands of unemployed left the country and went to America, but the majority of the poor people tried to eke out a living in one way or another, and struggled on without hope of better times. Van den Bosch organized a Benevolent Society that founded agricultural settlements in the less cultivated districts of the Netherlands, the northeastern provinces of Friesland and Drente. This Benevolent Society was doing good work when its leader was called by the king for a special mission to the West Indies. Upon his return and his submission to King William of a report on the economic conditions existing in those colonies, he received the order to proceed to the East Indies and reorganize its economic structure.

Van den Bosch did not believe in the liberal principle that people will always seek their economic advantage if they are only left free to do so. "Leave the Javanese peasant free to handle his own affairs," Muntinghe had said, "and he will adorn the hillsides with his rice fields." Van den Bosch did not believe in this pleasant theory. Neither did he believe in that other principle, put forward by Nederburgh fifty years before, when he discussed Hogendorp's views, that the Javanese peasant is too lazy to seek his own profit. He simply contended that the people of the Indies, however willing they might be, were too ignorant to make unaided progress. They must be guided by the authorities. They must be taught to work, and if they were unwilling out of ignorance, they must be ordered to work. Van den Bosch compared the conditions under which the Javanese farmer was living with those existing among the paupers of the Netherlands, and concluded that the former were much better off. Therefore, if the government "organized" Javanese agriculture to bring it to a higher level, it was but doing its duty. The realization of these plans would, in addition to other advantages, enable the government to balance its budget, both in Europe and in the Indies. From these theories sprang the so-called "Culture System," a name taken from the Dutch *Cultuur-stelsel*.[6]

[6] "System of Government-Controlled Agricultures" might be a better English term than "Culture System," but through the books of Clive Day and Furnivall the latter term has been introduced. On the System, see D. C. Steyn Parvé, *Het koloniaal monopoliestelsel getoetst aan geschiedenis en staathuishoudkunde* (Zalt Bommel, 1850), which forms

Van den Bosch now assured King William that he would find means to increase the production of export crops in Java to a value of twenty million guilders yearly. Special measures should give the Dutch merchants and Dutch shipping the first chances in handling the crop. He did not intend to put the whole burden of producing this wealth on the shoulders of the Javanese farmers. On the contrary, he hoped to be able to pay the Javanese their due share from the returns of the enterprise. Because Van den Bosch made the East Indian government once more the direct promoter of agricultural enterprises, he has been called an advocate of reaction who deliberately sought to return to the tyrannical system of the East India Company. This is wholly incorrect, for the East India Company had ordered the delivery of certain export crops as tribute. It had simply told the regents how much tribute and of what kind they had to pay, but it had not concerned itself with the organization of the production itself. In the days of the Company the Batavian government had ordered the restriction or the extension of production, but it did not care by whom the crop was produced or how the labor was organized. All this was a government concern under the Culture System.

Under this system the government demanded either payment of the land rent (normally two-fifths of the crop) or the cultivation of one-fifth of the rice fields in a crop indicated by the Director of Cultures. It was understood that labor spent on the cultivation should not exceed the amount needed for producing rice on the same acreage. If the crop produced exceeded in value the amount of land rent due before the introduction of the system, the surplus would be paid to the villagers. Some of the villagers were freed of the obligation to work on the government fields but could be requested to work in the factories where the crop, sugar and indigo for instance, was prepared for export. These factories were organized and managed by Europeans and Chinese to whom money was advanced by the government, and

---

the first in a long series of merciless criticism on the System. S. van Deventer, *Bijdragen tot de kennis van het Landelijk Stelsel op Java* (Zalt Bommel, 1865), is a publication of official documents, made public by order of Minister of Colonies Fransen van der Putte. N. G. Pierson, *Het cultuurstelsel* (Amsterdam, 1868), later published in revised form with the title *Koloniale Politiek*, is the classic book of the liberal school on the subject, by the leading economist of the Netherlands. See, further, G. H. van Soest, *Geschiedenis van het Kultuurstelsel*, 3 vols. (Rotterdam, 1869/71). An English version of the liberal tradition is represented by Clive Day, *op. cit.*, chs. vii and viii. J. S. Furnivall, ch. v, represents a broader and more modern view. One of the principal promoters of the System was J. C. Baud, governor-general 1833–1836, minister of colonies 1840–1848 (see P. Mijer, *Jean Chrétien Baud*, Utrecht, 1878). The rules of administration under the System were defined in the Administration Act of 1836; see P. Mijer, *op. cit.*, pp. 497 sq.

who received a fixed sum for handling the crop. For all work in these factories or in transporting the products the villagers were to be paid. Theoretically, all agreements concerning the fields, the labor, and the transport were to be made by free contract between the government officials and the village headmen. Since the contracting parties were rather unequal in power and economic strength, little liberty of choice was left to the weaker party.

The natural consequence of the system was the practical introduction of compulsory labor and the exploitation of Java as though it were one huge plantation owned by the government. The word "plantation" might perhaps evoke associations with slave-holding, but the government plantation of Java really resembled more closely a medieval manor.

Such a system required a new reform of the administration. Earlier in this book we have mentioned the appointment of "coffee-sergeants." In the days of the Company these officials were instructed to control the production and delivery of coffee in the Preanger districts. Their official title had become *opzieners*, i.e., inspectors. These officials gained, of course, new significance after the government enterprises had been extended. Since the government also badly needed the assistance of the regents for the organization of the native labor, Governor-General Van den Bosch in his reform of the administration gave a prominent place to the regents and "opzieners." To the former their attributes of rank and hereditary rights to the position were restored. The official title of the latter was changed to that of "controllers," and they were instructed not only to attend to the matters of government agriculture, but also to keep an eye on the administration of the regents and their subordinates.[7] This administration was made less arbitrary by introducing the custom of holding regular meetings of the officials. Once a month the regent gathered around him his *wedonos* or district heads. The wedonos in their turn had a monthly meeting with their assistant wedonos and village chiefs, while the assistant wedonos called the headmen of their villages together every week. The controllers were requested to attend a number of these meetings and thus to keep abreast of what was going on in the Javanese world. They also had control over those groups of the population that were not included in the administration of the regents, namely, the Chinese and the other "Foreign Asiatics." "Foreign Asiatics" is still the official

[7] On the development of the Civil Service in the Indies, see Furnivall, *op. cit.*, pp. 87 sq., 122 sq., 187 sq., 237 sq. On training of members of the civil service, A. Vandenbosch, *The Dutch East Indies* (sec. ed., Berkeley, 1941), pp. 158 sq.

term to indicate the non-Indonesian Asiatic inhabitants of the islands, such as the Chinese, the Indians, and the Arabs.[8] The number and influence of the latter had been growing ever since the beginning of the nineteenth century, when immigration from southern Arabia, especially Hadramaut, had begun to increase.

Sugar, coffee, and indigo were the main products provided by Java during the period of the Culture System. The coffee, mostly produced in the Preanger, was grown on government domains outside the rice fields of the people. Its production, therefore, was not, strictly speaking, a part of the system, because it was not produced by the people to meet tax payments. Van den Bosch, however, had reinstalled the monopoly of the produce, and the bulk of the revenue of the system actually came from this particular crop. The production costs of all the other crops were so high, in spite of the use of compulsory labor, that the government had difficulty in keeping them going. Working under this system the Javanese produced only one third of what they were able to produce by free labor. One of the reasons for this failure was, of course, the lack of experience of the controllers in purely agricultural affairs. The government tried to arouse their interest in production by allowing them a certain percentage of the returns (the same perquisite was granted to the regents), but this measure resulted only in greater demands by the controllers and regents on the population, and in vexatious extortions. Nevertheless, the coffee compensated for many other failures, and the greater part of the losses from agricultural experiments that miscarried was borne by the native population.[9]

The system not only brought big returns to the government exchequer, but also served the purpose of promoting Netherlands commerce and shipping. Until 1830 King William had vainly attempted to enable Dutch shipping to compete with the British in the Asiatic trade. Protective tariffs had helped, to some extent, to give Netherlands merchandise a chance on the Indonesian market, but the products of the Indies were handled for the most part by foreign merchants. After

[8] The differentiation among "Europeans," "Foreign Asiatics," and "Natives" was introduced into East Indian law by the Administration Act of 1854. The East India Company distinguished between Christians (subdivided into employees and citizens) and non-Christians. The development of this differentiation is one of the most complicated problems of East Indian constitutional history. See W. E. van Mastenbroek, *De historische ontwikkeling van de staatsrechtelijke indeeling der bevolking van Nederlandsch Indië* (Wageningen, 1934); ENI, under "Burger," "Christen-inlander," "Verdeeling der bewoners," "Vreemde Oosterlingen," etc.

[9] The economic aspects of the history of the Culture System are excellently described in Furnivall's *Netherlands India*, ch. v.

the Culture System was introduced, an agreement was made between the Netherlands government and the Netherlands Trading Company, a foundation of King William.[10] All products obtained by the government under the Culture System were consigned to this company to be brought to Amsterdam. In a few years the sales of tropical products held in that city had regained the importance they had held under the East India Company. The Trading Company in its turn promoted the use of Dutch shipping. The merchant fleet of the Netherlands rapidly became the third of its kind in the world, surpassed in size only by those of Britain and France.

The financial results of the Culture System are well known and have been very satisfactory for the Netherlands.[11] Between 1831 and 1877 the treasury received 823,000,000 guilders from the Indies. A small part of this sum was used for the amortization of the East Indian debts. The rest was spent in paying the debts of the Netherlands and the expenses of the war with Belgium (until 1839), and for the construction of railroads and public works. Since the yearly budget of the Netherlands did not exceed sixty million guilders in the years between 1840 and 1880, the contribution of the Indies, with an average of eighteen millions a year, was very considerable. Once the system began to yield results, the human tendency to profiteer as much as possible revealed itself in the Netherlands Ministry of Colonies, and for nearly twenty years government expenses in the Indies were pared to the bone, without regard for their educational or political needs, in order to raise the figure of the remittance from Batavia to Europe.[12] But as early as 1850 the deficiencies of the System from the economic point of view became apparent, and the administration began to relax its regulations. Liberalism, then prevailing in the Netherlands, opposed the System as inconsistent with the economic principles of the liberal trend of thought.

[10] W. F. M. Mansvelt, *Geschiedenis van de Nederlandsche Handelmaatschappij* (Haarlem, 1824), of which there is an abbreviated English version: *A Brief History of the Netherland Trading Society, 1824–1924* (The Hague, 1924).

[11] E. B. Kielstra, "De financiën van Nederlandsch Indië," *Koloniaal Economische Bijdragen*, vol. II (The Hague, 1904). Also H. van Kol, "Welk nut trekt Nederland van zijn koloniën?" IG, XXIX, 2 (1907), 989 sq.

[12] The *Algemeen verslag van den staat van het schoolwezen in Nederlandsch Indië* of 1833 stated that at that time 1800 children were attending schools, but in this figure the native Christian children who attended mission schools and the pupils of Mohammedan schools are not included. The next report is from the year 1845 and states that between 1833 and 1845 nineteen teachers were sent from Holland to the Indies. The report of 1849 gives a summary of the development of the East Indian school system after 1816. To save expenses the Home Government ordered the most stringent limitation of all military activities outside Java.

The reaction against the Culture System that began around 1848 found expression in a number of books in which the System and all its consequences is utterly condemned. Because of this reaction the effects of the system on the welfare and social conditions of the people of Java are difficult to ascertain. "The Culture System," writes a modern British historian, "was succeeded by a Liberal reaction, and the writers of this school depicted it in the darkest colors; since then it has never been critically re-examined, so that an attempt to gauge its effects on social economy is rather like trying to ascertain the truth about a heresy which survives only in the writings of the orthodox." [13]

The defects and evil consequences of the system were obvious enough and have been emphasized by scores of writers. Only 3 or 4 per cent of the arable soil of Java was used for growing the required crops, but the transportation of the produce bore heavily upon the whole people. In case of failure of the crop, the people were left responsible for the loss; an abuse that was contrary to the original orders of Van den Bosch. The villagers often had to walk many miles before they reached the fields where they were to work for the government. The production of the indigo often kept the population of whole villages away from home for months. The work for the sugar mills was exhausting. Contrary to the intention of Van den Bosch, the land rent was also demanded of the people who had already paid taxes by working under the Culture System. Thus the real demands made upon the people were far in excess of those envisaged by the original ordinances. Add to this the extortions resorted to by a number of regents and government officials and the sharp practices of the Chinese owners of sugar mills and of the Chinese farmers of tolls and market taxes, and the picture we get of conditions in Java around 1850 is far from bright. The controllers of Demak, Grobogan, and several districts of Cheribon reported that famine threatened the people of their districts because their rice fields had been used for the growing of export crops.

The drawbacks connected with the system were not so heavy, however, or the population of Java increased steadily. The importation of foreign goods also increased, which suggests an improvement in the purely economic situation of the Javanese as a whole. The area of land under cultivation expanded rapidly. Apparently the effects of the system were not always and everywhere so disastrous as some devoted defenders of the principles of liberal economy wanted to suggest. In reality the results were widely different in different areas of the island. If the net profit of the system had been used for the promotion of the

[13] Furnivall, *op. cit.*, p. 135.

welfare of the Indies there would probably have been little criticism. Moreover, the Batavian administration would have been less exacting in the execution of the system and consequently it would have been less oppressive.

One of the most beneficial results of the System was the introduction of many new export crops. The Direction of Agricultures took great pains in the years between 1830 and 1860 to experiment with foreign crops which yielded little immediate profit but later contributed considerably to the prosperity of the island when a more liberal system of economic exploitation had been introduced.[14] Most important among these experiments were those for the introduction of the tea plant. Tea had been a very profitable article of commerce since the end of the seventeenth century. It had been imported directly from China. That country and Japan were for a long time supposed to be the only lands of production. In 1825 a British officer discovered tea plants in Assam, but for years the leaves of this plant were considered unfit for the preparation of a beverage. In 1826 tea seeds were imported into Java from Japan and planted in the Botanic Garden of Buitenzorg. Better results were obtained when J. Jacobsen, a tea expert of the Netherlands Trading Company, imported seeds and plants from China, where he had studied the cultivation and preparation of tea for six years. In 1832 he returned to Java accompanied by several Chinese workers skilled in their job. Experiments with the production of tea were made in thirteen districts of Java. The beginnings of a new culture are always difficult and costly, and the government did not succeed in making the tea culture profitable. Hence the tea gardens were turned over to private promoters, and in 1860 the Director of Cultures decided to end all government participation in the new culture. The private planters succeeded no better than the government, and the tea culture made no progress until in 1873 the Assam tea plant was introduced. This variety prospered in the climate of the Indies much better than the China tea, and gradually all gardens planted with China tea were cut down and replaced by Assam tea plants. In our day Java and Sumatra produce nearly seventy thousand tons of tea yearly, or 18 per cent of the world export of this commodity.

Another product which, although not introduced, at least has been rendered profitable by the Culture System is tobacco. Probably tobacco was introduced into Asia by the Portuguese and became known in the

[14] K. W. van Gorkom, *De Oost Indische Cultures in betrekking tot handel en nijverheid*, third ed., 3 vols., ed. by H. C. Prinsen Geerlings (Amsterdam, 1917/19). For the history of the crops see also the respective articles in ENI.

Indies at the end of the sixteenth century, but the East India Company was never interested in its production. The Indonesians, however, rapidly became addicted to its use and produced a moderate amount for home consumption. Since the quality was not that demanded by Europeans, the Direction of Agricultures finally decided to send an expert to Cuba to study the possibilities of a reintroduction of the plant. The result of the experiments carried on in the district of Rembang was not satisfactory. A second mission to Cuba in 1854 succeeded no better, and in 1864 the government decided to give up the culture by which it had lost more than it had gained. But almost at the same time that the government stopped its experiments, private promoters succeeded in introducing the tobacco plant into northern Sumatra, near Deli.[15] Relentless energy and skill have combined to make this enterprise one of the greatest successes in the colonial agriculture of the Indies. When the period of the Culture System was drawing to its close and the Netherlands Trading Company accordingly began to change its activities into those of a bank subsidizing colonial ventures, it provided the capital that has helped to change Deli from a jungle district into a great and prosperous country.

The production of pepper could not be increased by forced cultivation, and that of cinnamon, introduced from Ceylon, gave only meagre results. The experiments made with silk were no more successful. Cotton grown in small quantities by the people of the Indies since the oldest times gave appreciable results only in Sumatra in the district of Palembang. As the population of Java increased, and the production of rice did not seem to keep up with the growing demand for food, the government decided to promote the cultivation of cassava, which could be planted as a second crop on the rice fields. The cassava plant was known to the Indies because it had been introduced from America by the Portuguese, but the variety grown in Java was of inferior quality. The government therefore imported another type from America and succeeded in persuading the Javanese to grow the crop in addition to rice, although it always remained of lesser importance. From Africa's west coast the oil palm was introduced in 1848, but until the beginning of the twentieth century it was utilized only for decorative purposes. Then an important industry developed for the preparation of the product, and the export of oil-palm products in our day amounts to nearly a million tons.

[15] P. J. Veth, "Het landschap Deli," *Tijdschrift Koninklijk Nederlandsch Aardrijkskundig Genootschap*, vol. II (1877). T. Volker, *From Primeval Forest to Cultivation. A Sketch of the Importance of . . . the East Coast of Sumatra* (n. p., 1928).

Late but excellent results brought the action taken by the East Indian government for the introduction of the chincona tree and the preparation of quinine. The medical value of this crop had been known for nearly two centuries, but South America had remained its only center of production. The price remained high, and the quality bad, so the project of starting plantations in other tropic countries was alluring. In 1852 the first chincona tree was brought to Java from Paris via the botanic garden of Leyden. It was fully thirteen years before the first fertile seeds could be obtained from these plants. The government did not await the result of this experiment, but in 1854 sent one of the officials of the Botanic Institute of Buitenzorg to South America. This emissary, J. K. Hasskarl, a German in Dutch service, returned to Java with seventy-five chincona trees, which became the basic stock of the first government plantation. After a few years Hasskarl retired because of illness, handing the direction of the chincona plantations over to his former compatriot, Franz W. Junghuhn, under whose direction the plantations began to yield their first results.[16] It was twenty years more, however, before the quinine of Java could be brought onto the world market.

Thus the Culture System must be thanked for the introduction of several new and economically valuable plants, and the advantages obtained by the people of the Indies from these acquisitions partly compensate for the demands made on them by the same system.

A typical aspect of the period of this system was the unwillingness of the Batavian government to interfere in Indonesian affairs outside Java unless it was absolutely necessary. Dutch colonial activity, which had been concentrated on Java for nearly a century before 1830, continued to be so for forty years after that year. The effects of that policy are marked, for the enormous differences in density of population and in economic development between Java and the other islands are partly, although of course not wholly, the result of this policy of concentration of effort. From our narrative it is plain that from the oldest times Java had been more favored than the other islands with the exception

[16] F. W. Jugnhuhn was born in Saxony. After an adventurous youth (escape from the fortress Ehrenbreitstein, service in the French Foreign Legion) he joined the Netherlands East Indian army as a surgeon. His works are *Licht und Schattenbildern aus dem Innern Javas* (Leiden and Amsterdam, 1854/55); *Die Battaländer auf Sumatra*, 2 vols. (Berlin, 1847); *Java, zijn gedaante, zijn plantentooi en inwendige bouw*, 4 vols. (Leiden, 1850/54). Biographies of Junghuhn include Max. C. P. Schmidt, *Franz Junghuhn* (Leipzig, 1909) and *Gedenkboek Franz Junghuhn*, published by the Junghuhn-Commissie (The Hague, 1910). An interesting story could be written about the Germans in the East Indian service. The existing book, A. Schwägerl, *Das Auslanddeutschtum im niederländischen Kolonialbereich* (Weimar, 1937), is nothing but a piece of Nazi propaganda.

of some districts of Sumatra. Nevertheless, the fact that the number of inhabitants of Java, which was perhaps double that of Sumatra at the end of the eighteenth century, now is five times that of its northwestern neighbor must have its cause in the greater concern of the Netherlands government with Javanese affairs than with the affairs of the other parts of Indonesia. The other islands of the archipelago had little significance for Batavia in the middle of the nineteenth century. Piracy was still rampant over all the Indonesian seas.[17] One punitive expedition after another was directed against the pirates of Tobelo in the Moluccas, against the rajas of Borneo's east coast, against the Atjenese, and even against the Moros in the Philippines, who were really under Spanish sovereignty. A hundred memoirs and stories narrate the adventures of the shipwrecked among these piratical tribes, and Joseph Conrad has pictured this world of strange adventures in his novels.

A prominent figure in this world was the Englishman James Brooke.[18] This officer of the English East India Company was born in Benares, India, and served with the armies of the Company. He was rewarded for his bravery in the first Burmese war and returned to England to restore his health. Having become a wealthy man through the inheritance of his father's estate, he decided to seek adventure in the eastern seas. In his yacht he sailed to Singapore, and from there proceeded to northern Borneo, the home of inveterate pirates. This particular part of Borneo's coast was nominally ruled by the sultan of Brunei. Earlier in this book we have told how a prince of this small town was the first to liberate his territory from the overlordship of Madjapahit and to seek protection from the Emperor of China, and how, later, Brunei became the radiating point from which Islam spread along the northern islands of the archipelago. James Brooke assisted the Sultan against his rebellious subjects in the interior, the Dyaks, who probably had good reason to resent the tyrannical domination of their Malay sultan. For his assistance James Brooke received the territory of Sarawak. From vassal he made himself sovereign and overlord of his former master. The island of Labuan was acquired by him for the British government, and he became its first governor in 1846. Thus the influence of the British rapidly extended along Borneo's

[17] Articles "Zeeroof in den Indischen archipel," TBG, vol. III (1855) and following volumes (until 1876).

[18] J. C. Templer, *The Private Letters of Sir James Brooke* (London, 1853); D. C. Steyn Parvé, *De handelingen van Sir James Brooke op Borneo* (Haarlem, 1859); R. Mundy, *Narrative of Events in Borneo and Celebes during the Occupation of Labuan from the Journals of James Brooke* (London, 1848); Sabine Baring-Gould, *A History of Sarawak under its Two White Rajahs* (London, 1909).

northern coast. Protests of the Netherlands government against this alleged infraction of the treaty of 1824 were not accepted. The British government stuck to a literal interpretation of the clause that guaranteed the Netherlands' rights *south* of Malacca Straits and Borneo's northern coast is indeed situated on a higher degree of northern latitude than Singapore. The acquisition of Borneo's northern coast appeared to the British government of primary importance since it completed the encirclement of the South China Sea after the occupation of Hong-Kong (1841). Thus Borneo was divided between the British and Dutch.

The same excuse for British territorial expansion could not be brought forward when a few years later another Englishman, Wilson, attempted the foundation of a British vassal state in Siak, one of the districts of northeastern Sumatra.[19] But his appeal to the British authorities in Singapore was in vain, for this time the treaty of 1824 was unequivocal; a British settlement south of the Strait of Malacca was expressly excluded, and there was no opposition from Singapore when in 1858 Netherlands troops occupied the territory. Although in 1837 the war with the Padris was brought to a successful conclusion, further extension of Dutch authority had been hampered by British protests because the oft-mentioned treaty of 1824 obliged the Netherlanders to respect the independence of Atjeh and the territory adjoining the Strait of Malacca.

For twenty years Dutch policy concerning Sumatra had been hesitating. But after the British occupation of Borneo's northern coast, the authorities in Batavia became more energetic. A military post had been established on the small island of Nias near Sumatra's west coast to protect the inhabitants from the slave hunters of Atjeh. Fierce fighting between the Dutch troops and the Atjenese led gradually to the occupation of most of the ports on Sumatra's west coast, where the piratical Atjenese chiefs had established bases for their predatory expeditions. The ports of Atjeh itself the Dutch were not allowed to occupy, although the obligation to curb piracy in these seas rested upon them. Many times European ships were attacked by the Atjenese, and the punitive expeditions undertaken by the navies of the insulted states were entirely ineffective. In 1831 a warship of the United States of America shelled one of the Atjenese coastal villages, and others were attacked by British men-of-war. The Netherlands government sought to obtain an improvement of the situation by sending a special envoy

[19] E. B. Netscher, "De Nederlanders in Djohore en Siak," VBG, vol. xxxv (Batavia, 1870).

to the sultan of Atjeh, but this mission revealed only that the power of that once famous prince had been reduced to the merely nominal leadership over the village and district leaders of the sultanate. The promises and agreements of the sultan were worthless because he had no power to force his subjects to observe them.

There were other reasons besides the fear of British competition that urged the government of Batavia to show more energy in respect to the inhabitants of the "outer possessions." The days of the old sailing vessels had passed. Steamships had taken their place, and as the maintenance of naval control was of primary importance for the government in the archipelago, explorations for coal fields were begun. These led to very satisfactory results. The archipelago has an abundance of coal. Immediately the exploitation of some of these fields was undertaken. The government exploited mines near Bandjermasin in southeastern Borneo, and a private company did the same in Kutei, on the east coast of that island. The working of the mines near Bandjermasin led to a conflict with the sultan of that city, and to a war that ended with the annexation of the sultanate to the Dutch territory. Other mining interests, this time in the tin deposits of Billiton, caused the founding of the great Billiton Tin Company, and the definite occupation by the Dutch of that island.[20]

The other parts of the Indonesian world suffered little change in the middle years of the nineteenth century. An expedition against the Chinese mining kongsis of Western Borneo restored order in the sultanates of Sambas and Pontianak, which by their eternal feuds kept that part of the country in permanent turmoil. Another expedition was directed against the kings of Bali, whose internecine wars finally, after two centuries of alternately friendly and hostile relations with the Dutch, forced a landing of Dutch troops on that island. Part of the island was summarily occupied. There was fighting also on Celebes, where a too-proud queen of the Buginese had ordered her skippers to display the Dutch flag upside down on their ships. This was an insult for which Batavia retaliated with armed force, and the campaign gave the Dutch the opportunity to renew the old alliance with the dynasty of the Aru Palaccas, whose first prince is well known from the campaigns of Cornelis Speelman.[21] On Timor there was some trouble with the Portuguese over the boundary which had never been clearly

[20] *Gedenkboek Billiton, 1852–1927*, 2 vols. (The Hague, 1927).

[21] G. Nypels, *De expeditiën naar Bali in 1846, 1848, 1849 en 1869* (Haarlem, 1897); M. Th. K. Perelaer, *De Bonische expeditiën, 1859–1860* (Leiden, 1872); W. A. van Rees, *De Bandjermasinsche krijg van 1859–1863* (Arnhem, 1865), and *Montrado, 1854, naar het dagboek van een Indisch officier* ('s Hertogenbosch, 1858).

established. A first treaty of delimitation could not meet with the approval of the Dutch parliament because of — last remnant of bygone times — a question of religion. The Portuguese demanded official recognition of freedom of worship for the Roman Catholics in Dutch territory. This was granted, but the Portuguese refused to give the same guarantee for the Calvinist Church in their territory. In 1860, however, a treaty was finally concluded.[22] Its terms were very vague and left ample score for misinterpretation.

The Moluccas finally were allowed to take another step towards their definite liberation from oppressive measures. In 1854 several ports of the islands were opened to all shipping. It was the first break in the system of monopoly that was doomed to disappear completely in a short time. The Indies were preparing for a new period in their history, but the revolt against the former autocratic and selfish system of government did not originate with the Indonesians, nor did it take place in the Indies. The whole movement developed in the Netherlands itself. The reforms of Daendels and Raffles had been followed by the revolt of Djocjakarta, those of the Commissaries General by numerous local uprisings in Java and the Moluccas, while the well-intentioned policy of Van der Capellen had led to the great revolt of Dipa Negara. But whereas the Culture System was accepted and maintained without resistance on the part of the Indonesians, the Dutch in the home country rose against its continuation.

It is necessary to review here the attitude taken even by thinking people in the Netherlands towards the Indies. To the masses the islands were only vaguely known as *de Oost*, the East, a country whither sailors and soldiers went when they had no other way to gain a living, or when the fatherland no longer appreciated their presence. To the East they went and in the East they died. The better-educated class had hardly more appreciation of the colonies until the middle of the nineteenth century. "To go to the East" was normally the last resource of a middle-class Netherlander. There was an appalling ignorance about the geography of the Indies and about their inhabitants. The odd-sounding Javanese geographical names usually aroused laughter even in Parliament before W. R. Van Hoevell's ceaseless efforts in the parliamentary debates made them more familiar to his listeners. When around 1840 economic conditions became unbearable for thousands of poor farmers in the Netherlands, and Albertus van Raalte, a minister

[22] H. E. K. Ezerman, "Timor en onze politieke verhouding tot Portugal sedert het herstel van het Nederlandsch Gezag in Oost Indië," *Koloniaal Tijdschrift*, VI, 2 (1917), 865 sq.

of the Church, planned to emigrate with hundreds of his religious followers, he asked permission to go to Java, believing that he would be able to found a Dutch settlement of farmers in the tropics. The government, unwilling to change its policy in respect to private ownership of land in Java, refused, but proposed that he found the colony on the smaller island of Ceram in the Moluccas. Van Raalte would not consider any place but Java. He did not understand that one of the lesser inhabited islands would have offered better chances of success, if such chances existed at all. Thoroughly disappointed, he renounced the idea of remaining under Dutch sovereignty and led his people to the United States, where they founded the town of Holland, in the state of Michigan.[23]

Van Raalte had figured that he and his friends would be able to spread the Christian religon among the people of Java. The attempts at Christianization of the Indies are among the first signs of unselfish interest shown by the Netherlands people. We have seen that the East India Company did not take the propagation of the Christian religion to heart. Because the Company's officials were ordered to supply a small quantity of rice to the native children who came to school, it became customary in later days to speak disdainfully of the Company's "rice Christians." The main objection the Company had against missionary work was that the Directors would not allow any other institution, even the Church, to exercise influence in its dominions. But when the Company had been doomed to disappear, a group of Calvinists in Rotterdam had founded in 1797 "The Netherlands Missionary Society." It was half a century before other missionary groups were formed. Thus the first society had the credit of reorganizing the Calvinist Church in the Indies after the restoration of Dutch rule. It paid especial attention to the groups of native Christians in the Moluccas, who were united and organized into a Church by their first minister, J. Kam. The greatest success obtained by the Society was the conversion of the people of the Minahassa. This was begun in 1827 and practically completed by 1860.[24] More than a hundred thousand Menadonese had accepted Christianity by that time. It was, however, a hindrance for the Protestant mission that King William insisted upon organizing the Church in the Indies according to his own ideas and made it practically into a department of the administration. He simply

[23] H. E. Dosker, *Albertus van Raalte* (Nijkerk, 1893), pp. 60 sq.

[24] Article "Zending (Protestantsche)," ENI, and literature indicated at the end of the article.

ordered all Protestants to unite into a single community and retained the power of appointment of all ministers and missionaries. The Catholics, who for the first time since the defeat of the Portuguese had enjoyed liberty of worship under General Daendels, might well be glad that they were allowed to organize some parishes among the Europeans of the cities. Real missionary work was for them out of the question. Interest in missionary work in the Indies remained limited to a small part of the Netherlands people. It showed a growing care for the spiritual welfare of individual Indonesians, but not for the Indies as a whole.

Nobody had objected when the Constitution of 1815 left the complete control over the colonies to the king, who could here govern autocratically without the interference of Parliament. When the Constitution was revised in 1840, this same clause concerning the colonies remained unchanged. When in 1848 King William II wisely gave way to a demand for greater popular control over government affairs, and the Constitution was revised once more with the power of government practically placed in the hands of the better-situated middle class, a clause was inserted to the effect that the king, through his Minister of Colonies, must report to Parliament yearly on the situation in the Indies.[25] Direct control by Parliament over the policy followed by the government in the Indies was only obtained when the Comptability Act had been voted in 1864. Under this act the budget for the East Indian administration had to be voted by the Parliament of the Netherlands.

Before the act was passed the Liberal party in the home country had interfered little with the policy followed by the government in the Indies. Both the Liberal and the Conservative parties in Parliament accepted the principle that the colonies ought to contribute to the material wellbeing of the home country. Neither objected to the remittance of the surplus of the Indonesian budget to the Netherlands. Both parties agreed, however, that these profits *should not be made at the expense of the welfare of the Indonesians*, but because the ignorance of Indonesian affairs was so great, all but a few representatives honestly believed that there was not much wrong with the administration and exploitation of the Indies.

The people of Java had a few devoted champions in the Dutch States General, and these, among whom W. R. van Hoevell was the most

[25] E. de Waal, *Nederlandsch Indië in de Staten Generaal sinds 1816*, 3 vols. (The Hague, 1860/61).

prominent man, demanded primarily justice and fairness in dealing with the Indonesians.[26] They made no objection to the exploitation of the colonies for the interest of the Netherlands once proper care had been taken of the interests of the native inhabitants. Consequently, the Ordinance arresting the Administration of the Indies, accepted by the Chambers of the States General in 1854, decreed that the existing government agricultures should be continued.[27] A provision in the Ordinance against their further extension was not intended as a criticism of the System but only as a safeguard of private enterprise originating in the well-known antipathy of the Liberal party toward the interference of the government with economic enterprises.

The main differences between Conservatives and Liberals concerning colonial policy sprang from this political principle. Both parties declared themselves to be seriously concerned about the fate of the poor Javanese peasants, and undoubtedly they were quite honest in this declaration, but it must be remembered that the period in which these political discussions took place held views on social welfare policy totally different from ours. The Netherlands Parliament looked after the interests of the Javanese farmers as it took care of the interests of the working people in the home country; that is, it sought to create work and the opportunity of earning wages, leaving the rest to the "laws of Nature" about which the political economists of the end of the eighteenth and beginning of the nineteenth century had written so beautifully and poetically. There were a few points, however, on which the Liberals did not tolerate compromise. One of these was the anti-slavery movement. The Liberal party demanded that slavery be abolished immediately in the West as in the East Indies. The Conservative party pleaded, but in vain, for a gradual redemption of the slaves. Slavery officially ceased to exist in the Indies — that is, in the territory directly controlled by Batavia — on January 1, 1860.[28]

In the long run, however, there was no escape from the conclusion that the principles of Liberalism were irreconcilable with a system of government enterprises based on compulsory labor and trade monopo-

[26] W. R. van Hoevell, *Parlementaire redevoeringen over koloniale belangen (1849–1862)*, 4 vols. (Zalt Bommel, 1862/65). Other books by van Hoevell: *Beschuldiging en Veroordeeling in Indië* (Zalt Bommel, 1851); *Dertienjarige beoordeeling van het Kultuurstelsel* (Zalt Bommel, 1881); *Reis over Java, Madura en Bali in het midden van 1847*, 3 vols. (Amsterdam, 1849/51), German version: *Aus dem indischen Leben* (Leipzig, 1868).

[27] L. W. C. Keuchenius, *De Handelingen der Regeering en Staten-Generaal betreffende het reglement op het beleid der Regeering in Nederlandsch Indië*, 3 vols. (Utrecht, 1857).

[28] W. van Hoevell, *De emancipatie der slaven in Nederlandsch Indië* (Groningen, 1848); Article "Slavernij," ENI.

lies. The principal defender of the rights of the Indonesian people was W. R. van Hoevell, a churchman who had been expelled from the Indies for criticizing the government. His constant efforts to spread a knowledge of Indian affairs finally bore result. Popular attention, however, was caught by the book of Eduard Douwes Dekker, who under the pseudonym of "Multatuli" published his *Max Havelaar*. Dekker had been a government official in the Indies, and as an assistant resident in West Java had been dismissed from his post because, if we accept his own version of the story, he had taken the interests of the people of Java to his heart and defended them against the extortions of the regents and other officials.[29]

His book was a merciless satire on a certain type of Dutch bourgeois, pious and even unctuous among his kind, but laying his hands on every penny he could acquire from the Indies while blandly ignoring the conditions under which the Indonesians toiled to produce this wealth. As a novel the book was successful, but few of its contemporary readers were willing to draw any economic or political conclusions from it. Even the author himself would gladly have returned to the Indies and accepted a high post in the administration under the prevailing system. Against the forced cultivation of export crops he had no objections whatsoever, but the force of his sentiments and expressions aroused in his readers a far more radical trend of thought than he himself cherished. The book helped to provide a popular background for those among the Liberals who desired to make a serious effort to introduce their principles into the administration of the Indies.

Although all these events and changes in political and social opinion occurred in the Netherlands themselves, their repercussion in the Indies was so strong that it is necessary for us to explain briefly their full significance. Once one of the younger Liberals had been appointed to the ministry of colonies, the effects on the Indies of these changes were to be enormously accelerated. This happened when Isaac Fransen van de Putte became minister of colonies. As an officer of the merchant marine and as an employee of one of the big sugar-refining plants in Java he had acquired a first-hand knowledge of Indonesian affairs. Back in the Netherlands he wrote pamphlets on colonial problems and in 1863 was asked to join the second cabinet formed by the great

[29] To cite only a few of the numerous books on Douwes Dekker: J. de Gruyter, *Het leven en werken van Ed. Douwes Dekker (Multatuli)*, 2 vols. (Amsterdam, 1920); J. Saks, *Ed. Douwes Dekker. Zijn jeugd en Indische jaren* (Rotterdam, 1937); P. M. S. de Bruyn Prince, *Officieele Bescheiden betreffende den dienst van Multatuli als Oost Indisch ambtenaar* (2nd ed., Amersfoort, 1910); C. Th. van Deventer, "Uit Multatuli's dienstjaren," *De Gids*, III (1901), 417 sq. and II (1910), 223 sq.

Liberal leader, Thorbecke.[30] Fransen van de Putte showed that he understood the trend of ideas prevailing among the majority of the representatives. His predecessor in the Cabinet, Uhlenbeck, had been so imprudent as to declare prematurely that it was high time that the Netherlands learned to get along without *any* contributions from the treasury of the Indies, and that the entire Culture System must be abolished at once! This attitude was far too radical for the majority of the members of Parliament, who vainly sought for an expedient that would justify a combination of continual remittances from Batavia with the Liberal policy. Fransen van de Putte proposed to abolish all government agricultures except the culture of sugar and coffee, to bring all monopolies to an end, and to introduce a new commercial policy based upon the principles of free trade. His proposals — which guaranteed for a brief period the returns from the sugar and coffee plantations, the only ones that still were profitable — were accepted. This decision marked among other things the definite end of the former economic oppression in the Moluccas. The restrictions put upon the spice production by the Company had been abolished by Governor-General Van der Capellen. The law of 1863 finally put an end to the obligatory planting of spice trees and to the monopoly of trade. The Comptability Act of 1864 brought the administration of the Indies under the control of the Dutch Parliament. Compulsory labor in the government forest districts was abolished one year later.

A new period had begun for the Indies. Van de Putte's attempt, however, to open new possibilities for private agricultural enterprises by a law regulating the conditions failed. Under the proposed regulations, soil and labor would have been made available for these enterprises. The opposition of the Conservative party increased in strength. This party objected to what it called the interference with "native Javanese customs and institutions," but it transformed its predilection for these institutions into a political argument for the maintenance of a system of economy controlled by the government. In spite of this, the movement toward reform prevailed. In 1870 two highly important laws were accepted by the States General. The law on the sugar culture abolished all government enterprises in this field. Of the whole Culture System only the compulsory production of coffee was left. It dragged

[30] I. D. Fransen van de Putte, *Parlementaire Redevoeringen 1862–1865* (Schiedam, 1872/73). A second series of his speeches has been published with the title *Atjeh, 1873–1885*. W. J. Van Welderen Rengers, *Schets eener parlementaire geschiedenis* (3rd ed., The Hague, 1917); S. L. van de Wal, *De motie Keuchenius. Koloniaal historische studie, 1854–1866* (Groningen, 1934).

on until January 1, 1917, when it finally came to an end in the last district where it still existed — the Preanger — the same district where it had been initiated two centuries earlier.

The other law, promulgated in 1870, was an attempt to formulate the rights of ownership to landed property in the Indies. The aim of this law was to establish a legal basis for future regulations under which private agricultural enterprises on native-owned land were to be permitted. The law, usually called the Agrarian Law, recognized the special character of Indonesian property rights and the variations of these rights existing in the different parts of the archipelago.[31] The law prohibited the selling of landed property by Indonesian members of communities to non-Indonesians, and claimed as government domain those lands to which no Indonesian held a claim.

The formulation unfortunately was very complicated and left many cases unclear because of the great variety of ownership rights in the different parts of the archipelago. It opened the possibility of converting the property titles held under Indonesian law into new ones defined according to western conceptions of property, but a later attempt to encourage the Indonesians, especially the Javanese, to accept individual landed property free of restriction met with very little success. Under the Agrarian Law the government had defined the Indonesian property rights to the best of its ability, but the thorough investigation into the whole complex material already ordered in 1867 could not be concluded in time to be utilized. It actually took twenty years for it to be completed! [32] In the meantime the Agrarian Law permitted private individuals and companies to hold an hereditary lease on government domains (uncultivated land) for seventy-five years. It also allowed them to arrange with the individual owners (actual possessors) of the village rice fields for a lease extending not over twenty years, or in certain cases, not over five years. The Liberal party hoped that in spite of the abolition of compulsory labor under the new system of free enterprise the Indies would continue to produce wealth in excess of their needs. They expected that the loss of the returns from the government agricultures would be compensated for by a far greater income from customs duties and taxes, and they confidently looked for-

[31] A. Mijer, *De agrarische verordeningen* (Batavia, 1880), text of the laws and comments. See A. Vandenbosch, *op. cit.*, ch. xv.

[32] By decree of June 10, 1867, an investigation into the rights of ownership of the soil was ordered by the government. The conclusion was published in *Eindresumé van het onderzoek naar de rechten van den inlander op den grond op Java en Madoera*, 3 vols. (Batavia, 1876–1896).

ward to the time when the Indies would not only be able to take care of their own needs concerning education and social welfare, but, on top of that, increase their remittances to the Netherlands. The events destroyed these illusions, and new and better conceptions began to prevail.

CHAPTER XIV

PLANTERS, SOLDIERS, AND PROFESSORS

FOR MANY YEARS the Liberal Reformers, as we have seen, had decried the system of government enterprises and compulsory labor. Time and again they had professed their belief in the beneficial results of the free play of economic forces. If the economic forces of the Indies were set free, they proclaimed, both the Indies and the Netherlands would see their wealth increased beyond all the expectations ever encouraged during the Culture System. The same forces that caused the rapid economic development of Europe and America in the nineteenth century would, if the same method was followed, set in motion the power of production of the east as well, for the liberal theory of the equality of men had led to a belief in the identity of man all over the world.

The first fifteen years under the new system did indeed seem to prove the Liberals right. The development of several of the agricultures was amazing. Between 1870 and 1885 the production of sugar doubled, not only through further extension of the area under cultivation, but also because the output per land unit was twice as high as in the days of the famous System. This fact alone seemed to prove irrefutably the superiority of free enterprise over government exploitation. Instead of 152,595 metric tons, the figure of 1870, Java in 1885 produced 380,346 tons of sugar. If we look back a moment at the figures of sugar production under the Company, we realize how the capacity to produce had increased in the nineteenth century. In 1637, the first days of the Batavian sugar industry, the output had amounted to a mere twelve metric tons. Even in 1779, when it reached its maximum under the old rule, it reached only the 100,000 picol mark, i.e., 6,250 metric tons. Under Raffles production fell to half that amount, but under the Culture System it had increased a hundredfold! [1] In addition, there was the growing export of tea and tobacco, two crops that could not prosper in the days of the System. In 1890 the value of the tobacco export had increased from 3,600,000 guilders to 32,300,000 guilders,

[1] Figures on sugar export: ENI, IV, 177, 179. The total export of sugar from the Indies in 1885 was 420,000 tons, with a value of 84,000,000 guilders (Furnivall, *op. cit.*, p. 207).

nearly tenfold.[2] Kapok had become an article of export too; more than 2,000 tons of this material were exported in 1891. But, when we note that the export of coffee, which had remained a government product, also rose in the same years, we realize that not only the application of liberal principles of economy but several other causes must be responsible for this efflorescence of commerce and industry.

Among these causes the outstanding one undoubtedly was the opening of the Suez Canal. In a history of the Indies this event must be mentioned as one of the highest importance. The communications with Europe were shortened not only in actual distance but still more in time. The new route emphasized the advantages of steamship connections over those maintained by sailing vessels. The costs of transportation fell, and the market for tropical products expanded accordingly, as prices could be reduced. The relations between Eastern Asia and Europe became closer. All these factors, combined with other ones — the economic expansion of Germany, the opening of Russia, the amazing development of North America — caused the great boom period of the end of the nineteenth and the beginning of the twentieth century. This time, the Netherlands people were prepared for the change. National energy appeared to have been revived after having been dormant for more than a century. In many fields of scientific and economic activity the Netherlanders succeeded in making up for the long years when they had been lagging behind other nations that were making rapid progress. The stigma attached to "The East" in the opinion of so many Netherlanders who had considered it a place fit only for people who had thrown away their chances in their own country was disappearing. Men of all ranks of society began to look upon the Indies in the same way as their ancestors had so long looked upon America; as a country that offered a fair chance to gain a good living to people who were willing to work hard.

Netherlands capital became more and more interested in Indonesian investment. Before 1845 investments were not very alluring on account of the great confusion in the monetary system, but between 1860 and 1880 a number of trading companies and banks were established with the purpose of purveying the necessary capital to private agricultural enterprises.[3] Among these the Netherlands-Indian Trading Bank, the "Handelsvereeniging Amsterdam," the "Koloniale Bank," and the bank of "Dorrepaal and Company," later the "Vorstenlanden," were

[2] Furnivall, *op. cit.*, p. 207, after the figures given by the *Statistiek van den Handel.*

[3] Em. Helfferich, *Die Niederländisch Indischen Kulturbanken* (Jena, 1914); Furnivall, *op. cit.*, pp. 196 sq.

especially important. Foremost, however, was the Netherlands Trading Company, the foundation of King William I. This institution had lost its former field of activity — taking the government products on consignment and selling them in Europe — when the Culture System came to an end. Then the Trading Company began to lend money to private promoters, and by 1875 it had already invested nearly ten million guilders in agricultural enterprises. The Deli Tobacco Company, among others, was promoted by the Trading Company. More and more it grew into a normal banking concern that spread its branch offices all over Eastern and Southern Asia, from Japan to Bombay, thus reviving, to a certain extent, the tradition of the East India Company's inter-Asiatic commerce.

The Liberals had contended that in the general prosperity of the Indies the government of Batavia would find the means to obtain sufficient substitute income to compensate for the loss of the returns from the government cultures. But here their expectations were not realized so quickly. A few figures will illustrate the financial situation of the Indies during the period between 1867 and 1897, when the Liberal system had things its own way.

In 1867 the total income of the government had amounted to about 137,500,000 guilders.[4] Since the expenses had run up to 96,000,000 guilders, a surplus of 41,983,000 was left, of which nearly fifteen millions were promptly remitted to the Netherlands treasury in Europe. From what source had this income been obtained? The state monopolies on the sale of salt and opium and the maintenance of pawnshops accounted for about 14,190,000. The land tax brought in 12,600,000, and the custom duties 7,500,000. These and all other taxes together turned in not more than 25,599,000 while the production of sugar, coffee, tin, etc., after the deduction of production costs, had rendered nearly 50,000,000. Evidently the government existed in 1867 on the returns of the Culture System. Coffee alone accounted for 37,736,000 guilders! Ten years later the situation had changed. The government culture of sugar was in liquidation, but the coffee production not only had maintained its former level but exceeded it by eleven millions. Thus, the total income from the government products amounted to 54,998,000 guilders. The income from taxes, however, had also increased from twenty-five to thirty-five millions. In spite of these increases, the budget closed with a loss of 4,239,000 guilders, a deficit for which the government in the Netherlands was partly responsible, for even while

[4] Figures in ENI, under "Geldmiddelen" (II, 750); N. P. van den Berg, *The Financial and Economic Condition of Netherlands India since 1870* (The Hague, 1895).

he saw the deficit coming the acting Minister of Finance had managed to siphon off for the home country two and a half million guilders from the Indies treasury.

This was, however, the last contribution the Netherlands received from the overseas territories. Since 1877 no remittances from the Indies to the Netherlands have been made and, after all, nobody ever complained that that time had definitely passed by. The deficit of 1877 and later, therefore, was caused largely by the rapid increase of government expenditures in the Indies. They had risen from 96,000,000 in 1867 to 159,000,000 in 1877. Another ten years later the development begun by the abolition of the Culture System clearly showed its results in the figures of the budget. In 1877 the income of the state had fallen to 143,351,000, of which 42,377,000 came from products, and 46,001,000 from taxes. For the first time in the history of the Batavian administration the income from taxes was larger than that from products. This development was further accentuated in 1897 when the taxes returned fifty-three millions and the products only ten millions. The expenditures, reduced to 117,896,000 in 1887, had risen again to 148,-626,000, and the deficit appeared as a normal entry on the budget. In 1897 it amounted to eighteen millions. The Liberal policy had led to an embarrassing situation. Outwardly, the Indies seemed to be prosperous, but the government could not make ends meet. Clearly the tax system was not yet adapted to the new circumstances. Three fourths of the taxes were paid by the Indonesians, and these had little with which to pay. The Indies, the islands of fabulous wealth, are in reality a very poor country. Only by introducing new sources of income, which meant introducing western skill and methods of production, could the income be raised. This measure would create a class of wealthy people, who automatically would become the principal taxpayers, and thus make other developments possible.

Before 1870 practically all Europeans living in the Indies had been government officials. After that year the Dutch "immigration" began. In 1872 there were 36,467 Europeans, including the Eurasians, living in the Indies.[5] These people of mixed blood, according to Dutch law, were and still are considered as Europeans. The number of Europeans increased to 43,738 in 1882 and another ten years later to 58,806. In twenty years the relative numerical strength of government officials had fallen far below that of the employees of private enterprises. A class of wealthy planters — a limited number — had also come into

[5] Figures: Vandenbosch, *op. cit.*, p. 7; statistics also in Report-Visman (see Chapter XVI, note 27, below), I, 53.

existence. It was only reasonable, of course, that this group, too, should contribute to the government expenses, and through various indirect taxes they were already doing so, but not sufficiently. Direct taxes on the European income were needed, but at the end of the nineteenth century people were not yet accustomed to the idea of direct taxes levied upon incomes. A regular income tax was not levied in the Netherlands before 1913, but in the Indies it dates from 1908. Therefore, the deficits of the last quarter of the nineteenth century had to be covered by loans totaling a hundred million guilders by 1898.

The solution of the problem could not be found in a reduction of expenditures, for the Liberal system called for expansion of the means of communication and for better policing of the countryside—both measures intended to facilitate the working of the private enterprises. The Liberal System is idealistic. It believes in progress, and in the Indies it demanded, according to its principles, extension of the educational facilities for the Indonesians, better local administration with supervision by European officials, etc. It holds the opinion that economic and cultural development must go hand in hand. Economic progress will provide the means for cultural development and the latter in its turn will promote the former. All these measures cost a great deal of money and most of them had the tendency to lay a naturally increasing burden on the government finances. Besides, the new policy would not permit leaving the outer possessions to take care of themselves with all the consequences bound to follow that policy: piracy, disorder, local wars, and the consequent hampering of commerce, especially of the Indonesian shipping. The new principles demanded that order and peace should be secured all over the Indies, that head hunting and tribal feuds fought by order of petty warlords should come to an end. But who was to pay the expenses for the expeditions that would be necessary to secure the pacification of the islands?

The period between 1870 and 1900 is clearly one of transition in which a new Indonesian world took shape. The results could only become apparent in another quarter of a century. No reform can endure unless it has been brought into existence after a long period of preparation and another of slow growth, and this time of transition is difficult and often painful. The Liberals of 1870 and '80 had hoped that this period of transition would be short and that, once over it, the Indies would be able to resume their remittances to the mother country without any damage to the interests of the Indonesian people, but when finally the finances of the Indies had overcome the difficulties all thoughts of colonial contributions had long since been given up.

To build up the new Indonesian world many nameless men of many different professions worked together. We may call them "nameless," for although perfectly well known the names of only a few are mentioned in the history books. There were the planters who introduced new crops and saved the older ones by perfecting the plants. There were the pioneers who turned the tiger-haunted jungles of Sumatra into cultivated land. There were the explorers of the oil fields and the builders of the mining works. There were the soldiers, the men of the rank and file, those always "nameless" men of all races, Javanese, Menadonese, Madurese, Amboinese, Buginese, and Dutch, and the officers, Dutch and Dutch-Indonesian, who made it possible to establish modern administration over the most forgotten corners of the archipelago, sometimes resisted fiercely by the inhabitants, sometimes welcomed by these people who were glad to be freed from their oppressive native rulers. Finally, there were the scholars. The part played by some very able University professors in the development of the Indies is of the greatest importance, for they taught the government and its officials to understand the people of the Indies and their institutions. Patient research-work, technical skill and courage created the new sources of wealth the Indies needed.

We have already mentioned that the production of sugar had increased under private industry, and how the experiments with tea plantations undertaken by the government had begun to bear fruit. When tobacco growing shifted to northern Sumatra, Java began to produce a new crop, quinine bark. After long years of experimentation the best variety of the plant was selected and planted in quantity. The government took the initiative in the matter and bore the expense of the first failures, but as soon as technical success had been achieved, private enterprise took up the production. From twenty-two tons in 1875 production rose to five hundred tons in 1885 and ten years later it reached 6000 tons. The quality had been improved to such an extent that the bark held an average percentage of quinine of 13.86.[6] In this same period, in the year 1883, the Botanic Garden of Buitenzorg received a few small specimens of the Brazilian rubber tree, the "Hevea Brasiliensis."[7] Rubber was already produced in Java and Sumatra from native rubber-bearing plants, but the quality and quantity were poor. Only after the introduction of the Brazilian species could the new culture become commercially important. It is interesting that as late as 1914,

[6] ENI, under "Kina."
[7] ENI, under "Caoutchouc."

Java and Sumatra together produced not more than 7500 tons of this commodity.

Tropical products are, however, an unstable foundation for the national welfare of a country. When the price of coffee fell, when there was overproduction of sugar, or when plant diseases or insects ruined the crop, the prosperity of Java disappeared overnight. A crisis was caused by the sudden fall of prices in 1885 and a financial debacle in which most of the banks would have been involved was avoided only with the greatest difficulty. After this economic crisis, the various cultures were threatened by blights. This led to the institution of several research bureaus for sugar and coffee, but the latter product could only be saved by the introduction of new varieties, first the Liberia coffee, after this too had failed, the Robusta coffee from the Congo. In this way the cultures of Java and Sumatra gradually reached a technical perfection that commanded the admiration of planters all over the world.

Even under the Liberal system the government remained unwilling to give up its share in several mining enterprises. The tin exploitation especially had its interest. Thanks to the modernization of the mining methods the production of the Bangka mines had increased tenfold since 1811, when it had not exceeded one thousand tons per annum. In 1870 the average yearly output was 2200 metric tons, but in 1900 it had increased to 10,000 metric tons. The neighboring island, Billiton, was perhaps even richer in tin than Bangka. The exploitation had been started by the Billiton Tin Company, of which Prince Hendrik of the Netherlands, a brother of King William III, had been the principal promoter. This company started with a capital of five million guilders, but it had already made a profit of fifty-four million at the end of thirty-two years! This seemed so excessive that the government of the Netherlands refused the renewal of the concession unless the company agreed to surrender five-eighths of the profits to the Treasury of the Indies.[8]

It had been known for many years that oil could be found in the soil of the Indies. The Indonesians knew of a great number of natural wells and used the oil for several purposes. But until 1885 the opinion prevailed that the quantity and quality of the oil made exploitation unprofitable. The first company founded for the exploitation of the oil wells was the "Dordtsche" (Dordrecht Oil Company), a small concern with only 75,000 guilders capital, which attempted to work the

[8] ENI, under "Tin."

oil fields in Java. Two years later, in 1889, another company began working in eastern Borneo, and in 1890 the famous Royal Dutch was founded.[9] The latter first concentrated its efforts on the oil fields of northern Sumatra, but its director, August J. Kessler, understood that the company was doomed to fail if it restricted its activities to a single field, however rich this might be. He formulated a plan to organize a transport service by which all southern and eastern Asia would be supplied with oil from the Sumatran as well as from the Russian fields. In these days oil for lamps, not fuel for engines, was, of course, the main product on which the companies kept going. The story of how oil lamps were introduced into all corners of Asia has often been told, by historians and by novelists. The main thing, from the point of view of the oil companies, was to organize the distribution of the oil and the sale of the products in the great emporia of Asiatic commerce—in Singapore, in Rangoon, in Penang, in Canton, in Shanghai, and in the ports of Japan. Kessler found an excellent collaborator in Henry Deterding, formerly an employee of the Netherlands Trading Company, stationed in Penang. Deterding was the man who made the Royal Dutch one of the big concerns of the world. Later, he became the leader of the combined Royal Dutch and Shell companies and, having been naturalized as a British citizen, was knighted for his services.

In 1893 the Royal Dutch was already involved in a deadly struggle with the then all-powerful Standard Oil Company. From this it emerged victorious because, owing to its lower costs of transportation, it could supply eastern Asia at far lower prices than the Standard. Once well on its way to success, the Royal Dutch was able to organize all the oil companies of the Indies into one concern, the Asiatic Petroleum Company, that would handle the sales of the products of all parties concerned. This led to the gradual absorption of most of the oil mining companies into the mighty Royal Dutch, which had become still stronger by combining with the Shell Transport and Trading Company, a British concern. In 1907 the new combination organized the production of the East Indian oil under three subsidiary companies. Of these the "Bataafsche Petroleum Maatschappij" was to take care of the exploration and exploitation of the oil fields in the Archipelago. In the meantime the yearly output of oil had risen from 300 metric tons (1889) to 363,000 metric tons in 1900. The government, however, could hardly approve of an economic development in which the natural

[9] C. Gerretson, *Geschiedenis der "Kominklijke,"* 2 vols. (Utrecht, 1937). ENI, under "Petroleum."

treasures of the Indies would be totally annexed by international enterprises. A mining law of 1899 decreed, therefore, that the government of Batavia should reserve certain oil fields for government exploitation. Not only economic but also political considerations urged the government to obtain control over the oil production of the Indies, as this production derives its main importance not from the size of its contribution to the world production but from the exceptional fact that eastern Asia is not very rich in oil and that practically the Indies are its only important producer. Later, when oil engines had been invented, the favorable situation of the fields near an all-important sea thoroughfare gave them their only too well known strategical significance.

These economic activities augured well for the future, but in the meantime left the government in Batavia with a great number of problems on its hands. Of these problems that of the finances was one of the most pressing, but there were others nearly as difficult, for instance that of the war with Atjeh. For half a century the policy of Batavia towards the "outer possessions" had been cautious and vacillating. We saw how Governor-General Rochussen (1845–1851) followed a stronger policy for a while, but later the attitude of the Home Government hindered further expansion. Times changed rapidly. After 1870 all the nations of the globe began to show an increasing interest in colonial expansion. Africa was totally occupied. The islands of Oceania were brought under American and European sovereignty. France broadened her sphere of influence in Indo-China and southern China. Japan conquered Formosa. Spain was ousted from the Philippines by the United States. A wave of imperialism swept over the world. In a short time all "free" territory would be occupied and the more powerful states were already looking for an opportunity to "alleviate the colonial burden resting on weak nations."

The Netherlands claims to the sovereignty over the Indonesian territories seemed well established by the treaties concluded in former centuries between the Indonesian princes and the Dutch East India Company. Its sphere of influence was well defined by the treaties with Great Britain of 1815 and 1824, but there remained one loophole, the undefined international position of the sultanate of Atjeh.[10] The treaty of 1824 had nullified the agreement concluded between Raffles and the candidate-sultan, promoted to the throne by that gentleman. The British government had promised not to establish any posts or to bring forward any claims to the Atjenese territory. On the other hand, the

[10] J. E. De Sturler, *Het grondgebied van Nederlandsch Oost Indië in verband met de tractaten met Spanje, Engeland en Portugal* (Leyden, 1881).

Netherlands had promised to respect the independence of Atjeh. It happened, however, that the Atjenese themselves caused a great number of incidents by their acts of piracy. English, Dutch, American, and Italian vessels were plundered by gangs from the small Atjenese ports. The government of Batavia was obliged to protect international shipping against Atjenese piratical activities, but it could not do so without occupying the principal ports of that country, which was forbidden by the treaty of 1824. The Atjenese were perfectly aware of these difficulties and tried to complicate matters further by offering an alliance to the sultan of Turkey, thus renewing old connections of the end of the seventeenth century. Even if he had been willing to do so the Padishah could hardly comply with this request. It was in the year 1868, and Turkey was very much under obligation to Britain and needed the help of the British Empire against possible attacks from Russia.

The Netherlands government considered it necessary to free its hands for all possible contingencies and concluded a new treaty with Britain under which the latter withdrew beforehand all objections to a possible occupation of Atjeh by the Dutch but in compensation received the small Dutch colony that still existed on Africa's Gold Coast (1871).[11] Thus liberated from all obligations, the government in Batavia seemed inclined to take drastic action, but it had to consider the opinions prevailing in The Hague. A war with Atjeh would be a far more important undertaking than any other expedition carried out in the Indies since the campaign of 1830 in Java. It would require a strong force and huge supplies. The Minister of Colonies urged caution, knowing only too well that the people of the Netherlands were extremely reluctant to undertake a war of that magnitude even if the acts of piracy in Malacca Strait called for immediate action.[12] Fresh acts of piracy by the Atjenese brought matters to a new crisis, but even these would perhaps not have resulted in open war had it not been for the constant fear of the Netherlands government that a foreign power might forestall the Dutch and acquire control over the half-civilized Sumatran sultanate. Turkey had definitely refused to interfere after having received an official request from Atjeh for protection; the Padishah had it communicated to the Dutch Minister at his court that he had no intention of interfering in Indonesian affairs. Shortly after-

[11] L. P. Jeekel, *Het Sumatra tractaat* (Leyden, 1881); E. S. de Klerck, *De Atjeh oorlog*, vol. 1 (only volume published), 283 sq. (The Hague, 1912).

[12] Under the treaty of 1824 the Netherlands government had undertaken to curb piracy in Sumatran waters and, therefore, could eventually be held responsible for the damage resulting from Atjenese piracy.

wards, however, there were rumors that the Sultan of Atjeh had sent an envoy to France and that a political group in the newly founded kingdom of Italy was planning the formation of a colonial empire and looking for a chance to occupy those parts of Borneo and Sumatra where the Dutch authority had not yet been established. Japan, too, was now in the running, and her ambitions from the beginning went very high.

The government of Batavia was continuing its efforts to come to a satisfactory agreement with the sultan of Atjeh, an agreement which would have left the sovereignty of that prince unimpaired, when a report of the Netherlands consul-general in Singapore precipitated events.[13] Atjenese envoys returning from Rhio, where they had been negotiating with the Dutch Resident, had halted at Singapore, where they entered into secret negotiations with the American and Italian consuls. The Italian immediately made it clear to the envoys that he had no power to conclude a political treaty and that he considered it unlikely that the Italian government would intervene in Atjenese affairs. The American consul-general, however, Mr. Studer, had several meetings with the Atjenese envoys and drafted an outline of a commercial treaty between the United States and Atjeh that would have given special protection and privileges to Americans who wanted to establish trading posts in Atjenese territory.

The Netherlands consul-general was informed of the proceedings and reported to Batavia that Studer had called upon Admiral Jenkins, commander of the United States naval squadron in the Asiatic seas, to dispatch warships to the Sumatran coast "to protect American interests." It is quite understandable that this report, which was afterwards proved untrue as far as the intended naval action was concerned, caused a sensation in Batavia. Telegrams were sent to The Hague requesting permission to take immediate steps to forestall the supposed intervention of the United States Navy. The government in The Hague approved of sending an ambassador extraordinary to Atjeh, who, backed by an expeditionary force, would request the sultan to conclude a definite treaty with the Netherlands. The ministers of King William in Rome and Washington were instructed to ask the opinion of the Italian and American governments concerning the "negotiations" carried on by their representatives in Singapore. The Italian

[13] On the negotiations between the representatives of Atjeh and the American consul-general in Singapore, see E. S. de Klerck, *op. cit.*, p. 385; documents (correspondence between Batavia and The Hague, reports from the Netherlands minister in Washington, etc.): *Officieele bescheiden betreffende het ontstaan van den oorlog met Atjeh in 1873* (The Hague, 1881).

Foreign Minister answered immediately that the consul had no power to conclude a political treaty or even to prepare its negotiation, and that, consequently, it was even superfluous to investigate into the matter, of which the Minister had never heard before he received the Dutch request. The American Secretary of State, Mr. Hamilton Fish, pointed out at great length that an American consul was perfectly free to ask for the help of the United States Navy when the protection of American interests might make this desirable and also that the United States Navy was free to visit the coast of Atjeh just as well as that of any other part of the world — rights which nobody had questioned — but that so far he had received no information on the subject and that the United States was not particularly interested in the sultanate of Atjeh and its relations with other powers. Paternally, he added that the Netherlands might well involve themselves in complications over this unimportant territory. Upon his request for information in Singapore he received a long report from the consul-general, "too long," the Secretary declared later, "to read," upon which he commented in a communication to the American minister in The Hague with the following remarkably short and plain words: "That man [the Consul General] is a fool!" [14] The American-Dutch "diplomatic incident" was closed. It is needless to say that there never had been any question of dispatching United States warships to Atjeh.

In the meantime the envoy of Batavia had entered into negotiations with the sultan of Atjeh in order to secure an agreement that would satisfy both parties by guaranteeing safety of shipping in Atjenese waters. Having received an unsatisfactory answer he officially declared war. A first expeditionary force landed in April 1873 and stormed some of the Atjenese fortifications but, being only 3000 strong, withdrew a few weeks later.[15] A second expedition undertaken with a force of nearly 7000 soldiers landed in December of the same year and conquered the Kraton of the sultan within eight weeks. Shortly afterwards the sultan died, and the government gave orders to suspend further military operations, expecting that the success of its army would in-

[14] Communication of the American minister to the Netherlands Minister of Foreign Affairs, *Officieele bescheiden*, p. 103.

[15] There exists a voluminous, but from the historical point of view not very satisfactory, literature on the Atjenese war. E. B. Kielstra, *Beschrijving van den Atjeh oorlog*, 3 vols. (1883/85), is the oldest book on the subject and necessarily incomplete. A compact story of the war in ENI, 1, 78, is identical with H. T. Damsté, "Atjeh historie," in *Koloniaal Tijdschrift*, 1 (1916), 318 sq. For articles in periodicals see *Repertorium op de literatuur betreffende Nederlandsche Koloniën in tijdschriften*, etc. (The Hague, 1895 sq.). On Atjeh, see C. Snouck Hurgronje, *De Atjehers*, 2 vols. (Leyden, 1893/94), published in English as *The Achinese*, 2 vols. (London, 1906).

fluence the new sultan to conclude a treaty in which the sovereignty of the Netherlands would be recognized under guarantee of independence in internal affairs. After all, the Netherlands authorities had only halfheartedly undertaken the expedition, vacillating between their desire to eliminate a source of permanent trouble and their wish to spare their country the losses in human lives and in money which are connected with war. It was really a shock for the gentlemen in Batavia when they learned that the sultan absolutely lacked the authority to make his subjects respect any treaty he might choose to conclude; that the war had to be fought out with the individual local leaders, the district chiefs, and the Imama, the religious leaders; and that because of the extension of the Atjenese territory and the fanaticism of its inhabitants this war would take at least five years. However, withdrawal was no longer possible, and the war was carried on, though without real vigor. Once the Kraton had been taken, it dissolved in scattered guerrilla fighting. Each time a few successes were gained the government ordered further attacks halted in the hope that the Atjenese would change their minds and come to terms, but the only effect of this half-hearted policy was to encourage resistance because it made the Atjenese guerrilla chiefs believe that the Dutch lacked courage and power. Year after year the war dragged on. The expeditionary force was decimated by illness, but instead of keeping the troops moving, of pursuing relentlessly the small guerrilla gangs after their defeats, orders were given to limit military activities as much as possible. In 1880, on the verge of obtaining definite success, just as the Atjenese really began to consider further resistance hopeless, the government decided to put authority into the hands of civil officials instead of into those of the military. This ill-considered move caused another outburst of violence. The war drained the Batavian treasury, and slowly the opinion began to prevail that the incapacity of some of the leaders was the main reason why the situation had turned for the worse.

There has never been — before 1941 — a war in the Indies that aroused so much public interest in the Netherlands as the Atjenese war did. The government was violently criticized, first for having started the war, then for not carrying it through vigorously, and yet again for not giving up the whole affair by evacuating the conquered positions. The critics agreed upon only one point: that the situation was embarrassing and that no solution was in sight. The most pessimistic ones saw "loss of the Indies" and "financial ruin" of the Netherlands near, an opinion which the most optimistic Atjenese did not dare to hold. The critics should really have agreed upon another point, namely, that none of them was qualified to judge Atjenese affairs because they did not know anything about them; but this was the last thing they would have conceded. Yet only profound knowledge of the characteristics of the Atjenese people and the motives behind their tenacious resistance could explain why the system of pacification that had been so successful in other parts of the archipelago failed completely in this country. This brings us to the discussion of certain aspects of Indonesian life and administration at the end of the nineteenth century.

The Liberal Party had broken with the theory that the Indies existed only for the Netherlands. It had limited government enterprises in the economic field, it had asked for the furthering of education among the Indonesians, it had demanded better care by the government for the poor and backward peoples of the Indies. It had done much good, but it was not progressive enough to break entirely with the old conceptions of colonial dependency. Nearly twenty years passed after the last remittances from Batavia before the principle that money from the Indies could be transmitted to the treasury of the mother country was given up in theory as well as in practice.[16] None of the political parties in the Netherlands mourned over the disappearance of that source of income, yet they postponed the official abolishment of the principle for a decade and more. Under the Liberal hegemony the Indonesians were considered to have equal rights with the Europeans, at least in principle, but they were to be "educated," and the word education was taken in a very strict paternal sense. Often it was understood to mean the education by the old-fashioned father who is very much convinced of the correctness of his own opinions, who loves his children but does not permit them to speak when not spoken to and punishes them when they do not behave exactly as he, for their own good, expects them to do. In the same way the administration of the Indies did its best to take care of the interests of the people, but being often very much convinced of the efficiency of European administration and the inefficiency of that carried on by Indonesian officials, it tried to bring the whole of Indonesian life under direct European supervision — a policy that often gave excellent results but sometimes ended in the local dictatorship of the lower official who dictated to the village people from minute to minute exactly what they should do.[17] There was never a

[16] The principle was first proclaimed by N. G. Pierson, then Netherlands Minister of Finance, in 1898. It was established in law in 1912 (L. H. J. F. van Bevervoorden, *De financieele verhouding van Nederland tot Indië*, Utrecht, 1895; H. A. Idema, *Parlementaire geschiedenis van Nederlandsch Indië, 1891–1918*, The Hague, 1924).

[17] See criticism of Snouck Hurgronje in *Verspreide Geschriften*, 10 vols. (Leipzig, 1932–1937), vol. IV, pt. 2, p. 421 sq.

deliberate attempt to force foreign conceptions of law upon them, but some officials seemed to believe that it took a European to explain to the Indonesian what his own laws and customs were. Very strong was the belief that the Indonesians must be protected against many of their own compatriots who abused their superstitiousness and credulity.

We must add, however, that this point of view found support in the traditional attitude of the Javanese farmer toward his ruler, of whom he expects paternal care, help, and advice in all matters of economy and social life. In this attitude some authors see the results of "centuries of European oppression," but this book has explained clearly enough that direct European control in the Indies is of rather recent origin and that this control aimed at stirring the people of Java into activity and succeeded in broadening the field of their agricultural activities by introducing new crops and new methods. The origin of the Javanese attitude goes much farther back. For the Javanese the "good king" of legendary times is the king who thinks and takes care of everything, not the one who leaves his subjects free to take care of their own affairs. It may be that the paternal administration went too far in its attempts to enlighten the backward Indonesian. It was excellent when the administration made heroic efforts to improve hygienic conditions and to protect the people against epidemic diseases, but the whole effect of these measures might well have been lost when a European official in charge of the work acted as if to show, and indeed, actually told the people, that Science and not Allah ruled the world.[18] The whole system was based upon excellent intentions but aimed too much at material improvements and complete assimilation of the Indonesian with the Westerner. The latter can never be an ideal, for it simply substitutes cultural for political imperialism. The time came when people understood that the Indies could only be truly ruled for the benefit of the Indonesians when those in charge knew the Indonesian world, not only from without but also from within, and began their work of civilization by penetrating into the Indonesian way of thinking without attempting to force their own western ideas upon the people of the East. This was the prerequisite for awakening confidence in the administration among the masses of the people. To have fostered the realization of this truth by expounding at length one of the principal factors in Indonesian life has been the great achievement of Christiaan Snouck Hurgronje, the great scholar of Arabia and Islam.[19]

[18] Example in Snouck Hurgronje, *Mekka*, 2 vols. (The Hague, 1888–1889, English version Leyden, 1931), II, 336.

[19] Snouck Hurgronje, nevertheless, wanted assimilation of the Indonesians to the Euro-

Snouck Hurgronje was born in 1857 at Oosterhout in the province of Brabant. He studied Arabic at the University of Leyden, continued his studies at the University of Strasbourg, and became professor of Islamitic Law and Religion at the Institute for Indological Studies at Leyden.[20] He had already published several important treatises on Islamitic problems when he decided to go and study his subject at the source, in Mecca itself. The Holy City of the Mohammedans is strictly forbidden to Infidels, and in Snouck's days it was extremely dangerous to hazard one's life inside its walls, but the professor showed then, as many times later, that he had no fear. He was confident that his knowledge of Arabic and his understanding of the customs and way of thinking of the people would safeguard him. In 1884 he landed at Jiddah, where he remained for nearly six months to get completely acquainted with the dialect of that part of Arabia and to pick up connections with important people in the Holy City. He posed as a Mohammedan scholar and mastered the extremely difficult pronunciation of the Arabic well enough to make people believe that he was an Arabian from the Maghreb, the part of North Africa on the Atlantic coast. Several other Europeans had already penetrated into the Holy City under the disguise of Mohammedan pilgrims, but Snouck was not content to see Mecca during the crowded period of the pilgrimage. He wanted to share the daily life of the Meccans outside those hectic months when the flood of pilgrims overwhelms the regular inhabitants. He wanted to study Islamitic Law with the Mohammedan students, to consult the collections of Arabic books in the possession of learned Meccans, and to discuss his problems with prominent Mohammedan scholars. Thus the Imam Abd al Gaffar, known in Holland under the name Snouck Hurgronje, set out for Mecca on February 21, 1885, with a small caravan of four camels and accompanied only by a Javanese servant. Two days later he entered the Holy City. For six months Abd al Gaffar lived as a Moslem among the Moslems. He seems to have convinced the guardians of the city that he had come with honorable intentions and that he wanted only to live as an Islamitic scholar among his colleagues. Like every other Mohammedan he took part in the religious services, and he won many friends among the Meccan

pean way of living, but not by the simple imposition of European conceptions and customs. See his *Nederland en de Islam* (Leyden, 1911).

[20] Snouck's chief publications (besides those mentioned above) are: *Het Mekkaansche feest* (Leyden, 1880); *Mohammedanism; Lectures on Its Origin, Its Religious and Political Growth and Its Present State* (New York, 1916); *Het Gajo-land en zijn bewoners* (Batavia, 1903).

scholars. These ties of friendship outlasted Snouck's stay in Mecca for scores of years. For ever after his departure he maintained correspondence with his Moslem friends. His stay in the Holy City was suddenly interrupted when the French vice-consul of Jiddah had the imprudence to spread the story that Snouck in reality had gone to Mecca for archeological discoveries but that he had kept his mission secret from the Arabians. No Arabian scholar had ever explored the ruins and stones of former ages, and therefore such an undertaking seemed highly suspicious. Moreover, the Turkish government, then ruling over Mecca, immediately suspected Abd al Gaffar of being a spy and ordered him out of Mecca at a few hours' notice. Further stay in Arabia was both useless and dangerous. Snouck returned to Europe in September 1885. This visit to Mecca had revealed to him quite new aspects of Indonesian life, for he found in the Holy City a very considerable colony of Indonesians and he had full opportunity of studying their relations with their native country.

In former chapters we have noted how in the seventeenth century the pilgrimage to Mecca began to win followers in Java and Sumatra, how sultans of Bantam undertook the far voyage, and how emissaries of the Meccan sharifs visited the sultans of Mataram. In those days the pilgrimage was perilous and expensive. This condition changed in the middle of the nineteenth century. European steamship companies undertook the transportation of the pilgrims and offered passage at very low prices. In 1859, two thousand pilgrims from the Indies made the trip to Mecca. Twenty-five years later, in the days when Snouck was in the Holy City, their yearly number amounted to seven thousand, while between 1911 and 1914 it rose to about twenty thousand or one fourth of the total number of all pilgrims from the whole Moslem world. The maximum number ever reached was that of 52,000 in the pilgrimage of 1926–1927.

Snouck has left us vivid descriptions of the Indonesian pilgrims of his time. In large groups they walked through the city, meekly following their sheiks (guides). The shrewd Meccans considered them honest but not very bright, and took good care to separate them from any pieces of silver or gold that they might possess. Nearly every Meccan salesman spoke a few words of Malay. There were special sheiks for the respective Indonesian countries — for the Atjenese and the Minangkabau Malays, for the men from Pontianak and those of Celebes, and for those of the different provinces of Java. Listening to the conversations of these pilgrims with their countrymen who lived steadily in Mecca, Snouck began to understand something of the attitude of the Indonesians towards the European government and something of the significance of Mecca as a center of learning for the Indies.[21]

For the most part violently anti-European, because anti-Christian and fanatically Moslem, were, as he noticed, the Atjenese. The fighting in Atjeh had already started, and the outbreak of this war had caused some sensation in the Islamitic world. We remember, of course, that in the same decade, between 1880 and 1890, the victories of the Mahdi of Kordofan over his Egyptian and British opponents had caused a revival of Moslem fanaticism in Africa and Arabia. The Padishah of Turkey still regarded the Pan-Islamitic idea as a useful factor in his system of foreign policy and rather encouraged than opposed it. Thus, the Atjenese war had become a common topic of conversation in Mecca and the "Djawah" (the Indonesians living in the Holy City) probably were much more interested in the war events than the people of Java or the Moluccas. The first question the Meccan Djawahs used to ask of the pilgrims from their homeland was about the progress of the war. Impatiently they inquired whether the Infidels were thrown back into the sea yet, when the yoke of the Christians was going to be thrown off, and so on. Snouck noticed that the pilgrims reacted very differently to these questions, and that apparently a great divergence of opinion existed among the peoples of the archipelago. The Atjenese used to boast of their successes. To be sure, the Netherlanders were not yet driven out, but this was going to happen, and they claimed to have sent already more than 17,000 of the hated Infidels to eternal damnation.

Among the pilgrims from Java many protested against this fanatical attitude. Snouck heard one of them point out that there never had been 17,000 Dutchmen in Atjeh, and that, therefore, the Atjenese were certainly exaggerating. Another one even expressed it as his opinion that the Atjenese were very unwise to resist the Dutch administration at the expense of so many human lives and so much money: If Allah had not wished the Netherlanders to rule the Indies, he would never have permitted it. Moreover, if the Dutch were driven out, the English might come in, and they were worse. Such a voice would be silenced, of course, for, in the Holy City, one was *bound* to be anti-Christian and therefore anti-European. The strict law of Islam calls all government exercised by non-Moslems over Mohammedans illegal, and at least in principle obliges the faithful to resist such "oppression." This law divides the world into two sections, that of Islam and that of the Holy

[21] Snouck Hurgronje, *Mekka*, II, 295 sq.

War for Islam. Where Islam prevails is peace, where the Infidels rule, Holy War is the normal state of affairs.[22]

The pilgrim to Mecca was bound to join the general outcry against the Infidel. In Mecca, a sentiment of loyalty towards an Infidel was treason against Mohammed. Simple pilgrims from Sumatra or Celebes might well come under the influence of these teachings. The common pilgrim, however, who stayed only a few weeks in Arabia, would not become deeply affected by these theories. The incitatory influence of the Meccan surroundings would wear off quickly enough once he had returned home. When the policy of the Liberal period began to show its full results in the Indies, and better living conditions began to prevail all over the islands, the teaching of Meccan fanatics rapidly lost all attraction for the Indonesians. They compared the situation at home with what they saw in Arabia and naturally concluded that life under the government of the Infidels was far better than that in the land of the Prophet. Snouck in his days heard such ideas propounded by a Malayan from Pontianak in Borneo, who argued that, after all, the Dutch were much better than the Chinese (there are numerous Chinese settlements near Pontianak) and that all Moslems of Pontianak would have been killed long ago by the Chinese kongsmen if the Dutch had not protected the followers of the Prophet.

Snouck did his best to convince his fellow countrymen in the Indies that the hadjis from Mecca would hardly ever try to apply, in practice, the theories they had heard in Arabia, unless they were treated with unjustified suspicion by officials who believed that to go to Mecca and to come back wearing Arabian dress and using Arabian names was the beginning of rebellion.[23] This had happened in isolated cases, and Snouck did his utmost to spread more knowledge about Moslem affairs to prevent such mistakes, which would only help the Meccan fanatics. Snouck understood that Mecca was not only a religious but also a political center for the Indonesian world, and that the best policy was to make friends with the leaders of Islam in the Holy City. This advice has been followed and has given excellent results. As long as the Atjenese war lasted, the relations remained difficult. Typical is Snouck's story of the Sumatran who wrote to his friend in Mecca that the war

[22] The interpreters of the law usually do not take this distinction in a literal sense. They explain the doctrine — which, by the way, is not found in the Koran itself — thus, that they understand by the "territory of the Holy War" all territory inhabited by non-Mohammedans, which gradually must be brought under the Islam. This leaves room for the indefinite postponement of the Holy War in all specific cases.

[23] Snouck Hurgronje, "Hadji-politiek?" *Verspreide Geschriften*, IV, 1, 353, and "De Hadji-politiek der Indische Regeering," *ibid*., IV, 2, 173.

in Atjeh was not going too well for the Dutch and that he felt bound in honor to help his Dutch friends. He intended to raise an auxiliary corps of 300 men and he asked his Meccan correspondent to send him a good Turkish sword and to dip it into the holy water of Zemzem so that its bearer might be victorious against the Atjenese. He received, of course, a reply with a violent diatribe against the Infidels and a lesson in the duties of the Holy War. The poor Sumatran hurriedly wrote back that he certainly would not commit the mortal sin of fighting side by side with the Infidels against the champions of the Prophet.

Later, when the Atjenese war came to a close, the relations between the Meccan leaders and the Batavian government improved greatly. The Meccans depended upon the profits earned from the pilgrimage, and when they saw that Batavia did nothing to discourage the Indonesians from the pilgrimage but on the contrary assisted them as much as possible, opinions rapidly swung around. In Snouck's days the Netherlands were hardly known to the Arabian scholars. The professor of Leyden had seen several Arabian textbooks on history and geography which used to describe Europe as a territory divided among six infidel kings who all paid regular tribute to the Padishah in Istambul. The Indonesians used to identify the Kingdom of the Netherlands with one of these six realms but when studying in Mecca they were told that the Netherlands was one of the smallest and least powerful states of Europe.[24] The Arabians of Hadramaut who went to the Indies as merchants and had been hampered there in their movements and commercial transactions by the government — which wished to protect the Indonesians from too sharp practices by the shrewder Chinese and Arabians — had also helped to spread animosity against the Netherlanders.

In the twentieth century, when peace and order prevailed all over the archipelago and consequently every trader had a fair chance to do business, the men of Hadramaut changed their minds. Thus it came about that after the First World War the prestige of the Netherlands stood very high in the Arabian world. At the present time, the Netherlands government is the only one that maintains a vice-consulate, with an Indonesian official in charge, in the Holy City of Mecca itself. King Ibn Saud sought the advice of Netherlanders in his work for the modernization of Arabia. In Hadramaut, Netherlanders succeeded after the last war in penetrating into regions never before visited by Europeans, and, to their great surprise, found themselves welcomed

[24] Snouck Hurgronje, "Een Rector der Mekkaansche Universiteit," BKI, xxxvi (1887), 357.

by wealthy Arabians in perfect Dutch, which they had learned in Java.[25]

We have continued the story of Netherlands and Indonesian contact with the Arabian world beyond the period of the Atjenese war, in order to show the enormous influence that went out from one single enterprising professor who succeeded in establishing lasting friendship between men from the West and men from the East, simply by assimilating himself to the Eastern world without expecting that the men from the East would be too glad to imitate his western way of living and thinking. Five years after his visit to Mecca, Snouck Hurgronje went to the Indies as an adviser of the Indies government on Moslem affairs. After a short stay in Java he visited Atjeh. For seven months he lived in the native quarter of the Atjenese capital, keeping away from his compatriots and devoting all his time to a thorough investigation into the manners, language, and political and religious institutions of the people. Then he made his report, in which he utterly condemned the tactics of waiting and appeasing that had been followed for so many years by the government. His experiences in Mecca helped him to understand that the fanatical Moslems of Atjeh would never coöperate freely with the Netherlands government, even if only because the Law of Islam forbade association with the Infidels. Even if the masses of the simple village people should be longing for peace, the religious leaders would not yield, and they would find enough adventurers and professional warriors among the village and district chiefs to carry on the war. But if force was met by force, and, at the same time, the simple people were assured that their religion and native customs would be secure under Dutch administration, Snouck was convinced that they would come to see that there were better chances for making a living under that administration than under the guerilla leaders who, whenever the Dutch left them alone, resorted to civil strife to continue the state of war. Once the adherence of the bulk of the population was secured, the war in Atjeh, although extremely difficult on account of the wild nature of the sparsely populated country, could undoubtedly be brought to a successful end.

Professor Snouck wrote his report in the spring of 1892 and it was published at government expense, slightly modified, in a two-volume work under the title of "De Atjehers." It is a masterpiece of ethnological research, but the authorities in Atjeh rejected his opinions haugh-

[25] L. W. C. van den Berg, *Le Hadramaut et les colonies arabes dans l'archipel indien* (Batavia, 1886); D. van der Meulen and H. von Wisseman, *Hadramaut: Some of Its Mysteries Unveiled* (Leyden, 1932).

tily.[26] "Professor Snouck," wrote the governor, "has made Islam his hobby and therefore he sees Islamitic influence and Holy War everywhere. The war in Atjeh is not a religious war of the Atjenese people, but only the gangsterism of lawless elements. The best tactics are not to pay too much attention to these gangsters. The people, once tired of the whole affair, will turn to us for protection and better government." This optimistic view of the local authorities suited the recalcitrant Atjenese very well. Fighting continued and the situation finally became almost disastrous for the Dutch, so much so that some high officials seriously recommended the withdrawal of all troops from Atjeh, since the principal aim of the expedition, the extirpation of piracy, had been obtained. That piracy would have started anew the moment the troops had left, seemed no point of consideration.

However, the tide was turning once more. In 1893 a new governor-general, C. H. A. Van der Wijck, arrived in the Indies and started immediately to pursue a more vigorous policy. In 1894 the Mohammedan inhabitants of the island of Lombok (Lesser Sunda Islands) implored the help of the Batavian government against their Balinese Hindu overlords, who oppressed them in a horrible way. The two groups of the population were continuously waging internecine wars. Finally a Netherlands expeditionary force put an end to these disorders. The island of Lombok was brought under direct Netherlands rule. Later, local self-government was restored.

The governor-general then turned his attention towards Atjeh. On the advice of Professor Snouck Hurgronje, Lieutenant Colonel Joannes B. van Heutsz was given the command of the army in Atjeh.[27] Van Heutsz had been in Atjeh before and there had gained a reputation for his bravery and for the sharpness of his tongue. He had never learned the Atjenese language, he did not understand much of Atjenese customs, and, as an officer, he had never cared for military science, but he knew how to fight. Several years before his appointment to Atjeh he had expounded his plans for ending the war in a much-discussed booklet. His opponents said that in practice he cared no more for his own theories than for the rules of scientific strategy. However this may have been, he was vivid and enterprising and free of cumbersome theoretical ideas, and was the right man to give back to the army of the Indies the self-confidence of which it had lost so much in the preceding

[26] H. T. Damsté, "Drie Atjeh-mannen: Snouck Hurgronje-van Heutsz-van Daalen," *Koloniaal Tijdschrift*, XXV (1936), 457 sq., continued in vols. XXVI and XXVII; J. W. Naarding, *Het conflict Snouck Hurgronje-van Heutsz-van Daalen* (Utrecht, 1938).

[27] Data on Van Heutsz: ENI Aanv. V, 265.

fifteen years. When asked by the governor of Atjeh to address the troops before an important attack, he simply said: "Boys, the governor wants me to say a few words. Do you see these *bentengs* (entrenchments)? Inside these are the Atjenese. They must get out and you must get in. Inside them there are tables loaded with military decorations. Go and pick them up!"

But to take entrenchments or to beat the Atjenese in the open field was only a trifle compared with the long exhausting marches through the jungles of Atjeh in pursuit of the guerillas. One after another the enemy leaders were cornered. Some of them fell sword in hand, others surrendered, sure of being treated well. But Van Heutsz, though an excellent soldier, was still only a soldier. His irrepressible tendency towards sarcasm made it very difficult to get along with him. The value of his achievement in restoring true fighting spirit to the army and in subduing Atjeh was evident, for after three years hesitation and the feeling of uncertainty in the army had been replaced by overconfidence, and most of the Atjenese leaders had offered submission. After that Professor Snouck, now official advisor of the East Indian government on native affairs, would have liked to see the administration of Atjeh placed in other hands, in those of an understanding man who would have an eye to the interests of the simple peasant of Atjeh and who would do his best to mitigate the sufferings that had befallen him in consequence of the guerilla warfare. The government of the Netherlands, however, elated by the unexpected successes of Van Heutsz, decided to promote that officer, who had already become a general, to the position of governor-general of the Indies and to appoint another military man governor of Atjeh. Van Heutsz held his office for five years, from 1904 to 1909, and surrendered the command in Atjeh to one of his best officers, Colonel Van Daalen. This officer was perhaps even a better soldier than Van Heutsz, but he lacked his wit and vivacity. He spoke the Atjenese language, he understood much of the Atjenese customs, and won fame by his marches through the deep interior of the country, through the Gajo and Alas lands into which no European had ever penetrated, but his lack of imagination made it impossible for him to take those measures that would have rapidly won over the inhabitants to the new administration.[28]

Snouck Hurgronje was not satisfied with the turn events had taken. He was a man of difficult character and considered himself ill rewarded for his services. Not that he expected great material rewards, but he

[28] Data on van Daalen: ENI Aanv. VI, 824. On his campaign, see J. C. J. Kempees, *De tocht van Overste van Daalen door de Gajo-, Alas en Bataklanden* (Amsterdam, 1905).

could not understand why the government did not always and everywhere follow his advice. He returned to Europe but remained most influential in Indonesian affairs, because the professorship in Islamitic affairs was once more entrusted to him, and the young men preparing for the civil service in the Indies followed his lectures without exception and were deeply impressed by his ideas.

His colleague was the no less famous Professor C. Van Vollenhoven, the great "discoverer" of Indonesian Law, the scholar who first understood the great difference between Islamitic and Indonesian institutions and that Indonesian Law was only superficially influenced by the rules of Mohammedanism.[29] He lectured for several generations at Leyden and, like Snouck, acted many times as advisor to the Netherlands government on Indonesian affairs. He always advocated allowing the Indonesian customs to subsist and building a new Indonesian society and civilization based upon the national institutions of the country. For him the *adat*, the code of national customs, was sacred. It should not be touched or modified unless there was an absolute necessity for doing so. But while Snouck as a young man had gone to Mecca to discover things for himself on the spot, Van Vollenhoven discovered his great theories at home, in his quiet study near the University of Leyden, and did not visit the Indies until he had built up his theories.

The same desire to learn to know the Indies that prompted Snouck and Van Vollenhoven promoted the exploration of other fields of research. Not only the institutions but also the languages, the ethnology, the archeology and the history of the Indies became a favorite topic among Netherlands scholars. First and one of the greatest of all was Johan Hendrik Kern, whose works we have often mentioned.

The growing interest in the monuments and inscriptions of the Hindu-Javanese period called for the foundation of a Department of Archeology in the bureaus of the Batavian administration.[30] A beginning was made in 1901. Dr. J. L. A. Brandes, another scholar of Old Javanese language and civilization, was appointed its first director. Now the remaining monuments of the Middle Ages were protected against further destruction by ignorant people, Dutch as well as Javanese, who sometimes were rather inclined to use the ruins as stone quarries when building sugar-factories. Brandes' successor was Professor N. J. Krom, the man who from scattered notices and inscriptions, from remnants of chronicles and obscure Chinese references, reconstructed and wrote the history of the Indies in the Middle Ages. Then, there

[29] Biography in ENI Aanv. VII, 1380.

[30] For the history of archeological research in the Indies: Krom, IHJK, vol. I, ch. i.

were the numerous scholars who dug up historical treasures from the archives of the East India Company, foremost among them Dr. De Haan, archivist of Batavia, who in his books pictured the social and economic conditions of Batavia and the countryside of Java during the seventeenth and eighteenth centuries. Indonesian scholars followed these examples and some of them reached the highest positions in the government service in the Indies, as for instance the philologist Prof. Dr. Pangeran Djajadiningrat, who became a member of the Council of the Indies.

But the history of the Indies in the Hindu and Mohammedan period can not be understood without a thorough knowledge of the primitive Indonesian world. To have contributed to this is the merit of missionaries such as Nicolaus Adriani and Albert C. Kruyt, who in central Celebes not only spread the gospel among the wild Toradja tribes but attended to their social needs and studied their religious beliefs and tribal customs.[31] They, and government officials like George A. Wilken, were the first Europeans to study scientifically these customs and beliefs, and their researches spread new light on the primitive society of Indonesia. Another missionary, Pieter Jansz, around 1872 published his books on the modern Javanese language which are still authoritative. The past of the Indies seemed revived. In the meanwhile, however, a new Indonesian world was being built.

While Van Daalen, who had succeeded Van Heutsz as governor of Atjeh, did his best to solve the problems of that particular territory, the governor-general himself turned his attention to the many districts where, until now, the Netherlanders had left the local rulers free to handle their own affairs completely to their liking.[32] To respect the independence of the native rulers was a noble principle, but what if the common people implored help, as the men of Lombok had done when they complained that they were "slaughtered like chickens" by their Balinese lords? Or what to do when the village men became so disgusted with oppressive rule that they stormed the kraton of their prince, as the people of Tidore did in 1904? What to do when the "princes" of the Borneo sultanates, the numerous descendants of the sultans of Pontianak, Bandjermasin, Kutei, and other districts, con-

[31] See Nic. Adriani, *Verspreide Geschriften*, 3 vols. (Haarlem, 1932); A. C. Kruijt, *Het animisme in den Indischen archipel* (The Hague, 1906) and *De West Toradja's op Midden Celebes* (Amsterdam, 1938).

[32] An excellent survey in E. B. Kielstra, *De vestiging van het Nederlandsche Gezag in den Indischen archipel* (Haarlem, 1920), also in Volume II of H. Colijn–D. G. Stibbe, *Nederlandsch Indië*, 2 vols. (Amsterdam, 1929); E. S. de Klerck, *History of the Netherlands East Indies*, 2 vols. (Rotterdam, 1938) vol. II, *passim*.

tinued to oppress the heathen tribes of the Dyaks in the interior? In 1896–97 and 1898–1900, A. Nieuwenhuis explored the interior of Borneo, making two voyages from the west to the east coast. He was the first European to come into contact with the primitive Dyak tribes of the far interior and he noticed that those Dyaks who remained outside the sphere of influence of the Malay coastal sultans were far better off than their compatriots who had been subdued by these princes. "The exploitation," he writes, "of these heathen tribes by the descendants of the Malay rulers has robbed these Dyaks of their relative welfare and civilization. The Malays made of these tribes a people which is scarcely able to provide its barest needs and which, generally speaking, is so degenerate that even a revolution in its existence would not be sufficient to raise it from its state of decay." "Just the presence," he writes of the Dyaks of Eastern Borneo, "of a controller and about fifty armed native policemen in a district twice as large as Holland was sufficient to awaken a feeling of peace, hitherto unknown, in the heart of every family; they were all able to work peacefully at their agricultural pursuits, and clothes and important items of their daily food have become much cheaper."[33] Here in Borneo the Dutch-Indonesian troops, in number not stronger than patrols, met only with the resistance of the descendants of the last sultan of Bandjermasin, who had to be pursued into the jungles of the Upper Barito River. A relatively small police force was sufficient to maintain order among the headhunting tribes, who, of course, might sometimes feel this interference with that age-old custom tyrannical, but the fact that an enormous island like Borneo could be occupied and maintained in a state of peace by a handful of Indonesian police with practically no difficulties shows clearly enough that the effects of the political change were beneficial.

Around the year 1900 the government of Batavia began to consider itself responsible for the system of "administration" carried on by local rulers under the protection of Batavia. It held the opinion that it was perfectly justified in interfering with these "administrations." It claimed overlordship over a great number of small sultanates in consequence of the treaties formerly concluded by the East India Company with the rulers of these sultanates. These contracts had been concluded for an indefinite period and, consequently, were considered to be still in force at the end of the nineteenth century if they had not been replaced by new conventions. In the nineteenth century, however, the instructions for the governors-general had expressly stated that the

[33] A. Nieuwenhuis in B. Schrieke, *The Effect of Western Influence on Native Civilization in the Malay Archipelago* (Batavia, 1929), p. 50.

independence of the Indonesian princes was to be respected unless the welfare of the inhabitants or the suppression of slavery demanded its curtailment.

During the period of the Culture System there had been no sufficient reasons for altering this attitude. This had changed in the years immediately following the arrival of Snouck Hurgronje in the Indies. The maintenance of the *complete* independence of the local rulers was hardly possible. Yet Professor Snouck advised leaving as much of their independence as possible but renewing the old treaties in a different form which would leave scope for the introduction of modern forms of administration in the semi-independent territories. This system was first introduced in Atjeh, under the governorship of Van Heutsz. The local rulers who wanted to come to terms with the government of Batavia signed the so-called *short declaration*.[34] This declaration was, in fact, a unilateral treaty in which they recognized the sovereignty of the Netherlands and promised to execute orders from Batavia concerning the internal administration of their territory. This form safeguarded native institutions but left ample scope for introducing such reforms as Batavia might think necessary. In a period of not more than ten years, more than 250 Indonesian rulers, petty district chiefs as well as powerful sultans, signed such a declaration. But though it was often easy to obtain the signature of the rulers in the eastern half of the archipelago, it was different in Atjeh and a few other districts of Sumatra, where Mohammedan fanaticism made some of the chiefs unwilling to conclude agreements with the "Infidels." In Atjeh the party hostile to the Dutch braced itself for a last stand when the news of the Japanese victories over the Russians first brought home to them that an eastern race might have a chance of success in war against the men of the west. After this last attempt armed resistance ceased.

In Celebes only the petty sultanates of the southwestern peninsula offered resistance. Here, in Gowa and Boni, and also in Buton near the southeastern peninsula, the aristocracy refused to accept a political change by which its power over the people would be curtailed. The civil wars and the slave-hunting expeditions into the interior among the tribes of the Toradjas had come to an end, and these were precisely the "liberties" the local aristocrats valued most. The great and glorious days when the Buginese had traded and plundered all over the archipelago had passed. A piratical excursion undertaken by them in 1903 into government territory on the island of Flores brought matters to a

[34] J. M. Somer, *De korte verklaring* (Breda, 1934), actually a history of the relations of Batavia with the native states during the nineteenth century.

head. After a few months the Buginese sultanates were forced to recognize the absolute sovereignty of Batavia. For the people living in the interior of the island of Celebes too, better times had now come. These tribes, the Toradjas, had so far remained outside the sphere of influence of the central administration. Their foreign enemies had been the Buginese and other coastal Mohammedans, but among themselves headhunting expeditions were quite common. Valiant missionaries had succeeded in obtaining a foothold among them, and the names of Adriani and Kruyt will always be remembered as those of the men who taught the Toradjas the first steps toward a better civilization. The Lesser Sunda Islands accepted the new situation with no more opposition than the island of Celebes. Only the petty war-lords among the tribespeople resented the introduction of a modern administration. The time had come for modern methods and new ideas.

In 1910 the Indies showed a very different picture from that which they had presented in 1870. Peace ruled everywhere, and the administration of Batavia had become highly efficient. Economically, the country had developed amazingly. In 1899 the Batavian government had seemed close to bankruptcy. Loans amounting to a hundred million guilders had been made to cover the deficits of the budget. In 1907 the budget had shown a surplus, in spite of the fact that the demands upon the Treasury had grown higher and higher. Time and again Professor Snouck pointed out that the best way to strengthen the foundation of the Netherlands Kingdom was to associate the Indonesians with Netherlands civilization, not by a foolish attempt to make them, overnight, into Indonesian Netherlanders, but by bringing within their reach the best results of Netherlands civilization. "The Indonesians," said Prof. Snouck, "are imploring us to give them instruction; by granting their wish we shall secure their loyalty for an unlimited time."

The only objection the government made to the realization of this idea was that it would cost too much to bring popular instruction within everybody's reach. Indeed, at that time, the costs of general instruction would have exceeded the total government income. It is undeniable that the government had neglected popular education in the days of the Culture System.[35] Until 1854 the only schools maintained from the public funds were elementary schools for European children. But then, we must remember that this was the year 1854, and what were the conditions in matters of education then existing in many

[35] See I. Brugmans, *Geschiedenis van het onderwijs in Nederlandsch-Indië* (Groningen-Batavia, 1938). On the development in the last twenty years, see I. Brugmans and Mr. Soenario, in Report-Visman, vol. 1, ch. iii.

other, non-colonial, territories in the world? These schools had been open to Indonesians until 1848, and then the principle of separate schools for Indonesians had been accepted. Aside from the foundation of two native teachers' colleges in 1866 and 1867 very little had been done towards establishing popular education at that time. With the Liberal period began the extension of elementary instruction for Indonesians. A reform of the Indonesian school system in 1893 made it possible, by lowering the general standard of instruction (not too regrettable, since it is one of the weaknesses of Netherlands elementary instruction to overburden the pupils), to enlarge the area in which instruction was given. Even in this modified form, however, the school system was too expensive. To establish these "second-class" schools (the official name) all over Java and Madura — not to mention the other islands — would have cost over sixty millions a year, or 50 per cent of the State income!

The urgent need for more and better education, combined with the desperate situation of the state finances, caused the publication of an article that stirred up public sentiment in the Netherlands. Under the title "A Debt of Honor," Mr. Conrad Th. Van Deventer published in the old and outstanding periodical *De Gids* of 1899 an article in which he argued that the Netherlands had acquired many millions from the Indies, and that, consequently, in a time when the Indies were in dire need of funds to provide education for their own people, the Netherlands were bound "in honor" to make restitution of those millions. He estimated the amount which should eventually be refunded as 187,000,000 guilders. With this sum, the school system of the Indies could be improved and many other works of public interest undertaken. Legally his argument was weak. But, if the Netherlands really believed in the principles of moral progress and civilization that they professed so feelingly in Europe they had a duty to provide for the needs of the Indonesians, not merely up to the limit of a certain amount of money, but to the best of their ability and with all resources at their disposal. Van Deventer's intention was excellent, but instead of advocating the restitution of money received many years ago from the Indies, he should simply have advocated the allocation of sufficient funds and made no allusions to the past. Even if the Netherlands never had obtained profits from the Indies, they still would have had obligations towards that country.

In this direction the solution of the problem was found. The "Debt of Honor" was paid in a different way; the new policy followed by the Netherlands government after 1900 practically reversed the relation between the two parts of the kingdom, and the "moral duty of the Netherlands toward the people of the Indies" was declared by the government in 1901 to be one of the principles upon which it would base its future policy.[36] In 1905 a sum of forty million was paid by the Netherlands treasury into that of the Indies for "the amelioration of economic conditions in Java and Madura." In 1912 the finances of the Netherlands and the Indies were definitely separated. In the meantime, the government of Batavia had managed to overcome its financial difficulties and to change the deficit into a surplus, and profits could once more have flowed into the home country, but nobody was in favor of the idea. The surplus belonged to the Indies and there it should be used. Because of the lack of a surplus since 1877 the question of the advisability of transferring money to the home country had not been raised, and therefore it was a mere formality that these remittances were now officially abolished.

Economic causes had brought about this change in part, but Governor-general Van Heutsz had been very able in making good use of every favorable circumstance. First there had occurred a general rise of prices for tropical products. A conference held at Brussels had given the cane sugar a better chance in its competition with beet sugar. This was the beginning of the golden age of the Javanese sugar plantations. The production rose from 700,000 tons (in 1900) to 1,400,000 tons in 1914. The production of tea increased fivefold, that of tobacco 50 per cent, that of rubber from practically nothing to 15,000 tons. Netherlands and foreign capital saw in the Indies a good place for investments. The government encouraged these investments, for the Indies did not command sufficient capital to finance their own agricultural enterprises and the foreign investments would create thousands of jobs and help to raise the income and the standard of living of the Indonesian peasants. The sugar production was almost wholly in the hands of the Dutch, but in the case of tea, rubber and tobacco, much foreign capital was involved, about 50 per cent, mostly English, if we may accept the statistics used by J. S. Furnivall.[37] Oil production rose from 360,000 tons in 1900 to 1,540,000 tons in 1914, increasing fourfold and drawing capital from all over the world. The Standard Oil Company was working side by side with the Royal Dutch, and had

[36] P. Broshooft, *De ethische koers in de koloniale politiek* (Amsterdam, 1901); A. D. A. De Kat Angelino, *Staatkundig beleid en bestuurszorg in Nederlandsch Indië*, 3 vols. (The Hague, 1929/30), abbreviated English version with the title *Colonial Policy*, 2 vols. (The Hague, 1930).

[37] Furnivall, *op. cit.*, p. 311.

founded the Netherlands Colonial Oil Company to exploit the rich fields near Palembang. The most remarkable feature of this development was the increasing share of the Outer Territories, especially of Sumatra, in this production. The value of exported goods had doubled in the period between 1900 and 1914, but although in 1900 only one-third of this export came from the islands outside of Java, the contribution of these territories had risen in 1914 to 50 per cent of the total exports.

Under these circumstances the government could expect better returns from the taxes and from its own enterprises, and indeed the total income of the state did double in the same fourteen years, but taxes still provided more than 50 per cent of it and the government enterprises, coffee and tin, only one-fourth. However, the European population which had increased to nearly 80,000 people, now began to bear an increasing share in the burden of taxes, as was expected. In 1907 Van Heutsz managed to obtain a government surplus and succeeded in maintaining a well balanced budget. The economic progress was such that the reformers saw most of the material obstacles to their plans removed. Thus, the period between 1900 and 1917 became an era of increasing care by the government for the native inhabitants of the Indies. Especially successful were the measures taken for the material well-being of the Indonesians.

In a human society like that of the Indies, one of the great problems of government is the protection of the Indonesians against western economic forces. It must see to it that the small but independent peasant is not ousted from his land and hampered in the production of food for himself and his family by the development of capitalist agricultural enterprises. This had been achieved by the agrarian laws and the prohibition of the alienation of Indonesian land to non-Indonesians, but with the increase of the population special attention had to be devoted to the extension of fields, especially irrigated fields, and to the introduction of new crops. The whole problem had been studied by a special committee "for enquiring into the causes of diminishing welfare in Java," appointed in 1902.[38] This enquiry was followed by others in later years. Not all experts drew the same conclusions from the mass of materials gathered by these committees. The general impression was that the Javanese peasant not only managed to subsist — which was all that could have been said in former centuries, as well under Indonesian as under Dutch rule — but that evidently his standard of living had

[38] Furnivall, *op. cit.*, pp. 393 sq.; C. Th. van Deventer, *Een overzicht van den economischen toestand der inlandsche bevolking van Java en Madoera* (The Hague, 1904).

risen. The first committee noted when enquiring into the "diminishment of welfare," that the welfare had *not* diminished. To have an exact idea of what this statement implies, we must take into consideration that the population of Java had increased fivefold or more since the beginning of the nineteenth century. The land upon which a century ago one family maintained itself now provided food for five. Apparently it was the task of the government to increase the area of arable land, and this was done by huge irrigation works. These works had already been undertaken in the days of the East India Company and the Culture System, but never on such an extensive scale. By these and other measures remarkable progress was accomplished, though there remained critics enough, even in the Netherlands Parliament, who urged the government to continue its endeavors and who pointed out that enough could never be accomplished.[39]

Another way out of the difficulties was emigration to thinly settled districts in the Outer Territories. But the Javanese only reluctantly undertook to leave their country for ever. The best system was to move whole villages, and especially in southern Sumatra in the Lampong districts suitable ground for settlements was found. Whatever the government planned, however, the rapid increase of the population of Java constantly created new tension in the small overpopulated island.

The total number of the inhabitants of Java and Madura rose from five millions in 1815 to eleven millions in 1860, twenty-eight millions in 1900, and thirty-four millions in 1920. In 1942 it reached the forty-eight million mark. These millions, practically all farmers or living on trades directly dependent upon agriculture, spread rapidly over the whole island, into the utmost corners and up the hills and mountains. Thus new problems rose every day. It was not enough to help the peasants by building irrigation works and promoting emigration. In the existing circumstances the individual Javanese might easily become the prey of the money-lender. In the Eastern world it is quite common for the farmer to sell his crop in advance. We saw how this system was practiced by the nutmeg growers of the Moluccas and how it was one of the causes of their destruction. The Javanese farmers followed the same custom and often became the victims of the Chinese money-lenders, who are usually advance buyers. The agrarian laws of the Netherlands government protected the Indonesian people against the worst consequences of this abuse, for the creditor could never seize

[39] H. van Kol, *Nederlandsch Indië in de Staten Generaal, 1897–1909* (The Hague, 1911).

land from the debtor, and "debtor bondage" had for decades already been abolished. To help the small farmers the government organized, at the beginning of the twentieth century, a number of institutions for popular credit.[40] Thus credit funds of the desas were instituted. These were foundations that advanced seeds and planting material to the farmers, who repaid both capital and interest in rice. In 1917 there were more than ten thousand of these institutions in Java and Madura alone, and in that single year they advanced materials to more than 1,300,000 farmers. Wherever the economic situation made it necessary and the single farmer became economically stronger, desa banks were established, sometimes working on coöperative lines. Of these banks there existed more than two thousand in 1917, and more than 600,000 people made use of them, a figure that increased by 50 per cent in the following ten years. The amount of the average loan was thirty-six guilders. Still more effective, perhaps, were the government pawnshops, taken over from the Chinese. These pawnshops purveyed in 1926 not less than 166,000 guilders on 48,000,000 pledges. All these measures were intended to help the Indonesian farmer economically and won a great measure of success. But he had enemies other than the money-lender.

Asia is, unhappily, the home of many epidemic diseases. From Asia the bubonic plague came to Europe in the Middle Ages, and, in the nineteenth century, the cholera. The latter disease caused great loss in human lives in the Indies too, but from the bubonic plague they had remained remarkably free. In May 1905, however, a report from eastern Sumatra caused great excitement in official circles. The story ran as follows. A Javanese coolie working in the rice storehouses of a big concern had won the high approval of his superiors because of his great skill as a rat-catcher. He spread a poison of his own making on the floor and over the sacks and each day he collected dozens of dead rats and caught a great number of others with his hands. Proud of his accomplishment, he guarded the secret of his poison with care, until he fell sick and died in two days.

The physicians became suspicious of the cause of his death and found that he had died of the bubonic plague, which, of course, had also been the cause of the death of the rats. The rice came from Rangoon, where the bubonic plague had manifested itself several times. At that time, at least, the plague did not spread; not more than two people died of it in that year. In 1911, however, a suspicious case was reported from Malang in eastern Java. Further investigations proved

[40] ENI, under "Volkscredietwezen"; A. Vandenbosch, *op. cit.*, p. 269.

that a number of people in this district had already died of the plague and that here, also, the disease had spread from the rice storehouses and had been carried inland from Batavia. In 1911 two thousand people died of the plague; in 1913 more than twelve thousand. The government devoted all its energy to the struggle against the spread of the disease. Most effective seemed the complete cleaning of the houses and farm barns, and as far as possible the destruction of all rats and other infected animals. Actually more than one and a half million houses of native farmers were destroyed and rebuilt, at an expense of thirty million guilders. Beside these sanitary measures, inoculation was carried out with great effect. In a struggle lasting twenty-five years, a struggle which truly may be called heroic, the epidemic was stopped and the country once more liberated from the plague.

Another disease which has been epidemic in the Indies since the oldest days is the *beri-beri*, an illness common in all tropical countries. Jacob Bontius described the symptoms in his book *De medicina indicorum*, published at Leyden in 1642. The peoples of the Malay race seem particularly susceptible, and in the Indies the disease every year caused the death of thousands. It was Prof. Dr. Christiaan Eykman who finally discovered the cause of the illness when he had found out that people who ate polished rice as their normal food easily fell a victim to it, while others who regularly consumed crude rice remained free of it. For a long time Eykman could not convince his colleagues of the truth and significance of his discoveries. The full meaning of his work became apparent when Funk, in 1911, working on the lines indicated by Eykman, discovered the significance of the vitamins, a discovery which has affected the whole of medical science. Eykman, now recognized as one of the pioneers of medical research, was honored at the Medical Congress of 1913 in the United States. The John Scott Medal was conferred upon him and he was nominated a member of the National Academy of Sciences at Washington. Finally, his merits were duly recognized before the whole world when, in 1929, the Nobel prize for medicine was conferred upon him.

It can hardly be said that the government did not take to heart the welfare of the people of the Indies once it had accepted the principles of government of modern, progressive times. But material welfare was not the only side of Indonesian life of which care had to be taken. The great demand of Snouck Hurgronje had been that the government should help the Indonesians to make the civilization of the Netherlands their own, and that popular instruction should be provided. Here too Van Heutsz had shown the way for new developments.

Realizing that for financial reasons it was impossible to give full elementary instruction to all Indonesian children — that, moreover, the teachers for that work were not available, and could not be made available for at least the next twenty years — he felt that the people of the Indies should acquire some instruction even before the scheme could be carried through on the full scale. His idea was to organize instruction of such a type that it would fit into the village surroundings, that, economically, it would not be too far above the people of the villages, and, therefore, that the schools would be a natural part of the village, not a foreign institution, imposed from above.

Village schools, therefore, were instituted, where, with government support, the people of each desa could organize elementary instruction for their children very cheaply. The government gave funds for the school buildings and provided the wood from which the village people could make the furniture for their school. It helped to find teachers, usually young people who had completed elementary instruction in a "second-class" school and whose salary it paid; but beyond this point the whole institution was maintained by village funds, with each child paying a few cents monthly for his or her education. The work was difficult, for, as a prominent Indonesian, Dr. Pangeran Husein Djajadiningrat, has written: "One of the hardest jobs of the East Indies government has been to persuade the natives that learning was desirable. Mild coercion frequently had to be employed to inveigle parents into sending their youngsters to school. And it often happened in primitive regions that a school would be set afire in the hope that this would offer an escape from the painful necessity of education!"[41] Nevertheless, it was a great scheme and will bear great results. Instead of donating a university to the Indies before providing grammar schools and thus trying to build the house downwards from the roof to the foundation, the government of Batavia decided to build instruction from the bottom upwards. It saw as its first object the teaching of reading and writing to as many children as possible, and these should be taught in the native tongue of the pupils. Then with the spread of knowledge and the increase of prosperity the secondary schools and finally higher education could follow in orderly fashion.

During this development a beginning was made with higher education in special fields. Vocational schools above the elementary school would serve the interests of the purely agricultural population of the

[41] Pang. A. A. Hoesein Djajadiningrat in *The Netherlands East Indies*, published by the Netherlands Information Bureau (New York, 1941), quotation on p. 24. On village schools, see De Kat Angelino, *op. cit.*, II, 241.

Indies. In 1903 there were not more than 1700 schools in the Indies, with 190,000 pupils. In 1913 there were 7000 schools, of which 3500 were desa schools, with a total of 227,000 pupils. Another ten years later the number of pupils had risen to 700,000 and in 1940 there were 18,000 desa schools with about two million pupils.[42] The number of schools increased yearly by about 800. More than half of the youngsters between six and ten years of age were then already receiving primary instruction and with the development of the scheme the rate of yearly increase of schools could have become steadily greater. The results of the system were not spectacular but the system itself was sound and, therefore, the results were expected to be durable. The Indies of 1914 were already widely different from those of 1900. The difference between the conditions existing in the country in 1914 and 1940 were still greater.

[42] For figures on education and schools, see Centraal Kantoor van Statistiek, *Onderwijsstatistiek* (latest volume, Batavia, 1941, covers the period 1938/39).

CHAPTER XV

THE END OF A COLONY AND THE BIRTH OF A NATION

For more than three centuries Netherlands influence had been predominant in the Indies when, after the first World War, the new colonial policy began to appear in full development in that territory. Netherlands control and government had completed a course of great historical interest. When the first Dutch merchants and sailors, honest according to their own lights, but rough; courageous and enterprising, but without understanding of foreign customs, had come to the island world of the Indies, they had been amazed by the variety of its nature and civilization, and the most observant among them had readily recognized that southern and eastern Asia were far ahead of western Europe in riches as well as in commercial ability and mercantile skill. The Netherlanders had imposed themselves upon this world, and especially upon the Indies, sometimes with the consent of the inhabitants, more often against their will; or better, perhaps, they had, once hospitably received into the midst of the Indonesians, refused to leave when their presence was no longer desired. For a century they had contented themselves with exploiting the existing natural wealth of the island. During the next century they had begun to bring in new sources of wealth which they exploited in the same way, by maintaining rigorous monopolies. Their work was commercial, their intercourse with the Indonesian world incidental. For two centuries the government of Batavia refused to occupy itself with purely Indonesian affairs. However it never questioned whether its economic measures might cause the disintegration of the native institutions. Before the interests of commerce, every other consideration had to give way.

Then came the French Revolution, and its ideals shaped, at least outwardly, the policy of the Netherlands for the next thirty years. The principle of liberty, equality, and fraternity was proclaimed in the Indies, but hypocritically interpreted; it led only to a theoretical equality between Europeans and Indonesians, an equality that tended toward the complete subjection of the economically weaker Indonesian groups of society to the stronger European and Chinese groups.

Raffles, more politician than statesman, did not alter this trend. The irony of history reserved to the commissaries of the restored Kingdom of the Netherlands, to those who well might be called the representatives of reaction, the task of applying to the government of the Indies the principle of justice for all, that is, the very essence of the theories of the Revolution. But it was a struggle against the prevailing ideas of the age and its complications caused the complete failure of Van der Capellen's well-intentioned administration. Nobody, neither Liberal nor Conservative, questioned the right of the conqueror to exploit economically the land of the conquered. Indeed, in this relation the word "justice" seemed to mean no more than the absence of arbitrary violence. With the end of Van der Capellen's administration the Netherlanders swung again to a different colonial policy, that of exploiting the Indies through the development and organization of their agricultural production under direct control of the government.

The Liberal Revolution of 1848 did not protest against the system of exploitation but only against economic participation in it by the government. It pleaded that private enterprise would do better than the government and that then the share of the Indonesians in general welfare also would increase. Once more "equal chances" in the economic field for both races were demanded without provision for guaranteeing the economic interests of the weaker groups of society — the Indonesians. And once more the Conservative — "conservative" only in internal Netherlands politics — group of the Netherlands statesmen corrected in time the well-intentioned but utopian policy of the Liberals and inserted in the Indonesian Laws the all important guarantee of Indonesian ownership of the soil. While Liberals and Conservatives struggled over the methods best suited to the economic development of the Indies, certain new groups in Netherlands politics, basing their views on religious tenets and drawing their sociological theories from the principles of Christianity, demanded that an end should be made of all forms of exploitation of the Indies, a demand repeated by the first Marxists in the Netherlands Parliament.

The expectations of the Liberals concerning the economic development of the country through private enterprise were only partly realized. Private enterprise worked wonders, but profits went chiefly to the promoters, not to the laborers. The slowly working but logical mind of the Netherlands people drew the unavoidable conclusions, namely, that private enterprise could justifiably be encouraged but that the share of the Indonesians should be enlarged; that they should be protected against economic exploitation and *that their country should be governed, not for the sake of the Netherlands, but for that of the Indies themselves.* This was the "ethical policy" of the beginning of the twentieth century. "Government of the Indies for the Indies" led unavoidably to "Self-government of the Indies," and consequently, after 1900 several political parties included this point in their programs. The program of the "ethical policy," therefore, shows a remarkable resemblance to what now is called "the American program of equality of opportunity in Asia." "This program," says Francis B. Sayre, United States High Commissioner to the Philippine Islands, "raises problems of great complexity. . . . The democratic faith does not mean the granting of independence to every people over night. But it does mean a vigorous program of education and training and preparation for the responsibilities of independence. It means self-government at the earliest practicable moment. It means the shaping of governmental measures primarily in the interest of the peoples themselves and not of those in control." [1]

This last point of the program was in 1901 definitely accepted by the Netherlands government and has been carried into execution since.[2] The other points were all accepted not later than 1922 as the officially acknowledged purpose of Netherlands rule in the Indies.

However, self-government can be understood in different ways. Was it to be self-government of the Indies by the upper classes, mainly of Dutch extraction and those pure Indonesians who had completely associated themselves with the Dutch? Or was it to be understood as self-government on a democratic basis, that is government by the masses of the Indonesian people; and in this case, would it mean the complete exclusion of all the numerous foreign elements of the population from taking an active part in the administration? Among these "foreigners" not only the Europeans but also the Arabians and the Chinese, together several million people of great economic importance, had to be included. Or would the goal of these endeavors be a commonwealth in which the diverse elements of the population, the minorities of foreign extraction as well as the minorities of Indonesian blood, would harmoniously coöperate and determine the character of the new state? The minorities of Indonesian blood included — it must be remembered — *all* Indonesians except the Javanese who represent, on 15 per cent of the surface of the Indies, 75 per cent of the inhabitants of the whole area! Another solution was that the Indies — or

[1] F. B. Sayre, in *New York Times Magazine*, July 5, 1942.

[2] Declaration of the Netherlands government in the speech from the throne, September 1901: "The Netherlands have a moral duty to fulfill towards the people of the Indies."

"Indonesia," a name preferred by many Indonesians though the word is just as unknown in the Malayan languages as the older term East Indies —[3] would become a partner with completely equal rights in the fourfold Netherlands kingdom, in which each of the four unities, the Netherlands, the East Indies, and the two parts of the West Indies, would determine its own affairs.

All these possibilities were given serious consideration. The first of these possible solutions, however, was upheld by only a minority of the Indonesian-born Netherlanders. In the first fifteen years of the twentieth century the government had taken an ever increasing interest in the material and spiritual welfare of the people. The results of this paternalism, however brilliant they might be in themselves, could content few in a progressive country like the Netherlands, where political theories flourished, and relatively few in the Indies, where progressive ideas spread rapidly.

The development was accelerated by the consequences of the first World War. The Netherlands and the Indies were lucky enough not to be actually involved in the conflict, but for several years the communications between the two parts of the empire were practically cut. The products of the Indies could not be shipped overseas, and for a while producers and native laborers had to cope with great difficulties. It is understandable that in the Indies other nations began to take the place of the Europeans as importers of industrial products and superseded them as buyers of the agricultural products.[4] In the ten years after 1914 the exports of the Indies to the United States of America increased sevenfold, that is, they rose from a pre-war percentage of two to 14 per cent of the total exports. Japan increased her imports fourfold, from nearly 2 to more than 8 per cent of the total Indies imports. The ground thus lost by the European nations could never be regained; on the contrary, the tendency of this development was strengthened by the effects of the great depression of 1929 and later years.

Yet this economic change was only one of the minor effects of the

[3] The name "Indonesia," which means, of course, "The Islands of India," was given to the islands of the Malay archipelago by a German student of ethnography, A. Bastian, and has been used since 1884. In our day the name has been used to indicate all territories where peoples live that are related to the Malays proper, thus including the Philippines, Formosa, part of Indo-china and even part of Madagascar. The nationalists in the Indies adopted the term for the territory of the Netherlands Indies, seen as a unity. Some Indonesians prefer a pure Malay name, "Nusantara," which means "Empire of the Islands."

[4] G. Gonggrijp, *Schets eener economische geschiedenis van Nederlandsch Indië* (Haarlem, 1928), ch. vii; Erich Voigt, *Wirtschaftsgeschichte Niederländisch Indiens* (Leipzig, 1931), chs. vii and viii; Furnivall, *op. cit.*, ch. x.

first World War on Indonesian life. The political turmoil in Europe that reached its climax between 1917 and 1920 caused opinions to prevail that before the war had been considered excessively radical. In the Netherlands modern conceptions of colonial policy made rapid headway, and in the Indies both international and nationalistic movements gained in strength. Let us first consider the origin of the Indonesian nationalist movement in order to see how this nationalism was influenced by internationalist tendencies and how political opinion in the Netherlands and among the majority of the Netherlanders in the Indies reacted upon it. While local political groups discussed the ultimate aim, or the greater or lesser desirability of the continuation of Netherlands rule, the government devoted its energy to the gradual development of institutions of self-rule in the Indies.

The awakening of national sentiment, or better, perhaps, the first signs of Indonesian national consciousness, are closely connected with the changes in Asiatic political affairs after 1900. The modernization of Japan had made a great impression on many Indonesians. We have already seen how the ex-sultan of Atjeh even hoped to obtain Japanese help in his resistance to Netherlands rule. This was an isolated case, but the example of Japan encouraged Indonesian leaders to seek equality of rights with the European inhabitants of their country. The government itself had in 1899 granted to Japanese citizens equality of status with the Europeans, and after 1909 a Japanese consul held office in Batavia, although the number of Japanese citizens residing in the Indies remained very small for years to come. (In 1923 the total number of Japanese in the archipelago did not exceed 4200, and even in 1940 it hardly exceeded 8000.)

The rights granted to the Japanese stirred the Chinese residents to action.[5] The number of Chinese residing in Java increased after 1860 from about 150,000 to nearly 280,000 in 1900 and continued after that year to increase rapidly, but on the other islands the increase was still more rapid. Here their number rose from 70,000 to 260,000 in the same period. After 1900 with the further extension of plantations in Sumatra and with the development of the mining concerns — which enterprises in those days made large use of Chinese labor — the number of Chinese

[5] On the Chinese and cultural and political trends among them, see H. Colijn-D. G. Stibbe, *Nederlandsch Indië*, I, 119 sq.; W. J. Cator, *Economic Position of the Chinese in the Netherlands Indies*, pp. 25 sq.; Nio Joe Lan, "De eigen onderwijsvoorziening der Chineezen," KS, XXIII (1939), 67 sq. On Chinese immigration see Ta Chen, "Chinese Migrations with Special References to Labor Conditions," U. S. Bureau of Labor Statistics, no. 40 (July 1923), pp. 51 sq. The issue of December 1936 (vol. XX) of KS is wholly devoted to the Chinese of the Indies.

residents of Java doubled and that of the other islands actually trebled in a period of twenty years. This increase of Chinese immigration in itself would have posed many political and social problems. First of all, the new immigrants of the twentieth century presented a type of Chinese totally different from the men who had come over in former times. The latter mostly came from the province of Fukien, of which Amoy is the port of emigration, and belonged to the merchant class. They knew something about, and therefore valued, the ancient civilization of their homeland. Once in the Indies they learned to value the Indonesian civilization as well. In preserving the cultural treasures of Java many Chinese, descendants of seventeenth- or eighteenth-century immigrants, had a part. The immigrants of the late nineteenth and early twentieth century mostly came from Canton and belonged to another class of people. They knew little of the treasures of Chinese culture and had no appreciation whatsoever for that of Java or Sumatra. They gained a bad reputation as being quarrelsome and greatly inclined to forming secret societies, the kongsis that in many towns of the earth made the Chinese quarters notorious. They were not interested in the Indies but always looked back towards China whither they hoped to return as soon as possible.

At this time the foreign policy of the Chinese government swung from complete indifference to the fate of its emigrants to deliberate promotion of Chinese national interests outside the empire. For centuries the emperors of the Manchu dynasty had forbidden emigration and had considered all Chinese outside the empire as having lost their nationality. The Imperial Ordinances even forbade the return of emigrants to their fatherland. In 1896, however, all these laws were repealed and the imperial government claimed that all people of Chinese blood, that is, descendants of a Chinese father, remained Chinese citizens. There were hundreds of thousands of Chinese in the Indies who had even forgotten their native tongue, most of them had racially ceased to be Chinese and had, through intermarriage for a hundred years or more, been assimilated to the Indonesians, but the cult of the ancestors had kept the Chinese tradition vivid among them. All these were now suddenly claimed by the imperial government as its subjects, while Dutch-Indonesian Law considered them subjects of Batavia. The moment of this political reversal coincided with a beginning discontent among the Indonesian-Chinese themselves with the Dutch administration. Before 1800 the Indonesian-Chinese had been favored by the East India Company; after 1800 they had been instrumental in the organization of the Culture System and the government monopolies of the opium trade, and the management of the pawnshops. In those days they had been outlawed by their own emperor and had been loathed by the Indonesians, but had found protection under the government of Batavia, while for many, many years they had been ruled by their own officers according to their own local customs until, around the middle of the nineteenth century, a civil code was given to them based upon the western principles of law. If they spoke Chinese at all it was the dialect of their homeland, Fukien, but most of them had adopted Malay, or, a few of them, even Dutch as their mother tongue.

When after 1900 the Batavian government began to devote great energy to the spreading of knowledge among the Indonesians and established Dutch and Indonesian schools side by side, the Chinese were admitted to the schools of either group only when, after all applications from Dutch and Indonesians had been received, there was sufficient room left. Thus no real provision was made for the Chinese, since no special schools were established where Chinese children should have preference. This was a symptom of the new policy of the Batavian administration, which now turned its attention primarily toward the Indonesian. By the Chinese it was felt as a setback from their former privileged position. It is understandable, therefore, that the new policy of the imperial government of Peking met with great approval among the Chinese circles in the Indies, both among the newcomers from Canton and among many Chinese whose ancestors had not seen China for a hundred years. The Chinese now started schools of their own, supported by funds collected among the Chinese themselves, and in these schools, Chinese, not one of the many dialects but the Mandarin-Chinese, was used as a language of instruction. If a foreign language was taught in these schools, it was English, because of its usefulness in business transactions. The imperial government of Peking saw its chance and sent several inspectors to unify the methods of instruction of these schools, and by this means, it tried to establish regular connections with the Chinese population of the Indies. In only ten years more than four hundred Chinese private schools were founded. Since most of the school teachers had studied in America or Japan, the ideas of reform and, later, of revolution against the old-fashioned empire were spread all through the Chinese settlements. The Chinese commercial societies established after 1901 helped this movement toward modernization to grow. The authority of the local Chinese "captains," who were recognized by the government as the leaders of the Chinese population, grew weaker. The Young China movement took the lead and organized the support of the revolutionaries, who in 1911 overthrew the imperial government in China and instituted the Republic.

Batavia had, of course, changed its policy under the influence of these events. The restrictions on the admittance of Chinese children to Dutch or Indonesian schools had been abolished. The government organized the so called "Dutch-Chinese" schools, especially intended for Chinese children but with Dutch as the language of instruction. Finally, once the Republic had been established, an agreement was reached with China under which that country gave up her claims upon the Indonesian-born Chinese and agreed to recognize them as Dutch subjects, while the Netherlands government admitted Chinese consuls to take care of the interests of the numerous Chinese-born immigrants who remained Chinese citizens. This agreement created a new situation full of the strangest complications. To understand these, which are highly illustrative of the complicated conditions of social life in the East Indies, we must review shortly the legal status of the different national groups in its development. The peculiarity of the position of the Chinese and the difficulty of finding a solution for the complicated problems connected with it then became apparent.

In a preceding chapter we have seen how the Dutch East India Company provided for the administration of justice among its subjects in its own territory. Its *own* territory, namely that ruled directly by the Company, was for a long time extremely limited. It did not extend farther than the city walls of Batavia and a few dozen fortresses scattered over the islands. In this territory the Company rendered justice, it appointed courts and issued a code of laws. All people residing within the area directly ruled by the Company were subjected to that same code, which was, by the way, based upon the Roman-Dutch conceptions of law. We have seen how the government of Batavia was quick to discover that it was impossible to apply this principle rigorously. How could a Chinese be convinced that he had to bequeath his property to his heirs, that he had to marry — never divorce! — in accordance with the ideas on these subjects existing in the western world of the seventeenth century? The same difficulty existed where other nationalities of the Far and Near East were concerned. Therefore the rule was instituted that the national groups of the East, even if living on the territory and under direct administration of the Company, should follow their own national customs concerning civil law. Criminal law remained identical for all groups of the population.

Later, after the conquest of a large part of Java in the first half of the eighteenth century, the Directors of the Company ruled immediately that in the newly acquired territories where the Company held only the overlordship over the Javanese regencies, the local customary law should remain in force for the non-Christians. The judiciary was organized on this basis when the Ordinance for the Administration of the Indies (1854) was promulgated. Criminal law remained the same for all groups of the population but the lawbreakers from the different groups of the population were to be arraigned before different courts. For the Netherlanders and those identified with Netherlanders — other Europeans and non-Europeans of *Christian* countries (the United States, South Africa, Australia, South America) — there were the European courts; for the Indonesians and other "Oosterlingen" (Easterners) — nationals of non Christian countries (Egypt, Persia, Arabia, China, Siam) — there were the Indonesian courts. In civil law not only the court but also the content of the law differed. Here every nation was, roughly speaking, judged according to its own customs and institutions. The idea behind this arrangement was not to create discrimination but rather to apply the principle that everybody should be judged by his own peers. There could be no question of racial discrimination, for the factor *race* did not appear.[6] On the contrary, Indonesians could obtain by a procedure the same legal status and the same rights (and obligations!) as Europeans and, consequently, could be appointed as judges to European courts, while Europeans could never be appointed to Indonesian courts.[7]

So far the whole organization was relatively simple. Under its rules the Indonesian-Chinese, while retaining their own legal code, came eventually before the Indonesian courts. The whole arrangement was somewhat disturbed, however, to say no more, when the division into the two groups could no longer be founded upon the antithesis of basically Christian vs. basically non-Christian. This happened when the Japanese, by the agreement of 1899 between the Netherlands and Japan, were put on a legal footing with the "Europeans." A new factor was now introduced into the problem. Nationals of a foreign state which was ruled according to European conceptions of administration were considered to have the same status before the law as the nationals

[6] W. E. van Mastenbroek, *De historische ontwikkeling van de staatsrechtelijke indeeling der bevolking van Nederlandsch Indië* (Wageningen, 1934); J. H. Carpentier Alting, *Grondslagen der rechtsbedeeling in Nederlandsch Indië* (The Hague, 1926).

[7] The consequences of this change of status are manifold. Indonesian law permits polygamy, but Dutch law prohibits it. Nevertheless, thousands of Indonesians have received the status of "European." Indeed it happened in the city of Semarang in the last decade that the majority of the members of the "European" court racially were Indonesian.

of "Christian" states.[8] The question instantly arose: why the Japanese and not the Turks or the Egyptians or the Chinese?

There were, really, no reasons why the Turks or Persians or Siamese should not, in their quality of nationals of a foreign state, be grouped with the Europeans, Americans, and Japanese. This was eventually done, though the Turks did not obtain the same status until after the first World War and the Siamese (or Thai) not before 1938. As far as the Chinese were concerned, there arose difficulties.

First, who were the Chinese who would be subject to the new regulations? All of them? But a great number of them were only Chinese by tradition, not by nationality. They clung to certain Chinese customs but could not claim to be treated differently from the other native inhabitants of the Indies. Only the Chinese who were Chinese citizens? This would split the Chinese population into two groups as far as arraignment in court was concerned, while they would still remain a separate entity as affected by certain points of civil law.[9]

For many Chinese, equal legal status with the Europeans was simply a matter of prestige. Under the present regulations they considered themselves in a position of inferiority as compared with the Japanese, for whom they had never any love. Apparently, the whole question of civil and criminal procedure for the Chinese could only be settled by a total reorganization of the judiciary in the Indies, a reform which was well on its way when the war broke out in 1941. Thus, between 1911 and 1940 the Chinese part of the population hesitated between the old country, China, which had been revived to new strength by the revolution of 1911, and the new country, Indonesia, with which many of the cultivated Chinese felt closely connected by a tradition of centuries. However, one conclusion could already be drawn: the privileged position of the Chinese as it existed in the Indies in the old days had definitely come to an end, for the rising tide of national feeling among the Indonesians was not in the last place directed against them. For the Indonesians the political events in China and Japan had not the

[8] Ph. Kleintjes, *Staatsinstellingen van Nederlandsch Indië*, etc., I, 95, gives a definition of the legal term "European." Five criteria are involved: nationality, European origin, legal principles of private law, descent, and existing status. The matter is one of the most complicated in East Indian constitutional law.

[9] In nearly all matters of civil law the Chinese had been brought under the same statutes as the Europeans as early as 1855. The most difficult points were those regulating inheritance and adoption. Further progress was made in 1925, but then many Chinese did not fulfill the obligations connected with their new status and, for instance, failed to comply with the regulations of the law concerning the registering of marriages and divorces (to which the Europeans always had been subjected) and thus created new and horrible confusion.

same importance as for their countrymen of Chinese descent. Once the national feeling of the Indonesians began to manifest itself, it looked more toward the west than toward the north, which after all only confirms the historical tendency of the East Indies to maintain contact with India and the Near East.[10]

In 1906 a Javanese physician, Mas Wahidin Sudiro Husodo, traveled all over Java to collect money for the establishment of scholarships for Javanese boys. The initiative for this movement came from the pupils of the Javanese Medical School. One of them, Raden Sutomo, who afterwards became one of the most prominent leaders of Indonesian nationalism, founded the Society "Budi Utomo" ("High Endeavor") in 1908 which, within a year, counted more than ten thousand members. The society limited its activities to Java and Madura and strove for the organization of schools on a national basis. Politically it was, in the first years of its existence, nearly always unpartisan. The character of the organization and the statements of its leaders seemed to confirm the opinions, held by nearly all European experts on the Indies, that even after centuries of Mohammedan supremacy, the Javanese outlook on life had changed very little from its basically Indonesian prototype and that the Islamitic ideals never had substantially modified that spiritual attitude.

Budi Utomo found its first adherents among the Javanese aristocracy, government officials and other intellectuals. That the views held by these social groups were not identical with those of the mass of the people was shown a few years later. The members of Budi Utomo indeed looked toward India, from which country they hoped at some time to obtain teachers for their schools. India's leaders, Tagore, and later Gandhi, they for a while greatly admired. The masses, however, were much more easily influenced by ideals taken from the Islamitic world. "Revival of Islam" had become a common ideal for millions of Mohammedans. The average Indonesian is Moslem only by name. Except in a few districts of Sumatra and western Java the commands of the Koran hardly influence public and private life of the Indonesian. But in the same way as the Christian churches had their missions

[10] There is no satisfactory history or even survey of Indonesian nationalism. A short survey appears in Colijn-Stibbe, *op. cit.*, pp. 339 sq. J. Th. P. Blumberger, *De nationalistische beweging in Nederlandsch Indië* (The Hague, 1931), is written from a strictly conservative point of view. The same author wrote the articles in ENI. Interesting is Noto Suroto, *Van overheersching tot zelfbestuur* (The Hague, 1931). The article by Virginia Thompson in Emerson's *Government and Nationalism in Southeast Asia* (I. P. R. Inquiry series, New York, 1942) is based solely upon the books of Vandenbosch and Furnivall. In the *Koloniale Studiën*, *Koloniaal Tijdschrift*, and *Indische Gids* several articles on nationalism have been published.

among the Indonesians to convert them to Christianity, the Mohammedans of India and Arabia kept working for the intensification of Islam among its nominal adherents in the East. The Indonesians did not care for the Pan-Islamitic ideals as propounded from Stambul and Mecca in the first decades of the twentieth century but they found Islam a well-chosen rallying point against foreign influence.[11] Protestant and Catholic missions in Java and Sumatra met only with very limited success; their real chances lay in Borneo and the Lesser Sunda Islands where the Catholics, and in Celebes and the Moluccas where the Protestants made good progress. In Sumatra only part of the people of the Bataks — who had never accepted Islam — could be converted. The great majority of the Sumatrans and Javanese rallied, however, around the banner of the Prophet in an instinctive reaction against the attempts to bring them new religious beliefs. Powerful Islamitic organizations sprang up overnight but often disappeared as rapidly as they had developed, unless they had learned from the opponent and used the same methods as the missions to keep their flock together, namely by the exertion of relentless efforts to bring about social improvements.

In a certain sense these Islamitic organizations were purely reactionary, which fact marks the difference between them and the societies based upon Javanese idealism like the Budi Utomo.

The reactionary character of the Islamitic mass movement became apparent from the beginning, for it made its first appearance as a reaction against the growing economic influence of the Chinese. Once the Chinese in Java had been freed from a legal restriction in matters of traveling and residence they began to exercise a disproportionate economic influence in every corner of the country, even in the most remote desas. The middle-class Javanese were badly hurt in their economic interests by the Chinese competition in the retail trade, and were reacting by forming economic organizations. These middle-class people, however, are exactly the ones who are the most conscious believers in Islam in the island of Java. Under the leadership of Hadji Samanhudi of Surakarta they began to organize coöperative societies, a counter action which in consequence of the character of the Javanese people in general and especially of the class of people concerned rapidly took the form of a religious social movement. Thus, in 1911 the Sarekat Dagang Islam was founded. The intentions of the founders of the society were undoubtedly peaceful, but the anti-Chinese sentiments

[11] G. H. Bousquet, *La Politique musulmane des Pays Bas* (Paris, 1938); English version: *Dutch Colonial Policy through French Eyes* (New York, 1940).

had risen to such heights that the founding of the organizations coincided with numerous anti-Chinese riots, both in Surabaya and in Surakarta. For this reason the society was for a short while forbidden by the government. It was reorganized as the Sarekat Islam in 1912.[12] The program of the new organization included the following points:

(1) The promotion of commercial enterprise among the Indonesians,
(2) The organization of mutual economic support,
(3) The promotion of the intellectual and material well-being of the Indonesians, and finally,
(4) The promotion of the true Islamitic religion.

At the first Congress, Omar Said Tjokro Aminoto, its new leader, pointed out at length that the Sarekat Islam was not intended to be a political party and that unwavering loyalty toward the government would be maintained. Neither was it to be its intention to stir up the religious feelings of the Mohammedans against the followers of other religions.

In an incredibly short time the Sarekat grew to be the first mass organization in the Indies. Within five years it counted 800,000 members. The religious character of the association was accentuated. Hence, when here and there the rather primitive Islamitic enthusiasts of Borneo and Celebes understood the forming of the society as an instigation of the people to "holy war," the leadership could hardly be blamed for these events. Actually, the amazingly rapid development of the society surprised even its own leaders and caused them to be over-confident. The masses flocked to join, but except for its general religious aspect, hardly knew what the movement stood for. In a quarter of a century the membership fluctuated between two million and a few thousand.

While the partly economic, partly religious program of the Sarekat Islam appealed to the masses, the purely religious Islamitic movement of Muhammadyah, started by Kjahi Hadji Ahmad Dahlan at Djocjakarta in 1912, developed much more slowly.[13] This movement is connected with the trend toward religious reform in Islam that originated in Egypt and spread over all Islamitic countries. It is a trend toward the modernization of the Mohammedan rules of society, toward a return to the original commands of the Koran. Mohammedan life everywhere had been ruled rather by the commands of the four schools of Mohammedan Law than by an attempt to conform directly to the

[12] See article "Sarekat Islam," ENI, III, 694, and Aanv. 15, 196 and 945 (all by Blumberger), and literature indicated there.

[13] Bousquet, *op. cit.*, pp. 11 sq.

original rules of the Koran. To clear away all later interpretations, to abolish all superstitious customs, mostly relics of pre-Islamitic times, and to loosen the stiff bonds of tradition that tended to strangle all cultural life in the Islamitic world was the aim of the reformists, among whom the adherents of Muhammadyah could also be counted. Its task was difficult, for in the Indies perhaps more than anywhere else pre-Islamitic customs, tolerated by the traditionalist interpreters of Mohammedan law, had remained in force. The membership of Muhammadyah grew steadily and the organization took the lead in Islamitic affairs when it became apparent, even to the ignorant masses, that the great movement of Sarekat Islam had miscarried. This had happened when its leaders shifted their aims from the religious and cultural to the political and social-economic field. Doing so they had come under the influence of the international socialist movement.

The city of Semarang on Java's north coast has been the center from which socialist ideas spread over the Indies. From the first moment that modern political life sprang into existence in the archipelago—this was when the first elections for city councils were held in 1903—the Semarangsche Kiesvereeniging (Club of Franchise-holders of Semarang) was very radical in its political opinions.[14] Socialism, that is to say, Marxism, obtained a foothold there, especially among the Indos, the Europeans of mixed blood. Many of the Indos followed the leadership of Eduard F. E. Douwes Dekker, an Indo himself and a distant relative of the author of the *Max Havelaar* whom we mentioned in connection with the Culture System. From a racial point of view Douwes Dekker is certainly an example of internationalism. His father was a Netherlander, son of a Dutch father and French mother. His mother was an Indo, daughter of a German father and a Javanese mother. Born in the Indies and considering the Indies his true fatherland, he initiated a movement the slogan of which, "The Indies for those who make their home there," was directed against the growing number of Netherlanders who emigrated to the Indies with the sole intention of returning to Europe as soon as circumstances would allow. Douwes Dekker's party was, consequently, intended to be inter-racial. Dutch-Indonesian, pure Dutch as well as Indos, Indo-Chinese, Indo-Arabians, and pure Indonesians were asked to join in united opposition to the Netherlands. It was inevitable that his group should fall more and more under the influence of the pure Indonesians, who after all represent fully 95 per cent of the total number of inhabitants. At the

[14] A. C. van den Bijllaardt, *Ontstaan en ontwikkeling der staatkundige partijen in Nederlandsch Indië* (Batavia, 1933).

same time Douwes Dekker himself shifted steadily toward radical socialism.

In this field other leaders forestalled him. That part of the Semarangsche Kiesvereeniging that had not followed Douwes Dekker joined Hendrik Sneevliet, a former member of the Social Democrat Party in Holland, who had moved to the Indies and there founded the Indian Social Democratic Club, a political group whose principles rapidly developed into those of very radical Marxism. From the beginning, Sneevliet [15] showed great sympathy for the Russian revolution and its leaders. To start the revolutionary movement in the Indies and to join hands with the Soviet became his aim. As long, however, as the movement remained restricted to the European and Indo-European section of the population, it had little chance of success, or even of gaining great importance. It was necessary for his purpose to win over the Indonesians to his social-political ideals. To accomplish this he had to solve the problem of how to combine radical Marxism with its anti-religious tendencies and the Islamitic ideals of the principal Indonesian groups. Nearly all the Marxists were Netherlanders, and this fact confronted him with another problem, namely, how to gain the confidence of the Indonesians. Here a young Javanese offered himself as an intermediary. This young man, with the name of Semaun, was an active member of the Semarang section of the Sarekat Islam and at the same time an enthusiastic supporter of the Marxist theories. He began to influence the local Sarekat Islam groups toward acceptance of Marxist slogans.

The development that followed is highly instructive. The executive committee of the Sarekat Islam, under the leadership of Tjokro Aminoto and Abdul Muis, remained very moderate in its political demands until 1917. At its first congress in 1913 the leaders rejected all ideas of anti-Dutch activity. At the first National Congress, June 1916, a demand for self-government had been formulated, but the slogan had been: "Coöperation with the Government for the welfare of the Indies!" Self-government, it was said, would unify the Netherlands and the Indies. The Indo Party of Douwes Dekker had sought the coöperation of the Sarekat Islam in its demand for Indonesian independence but their religious differences were far too great to permit coöperation on any platform whatsoever. At the Congress of Batavia in 1917, the leaders of the Sarekat Islam were already speaking in a quite different tone. Violently they attacked the administration, and if they did not

[15] In the spring of 1942 Sneevliet was executed by a Gestapo firing squad in occupied Holland.

mention the government as such they mercilessly criticized its officials. A demand for independence was brought up, although this was to be obtained "by evolution, not by revolution." Consequently, the leaders of the group did not refuse to take part in the newly established People's Council. Very significant, however, was a new plank in the platform, presented as the fight against "sinful capitalism."

This is the first time that a Marxist slogan was introduced into the speeches of the Sarekat Islam Congress, but its true Marxian character was curiously modified by a local interpretation. "*Sinful* capitalism" is, from a Marxist point of view, of course, a contradiction in terms, for it leaves open the possibility of *righteous capitalism*, which does not find a place in Marx's theories. Tjokro Aminoto was asked to explain *when* capitalism is sinful, and his reply was, "Foreign capitalism is always sinful." This clarified the expression so far that apparently only non-Mohammedan capitalism was to be condemned. In a further attempt to reconcile Islam and Marxism the theory was propounded that, after all, Mohammed in his Koran had been the first propagandist for a socialistic human community.

Events moved rapidly after 1917. Urged on by the socialist competition for the support of the masses, feeling that the Marxist slogans were extremely useful in capturing the masses for their party, and, finally, strongly encouraged by the course of events in Europe, the Sarekat Islam shifted from political, non-violent opposition to open hostility toward the government. It demanded immediate provisions for the masses of the laborers, supported the strikes that broke out time and again in the larger cities of Java, and refused further coöperation with the government in parliamentary work. A Javanese nobleman organized the "Revolutionary Socialistic Trade Union," an organization that entered into conflict with the sugar planters over labor conditions and the lease of farmlands.[16] The founder of the organization expressly stated, however, that the words "Revolutionary" and "Socialistic" should not be taken in their strict sense but were only used for propagandist purposes. The Sarekat Islam and its affiliated organizations still adhered to a policy of "moral violence," which can be best translated by "passive resistance." No wonder that the Marxist organizations of Semarang under the leadership of the energetic Semaun were far from satisfied with their Revolutionary Socialistic allies. Semaun tried to win over the Trade Union to communist principles, and when this attempt failed, succeeded in founding a rival organization, the Revolutionary Trade Union, a name in which the term "Revolutionary" was

[16] For labor unions in the Indies, see ENI Aanv. 961, under "Vakbeweging."

this time to be taken quite seriously. Surjopranoto, the founder of the Revolutionary Socialistic Trade Union, thereupon reorganized his group into the "Personeel Fabriek Bond" ("Union of Industrial Workers") and continued the struggle against the sugar magnates. The Sarekat Islam, grown into an organization that boasted two million and a half members, was now politically in the greatest difficulties. The Javanese intellectuals and aristocrats held aloof and stuck to their Budi Utomo Society. Most of the regents organized a separate Regents Union, and other groups of Javanese government officials, sincerely believing in the constructive value of their work and averse to revolutionary movements, did the same. Douwes Dekker and his adherents now demanded a reorganization on purely nationalistic lines and urged the leaders not to become involved in purely economic struggles. The socialist and communist groups of Semarang urged them to throw overboard the purely Islamitic points of the platform and to join the International Workers Organizations headed by Moscow.

Sneevliet had been ordered to leave the Indies after he had — in his enthusiasm for the cause of world revolution — endeavored to bring about a revolution among the soldiers and sailors of the East Indian Army and Navy. But his successors, among whom Semaun was prominent, stuck to the principles he had taught. On May 23, 1920, the Social Democrat Club of Semarang decided to take the name of Communist Party of the Indies, in Malayan, *Perserikatan Kommunist di India* (P.K.I.).[17] On December 25 of the same year the group decided to join the Third International of Moscow. Before this was done, the Indies had already been represented at the Second Congress of the Komintern (July-August 1920) by Sneevliet, who took it upon himself to represent the masses of the Indonesian peoples, although they undoubtedly never had heard his name. The Komintern had at that time already issued several statements regarding the policy of the organization of the International Union toward colonial problems. Of course it had written into its program the indiscriminate abolishment of all Western European and American governments over foreign dependencies, but the point of chief interest in these statements of policy concerned the tactics which the local organizations were ordered to follow. Should the communists coöperate temporarily with the national anticolonial movements, for instance with Moslem and Hindu groups of India, even if they were opposed to the principles of Marxism? The second Congress of 1920 stated definitely that communism was just as

[17] J. Th. P. Blumberger, *De communistische beweging in Nederlandsch Indië* (Haarlem, 1928).

much opposed to Pan-Islamism as it was to European (or American) domination; both were considered as merely different forms of capitalism. "Pan-Islamitic and identical movements that aim at combining the struggle for freedom against European and American Imperialism with the strengthening of the power of the Khans, the wealthy landowners, the Mullahs and so on, must be opposed," was the resolution of the Congress. This point in the platform caused some embarrassment in Java among the new communist leaders because their only chance for success lay in coöperation with the outspokenly Pan-Islamitic Sarekat Islam. A way out was found when the group declared the "dictatorship of the proletariat" to be the ultimate goal of the party, a goal which should be attained "by using all methods sanctioned by communist principles." Not only Pan-Islamism, but also the racial problem offered difficulties to communist organization, for communism knew, of course, no racial differentiation among its adherents, while the Indonesian organizations were strictly based upon the distinction European vs. Indonesian. The tactics indicated for the local communist party were to undermine the influence of the leaders of the Sarekat Islam and to bring the whole organization, slowly and if necessary without fully informing the members, into its own camp. To this task the communists devoted their quite uncommon energy and intelligence.

One of their first successes was the taking over of the Union of Railroad Employees, which had both European and Indonesian members. In 1921 they seemed to have maneuvered the leaders of the Sarekat Islam into a hopeless position. The hesitating and wavering Tjokro Aminoto saw the prestige of his party diminish, and the communists contributed to the decline by violently attacking the leader in person and by insinuating that the financial management of the party was far from blameless. In the hope of retaining the sympathy of the masses, Tjokro swung over once more to the Marxist side. The fifth Congress of the Sarekat brought the official declaration of the party on the relations between the Netherlands and the Indies. The origin and development of these relations were explained to the people according to the theories of the Marxian historical materialism. The social doctrines of Marxism were accepted, though with the rather weak qualification that this did not imply coöperation with foreign socialist political organizations. Of course the Komintern was meant. The attitude toward the government of Batavia was revised and took gradually more unpleasant forms.

All these attempts to keep the Sarekat in its place as the foremost

Indonesian organization were in vain. Resentment against the leaders rose even higher. The Arabic supporters of the group, mostly traders from Hadramaut who had come to the Indies to make their fortune, not to share their wealth with others, left the organization in protest. When the state employees of the government pawnshops went on strike, the Sarekat Islam supported their action and shared consequently in their defeat. Semaun reaped the harvest and succeeded in winning over most Indonesian trade unions for his party. Another member of the executive committee of the communist group, Tan Malaka, had been exiled by the government after the pawnshop strike and had gone to Moscow where he defended a change in the tactics of the Komintern towards Pan-Islamism and other anti-European movements. Pan-Islamism he said, does not mean anything but the joint resistance of all Moslems to colonial governments. Therefore, he brought a motion that the Komintern should give full support to that movement.

But at the very same time that he propounded this theory, the leaders of the Sarekat Islam were rallying once more around the banner of Pan-Islam to stem the rising tide of communist propaganda. At the sixth national congress of October 1921, where Abdul Muis and Hadji Agus Salim presided over the meetings, a motion was brought by the committee to introduce party discipline, that is, a rule that none of the members of the Sarekat would be allowed to be, at the same time, a member of another political party. This was directed at crushing the influence of the communist group. By throwing them out of the main organization, their small number would be revealed and their prestige annihilated. The communists retorted by accusing the Sarekat of being a "capitalist" institution, by ridiculing the notion of "sinful" capitalism, and by demanding organization of the people along the line of class distinction, not along that of religion. Hadji Agus Salim protested against the defamation of the Sarekat and of Islam in general, and, by boldly asserting that Mohammed had taught the doctrine of historical materialism in his Koran twelve centuries before Marx was born, carried the day. The communists were forced to withdraw from the Sarekat.

This was the first turning point in the history of national movements in the Indies. For five years more the Sarekat fought a losing battle against the communist group, which in the meantime organized Sarekats of its own, especially near Semarang, supported a strike of railroad workers, and, finally, in several districts of northern and western Java, organized fighting squads among the lawless elements of the population. Of course, the large organizations of Sarekat Islam, Budi Utomo, and the P.K.I. had not remained the only ones in the field. The Indies are a land of many peoples and languages and also of many religions, and many of these local racial and religious groups also asserted themselves by forming popular organizations. In a few years after the foundation of Budi Utomo there were national clubs of the "Sumatrans" (actually only the Menangkabauers), of the Madurese and Sundanese, of the men from Amboina and the Minahassa, and even of the Timorese. It is noticeable, however, that all these organizations, except that of the Timorese, were founded by national groups living in *Java*, not in their own territories. From Java they spread to the districts inhabited by their own people. Only the Timorese club originated outside Java, but even so, it was founded in Celebes, at Macassar, not at Timor. This proves that the national societies originated directly from the contact with the western world, and that more especially, they found their first adherents among men cut loose from their normal surroundings.

A special feature of the Indonesian movement was the formation of women's societies. Among many Indonesian peoples the women held a position of equality with men. Mohammedan Law had brought little change in the old customs in this respect. Therefore, even the franchise for women was seriously taken under deliberation when the People's Council was instituted. The committee that reported on the matter stated that in Amboina and the Minahassa the franchise for women would be considered by the native inhabitants the most natural thing in the world, and that even in central and eastern Java there would be no objection to it. The women's movement dated back to the beginning of the twentieth century. In the first four years of the century the noble Raden Adjeng Kartini, daughter of the regent of Japara and wife of the regent of Rembang, began to call the attention of her Dutch friends to the situation of the Javanese women and in her letters gave expression to the ideas prevailing among the girls and young women of the educated class in Java.[18] She died in 1904 when she was only twenty-five years old, but her ideas were made known in 1911 when a selection of her letters was published. Thus she has remained the shining example of Javanese womanhood, and when the men of Java began to organize, the women followed in a very short time. A special center of this very dignified movement was the small Javanese principality of

[18] R. A. Kartini, *Door duisternis tot licht. Gedachten over en voor het Javaansche volk* (4th ed., 1923); English version: *Letters of a Javanese Princess by Raden Adeng Kartini* (New York, 1920).

the Paku Alam (separated in 1811 from the Sultanate of Djocjakarta). One of the main aims of the movement was, of course, to provide adequate education for Javanese girls, and a number of so-called "Kartini schools" were established. Coöperation between Netherlanders and Indonesians brought into existence the "Van Deventer schools" which were also organized for the education of Javanese girls and called after the great friend of the Indonesians, C. Th. Van Deventer.

The variety of the Indonesian organizations was great as it should be, for, after all, the Indies are a vast and varied territory. But however great the differences might be, a feeling of national unity, based not only upon common interests but also upon common traditions and on a basic unity of language, steadily developed. The Netherlands had built the framework of this unity; through them the different tribes and peoples, the thousands of islands, had become one single coördinated body politic; and this is an achievement of their European rulers which the Indonesian nationalists will never surrender. There were some Netherlanders, among them Hendrik Colijn, ex-officer of the army of the Indies, ex-chairman of the Bataafsche Petroleum Company, and several times prime minister of the Netherlands, who began to think that it would perhaps be wise to undo what had been accomplished in this respect after three centuries of effort. Colijn advocated the organization of limited self-government in the Indies separately for each of the larger islands and of the island groups.[19] This policy, however, was too reactionary to be accepted by public opinion. Self-government of the Indies as a political *unity* could be the only proper aim of the Netherlands government. Later, Colijn himself understood that he had been wrong for, when he became a minister again, he never even alluded to the ideas he had professed in his book.

While the first signs of an Indonesian movement revealed themselves, the first important step in the development toward autonomy was taken by the institution of the "Volksraad," the People's Council. The law of 1903 dealing with the decentralization of the Indonesian administration had provided for the establishment of local and city councils with limited authority.[20] Another step in the right direction was the introduction of a certain amount of self-government for the desa, the Javanese village. The desas always had been more or less autonomous unities; we have seen how little the organization of the

[19] H. Colijn, *Koloniale vraagstukken van heden en morgen* (Amsterdam, 1928). Against this book see C. Snouck Hurgronje, *Colijn over Indië* (Amsterdam, 1928).

[20] Furnivall, *op. cit.*, p. 225. For details see Ph. Kleintjes, *Staatsinstellingen van Nederlandsch Indië*, vol. II, where also is listed literature on the subject; Report-Visman, I, 134 sq. and II, 148 sq.

village administration changed from early times to the nineteenth century. The "Desa Ordinance" of 1906 tried to revive this type of local autonomy. This first, very modest experiment in self-government for small areas was a success, but its importance was not great. The administration by the central government and that by the local councils were still too much intermingled to permit a clear appreciation of the efficiency of self-government as a working principle. Proposals were made for the reorganization of the system, but the Netherlands government preferred to start on a new line by first introducing limited self-government for the Indies as a whole. From the early days of parliamentary control over the Indonesian administration, some Liberal members of the Netherlands Parliament had objected to the interference of a Netherlands House of Representatives, elected by Netherlanders in Europe and destined to rule the country in Europe, with the affairs of the people of the Indies who were not represented in the same house.[21] It was the old question, of course, of "no taxation without representation," but here it was not so much that representation was demanded as it was that the power to enforce taxation and other matters of government was found objectionable. The large majority of the House had never concerned themselves with these distinctions, but the Europeans in the Indies had often grown very impatient while reading the debates in the House, where one hundred people, of whom only a few could be considered experts on colonial affairs, were asked to decide upon all matters, large and small, connected with the Batavian administration. In 1893 and 1907 weak attempts at changing the situation were made, but without effect. In 1913 the matter of greater participation of the inhabitants of the Indies in the affairs of government was revived and in 1916 brought to a successful conclusion by the institution of the People's Council, composed of Europeans, Indo-Arabians, Indo-Chinese, and Indonesians.[22] On May 18, 1918, the first meeting of the Council was opened by Governor-General Van Limburg Stirum.

The institution of the People's Council was an *experiment* in self-government. It could not be otherwise, for under the constitution in force in the Netherlands the Indies were governed in The Hague and not in Batavia. The People's Council was composed of elected and appointed members, the latter appointed by the governor-general. This

[21] For debates on the Indies in the Netherlands Parliament, see H. A. Idema, *Parlementaire Geschiedenis van Indië, 1891–1918* (The Hague, 1924).

[22] On the People's Council: Kleintjes, *op. cit.*, I, 212; Report-Visman, I, 76–124; American opinions: Vandenbosch, *op. cit.*, pp. 111 sq. and Lennox A. Mills in Emerson's *Government and Natonalism*, pp. 100 and 105.

provision was intended as a corrective measure for possible injustice of elections. As the elected members were chosen through intermediary elections of the local and city councils and the franchise was still very limited, several political groups, especially those of the opposition, would have slight chance to see one of their group in the Council. In such a case the governor-general could, if he deemed the group important enough, give one of its members a seat in the House. Actually, several of the most bitter critics of the government were in the following years appointed by the government. Because the governor-general could not act independently of the government in The Hague, the Council received only advisory powers and the right to suggest to the governor-general reforms it might consider necessary. In 1918 the majority of the members were Europeans. The experiment was a success beyond all expectation and a lively political activity immediately developed.[23] The events in Europe in November 1918 moved the governor-general to promise extension of rights to the People's Council, and in 1920 the number of Indonesian members was increased. Far more important were the reforms of 1922 and 1925, which marked the end, from a political point of view, of the centuries-old development of Netherlands rule in the Indies and the beginning of a new period.

The constitution of the Netherlands was revised in 1922 to make possible the introduction of the democratic reforms that apparently were necessitated by the political development of post-war Europe. The relations between the home country and the colonies were also discussed and brought in accordance with the prevailing view of the representatives that *colonial government finds its sole justification in the duty of the mother country to promote the interests of the governed peoples and to develop their social and political institutions according to their own ideals* (and not according to *our* conceptions!). The resolution was taken to omit from the constitution of the Netherlands the words *Colonies and Overseas possessions*. In the future the territories forming part of the kingdom should be treated as separate entities. This was not only a change of words, it meant that the constitution recognized in principle the equality of the four territorial units into which the kingdom is divided: the Netherlands, the Netherlands East Indies, Surinam, and Curaçao with dependencies.[24] The way was pre-

[23] W. H. van Helsdingen, *Tien jaar Volksraadarbeid, 1918–1928* (Weltevreden, 1928), continued in a second volume for the period 1928–1938. The issue of June 1938 of KS contains a series of articles on the People's Council.

[24] A discussion of this constitutional change in the Report-Visman, *passim*. See J. A. Eigeman, *Indië en het Koninkrijk* (The Hague, 1928).

pared for the transformation of the undivided Netherlands kingdom into a federation of states.

Once this principle had been adopted the government of Batavia could no longer be kept in a strictly dependent position toward the government in The Hague.[25] The "Regeeringsreglement" (the Act for the Administration of the East Indies) was replaced by a constitution under which the executive and legislative powers in the Indies were given to the governor-general, who only in certain well-defined cases needs the approval of The Hague on his decisions, while in many others he must consult, and often have the approval of, the People's Council. The details of the yearly budget, for instance, are fixed by the common consent of the governor-general and the Council, while the Netherlands Parliament has only the authority to reject the budget *en bloc* but not to make any changes in details. The number of members of the Council was fixed at sixty, of whom, according to the Constitution of 1925, thirty had to be Netherlanders, twenty-five Indonesians, and five Indo-Arabians and Indo-Chinese.[26] This was changed as early as 1928, when a definite majority was given to non-European members, the figures being reversed so that thirty Indonesians, twenty-five Netherlanders, and five Indo-Arabians and Indo-Chinese would be admitted. By these laws the foundations were laid for Indonesian self-government.

The administrative reforms of 1922 and 1925 helped toward the further development of local self-government. These reforms created, at least in the island of Java, provincial and regency councils. As these councils elect a board of deputies or commissaries, which board is charged with the handling of all affairs of the daily administration, the reform actually took away the administration of the provinces from the high Netherlands officials and entrusted it to the representatives of the people, leaving to the officials only the task of general supervision. Thus the people of Java obtained a chance to get fully acquainted with all details of local administration in preparation for self-government on a national scale.

[25] On the preparation of the new Constitution: *Verslag van de Commissie tot herziening van de staatsinrichting van Nederlandsch Indië* (Weltevreden, 1920), *Verslag der Kiesrechtcommissie, ingesteld bij besluit van 16 November 1921* (Weltevreden, 1922); J. Oppenheim and others, *Proeve eener staatsregeling voor Nederlandsch Indië* (Leyden, 1922), *Memorie van aanvulling* of the same (Leyden, 1923).

[26] The original bill provided for an Indonesian majority, but the Lower Chamber of Parliament by amendment reversed the figures (Report-Visman, I, 98 sq. and II, 205 sq.). On the new Constitution and East Indian administration, see H. J. van Mook, *De organizatie van de Indische Regeering* (Batavia, 1932); J. H. Heslinga, *De nieuwe Indische staatsinrichting* (Weltevreden, 1926).

It proved more difficult to create an administrative system of the same character for the other islands because of the great divergencies of the local tribes in matters of customary law and religion and of the great number of native states with their widely diverse political forms and languages. The Ordinances regulating the administration of the governments of Sumatra, Borneo, and the "Great East" were not published until 1938. They created self-government for regional communities, territories where the villages were connected by tradition, customs, and language. In Sumatra, for instance, the territory of the Menangkabau was reconstituted as a self-governing unit. These measures met with great success.

The laws of 1918, 1922, and 1925 left a great number of problems to be solved, of course, and the solution of these problems could undoubtedly only be found after new experiments in legislation and administration. If all parties concerned were willing to coöperate to this end — and if this can not be said of all Netherlanders, it was certainly true for the Netherlands government — then the evolution of the Indies could be rapid.[27] If not, all parties concerned would have to suffer. From this point of view it was extremely deplorable that by the year 1923 a large part of the Indonesian movement had fallen under the influence of totally foreign powers and organizations. Between evolution, as meant by the government and the majority of the liberal-minded part of the inhabitants of the Indies, and revolution, as schemed under the influence of the Komintern, no reconciliation was possible. The conflict that was growing from this antithesis could only be to the interest of the reactionary part of the inhabitants of the Indies, especially those Europeans who were used to think in terms of dividends and investments only.

The communist group, however, dreamt of easy and speedy successes. The leaders had not shrunk back from enlisting in the ranks of their party hundreds of gangsters, professional thieves, and bandits, of whom there have always been a certain number in the rural districts of Java, by which means they succeeded in intimidating the people of the countryside but made themselves detested by the better elements. The government hesitated to take action, afraid of being called reactionary and dictatorial, a hesitation not unlike that of moderate governments of Germany when faced with the problem either of using force against Nazi gangsterism and incurring the blame of being "dictatorial" or of permitting the organization of political crime until it

[27] J. Kielstra, *Taak en toekomst van het Nederlandsch Gezag in Oost Indië* (Utrecht, 1927), and *Het koloniale vraagstuk van dezen tijd* (Haarlem, 1928); D. van der Zee,

had become too strong to be dealt with. It should have been a warning to the communist leaders that the Sarekat Islam became increasingly hostile against communism, and that anti-communist organizations were formed by the population of the Preanger districts. The people of Java began to organize their own defense against lawlessness. In central Java the adherents of the Sarekat Islam and Muhammadyah broke up the meetings of the communists. Several leaders were so compromised that they emigrated to the Straits Settlements. But nothing could stop their revolutionary scheming. The Sarekat Islam leaders, disgusted with the proceedings of the communist group, succeeded in having the congress of their party, held at Madiun in October 1922, renew the stipulations against simultaneous membership in both groups. To retain the favor of the masses the Sarekat Islam turned once more, and with renewed energy, towards Pan-Islamism. Several "All Islam Congresses" were held. The question of the Chalifat, opened by Mustafa Kemal's drastic measures toward the last Turkish sultan, was discussed, and, when Ibn Saud of Arabia seemed willing to establish a new Chalifat in Mecca, Tjokro Aminoto was sent to the congress held in the Holy City.

Not quite in harmony with this tendency was another scheme of the leaders, namely to group together all Indonesians, regardless of religious distinctions. A plan was made to organize an "Insular Congress" in every island or island group of the archipelago and to unite the deputies of all these insular congresses in a Pan-Indonesian Congress. However, the difficulties were insurmountable. On a visit to Celebes, Tjokro Aminoto had to recognize that it would be impossible to win over the masses of the Christian Menadonese to the cause of the Sarekat and its Congress. At Menado the local Indonesian leaders made it perfectly clear to him that they were more interested in the legal development of the Dutch-Indonesian relations than in any radical movement. A last resort for the Sarekat was to throw all its energy into the problems of education in the hope of gaining a better hold over the future generations; but in the midst of their activities a revolutionary agitation of the communist group overthrew all their plans and schemes.

When the Indonesian communist movement began, Soviet Russia was still a state whose chances of survival were very precarious, hard-pressed as she was by a host of enemies. These difficulties were overcome and Russia developed steadily into one of the strongest powers

---

De S. D. A. P. en Indonesië (Amsterdam, 1929). See the issues of *De Stuw*, a periodical published by progressive groups, 1929 and following years. A retrospect: J. Meijer Ranneft, "Hollands fout in Indië," in *De Gids* (1937), I, 305 sq.

on earth. The interests of Russia and of the Komintern are not always identical, as is well known, but it is understandable that the Indonesian leaders took the promises of assistance given by Zinoviev in 1925 and Bucharin in 1926 very seriously. "The people of the Indies may be assured of our help," declared the latter at the Congress of the Executive Committee of the Komintern. At that very time the smouldering revolutionary movement in the Indies had already burst into flame. Armed gangs of communists and, in still greater number, of bandits and professional troublemakers incited to revolt by communist leaders, had attacked Javanese officials in the western province of Java, and a group of them had even seized by surprise and for a few hours occupied the central telephone office of Batavia. No special military measures were necessary to restore order. The great mass of the people remained quiet, and the Indonesian officials showed admirable diligence in checking the movement. More serious was an outburst on Sumatra's west coast, but here also the revolt was crushed without difficulty.[28]

The government immediately took steps to prevent further disturbances, and prohibited communist meetings and banned the Communist Party. About 1300 adherents of the group were arrested and interned in New Guinea. Against these measures most of the Indonesian organizations protested, but at the same time a number of prominent leaders declared their disapproval of the tactics of the Communist Party. The influence of the Komintern did not at once cease to exist, but it never regained its former strength. This was not only the consequence of repression by the government but also of the changing times. A second period in the national Indonesian movement had begun.

Before the war of 1914 only a few Indonesian students had found their way to the Netherlands Universities. After the war their number increased rapidly. Several organizations had been planned to bring these young Indonesians into closer association with their Dutch fellows, and in this purpose they succeeded fairly well until revolutionary sentiments got a hold over the larger part of the younger Indonesian students. Notwithstanding the example set by prominent Indonesians, such as for example the poet Noto Suroto, a prince of the house of Paku Alam, who devoted all his energy to fostering better understanding between Netherlanders and Indonesians, the majority of the younger generation was easily enticed by revolutionary ideals.

[28] For an American view on these events, see R. Kennedy, *The Ageless Indies*, pp. 126 sq.

Strong nationalist tendencies revealed themselves in Europe in those days. The successful liberation of Poland by Pilsudski and others, of Czechoslovakia by Masaryk, of Finland and the Baltic States, and especially the war waged by the Irish Sinn Fein against the British kingdom, stirred the feelings of the younger generation in nearly every country of Europe. The Congress of Paris had sanctified the principle of self-determination of peoples, and a number of smaller nationalities began to apply that principle in a way highly inconvenient for the established powers, especially for those very powers who had promulgated the principle at Paris. The Komintern made use of the opportunity to claim the leadership of the movements for liberation. Certain groups in Germany, some of which later became closely connected with Nazism, proclaimed the identity of the interests of the "oppressed people of Germany with those of the colonial peoples." Students who came from the Indies could hardly escape this trend of thought. The "Indische Vereeniging," an association of students coming from or bound for the Indies, irrespective of race, which in 1922 already had an Indonesian majority among its members, in that year closed its doors to non-Indonesians and changed its name into "Perhimpunan Indonesia" (The Indonesian Club). This club established contact with the Komintern, and some of its leaders even resided for a time in Moscow. They accepted the coöperation of the Komintern without, however, proclaiming adherence to the Communist Internationale. In reality, each group hoped to use the other for its own purposes.

Once returned to the Indies, these young men sought connection with the existing Indonesian groups in the hope of bringing all of them together under their leadership. First, they founded an organization of their own, the "Perserikatan Nasional Indonesia" ("National Indonesian Party"), in which Sukarno and Tjipto Mangunkusumo played an important part, and then they gradually rallied to their banner the other organizations, including the Budi Utomo, the Sundanese Club, the Sarekat Islam, the League of Sumatrans and the Indonesian Study Club (for the study of social, economic and political problems). However, the political ideals of these groups were widely different. It was the intention of Sukarno and his friends to persuade all these groups to accept the principle of non-coöperation and then to refuse to coöperate with the Dutch government by taking part in the People's Council and the local and provincial councils. This idea was, by the way, adopted from the program of Gandhi, but it could hardly be as effective in the Netherlands Indies as in British India, where the government depended far more upon the Indian help to carry on its task than did the government of Batavia in the archipelago. Moreover, several of the groups, for example the Budi Utomo and the Sundanese party, refused to accept the principle. It was undoubtedly a success for Sukarno that he had succeeded in grouping all these organizations together, even if only in a loose federation. The success was slightly marred by the fact that the chairmanship of the federation had not fallen to himself, the leader of the extreme nationalists, but to the founder of Budi Utomo, Dr. Sutomo, the chairman of the Study Club of Surabaya, a man who considered service to his people, not political agitation, his sole aim and who, consequently, was far more moderate in his views than Sukarno. The latter, however, hoped that by strenuous campaigning he could win the masses over to his special party, the Perhimpunan Indonesia.

His attempts failed. Not only the great divergencies of ideals among the different groups but also his own shortcomings prevented Sukarno from building one great nationalist organization. Although a wonderful orator, he lacked the sense of responsibility and the unflinching energy needed in a great political leader. In his speeches Sukarno hit upon excellent slogans for his political propaganda. A flag, red and white with a buffalo head, was devised for the party. A "national song" was composed. As an explanation — really a condemnation — of the Dutch governmental methods, the history of the Indies was explained according to the theories of historical materialism. Nevertheless, Sukarno did not meet with the success he expected. His methods were perhaps a little bit too western, too remote from the real Indonesia. The Marxist philosophy of history is, after all, not suited to the Indonesian mentality. His national song was too much of a western music-hall song to capture the ears of a people that has its own wonderful music. Although every slogan fit to excite the masses was dug up, the congresses of the Nationalist Party and the meetings of its federation remained small affairs when compared with the mass demonstrations organized at the same time by the Muhammadyah. This organization had continued to base itself upon purely religious principles and had accomplished very important social work. It openly proclaimed its loyalty to the government. The same was true of the tens of thousands of Indonesian government officials who, believing in the usefulness of their work and seeing the progress made in social welfare, continued their tasks without paying attention to the incitatory language of Sukarno. Even the mass of the people showed clearly that an agitation with revolutionary aims was not to their liking. Most Javanese, and it was they who would have to form the vanguard of the movement, clung to their traditional ideals of *toto tentrem*, "peace and order in harmony." They wished to see many reforms introduced, they cherished the memory of the times of Javanese greatness in civilization and hoped for their return, but the agitation of the masses after western revolutionary models had no appeal for them.

Thus Sukarno tried in vain to gather the masses around his banner. Finally, he resorted to the methods of the former communist party and tried to intimidate the village people and to force them to join by enrolling the professional criminals in the rural districts as his propagandists. The extreme nationalists indeed needed some help, for in several districts the people, tired of their agitation, had turned against them. The government, trying to be fair — the Law protects equally *all* citizens, even those who profess to be enemies of the Law — had some of these opponents of the political agitators arrested and punished, but soon enough it had to turn against Sukarno and his helpers who, while calling for the protection of the government, organized "fighting squads" against that same government. After Sukarno and two of his helpers who were especially responsible for the enlistment of lawless elements had been arrested and sentenced to imprisonment by the native tribunal — the governor-general halved the sentence — the whole extremist organization crumbled. This proved a happy event even for the nationalist movement, for it gave an opportunity for Dr. Sutomo and other serious workers for the cause of the Indonesian to come to the front.

Again the Indonesian national movement was approaching a turning point.[29] The self-appointed "leaders" who tried to arouse the masses with slogans taken from foreign countries and foreign philosophies had had their say and they had failed to rally the people. It had not been the action of the government that had been the cause of their failure, but the attitude of the mass of the people. The government took action only when disappointed leaders, in frantic attempts to swing over the people to their ideas by all means, good or bad, had resorted to direct violence. After the disappearance of Sukarno, other men, who had been working earnestly for years while the radicals had been making propaganda for purely Marxist ideals, now began to build a new movement based upon truly national ideals.

Foremost among these men was Raden Mas Suwardi Suryaningrat who afterwards called himself Ki Hadjar Dewantoro (which means the "teacher of all the Gods," a name typical of Javanese religious

[29] See Kennedy, *op. cit.*, pp. 128 sq. Ch. O. van der Plas, *Recent Developments in the Netherlands East Indies* (no pl., 1942), pp. 7 sq.

syncretism). This Javanese of noble birth — he belonged to the princely house of Paku Alam — had been a member of the revolutionary party of Douwes Dekker and had been exiled from the Indies. For several years he had lived in Holland, and here he studied educational problems and planned a system of national Indonesian education. He gave up all ideas of revolutionary action and, having returned to the Indies, started his "Taman Siswa" schools (Taman Siswa means "The Children's Garden" but is *not* to be translated by "Kindergarten"!).[30] His ideal had become to make his compatriots turn away from the purely intellectual and too materialistic western conception of education, which, in his opinion, could never give satisfaction to the people of Java. "No imitation of the western world, but construction from the bottom up of a civilization initially Javanese, later Indonesian," was his principle. Outside Java his schools should adapt themselves to the local character of the region where they were established. He maintained the principle that the national culture of a nation, in its development through the ages, could be bent but never should be *broken*. Wisdom, beauty, art, and science from abroad were welcome. To get acquainted with them was necessary. "Everybody," he said, "who learns a foreign language, gains access to a new world!" But all these foreign elements should be absorbed into national life. They should become nationalized, thus enriching the already existing treasures of national civilization. They should never be imposed on top of that civilization. To educate the people to be men and women of independent judgment and understanding for the harmony that must exist in human society, if *toto tentrem*, the harmony of peace, is to rule, is his ideal.

For many years Dewantoro had the greatest difficulties to overcome, for he refused financial help and stuck to his theory that the people of the Indies should build their own schools and that a system of education too expensive to be maintained by the people themselves could not bear good fruit. It would not be part of the national life, it would be a superimposed structure without roots in the community. The government showed the greatest sympathy for his work, but he insisted upon maintaining his complete independence, though he highly appreciated the measures taken by the government for public education. By 1940 there were two hundred and fifty Taman Siswa schools in the Indies.

It will be understood from the foregoing that this movement did not spring from contempt for Western civilization. On the contrary, as the

[30] S. Mangoensarkoro, "Het nationalisme in de Taman Siswabeweging," KS, XXVI (1937), 287 sq., and the same, "Leidende Gedachten bij het z.g. amongsysteem van de Taman Siswa scholen," KS, XXVII (1938), 595 sq.

Javanese leaders grew more and more conscious of their national characteristics and less inclined to follow blindly imported ideas and political movements, they began to show an increasing interest in the Netherlands cultural life. The artistic temperament of the Javanese made the educated men and women among the people more and more appreciative of the products of Netherlands — and in general European — arts and literature which flourished after the First World War.[31] There was an increasing demand on the part of the Indonesians that instruction in the Dutch language should be made more general. We have seen how the Commissaries General ordered, in the beginning of the nineteenth century, that the Netherlanders in the Indies should acquire a thorough knowledge of the Indonesian languages. This and other measures had happily prevented the promotion of the study of the Dutch language in the Indonesian schools at the expense of the native tongues, but once the Indonesians had become conscious of the value of their own languages and civilization and had begun to develop their own educational system, the spreading of Dutch as the *second* language in Indonesian schools became highly desirable for all parties concerned. Some Netherlanders in the Indies, interpreting wrongly the ordinances of the Commissaries General, protested against the spreading of the knowledge of Dutch, in the vain hope that by preserving the language of the ruling nation to members of that nation alone they would be able to strengthen its privileged position. It was a hopeless attempt to stem the tide of a cultural and political movement that already had received the high approval of the government and of the majority of the Netherlands people.

If Dewantoro was the most prominent man in matters of education, Dr. Sutomo was the great promoter of social justice.[32] Dr. Sutomo, a Javanese physician, who when a student had founded the Budi Utomo and later became a professor at the Medical School and a specialist of great reputation, was the great promoter of the Indonesian Study Club, founded in 1924. He was constantly active in all kinds of social work. The Club, of which he was the principal leader, established schools, coöperative societies, a bank; helped in the organization of Trade Unions, and advised the leaders of these Unions. It undertook the struggle against the practices of usurers among the village people. From the beginning Dr. Sutomo held political views that were widely

[31] Foreign forms of poetry were adopted by Malay writers. Rustam Effendi and Mohammed Yamin, for instance, wrote beautiful Malay sonnets.

[32] "Social justice" is an excellent term, although it has, unfortunately, been made a political slogan.

different from those of the radical socialist leaders. Especially concerning the means to be used, he disagreed completely with Sukarno and others who expected immediate results from assuming an irreconcilable attitude toward the Netherlands authorities. For Dr. Sutomo, non-coöperation was not a principle, but merely a weapon in the political struggle, which ought to be taken up only when the interests of the Indonesian people demanded it. Looking at the nationalist movement from an idealistic point of view, he scorned the rather cheap political propaganda of the radicals and demanded of his compatriots that they should *work* for the interests of the people, and that the work should start immediately and not be postponed until a political utopia had been reached. Between men like Dewantoro and Sutomo on one side and Netherlands idealists on the other an understanding could be reached without any difficulty. An understanding between these two groups in the Indonesian world was able to contribute infinitely more to the well-being of the mass of the people than political theories and propaganda. Indeed, the mutual understanding grew to be a mutual friendship and respect which prepared the way for straightening out the existing political difficulties.

After the arrest of Sukarno and the downfall of his party, the new tendency in Indonesian nationalism began more and more to assert itself.[33] The Indonesian Study Clubs, which had formed a federation, reorganized as the *Partai Bangsa Indonesia* (Party of the Indonesian Nation). The more radical elements of the former Nationalist Party still refused to accept the leadership of Sutomo and formed a group of their own, but with little success. The groups based on religious principles continued their activities, but the Sarekat Islam was definitely on the decline, registering not more than 12,000 members in 1930 against two million a few years before. It was losing ground to the Muhammadyah and even a more fanatical Mohammedan attitude taken by the leaders of the party could not revive its strength. Only a few of the early leaders in this movement proved to have the capacity to play a part, once the political and religious groups began to show more clearly their particular character.

In the meanwhile a Netherlands political movement had begun to develop, either side by side with or in opposition to the Indonesian currents of thought. To understand this political activity under the Netherlanders in the Indies we must review once more the general situation in the country as it developed after the First World War.

[33] The *Indisch Verslag* gives a succinct yearly report on the outward development of political groups in the Indies.

The period between 1920 and 1940 marks the end of the old Indonesian world and the beginning of a new one. The dividing line itself coincides with the great depression of 1931.[34] In the first half of the period the production and outward prosperity of the Indies reached unparalleled heights. The production of tin increased in the ten years between 1920 and 1930 by 50 per cent, that of coal and oil by nearly 100 per cent. Of the agricultural products, coffee remained at its old production level of around 60,000 tons a year, but sugar and tea rose by 100 per cent, copra increased by 50 per cent, and rubber by 200 per cent! The income of the government, from all its sources together, rose to more than 500,000,000 guilders, of which around 20 per cent were derived from enterprises and products, while taxes, paid chiefly by the European section of the population, yielded 114,000,000 guilders. The situation had totally changed since the early days of the twentieth century, when products and land-rent had yielded the bulk of the state revenue. Yet the Indies were not a country of millionnaires. Among the Europeans hardly 3 per cent enjoyed an income of more than ten thousand dollars yearly. Of course, further large incomes were derived from the Indonesian production by the shareholders of the agricultural and mining enterprises who lived all over the world (especially the shareholders of the oil companies), though the majority of these shareholders were still to be found in the Netherlands. In 1929 the total investments of international capital in the Indies amounted to about 4,000 million guilders, and in that year of seemingly great prosperity the income derived from that capital was probably less than half a billion.

The consequence of this development was that a great number of Europeans, and especially Netherlanders, came to the Indies. The number of Europeans (including the Indo-Europeans of mixed blood) had already risen to about 170,000 in 1920, but in the next ten years it jumped to 242,000. Of these about 40,000 had been born in the Netherlands, while the others were natives of the Indies. This influx of European-born Netherlanders caused a considerable change in the social structure of Java, for most of these immigrants came with no intention of settling permanently in the tropics. They hoped to serve their term (the average was twenty years) and then to return to enjoy their pension for another twenty years or more. The days when a large fortune could be collected in the Indies in a relatively short time had

[34] A. Neytzell de Wilde and J. Th. Moll, *The Netherlands Indies during the Depression* (Amsterdam, 1936); Jan O. M. Broek, *Economic Development of the Netherlands Indies* (New York, 1942), I. P. R. Inquiry series; Furnivall, *op. cit.*, chs. x, xi, and xii.

passed, but the right to a pension, a very modest one if figured in American money but quite handsome for Dutch conditions, made the service in the Indies still very attractive. These "trekkers" added a new element to Indonesian society. They did not intend to become a part of that society; they looked forward to their furloughs as to an escape from exile, and hence quite naturally emphasized the contrast between the European and the Indonesian sections of the population.

In the older days, the planters in the interior of the country, isolated from the larger settlements of Europeans, had made friends with the Javanese aristocracy. Through this daily contact mutual understanding had been fostered. For racial antagonism there was no place in these surroundings.

The newcomers, however, did not care to acquire a thorough knowledge of Indonesian languages. They did not understand the Indonesian customs and were not much interested in understanding them. Outward circumstances no longer forced the Europeans living in the interior to stay away from the centers of European life. Motor transport over the highly improved roads made it possible for them to spend the evening in the clubs of the principal towns, where people of their own race could always be found. This period did not last very long, but in the meantime, the Indies went through a difficult time. Not only the differences between the Europeans and the Indonesians, but also those between the Europeans and the Indos, had been intensified.[35]

The Indos, the people of mixed blood, formed, politically, a powerful group after the elections for the People's Council had offered them a possibility of expressing their views. The Indo-European League, founded in 1919, had enrolled within ten years of its foundation more than 14,000 members, it had founded a great number of institutions for social help and the promotion of education, and, finally, it had seen six of its members elected to the People's Council. This group was, politically and economically, in a rather difficult position. Economically, it was not quite on the same level as the European-born section, but, on the other hand, it was separated from the purely Indonesian section by the laws that restricted the ownership of the soil to Indonesians alone. The Indo-European was, by law, a European, but this very privilege of being a European by law hindered him from acquiring land and from founding agricultural Indo-European settlements. Most Indo-Europeans had clerical positions, and consequently their political ideal was a semi-independent state in which the actual power would remain in the hands of the Europeans. Later they formulated the demand for an

[35] On the people of mixed blood, see J. Th. Koks, *De Indo* (Amsterdam, 1936).

Indies citizenship, open to all those members of the European or Europeanized society who considered the Indies their real home. In some points this group found support for its political ideals with several other political groups of Europeans, such as the Catholic Party and the Democratic Liberal Group. The "Sociaal-Democratische Partij" (moderate Marxist socialists) for some time proclaimed its willingness to support in principle even the more radical demand for complete Indonesian independence, but later reacted against this idea.

Against these parties, however, rose a powerful European union, that of the "Vaderlandsche Club" (the Patriotic Club), which vigorously defended the maintenance of close political connections between the Netherlands and the Indies. At the end of the first half of the period under discussion, about 25,000 Europeans and 50,000 Indonesians were politically organized, and a large majority of these 75,000 had made either Indonesian self-government or independence, though nearly always within the limits of a Netherlands "Empire," their political goal. The Chinese, more or less crushed between the European and Indonesian elements, formed political organizations of their own. Part of the Chinese, composed of *peranakans* (Indonesian-born Chinese), declared themselves for constitutional evolution, others proclaimed their sympathy for Indonesian nationalism, while a third group turned toward China and advocated a return to Chinese citizenship and coöperation with modern Chinese cultural movements. If political development had continued along these lines, a deadlock would have followed. The Indonesian parties for a while turned more and more towards the tactics of non-coöperation until the downfall of Sukarno's party put a stop to this tendency. The European parties of the center were practically wiped out in the elections, and only the denominational and socialist parties were able to maintain themselves in the rising tide of national antagonism. Then the depression of 1930 and the following years brought a momentary respite in the political struggle.

J. S. Furnivall has said that the depression of 1929 marked the close of a period in the history of the Indies, of the period "beginning with the opening of the Suez Canal, or even of the period of four hundred years from the first landing of Vasco da Gama in Calicut.[36] There is much truth in this statement. We have pointed out many times in this history that economic conditions in the Indies were never very stable because in this purely agricultural empire the value of its exports, and hence the possibilities of import, depended largely on the market price of such products as coffee in the eighteenth and nineteenth centuries

[36] Furnivall, *op. cit.*, p. 428.

and of sugar and rubber from the beginning of the twentieth century. The market price of these commodities goes up and down in a highly unnerving way for the producers, and every time there was a slump on the market the East Indies faced economic disaster. Whenever this happened the Indonesians had to fall back on the production of food, turning the area cultivated to sugar cane back into rice fields and deserting, en masse, the plantations and European communities for their native villages. The European producers had to see it through, living on the reserves built up in more prosperous years.

The Indies had never before reached a degree of prosperity and economic expansion such as that in the second decade of the twentieth century. Consequently, the country had never before experienced such a reverse as it suffered after 1930. Professor J. Van Gelderen, describing this crisis, has explained that all important products of the Indies, except rice, were produced for export.[37] Of the gasoline produced by the oil refineries and oil wells only 10 per cent was for home consumption; of the rubber, practically nothing; of the tea 10 per cent; of the sugar 20 per cent; of the copra and coffee 30 per cent; of the quinine only 12 per cent; and, finally, of the tobacco no more than 4 per cent. Suddenly foreign nations stopped buying these products. By cutting down prices to the minimum, a market could be regained for part of the output, but while the amount of the produce fell by 50 per cent the value of the exports was reduced to 25 per cent! The Batavian government, always one of the greatest agricultural producers, had in 1928 made a profit of fifty-four million guilders in this field, but in 1932 its agricultural enterprises showed a *loss* of nine millions! Its other enterprises, especially mining, brought a profit of twenty millions instead of fifty. The European-owned and -managed joint-stock companies saw their profits reduced to nothing. No dividends were paid, employees were dismissed, and the general welfare of the European section of the nation deteriorated so rapidly that the revenue from the income tax, paid almost entirely by the Europeans (with a few Chinese), dropped to 50 per cent of its former level in spite of a sharp increase in the tax rates. There had always been a large surplus of exports over imports, but when the European and American customers could no longer buy from the Indies, the Indonesians were unable to buy from Europe and America. At this moment the Japanese stepped in to look for nooks and corners where they could settle comfortably amidst the ruins.

After the First World War commerce between Japan and the Indies

[37] J. J. van Gelderen, *The Recent Development of Economic Foreign Policy in the Netherlands East Indies* (London, 1939).

had increased, which was only natural because of the growing importance of inter-Pacific trade.[38] Japan's imports into the Indies had increased to 14 per cent of the total, but exports from the Indies to Japan had remained insignificant, and only a small amount of Japanese capital had been invested in the Indies. There were no more restrictions on Japanese commerce and Japanese investments than on those of any other country, including the Netherlands. Once the system of monopoly had definitely been abolished, around 1870, and, a few years later, custom duties had been lowered to make the Indies practically a free-trade area, all nations had had equal opportunities in economic ventures. The Netherlands government and nation had always been proud of having maintained for sixty years the policy of the "open door," even when nearly all other nations had protected their commercial and industrial interests by levying high duties on imports. There had been not only liberty of trade and industrial enterprise but also liberty of immigration.[39] The foreign immigrant, once admitted, had practically the same rights in the economic field as the Dutch nationals living in the Indies. After the depression set in, however, all these advantages seemed suddenly to serve the interests of only a single nation, the Japanese.

It would perhaps be more accurate not to speak of the Japanese, but only of Japan, for the part played by free Japanese enterprise in the affair was small compared with that played by the Japanese government and the men directly behind it. Although the individual Japanese had exactly the same right, and apparently the same opportunity, as the individual Chinese to come to the Indies and to make his living there, few of them made the attempt. Around 1930 there were not more than 7000 Japanese living in the whole area of the archipelago, compared with more than a million Chinese. Yet it was a subject of concern to the government that so many of these 7000 had come with other intentions than those they professed. Their number did not increase to any considerable extent during the next ten years. The Japanese, far less inclined to emigrate than the Chinese, clung stubbornly to their relatively small islands while their government complained that European and American "imperalism" had denied to its people all chances to spread over more thinly populated areas. It may well be that the over population of their country served the purposes of its leaders very well.

[38] E. D. van Walree, *Economic Relations of the Netherlands Indies with Other Far Eastern Countries* (Amsterdam, 1935).

[39] On immigration: ENI. Aanv. 292 and 766 (index gives 676, erroneously, as the page number).

It enabled them to build up an industrial organization in which the producers combined the advantages of the technical skill and equipment of the twentieth century with those offered by a social structure not unlike that of the early nineteenth century in Europe and even reminiscent of serfdom. Thus an industrial organization was built up that could outbid every other nation on earth in all areas of free trade in purveying cheap mass products. The system left, of course, no place for imports into Japan other than raw materials and the most necessary foodstuffs.

Immediately after 1930 Japan began to flood the Indies as well as the rest of the world with its products, and at the same time built up wherever it could an agricultural production in competition with that of the Indies. Furnivall gives a list of Japanese products imported into the Indies, before and after the depression.[40] Before the depression the list contains only ten items; after it, it reads like a Sears Roebuck catalogue, running from electric bulbs, sheet iron, bicycles, through beer, fish preserves, sweets, and toilet soap to paper, earthenware and haberdashery. In 1934 the imports of the Indies from Japan exceeded the exports to Japan by seventy-four million guilders; or, in proportional figures, 31 per cent of the imports came from Japan and only 5 per cent of the exports went to that country. Van Gelderen quotes the words of an East Indian official who said, "The open door has become the entrance to the Japanese house!"

The Japanese, moreover, tried to get hold of all the links in the economic chain. They tried to monopolize the shipping, the handling of the imports and exports in their commerce with the Indies, the storing of their goods in the Indonesian ports, the wholesale and retail trade in their products. Because of these methods of trading the Japanese became a grave threat to the Indonesian middlemen in commerce. Consequently they incurred the hatred of this class of people. But, while Japanese industry thus tried to monopolize the Indonesian market, it protected its own sugar production on Formosa against the competition of the Javanese sugar, thereby depriving the Indies of a market for one of their main products. Doubtless the best days of European economic activity in the Indies had passed, but whereas the Europeans had always, even in the days of the East India Company, brought large sums into the Indies for the purchase of their products, the Japanese hegemony of commerce tended to drain the Indies by unloading Japanese-produced goods and taking out the money. If this process had gone on, the Indonesians would have become completely subservient to Japan in the

[40] Furnivall, *op. cit.*, p. 432.

economic field, and the development toward economic independence that began to show itself before 1930 and gathered momentum immediately after that year would have been stopped.

The depression had indeed caused an increase of native production; that is to say, on native-owned land without the employment of foreign capital. A few figures given by Van Gelderen illustrate this tendency. In 1890 the foreign-owned estates supplied 90 per cent of the exported agricultural produce; in 1913 this contribution had decreased to 76 per cent, in 1930 to 69 per cent, but in the next seven years it fell to 54 per cent. By 1937, pepper, maize, and spices were produced only by natives. Copra and kapok were practically native products. Half of the rubber output came from native rubber gardens. The government hoped that this shifting of production would tend to form an Indonesian middle class. The economic structure of Indonesian society would thus become stronger and the foundations be laid for the building up of small Indonesian business and industry. Native industry would, however, be crushed beyond hope of recovery if the Japanese importers could have things their own way. A change in foreign economic policy was indicated. The balance between imports and exports had to be restored by securing a larger share in the Indonesian import market to those nations who were willing to buy a corresponding share of the exported goods. Greater economic stability had also to be assured by the building up of an Indonesian industry that would put an end to the unbalanced character of Indonesian economic life. This policy would anger the Japanese government, and public opinion might well oppose it on the grounds that it might involve the Indies in grave political dangers. Fortunately the Japanese government made its adoption easier by doing all in its power to enflame Asiatic public opinion. At the same time that the Indies were preparing their economic defense, the Japanese started their military attack on China proper. The policy of conquest carried out in Manchuria and Northern China had already caused serious repercussions in the Indies, especially among its one million and a quarter of Chinese inhabitants, but the attack on Shanghai — where hundreds of Indo-Chinese students were following courses — and the brutality of the Japanese military, combined with the coarse and overbearing attitude taken by nearly all Japanese living in the Indies, destroyed any possible sympathy with the "liberators of Asia." Thus, not only a new economic period began in the Indies, but also a new period in their political life.[41]

[41] G. H. C. Hart, *Towards Economic Democracy in the Netherlands Indies* (New York, 1942).

The economic defense of the Indies began with the introduction of a regulation of imports and exports on a quota system. By 1937 the Japanese share in the increasing imports was reduced to 25 per cent of the total. To strengthen and promote native economic enterprises, to further colonization by landless Javanese of the thinly settled districts of southern Sumatra, and to promote measures for social welfare, the government of the mother country offered a gift to that of the Indies of twenty-five million guilders. Further assistance was given through the drawing up of international economic conventions. Sumatra tobacco was able to maintain its market in Germany because the Netherlands government agreed to place orders with German shipbuilders. It also reserved a Dutch market for the Java sugar.

In the matter of wider dissemination of industry in the Indies the government gave most attention to the furthering of small businesses employing between twenty-five and one hundred workers and manufacturing low-priced articles for the domestic market. One of the basic Indonesian industries is the fabrication of textiles. There was a local traditional weaving industry on native handlooms, and the true interest of the people called rather for the improvement of this native industry than for the establishment of large factories. This end was attained by introducing a standard model of improved handloom with a capacity ten times greater than that of the old loom. The introduction proved a great success, for whereas in 1931 only 500 of these modern looms were in use, in 1938 their number had increased to 25,000! This native industry was able to compete effectively with the Japanese textile industry. The increase in weaving stimulated the native woodworking because of the large number of handlooms required, and the cultivation of indigo for the production of dyestuffs was also revived. The great natural ability of the Indonesians, especially the Javanese, in skilled handcrafts fitted them ideally for the production of leatherwork, all manner of utensils, and articles of furniture. The cigarette industry was also reserved as much as possible for native workers. Upon these smaller industries, other more highly developed ones could be built.

These measures, all aimed at the stimulation of industrial production, were not sufficient to secure better economic conditions for the people. Supervision of the wage-scale was imperative. It was out of the question for the Javanese and Sumatran working people themselves to form trade unions strong enough to secure higher wages. It was the duty of the authorities to take care that the still primitive economic conditions existing among the people should not be abused as was done in Japan. Laws were passed which gave the authorities the power to enforce minimum wages in favor of the workers, laws which, at the same time, guaranteed other countries around the Pacific against unfair competition. The government also promoted the growing tendency to give more important economic positions to Indonesians and tried to secure for the Indonesians a reasonable share in the investment of capital in the new industries.

In order to establish the new industries, it was necessary to strengthen the buying power of the mass of the people. Most important of all was to increase for the primary producer his share in the returns of production. Several measures were taken to obtain this result: the promotion of native agricultural production, the stabilization of the price of rice — the chief product of the Indonesian farmer, the lowering of the land rent, and others. The government could not afford to lose part of its income, the unavoidable result of the lowering of taxes on the native population; it therefore made up for this loss by raising the tax on higher incomes, that is, in practice, the tax on Europeans. This financial policy tended to level the different classes of the Indonesian society and thus contributed toward the abolishment of the last traces of the old colonial system of former centuries.

Thus the Indies were able at last to look forward confidently to a better future in which an ever increasing share of the "fabulous," but alas, fabled, wealth of the islands would be their own. At the same time this development helped to create resources upon which the government was able to start a policy of enormous increase of the means of popular education. Dewantoro, the founder of the Taman Siswa schools, had said, "The Indies can not expect to obtain satisfactory results from a system of education for which they can not pay themselves." But now the time had come when the simple desa schools could be organized in every corner of the archipelago, and if another ten years of peaceful development had been granted to the islands, the results of the new policy would have become apparent.

A development like this which brings material prosperity to so many and bridges the differences between classes and races always helps to overcome such political difficulties as are unavoidable when a backward community begins to make rapid social and economic progress. The attitude of all groups of Indonesian society changed considerably. There developed a growing faith in coöperation with the government, and, on the side of the Netherlanders, a growing understanding of the political and social problems of the Indonesians. The Dutch in the Indies began more and more to consider their tropical country as their home, and the amazing development of the means of communication made this easier every year. In 1924 the first flight between Amsterdam and Batavia was accomplished, but it took fifty-four days! Ten years later, the same course was flown in seven days, and a year later in only five days and a half. All mail was carried by plane. Periodicals and weekly papers could be brought over before they had lost all news interest. Helped by the establishment of an intercontinental broadcasting service, the newspapers of the Indies could publish the most recent news.[42] More closely linked with the home country, the Netherlanders felt happier and, missing less what they had left behind, appreciated better what they had found abroad. The technical skill of the twentieth century made it possible to convert the high mountain districts of Java into easily accessible and very pleasant residential districts for Europeans. After 1920 many pensioned government officials and employees preferred to stay in the Indies instead of returning to Holland and thus added considerably to the number of permanent European settlers in the East. The automobiles which at their first appearance had helped to destroy the balance of Indonesian-Dutch society later contributed to a reversal of that tendency by bringing the European townspeople back to the countryside.

The revival of trade and production in the late thirties also contributed toward the development of better feeling among the population groups of the Indies, for, although the commerce of the islands in 1938 was still far below the level of 1928, the revival had been sufficient to bring back general welfare and content. It is no wonder that under these circumstances the political situation became less complicated. We have seen how around 1930 extreme radicalism under the nationalists began to disappear and made place for more coöperative tendencies. This process gained momentum in 1936 and after. Idealism took the place of radicalism, and the desire for harmonious development, *toto tentrem*, prevailed over revolutionary tendencies. The Indonesians on the one side began to overcome their "inferiority complex" and became more confident of themselves once they had found in the movement for national culture and social revival safe ground to tread on. The Netherlanders, on the other hand, showed an increasing appreciation for the Indonesians. A color bar had never existed between the two peoples. Men of mixed blood were admitted to the highest position both in the Indies and in the Netherlands. Raden Mas Noto Suroto

[42] Some of these newspapers are of quite venerable age and have survived since the days when it took six months to receive the news from Europe. The *Surabaya Courant*, for example, was founded in 1831, fully twenty years before the *New York Times* began its momentous career. *De Locomotief*, one of the most prominent papers in the East Indies, dates back to 1845.

had served, during the First World War, as an officer in the Netherlands army in Europe. So had the present ruler of the House of the Mangkunegara. The son of a Javanese mother, William F. van Leeuwen, became burgomaster of Amsterdam and vice-president of the Council of State of the Netherlands, the highest position existing in that country. In the eighteenth century the Protestant ministers of Batavia had protested — an isolated case, however, — against the admittance of Meester Cornelis, the Amboinese, to the ministry of the church in Batavia, but in the twentieth century Javanese students were the pride of the theological schools of the Netherlands. This complete absence of racial prejudice among the majority of the Netherlanders made coöperation much easier.

In 1935 Dr. Sutomo succeeded in uniting his Partai Bangsa Indonesia with the oldest of the Indonesian societies, the Budi Utomo. The new party took the name of "Partai Indonesia Raja" and was commonly called the "Parindra." The party decided to work with the government for the amelioration of Indonesian conditions and to make its further attitude concerning coöperation dependent on the results achieved by the government in its work for the welfare of the people. The other remnants of the Partai Indonesia regrouped themselves in the "Gerakan Rakjat Indonesia" or, abbreviated, the "Gerindo," which for the time being also rejected non-coöperation as a political weapon. Thus, the East Indies, who looked toward India as their political model, had succeeded in overcoming first the initial stage of political maturity, that of mere reaction against the ruling power. The tendency toward nihilism, toward self-destruction, that had played so great a part in the cultural development of India could not maintain for long a hold over the more realistic Indonesians.

The political groups showed more and more inclination toward a coöperative policy. To be correct, we must add that the political parties always had only a limited number of members and that they attracted attention far in excess of the proportion of the Indonesian people they enlisted. In the early days of nationalism the parties stood and fell with their leaders. Even after a period of twenty years of political activity a party such as the Parindra had a year after its foundation not even three thousand registered members. This does not mean that the political opinions propounded by these small groups did not deserve and receive full consideration, but at the same time the purely Islamitic organizations numbered their adherents by tens of thousands. The Sarekat Islam had lost much of its importance, but the Muhammadyah was still very active; and against the Muhammadyah, which stood for

Reformist Mohammedanism, a loose organization of orthodox Mohammedans had been founded, numbering in 1937 not less than 67,000 members. This was a purely religious organization, and its meetings were solely devoted to questions of the Mohammedan religion. These figures clearly show what kind of problems the mass of the Indonesians took most to heart. The Mohammedan organizations showed no animosity against the government, nor did they concern themselves with politics except in cases where they considered it necessary to defend Mohammedan customs and rights.

Thus, after the first ten years of violent agitation had passed, a more quiet political development began to prevail. This policy of coöperation brought more immediate results than that of violent action had accomplished. In 1936 a motion was brought in the People's Council by some Indonesian representatives in which the government of the Netherlands was asked to call an Imperial Conference to discuss the best methods by which self-government of the Indies, always within the limits of Article One of the Netherlands Constitution, could be realized, and to fix a time limit within which this self-government should become effective.[43] Article One of the Constitution indicates by its wording that the Netherlands in Europe and the Territories in the East and the West Indies were considered separate entities with equal rights. This motion was accepted in Council by a majority composed of both Dutch and Indonesian members. Thus, economic self-sufficiency and political self-government, which were the goals of the Indonesian movement, seemed well on their way to realization, and the decision, taken by the Netherlands government in London and announced by H.M. Queen Wilhelmina on July 30, 1941, to hold such a conference immediately after the war, was not a mere war measure dictated by circumstances but the logical consequence of a policy followed since 1922.

After 1930, two seats in the Council of the Indies had been given to Indonesians. When the Japanese invasion came, Raden A. A. Sujono and Prof. Dr. Pangeran A. A. Husein Djajadiningrat held these offices. Before becoming a member of the Council of the Indies, Pangeran Djajadiningrat had held the office of director of the department of education, and in this capacity he had been the great promoter of education in the Indies. Several separate schools for higher education already existed in the Indies, but it was Pangeran Djajadiningrat who took the initiative in combining these schools into a university with all faculties completed. He founded a Faculty for Agricultural Sciences

[43] Report-Visman, I, 108.

and a Faculty of Philosophy, Literature, and Sociology. He hoped to be able to develop this last faculty in such a way that it should become the preëminent center of learning for Indonesian philology and literature. Even if the memory is saddening, we must not forget to mention that the Indies, together with the Netherlands, coöperated to the best of their abilities in the work of the League of Nations. Several times Indonesians were among the members of the Netherlands delegation.

One major problem remained very difficult to solve, that of the Indonesian Chinese. The establishment of coöperative societies among the Indonesians would undoubtedly have been of great help to the people but it might well have stirred up new difficulties, since these societies tended to eliminate, or at least limit, the economic role of the Indonesian Chinese. And at this very moment, these Chinese turned their attention more and more from the Indies to China. The dramatic events taking place there since 1931 aroused a lively interest in the land of their origin — especially, of course, among the Chinese-born immigrants. The Chinese National Government did its best to encourage these nationalist sentiments. A number of high officials from Nanking were sent to the Indies, either to investigate into the social and educational conditions existing among the Chinese abroad or to study economic and technical problems. When the catastrophe overwhelmed China, anti-Japanese resentment rose tremendously. The government saw to it that more than two hundred Indonesian-Chinese students who had been studying in Shanghai were able to return safely to the Indies, and the story they had to tell contributed to arouse hatred for the Japanese policy. In one form or another the Indonesian Chinese contributed about four million (U. S.) dollars to the Chinese war effort. This growing tendency of the Indonesian Chinese to turn their attention towards China constituted, however, one of the problems of the Indies. Before 1942 it mattered little, as a common aversion toward Japanese violence united all the inhabitants of the Indies — Dutch, Chinese, and Indonesian.

All attempts of the Japanese leaders to follow up their economic penetration by a political one remained of little avail. Japanese bankers and shipping magnates tried — with the help of Japanese consular officials — to buy the support of Indonesian and Chinese publishers, and offered large sums in the form of advertising contracts to papers in the Indonesian, Dutch, or Chinese languages that were willing to accept Japanese propaganda material. Indonesian students were encouraged to go to Japan to complete their education, but only a few of them could be induced to accept, along with the purely technical knowledge, the

Japanese views on Asiatic "co-prosperity" then already in the making. Even a Japanese Islamitic movement was started and the theory propounded that Japan was going to save Islam! This ridiculous move met with no success. Facts spoke too loudly for propaganda to muffle, and the bombing of Chinese cities caused horror in the Indies. When Nipponese agents succeeded in buying a Chinese newspaper in Surabaya, the indignant inhabitants, especially the Chinese, stormed and sacked the building.

In spite of every type of undercover activity, the Japanese could make no headway in fomenting dissension among the peoples of the Indies; indeed, their tireless attempts to "bore from within" resulted in a tendency to even closer unity among the people and a quickening of the pace of social and political evolution. Thus it is not in any way astonishing that the invasion and occupation of the Netherlands in May 1940 did not lead to a disintegration of the East Indian state but rather to a strengthening of its hard-won consciousness of unity and independence.

CHAPTER XVI

WAR COMES TO THE INDIES

ON MAY 10, BEFORE DAWN, the armies of Adolf Hitler invaded the Netherlands and Belgium. From the beginning of the attack until the last Dutch soldier had either been driven from his native soil or forced to capitulate, the German Luftwaffe held complete control of the air. Thus the defense was hopeless from the start. Thousands of parachutists landed behind the Dutch line of defense and engaged the Netherlands army reserves, while armored divisions and infantry attacked the troops of the line in the front. The Germans really did not depend upon the assistance of a Fifth Column within the ranks of the Dutch civilians in order to secure victory in a few days. In fact, the treacherous behavior of a small group of Dutch Nazis did little more than hamper and annoy the Netherlands authorities in the fulfilment of their task; from the military point of view it was of little consequence.

However, the exaggerated reports of multiple acts of treason spread by foreign newspapermen caused irreparable damage to the reputation of the Dutch name among foreign nations. People all over the world who had been reading the stories of treason which — to the great joy of Goebbels' propagandists — were spread by newspapers in neutral countries wondered what might happen in the Indies now that Holland had succumbed after no more than ten days of resistance.[1] If the Netherlanders at home were not loyal to the government, how could the Indonesians be?

Some people predicted that the Netherlands authorities might have to face a revolt in the Indies and that the whole structure of the East Indian government might crumble as soon as it was threatened by a foreign power, but these prophets were mistaken. It is true that the outbreak of the war in Holland put the government and people of the Indies to a severe test. Now the world was to find out whether the

[1] The main part of the Netherlands Army capitulated on May 14, the troops in Zeeland on May 19. It is, therefore, incorrect to speak of a "five-days" war in Holland. The best book on the war in Holland is still that of the Netherlands Minister of Foreign Affairs, E. N. van Kleffens, *Juggernaut over Holland* (New York, 1941) (British ed., *The Rape of the Netherlands*). See also H. S. Ashton, *The Netherlands at War* (London, 1941), which also deals with the overseas territories.

social and political edifice which Netherlanders and Indonesians had been building in the archipelago throughout the last half century really possessed the durability and power of resistance which the builders claimed for it.

Immediately after the invasion of Holland the leaders of all parties, the Indonesian nationalists included, and of all groups of the population expressed their loyalty to the cause of the Netherlands and promised their support for the recovery of its territory in Europe.[2] The East Indian government, and consequently also the Netherlands government which had moved to London, could be assured of the coöperation of the whole country in organizing resistance against the aggressors. In this undertaking there were enormous difficulties to be faced.

During the First World War, Batavia had gone through a similar experience. Then, also, communications between Holland and the Indies had been cut for several years. But then the Pacific had been safe for Dutch shipping, Holland had not become involved in the war, and Japan had been friendly to the United States and Britain. All this was different in 1940. Now the East Indies had to prepare themselves for defense against an attack by an alliance of powers which had already conquered the European portion of the kingdom. The market of Amsterdam was closed to the East Indian treasury, which would have to find the large sums necessary for the equipment and reinforcement of the army and navy in the Indies themselves. Reinforcements from Holland, especially officers, could no longer be expected.

Many of these problems were satisfactorily solved. The government succeeded in collecting the millions needed for war expenditures. The people of the Indies — and here the European portion carried at least 60 per cent of the burden — willingly paid the increased taxes.[3] In addition they contributed millions voluntarily to the Netherlands government in London and to the British government.[4]

The war created a boom in the market for raw materials, and this somewhat eased the financial situation. The production of tin and

[2] See for instance the radio address of Hadji Agus Salim in January 1941 (Reported by *Vrij Nederland* (Dutch weekly published in London), issue of Jan. 25, 1941, I, 601). For a translation, see Ashton, *op. cit.*, p. 29.

[3] The tax rates in the Indies were — even before 1940 — higher than the federal income-tax rates in the United States in 1943.

[4] The people of the Indies offered, among other gifts, $2,000,000 to the Netherlands government for a new destroyer and a total of $9,000,000 for the "Spitfire fund" presented to the British government for the air defenses of London. See *Netherlands News*, published by the Netherlands Information Bureau, New York, I, 316, and II, 61.

other commodities was increased to the utmost limit.[5] There were buyers enough in the market, but the government immediately established a rigid control over the export trade and foreign exchange.[6] To Japan a certain amount of merchandise had to be delivered as long as the other democratic nations maintained normal trade with that country. Some of the exports still went to Great Britain and Australia, but the bulk of the production was bound for the United States.[7] The export would have been even more voluminous had it not been for the lack of cargo space. The whole Netherlands merchant marine, over two million tons, now served with the allied merchant fleets in carrying war materials to Great Britain and other important theaters of war. Losses were terrific, especially in the first half year after the fall of France. It was not long before the Pacific too became unsafe for Dutch ships. Mysterious so-called "German" raiders operated on the sea lanes between the Indies and the United States, and many ships left the Indies never to be heard of any more.

The Indies had valuable goods to sell but they also needed to buy. The United States was practically the only source of war equipment. If the Indies were not adequately equipped, the flow of rubber, tin, quinine, and other goods might soon be stopped. Even before the invasion of Holland it was already evident that this time the Indies too would be involved in the conflict. There was no doubt, of course, about the general schemes of expansion fostered by the Japanese war lords. Neither was there any doubt about their desire to appropriate the resources of the Indies for the building up of the future world empire of which they were dreaming. Yosuke Matsuoka had made it perfectly clear, as early as 1932, that New Guinea was to become a "New Japan," and since that time Japanese authorities had under one form or another continued their efforts toward penetration.[8] Japanese government-controlled "developing companies" had started working, though with very small financial returns, in strategic areas like the Minahassa.

[5] See *Netherlands News*, I, 196, 281; also T. A. Bisson, *The Netherlands Indies at War* (Foreign Policy Reports, November 1, 1941), p. 201.

[6] E. van Zyll de Jong, "Economic Mobilization in Netherlands India," *Far Eastern Survey*, November 6, 1940 and B. Landheer, "Financial Policy of the Dutch East Indies," Far Eastern Survey, September 8, 1941.

[7] Bisson, *op. cit.*, following the figures presented by the Department of Economic Affairs of the East Indies, gives the total value of exports for the first four months of 1941 as 287,500,000 guilders, of which 114,600,000 guilders were to the United States.

[8] In 1934 negotiations between the Netherlands and Japan had to be broken off because of the exaggerated demands of the Japanese, who requested a share in the exploration and exploitation of the Outer Territories. See for these negotiations A. Vandenbosch, *The Dutch East Indies*, p. 400. In 1933 the "Great Asiatic Society" had been founded in Tokyo of which Prince Fuminaro Konoye was one of the founders (*Ten Years of Japanese Bur-*

As long as Europe kept the peace, the Nipponese had to satisfy their lust for conquest in China, a sufficiently difficult and hazardous enterprise. After the outbreak of the war in 1939 they ventured to come out into the open with still more ambitious schemes. Special "economic" missions from Tokyo visited the Axis partners in Berlin and Rome, where they were treated as distinguished guests. If documents dealing with these diplomatic intrigues have not all been destroyed at the close of the war, the archives may later reveal that in these conferences during the winter of 1939/40 the world was divided into spheres of interest among the Axis partners. The first signs of the coming storm could be noticed by the beginning of 1940. On February 13, 1940, two months and a half before the invasion of Holland, Japan denounced her treaty of arbitration with the Netherlands. This treaty would have lapsed during the following August. The treaty, the Tokyo Foreign Office said, provided for arbitration by the Permanent Court of International Justice, and Japan had no longer any part in this institution. Therefore, a new treaty would have to be negotiated. On April 8 the Italian news agency Stefani circulated a story, allegedly originating from Amsterdam, that *in the event of the Netherlands becoming involved in the war*, the East Indies would be placed under the protection of a great power which should be neither Germany nor Great Britain.[9]

This rumor gave, and probably was meant to give, an opportunity to the Japanese Minister of Foreign Affairs, Arita, to state his concern over a possible change in the political status of the Indies. The whole procedure was clearly meant as a definite warning to the Netherlands that if she resisted a German attack, she risked the loss of her Asiatic territories to Japan. The Secretary of State of the United States immediately reacted to Arita's statement by calling the attention of the Japanese government to existing agreements which explicitly guaranteed the integrity of the East Indian territory.[10] Arita preferred not to reply. The real Japanese views were bluntly expressed in a letter published in the Army paper, *Kokumin Shimbun*, in which the Netherlands were called "a rotten spot on earth" (April 24); and the *Hochi Shimbun* of Tokyo even demanded that Japan should seize the initiative and invade the Indies without further delay.[11]

---

rowing in the Netherlands East Indies, Official report of the Netherlands East Indies Government, New York, 1942, p. 22).

[9] Vandenbosch, *op. cit.*, p. 406. *Contemporary Japan*, a periodical published under the auspices of the Japanese Foreign Office, IX, 1 (1940), 366.

[10] Vandenbosch, p. 405; *The Netherlands Overseas Territories*, Information Papers, No. 28 of the Royal Institute of International Affairs (London, 1941), p. 5.

[11] *Ten Years of Japanese Burrowing*, p. 58.

After May 10, the Japanese Foreign Office once more expressed its concern over the status of the Indies. British and French troops had been landed on the Dutch island of Curaçao in the West Indies to safeguard that important oil center from acts of sabotage. Japan declared that it could not permit the same development to occur in the East Indies. The ambassadors of Great Britain, France, and the United States were instructed to notify Tokyo that their governments had no intention whatsoever of sending troops to the archipelago, and the Netherlands Minister added that his government had no reason and no intention to ask for similar aid in the East Indies. The German ambassador struck a different note when he declared that his master was not interested at all in the fate of the Indies. Thus Hitler stated publicly (what undoubtedly had been agreed upon in preceding secret conventions of the Axis) that the Netherlands Indies were to be the private hunting ground of the Mikado.[12]

The Netherlands government stood before a momentous decision. With inadequate forces the Netherlands had undertaken to resist Hitler's army, at that time the best in the world. Defeat had been the unavoidable consequence, but the sacrifice had to be made in order to preserve the right of the Netherlands to national independence. Was the same sacrifice to be made once more in the Far East? Japan apparently was resolved to make full use of the opportunities created by the defeat of Holland, the downfall of France, the seemingly hopeless position of Great Britain, and the internal dissensions in the United States. The prize was hers if she was willing to grab it. It may be asked why, in the summer of 1940, Japan did not invade Malaya and the Indies. There were no defenses worth mentioning. Britain had not a single ship, not a single gun, to spare for Singapore. There was no air force except the antiquated bombers and fighters of the Indies, a few hundred at most. Finally, there was no promise of help from the United States and no indication whatsoever that such help might ever be forthcoming. Public opinion in the United States was not ripe for it, to express it mildly. Why, then, did Japan not strike? In one or two months the prize might have been conquered, and undamaged. Preparations for scorched-earth tactics had hardly been begun.

The exact reasons will perhaps never be known, though some of them seem rather obvious. First of all, Japan herself was not ready. She had no military bases near enough to the object of her expedition. Her air force probably needed modernization in the light of the experiences gained by the British and Germans in Western Europe. Of

[12] *Contemporary Japan*, IX (1940), 779.

course she could never be sure that the United States would not intervene at the last moment, but far greater was the danger to her from Russia. In the summer of 1940 the Soviet Republic was free to act and it was fully prepared to do so. It is more than probable that the Soviet air force was superior to the Japanese at that time. If Japan moved southward, Stalin might be tempted to make use of this opportunity to crush one of his possible opponents before the other one, Germany, could act. And with Russian planes bombing Japanese cities and docks, the United States might revise her attitude, and that would be the end for Japan. Evidently Japan could not well move until Russia's hands were tied in Europe, and this was Germany's task. But Adolf Hitler was still dreaming of conquering Britain. If he succeeded, Japan might consider herself free to attack. If not, she must wait until her ally turned his armies east, and this could not be done before the summer of 1941. Meanwhile the situation had its advantages for all parties concerned. It enabled both Russia and Germany, the enemies of tomorrow, to draw for a few months more on the resources of East Asia for their war materials. Rubber, bought by Japan in Singapore and Batavia, could find its way, though in limited quantities, to Moscow and Berlin.

Thus the Netherlands Indies obtained a breathing space. But not for long. Tokyo was resolved to draw *some* profits from the favorable constellation of affairs. If Japan could not strike now, it could at least prepare the attack to come and feel out the point of weakest resistance. This was done in August 1940. At that time the Foreign Office of Tokyo put a question before the governments of Saigon and Batavia: were these governments willing to coöperate with Japan in the new Asiatic Co-prosperity Sphere? There were no specific demands made, only a principle of policy to be decided upon. French Indo-China, after referring to Vichy, answered in the affirmative; Batavia, after conference with the Netherlands government in London, in the negative. This refusal was emphatically underlined by official statements of November 1940 and February 1941. The die was cast. Japan had gained the coöperation of Indo-China and with this her advanced bases near to Singapore, while the Netherlands Indies had pledged themselves to fight Nipponese penetration.[13]

With their inadequate defenses the Indies were about to face militarist Japan and the third largest army and navy of the world. The resolution of the Netherlands government might be called suicidal. Yet what other course could it follow? For fifty years the Batavian administration had been working at the methodical construction of a new

[13] *Netherlands Overseas Territories*, p. 7.

national community in the Indies and to surrender now to Japan would be desertion of that community in the hour of need.[14]

In the meantime the leading men in Tokyo were eagerly waiting for the great news from Europe. Would Britain fall? If Britain did not fall soon, Japan would have to prepare an attack on the Indies. During the interval of waiting, supplies of raw materials might be obtained from the Indies themselves by negotiating a temporary trade agreement with them. These considerations resulted in the sending of a Japanese economic mission to Batavia.[15]

In the same month in which the alliance of Germany, Italy, and Japan was renewed [16] and in which the Japanese government, with the consent of Vichy France, sent its troops into Tonkin, Schizo Kobayashi, minister of commerce and industry of the Tokyo government, arrived in Batavia "to carry on the economic negotiations which until the invasion of the Netherlands had been conducted at the Hague by Minister Ishii." [17]

Kobayashi was accompanied by a large staff of "technicians," all provided with diplomatic passports which gave them great freedom of movement and ample opportunity to complete their studies of geographic conditions and points of strategic importance in the Indies through personal observation. From many Japanese sources messages were cabled to Kobayashi, exhorting him to take a strong line with the recalcitrant Dutch and to make it clear to them that it was the "Will of Heaven" that Japan should lead in Eastern Asia. The same note was

[14] Under the circumstances the Netherlanders had only to lose whether they accepted Japanese protection or decided to take the risks of war, but the latter decision definitely presented the greater risk as far as financial losses were concerned.

[15] On June 28, the Japanese government had first announced its intentions to bring about a more favorable trade agreement with the Indies (*Netherland Overseas Territories*, p. 7). On June 29, 1940, Foreign Minister Arita said in a radio address: "The countries of East Asia and the Regions of the South Sea are geographically, historically, racially, and economically very closely related to one another. They are destined to coöperate and minister to one another's needs for their common well being and prosperity. The uniting of all these regions under a single sphere on the basis of common existence and insuring thereby the stability of that sphere is, I think, a natural conclusion." — *Contemporary Japan*, IX (1940), 1077.

A month later, on July 23, Prince Konoye said over the radio: "In order to carry out this foreign policy, it is important to forge close ties of economic coöperation with China and Manchukuo and to plan further advance in the South Seas." — *Contemporary Japan*, IX (1940), p. 1080.

[16] Text of the Tripartite Alliance as published: *Contemporary Japan*, IX, 2 (1940), 1493. The public treaty probably was accompanied by secret arrangements about the division of the spoils of war, and the means to be used. The treaty mentions separate agreements in which "technical details" are settled.

[17] *Ten Years of Burrowing*, p. 53.

struck by the new minister of foreign affairs, Yosuke Matsuoka, when in a public address he spoke of "liberating the peoples of the Far East from their fetters." [18] But Kobayashi was not in a hurry. He devoted much of his time to making social contacts. "The negotiations," said a Dutch weekly paper, "are carried on among many festivities. One cocktail party follows another." Two weeks later the same paper said: "Japanese and Dutch are still combining business and pleasure." Yet the only result of these weeks of negotiating was a contract for the export of one hundred thousand tons of salt to Japan.[19] Kobayashi was simply biding his time. Sooner or later, he hoped, the report would come that Britain had capitulated under the blows of the Luftwaffe, and then he would present the real object of his mission: the forced acceptance of a Japanese protectorate and a reorientation of the economy of the Indies towards coöperation with Japan and Japan alone. A Japanese diplomat, well acquainted with both the Netherlands and the Netherlands Indies, had neatly formulated this program: "It will be only a matter of time," he wrote,[20] "before Germany attacks England. And if this observation should prove correct, it may be no exaggeration to say that the future of the Netherlands East Indies must be considered with Germany as the central figure. . . . But, although Germany will become the central figure, she has made it clear that she has no interest in the Netherlands East Indies. Therefore, there shall be no change in the status of the Indies and . . . in Japan's concern for the maintenance of economic relations based on the principles of mutual aid, co-existence and co-prosperity." This generous offer to spare the lives and property of the East Indian peoples on the condition that they would fully coöperate within the famous Japanese co-prosperity sphere was hidden under a great display of complimentary remarks on the efficiency of the Dutch administration.

The truth was that the Japanese not only wanted the prize promised to them under the Tripartite Alliance but wanted it cheap and unscathed. "The great need is," wrote another Japanese commentator, "to win and consolidate the confidence of the one hundred and twenty millions of the South Sea regions in such a way that they will welcome us Japanese." The people of the Philippines, both officials and private individuals, including President Manuel Quezon himself, were now well disposed towards the Japanese, he asserted. "But, at the same

[18] *Ibid.*, p. 56.

[19] *Vrij Nederland* of Oct. 5 and Oct. 14, I, 221 and 275.

[20] Tetsuichiro Miyaké, "The Dutch East Indies and Japan," *Contemporary Japan*, IX, 2 (1940), 834 sq.

time," he continued, "there must be as little sacrifice as possible. . . . Plans in regard to French Indo-China and the Netherlands Indies must be mapped with the utmost caution." [21]

Kobayashi temporarily returned to Japan in October. Britain had not fallen. Consequently the Japanese envoy kept in his pocket the ultimatum he was to present in case of a complete German victory, and changed his tactics. The threatening statements made by official and semi-official Japanese spokesmen had stiffened the Dutch in the Indies in their resistance. They were feverishly working to strengthen their defenses. There was talk of destroying the equipment of the oil fields rather than surrendering it to Japan. "Plans must be mapped with the utmost caution," Kijujoro Hayashi had written. Therefore, Kobayashi's instruction had been twofold. To make the Netherlands come to an agreement he would have to allay their fears and to foster in them a false sense of security.[22] Thus the arming of the Indies might be delayed, the preparations for the destruction of the oil industry retarded, and a fair amount of raw materials secured for Japan. This was the reason the Japanese delegation suddenly agreed to issue a joint Dutch-Japanese communiqué in which it was recognized that the East Indies were not considered within the so-called "Greater East Asia sphere" over which Japan planned to assume full leadership under the Tripartite Alliance.

This declaration, published October 26, 1940, was followed by the conclusion of an agreement in which the Japanese quota of oil to be exported from the Indies was fixed at 1,800,000 tons for the next twelve months.[23] This agreement was signed on November 12. Negotiations then came to a standstill when Kobayashi left for Japan (December 1940) and were not resumed until his successor, Kenkichi Yoshizava (appointed December 14, 1940), had arrived in Batavia on January 11, 1941.

It could easily be foreseen that Yoshizava would take a less conciliatory attitude than Kobayashi. The Indies had refused to coöperate with Japan, and Hitler had failed to deliver them into the hands of his allies by dealing a knockout blow to Britain. Japan would have to fight for

[21] Kijujoro Hayashi, "Glimpses of the South Sea Regions," *Contemporary Japan*, IX (October 1940), 1293 sq.

[22] Secret instructions to the Kobayashi mission included the injunction "to give peaceful assurances so as to delay armaments as much as possible" (*Ten Years of Burrowing*, p. 54).

[23] T. A. Bisson (*The Netherlands Indies at War*, p. 205) points out that all the high octane gas for aviation fuel had already been sold to Britain and the East Indian Government in order that the Japanese share in this special commodity could not be increased!

her share in the booty and was already mapping her attack and concentrating her forces. Reports came from China that a number of veteran divisions had been withdrawn from the Chinese front and concentrated on the islands of Formosa and Hainan. These reports spoke of forces numbering a hundred to a hundred and fifty thousand men. A Japanese military mission, headed by Lieutenant-General Tomoyuki Yamashita, later commander-in-chief of the expeditionary force to Malaya and the Indies, visited Berlin to confer with German commander-in-chief Field Marshal Von Brauchitsch.[24] In Indo-China the ground was prepared for further Japanese penetration when Tokyo first incited, and then brought to an end, an armed conflict between France and Thailand.[25] Now, to appease the United States, Admiral Nomura was sent to Washington.

The government of Batavia had decided upon its course. It set to work to prepare the resistance. From the military point of view the situation was alarming. There was need of rifles, guns, and modern planes, and there were no plants in which this equipment could be fabricated. Everything had to be imported from abroad. Equally important with the military preparations was the strengthening of the spirit of resistance on the home front. This brings us to the internal political development in the Indies during the fateful years 1940 and 1941.

Faced by the grave danger of a Japanese attack, the government of Batavia needed the full coöperation of all classes and all racial groups in the Indies. Unless all these groups were united by a feeling of solidarity strong enough to outweigh the counteracting influence of social and racial differences, defense was impossible. The administration had endeavored to develop this feeling of solidarity. During the twentieth century, and especially after 1930, enormous progress had been made in putting the social and political theories of 1901 and 1922 into practice, but there was still much to do. In many matters the outlook on life of thousands of Netherlanders was suddenly changed by the war, whereas in normal circumstances this development would have required a decade or more. From the first days of the war it had become clear to the people of the Indies that they would have to defend themselves in a very unequal struggle. In this common defense, Dutch,

[24] In Dutch newspapers in occupied Holland, photographs of Von Brauchitsch and Yamashita conferring were published on January 23, 1941.

[25] The conclusion of the Thai-Japanese pact in December 1940 was immediately followed by military action from the side of Thailand. On January 22, 1941, Japan offered mediation. Eight days later an armistice was signed aboard a Japanese cruiser. The peace conference was opened in Tokyo February 7 and came to a conclusion March 11.

Chinese, Indonesians, whether belonging to parties of the right or of the left, were willing to take their share. Class barriers that had existed for decades broke down overnight when men of all classes and different races served side by side in the Home Guard and in the civil air defense, to which after a few weeks practically every Netherlander and a number of the Chinese and Indonesians belonged. The society of the Indies is a very complex one, but when put to the test of threat from without it showed a tendency to coalesce and not, in spite of all racial and economic antagonism and of all political differences, to fall apart. This meant that in principle the policy of education towards self-government, carried out since 1916, had been successful.

The outstanding feature of the history of the two years of tension and anxiety that elapsed between the invasion of Holland and the fall of Bandung is the complete absence of Fifth-Column activities. In every other country invaded by the Axis troops there had been some degree of coöperation with the invaders before and during the attack, but not in the Indies. No extraordinary measures were necessary in order to secure the loyalty of the sixty million Indonesians. Only among the Chinese were there some adherents to the Japanese puppet government of Nanking who might have become dangerous if not closely watched.[26] The army and navy of the Indies were never hampered in their preparations for war by acts of sabotage. The government of Batavia had ordered all male German nationals to be rounded up and interned, while the women and children were allowed to leave for Japan and Germany.

The war had forced the Netherlands Indies to rely for their defense solely upon their own forces. The Netherlands government in London continued to direct the international relations, but necessarily the influence of the Batavian government on the handling of general affairs had increased enormously. Actually, the Indies were now if not an independent *state*, at least an autonomous unit with their sovereign residing in London. From the beginning there was no doubt about the necessity of giving, sooner or later, a legal expression to an existing state of affairs. The Constitution of the Indies, promulgated in 1925, had to be revised. But along what lines? Once that was determined, the second question would be: when could the revision be put into effect?

The government of Batavia decided to appoint a committee for in-

[26] For agitation among Nankingite Chinese, see *Netherlands News*, I, 239. Of the Dutch nationals only a few belonging to the small National Socialist Party were arrested. The internees did not number more than four hundred.

vestigation into the political aspirations of the people of the Indies. This committee was instructed to hold hearings in the principal centers of the country and to invite all people interested in political affairs to submit their ideas on the subject orally or in writing. Dr. F. H. Visman, a member of the Council of the Indies, was appointed chairman of the committee.[27]

The report on this investigation consists of two parts. The first deals with the development of political, social, and economic conditions in the Indies between the two wars. The second part contains the aspirations of the people. It deals with a series of problems, such as racial problems, those of a common Indonesian citizenship, of the eventual reorganization of the administration on a federal basis, of local self-government and its future development, of the reform of the People's Council and extension of the franchise, of readjustment of the relations between the Netherlands and the Indies, and finally, of the establishment of a joint Imperial Council for all parts of the Netherlands kingdom, in Europe, in Asia, and in America. It was to be expected that opinions would differ widely. It even seemed questionable whether there would be found enough ground common to all groups to afford a base upon which to build the new Netherlands-Indian state.

It became clear, however, from the hearings of the committee, that this common ground did exist, and that even among the most extreme groups to the left and to the right there was willingness to coöperate. Neither the termination of the connection between the Netherlands and the Indies nor the destruction of the political and social edifice constructed by the Netherlands administration during the last century was advocated by a single one of the informants who appeared before the committee.

The prerequisite for a healthy future development of the Indies,

[27] The Committee was appointed by decree of September 14, 1940. Its task was formulated as follows:

(a) to investigate into the wishes, opinions, and trends of thought existing in the different racial and social groups of the Netherlands Indian society on the political development of the Indies;

(b) to render a report of this investigation reproducing the opinions presented with a commentary by the Committee;

(c) to investigate into the problems connected with the institution of a "citizenship" of the Indies with its consequences, and into the possibility of substituting other terms for those of "Natives" and "Native" commonly used in law until now.

The Committee finished its report on December 9, 1941. It is divided into two volumes, the first one dealing with the development of the Indies between the two wars and the second containing the result of the investigation. It was printed a few days before the fall of Batavia, and consequently only very few copies are available. It will be referred to as Report-Visman.

many Indonesian spokesmen said, was that the last traces of racial discrimination, both in law and in practice as well as in social life, should disappear. They cited certain examples of this discrimination, and in the light of these the committee found it advisable to list all cases in which the law continued to differentiate between Europeans and Indonesians.[28] Fifteen such instances were found, but it would be incorrect to list all fifteen as instances of discrimination against the native population. The committee considered first cases of differentiation as far as private law was concerned. The limitation of ownership of the soil to Indonesians alone is of course the very opposite of discrimination against them. The same could be said of the regulations for the coastal fishing, which practically reserved to Indonesians the right to engage in this special trade. Other differences in treatment were the result of special circumstances; an example of this type is the regulation which gave to European officials long-term leaves of absence with traveling expenses to Europe paid. This regulation did not apply to Indonesian civil servants, simply because they had not left their country when entering the civil service. Then, too, military service was compulsory for all Europeans, whereas only a few of the Indonesians were under the same obligation. Differentiation but not segregation existed in elementary education.[29]

The "Heerendiensten" (periods of forced labor on public roads), from which all non-Indonesians and most of the Indonesians were exempt,[30] were once keenly felt as a case of unjustifiable discrimination against the native population, but they had been abolished in 1941, before the Report was published. Other, real cases of discrimination included different treatment in the matter of food and clothing in state prisons and state hospitals, and the inequality of franchise whereby the Europeans elected proportionately more representatives to the People's Council than the Indonesians.

The problem of the franchise was one that really belonged to the

[28] The term "European" must always be understood in the sense given to it by the Constitution of the Indies as explained in the preceding chapter and never as an indication of *race*.

[29] To the "European Elementary schools" were admitted children whose conversational language at home was Dutch. Thus Chinese and Indonesian children had access to the "European" school if they could give sufficient guarantees that they would be able to follow the instruction given in Dutch. See Raden Loekman Djajadiningrat, "Educational Developments in the Netherlands Indies," paper read at the eighth Congress of the Institute of Pacific Relations, December 1942, pp. 13 sq. In 1937, 20 per cent of the children attending European schools were Indonesians or Indonesian-Chinese. (Figures in *Indisch Verslag 1938*, The Hague, 1939, p. 287.)

[30] Vandenbosch, *op. cit.*, pp. 293–294.

political field. Few speakers — in fact only a small minority among the Chinese — wanted to abolish the existing differentiation in matters of private law. Some Indonesians complained, however, that although the existing discrimination was of minor importance legally, it was more serious in practice and in social life. In support of this contention they cited cases in which government officials had successfully obstructed the promotion of Indonesians by arbitrarily raising the qualifications for holding a government position. It was easy enough, they pointed out, to demand such a perfect knowledge of the Dutch language that only native Hollanders could meet the required tests and obtain the position. They especially criticized the tactics followed by the big business concerns, who not only rejected Indonesians but even Indian-born Dutch in favor of native Europeans.

The same people, these Indonesians contended, laid down the regulations observed in hotels, clubs, and social gatherings, and prevented Indonesians, even those of high rank, from free association with white people. They recognized, however, that high government officials had several times taken a strong attitude in these matters and even forced the leading members of these European circles to adopt a different attitude.[31]

Apparently, these "racial" difficulties could be overcome without much trouble. Here the war was able to do more to bridge the distance between the whites and the Asiatics than all government regulations had accomplished in a hundred years. The rapid spread of education and the improvement of the standards of native education would do the rest.

The committee correctly concluded that racial discrimination and racial differentiation had to disappear. However, since in some cases the discrimination was social rather than racial and since the differentiation in matters of private law was often helpful to the Indonesians, the committee concluded that it would be best to abolish the terms "Europeans, Foreign Asiatics, and Natives," introduced by the Constitution of 1854, and to base such differentiation as was inescapable on other than racial criteria. A sounder foundation might thus be created for a national unity of all racial and social groups.

Much time was devoted by the committee and the speakers who appeared before it to the problem of what the exact legal expression of this new national unity should be. In other words, should all inhabitants of the Indies be given the same internationally recognized legal status, as for instance, that of "citizen of the Indies"? If so, what would

[31] Report-Visman, II, 84–88.

be the rights conferred by that citizenship? Should every citizen have the franchise? Should all citizens have equal franchise? It is simple enough to draw up a democratic constitution in theory, but in practice difficulties may arise which, unforeseen or ignored, might ruin the whole structure.

A certain level of general education is required to bring a democratic system of government to its full development. In the Indies, education had not yet reached the mass of the people. Although 40 per cent of the children between six and nine years of age went to school in 1940, more than 80 per cent of the population was still illiterate. The level of civilization varied from that of the neolithic stage (in the interior of New Guinea) to the highest forms of European and Asiatic culture. Peoples on the same level of civilization differed in customs, religion, and language. Of these peoples, one, the Javanese, outnumbered all others.[32] It was necessary to work out a system of self-government which would be satisfactory to all the peoples, which would not result in domination by the numerically strongest group, and which would provide at least some safeguards against the dangers of demagogic excesses.

These were the problems which had to be faced in revising the Constitution of the Indies on a more democratic basis, and it was these problems for which the committee sought a solution from its informants.

One of the solutions suggested was that of a gradual transformation of the Netherlands Indies territory into a self-governing democratic state. Self-government, the advocates of this program said, could be introduced immediately, but its administration should be entrusted temporarily to a part of the population.[33] This group would be composed of all those who possessed certain educational and social qualifications, without of course any discrimination of a racial character. These "full citizens"[34] would gradually absorb the non-voting class, as the latter advanced in education and economic stability.

This system, which, if liberally applied, might present great advantages, was vigorously opposed by other speakers.[35] Some of these

[32] In 1939 Java had 40,891,000 inhabitants, of whom 27,036,000 were Javanese, 8,468,000 Sundanese, 4,321,000 Madurese, and 958,000 Batavians (Lekkerkerker, *Land en Volk van Java*, I, 226, 108, 124).

[33] See Report-Visman, vol. II, "Petitie voorstel-Roep," and on the extension of franchise to the same category of inhabitants, II, 221.

[34] Term of the author of this book.

[35] Report-Visman, II, 214. It should be remembered that the report never gives the names of the people whose views it reproduces but only indicates their social and racial background.

defended universal suffrage for all male residents of the Indies, but with the restriction that the illiterate section of the population should exercise its right by electing local spokesmen who would then vote for the candidate for the Parliament. Others wanted universal suffrage for the election of provincial or district councils, the members of which would elect the representatives for the People's Council.

Under a democratic system with universal suffrage the problem of guaranteeing the rights of minorities would immediately arise. Suppose the Indies were divided into a number of electoral districts with roughly the same number of inhabitants, would not the Javanese[36] automatically obtain a permanent majority in a House of Representatives? This possibility was the reason why many speakers before the committee, and not only the European ones, preferred to see the existing composition of the People's Council maintained. Two solutions were presented. One was the organization of the Indies into a federation of semi-autonomous territories. The other was the institution of a Parliament with two Chambers. One of these, comparable to the Senate in the United States, would simply be a continuation of the present People's Council with a certain number of seats reserved for representatives elected by the different sections of the population, while the House of Representatives would be elected by the electorate as a whole.

The importance of suffrage and representation is directly related to the degree of power which the new Parliament might receive and the future relations between the government of the Indies and that of Holland. Here there were two main trends of thought.

One group declared itself satisfied in principle with the existing relations and division of authority between the government in Europe, that in the Indies, and the People's Council, but desired a limitation of the influence still exercised by the Dutch Parliament. The main idea of these speakers was to substitute an Imperial Council for the Dutch ministry of colonies, to exercise such supervision over the affairs of the Indies as might be necessary.

The other group demanded the organization of a parliamentary government in the Indies in which the governor-general would represent the king of the Netherlands but the actual management of affairs would be in the hands of a council of ministers responsible to Parliament. It was incumbent on this group to explain, of course, the character of the relations between the Netherlands and the Indies which would develop if the whole administrative responsibility were to be transferred to Batavia. Here again opinions differed, but on one point

[36] Here, all inhabitants of Java.

all speakers agreed: that under any form the connection between the Netherlands and the Indies must be maintained. Some thought of a relation like that between Britain and her Dominions. Others preferred to see both the Indies and the Netherlands organized as interdependent states bound together in a permanent federation, in which the Dutch West Indies would be a third member. Especially in the details suggestions differed widely, and most of them lacked clearness and precision. A large majority of the speakers appeared willing to accept a reorganization in which a central government with definite powers over both the Netherlands and the Netherlands Overseas Territories should be maintained. These powers were to be entrusted to a council composed of members from *all* the territories. This was referred to as the "Imperial Council." [37]

The project of the institution of an Imperial Council was one of the most constructive ideas that resulted from the hearings of the committee. There were three main trends of thought concerning the functions of this institution. That of the more conservative group envisaged it as a purely advisory body which would concern itself with all matters of joint interest for all parts of the kingdom. Its meetings were to be open to the public, but the central government in the Netherlands would be in no way bound to accept the suggestions of the Imperial Council.

A second group saw the new Council as a kind of super-parliament which would have legislative power for *all* territories of the kingdom, in Europe as well as in Asia and America. This was the preference of many Indonesians as well as Europeans. This scheme, however interesting it might have been, had one drawback: it would not free either of the two overseas territories from interference with their purely internal affairs; it would only restrict the freedom of action of the Netherlands home government by the presence of a super-parliament in The Hague. For this reason a third group advocated an Imperial Council, composed of a limited number of members, possessing legislative as well as advisory powers in matters of purely imperial character. These would include foreign relations and defense of the empire. The imperial government would reside in The Hague, and the spokesmen of this group saw no objection to the proposal that in the event of matters of extreme urgency arising when the Imperial Council was not in session the Netherlands government should be entitled to act in the name of the empire. This scheme was supported by one of the most influential groups of Indonesian nationalists.

[37] The Report-Visman, II, 331–337, gives a survey of the historical development of the idea of instituting an Imperial Council and the different opinions presented on the subject.

Only a small minority among the Indonesian nationalists demanded full dominion status for the Indies with the Imperial Council acting in the same capacity as the Imperial Conferences of the British Commonwealth.

These were the main suggestions presented to the Committee of Investigation. Between extreme right and extreme left there was a wide range of divergent opinion, but the obstacles to a solution of the constitutional problems apparently were not insurmountable. On the basis of the hearings conducted by the committee, it appeared that a solution could be found and a constitution worked out which would prove satisfactory to nearly all Indonesians and Netherlanders.

The Netherlands government residing in London had not waited for the results of the investigation to be published to take certain preliminary steps towards the political reform of the kingdom. These steps were officially announced in an address of H.M. Queen Wilhelmina broadcast to the East and the West Indies. In this message (July 30, 1941) the Queen declared:

> As soon as the Netherlands are liberated from the oppressor, a new Cabinet will be formed. . . . This new Cabinet must immediately prepare a revision of the Constitution . . . a revision by which (among other matters) the relations between the mother country and the other parts of the Kingdom shall be reorganized. To prepare this revision a Board constituted by representatives of all parts of the Kingdom will be appointed. Beside the revision of the Kingdom, that of the Administrative Acts now in force for each part of the Kingdom must be undertaken. This will be done in common agreement with representatives of these territories. In this manner we can lay the foundation for a happier and more prosperous future for the entire Kingdom.[38]

These words seem to indicate that the Netherlands government plans a reorganization of the kingdom into four completely autonomous parts whose common affairs are to be administered by a government composed of representatives from the four territories. This solution of the "colonial" problem appears most in keeping with the attempt to build a free yet interdependent world.

The proclamation of the Queen was well received in the Indies. All political leaders expressed their sympathy with the broad outlines of the political plan.[39] Differences of opinion manifested themselves, how-

[38] Complete text of the radio address of Queen Wilhelmina in *Vrij Nederland*, issue of August 9, 1941, p. 35.

[39] The "Gabungan Politiek Indonesia" ("Gapi"), a federation of all nationalist political parties, founded in 1939, drew up a "memorandum concerning the political construction of Indonesia" which was published in the middle of 1939. In this memorandum was set forth the organization of an autonomous state which would form a "Union" with the Netherlands and the Netherlands West Indies. In the autonomous state of the

ever, in regard to the time when this political reorganization should be put into effect. Most Indonesian nationalists wanted the reform to be initiated immediately. "We do not demand the impossible or the unreasonable," said Mr. Wirjapranoto, leader of the nationalist Parindra group in the People's Council. "Proof of the Queen's desire for a change in the general structure of the Netherlands Empire and the final steps toward this goal have been gratefully received." The nationalist leader contended, however, that the concentration of all power in the hands of the high officials (which was unavoidable in view of the imminent threat of war) tended to widen the gulf between the government and people, and this situation he wanted remedied immediately. Other Indonesians expressed the same ideas though in more moderate form, and stressed the point that the moral preparedness of the country would be immeasurably strengthened if at least the outlines of the plan which was to be proposed after the war to the Imperial Board mentioned by the Queen should be fixed without delay.[40]

On July 11, 1941, the People's Council had passed a bill which instituted a native militia, a desideratum of the Indonesian leaders since 1916. The bill was passed by a majority of 43 to 4, the dissenting votes were those of the members of the Parindra party who contended that political reforms ought to precede the imposition of military service on the Indonesian section of the population.[41] Against this opinion the Netherlands government in London maintained its point of view that, while reforms could be prepared during the war, no definite changes could be made until the people of the Netherlands was able to express its opinion on the subject and to take part in the revision of the Consti-

East Indies the executive power would be entrusted to a "Head of the State" who would have about the same authority as a constitutional king. The Head of the State would be assisted by an Indonesian Lieutenant-Governor and by a Council of Ministers responsible to a Parliament of two Chambers. The Upper Chamber would be composed of the representatives of the different cultural groups, the Lower Chamber would be a direct representation of the people elected by universal suffrage. In this plan foreign affairs and national defense would remain in the hands of the "Highest Authority," which apparently meant the Union of States including the Netherlands and the Indies. Much remains vague, however, in these plans presented by the Indonesian nationalists. They lack precision and clearness of detail.

[40] For comments on the Queen's address in the People's Council see *Netherlands News*, I, 106.

[41] Letter of the Parindra group of the People's Council, July 4, 1941. The letter explicitly stated that the attitude of the group should *not* be understood as a refusal to do its share in the defense of the Indies. On July 15, 1941, several nationalist groups in the People's Council announced that they had merged their parties into one, the "Fraktie National Indonesia." Announcing this merger, the nationalist spokesman, Suroso, declared that the new party would work for "Indonesia Merdika" (Free Indonesia), but that this did not involve separation of the Indies from the Netherlands.

tution. In other words, the government did not feel justified in taking a decision of such importance by simple decree, as long as the possibility remained that within two or three years the reforms could be introduced according to the legal procedure fixed in the Constitution itself. The majority of the people of the Indies, in so far as it took part in political affairs, felt this attitude to be a reasonable one, although most Indonesians deplored the delay.

In one respect, however, there was unanimity; none of the political leaders for a moment considered the possibility of appeasing or even of making terms with foreign aggression. "Beware of the Japanese" had been the last warning of Dr. Sutomo to his followers before his death, and the leaders of the opposition were those who most actively urged the speeding of defense preparations. The leftist Gerindo party neatly labeled the "Greater East Asia co-prosperity sphere" a "fabrication of and for Japanese fascists," and in its statement of August 4, 1941, it said: "The Greater East Asia idea as propagated by Japan is exclusively designed to deprive other peoples of their freedom by Japanese domination as happened in Manchukuo, China, and Indo-China." The bombs that fell on Pearl Harbor immediately brought the representatives of the Parindra party back into the People's Council to coöperate with the government in the common defense of the country.

Meanwhile the danger of Japanese attack had grown. Yoshizava had come to Batavia to continue the trade negotiations but met with little success. The talks between the Japanese delegation and the Dutch representatives, headed by Mr. H. J. van Mook, dragged on until June. Matsuoka's speech at the opening of the Diet in Tokyo (January 21), in which the foreign minister of Japan mentioned the Netherlands Indies in one breath with Indo-China and Thailand as belonging to the Japanese co-prosperity sphere, caused general resentment in the Indies. A sharp Dutch protest followed.[42] The excessive demands presented by Yoshizava left no doubt about the real meaning of the term "co-prosperity." Some of these demands were the following: unlimited immigration of Japanese to islands other than Java, enormous increase (fourfold) of Japanese imports into the Indies, the handling of the imported Japanese goods by Japanese merchants who were to receive unlimited freedom of action, and, in connection with this increased

[42] The Netherlands Indies and Indo-China ought to be brought into close and inseparable contact with Japan, if only for geographical reasons." The Netherlands government ordered its minister in Tokyo to notify the Japanese Foreign Office that the Netherlands rejected all schemes that tended to make the Indies part of a "New Order-sphere" in East Asia, and also leadership of any other nation. (*Vrij Nederland*, February 8, 1941, p. 34.)

importation, the construction of railroads and port facilities by the Japanese, the exploitation of these installations under Japanese management and by Japanese engineers, the removal of all restrictions on fishing for Japanese fishermen (who, if uncontrolled, ruin the fishing grounds by their ruthless methods), abolishment of all restrictions on the establishment of new industries in favor of Japanese industrialists but of them alone, the exploration and exploitation of the less populated outer islands by Japanese companies and settlers.[43] It would have been simpler if Yoshizava had demanded the surrender of the Indies, lock, stock, and barrel, to Japan, instead of presenting his long-winded request for economic "coöperation."

The Netherlands delegation made counterproposals and Yoshizava complained that the Netherlanders were not "coöperative." Gradually the discussions lost all meaning. Both parties knew that an agreement was impossible. Moreover, Yosuke Matsuoka had gone to Berlin and Moscow and the future policy of Japan had been irretrievably fixed. The story of Matsuoka's trip to Europe in March and April of 1941 [44] does not belong to the subject of this book. We can only guess what was discussed in the capitals of Nazi Germany and Soviet Russia. But there is little doubt that in Berlin the active participation of Japan in the war was decided upon and the time for it set. When Matsuoka came to Moscow both he and Stalin must have known that war between Germany and Russia was coming. Neither Russia nor Japan wanted to fight a war on two fronts. From this may have resulted a protective agreement that neither of them would, simply for the sake of their respective allies, permit himself to be dragged into a conflict with the other. Shortly after Matsuoka's return Prince Konoye, who had promised the people of Japan that under his leadership they would have a minimum of luxury but a maximum of glory, retired to make place, as he expressed it, for a stronger government, of which his country was now supposed to be in need.

This new and stronger, i.e. military, government did not waste much time in taking action. Within a week Japanese troops marched into southern Indo-China. The reaction of the United States to this aggression was the freezing of Japanese assets in that country. The Netherlands Indies followed the American example without delay (July 26).[45] War had become inevitable. A few months more were

[43] *Vrij Nederland*, February 15, 1941, p. 72 and private information.

[44] Matsuoka arrived in Berlin on March 26; the Russian-Japanese neutrality pact was signed on April 13.

[45] *Netherlands News*, I, 69.

spent in sparring for time while the Japanese hurriedly established the advance bases from which they planned to strike.

The Japanese government gave warning to residents of Japanese nationality in the Indies that they were advised to leave the country. Dutch women and children began to move out of Japan. A United States military mission arrived in Batavia in August, and staff talks among the military commanders in Singapore, Batavia, and Manila took place in rapid succession. The Japanese ambassador in Berlin, General Oshima, paid a visit to General Christiansen, commander of the German occupation troops in Holland, possibly to collect further material on the military and political situation in the Indies from documents in the Dutch Department of Colonies in the Hague. While the Japanese government boldly asserted that it had never more than 35,000 men in Indo-China, it really was massing strong forces along the boundary of Thailand and near its new naval bases in the neighborhood of Saigon. It was massing air fleets at the bases northeast of the Indies, in the archipelago of the Caroline Islands. An imposing force was concentrating for the attack on the Indies.

In view of this threat of war the democratic nations sought to coordinate their efforts. The Indies increased their production of raw materials, essential for the war production in the United States. Rubber production was fixed at 120 per cent of the normal quota (650,000 tons), and the rubber planters succeeded in producing that amount. In August 1941 alone, 52,886 tons of rubber were shipped overseas.[46] The export of quinine was more than double the normal amount. The United States feverishly increased its production of war equipment. But the Indies were not the only customer in the American market. Russia too was in dire need of help, and there furious battles were fought while the war in the Far East had not yet started. Only part of the large orders placed by the Indies in the United States could be executed. Shipping difficulties steadily increased because more and more ships were sunk by "German" raiders in the far Pacific.[47] In September 1941 the first Catalina flying boats arrived in the Indies. The badly needed modern fighter planes unfortunately could never be delivered.

There were men enough in the Indies willing to fight for their country, but there was not enough equipment to arm them. The native

[46] Figures on exports from the Indies: *Vrij Nederland*, June 28, 1941, p. 678. The export of rubber in 1940 exceeded that of 1939 by 42 per cent.

[47] Figures on delivery of ammunition and arms from the United States to the East Indies: *Bulletin* of the United States Department of State, May 31, 1941. Over the first four months of 1941 only 10 per cent of the goods, for the export of which the Netherlands Indies held license (and paid for), were actually exported.

militia had been instituted in Java, Amboina, and the Minahassa, and the response on the part of the population had been magnificent. Although it was announced that only eighteen thousand men were to be drafted, one hundred thousand volunteers presented themselves. However, when a selection of eighteen thousand had been made, only six thousand could be inducted because of lack of arms.[48] The Home and City Guards finally received rifles, but these were Italian rifles, captured by General Wavell in the Western Desert of Egypt, most of which were spoiled by erosion and had to be reconditioned.

The total strength of the East Indian forces at the outbreak of the war was the following: The East Indian squadron of the Dutch navy consisted of three cruisers, the *Java*, the *De Ruyter*, and the *Sumatra*.[49] Of these the *Sumatra* was under repair at the Surabaya navy yard. There were five destroyers, the *Evertsen*, the *Piet Hein*, the *Kortenaer*, the *Witte de With*, and the *Tromp*. The latter, a flotilla leader of 3,350 tons, might be called a light cruiser. The small but efficient submarines numbered about fifteen. Add to these ships a number of small craft and auxiliary vessels and we have the whole East Indian squadron of the Netherlands Navy. The squadron was entrusted to the command of Admiral Coenraad E. L. Helfrich. The cruisers were fast but only lightly armored. Only the *De Ruyter* was of modern construction. It is needless to say that these ships were no match even for a small part of the Japanese navy.

The air force which was destined to gain immortal glory in the next months was even further outclassed by the enemy. Reports indicate that all together the air force included ninety-seven old Glenn Martin bombers, some recently acquired Brewster Buffalos (which proved absolutely useless against the Japanese aircraft), a dozen modern pursuit planes, a few obsolescent fighters of Dutch construction, about forty modern seaplanes, and a number of training and transport planes. The total number of all aircraft together was about five hundred, but only

[48] Most critics who pretend to know that the people of the Indies were unwilling to fight overlook the fact that it is rather difficult to resist the Japanese army if the defenders have not even rifles. On the value of well-equipped professional soldiers compared to that of a poorly armed militia, see Hanson W. Baldwin on the campaign in the Philippines (*Foreign Affairs*, July 1942).

[49] The *De Ruyter*, built in 1935, was a cruiser of 6,450 standard tons with seven guns of 5.9 inches. The *Java* and *Sumatra*, built respectively in 1921 and 1920, were ships of 6,670 standard tons with ten 5.9 inch guns. The destroyers, except the *Tromp*, were ships of 1,300 standard tons. In 1939 the Netherlands Parliament had passed a bill permitting the construction of three battleships of 27,000 tons each, two cruisers of 8,250 tons, and a number of additional vessels. Some of these ships were under construction at the time of the German invasion and were destroyed on the slips.

part of these were fit for combat duty. Commanded by Major General L. H. van Oyen, this weak force succeeded in destroying scores of enemy ships and transports before it was annihilated by the enemy, who had overwhelming superiority not only in quantity but also in quality of aircraft.

The army was better equipped, but too small. Before the war it numbered 35,000 soldiers, some Dutch, some Indonesian. Among the Indonesians there were men from many peoples, from Java and Sumatra as well as from the Minahassa and Amboina. This standing army had been increased by a few thousand men. After the death of Lieutenant-General J. Berenschot, killed in an airplane accident near Batavia in October 1941, its command had been entrusted to Lieutenant-General Hein ter Poorten. It was furthermore reinforced by about 30,000 Home and City Guards and by 6,000 men of the Native Militia. The latter, however, had been in training for only a few months when the war broke out. With all auxiliary troops, the total number of enlisted men — the majority of these were only partly trained and poorly equipped — was about one hundred thousand. The tank force was insignificant. The anti-aircraft artillery was not sufficient to protect even the most important points, and, consequently, could provide no protection for the numerous small cities. The larger part of the army was concentrated on Java. Weak garrisons were scattered over the other islands, chiefly for protection of the advance air bases and some points of special strategic value such as the oil fields of Borneo. There was no hope of defending these oil fields for any length of time; the main task of the garrisons was to gain time to permit the destruction of the installations before the enemy could seize them. Only Amboina was better guarded, thanks to the militia and companies of ex-service men of that oldest of all Dutch strongholds in the Far East.

The armed forces were weak, but they were alert. At the end of November 1941 it was announced that Dr. H. J. Van Mook, who had planned to leave for London because of his appointment to the Ministry of Colonies (November 20), had suddenly decided to await the further development of events before leaving the Indies. On November 30 a number of Dutch warships, cruisers, destroyers, and submarines quietly slipped out of port to take up their positions in the northern waters of the archipelago. Some of the submarines progressed as far as the Gulf of Siam, where they remained in hiding. On December 2 the mobilization of all armed forces was completed. By December 6 it had become clear that war would break out in the next few days, and the Batavian government decided to allow Australian flyers to join the

Dutch at the base of Amboina and to admit Australian troops into Timor. On December 8, about three o'clock in the morning,[50] the news of the Japanese attack on Pearl Harbor was communicated to the governor-general and his chief advisors. Only four hours later, at 6:30 in the morning of this same day, Monday December 8, after telephone communication with London, the governor-general addressed the people of the Indies over the radio and announced that from that time a state of war existed with Japan.

The news of the attack came to the Netherlands government in London about eleven-thirty Sunday evening. In the middle of the night Queen Wilhelmina was notified by telephone of what had happened. "A bomb on Pearl Harbor is a bomb on Java," was her comment. The issue was settled. In the early hours of Monday (London time), the Cabinet of Ministers met and decided to submit for the Queen's approval an official declaration of war upon Japan. This declaration was immediately cabled to the Netherlands Minister in Tokyo, who without delay communicated it to the Japanese war lords.[51]

The Japanese attack fused the national unity of the Indies. On December 12, 1941, the Executive Board of the Madjelis Rakjat Indonesia (Council of the Indonesian People), together with the secretariat of the Gabungan Politiek Indonesia — and these two organizations included all nationalist groups — declared it to be the duty of every self-respecting people to resist any attack from the outside. They urged the people of the Indies to give complete support to the authorities in the maintenance of order and to obey promptly and to the letter the orders and requests of the authorities. Most striking of all similar statements was the appeal of Mohammed Hatta, former revolutionary leader: "Our people, with the exception of a small minority now in the armed forces, has not learned to use arms and bears no responsibility for its own fate. Yet it should not think that this war does not affect us. . . . If we are convinced that the Japanese aggression endangers our ideals, then we must resist Japanese imperialism. Even if we believe that Japan will probably win, it remains our duty to come to the defense of our en-

[50] For a report on the exact time when the Netherlands government in London received the news, and on its subsequent actions, see *Knickerbocker Weekly*, December 7, 1942: H. George Franks, "The Inside Story of December 7, 1941."

[51] By attacking United States territory instead of continuing their expansion by direct aggression in the Netherlands Indies, side-stepping the Philippines, Japan made perhaps the greatest blunder in her history. There was never a definite guarantee given that the United States would come to the assistance of the Indies or Singapore in case of a Japanese attack, and such a guarantee could not be given. Japan destroyed a few battleships at Pearl Harbor but unified the American people. It seems to be a typical example of purely military thinking.

dangered ideals. It is better to die standing than to live kneeling. . . ."[52]

The first measure taken by the commander-in-chief was to round up all Japanese nationals still in the Indies. Of these there were still about 1300. Netherlands troops were also sent to British North Borneo to clean up a Japanese settlement on the east coast of that territory. The second step was to eliminate the danger of Japanese infiltration through neutral but unprotected territory. This led to the landing of Dutch and Australian troops near Dilli, the capital of Portuguese Timor.

This occupation was part of the scheme of defense planned months before by the joint Dutch-Australian-British general staffs and approved by their respective governments. Britain, for two centuries the ally of Portugal, had approached the Portuguese government as early as November 4.[53] The talks were speeded up, a British statement declared, after Pearl Harbor, and on December 15 the British proposals of Dutch-Australian assistance for the defense of Timor were definitely *accepted* by Portugal (if we believe the British statement) or *rejected* (if we accept Salazar's version of the negotiations).[54] Both parties agreed that Portugal had promised to send reinforcements to bolster the defense of the colony. These reinforcements were already being concentrated in Portuguese East Africa. The apparent contradiction between the two statements and the rest of the contents of the British statement suggest that some understanding between the two governments existed, but that Portugal had refused to give *official* permission for an occupation of her territory by Allied troops for fear that the Axis partners in Europe might take drastic steps in retaliation.[55]

The actual occupation was carried out under (*pro forma?*) protest of the Portuguese governor, but without incident. The Japanese found in Portuguese territory — there was, for instance, a vice-consul with no less than thirty employees — were interned. The civil administration continued to function as before, while guarantees were given to Lisbon that as soon as the war situation would permit, the Allied troops would be withdrawn. These assurances by the Allies apparently satisfied the Portuguese government.

[52] Article in the Malay newspaper *Pemandangan* of December 22, 1941.

[53] According to Dr. Salazar's speech in the National Assembly on December 19, 1941.

[54] Compare the British statement, released December 21, 1941, with the speech of Salazar of December 19.

[55] In his statement of February 22, 1942, on the Japanese occupation of parts of Portuguese Timor, Salazar pointed out "the most determined good will on Britain's part, good will in which the Netherlands and Australian Governments joined." In the same speech he severely criticized the Japanese action. "Unlike Britain," he said, "the Japanese Empire could not even invoke obligations of help, rightly or wrongly interpreted. . . ." The marked difference in his attitude towards Japan and towards Britain is noteworthy.

Meanwhile the desperate struggle against the overwhelmingly superior Japanese forces had begun. Strategically, the Japanese held all trumps. They had strong forces concentrated in Southern Indo-China, from where they could drive a wedge between the British in Malaya and the Americans in the Philippines. General MacArthur held the advance positions of the Allied lines, but he was practically encircled by Japanese forces in Northern Indo-China, Hainan, Formosa, and the Caroline Islands. From their outpost on Yap and in the small Palau Archipelago east of Mindanao the Japanese even threatened his communications to the south with the Netherlands Indies. The annihilation of the American air force on Luzon in the first hours of the war made the Philippines a lost outpost, doomed to fall instead of being a possible base for counter attacks on the Japanese communication lines. It left the war lords of Tokyo free to throw the bulk of their forces against the key stronghold of the Allies, Singapore, from where all sea lanes between the Indian Ocean and the Pacific, except the distant route around Australia, could be controlled.

The strategy of the Japanese was clear from the beginning. While strong forces would draw the circle around MacArthur's troops closer and closer until finally he would be thrown back into the fortress of Corregidor, the main army would proceed to Malaya, both overland and by sea. The village of Patani, once the famous trading port of the sixteenth and seventeenth centuries, so often mentioned in former chapters, would be the starting point for the march to the south. As soon as the drive towards Singapore was well under way, a second attack would develop, southward from newly conquered bases in Mindanao, and proceed east and west of Celebes towards Timor. This would cut off the Dutch from their allies in Australia and, consequently, in the United States.

If the Japanese were permitted to proceed with this plan to conquer further advanced bases and to gain a foothold in Singapore, the first round — and quite possibly the last one, too — of the war in the Pacific was lost. Their plans had to be disrupted before they could fully develop their forces. The American-Philippine army could not do this; neither could the British in Singapore who lacked even the planes necessary for their own defense. The United States Pacific fleet, upon which the Allies in all their plans had figured as one of the principal factors in the disruption of the Japanese plans of attack, was temporarily out of action. The only ones of the allies who at the moment were in a position to attack were the Netherlanders. They were willing enough to do it; Admiral Helfrich's whole strategy was based upon the assumption that all available forces of the Allies would be concentrated to strike at the widely spread Japanese naval forces; but where was the material to carry out that strategy? The very first attempt of the Allies to strike out, this time in defense of Singapore, had ended with the loss of the *Repulse* and *Prince of Wales*, the only two capital ships they had. This was nothing less than a disaster, nearly equal to that of Pearl Harbor, since it gave the Japanese complete mastery over the South China Sea. It badly reduced the striking power of the Dutch and American squadrons because they had now to take an increasing part in the protection of convoys bound for Singapore.

Consequently the Japanese operations could develop according to schedule. The Japanese suffered setbacks, chiefly through daring submarine attacks by the Allies in which the Dutch took a prominent part. Dutch flyers also made the enemy pay dearly in men and ships for the occupation of the practically undefended British protectorate of Sarawak. On December 21 a Japanese force approached Davao and began to land troops. General W. F. Sharp had only poorly equipped Philippine troops with which to oppose the invaders. Dutch planes violently attacked the Japanese ships in Davao Gulf and scored a number of hits, but, of course, without being able to stop the enemy's advance. Here the Allied navies might have had a chance to score a local success, but Admiral Hart's Asiatic fleet was not able to take part in offensive operations until it had received new supplies from the United States.[56]

For a month the war hardly touched the territory of the Indies, though Japanese planes intermittently bombed air fields and ports in the northern section of the archipelago in order to reduce the efficiency of the Netherlands navy and air force. Pontianak, an unprotected open city in West Borneo, was cruelly bombed on December 19, when many civilians were killed and part of the town was set afire. Enemy planes came scouting over the Java Sea, but no serious attacks were made against any part of the Dutch territory until January 10. During these months the Japanese continued their efforts to drive a wedge into the united front of the allies and to persuade the Dutch to give up a struggle that from the beginning was hopeless. Even the Japanese communiqués suggested that Japanese attacks on Dutch territory only took place "in retaliation for repeated hostile acts on the part of the Nether-

[56] The Asiatic Fleet consisted of the cruisers *Houston* and *Marblehead*, thirteen destroyers, and twenty-seven submarines, but only part of the destroyer squadron is mentioned in the battles. The United States Navy so far has not released information concerning the submarine warfare.

lands forces" and "to eliminate enemy air bases obstructing the Japanese campaign against the Philippines and British Borneo." On January 1 the Netherlands government received through Swedish diplomatic channels an official proposal of the Japanese government that "in the name of humanity" (*sic!*) bloodshed and any sort of hostile action against the Japanese forces should be avoided.[57] The answer was "No." There was no chance of separating the Netherlanders from their allies in this war, which was truly regarded as a war of principles. Dutch, Chinese, and Indonesians remained strongly united in opposition against Japanese aggression. The Malay newspapers, many of them nationalist, and the Indonesian-managed broadcast for the Orient attacked the war lords of Tokyo so violently that the Japanese radio retorted by threatening reprisals on the spokesmen and their families once the Indies should be conquered.

In the second week of January the Japanese had turned conquered Davao into a base for further attacks and started on their drive southward toward Timor Sea. Java had then (since January 6, 1942) become the headquarters of the new commander-in-chief of the Allied forces in the Southwest Pacific, General Wavell, but this did not mean that strong reinforcements for that area were to be expected soon. Even if the troops, the planes, and further equipment were ready for shipment in the United States, the transport would take at least two months and a half. This meant that substantial help could not arrive before the end of February. The slightest delay might retard its arrival for another month.[58] The Dutch had scored successes in their attacks on Japanese shipping and communications; they had also taken an important part in the defense of Malaya by sending part of their air force to that war theater; but they had paid dearly for the reputation these offensive actions had gained for them.

Before a single Japanese set foot on Indonesian soil, 50 per cent of the Dutch planes had been lost. Numbers of submarines had been sunk by the enemy or had struck mines. The remaining aircraft were no longer in the best of condition, and supplies were running low. Thus, the defenses of the islands had already been considerably weakened when on January 10 the first Japanese landings took place. A transport fleet of fourteen ships landed troops on the island of Tarakan, impor-

[57] H. George Franks, for Aneta News Agency, in *Knickerbocker Weekly*, December 7, 1942, p. 15.

[58] Arrival of these troops and planes in Australia was announced in Washington on March 16, 1942, three months and one week after Pearl Harbor. If we bear in mind that the communication lines between Hawaii and Australia first had to be made safe, we may call this an excellent accomplishment.

tant for its oil wells. Five hundred parachutists came down near the airfields of the Minahassa, while another transport fleet brought a force of six to seven thousand Japanese ashore in the same district. The strategic points fell quickly to the Japanese. Fighting in the hills continued for three weeks and more, and to crush this resistance the enemy finally was forced to bring in a whole division.

The second half of January was decisive for the campaign in the Indies. On January 20 Japanese and British engaged in a furious battle along the Endau–Muar line north of Johore. Without waiting for the outcome of this battle, the Japanese started an encircling movement to cut the communications between Singapore and Batavia. From Kuching in Sarawak they moved southward to Sambas. Troops landed near Pontianak on February 1 occupied that city. While Japanese bombers penetrated farther and farther into the Dutch area, attacking Sabang on Sumatra's northern point, Medan and Palembang on the same island, and the naval base of Amboina in the east, a strongly protected convoy moved down Macassar Strait. From January 23 on, the Japanese were attacked — first by Dutch planes, then by combined Dutch-American forces. Flying Fortresses, the first reinforcements for the Allied troops fighting in the Indies, had arrived and immediately took part in the battle. During the night of January 23–24 American destroyers commanded by Commander F. R. Talbot executed a daring and brilliant attack upon the Japanese. Neither the allied air force nor the weak naval forces, however, were able to stop the advance of the enemy, who safely reached Balik Papan with the greater part of his ships and men.[59]

Balik Papan, the most important oil center of Borneo, was in flames when the Japanese sighted it. To prevent mistakes or oversights in the application of the scorched-earth policy, the oil installations were destroyed before the enemy arrived. The landing of his troops was opposed by the garrison, which then withdrew into the interior. After sending part of their troops north to occupy the oil and coal fields near

[59] Exaggerated reports of sinkings of Japanese ships were circulated through the press at the time of the battle of Macassar Straits. Confusion was created when newspapers listed as sunk enemy ships which were reported "left in sinking condition" or "hit." In reality the Netherlands communiqué's claim for the first two days of the battle (Dutch airforce alone attacking) was *one* ship sunk by bombing, and *one* through submarine attack. The United States communiqué's claim was *two* ships destroyed by the destroyer attack and *four* through bombing in the last three days (Flying Fortresses attacking), which would give a total of *eight* ships destroyed. If there really was some confusion of facts in the United States communiqués of February 28 and 29, as seems to be the case, the total number would be only *seven*. Even moderate newspaper reports of February 28 claimed fourteen ships sunk.

Samarinda, the Japanese began to march overland to Bandjermasin. The possession of that town and its airfield would provide them with an excellent air base for their attack on Java.

Three days after the fall of Balik Papan, the Japanese penetrated into the Banda Sea. They prepared their attack with repeated and violent bombardments of the naval base of Amboina, then landed at Kendari (January 25) and overran that small place, only important because of its airfield. Thus protected in the rear, they moved eastward toward Amboina. In the evening of January 30 they began to land on its shores. On this small island, of only 286 square miles and with a population of no more than 240,000 inhabitants, the fighting lasted for three weeks. Japanese reports of February 23 finally claimed the conquest of the island and the capture of 2300 prisoners, a figure which they can only have reached by including in the figure every European on the island.

After the Japanese landing at Amboina the situation became desperate. In the western section Dutch territory was still untouched except for the districts of Sambas and Pontianak, but the British had been driven back on the island of Singapore. That key fortress of the East Indies was practically besieged and no longer hindered further Japanese progress. The Nipponese squadron of Macassar Strait, having overcome the violent Dutch-American resistance from the air, penetrated into the Java Sea, and carrier-borne aircraft appeared over the Surabaya naval base. Forty bombers escorted by fighters bombed the naval installations (February 5), but without putting them definitely out of action. Other carriers sailed southward over the Banda Sea, and from this time on Japanese fighters harassed the allied communications between Australia and Java. On February 7 the airfield of Kupang on Timor was bombed for the first time. This airfield was of primary importance to the Allies. Once Timor was lost or its airfields put out of action, the connections between the Dutch and their Allies would be severed. Then, fighter planes could only be *shipped* to Java (through waters controlled by the enemy), and no longer flown. All forces should have been concentrated to protect this vital spot from enemy occupation. Yet there were no troops to do it. Although only a relatively small force, perhaps one division, would have been sufficient to guard the island from immediate enemy occupation, it seemed impossible to collect even that small number of Allied soldiers with the necessary equipment and air support. The main burden of the task would have fallen on the Australians, and Australia was so much impressed by the defeat of the Imperial army in Malaya that only one thought seemed to prevail in her councils, that of concentrating all available troops for the purely local defense of the home country.

It was a slight consolation that a few American fighter planes and Flying Fortresses arrived in Java, together with small units of American troops.[60] The latter never numbered more than a few hundred men. The Japanese advance could not be stopped. The enemy took control over the eastern sector of the Java Sea and pushed on, both by sea and by land, towards Bandjermasin in Borneo and Macassar in Celebes. When these two towns had been occupied (February 10–13), the Japanese made ready for the final onslaught. They already claimed the mastery over the Java Sea and in their communiqué of February 6 they boasted as having sunk or put out of action the *Java*, the *Tromp*, and the *Marblehead*. "The Dutch Navy was practically wiped out," they said. What really had happened was that the *Marblehead* had been damaged severely and was forced to leave the war zone. The other ships were still there and bravely carried on in spite of Japanese air superiority.

To the west the enemy completed the encirclement of Singapore by an air- and sea-borne invasion of southern Sumatra. Eight hundred parachutists came down near the oil installations of Palembang, the largest ones of the Indies. These eight hundred were annihilated by the Menadonese soldiers of the East Indian Army, but in their place thousands came by sea. The burning oil plants had to be left to the enemy, who lost no time but immediately started on his march to the south, to the port of Telokbetong, whence he could control the narrows of Sunda Strait. Singapore fell on February 15, and in addition to this blow, numerous transports were seen leaving Formosa and South China to bring still more invaders to the battered Indies.

Between February 20 and February 22 the Japanese scored two momentous successes which made them virtually the masters of Southeast Asia. They landed troops on both Timor and Bali, occupied the air field of Kupang and Den Pasar, and thus cut the communication line with Australia, the importance of which has been indicated. Far to the northwest they cut the Burma road by the conquest of the town of Pegu. The fighting continued, and the allies defended themselves with ever growing fury, but it was the beginning of the end. Disaster could no longer be avoided.

[60] A Texan field artillery unit and a battalion of the 131st regiment of infantry were the only American troops reported in Java, besides the crews of the Flying Fortresses and some technicians. On April 9 the Japanese made known that they had taken 883 American prisoners in the land battle for Java.

The last three weeks of the campaign of the Indies had begun. The Allied forces were now reduced to a few American planes, a British-Dutch-American fleet of five cruisers, twelve or thirteen destroyers, and a number of submarines, and an army of about five thousand American and British[61] and perhaps twenty-five thousand regular Netherlands soldiers. The Netherlands East Indian air force practically did not exist any more. Of the army, part was tied down to the coastal batteries and other fixed works of defense. For maneuvering and opposing the enemy in force once he had landed there were only eighteen weak battalions disposable. There was only one thing left to do for the stubborn defenders, who were now cornered in the relatively small island of Java. They could make the enemy pay high in men and material for his conquest. They could buy time at the cost of their lives — time for the Allies in Australia and in India, in Alaska and Hawaii. Moreover, they could set an example of undaunted courage, of resistance to the bitter end, even though there was no doubt that death and destruction would be the inevitable outcome. The Allies in Java were defending the pass that gave access to Australia. Their position was hopeless, the enemy was already in the rear of their lines, but they sallied forth from their last bulwark to strike at the host of invaders wherever a chance offered itself. By the same sacrifice King Leonidas of Sparta saved ancient Greece from foreign domination.

The Allied leaders in Java have often been blamed because they did not retreat with as many ships and men as possible to Australia, but for the Dutch there was no retreat without giving the lie to all they had said and proclaimed their ideal in the Indies during the last twenty years.[62] The British and Americans probably did not want to go and leave the Dutch to the "mercy" of Nipponese "Bushido." By making a last stand before Java the United Nations lost a few old ships, and, what was infinitely worse, the lives of several thousands of brave sailors, but inspired a grim determination in those who came to avenge them. The history of the invasion of the Indies without the battle of the Java Sea would be like that of the defense of the Philippines without Bataan.

[61] On March 9 the Japanese claimed 5,000 American and British prisoners in Java, but on April 9 they gave other figures, including 10,636 British and 4,890 Australians. The number of British prisoners seems exaggerated, even if they included every British civilian in the number.

[62] This is not an idea peculiar to the year 1942. Compare Pieter van Hoorn's "Consideratiën" of 1675: "It is a grave dishonor to desert a colony once it has been established, for, besides being dishonorable, it is a true betrayal causing the death of many helpless people" (De Jonge, *op. cit.*, VI, 134).

And it may well be that Bataan was the first step towards winning the war.

The first sally of the United Nations fleet against the invaders was successful. On the night of February 19 a squadron composed of the cruisers *De Ruyter* and *Java*, of the Dutch destroyers *Piet Hein* and *Tromp* and six American destroyers, the whole force under the command of Rear Admiral Karel Doorman of the Netherlands Navy, executed a rapid sweep around the island of Bali. The surprise attack was a complete success. The two cruisers and the *Piet Hein* with two American destroyers dashed into a Japanese fleet of warships and transports off the southern coast of Bali. With her first salvo the *Piet Hein* hit and set afire a transport. Caught in the flares of a Japanese cruiser, the Dutch ship rushed forward and launched her torpedoes before being hit and sunk. The enemy shared her fate. The other ships rushed on, swung north around Bali, and left the Japanese shooting it out among themselves. Then the other American destroyers charged in, inflicting further losses and damage upon the invaders, and last of all the *Tromp* came up to cover the retreat of the Allies by a final daring onslaught. Regardless of the losses suffered the Japanese navy and air force pressed forward. Now they had the Allies completely encircled, and the sinking of the United States carrier *Langley* south of Java indicated that even the round-about approach to the beleaguered island had become unsafe.

So far the Japanese held only a few thousand square miles of territory in the Indies. That area, however, included most of the strategic points in the Outer Islands. The enemy held the keys to the Allied positions. In many places he had only a precarious foothold, but unfortunately there was no possibility of ever exploiting the weaknesses in his far-flung communication lines. In the interior of Timor hundreds of Dutch and Australian soldiers were holding their own and thus offering the Allies an opening for counter attack. No Allied force felt itself in a position to make use of the opportunity. War correspondents reported over the radio, for the whole world to hear, that they had found great confusion among Australia's leaders, that all efforts were to be concentrated upon the defense of Australia alone, and that the Indies must be given up. Thus the Japanese were assured that their communications would not be threatened, not even at their most vulnerable point in the southeastern archipelago.

They threw all available force in the Indies against Java for a general attack in which the defenders were outnumbered to such an extent that prolonged defense was impossible. The last Dutch and American bombers, which had continued to harass the enemy at Palembang and at Macassar, where he had concentrated strong forces, were destroyed by Japanese planes which attacked with a superiority of a hundred to one. The air fields were bombed out of action. A few Flying Fortresses escaped to Australia. Transport planes continuously made the hazardous trip from Java to Darwin, carrying refugees and United States and British officials.

On February 26, reconnaissance planes reported the movement of new strong invasion fleets, emerging from Macassar Strait and heading for Java. The Allied naval forces were concentrated off Surabaya. Three British destroyers had taken the place of the Dutch ships that had been sunk and of the American vessels that had been destroyed or so badly damaged that they had been forced to leave the area of action. An Australian cruiser, the *Perth*, and the British cruiser *Exeter*, the victor in the epic battle with the German *Graf Spee* off Montevideo, were added to the force. This fleet, with the damaged United States cruiser *Houston*, fought the battle of the Java Sea in the afternoon of February 27.[63]

For two hours the Allied fleet fought the far superior enemy, not only holding him at bay but inflicting such damage that he withdrew. Doorman tried to follow, and (in the wording of the British–United States communiqué of March 14) "chased the enemy to the northeast." His own forces had suffered badly. The *Exeter* was crippled. The Dutch destroyer *Kortenaer* had been torpedoed and sunk in fifteen seconds. The British destroyer *Electra* had charged into the smoke screen of the Japanese destroyers and never appeared again.

Now Doorman turned back to locate other sections of the enemy convoy. He sighted four ships but could not overhaul them. Then enemy attacks in the darkness began to take their toll. First the British destroyer *Jupiter* was sunk not far from the coast of Java, probably by a torpedo. Shortly before midnight Doorman with his remaining force, the two Dutch cruisers, and the *Houston* and the *Perth*, attacked once more. Two Japanese cruisers had been sighted near Rembang. This time the Allies lacked destroyer protection. Within a few minutes both Dutch cruisers sank, hit by Japanese torpedoes.

The Allied fleet had done all it could do to save Java. The remaining

[63] In *Harper's Magazine*, November 1942, pp. 561–574, Fletcher Pratt gives an account of the naval operations in which especially the battle of the Java Sea is discussed. Although prepared with the help of material provided by the United States Navy Department the article brings little more information than the joint British and American naval communiqué of March 14, 1942. See also the statements of one of the survivors of the *Kortenaer*, apparently also used by Fletcher Pratt (*Vrij Nederland*, June 27, 1942), and

ships were ordered to try to escape, either to the east or west of Java. This was not an impossibility, as was shown by the experience of three British cruisers which during the night of February 27 safely passed Sunda Strait without sighting enemy ships. The following night, the night after the battle, four United States destroyers fought their way through Bali Strait and reached Australia safely. A Dutch warship even left Surabaya as late as March 6, and, protected by expert camouflage, reached Australia undamaged through Bali Strait. But the night of February 28 was an ill-fated one. A fierce sea battle, the details of which we still have to learn from Japanese sources, was fought in Sunda Strait. Here the *Houston*, the *Perth*, and the Dutch destroyer *Evertsen* went down. There was another encounter between the damaged cruiser *Exeter* with two destroyers and three Japanese cruisers off the coast of Madura. Here, too, only Japanese sources can tell us of the details of the disaster that followed.

The Allied fleet was wiped out. The Japanese had suffered heavy losses but had accomplished their task. While their fleet fought the Allies their transports safely landed their invasion troops near Rembang, and farther to the west, near Indramayu and near Bantam. From the west and from the east Japanese columns closed in upon Batavia, which was taken on March 5, while General ter Poorten, in sole command since March 2, fought a desperate battle near Subang in defense of the approaches to the fortified sector of Bandung.[64] In a few days the Japanese outnumbered his troops, a single division, seven to one. On March 8, they entered Bandung and captured the high command of the Allied troops and the bulk of their army. In the east of Java, the invaders had driven on to Djocjakarta without meeting much resistance. The Dutch had concentrated on the defense of Surabaya, which was taken on the same day as Bandung. With the Allied Command the governor-general, Jhr. A. W. L. Tjarda van Starkenborgh Stachouwer, had fallen into the hands of the enemy. He had decided to stay at his post while by order of the government the lieutenant governor-general, H. J. van Mook, had left Java a few hours before the fall of Bandung with a group of officials to carry on from Australia.

The Japanese now faced the task of completing their occupation of the islands. On March 18 they claimed to have reached Padang on Sumatra's west coast after a five-day march through the country. On

---

the statement of Admiral Helfrich on the loss of the Dutch cruisers (*Vrij Nederland*, December 12, 1942).

[64] On March 2, General Sir Archibald Wavell left Java to take command in India. On February 11, Admiral Thomas Hart had already handed over the supreme command of the naval forces to Admiral Helfrich.

March 27 they announced the "complete occupation" of Sumatra. But fighting was going on everywhere, even on Java. Some units of the Java Army succeeded in escaping to Australia in the second week of April. Others, under the command of Major-General A. Pesman, were reported by Japanese sources to have continued resistance until June. The troops of Major-General Schillings, in East Java, held out several weeks longer. In June, Dutch troops surprised the Japanese by an attack on the small Natuna Islands, northwest of Borneo, where they destroyed the radio station. In July the Japanese claimed to have brought resistance to an end in Central Borneo, but they contradicted their own statement by putting forth an identical claim in October, when they claimed to have captured the remnants of an American-British-Dutch force four hundred miles north of Balik Papan. Only sixty-six men of this force were left when finally they were forced to surrender. In the beginning of September, Lieutenant De Jong, who commanded an army unit in Central Celebes, was reported captured. For six months he had resisted the Japanese and even succeeded in reconquering the port of Kolonodale on Celebes' east coast.

In June the Tokyo radio reported that all the Moluccas were occupied, but it was not before July that the Nipponese appeared off the Kei and Tanimbar Islands. They occupied these after some resistance, which apparently irritated the local Japanese commander to such an extent that he ordered the execution of the sixty-two-year-old Catholic missionary, Bishop Johannes Aerts, and seven of his priests. Slowly the invaders pushed on along the southwestern coast of New Guinea, but here they never reached their goal. On Timor, too, their advance had been checked. Strong United States army and air force units had come to Australia a few weeks too late to save Java but in time to prevent an invasion of Australia. Their arrival in Australia had been announced by United States authorities on March 16. The growing strength of the Allied air force in Northern Australia permitted the Australian and Dutch guerilla fighters of Timor to continue the fight for twelve months longer, until, unconquered, they were evacuated to Australia. Soon the counter attacks from the air on Japanese air and naval bases were to begin. Thus the enemy never succeeded in completing the conquest of the Indies. In Merauke, capital of the district of South West New Guinea, the Dutch flag was still flying when these lines were written, well guarded by soldiers of the Netherlands Indies and of the United States Army, and protected from the air by the planes of General Douglas MacArthur's forces. The epic of the Indies has not come to an end. The second episode may begin any day.

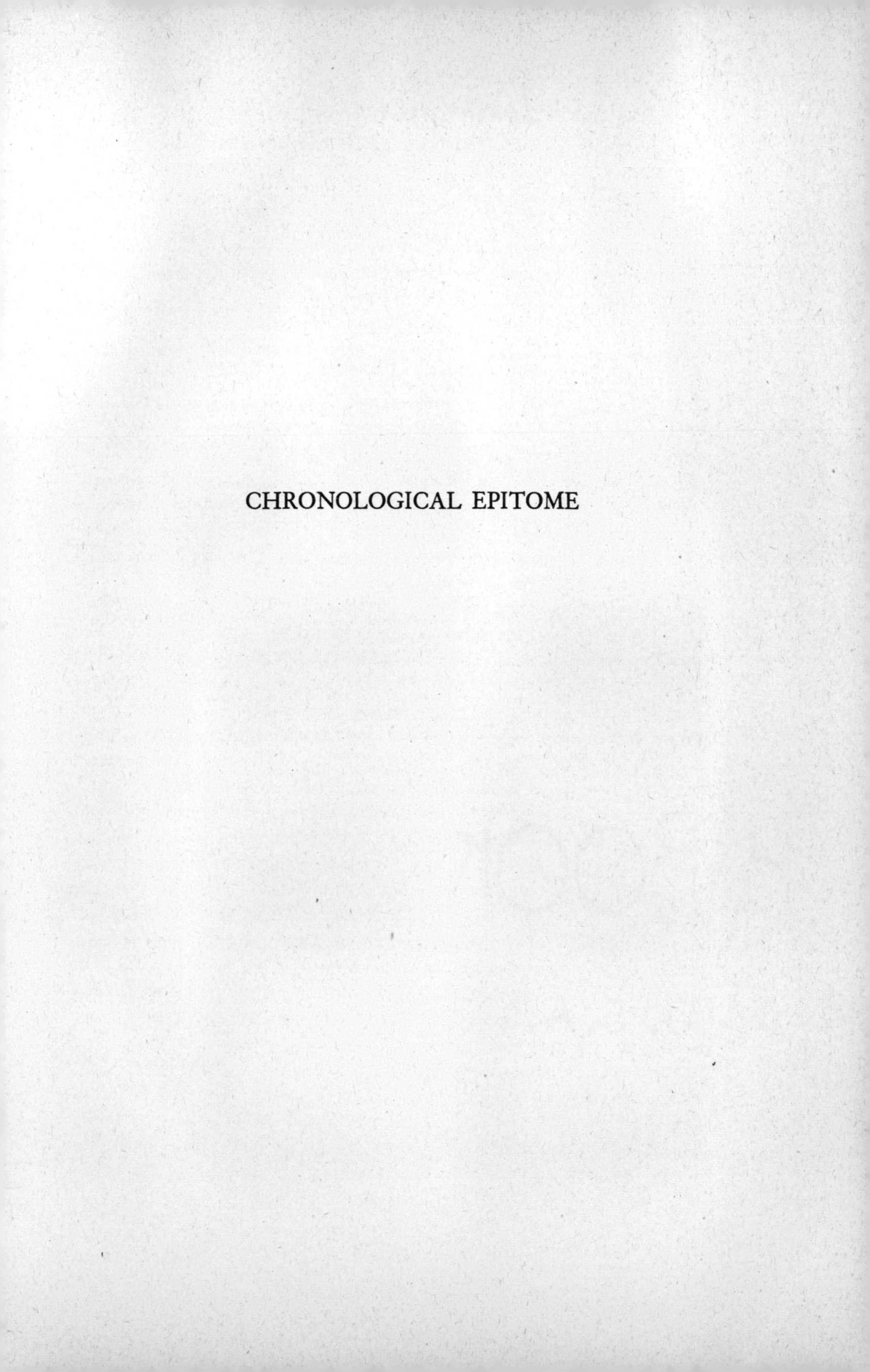

CHRONOLOGICAL EPITOME

CHRONOLOGICAL EPITOME

I. HINDU–INDONESIAN PERIOD

PRINCIPAL EVENTS

Outside the Archipelago	*In the Archipelago*
	c.1–700 A.D. Hindu immigration into the East Indian islands.
25–220. The Later Han Dynasty rules in China and establishes connections with the archipelago and the western world.	132. An embassy of King Tiao-Pien of Yavadvipa pays tribute to China. c.160. Ptolemy of Alexandria, for the first time in western literature, describes the East Indian islands.
200–600. Buddhism flourishes in China. Numerous Chinese pilgrimages to India.	c.400. Oldest Sanskrit inscriptions (at Muara Kaman) prove the existence of a Hindu-Indonesian state in East Borneo. 414. The Chinese pilgrim Fah-hien reports Brahmanism to be the prevailing religion in Java and Sumatra. 424. Prince Gunavarman of Kashmir preaches Buddhism in Sumatra.
671–685. Pilgrimage of I-tsing through Indonesia and India.	c.670. First reports on the Sumatran kingdom of Shrivijaya. The religion of its kings is Mahayana-Buddhist.
	c.750. Construction of the Shivaist temples of the Dieng plateau. c.770–800. Mahayana-Buddhism becomes the official religion of the kingdom of Central Java. Construction of Borobudur and Tjandi Mendut, etc.
800–900. The transfer of the capital of the Arabian empire to Baghdad (817) and the opening of the port of Canton to foreign trade by the emperors of the Sung dynasty result in greatly increased commercial connections between western and eastern Asia.	c.800. Shrivijaya is the predominant naval power in the archipelago. c.870. Return of the Shivaist kings of East Java to Central Java (Mataram). c.900. Construction of the Lara Djonggrang temple group at Prambanan. c.930. Central Java deserted by its kings and most of its inhabitants. 990–1007. First war between East Java and Shrivijaya, ending with complete defeat of Java.
	c.1025. Indian pirates occupy briefly the territory of Shrivijaya. 1102. Moslem inscriptions at Leran, Java, the first indication of Islam in the archipelago.

c.415. King Purnavarman of West Java mentioned by Sanskrit inscriptions.

732. Sanjaya, king of Mataram, a Shivaist ruler of Central Java, is mentioned by inscriptions.

778–870. The Buddhist House of Shailendra rules Central Java. The Shivaist kings of Mataram find refuge in East Java.

c.870. The House of Shailendra ceases to rule in Java but continues to rule Shrivijaya.
928–947. Sindok, king of East Java.

c.989–1007. Dharmavangça, king of East Java, extends his power over Bali, promulgates laws, causes the *Mahabharata* to be translated into Old Javanese.

1019–1049. Airlangga, king of East Java. After his death the kingdom is divided into the states of Kadiri and Janggala.

1135–1160. Jayabhaya, king of Kadiri, orders the composing of the *Bharatayuddha*.
1190–1222. Kertajaya, last king of Kadiri, defeated by Angrok.

Kings of Singhasari

1222–1227. Rajasa (Angrok).
1227–1248. Anusapati.

CHRONOLOGICAL EPITOME

PRINCIPAL EVENTS

Outside the Archipelago	*In the Archipelago*
	1251. By attacking Ceylon, Shrivijaya makes a last effort to retain control of the seas.
c.1260. Islam penetrates into Gujerat, main trading center of India for the archipelago.	
1260–1295. China is united under the rule of the Mongol emperor Kublai Khan. First Chinese expansion to the south.	c.1290. First town in the Indies (Perlak in northern Sumatra) converted to Islam. 1292. Marco Polo visits Sumatra. 1293. Chinese expedition against Kertanagara arrives in Java. 1294. Prince Vijaya expels the Chinese from Java and founds the kingdom of Madjapahit. 1294–1307. Vijaya extends the authority of Madjapahit over East Java, Madura, and Bali.
1307–1368. Revolt of China against the Mongols, followed by the founding of the Ming dynasty.	1331–1364. Gajah Mada, patih of Madjapahit, extends the authority of his kings over all coastlands between Malaya and the Moluccas. c.1350. Refugees from Java found the port of Malacca.
1403. The emperors of the Ming dynasty begin a policy of expansion towards the south.	1405. Cheng-Ho, ambassador of the Chinese emperor, visits Malaya. Later embassies force all princes of Sumatra and Java to recognize Chinese overlordship. 1414. Malacca accepts Islam. 1419. First Moslem graves at Gresik, Java.
	1465–1486. Marhum, first sultan of Ternate, spreads Islam in the Moluccas. 1478. Traditional date of the fall of Madjapahit. The kingdom probably subsisted fifty years longer.
1498. Vasco Da Gama arrives in India.	

II. MOHAMMEDAN–PORTUGUESE PERIOD

	1509. The first Portuguese ship arrives at Malacca. 1511. The Portuguese under Albuquerque conquer Malacca. D'Abreu visits the Moluccas. 1518. Final destruction of Madjapahit by the sultan of Demak.
1519–1522. First circumnavigation of the world. 1529. First French attempt to open trade connections with the East Indies.	c.1515–1530. Ali Mughajat Shah founds the sultanate of Atjeh. 1521. Spaniards aboard Magellan's ship *Victoria* pass through the Moluccas. 1522. Antonio de Brito builds a fort on Ternate. 1526. Bantam and Jacatra (now Batavia) conquered by the Mohammedans.

RULERS OF JAVA

1248–1268. Visnuvarddhana.

1268–1292. Kertanagara.

Kings of Madjapahit

1294–1309. Kertarajasa (Vijaya).

1309–1328. Jayanagara.
1329–1350. Tribhuvana.
1350–1389. Rajasanagara (Hayam Wuruk).

1389–1429. Vikramarddhana.

1429–1447. Suhita.

1447–1451. Bhre Tumapel.
1451–1453. Bhre Pamotan.
(Interregnum).
1456–1466. Bhre Vengker.
1466–1478. Bhre Pandan Salar.

Sultans of Demak

1511. Patih Yunus conquers Japara and becomes first sultan of Demak.

1521 1550. Pangeran Trangganan, ruler of Demak, conquers Singhasari.

Principal Events	
Outside the Archipelago	*In the Archipelago*
	1536–1540. Antonio Galvao firmly establishes Portuguese authority in the Moluccas. 1546. Faletahan of Bantam converts Cheribon to Islam. Francis Xavier converts thousands of Amboinese to Christianity.
1571. Spaniards from Mexico occupy the Philippines and found Manila. 1572. The Netherlands revolt against the authority of Philip II of Spain. 1579. Francis Drake visits the archipelago. 1580. Portugal is forced to accept Philip II of Spain as king.	1570. Sultan Hairun of Ternate is murdered by the Portuguese. General revolt under his son Baabullah (1570–1584). 1574. The Portuguese are driven from Ternate but maintain a foothold on Amboina. Four years later they build a fort on Tidore. 1579/1580. The last stronghold of Shivaism in West Java is conquered by the Mohammedans. In East Java, Shivaists maintain themselves in Balambangan.

III. THE DUTCH EAST INDIA COMPANY

1594–1596. Dutch expeditions to find the North-East Passage. 1595. Cornelis de Houtman sails for the Indies, arriving on June 23, 1596.	1596. First treaty between the Dutch and an Indonesian prince (Bantam).
	1599. First Dutch ships arrive in the Moluccas.
1602. The Dutch East India Company is founded.	1605. The Amboinese accept the suzerainty of the Dutch Company. The Portuguese leave the Moluccas. 1606. Spaniards from the Philippines occupy the deserted Portuguese fort of Tidore. 1607. Alliance between the Dutch and the sultan of Ternate. 1609–1636. Iskandar Muda, sultan of Atjeh, then at the summit of its power, threatens the Portuguese in Malacca.
1619. July 17, The Dutch and English East India Companies conclude a treaty of friendship and coöperation.	1619. Under Coen's administration rivalry between Dutch and English leads to actual war. Naval battle off Jacatra. May 30, Dutch fort at Jacatra, besieged by Bantamese, liberated by Coen. Founding of Batavia. 1621. Coen conquers the Banda Islands, center of the nutmeg production. 1623. The "massacre of Amboina" brings the British-Dutch coöperation to a close. 1629. Second siege of Batavia. 1635–1638. First war in the Moluccas to enforce restriction of the production of spices.
1641. The Dutch Republic and Portugal conclude a ten years' truce.	1641. Conquest of Malacca. 1642. The "Statutes of Batavia" promulgated.

CHRONOLOGICAL EPITOME

Rulers of Java

Sultans of Bantam	*Sultans of Demak*
1526–1552. Faletahan (Sunan Gunung Djati), first sultan of Bantam.	
	After 1550 Demak cedes first place to Padjang.
1552–1570. Hasanuddin, second sultan of Bantam. 1570–1580. Maulana Jusup, third sultan of Bantam.	
	Sultans of Mataram
1580–1596. Maulana Mohammed, fourth sultan of Bantam.	1582. Sutavijaya Senopati, ruler of Mataram, replaces the rulers of Demak as overlord of East Java and founds the Mohammedan empire of Mataram (now Surakarta).

Governors-General	
	1582–1601. Senopati. Conquest of East and Central Java.
	1601–1613. Mas Djolang.
1609–1614. Pieter Both. 1614–1616. Gerard Reynst. 1616–1618. Laurens Reaal. 1618–1623. Jan Pieterszoon Coen.	1613–1645. Tjakrakusuma Ngabdurrahman (Sultan Agung), after 1625 with the title of susuhunan.
1623–1627. Pieter de Carpentier. 1627–1629. Jan Pieterszoon Coen. 1629–1632. Jacques Specx, acting governor-general. 1632–1636. Hendrik Brouwer. 1636–1645. Anthony van Diemen.	

CHRONOLOGICAL EPITOME

PRINCIPAL EVENTS

Outside the Archipelago	*In the Archipelago*
1642. Van Diemen orders the exploration of the southern and northeastern oceans (voyages of Tasman around Australia and of De Vries to Kamchatka).	
1648. Peace with Spain.	
1651. The war with Portugal is renewed.	1650–1656. Second war in the Moluccas.
1652. The East India Company establishes an outpost at the Cape of Good Hope.	1651–1683. Sultan Abulfath Abulfatah (Agung) of Bantam makes his capital into a center of international trade.
1661. Peace with Portugal.	
	1662. The treaty of Painan breaks the power of Atjeh on Sumatra's west coast.
	1663. The Spaniards depart from the Moluccas.
	1667. Speelman forces the sultans of Ternate and Tidore to make peace. The treaty of Bongaya secures the submission of Macassar.
1672. The Dutch Republic, attacked by France, Britain, and others, on the verge of destruction.	1674. The revolt of Trunajaya of Madura breaks the power of the sultan of Mataram.
	1677. Treaty between Mataram and Batavia in which the sultan recognizes Dutch overlordship.
	1679–1683. The third war in the Moluccas ends with complete submission of Ternate.
	1682–1684. War of succession in Bantam which results in loss of independence.
	1696. The coffee tree is introduced into Java from India.
	1704–1708. A revolt among the vassals of the sultan of Mataram causes his deposition by the Dutch, hence the first Javanese war of succession.
	1717–1723. Second war of succession; like the first, principally a revolt of the vassals against the weakened authority of the sultan.
	1740. Revolt of the Chinese in Batavia, and subsequent massacre. This causes a new war in Mataram which is closed in 1743 by a treaty.
	1743. Nov. 11, treaty between Batavia and the susuhunan, who becomes a vassal of the Company and cedes the northern and eastern provinces of his territory.
	1747. First attempt to open direct trade connections between Batavia and America.
	1749–1755. Third Javanese war of succession, ending with the division of Mataram into the states of Surakarta and Djocjakarta.

CHRONOLOGICAL EPITOME

Rulers of Java

Governors-General	*Sultans of Mataram*
1645–1650. Cornelis van de Lijn.	1645–1677. Prabu Amangkurat I (Sunan Tegalwangi).
1650–1653. Carel Reyniersz.	
1653–1678. Johan Maetsuycker.	
	1677–1703. Amangkurat II.
1678–1681. Rijklof van Goens.	
1681–1684. Cornelis Speelman.	
1684–1691. Johannes Camphuijs.	
1691–1704. Willem van Outhoorn.	1703–1705. Amangkurat III (Sunan Mas).
1704–1709. Johan van Hoorn.	1705–1719. Pakubuwana I (Sunan Puger).
1709–1713. Abraham van Riebeeck.	
1713–1718. Christoffel van Swoll.	
1718–1725. Henricus Zwaardecroon.	1719–1725. Amangkurat IV.
1725–1729. Matheus de Haan.	
1729–1732. Dirk Durven.	1725–1749. Pakubuwana II.
1732–1735. Dirk van Cloon.	
1735–1737. Abraham Patras.	
1737–1741. Adriaan Valckenier.	
1741–1743. Johannes Thedens.	
1743–1750. Gustaaf W. van Imhoff.	1749–1788. Pakubuwana III.
1750–1761. Jacob Mossel.	

CHRONOLOGICAL EPITOME

PRINCIPAL EVENTS

Outside the Archipelago	*In the Archipelago*
	1757. Within the territory of Surakarta, the vassal state of the Mangkunegaras is created.
1780–1784. The Dutch Republic joins the allies in the war against Britain.	1778. The Batavian Society of Sciences is founded. 1791. Losses resulting from the war with Britain bring the East India Company to the verge of bankruptcy. S. C. Nederburgh investigates the existing system of commerce and administration.
1795. The Dutch Republic conquered by French troops. Democratic revolution, bringing the oligarchic system of government, and with it the East India Company, to an end.	1796. A democratic movement in Batavia is suppressed by Nederburgh. All trading posts and territories are lost to the British, except Java and the territories to the east.
1799. Dec. 31, The East India Company dissolved.	
1802. The peace treaty of Amiens restores all territories in the archipelago to the Dutch government.	1800–1808. Frequent trade relations with the United States of America. 1803. All territory except Java, Macassar, Timor, and Palembang lost to the British.
1803. War with Britain breaks out again.	
1804. A "Charter for the East Indies" is adopted by the Dutch legislature (revised in 1806).	
1810. The Netherlands are annexed by Napoleon Bonaparte.	1811. Java becomes French territory. A British attack brings this situation quickly to an end. 1813. Raffles introduces the land rent.

IV. THE INDIES UNDER THE KINGDOM OF THE NETHERLANDS

1813. Independence of the Netherlands restored. 1814. Treaty of London guarantees restitution of overseas territories.	1813. The sultanate of Bantam ceases to exist. The principality of the Paku Alam is founded within the territory of the sultanate of Djocjakarta.
	1819. Raffles, back in the Indies, founds Singapore.
1824. Treaty of London concerning Singapore and Sumatra.	
	1825–1830. Revolts of Dipa Negara, prince of Djocjakarta.
1830. Revolution in Belgium against the administration of King William of the Netherlands.	1830. The Culture System is introduced. 1840. James Brooke settles on the northern coast of Borneo (Sarawak).

CHRONOLOGICAL EPITOME

Rulers of Java		
Governors-General	*Princes of Surakarta*	*Sultans of Djocjakarta*
1761–1775. P. A. van der Parra.		1755–1792. Abdurrahman Amangkubuwana I (Mangkubumi).
1775–1777. Jeremias van Riemsdijk.		
1777–1780. Reinier de Klerk.		
1780–1796. Willam A. Alting.	1788–1820. Pakubuwana IV.	1792–1810. A. Amangkubuwana II (Sultan Sepuh).
1796–1801. Pieter van Overstraten.		
1801–1805. Johannes Siberg.		
1805–1808. Albert H. Wiese.		
1808–1811. Herman W. Daendels.		
1811. Jan Willem Janssens.		
1811–1816. Thomas S. Raffles (Lieutenant-Governor for the English East India Company).		1810–1814. A. Amangkubuwana III.
		1814–1822. A. Amangkubuwana IV.
1816. John Fendall (Lt. Gov.).		
1816–1818. Commissaries General of King William I of the Netherlands.		
1818–1826. G. A. Baron van der Capellen.	1820–1823. Pakubuwana V.	
	1823–1830. Pakubuwana VI.	1822–1855. A. Amangkubuwana V.
1826–1830. L. P. J. Viscount Du Bus de Ghisignies (Commissary General).		
1830–1833. J. Count van den Bosch.	1830–1858. Pakubuwana VII.	
1833–1836. J. C. Baud.		
1836–1840. D. J. de Eerens.		
1840–1844. P. Merkus.		

CHRONOLOGICAL EPITOME

Principal Events	
Outside the Archipelago	*In the Archipelago*
1848. A liberal constitution introduced in the Netherlands.	1845–1860. The British intervention in North Borneo causes a more vigorous policy of expansion from Batavia.
1860. Douwes Dekker publishes his book *Max Havelaar.*	1863. Beginning of the tobacco culture in northeastern Sumatra, the first step towards development of the outer islands.
1869. Opening of the Suez Canal.	
1870. Netherlands Parliament abolishes obligatory production of sugar.	1870–1880. Private enterprise takes the place of government-controlled agriculture. Sugar becomes the main export crop of Java.
1870. Agrarian Law promulgated.	
1871. Great Britain and the Netherlands revise their treaty regarding Sumatra.	1873. War declared on Atjeh. This war lasts until 1904.
	1900–1910. Vigorous action is undertaken to extend effective administration over the remotest corners of the archipelago.
1904–1905. Russo-Japanese War.	1908. The "Budi Utomo" is founded by Javanese intellectuals.
	1912. The "Sarekat Islam," Mohammedan mass movement, is founded in Surakarta.
1914–1918. First World War.	1916. Institution of the People's Council; first session May 18, 1918.
1922. Revision of the constitution of the Netherlands. The term "colonies" is barred from the constitution.	1922. Beginning of Communist agitation. 1925. The "East Indian Constitution" is promulgated (revised in 1927 to guarantee a majority in the People's Council to the Indonesians).
1929. Beginning of the economic depression.	1926. Communist agitation leads to an outbreak of violence in West Java and West Sumatra. 1930. The depression causes enormous losses in the Indies. Japan makes use of the existing conditions to try to gain economic control. 1933. Stringent measures taken to prevent sole predominance of Japanese industry and commerce.
1939. War breaks out in Europe.	1938. A large-scale program of industrialization is started to improve the standard of living of the Indonesians.
1940. May 10, Invasion of the Netherlands.	
1941. Dec. 7, Attack on Pearl Harbor.	1941. Dec. 8 (west of the date line): the Netherlands declare war on Japan; ships of the East Indian squadron attack Japanese convoys. 1942. Jan. 10, First Japanese landings on Netherlands-Indian soil (Tarakan). 1942. Feb. 28, Battle of the Java Sea. 1942. March 8, Fall of Bandung.

CHRONOLOGICAL EPITOME

Rulers of Java		
Governors-General	*Princes of Surakarta*	*Princes of Djocjakarta*
1844–1845. J. C. Reynst.		
1845–1851. J. J. Rochussen.		
1851–1856. A. J. Duymaer van Twist.		
1856–1861. C. F. Pahud.	1858–1861. Pakubuwana VIII.	1855–1877. A. Amangkubuwana VI.
1861–1866. L. A. J. W. Baron Sloet van den Beele.	1861–1893. Pakubuwana IX.	
1866–1872. P. Mijer.		
1872–1875. J. Loudon.		
1875–1881. J. W. van Lansberge.		1877–1921. A. Amangkubuwana VII.
1881–1884. F. 's Jacob.		
1884–1888. O. van Rees.		
1888–1893. C. Pijnacker Hordijk.		
1893–1899. C. H. J. van der Wijck.	1893. Pakubuwana X.	
1899–1904. W. Rooseboom.		
1904–1909. J. B. van Heutsz.		
1909–1916. A. F. van Idenburg.		
1916–1921. J. P. Count of Limburg Stirum.		1921– . A. Amangkubuwana VIII.
1921–1926. D. Fock.		
1926–1931. A. C. D. de Graeff.		
1931–1936. B. C. de Jonge.		
1936– . A. W. L. Tjarda van Starkenborgh Stachouwer.		

INDEX

(For double names in Dutch, look under first name; for instance, for Snouck Hurgronje, *see* Snouck.)